	DATE DUE		

CHLOE PLUS OLIVIA

COMPILED AND EDITED BY

Lillian Faderman

CHLOE PLUS OLIVIA

An Anthology of

Lesbian Literature from

the Seventeenth Century

to the Present

Viking

VIKING
Published by the Penguin Group
Penguin Books USA Inc., 375 Hudson Street,
New York, New York 10014, U.S.A.
Penguin Books Ltd, 27 Wrights Lane, London W8 5TZ, England
Penguin Books Australia Ltd, Ringwood, Victoria, Australia
Penguin Books Canada Ltd, 10 Alcorn Avenue,
Toronto, Ontario, Canada M4V 3B2
Penguin Books (N.Z.) Ltd, 182–190 Wairau Road,
Auckland 10, New Zealand

Penguin Books Ltd, Registered Offices:
Harmondsworth, Middlesex, England

First published in 1994 by Viking Penguin,
a division of Penguin Books USA Inc.

1   3   5   7   9   10   8   6   4   2

PUBLISHER'S NOTE
Some of the selections in this book are works of fiction. Names,
characters, places, and incidents either are the product of the authors'
imagination or are used fictitiously, and any resemblance to actual
persons, living or dead, events, or locales is entirely coincidental.

Pages 807–812 constitute an extension of this copyright page.

LIBRARY OF CONGRESS CATALOGING IN PUBLICATION DATA
Chloe plus Olivia : an anthology of lesbian literature
from the seventeenth century to the present / [compiled by] Lillian
Faderman.
p.   cm.
ISBN 0–670–84638–4
1. Lesbians—Literary collections. 2. Bisexuality—Literary
collections. 3. Lesbians' writings, American. 4. Lesbians'
writings, English. 5. Lesbians' writings—Translations into
English.   I. Faderman, Lillian.
PS509.L47C47   1994
810.8'09206643—dc20   93–45750

Printed in the United States of America
Set in Sabon
Designed by Kate Nichols

I turned the page and read. . . . I am sorry to break off so abruptly. Are there no men present? Do you promise me that behind that curtain over there the figure of Sir Chartres Biron is not concealed? We are all women, you assure me? Then I may tell you that the very next words I read were these—"Chloe liked Olivia. . . ." Do not start. Do not blush. Let us admit in the privacy of our own society that these things sometimes happen. Sometimes women do like women.

—Virginia Woolf,
A Room of One's Own, 1929

PREFACE

In 1956, as a teenager, I began to consider myself a lesbian. Almost as soon as I claimed that identity, being already enamored of books, of course I looked around for literary representations that would help explain me to myself. I did not have far to look, because the pulp book racks at the local drugstore exhibited a dizzying array of titles like *Odd Girl*, *Twisted Sisters*, *Twilight Lovers*, *We Walk in Shadows*, and *Whisper Their Love*. I was fascinated by their lurid covers and astonishingly graphic sexual scenes, I was depressed by their pathos and bathos, and—intellectual snob that I was at the age of sixteen—I was bored by their heavy-handed prose, stock characters, and predictability.

I wanted "real literature," the kind I read in my English classes, to comment on the lifestyle I had just recently discovered with such enthusiasm, to reveal me to myself, to acknowledge the lesbian to the world. Naturally, my high school English teachers never gave me a hint about where to look for such literature. As an undergraduate in college I was an English literature major, but the only time I learned about a lesbian book was in an Abnormal Psych class, where *The Well of Loneliness* was mentioned. As a graduate student, although I read Emily Dickinson, Sara Orne Jewett, Willa Cather, Virginia Woolf, Carson McCullers, Elizabeth Bishop, and even Sappho, I never had a professor who mentioned the word "lesbian" or acknowledged that love between women had ever been a subject of literary focus. In 1967 I received a Ph.D. in English without the slightest notion that lesbian literature had a rich history and that many of the writers I admired—in fact almost all of those few women writers who were studied in graduate school—had contributed to that history.

More than a quarter of a century later lesbianism is no longer the love that dares not speak its name—but there has not yet been a literary anthology that collects the work of a variety of "lesbian" writers of the past and present and offers it in a historical and theoretical framework. *Chloe Plus Olivia* is an attempt to fill that gap.

The title of this book derives from a passage in Virginia Woolf's *A Room of One's Own* (1929). Woolf, imagining a woman novelist of the future, speculates that she would be able to examine what Woolf believed to be hitherto unexplored territory: It would be possible for her to write about women's relationships with each other. "Chloe liked Olivia" is the sentence Woolf attributes to the pen of this fictive woman writer. However, before Woolf can articulate even that sentence she must check out her audience. Are men observing? Is anyone prone to blushing over blunt facts? "Let us admit in the privacy of our own society," Woolf states after looking around the room, "that these things sometimes happen. Sometimes women do like women."

The year before Woolf undertook *A Room of One's Own* she wrote what has been described as the longest and most charming love letter in literature, the novel *Orlando,* to (and about) her sometime lover, Vita Sackville-West. Woolf masked the lesbian content of *Orlando* by manipulating the gender of her eponymous character, and she was also careful not to step beyond the boundaries of her era in *A Room of One's Own.* But in attributing to the fictive woman novelist the declaration "Chloe liked Olivia" surely she meant to indicate an emotion far more intense than mere "liking." Imagining a novel of the future about Chloe and Olivia (whose relationship is not explained away as "congenital sexual inversion"), Woolf was predicting what must have seemed all but impossible in her day: a nonmedical literature that would unmask the subject of love between women. She was not aware, apparently, that there had already been such a literature in the centuries before Krafft-Ebing and Freud. This anthology attempts to bring together not only the works Woolf predicted would someday be written but also those works about female-female relationships that preceded her and that her era had forgotten or lacked the knowledge to decode.

In subtitling this book *An Anthology of Lesbian Literature from the Seventeenth Century to the Present* I have been anachronistic. Many of the women writers of the seventeenth, eighteenth, and even nineteenth centuries who are included here would not have considered themselves lesbian—even had that word been available to them. They would have recognized themselves instead as belonging to other categories with which they were familiar, and which do not exist today. Characters created in other centuries, that we would be tempted to identify as lesbian, also were not described with that term by their authors. Therefore, a woman writer of the eighteenth century, for example, who wrote passionate love letters to another woman, might have considered her correspondent her "romantic friend." Or a character in a nineteenth-century work of fiction who dressed as a man and desired to make love to other women would probably have been considered by the author a "female sexual invert." By dubbing such writers and characters "lesbian," I am employing the word most familiar to our era to signal content about female same-sex emotional and physical relationships—though it is not a word other eras would have been likely to employ.

Nor would "bisexual" have been a recognized category in most of the eras in which the literature included in this book was written—although many of the writers and subjects of these works had affectional and sexual relations with both women and men. The term "bisexual" has become current only in the twentieth century; nevertheless, it is very apt as a descriptive term for many women of other eras. Social and economic realities before the successes of the first wave of feminism in the latter part of the nineteenth century mandated that women marry if they could, regardless of their affectional preference. The seventeenth-century poet Katherine Philips, for example, who wrote her beloved friend Lucasia, "thou art all that I can prize,/ My joy, my life, my rest," had a husband from the time she was sixteen years old.

But even after feminism succeeded in opening careers to large numbers of middle-class females, which permitted them to be economically self-sufficient and geographically more mobile, many women who loved other women continued to marry or take male lovers. Their reasons for doing so were varied and complex. It was not easy, even through much of the twentieth century, to assume a lesbian identity, and for some of these females it would not have been appropriate. Many women who had lesbian affairs, such as Vita Sackville-West, Virginia Woolf, Jane Bowles, and Carson McCullers, believed they also needed to be married to a man—for the sake of appearances, for the promise of permanent companionship (which they despaired of achieving with other women in a world that was hostile to homosexuality), in order to have children, or simply because of a profound attachment to a particular male. Others, such as Katherine Mansfield and Edna St. Vincent Millay, were genuinely bisexual, believing that they needed sexual and emotional relationships with both men and women in order to complete themselves. The selections in this anthology from "bisexual" writers of various centuries are concerned primarily with the "lesbian" side of their psychosexuality.

In this collection I have chosen to focus on literature about love between women from the seventeenth century through the present, although there are isolated instances of rich material that dates well before the seventeenth century. The earliest extant example of a lyric poem of lesbian love antedates heterosexual lyric poetry. Sappho of Lesbos, born circa 630 B.C., wrote of her desire for another woman:

> I think that man is like the gods
> who is privileged to sit close to you and gaze
> into your eyes and hear your voice softly and
> sweetly murmuring in love and in laughter. All is for
> him.

> But it breaks me. The heart in my breast is shaken.
> When I glance at you I can only stutter or am stricken
> dumb. A delicate fire runs under my skin. I become
> like one who is blinded. My ears are ringing.

> Sweat runs down me, fever shakes me. I become as pale,
> as green as the grass is. I feel that death has
> touched me.

Even the Old Testament is not without a beautiful passage of "lesbian" love—such a moving statement of deep emotional commitment, in fact, that it has often been appropriated for the heterosexual wedding ceremony. In the Book of Ruth, it is a woman, Ruth, who says to another woman, Naomi, "Entreat me not to leave you or to cease following you. Whither thou goest I will go, and whither thou stayest I will stay. Your people will be my people, and your God will be my God. Whither thou diest, I will die, and there will I be buried. May the Lord deal with me severely if I allow anything but death to separate us."

But these important early expressions of love between women, that date centuries before Christ, cannot be presented with any certainty as representative of "lesbian" literature of their eras since nothing else comparable from those eras has survived. Beginning in the seventeenth century, however, there is a tremendous literature that focuses on love between women in the form of "romantic friendship," a relationship no less intense and passionate than what our era has called "lesbian" love. It is with the literature of romantic friendship that this anthology begins.

I have chosen to collect in this book only work that was written by Europeans or North Americans (inclusive of European or North American lesbians of color) because I wished to trace a particular set of literary traditions through my selections. African, Asian, or Latin American writing that deals with love and sex between women may have some concerns similar to the work included here. But I believed it would be instructive to illustrate influences and evolutions through my selections, and works that were conceived outside of Euro-America cannot clearly be shown to partake of the same traditions.

Although I have included a good deal of material by twentieth-century European and American lesbians of color (they are producing some of the most vital writing today), I regret that I have been able to locate virtually no pre-twentieth-century work by lesbians of color. I suspect that because of the immigration and literacy patterns before the twentieth century not much was written that would be pertinent for this collection.

I have also elected not to include gay male literature in this book. I believe that while presently gay men and lesbians share many social problems as well as achievements and joys, their histories have been quite different, and their literature often reflects that difference. For example, the nineteenth century saw the birth of the genre of Decadent literature, which often presented lesbianism as an objective correlative that would best portray certain male writers' shock and fascination with the corruption of their era. The exotic literary images of female same-sex relationships they created in order to warn and/or titillate were later taken up by lesbian writers and ultimately rescued from their moralistic and male voyeuristic uses. In recent years they have been transformed into pro-sex literary statements for lesbian delectation. (See, for example, Pat Califia's "The Finishing School," p. 749.) Gay male literature has no history that is precisely comparable. Nor is there an analogue in the work of gay male writers to the fiction and poetry that came out of the lesbian-feminist movement of the 1970s. It seemed to me important to focus on such patterns in the development of lesbian literature, and I feared that an anthology that combined both lesbian writing and gay male writing would detract from the clear illustration of the lines of development. It is my hope that other scholars will soon compile anthologies, which could be read as companions to this volume, that trace the developments of literary representations of homosexual men and non-Western lesbians.

Chloe Plus Olivia does contain some writing by men who focused on women's relationships. I have included such works in the early sections of the book because I believe they were in various ways important to the development of lesbian literature. Men were far more likely than women to achieve publication in other centuries. Thus, it was often the ideas they generated through their writing, whether true or false, that became influential in social perceptions. For example, it was initially male writing that defined the "female sexual invert" as a medical specimen and influenced the development of such a literary character.

It has already been well observed among critics that literature is far more likely to mirror other literary models than to reflect real life. Therefore, it is to be expected that numerous women writers, having turned their attention to lesbianism, imitated for a period of time the male-generated models that had been promulgated by their predecessors. One striking example of this is the echoes of Krafft-Ebing's account of Countess Sarolta's lament (see p. 157) in the denouement of Radclyffe Hall's *The Well of Loneliness*. Hall's reading of the sexologist was more influential in her depiction of Stephen Gordon than were her observations of the lively lesbian society around her.

Publishers also would have pressured writers to present their subject in a way that was consonant with public knowledge and expectations—which were formed by earlier male representations. Later in literary history, in the context of different times, women writers were able to modify some of those earlier literary images to reflect more closely the realities they had observed. The material by male writers that has been included in this anthology not only provides examples of the literary sources available to earlier lesbian writers but also serves to illustrate by comparison the ways that later lesbian writers transformed those sources.

In recent years a number of critics have tried valiantly to categorize and define lesbian literature. Such literature is resistant to easy definition since the very term "lesbian" may be confusing. Is a lesbian a woman who has sex with other women? (Recent sexological writing tells us that in long-term "lesbian" relationships sexual contact is often infrequent though the two women have committed themselves to one another.) Is a lesbian a woman who is committed to another woman? (What of those women who have sexual and emotional relations with other females but are committed in a heterosexual marriage?) Can a woman be considered a "lesbian" because she wrote passionate, erotic letters to another woman—as Emily Dickinson did to Sue Gilbert, for example—if she would not have used that term to describe herself and it was probably not even in her vocabulary? For the purpose of inclusion in this anthology I have chosen to define "lesbian" in the very broadest descriptive sense and include the work of women who fall into any of these categories or who focus on any of them, as long as their writing contributes meaningfully to an illustration of the various genres in which love between women has been treated.

My classifications of "lesbian" literature diverge to a greater or lesser extent from those of other critics. Elaine Marks, for example, in her essay "Lesbian Intertextuality" defines two primary categories of lesbian literature: the mother-daughter model and the amazonian model. Catharine Stimpson in "Zero Degree Deviancy: The Lesbian Novel in English"[1] has also identified two patterns: a narrative of damnation, which shows the lesbian's suffering as a lonely outcast, and a narrative of the enabling escape, which depicts the lesbian's rebellion against social stigma. While both of those critical classifications are useful, it has seemed to me that lesbian literature has fallen into other major categories as well. *Chloe Plus Olivia* delineates six categories:

1. Kindred spirits: the literature of romantic friendship
2. A man trapped in a woman's body: the literature of sexual inversion
3. Carnivorous flowers: the literature of exotic and evil lesbians
4. In the closet: the literature of lesbian encoding
5. Amazons: the literature of lesbian feminism
6. Flowerings: post–lesbian-feminist literature

This anthology also engages with the critical dialogue that attempts to identify a "lesbian aesthetic" or "lesbian sensibility." I argue through these selections that any generalization about what is distinctly "lesbian" in writing is easily contradicted by numerous counterexamples. The fact that many early-twentieth-century lesbian writers were modernists, for instance, and experimented with form might tempt a critic to suggest that lesbian writing is often nonlinear. But those modernist lesbian writers also had contemporaries who wrote lesbian literature in the most linear of styles, as did Radclyffe Hall. And, of course, nonlinearity often characterized the writing of modernist men, such as James Joyce.

Other attempts to define a lesbian aesthetic or sensibility are equally specious or arbitrary. For example, Bertha Harris has suggested in her essay "What We Mean to Say: Notes Toward Defining the Nature of Lesbian Literature"[2] that the lesbian hero is an outsider, a "monster," a self-creation in a hostile world. Her depiction of the lesbian sensibility becomes confusing when she suggests, not with total facetiousness, that F. Scott Fitzgerald's *The Great Gatsby* may be considered through her definition the lesbian novel par excellence. But even without such an outrageous critical assessment, Harris's definition of lesbian sensibility is persuasive only as it applies to a limited kind of "lesbian" literature. Most women who wrote about their love for other women in the seventeenth, eighteenth, and nineteenth centuries would not have recognized themselves or their characters in her description. Nor would many twentieth-century lesbian authors, such as Helen Hull, have recognized themselves or their characters as possessing Harris's "lesbian sensibility."

Other critics have suggested that lesbian writing is powerfully feminist, dramatizing, for example, the moral superiority of women. That observation applies well to those authors who wrote of romantic friendship or to the lesbian-feminist authors of the 1970s. But writers from the Baroness von Puttkamer, who adopted the carnivorous-flower image in her late-nineteenth-century writing (see p. 363), to Pat Califia, who *adapted* that image a hundred years later (see p. 748), have had little interest in depicting such feminist principles in their works, though they focus on women's relationships.

Still other critics have attempted to define as lesbian any writing that depicts intense friendships between women. Barbara Smith, for example, has suggested that Toni Morrison's *Sula* is a lesbian novel because the two main female characters are central to each other. It may, in fact, be appropriate to include in the "lesbian" literary canon works about intense female friendship that were written before the sexologists promulgated an awareness of "the lesbian" as a species in the second half of the nineteenth century. But it is perhaps less convincing to present as lesbian a work of the late twentieth century that does not address the issue of lesbianism with some measure of directness, unless there is reason to believe (because of clues such as the author's own lesbianism) that she has encoded the lesbian material.

Bonnie Zimmerman, in her essay "What Has Never Been: An Overview of Lesbian Feminist Criticism"[3] has offered a number of interesting criteria by which critics might wish to define lesbian literature. But none of these criteria can be inclusive of the whole of lesbian literature. Zimmerman is somewhat persuasive, for example, in suggesting that lesbian literature deals with flexibility of gender roles and a fascination with costuming as an expression of gender roles. However, her observation is not applicable to a good deal of literature that depicts passionate love between women. For example, much of the "lesbian" literature that emerges out of the institution of romantic friendship presents females and their pursuits as superior to men, who are mucked up in the battles of the world. Those writers have no interest in challenging gender roles or assuming male "costume" in any way.

Perhaps the "lesbian aesthetic" defies easy definition because lesbian literature has developed over so long a period of time and is so diverse. Lesbian literature has been in constant metamorphosis, reflecting the social attitudes of the eras in which it was written, the timidity or power of women's voices at a given time, who felt free to write, and who and what would be published.

1. Catharine Stimpson, "Zero Degree Deviancy: The Lesbian Novel in English," in Elizabeth Abel, ed., *Writing and Sexual Difference* (Chicago: University of Chicago Press, 1982).
2. Bertha Harris, "What We Mean to Say: Notes Toward Defining the Nature of Lesbian Literature," *Heresies* (3) 1977.
3. Bonnie Zimmerman, "What Has Never Been: An Overview of Lesbian Feminist Criticism," *Feminist Studies* (7:3) 1981.

ACKNOWLEDGMENTS

An anthology as ambitious as this one could not be produced without the gracious support of many people over a period of many years. I am grateful for the help and good will I have received from my colleagues at California State University, Fresno, not only on this project but throughout my writing career. They supported me long before it became fashionable in academia to look kindly on lesbian studies. I am especially grateful for the encouragement and practical support I received on this project from my chair, Craig Bernthal, and my dean, Luis Costa.

I would also like to thank those many friends and colleagues who recommended materials or assisted me in translations and poetic renderings of Spanish and German works. My special thanks go to Martin Paul, Jose Elgorriaga, Brigitte Eriksson, Frankie Hucklenbroich, Electa Arenal, Amanda Powell, Deborah Oller, Antoinette Gonzales, and Rosie Pegueros.

Profuse thanks to my very competent research assistants, Graciela Garcia, Shannon Wentworth, and Kim Willis, for their invaluable help in locating, ordering, and duplicating material for me, and to the interlibrary loan librarians at California State University, Fresno, for their great diligence and patience.

My special thanks go to Phyllis Irwin, Frankie Hucklenbroich, Degania Golove, and Harriet Perl for their helpful and honest responses to whatever I tried out on them, and to my son, Avrom Faderman, for making me think I know how to use a computer.

CONTENTS

PREFACE   vii

I. KINDRED SPIRITS: THE LITERATURE OF ROMANTIC FRIENDSHIP

INTRODUCTION   3

MEN'S WRITING ON ROMANTIC FRIENDSHIP   9

Michel de Montaigne
From *On Friendship*   9

Jean Jacques Rousseau
From *La Nouvelle Héloïse*   12

William Cullen Bryant
To the *Evening Post*   13

William Rounseville Alger
From *The Friendships of Women*   14

WOMEN'S WRITING ON ROMANTIC FRIENDSHIP 17

Katherine Fowler Philips 17
To Mrs. Mary Awbrey 19
To Mrs. M. A. at Parting 20
Friendships Mystery, To my dearest Lucasia 22
To My Excellent Lucasia, on Our Friendship 23

Aphra Behn 24
To My Lady Morland at Tunbridge 25
A Song 26
To the fair Clarinda, who made Love to me,
  imagin'd more than Woman 27

Sor Juana Inés de la Cruz 28
My Divine Lysi 30
Happy Easter, My Lady 31

The Ladies of Llangollen [Lady Eleanor Butler and The Honourable Sarah Ponsonby] 32
From *The Hamwood Papers of the Ladies of Llangollen* 35

Anna Seward 37
Elegy 39
Sonnet XII 40
Sonnet XIII 40
Sonnet XIX 41
Sonnet XXXI 41
Sonnet XXXII 42
To the Right Honourable Lady Eleanor Butler 42
To Miss Ponsonby 43

Emily Dickinson 43
From *The Letters of Emily Dickinson* 46
From *The Poems of Emily Dickinson* 56
  Her breast is fit for pearls 56
  The Lady feeds Her little Bird 56
  I showed her Hights she never saw 56
  You love me—you are sure 57

Like Eyes that looked on Wastes   57
Ourselves were wed one summer—dear   58
Be Mine the Doom   58
Now I knew I lost her   58
Her sweet Weight on my Heart   59
Frigid and sweet Her parting Face   59
That she forgot me was the least   60
To see her is a picture   60

Christina Rossetti   60
Goblin Market   62

Mary E. Wilkins (Freeman)   76
Two Friends   77

*"Michael Field" [Katharine Bradley and
Edith Cooper]*   88
Prologue   91
Constancy   91
A gray mob-cap   91
A Girl   92
Unbosoming   92
My lady has a lovely rite   93
My Darling   93
Methinks my love to thee doth grow   93
Beloved, now I love God first   94
Lovers   95
Beloved, my glory in thee is not ceased   95
She is singing to thee, *Domine!*   95
Caput Tuum Ut Carmelus   96

Sarah Orne Jewett   96
Together   98
Martha's Lady   99

Katharine Lee Bates   113
If you could come   115
Yellow Clover   115
To One Who Waits   117

Helen Rose Hull   118
  The Fire   121

II. A MAN TRAPPED IN A WOMAN'S BODY: THE LITERATURE OF SEXUAL INVERSION

INTRODUCTION   135

MEN'S WRITING ON A MAN TRAPPED IN A WOMAN'S BODY   143

Henry Fielding
  The Female Husband   143

Richard von Krafft-Ebing
  From *Psychopathia Sexualis*   157

Sigmund Freud
  From *The Psychogenesis of a Case of
  Homosexuality in a Woman*   164

WOMEN'S WRITING ON A MAN TRAPPED
IN A WOMAN'S BODY   179

Charlotte Cibber Charke   179
  From *A Narrative of the Life of Mrs. Charlotte
  Charke*   181

Maria Edgeworth   190
  From *Belinda*: "Rights of Woman"   192

Anne Lister   198
  From *The Journal of Anne Lister*   199

Constance Fenimore Woolson   207
  Felipa   209

[Sidonie Gabrielle] Colette   226
    From *The Pure and the Impure*   228

Willa Cather   234
    Tommy, the Unsentimental   236

Henry Handel Richardson [Ethel Florence
Lindesay Richardson]   243
    Two Hanged Women   244

Radclyffe Hall   248
    Letters   252

Vita Sackville-West   268
    From Vita Sackville-West's *Journals*   270

III. CARNIVOROUS FLOWERS: THE LITERATURE OF EXOTIC AND EVIL LESBIANS

INTRODUCTION   293

MEN'S WRITING ON THE "CARNIVOROUS FLOWER"   299

Charles Baudelaire   299
    Femmes Damnées   299

Sheridan Le Fanu   303
    Carmilla   303

WOMEN'S WRITING ON THE "CARNIVOROUS FLOWER"   363

Marie-Madeleine, Baroness von Puttkamer   363
    Words of Old Age   364
    Crucifixa   365
    Sappho   365
    Vagabonds   366

Renée Vivien (Pauline Tarn)   367
    Chanson   369
    Undine   370
    Your Strange Hair   370
    Sad Words   370
    Roses Rising   371

Mary E. Wilkins Freeman   372
    The Long Arm   373

Rose O'Neill   398
    The Master-Mistress   399
    Lee   399
    A Dream of Sappho   400
    The Sister   401

Clemence Dane (Winifred Ashton)   402
    From *Regiment of Women*   404

Djuna Barnes   411
    From *Nightwood*   412

Anaïs Nin   419
    From *House of Incest*   420

Jewelle Gomez   425
    From *The Gilda Stories*: "Louisiana: 1850"   426

IV. IN THE CLOSET: THE LITERATURE OF LESBIAN ENCODING

INTRODUCTION   441

Charlotte Mew   446
    Monsieur Qui Passe   449
    My Heart Is Lame   450

Absence 450
On the Road to the Sea 451

Gertrude Stein 452
Miss Furr and Miss Skeene 455

Amy Lowell 460
From "Two Speak Together" 462
The Letter 462
Venus Transiens 463
Madonna of the Evening Flowers 464
The Weather-Cock Points South 464
The Artist 465
The Garden by Moonlight 465
Bullion . 466
A Shower 466
Summer Rain 467
April 467
Left Behind 467
A Sprig of Rosemary 468
Preparation 468
A Decade 469
Frimaire 469

Katherine Mansfield 470
Bliss 473

Angelina Weld Grimké 483
When the Green Lies Over the Earth 485
A Triolet 486
Brown Girl 486
You 487
Your Eyes 487
Naughty Nan 488

Virginia Woolf 489
Moments of Being: "Slater's Pins Have No Points" 492

H.D. (Hilda Doolittle) 498
  Fragment Thirty-six 501
  The Gift 503
  At Baia 505

Carson McCullers 506
  Like That 509

Jane (Auer) Bowles 516
  Selected Letters 520
  Everything Is Nice 526

Muriel Rukeyser 531
  Despisals 533
  Looking at Each Other 534
  Cries from Chiapas 535

May Swenson 536
  Poet to Tiger 537
  A Trellis For R. 540
  You Are 541

V. AMAZONS: THE LITERATURE OF LESBIAN-FEMINISM

INTRODUCTION 547

Rita Mae Brown 552
  From *Rubyfruit Jungle* 553

Audre Lorde 560
  From *Zami* 561
  Meet 566
  Love Poem 567
  On a Night of the Full Moon 568

Adrienne Rich   569
   From *Twenty-one Love Poems*   570

Judy Grahn   573
   A Woman Is Talking to Death   575

Joanna Russ   588
   When It Changed   589

Jane Chambers   596
   Last Summer at Bluefish Cove   596

Jane Rule   655
   In the Attic of the House   656

Monique Wittig   664
   From *The Lesbian Body*   665

Olga Broumas   668
   Amazon Twins   669
   Sleeping Beauty   670
   Rapunzel   671
   Snow White   672

Irena Klepfisz   674
   They Did Not Build Wings For Them   675
   dinosaurs and larger issues   677
   Etlekhe verter oyf mame-loshn / A few words in the
      mother tongue   677

Pat Parker   680
   For Willyce   681
   My Lady Ain't No Lady   681
   Have You Ever Tried to Hide   682
   Brother   682

VI. FLOWERINGS: POST–LESBIAN-FEMINIST LITERATURE

INTRODUCTION   689

Chrystos   693
   For Sharol Graves   694
   Dream Lesbian Lover   695
   Getting Down   695
   Your Tongue Sparkles   696
   Night Visits   697

Beth Brant (Degonwadonti)   697
   Her Name Is Helen   698

Kitty Tsui   700
   A Chinese Banquet   701
   How Can I Show This Poem to Geraldine?   702
   It's in the Name   704

Suniti Namjoshi and Gillian Hanscombe   707
   Was It Quite Like That?   708
   In That Particular Temple   709
   Because of India   710
   We Can Compose Ourselves   711

Cherríe (Lawrence) Moraga   711
   Later, She Met Joyce   712
   La Dulce Culpa   714
   Loving in the War Years   715

Emma Pérez   717
   Gulf Dreams   717

Jeanette Winterson   728
   From *The Passion*: "The Queen of Spades"   729

Sarah Schulman 737
  The Penis Story 739

Marilyn Hacker 745
  Runaways Café I 746
  February 25 746
  Future Conditional 747
  Saturday Morning 748
  Bloomingdale's I 748

Pat Califia 748
  The Finishing School 749

Cheryl Clarke 767
  Kittatinny 768
  what goes around comes around, or the proof is in
    the pudding 768
  San Juan: 1979 769

Frankie Hucklenbroich 770
  A Crystal Diary 771

Dorothy Allison 786
  the women who hate me 787

Minnie Bruce Pratt 792
  All the Women Caught in Flaring Light 793
  A Waving Hand 796
  The Place Lost and Gone, the Place Found 797
  The Laughing Place 798

Jackie Kay 799
  Photo in the Locket 800
  He Told Us He Wanted a Black Coffin 804
  Mummy and Donor and Deirdre 805
  Dressing Up 806

Part I

Kindred Spirits:
The Literature of
Romantic
Friendship

INTRODUCTION

For centuries before the successes of the first wave of feminism a little over
a hundred years ago, much of social life in the Western world, especially
for the middle and upper classes, was carried on in homosocial environments. Males and females were educated separately, performed their paid
or unpaid employments separately, and before (and often even after) marriage engaged in various diversions separately. They generally inhabited, as
a nineteenth-century phrase aptly characterized it, "separate spheres."

Not only did the differences in their socialization often make friendship
between men and women difficult, but during many eras in the Western
world an enormous importance was placed on female chastity among the
middle and upper classes, which meant that outside of marriage close intercourse between males and females was potentially dangerous. It could
introduce a threat to what was the sine qua non of a woman's social value.
Thus, if males and females had so little in common and their relationships
were even potentially unsafe, how could they be intimate friends?

Men who lived in an era such as the Renaissance, which prized the
literature and the culture of the ancients, had models of close friendship
that could be far more meaningful to them than social relations with the
alien creatures that women were. As Michel de Montaigne pointed out in
his sixteenth-century essay "On Friendship," early Greeks and Romans understood that the most intimate, important, and even passionate friendships
were between men rather than men and women. Montaigne himself carried
on such a passionate friendship with Étienne de la Boëtie, with whom, he
said, he fell in love at their first meeting: "From that time on nothing was
so close to us as each other. . . . Each one gives himself so wholly to his
friend that he has nothing left to distribute elsewhere." Similar sentiments

about male-male friendship pervaded Western literature over the next three centuries.

Perhaps because male friendship was so important, men believed it was to their benefit not to interfere in women's equivalent passions with each other, though much else was forbidden women by male-controlled society. Intense, emotional, affectionate relations between females not only left men freer for their homosociality, but it posed little threat to heterosexual institutions. It was assumed that most women would and even must marry men. How else could a middle- or upper-class female support herself in centuries when few nondrudgery jobs were open to women and inheritance followed the laws of primogeniture? The American writer Henry Wadsworth Longfellow characterized perfectly the male view of women's intense, emotional relations with each other in his 1849 novel, *Kavanagh*. Such relations were seen by society to be merely "a rehearsal in girlhood for the great drama of woman's life," marriage. But until she married, women were socially permitted, and took that permission gladly, to fall in love with each other. Some women's letters, diaries, poetry, and fiction beginning in the seventeenth century showed they continued their romantic friendships even after marriage.

Men may have also looked kindly on women's passion for each other because it stimulated a perhaps unconscious voyeurism. As Jean Jacques Rousseau has his hero, Saint Preux, admit to Claire and Julie in *La nouvelle Héloïse,* "Nothing, no, nothing on earth is capable of exciting such a voluptuous sensibility as your mutual caresses; and the spectacle of two lovers has not offered my eyes a more delicious sensation." In addition, to permit females their affectional relationships with each other was practical during eras in which they far outnumbered men because a devastating war had recently taken place. In 1867, for example, after the American Civil War, William Alger recognized in his popular book *The Friendships of Women* that the man shortage would leave many women "old maids," and that society had an obligation to alleviate their loneliness by encouraging their same-sex emotional relationships.

Moreover, most men would not have felt threatened by such relationships because common wisdom had it, at various times, that well-brought-up middle- and upper-class women had no autonomous sexuality, that they were sexual only to fulfill connubial duties or for the sake of procreation, or that anything two women might do together was *faute de mieux* or insignificant, that without penetration by a penis nothing "sexual" could take place. Although there are occasional records of male-identified women in earlier centuries, the sexologists, such as Krafft-Ebing, did not define the category of the female sexual invert (the woman who, as a man trapped in a woman's body, actively sought sexual relations with other women) until the second half of the nineteenth century, and the possibility of there being such creatures was largely considered inconceivable. Usually patriarchal chauvinism could not conceive of a satisfying female sexual agency, though there are occasional works such as *Satan's Harvest Home* (1749), whose anonymous author complained that when he saw "two Ladies Kissing and Slopping each other, in a lascivious Manner, and frequently repeating it, I am shocked to the last Degree." But such moral outrage over the embraces of two females was rare. Therefore, though so much was denied to women during these centuries by men who were the authors and arbiters of the standards of social behavior, intense, passionate female-female relationships were allowed to flourish unmolested by social proscriptions. Such relationships were so common in the eighteenth century that the term "romantic friendship" was coined to describe them.

But what did these romantic friendships mean to the women who experienced them? The literature reflects that for many women romantic friendship was not simply a "rehearsal" for heterosexuality but rather the most important relationship of their lives. In the seventeenth and eighteenth centuries females of "good birth" were often married off by their families not to a man with whom they could fall in love but to a suitable estate. The tastes of the young woman were not taken into consideration. The seventeenth-century poet Katherine Philips, for instance, was married when she was sixteen to a wealthy man of fifty-four. Her own sentiments in the matter were not inquired into. However, her primary emotional outlet after marriage was not with him but with the many women whom she loved and took as her muse for her poetry.

Bluestockings, women who took themselves seriously as intellectuals in the seventeenth, eighteenth, and nineteenth centuries, when men usually thought that the female intellectual was a contradiction in terms, also often turned to other women for encouragement, dialogue, respect, and affection. A whole culture of romantic friendship sprang up around them, as the correspondence, poetry, and fiction of writers such as Anna Seward (see p. 37), Elizabeth Carter, Sarah Scott, and Elizabeth Montagu illustrate. *A Description of Millennium Hall* (1762), a novel by the bluestocking Sarah Scott, even presents a utopian blueprint for romantic friends who manage to live their lives together in a perfect relationship and to assist others in leading happy and productive lives.

Whether or not their relationships were sexual, romantic friends, in both the eighteenth and nineteenth centuries, often liked to compare the "purity" of their love for each other with the impure lusts they associated with heterosexuality. The Ladies of Llangollen, for instance, claimed to eschew "Vulgar Eros" while still enjoying the pleasures of "mighty Love." Katharine Bradley and Edith Cooper, the two poets who collaborated under the name of Michael Field, contrasted the smiting darts of Eros with their own gentle romantic friendship. Perhaps some of these romantic friends felt free to indulge in eroticism together but, like men, did not consider their lovemaking sexual because no penis was present. Regardless, in the centuries before the sexologists defined "the lesbian" and thus helped call her into popular consciousness and being, romantic friends would have had the luxury of not having to fear they were "abnormal" or diseased because they loved each other. Their secret sexual exchanges, if they took place, could be seen perhaps as anomalous but not cause for fear that those exchanges rendered them innately and irrevocably different from the rest of the female population.

With the initial successes of the feminist movement, which helped to usher women into higher education and the middle-class work force, romantic friendship did not lose its importance for a long time. Females in the first women's colleges of the nineteenth century not only found themselves in an entirely sexually segregated setting but they also discovered that they could become heroes—socially, athletically, intellectually—to one another and thrive in each other's regard. Such admiration and desire often led them to love. There is a considerable literature of the second half of the nineteenth century and the early twentieth century that reflects college women's "raves," "spoons," "smashes," "crushes" (all terms coined to describe a college female's falling in love with a woman professor or fellow student).

The pioneering women who entered the professions during this time also found, as Florence Converse's novel *Diana Victrix* (1897) dramatizes, that a woman who is serious about her career must not get involved in the distractions of birthing and raising multiple children and, before the days of labor-saving domestic devices, the full-time job of running a house. The most satisfactory domestic situation a serious career woman could arrange was to live with another career woman in an egalitarian relationship in which finances, household duties and responsibilities, and affection and even passion might be shared. The term "Boston marriage" was coined in the late nineteenth century to describe these new relationships, which had become ubiquitous, not only in Boston but in all big cities in America and Europe where employment opportunities were expanding for middle-class women.

Little record has been left to tell us whether working-class women also enjoyed romantic friendships, crushes, smashes, or Boston marriages. They were not often the subject of the (generally genteel) novels that described those passionate relationships between women, and since working-class women usually had little education, they seldom recorded their own experiences in letters, diaries, fiction, and poetry as those women of the middle and upper classes did. Romantic friendship, as it was played out in the course of several centuries, however, usually appears to have required some degree of leisure, the luxury of long-letter writing, for example, and the time to develop shared sensibilities and "refinements," time that working-class women in the confines of the factory or domestic drudgery did not have. But in "Martha's Lady" Sarah Orne Jewett, who was herself in a Boston marriage with Annie Fields for almost thirty years, describes a romantic friendship, lived mostly in imagination, between a servant and a woman of the wealthier classes. Unfortunately, we will never know how common such sentiments were among working-class women.

Romantic friendship and its later nineteenth-century equivalents disappeared as a social institution by the 1920s. Its disappearance may be attributed to a number of factors. First of all, it had the potential to become threatening to the fabric of society by the twentieth century as it could not in earlier eras. Feminism had succeeded "too well." Large numbers of women had become self-supporting, and economic factors would no longer assure that a woman would feel obliged to marry regardless of where her heart lay. The 1920s also saw the rise of "companionate marriage," an ideal that suggested that husbands and wives could be equals and friends. If men could now conceive of taking a woman as a friend, earlier homosocial arrangements lost a good deal of their practicality and charm. Finally, and perhaps most important, the writings of the sexologists that defined love between women as abnormal by now had filtered down into mass consciousness, thanks particularly to the wide dissemination of the ideas of Sigmund Freud. Passionate "romantic friendship" would now be looked on with suspicion. Intense same-sex relationships that could be experienced without self-consciousness during the previous centuries would be examined for the "taint of homosexuality" by the 1920s.

MEN'S WRITING

ON ROMANTIC FRIENDSHIP

From *On Friendship* by Michel de Montaigne

What we ordinarily call friends and friendships are nothing but acquaintanceships and familiarities formed by some chance or convenience, by means of which our souls are bound to each other. In the friendship I speak of, our souls mingle and blend with each other so completely that they efface the seam that joined them, and cannot find it again. If you press me to tell why I loved him,* I feel that this cannot be expressed, except by answering: Because it was he, because it was I.

Beyond all my understanding, beyond what I can say about this in particular, there was I know not what inexplicable and fateful force that was the mediator of this union. We sought each other before we met because of the reports we heard of each other, which had more effect on our affection than such reports would reasonably have; I think it was by some ordinance from heaven. We embraced each other by our names. And at our first meeting, which by chance came at a great feast and gathering in the city, we found ourselves so taken with each other, so well acquainted, so bound together, that from that time on nothing was so close to us as each other. He wrote an excellent Latin satire, which is published, in which he excuses and explains the precipitancy of our mutual understanding, so promptly grown to its perfection. Having so little time to last, and having begun so late, for we were both grown men, and he a few years older than I, it could not lose time and conform to the pattern of mild and regular

*Étienne de la Boétie.

9

friendships, which need so many precautions in the form of long preliminary association. Our friendship has no other model than itself, and can be compared only with itself. It is not one special consideration, nor two, nor three, nor four, nor a thousand: it is I know not what quintessence of all this mixture, which, having seized my whole will, led it to plunge and lose itself in his; which, having seized his whole will, led it to plunge and lose itself in mine, with equal hunger, equal rivalry. I say lose, in truth, for neither of us reserved anything for himself, nor was anything either his or mine. . . .

This perfect friendship I speak of is indivisible: each one gives himself so wholly to his friend that he has nothing left to distribute elsewhere; on the contrary, he is sorry that he is not double, triple, or quadruple, and that he has not several souls and several wills, to confer them all on this one object. Common friendships can be divided up: one may love in one man his beauty, in another his easygoing ways, in another liberality, in one paternal love, in another brotherly love, and so forth; but this friendship that possesses the soul and rules it with absolute sovereignty cannot possibly be double. If two called for help at the same time, which one would you run to? If they demanded conflicting service of you, how would you arrange it? If one confided to your silence a thing that would be useful for the other to know, how would you extricate yourself? A single dominant friendship dissolves all other obligations. The secret I have sworn to reveal to no other man, I can impart without perjury to the one who is not another man: he is myself. It is a great enough miracle to be doubled, and those who talk of tripling themselves do not realize the loftiness of the thing: nothing is extreme that can be matched. And he who supposes that of two men I love one just as much as the other, and that they love each other and me just as much as I love them, multiplies into a fraternity the most singular and unified of all things, of which even a single one is the rarest thing in the world to find. . . .

The ancient Menander declared that man happy who had been able to meet even the shadow of a friend. He was certainly right to say so, especially if he spoke from experience. For in truth, if I compare all the rest of my life—though by the grace of God I have spent it pleasantly, comfortably, and, except for the loss of such a friend, free from any grievous affliction, and full of tranquillity of mind, having accepted my natural and original advantages without seeking other ones—if I compare it all, I say, with the four years which were granted me to enjoy the sweet company and society of that man, it is nothing but smoke, nothing but dark and dreary night. Since the day I lost him,

> Which I shall ever recall with pain,
> Ever with reverence—thus, Gods, did you ordain—
>
> VIRGIL

I only drag on a weary life. And the very pleasures that come my way, instead of consoling me, redouble my grief for his loss. We went halves in everything; it seems to me that I am robbing him of his share,

> Nor may I rightly taste of pleasures here alone,
> —So I resolved—when he who shared my life is gone.
>
> TERENCE

I was already so formed and accustomed to being a second self everywhere that only half of me seems to be alive now.

> Since an untimely blow has snatched away
> Part of my soul, why then do I delay,
> I the remaining part, less dear than he,
> And not entire surviving? The same day
> Brought ruin equally to him and me.
>
> HORACE

There is no action or thought in which I do not miss him, as indeed he would have missed me. For just as he surpassed me infinitely in every other ability and virtue, so he did in the duty of friendship.

> Why should I be ashamed or exercise control
> Mourning so dear a soul?
> Brother, your death has left me sad and lone;
> Since you departed all our joys have gone,
> Which while you lived your sweet affection fed;
> My pleasures all lie shattered, with you dead.
> Our soul is buried, mine with yours entwined;
> And since then I have banished from my mind
> My studies, and my spirit's dearest joys.
> Shall I ne'er speak to you, or hear your voice?
> Or see your face, more dear than life to me?
> At least I'll love you to eternity.
>
> CATULLUS
> *(Trans. Donald Frame)*

From *La Nouvelle Héloïse* by Jean Jacques Rousseau

Claire to her fiancé, Monsieur d'Orbe:

My father told me this morning about the conversation he had with you yesterday. It pleases me that all is proceeding in the direction of what you call your good fortune. You know that I hope it will also be mine. You have won my regard and my amity, and the tenderest sentiments of my heart are also yours. But do not be deceived in this; as a female I am a sort of monster, and I know not why my nature is so capricious, but my friendship outweighs my love. Whenever I say that my Julie is dearer to me than you are, you merely laugh—despite the fact that nothing could be truer. Julie understands this so well that she feels more jealousy for your sake than you do, and while you seem perfectly happy, she always complains that I do not love you enough. Moreover, I have such deep affection for anyone that is dear to her that you and her lover both occupy almost an identical spot in my heart, although there is some distinction: I feel only friendship for him though it is more intense; while for you I believe I feel some love, though it is more calm. All of this must seem so ambiguous that it would upset the composure of a man who is given to jealousy, but I imagine that you will not be extremely upset. . . .

Whatever happens, I tell you I will not discuss marriage until I see that Julie has peace of mind and that her tears will not irrigate the knot that binds us. Therefore, sir, if you really love me, your interest in this situation will give way to your generosity. . . .

Claire to Julie:

. . . If Monsieur d'Orbe loves me, he must console himself. I feel great esteem for his character and I also have some affection for his person. But although I would be sorry to lose such an honest gentleman, compared to my Julie, he is as nothing to me. Tell me, my child, does the soul have a sex? Truly, I hardly feel that mine does. Perhaps I have fancies, but not much love. A husband might be useful, but to me he would always be nothing more than a husband, and as long as I am free and not too unattractive, I can find one of those anywhere in the world.

Since my childhood I have felt attached to you by a habit that has been as sweet as it has been unconquerable. There is no one else that I love perfectly, and if I must break a few ties by following you, your example will encourage me. I will say to myself, "I do as Julie does," and I will think I am justified.

Julie to Claire:

My cousin, my benefactor, my friend, I come from the ends of the earth, and the heart I bring back is full of you. Four times I have crossed the equator. Two hemispheres I have passed. Four quarters of the world I have seen. The distance of its diameter I have put between us. I have circled the whole globe, but I have not been able to escape you for an instant. We can try as much as we like to run away from what we hold dear; but its image, which is far quicker than the oceans and the winds, will follow us to the ends of the universe, and wherever we go we carry with us that which gives us life. I have suffered exceedingly. I have seen others suffer even more. How many unfortunate ones have I seen die! Alas, they held life so dear! And I, I have survived them all. Perhaps there is really not much reason to pity me. I felt the miseries of my companions more than my own. I saw them completely devastated. Their suffering was much greater than mine, for I was able to tell myself, "I may be wretched here, but there is a corner of the earth where I am happy and in peace."

To the *Evening Post* by William Cullen Bryant
Keene, New Hampshire, July 13, 1843

I passed a few days in the valley of one of those streams of northern Vermont, which find their way into Champlain. If I were permitted to draw aside the veil of private life, I would briefly give you the singular and to me most interesting history of two maiden ladies who dwell in this valley. I would tell you how, in their youthful days, they took each other as companions for life, and how this union, no less sacred to them than the tie of marriage, has subsisted, in uninterrupted harmony, for forty years, during which they have shared each other's occupations and pleasures and works of charity while in health, and watched over each other tenderly in sickness; for sickness has made long and frequent visits to their dwelling. I could tell you how they slept on the same pillow and had a common purse, and adopted each other's relations, and how one of them, more enterprising and spirited in her temper than the other, might be said to represent the male head of the family, and took upon herself their transactions with the world without, until her health failed, and she was tended by her gentle companion, as a fond wife attends her invalid husband. I would tell you of their dwelling, encircled with roses, which now in the days of their broken health, bloom wild without their tendance, and I would speak of the friendly attentions which their neighbors, people of kind hearts and simple manners, seem to take pleasure in bestowing upon them, but I have already said more than I fear they will forgive me for, if this should ever meet their eyes, and I must leave the subject.

From *The Friendships of Women* (1867) by William Rounseville Alger

School-girl friendships are a proverb in all mouths. They form one of the largest classes of those human attachments whose idealizing power and sympathetic interfusions glorify the world and sweeten existence. With what quick trust and ardor, what eager relish, these susceptible creatures, before whom heavenly illusions float, surrender themselves to each other, taste all the raptures of confidential conversation, lift veil after veil till every secret is bare, and, hand in hand, with glowing feet, tread the paths of paradise! Perhaps a more impassioned portrayal of this kind of union is not to be found in literature than the picture in *A Midsummer Night's Dream,* which Shakespeare makes Helena hold before Hermia, when the death of their love was threatened by the appearance of Lysander and Demetrius:

> Is all the counsel that we two have shared,
> The sisters' vows, the hours that we have spent,
> When we have chid the hasty-footed time
> For parting us,—O! is all forgot?
> All school-days' friendship, childhood innocence?
> We, Hermia, like two artificial gods,
> Have with our needles created both one flower,
> Both on one sampler, sitting on one cushion,
> Both warbling of one song, both in one key,
> As if our hands, our sides, voices, and minds
> Had been incorporate. So we grew together,
> Like to a double cherry, seeming parted,
> But yet an union in partition,
> Two lovely berries moulded on one stem:
> So with two seeming bodies, but one heart;
> Two of the first, like coats in heraldry,
> Due but to one and crowned with one crest.
> And will you rend our ancient love asunder,
> To join with men in scorning your poor friend?

Romantically warm and generous as the friendships of school-boys are, those of school-girls are much more so. They are more purposed and absorbing, more sedulously cultivated and consciously important. School-girls often have their distinctly defined and well-understood degrees of intimacy,—their first, their second, their third, friend. Thus a thousand little dramas are daily played, full of delights and woes, of which outsiders, who have no key to them, never so much as dream. Probably no chapter of sentiment in modern fashionable life is so intense and rich as that which covers the experience of budding maidens at school. In their mental caresses, spiritual nuptials, their thoughts kiss each other, and more than all the blessedness the world will ever give them is foreshadowed. They have not yet reached the age for a public record or confession of their pangs and raptures; so these dramas are for the most part only guessed at. But keener agonies, more delicious passages, are nowhere else known than in the bosoms of innocent school-girls, in the lacerations or fruitions of their first consciously given affections. A startling illustration has come to the knowledge of the writer just as he is penning these words. Two girls, about sixteen years old, attending a private school together, in one of the chief cities of the United States, formed a strong attachment to each other, and were almost inseparable. The father of one of the girls, for some reason, had a dislike for the other, and forbade his daughter to associate with her. The two friends preferred death to separation. They took laudanum, and were found dead in each other's arms. What element of romance or tragedy ever known, is not every day experienced, all about us, under the thin disguise of commonplace?

No doubt there is often something a little grotesque or laughable in these youthful relations. An anecdote will illustrate it, and, at the same time, convey the corrective moral. There were a couple of school-girl friends, each of whom loved to do and experience whatever the other did or experienced. One of them accidentally set fire to the window-curtains in her chamber, and the house came near being burned down. She wrote word to her friend of the dangerous accident. The other at once proceeded carefully to set fire to the curtains in her chamber, so as to be just like her friend in every thing. One may well reprove, with a complacent smile of superiority, the folly of the act; but the sentiment underneath should never be ridiculed.

A harrowing instance of the suffering consequent on the overstrung feelings of girls is furnished by Margaret Fuller in the story of "Mariana," a vivid autobiographic leaf inserted in her *Summer on the Lakes*. Much precious wisdom is learned, many cruel scars are received, in these sincere, though often fickle, connections,—these inebriating preludes to the sober strain of existence. There is a touch of sadness in the thought that the earliest friendship of youth must so frequently fade and cease. But there is comfort for that sadness in the knowledge that the fair flowers of April are but precursors of those which June shall fill with the richer fragrance of a more royal fire.

WOMEN'S WRITING
ON ROMANTIC FRIENDSHIP

Katherine Fowler Philips
(1631–64)

When Katherine Fowler was sixteen years old her family married her to a man of fifty-four, a not-uncommon arrangement in the seventeenth and eighteenth centuries. Fortunately for her, her husband was indulgent and even encouraging of her literary interests. He also did not demand her presence a great deal. James Philips lived much of the time on the remote west coast of Wales while his young wife went off to London and even spent a year in Dublin without him in order to be near a female friend. All of her most important emotional relationships appear to have been with other women.

In keeping with a neoclassical tradition Philips gave herself and her friends pastoral names in her poetry. She appears as Orinda. Her first love, Mary Awbrey, the subject of many of her poems, is Rosania. Rosania's successor, Anne Owen, is Lucasia. Elizabeth Boyle, with whom she began a relationship shortly before her death, is Celimena. The men of her literary circle who read these love poems from woman to woman admired them greatly. Jeremy Taylor dedicated his discourse "Offices and Measures of Friendship" to her. Abraham Cowley celebrated her relationship with Lucasia in a poem of praise to "Orinda":

> The fame of friendship which so long had told
> Of three or four illustrious Names of old,
> Till hoarse and weary of the tale she grew,

Rejoyces now to have got a new,
A new and more surprising story,
Of fair Lucasia's and Orinda's glory.

More than a century later, in 1817 (when romantic friendship was still an accepted social institution), John Keats was so impressed with Philips's poem to Rosania, "To Mrs. M.A. at Parting," that he copied it out and sent it to his friend John Reynolds with praise for Philips's delicacy of thought and mastery of seventeenth-century rhythm.

Katherine Philips's first great love, "Rosania," was the "Soul of my Soul, my Crown, my Joy, my Friend," to whom she had been close since girlhood. When Rosania married, the relationship cooled though they maintained amicable contact. Philips speaks of her loss of Mary Awbrey Montague in "To Rosania, now Mrs. Montague, Being with Her," describing her frustrations with their occasional visits and in effect putting an end to their love because of Rosania's betrayal: "Thy absence I could easier find,/ Provided thou wert well and kind,/ Than such a Presence as is this,/ Made up of snatches of my bliss."

Philips soon found another romantic friend, as she says in "On Rosania's Apostasy and Lucasia's Friendship," in which she specifically depicts Lucasia as a replacement for her old love and vows even more devotion to the new: "Hail, Great Lucasia, thou shalt doubly shine,/ What was Rosania's own is now twice thine." Another poem about Lucasia, "To the Truly Noble Mrs. Anne Owen, on my First Approaches" uses the language of seduction to describe Philips's wooing of the other woman. In a poem written when they were to be separated for a time, "Orinda to Lucasia Parting, October 1661, London," Philips laments: "Adieu, dear Object of my Love's excess,/ And with thee all my hopes of happiness." Many of these poems that were seen by Philips's contemporaries as pure expressions of idealized, platonic love are imbued with ambivalence, anger, jealousy, and sensuality such as is generally more consonant with eros than friendship as we conceive such a relationship in our era. But it is apparent that the seventeenth century did not make the kinds of distinctions that have been common to the twentieth century.

Philips's relationship with Lucasia continued for ten years until, like Mary Awbrey, Lucasia decided to marry. Philips made no secret about her displeasure over yet another desertion by a beloved woman. She had been shocked to discover that Lucasia's husband was not charmed by their friendship (though he was tolerant enough to permit her to accompany them to Ireland, where she stayed for a year in order to be near Lucasia). She wrote to a male friend, Sir Charles Cotterell, about her annoyance over Lucasia's marriage:

I see now by Experience that one may love too much, and offend more by a too fond Sincerity, than by a careless Indifferency. . . . I find too there are few Friendships in the World Marriage-proof; especially when the Person our Friend marries has not a Soul particularly capable of the Tenderness of that Endearment, and solicitous of advancing the noble Instances of it. . . . [S]uch a Temper is so rarely found, that we may generally conclude the Marriage of a Friend to be the Funeral of a Friendship.

As upset as she was over Lucasia's breach of their dyad, Philips eventually "fell in love" yet again, in 1664, with "Celimena," to whom, in her poem "To the Lady E. Boyle" she offered her "trivial heart" with self-pity and trepidation:

> For it has been by tenderness
> Already so much bruis'd,
> That at your Altars I may guess
> It will be but refus'd.
> For never Deity did prize
> A torn and maimed Sacrifice.

There was no time for the relationship to come to fruition. Philips died that year of smallpox, at the age of thirty-three.

FURTHER READING: *Poems by the Most Deservedly Admired Mrs. Katherine Philips, The Matchless Orinda* . . . (London: Herringman, 1667). Harriette Andreadis, "The Sapphic-Platonics of Katherine Philips," *Signs*, 15: I (Autumn 1989), 34–60. Elaine Hobby, "Katherine Philips: Seventeenth Century Lesbian Poet," *What Lesbians Do in Books*, eds. Elaine Hobby and Chris White (London: The Women's Press, 1991), pp. 183–204. Philip Webster Souers, *The Matchless Orinda* (Cambridge: Harvard University Press, 1931).

TO MRS. MARY AWBREY

> Soul of my Soul, my Joy, my Crown, my Friend,
> A name which all the rest doth comprehend;
> How happy are we now, whose Souls are grown,
> By an incomparable mixture, one:
> Whose well-acquainted Minds are now so near
> As Love, or Vows, or Friendship can endear?
> I have no thought but what's to thee reveal'd,
> Nor thou desire that is from me conceal'd.

Thy Heart locks up my Secrets richly set,
And my Breast is thy private Cabinet.
Thou shed'st no tear but what my moisture lent,
And if I sigh, it is thy breath is spent.
United thus, what Horrour can appear
Worthy our Sorrow, Anger, or our Fear?
Let the dull World alone to talk and fight,
And with their vast Ambitions Nature fright;
Let them despise so Innocent a Flame,
While Envy, Pride, and Faction play their game:
But we by Love sublim'd so high shall rise,
To pity Kings and Conquerours despise,
Since we that Sacred Union have engrost,
Which they and all the factious World have lost.

TO MRS. M. A. AT PARTING

1

I have examin'd and do find,
   Of all that favour me,
There's none I grieve to leave behind
   But only, only thee.
To part with thee I needs must die,
Could parting sep'rate thee and I.

2

But neither Chance nor Complement
   did element our Love;
'Twas sacred Sympathy was lent
   Us from the Quire above.
That Friendship Fortune did create,
Still fears a wound from Time or Fate.

3

Our chang'd and mingled Souls are grown
   To such acquaintance now,
That if each would resume their own,
   Alas! we know not how.
We have each other so engrost,
That each is in the Union lost.

4

And thus we can no Absence know,
　Nor shall we be confin'd;
Our active Souls will daily go
　To learn each other's mind.
Nay, should we never meet to Sense,
Our Souls would hold Intelligence.

5

Inspired with a Flame Divine,
　I scorn to court a stay;
For from that noble Soul of thine
　I ne'er can be away.
But I shall weep when thou dost grieve;
Nor can I die whilst thou dost live.

6

By my own temper I shall guess
　At thy felicity,
And only like my happiness
　Because it pleaseth thee.
Our hearts at any time will tell,
If thou, or I, be sick, or well.

7

All Honour sure I must pretend,
　All that is Good or Great;
She that would be Rosania's Friend,
　Must be at least compleat.
If I have any bravery,
'Tis cause I have so much of thee.

8

Thy Liege Soul in me shall lie,
　And all thy thoughts reveal;
Then back again with mine shall flie,
　And thence to me shall steal.
Thus still to one another tend;
Such is the sacred Name of Friend.

9

Thus our twin-Souls in one shall grow,
　And teach the World new Love,
Redeem the Age and Sex, and shew

A Flame Fate dares not move:
And courting Death to be our friend,
Our Lives together too shall end.

10

A Dew shall dwell upon our Tomb
 Of such a quality,
That fighting Armies, thither come,
 Shall reconciled be.
We'll ask no Epitaph, but say
 ORINDA and ROSANIA.

FRIENDSHIPS MYSTERY,
TO MY DEAREST LUCASIA

Come, my Lucasia, since we see
 That Miracles Men's Faith do move,
By wonder and by prodigy
 To the dull angry World let's prove
 There's a Religion in our Love.

2

For though we were design'd t' agree,
 That Fate no liberty destroys,
But our Election is as free
 As Angels, who with greedy choice
 Are yet determin'd to their joys.

3

Our hearts are doubled by the loss,
 Here Mixture is Addition grown;
We both diffuse, and both ingross:
 And we whose minds are so much one,
 Never, yet ever are alone.

4

We court our own Captivity
 Than Thrones more great and innocent:
'Twere banishment to be set free,
Since we wear fetters whose intent
Not Bondage is but Ornament.

5

Divided joys are tedious found,
 And griefs united easier grow:

We are our selves but by rebound,
    And all our Titles shuffled so,
Both Princes, and both Subjects too.

6

Our Hearts are mutual Victims laid,
    While they (such power in Friendship lies)
Are Altars, Priests, and Off'rings made:
    And each Heart which thus kindly dies,
    Grows deathless by the Sacrifice.

TO MY EXCELLENT LUCASIA,
ON OUR FRIENDSHIP

I did not live until this time
    Crown'd my felicity,
When I could say without a crime,
    I am not thine, but thee.

This carcass breath'd, and walkt, and slept,
    So that the world believ'd
There was a soul the motions kept;
    But they were all deceiv'd.

For as a watch by art is wound
    To motion, such was mine:
But never had Orinda found
    A soul till she found thine;

Which now inspires, cures and supplies,
    And guides my darkened breast:
For thou art all that I can prize,
    My joy, my life, my rest.

No bridegroom's nor crown-conqueror's mirth
    To mine compar'd can be:
They have but pieces of the earth,
    I've all the world in thee.

Then let our flames still light and shine,
    And no false fear controul,
As innocent as our design,
    Immortal as our soul.

Aphra Behn
(1640–89)

Little is known for certain of the life of the mysterious Aphra Behn, the first woman in England to have made her living by her pen. She was married briefly but widowed at the age of twenty-five. She spent some time in Surinam, where she observed the injustices of slavery. In 1666 she worked as a spy in Belgium for the Restoration court of Charles II. In 1668 she was thrown into debtors' prison in London.

By 1670 Behn began making money through her writing with the production of her first play, *The Forc'd Marriage.* This was followed by more than a dozen successful plays, though she also demanded, as she said in one poem, to assert "my masculine part, the poet in me." In addition to writing drama and poetry she was the author of what some critics deem to be the first novel in English, *Oroonoko; or The Royal Slave* (1688).

Her work, and apparently her life too, often challenged convention to such an extent that her contemporaries described her as "not a lady" and "among the rakes of her day." Her writing was often concerned with feminist themes, including pleas for the more serious education of women and the acceptance of women writers, as well as witty insistences, in poems such as "The Willing Mistress" and "The Disappointment," on a woman's right to (hetero)sexual pleasure.

Her love poems to other women, however, which appeared especially in her volume *Lycidus* (1688), may not have been viewed as presenting particularly significant challenges to the prejudices of her day. Her poem "To My Lady Morland at Tunbridge" was even rewritten with only slight alterations as "To Mrs. Harsenet . . . ," suggesting that Behn really saw such an address of intense admiration from one woman to another, in which the speaker "much a Lover grew," as being consonant with socially approved behavior and in no way unconventional.

Yet Behn also seems to play with such conventions of romantic friendship in her poetry by hinting at the possibility of going beyond them. In "A Song. By Mrs. A.B." in which the speaker identifies herself as female through the title, she asks for the same intimacies that Iris allows her male lover. In her poetic address to the hermaphroditic Clarinda, Behn teasingly suggests why she could so boldly request such favors. After all, society agreed that two women "might Love, and yet be innocent/ For sure no crime [that is, illicit sexual congress]" could be committed if no male was involved. "To the Fair Clarinda . . ." provides a provocative hint that

"romantic friends" may have sometimes laughed at the shield that convention allowed them in relationships that we would describe as "lesbian."

FURTHER READING: *The Works of Aphra Behn*, 6 vols., ed. Montague Summers
(1915; reprint, New York: Benjamin Blom, 1967). Judith Kagan Gardiner, "Aphra Behn:
Sexuality and Self-Respect," *Women's Studies*, 7: 1/2 (1980). Angeline Goreau,
Reconstructing Aphra: A Social Biography of Aphra Behn (New York: Dial, 1980).

TO MY LADY MORLAND AT TUNBRIDGE

As when a Conqu'rour does in Triumph come,
And proudly leads the vanquish'd Captives home,
The Joyful People croud in ev'ry Street,
And with loud shouts of Praise the Victor greet;
While some whom Chance or Fortune kept away,
Desire at least the Story of the Day;
How brave the Prince, how gay the Chariot was,
How beautiful he look'd, with what a Grace;
Whether upon his Head he Plumes did wear;
Or if a Wreath of Bays adorn'd his Hair:
They hear 'tis wondrous fine, and long much more
To see the *Hero* then they did before.
So when the Marvels by Report I knew,
Of how much Beauty, *Cloris,* dwelt in you;
How many *Slaves* your Conqu'ring Eyes had won,
And how the gazing Crowd admiring throng:
I wish'd to see, and much a Lover grew
Of so much Beauty, though my Rival too.
I came and saw, and blest my Destiny;
I found it Just you should out-Rival me.
'Twas at the Altar, where more Hearts were giv'n
To you that day, than were address'd to Heav'n.
The Rev'rend Man whose Age and Mystery
Had rendred Youth and Beauty Vanity,
By fatal Chance casting his Eyes your way,
Mistook the duller Bus'ness of the Day,
Forgot the Gospel, and began to Pray.
Whilst the Enamour'd Crowd that near you prest,
Receiving *Darts* which none could e'er resist,
Neglected the Mistake o'th' Love-sick Priest.
Ev'n my Devotion, *Cloris,* you betray'd,
And I to Heaven no other Petition made,

But that you might all other Nymphs out-do
In Cruelty as well as Beauty too.
I call'd *Amyntas* Faithless *Swain* before,
But now I find 'tis Just he should Adore.
Not to love you, a wonder sure would be,
Greater then all his Perjuries to me.
And whilst I Blame him, I Excuse him too;
Who would not venture Heav'n to purchase you?
But Charming *Cloris,* you too meanly prize
The more deserving Glories of your Eyes,
If you permit him on an Amorous score,
To be your *Slave,* who was my *Slave* before.
He oft has Fetters worn, and can with ease
Admit 'em or dismiss 'em when he please.
A Virgin-Heart you merit, that ne'er found
It could receive, till from your Eyes, the *Wound;*
A Heart that nothing but your Force can fear,
And own a *Soul* as Great as you are Fair.

A SONG.
By Mrs. A. B.

While, *Iris,* I at distance gaze,
    And feed my greedy eyes,
That wounded heart, that dyes for you,
    Dull gazing can't suffice;
Hope is the Food of Love-sick minds,
    On that alone 'twill Feast,
The nobler part which Loves refines,
    No other can digest.

In vain, too nice and Charming Maid,
    I did suppress my Cares;
In vain my rising sighs I stay'd,
    And stop'd my falling tears;
The Flood would swell, the Tempest rise,
    As my despair came on;
When from her Lovely cruel Eyes,
    I found I was undone.

Yet at your feet while thus I lye,
    And languish by your Eyes,

'Tis far more glorious here to dye,
　　Than gain another Prize.
Here let me sigh, here let me gaze,
　　And wish at least to find
As raptur'd nights, and tender days,
　　As he to whom you're kind.

TO THE FAIR CLARINDA,
WHO MADE LOVE TO ME,
IMAGIN'D MORE THAN WOMAN.
BY MRS. B.

Fair lovely Maid, or if that Title be
Too weak, too Feminine for Nobler thee,
Permit a Name that more Approaches Truth:
And let me call thee, Lovely Charming Youth.
This last will justifie my soft complaint,
While that may serve to lessen my constraint;
And without Blushes I the Youth persue,
When so much beauteous Woman is in view.
Against thy Charms we struggle but in vain
With thy deluding Form thou giv'st us pain,
While the bright Nymph betrays us to the Swain.
In pity to our Sex sure thou wert sent,
That we might Love, and yet be Innocent:
For sure no Crime with thee we can commit;
Or if we shou'd—thy Form excuses it.
For who, that gathers fairest Flowers believes
A Snake lies hid beneath the Fragrant Leaves.

　　Thou beauteous Wonder of a different kind,
Soft *Cloris* with the dear *Alexis* join'd;
When e'r the Manly part of thee, wou'd plead
Thou tempts us with the Image of the Maid,
While we the noblest Passions do extend
The Love to *Hermes, Aphrodite* the Friend.

Sor Juana Inés de la Cruz
[Juana de Asbaje y Ramírez de Santillana]
(c. 1648–95)

The seventeenth-century Colonial Mexican writer Sor Juana Inés de la Cruz was a nun of the Order of St. Jerome. She appears to have entered the convent at least partly because life as a nun gave her the leisure and opportunity to study and write, which she would not have had had she chosen to marry. She was able to keep a library of some 4,000 volumes, one of the largest private libraries in Colonial Mexico, and to conduct scientific experiments and write poetry in her cell. She was even able to conduct a literary salon in her convent that included members of the court.

Sor Juana Inés's intellectual enthusiasm as well as her feminism and social conscience began early. She had learned to read at the age of three, and when she was seven years old she had fantasies of entering the university in male disguise. The traditional female role was never comfortable for her. In one poem she proclaimed, with regard to her entrance into the convent:

> . . . I came here
> So that, even if I am a woman,
> No one could discover it.
> . . . In Latin,
> Married women alone are called
> *Uxor,* or woman,
> And *virgin* is said of both men and women;
> The word is neither masculine nor feminine.
> Therefore, it is not just
> To deem me "woman."
> I am not a woman,
> For I will serve as wife to no one.
> I know only that my body
> Is neither one gender nor the other,
> But is neuter or abstract,
> The dwelling of my soul.

Injustice or forced servility, whether of wives or the socially powerless, disturbed her greatly. Her prose writing is concerned with the rights not only of women but also of slaves and Indians.

Sor Juana Inés's remarkable love poetry was written primarily to two women. Her first beloved was Leonor Carreto, the Marquise de Mancera, whose husband, the Viceroy of Mexico, reported, without rancor, that the Marquise "could scarcely live a moment without her Juana Inés." The Marquise de Mancera is "Laura" in many of Sor Juana Inés's love poems. Some time after the Marquise de Mancera's death, Sor Juana Inés wrote love poetry to Luisa Manrique de Lara y Gonzaga, who was the Marquise de la Laguna and the Countess of Paredes. She appears under the pastoral names of "Lysi" or "Filis" in Sor Juana Inés's poetry. It was she who arranged for Sor Juana Inés's volume of poems *Castalian Inundation* to be published in Spain in 1689. The book, an homage to "Filis," made Sor Juana Inés a well-known literary figure in her day. She came to be called "the tenth muse."

Contemporary literary historians are sometimes perplexed about the nature of the passionate poetry Sor Juana Inés wrote to other women, since it is hard to imagine an affectional and sensual space, such as romantic friendship, that no longer exists today. Octavio Paz, for example, attempts to explain that Sor Juana Inés's expressions of same-sex love may be seen as merely polite compliments to the noblewomen who were her patrons—though he is forced to admit that the poems "achieve the intensity that distinguishes authentic passion from rhetorical affect." Other scholars place Sor Juana Inés's love poetry in the Provençal troubadour tradition. They point out that the social distance between Sor Juana Inés and her beloved noblewomen would have signaled a guarantee that whatever passion Sor Juana Inés was expressing in words would probably never be consummated carnally.

However, there is another way to read this verse, one which Sor Juana Inés apparently hoped her audience would employ. It is, of course, impossible to know whether she was worried that her society would see her love poems to the noblewomen as expressions of actual or potential carnality. But writing in a century that preceded the one in which terms such as "romantic friendship" and "*l'amitié amoureuse*" were coined, she characterized the poetry as being in the "neoplatonic" tradition—an explanation that Renaissance male authors such as Montaigne depended on in their presentation of their own writing about same-sex love. The anonymous author of the "Prologue to the Reader" of her first published volume *Castalian Inundation* (Paz speculates he was a Jesuit priest) emphasizes that explanation by observing that the women to whom Sor Juana Inés wrote her passionate verse "generated in the poet a love utterly pure and ardent."

FURTHER READING: Sor Juana Inés de la Cruz, *The Answer/ La Respuesta*, commentary and translation by Electa Arenal and Amanda Powell (New York: The Feminist Press, 1994). Fredo Arias de la Canal, *Intento de Psicoanalisis de Juana Inés y Otros*

Ensayos Sorjuanistas (Mexico: Frente de Afirmación Hispanista, 1988). Stephanie Merrim, *Feminist Perspectives on Sor Juana Inés de la Cruz* (Detroit: Wayne State University Press, 1991). Octavio Paz, *Sor Juana, or The Traps of Faith* (Cambridge, MA: Harvard University Press, 1988).

MY DIVINE LYSI
To the Marquise de la Laguna

Divine one, my Lysi:
Forgive me if I dare
To call you mine
Though I do not merit to be called "yours."

I believe it is not presumption
To address you thus—
For you are so radiant
That my daring could not dim you.

It is merely the tongue that misspeaks
When one states that the master's empire,
His very domain,
Belongs to the slave.

"My King," says the vassal;
"My jail," says the prisoner;
And the humblest of slaves
Calls his master "his" without offense.

So, when I call you mine
I have no pretense
That all will think you are mine.
It means only that I want to be yours.

I saw you; but that is enough:
In discoursing of fires
It is enough to point to the cause
Without dwelling on the blame of the effect.

To see you so distant
Does not deter my daring;
No deity is secure
From the arrogant flight of the mind.

And though there may be others more deserving,
The most humble valley

And the loftiest mountain
Are equidistant from Heaven.

Finally, I plead guilty
Of adoring you;
If you wish to punish me
That punishment will be my reward.

HAPPY EASTER, MY LADY

To convey my Happy Easter wishes to the excellent
Countess of Paredes, on the occasion of the birthday
of the reigning queen.

Happy Easter, my Lady,
Only your mirror can reflect your splendor,
For you are the proof of such heaven
Which only God can grant in its entirety.

Since your sun and your reflection
Cover the moon and not me, poor me.
Poor me, who has not seen you in so long,
Who feels such emptiness for want of you,

The anguish of desire,
The fasting of the mind.
My sense of touch, of taste,
Of sight have no object.

Truly, my sweet love,
I do not exaggerate:
Without you, even my own speech
Seems foreign to me.

For the wanting of you
Exceeds all the torture
That cruelty abetted by skill
Could invent.

If Tyranny had knowledge
Of so beautiful an instrument
She would need neither tenterhooks,
Straps, nor chains.

Knives would be useless,
The rope superfluous,

Lashes bland
And fires lukewarm.

But if you dwelled
Among the condemned,
They would find heaven in your presence
And in your absence, hell.

Enough! Easter does not call
For such laments;
One might think that the Service
Is embedded in my body.

May you live long, my Lady,
May you rejoice in your years, as I wish you to;
This is, though a common phrase,
The greatest praise.

Because the cycle of years and Easters
Are alike,
For all of us
Easter is a renewal.

I give to my two sovereigns
Whose feet I kiss
Simply
The purest affection,

And to God, my Lady,
Until the vision of your heaven
Revives me, for it is Easter
When the dead are brought back to life.

The Ladies of Llangollen
[Lady Eleanor Butler (1737–1829)]
[The Honourable Sarah Ponsonby (1755–1831)]

Lady Eleanor Butler and the Honourable Sarah Ponsonby are one of the great "success stories" of eighteenth-century romantic friendship. Unlike most romantic friends of their era, they not only dreamed of a life devoted to each other, but they were able to live it. They resisted their families' attempts to marry them off, commit them to a convent, imprison them until they relented, and starve them into submission. They donned men's clothing to escape the major dangers to which women were prone on the road, and they fled their native Ireland for Llangollen Vale in North Wales. They managed finally to get small stipends from their families, and Sarah eventually received a pension from the King. In Llangollen they built a shrine to romantic friendship—a charming cottage and garden—where they lived together for more than fifty years, until Eleanor's death at the age of ninety-two.

They were the Gertrude Stein and Alice B. Toklas of their age. Luminaries came from all over Great Britain and the Continent to pay homage to their brilliant conversational wit and extraordinary housekeeping. They numbered among their distinguished guests and friends William Wordsworth, Sir Walter Scott, Edmund Burke, Hester Thrale Piozzi, Comtesse de Genlis, Lady Caroline Lamb, and the Duke of Wellington. Their poet friends were moved to pen verse tributes to their relationship. Wordsworth, for example, after visiting them in 1824, wrote:

> Glyn Cafaillgaroch, in the Cambrian tongue,
> In ours the Vale of Friendship, let this spot
> Be nam'd where faithful to a low roof'd Cot
> On Deva's banks, ye have abode so long,
> Sisters in love, a love allowed to climb
> Ev'n on this earth, above the reach of time.

From 1785 to 1821 Eleanor kept a diary of their daily life together. References to Sarah as "my Heart's darling," "my sweet love," "my Sally," "my Beloved" abound. Might their relationship have been sexual? Specific evidence of that is lacking from the diary, though some biographers have suggested that the subject of illnesses, such as headaches, may have served as conscious or unconscious encoding for sexuality, as in Eleanor's journal entry, "I kept my bed all day with one of my dreadful Headaches. My Sally, my Tender, my Sweet Love, lay beside me holding and supporting my Head." Those scholars who argue for erotic possibilities in the Ladies' relationship also suggest that their contemporaries suspected that they were sapphists (and of the "butch and femme" variety). They point to the innuendo in a newspaper article, entitled "Extraordinary Female Affection," that appeared in a Welsh paper in 1790:

> Miss Butler, who is of the Ormonde family, had several offers of
> marriage, all of which she rejected. Miss Ponsonby, her particular
> friend and companion, was supposed to be the bar to all matri-

monial union, it was thought proper to separate them, and Miss Butler was confined.

The two Ladies, however, found means to elope together. . . .

Miss Butler is tall and masculine, she wears always a riding habit, hangs her hat with the air of a sportsman in the hall, and appears in all respects as a young man, if we except the petticoats which she still retains.

Miss Ponsonby, on the contrary, is polite and effeminate, fair and beautiful.

Most of the Ladies' friends and acquaintances, however, preferred to see Eleanor and Sarah as the embodiment of the highest ideals of purely spiritual love. Edmund Burke described them as the esteemed "of all who know how to esteem honour, friendship, principle, and dignity of thinking." Hester Thrale (an eighteenth-century "homophobe" who wished in her diary that the French sapphists might be thrown "into Mount Vesuvius") called the Ladies "fair and noble recluses" and "charming cottagers."

Of course, the opinions of their contemporaries do little to establish one way or another the true nature of their relationship. Perhaps somewhat more conclusive is a poem by Sarah Ponsonby, in which she attempted to distinguish between sexual love and romantic friendship and identified her own feelings with the latter:

By Vulgar Eros long misled
I call'd thee Tyrant, mighty Love!
With idle fear my fancy fled
Nor ev'n thy pleasures wish'd to prove.

Condemn'd at length to wear thy chains,
Trembling I felt and ow'd thy might;
But soon I found my fears were vain,
Soon hugged my chain, and thought it light.

Sarah Ponsonby saw herself, apparently, as a prisoner of "mighty Love," but her beloved jailer bestowed pleasures to be contrasted to those too heavy and frightening pleasures of "Vulgar Eros." Such a distinction is common in the literature of eighteenth-century romantic friendship.

FURTHER READING: *The Hamwood Papers of the Ladies of Llangollen and Caroline Hamilton*, ed. Mrs. G. H. Bell (London: Macmillan, 1930). Colette, *The Pure and the Impure* (1932; Farrar, Straus and Giroux, 1967). Mary Gordon, *Chase of the Wild Goose* (1936; reprint, New York: Arno Press, 1975). Elizabeth Mavor, *The Ladies of Llangollen: A Study in Romantic Friendship* (London: Michael Joseph, 1971).

From *The Hamwood Papers of the Ladies of Llangollen*

1785:

Wednesday, October 12th.—An excellent fire in the Library, candles lighted and an appearance of Content and cheerfulness never to be found but in a Cottage.

Monday, October 17th.—My Love and I spent from Five till Seven in the shrubbery and in the Field endeavouring to talk and walk away our little Sorrows. Sent the woman of Pen-y-coed to Ruabon for our Winter provision of groceries. At seven walked to the Hand to see Mrs. Myddelton. The Company Col. and Mrs. Myddelton, Mr. and Mrs. and Miss Carter, Mr. Robert Myddelton (little Mrs. Jones' elder brother), Miss Lloydde. Declined supping with them.

. . . *Thursday, January 31st. (1788)—* . . . My beloved and I went to the new garden. Reading. Drawing. Read "Davila." Then my beloved read "La Morte d'Abel." Nine till twelve in the bedchamber reading. Old Parkes of the Lyon came up to inform us that Mr. Palmer, my brother's chaplain, had been at their House for a moment on his way to Ireland. Had sent his compliments to us and Butler's Love and Duty, who was settled at Maudlin College, liked it very much and was to dine in the Hall yesterday. Very impertinent in them not to Deliver this message yesterday morning. A day of sweet and delicious retirement.

February 1st.—Three o'clock dinner. Boiled Pork. Peas pudding. Half-past three my beloved and I went to the new garden. Freezing hard. I am much mistaken if there be not a quantity of snow in the sky. I read to my beloved No. 97 of the Rambler written by Richardson, author of those inimitable Books "Pamela," "Clarissa," and "Sir Charles Grandison."

Thursday, April 10th.—Fine evening. Gentle wandering light on the mountains. . . . My beloved and I took a delightful walk, ascended the Hill then descended into the narrow deep valley which leads to Llansantffraid. Steep hills on either side clothed to the summit with wood. The Cyflymen gushing rapidly over the Rocks and hastening to the little Mill of Pengwern. That mill, a wooden bridge, our Landlord's cottage closing the scene at one end, the other terminated by the small hamlet of Blaen Bache, the Berwyn Mountains rising behind. Walked by the brook side to Pengwern. Our Landlady came out with great expectation of joy in her countenance, said she was rejoiced to see us, that she thought it a long while since she had that satisfaction. When we had returned her greeting crossed the large wheatfield, then the Miller's field of Peas, the meadow, crossed the lane, returned hence by our own field.

Wednesday, July 30th.—Writing. Drawing. My beloved and I went the home circuit then visited the waterfall. . . . Met a child gathering wild flowers on a bank. Looked in a Cottage by the brook side. A young woman winding thread, a little boy beside her rocking a Cradle.

Three dinner, boiled mutton. Cauliflowers, mushrooms. Potatoes. Just as we had dined the Letters were brought by Mrs. Kynaston's servant from Mrs. Kynaston, dated The Lyon, to say she and Mr. Kynaston would wait on us this evening, and desiring permission to introduce their friends Mr. and Mrs. Smith. Letter from Mrs. Mytton to say that she and Miss Mytton would dine here to-morrow. Returned our Compliments to Mr. and Mrs. Kynaston. Shall be happy to see them and any of their friends. Evening delicious. While we were expecting them, note from Mr. Lewis of Shrewsbury, acquaintance of the Pigotts, desiring permission for himself and a friend to see this place. Permitted on condition they came immediately. They came. Saw them through the window. One a clergyman, the other a shabby dirty officer. My beloved and I went to meet the Kynastons. They were coming down the street as we were coming up. They introduced Mr. and Mrs. Smith of Havering at Bower in Essex. Conducted them by the Vicar's to Cottage. Lewis and his drunken friend still in the shrubbery. Sat in the Library till this ill-behaved couple were gone.

1807:
. . . *Thursday, October 21st*—My Better half and I rose at five. Went at six to Oswestry. Stopped at the Cross Keys. Sent a messenger to Porkington. Mrs. R. Wingfield came and we three went off. Arrived at the Hall before ten. Were kindly received in the handsome and ancient mansion. Breakfast. Then a tour of the House, office, gardens. Saw the Canary Birds. My Better half and I set out and met Mrs. Powys near the Bridge. Got into her Carriage. Went to Vaughans, then to Eddowes, then to two other filthy Booksellers shops. Then drove to the Council House. Did not alight. Went on to Berwick. Lady Feilding, Miss Powys, Miss Mytton. Luncheon. Mr. Jones powdered and dressed our hair. Mr., Mrs., Miss, Mr. R. and Mr. Charles Wingfield came. Dinner. At twelve Mrs. R. Wingfield and we set out in darkness and rain. One wheel flew off near Aston. Called to the Lodge near the gate. Terrified by the noise, and we made amends. Wheel right, we got to Oswestry. Sat in the parlour of the Cross Keys till the chaise which was to convey Mrs. Wingfield to Porkington was ready. Got home at five in the morning.

Anna Seward
(1747–1809)

As the daughter of a widowed clergyman, Anna Seward's filial obligations gave her an excuse not to marry until her father's death, at which time she was in her forties and therefore excused from matrimony because of her age. From her youth she scoffed at marriage and preferred the company of her female friends and their bluestocking pursuits. As she wrote one girl-hood intimate who was contemplating what Seward thought would be a dubious match, "If he should treat you after marriage with tolerable kind-ness and good nature, it is the best you have reasonably to expect. What counterpoise, in the scale of happiness, can be formed by that *best* against the delights you must renounce in the morning of your youth?" Seward offered her friend what she believed to be a tempting lure to pull her out of the matrimonial snare:

> Return to Lichfield to me for the remainder of the winter! We will banish all mention of Mr. L——. . . . We will read ingenious au-thors, who shall rather give our minds new ideas from the stores of science and observations, than increase the susceptibility of our hearts.

Seward's literary productions brought the attention of several notable admirers in her own day. Sir Walter Scott edited a six-volume edition of her letters and a three-volume edition of her poetry after her death. Erasmus Darwin, who dubbed her "the inventress of the epic elegy," quoted from her poetry at length in his *Botanic Garden*. They accepted the indications in her work of her passionate love of other women as being consonant with the institution of romantic friendship. Seward's writing hints at close at-tachments to Elizabeth Cornwallis, Mrs. Mompesson, Penelope Weston, and a Miss Fern, with whom she lived for several years before her death, and to whom she wrote in 1806, "My health and my heart have need of you."

But the ruling passion (perhaps even obsession) of her life was Honora Sneyd. Honora, who was nine years younger than Anna, lived in the Sew-ard household from childhood to young adulthood, her widowed father having been unable to care for her. When Honora was nineteen her father's circumstances changed, and she went to live with him. Anna observed of that period, "The domestic separation proved very grievous; but still she was in the same town; we were often together; and her heart was unchanged."

Two years later, however, despite Anna's attempts to dissuade her, Honora married Robert Edgeworth, an older recent widower, and all did change between Anna and Honora. One of Anna's twentieth-century biographers, unable to understand eighteenth-century romantic friendship (and unwilling to deal with any implications of lesbian feeling), speculated that Anna was upset over Honora's marriage because she may have desired "to marry Edgeworth herself. She was thirty years old—better suited to him in age and experience than Honora. Was she jealous of the easy success of her foster sister? Would she have snatched away, if she could have done so, the mature yet youthful bridegroom, so providentially released from his years of bondage?" The speculation ignores all the evidence of the letters and poems, which suggest that Anna was upset with Honora's marriage not because she desired Edgeworth but because she was in love with Honora. Her obsession continued long after the younger woman's death in 1780 from consumption. Even thirty years later, and not long before Anna's own death, she was still writing that she wept because her eyes would never again see Honora's "speaking eyes, that cheer'd my soul."

Seward's poetry has been largely neglected in our century, receiving no attention even in historically based anthologies devoted to women's writing, such as Sandra Gilbert and Susan Gubar's *Norton Anthology of Literature by Women* and Louise Bernikow's *The World Split Open: Four Centuries of Women Poets in England and America*. But such neglect is not entirely deserved. While Seward's poems are not striking in their originality of language or imagery, they do express deep feeling motivated by an all-consuming passion that is often very moving, and as literary evidence of eighteenth-century romantic friendship they are historically important.

Despite the admiration of her work by other poets of her era, her neglect began soon after her death. It was due at least in part to the fact that she was associated with a tribe of "women scribblers" at whom it became fashionable to laugh, as Horace Walpole did in characterizing her and fellow "old maid" writers as "harmonious virgins [whose] thoughts and phrases are like their gowns, old remnants cut and turned." Walpole and others criticized her for her lack of "novelty," but a contemporary reader might find considerable novelty in the discovery of her sonnets that trace her pain at the loss (to heterosexual marriage) of a woman with whom she hoped to spend her life. The sonnets tell an impassioned story, from the anger at Honora, her "false friend," for having betrayed her by desertion, to her horror at having learned that the married Honora was dying of consumption, to her romantic idealization of Honora once more and her villainization of Robert Edgeworth, Honora's husband, who is depicted in these poems as being uncaring and superficial.

In 1795 Seward began a friendship with the Ladies of Llangollen, which continued until her death. Her letters and poems suggest her admiration of their romantic friendship, which enjoyed the permanence Anna had craved. In 1797 she discovered a picture by Romney, "Serena, Reading by Candlelight," which, she claimed, "accidentally formed a perfect similitude of my lost Honora Sneyd's face and figure." She purchased the portrait and sent it to Llangollen, writing the Ladies of her desire that Honora's "form should be enshrined in the receptacle of grace and beauty and appear there distinctly, as those of Lady E. Butler and Miss Ponsonby are engraved on [my] heart." The gesture was touchingly symbolic—Anna, as her Llangollen poetry suggests, identified with the Ladies and lived in spirit at the Vale (that temple dedicated to love between women) together with the artistic embodiment of her lost Honora.

FURTHER READING: *Letters of Anna Seward: Written Between the Years 1784 and 1807*, 6 vols., ed. Walter Scott (Edinburgh: Constable and Co., 1811). *The Poetical Works of Anna Seward; With Extracts from Her Literary Correspondence*, 3 vols., ed. Walter Scott (Edinburgh: John Ballantyne and Co., 1810). Margaret Ashmun, *The Singing Swan: An Account of Anna Seward and Her Acquaintance with Dr. Johnson, Boswell, and Others of Their Time* (New Haven: Yale University Press, 1931). Lillian Faderman, *Surpassing the Love of Men: Romantic Friendship and Love Between Women from the Renaissance to the Present* (New York: William Morrow, 1981), pp. 132–38 and passim.

ELEGY
Written at the Sea-Side, and Addressed to
Miss Honora Sneyd

I write, HONORA, on the sparkling sand!—
The envious waves forbid the trace to stay:
HONORA's name again adorns the strand!
Again the waters bear their prize away!

So Nature wrote her charms upon thy face,
The cheek's light bloom, the lip's envermeil'd dye,
And every gay, and every witching grace,
That Youth's warm hours, and Beauty's stores supply.

But Time's stern tide, with cold Oblivion's wave,
Shall soon dissolve each fair, each fading charm;

E'en Nature's self, so powerful, cannot save
Her own rich gifts from this o'erwhelming harm.

Love and the Muse can boast superior power,
Indelible the letters they shall frame;
They yield to no inevitable hour,
But will on lasting tablets write thy name.

SONNET XII
July 1773

Chill'd by unkind HONORA's alter'd eye,
  "Why droops my heart with pining woe forlorn,"
  Thankless for much of good?—what thousands, born
  To ceaseless toil beneath this wintry sky,
Or to brave deathful oceans surging high,
  Or fell Disease's fever'd rage to mourn,
  How blest to them would seem my destiny!
  How dear the comforts my rash sorrows scorn!—
Affection is repaid by causeless hate!
  A plighted love is changed to cold disdain!
  Yet suffer not thy wrongs to shroud thy fate,
But turn, my soul, to blessings which remain;
  And let this truth the wise resolve create,
  The Heart estranged no anguish can regain.

SONNET XIII
July 1773

Thou child of Night and Silence, balmy Sleep,
  Shed thy soft poppies on my aching brow!
  And charm to rest the thoughts of whence, or how
  Vanish'd that priz'd Affection, wont to keep
Each grief of mine from rankling into woe.
  Then stern Misfortune from her bended bow
  Loos'd the dire strings;—and Care, and anxious Dread
  From my cheer'd heart, on sullen pinion fled.
But now, the spell dissolv'd, th' enchantress gone,
  Ceaseless those cruel fiends infest my day,
  And sunny hours but light them to their prey.
Then welcome midnight shades, when thy wish'd boon

May in oblivious dews my eye-lids steep,
Thou child of Night and Silence, balmy Sleep!

SONNET XIX
To ——

Farewell, false Friend!—our scenes of kindness close!
  To cordial looks, to sunny smiles farewell!
  To sweet consolings, that can grief expel,
  And every joy soft sympathy bestows!
For alter'd looks, where truth no longer glows,
  Thou hast prepared my heart;—and it was well
  To bid thy pen th' unlook'd-for story tell,
  Falsehood avow'd, that shame, nor sorrow knows.
O! when we meet,—(to meet we're destin'd, try
  To avoid it as thou may'st) on either brow,
  Nor in the stealing consciousness of eye,
Be seen the slightest trace of what, or how
  We once were to each other;—nor one sigh
  Flatter with weak regret a broken vow!

SONNET XXXI
To the Departing Spirit of an Alienated Friend

O, ever dear! thy precious, vital powers
  Sink rapidly!—the long and dreary night
  Brings scarce an hope that morn's returning light
  Shall dawn for thee!—In such terrific hours,
When yearning fondness eagerly devours
  Each moment of protracted life, his flight
  The rashly-chosen of thy heart has ta'en
  Where dances, songs, and theatres invite.
Expiring Sweetness! with indignant pain
  I see him in the scenes where laughing glide
  Pleasure's light forms;—see his eyes gaily glow,
Regardless of thy life's fast ebbing tide;
  I hear him, who should droop in silent woe,
  Declaim on actors, and on taste decide!

SONNET XXXII
Subject of the Preceding Sonnet Continued

Behold him now his genuine colours wear,
   That specious false-one, by whose cruel wiles
   I lost thy amity; saw thy dear smiles
   Eclips'd; those smiles, that used my heart to cheer,
Wak'd by thy grateful sense of many a year
   When rose thy youth, by Friendship's pleasing toils
   Cultured;—but Dying!—O! for ever fade
   The angry fires.—Each thought, that might upbraid
Thy broken faith, which yet my soul deplores,
   Now as eternally is past and gone
   As are the interesting, the happy hours,
Days, years, we shared together. They are flown!
   Yet long must I lament thy hapless doom,
   Thy lavish'd life and early-hasten'd tomb.

To the Right Honourable
LADY ELEANOR BUTLER
With the Same Present

Thou, who with firm, free step, as life arose,
Led thy loved friend where sacred Deva flows,
On Wisdom's cloudless sun with thee to gaze,
And build your eyrie on that rocky maze;
Ah, ELEANORA! wilt thou gently deign
To bid these nets the tribute lines contain,
When Virtue, Genius, Rank, and Wealth, combine,
To pay ow'd homage at so pure a shrine?
And O! when kindling with the lovely theme,
The blest reality of Hope's fond dream,
Friendship, that bliss unshar'd disdains to know,
Nor sees, nor feels one unpartaken woe;
When for such worth, in each exalted mind,
Resolv'd as man, and more than woman kind,
Their warm admirers ask a length of years,
Unchill'd by terror, and unstain'd by tears,
Then may the fervent benedictions lie!
And long, long hence meet ELEANORA's eye,
While with her ZARA's it shall frequent rove
The treasur'd records of esteem, and love!

TO MISS PONSONBY

Seek, roseate net, inchanting ZARA's hand,
And, tho' unworthy, say thy fold aspires
To guard the gentle scriptures, where expand
Deserved attachment's tributary fires!

Say, that in no charm'd spirit livelier dwells,
Than hers who wove thee, each ingenuous trace
Of the fair story this retirement tells,
The minds that sought it, and the forms that grace;

Davidean friendship, emulation warm,
Coy blossoms, perishing in courtly air,
Its vain parade, restraint, and irksome form,
Cold as the ice, tho' with the comet's glare.

By firmness won, by constancy secured,
Ye nobler pleasures, be ye long their meed,
Theirs, who, each meteor vanity abjured,
The life of Angels in an Eden lead.

Emily Dickinson
(1830–86)

Emily Dickinson, perhaps the most famous poet in American literary history, has also been considered its most enigmatic figure, partly because until recently most literary critics have refused to acknowledge her love for other women. Throughout much of the twentieth century a whole industry of scholarship was built around the quest for the identity of this "reclusive spinster's" elusive (male) lover, her male muse. Although a dozen men have been named as candidates, no researcher has been able to construct a convincing case for any of them because concrete evidence of her emotional or physical involvement with a man is scanty. Her voluminous extant correspondence, with the exception of three letters addressed to "Master" (which may never have been sent), shows no significant heterosexual involvements until she was well into middle age, at which time she may have had a relationship with a friend of her father's, Judge Otis Lord, a man many years her senior. The letters of her earlier years do, however, reveal intense romantic friendships with other women, including Emily Fowler, Kate Anthon, and Sue Gilbert. While it is impossible to say, because of the lack of concrete evidence, that Dickinson was never involved with a man during her peak poetry-writing years, it is also impossible to say, in view of the evidence that does exist, that she was not a passionate lover of women during those years.

As the following letters will indicate, one of Dickinson's most important emotional involvements was with Sue Gilbert, who eventually married Dickinson's brother, Austin. By 1851, Emily had fallen in love with Sue, a young woman in circumstances of genteel poverty, who was forced to support herself as a schoolteacher. Numerous letters passed between them, though those written by Sue were destroyed at Emily's death. When Sue became engaged to marry Emily's brother (she wrote her siblings that he "will take care of me. . . . We shall have a cozy place some-where, where the long-cherished wish of my heart to have a home . . . will be realized)," the relationship between Sue and Emily became stormy. The correspondence between them ceased, and it was at this time, many Dickinson biographers have speculated, that Emily may have had a nervous breakdown. They have found little trace of her life during those years.

In 1858, two years after Sue and Austin were married, Emily resurfaced and began writing poetry seriously. Her reconciliation with Sue, judging from extant notes, came at about the same time. Her early poems were invariably sent to Sue for criticism. It was as though Emily had found a way to be after a dark period. If she could not share her life with Sue, she would share her art. There are 128 extant letters and 276 poems that she sent to her sister-in-law.

Many of Dickinson's poems appear to be love lyrics to a female. Perhaps she was somewhat self-conscious about this poetry, not because she formulated it specifically as lesbian (she would have seen it as an expression of romantic friendship), but because it revealed so much of her. At one point, when she briefly entertained the idea of publication, Dickinson sent her poems to the editor of *Atlantic Monthly*, Thomas Wentworth Higginson, explaining, "When I state myself as the Representative of the Verse—it does not mean me—but a supposed person." But the poems do, indeed, appear to be autobiographical because they are without a characterized persona or plot, and they seem to refer to specific incidents that are not described in the poems and hence have no dramatic value for the reader. Their autobiographical nature is also confirmed because they often echo the sentiments of Dickinson's letters. Compare, for example, a letter to Sue Gilbert: "The wind blows and it rains. . . . I hardly know which falls fastest, the rain without, or within—Oh, Susie, I would nestle close to your warm heart, and never hear the wind blow, or the storm beat, again. Is there any room there for me, or shall I wander all homeless and alone?" with her poem:

Wild nights! Wild nights!
Were I with thee,
Wild nights should be
Our luxury!

Futile the winds
To a heart in port,—
Done with the compass,
Done with the chart.

Rowing in Eden!
Ah! the sea!
Might I but moor
To-night in thee!

Or compare her brief note to Sue: "To the faithful Absence is condensed presence," with her poem:

The Day she goes
Or Day she stays
Are equally supreme—
Existence has a stated width
Departed, or at Home—

For years twentieth-century Dickinson critics, unfamiliar with the earlier institution of romantic friendship and uncomfortable with the idea that a poet of Dickinson's stature was a "lesbian," have gone to great lengths to explain away the content of same-sex love in her poems. For example, one critic wrote of Dickinson's poem "Her breast is fit for pearls" (see p. 56) that "the persona is a male [!] sparrow." Another explained of "Her sweet Weight on my Heart a Night" (see p. 59) that it was an elegy for Elizabeth Barrett Browning, whose writing Dickinson admired. (Surely such an explanation takes far too literally the notion of curling up in bed with a good book.)

Only in recent decades have critics been less hysterical in their attempts to obfuscate what appear to be hints of Dickinson's same-sex love interests in her poetry. Paula Bennett has even suggested that much of Dickinson's imagery is clitoral (and hence demonstrates an awareness of lesbian sexuality): jewels, gems, pearls, peas, berries, nuts, buds, crumbs, and beads abound in Dickinson's poetry. But whether or not the reader can accept the idea that so much of Dickinson's poetry deals symbolically with lesbian sexuality, it is hard to refute that the poems demonstrate that at some points in her life Dickinson passionately loved women.

FURTHER READING: Thomas Johnson and Theodora Ward, *The Letters of Emily Dickinson*, 3 vols. (Cambridge: Harvard University Press, 1958). *The Poems of Emily Dickinson*, 3 vols., ed. Thomas H. Johnson (Cambridge: Harvard University Press, 1955). Paula Bennett, "The Language of Love: Emily Dickinson's Homoerotic Poetry," *Gai Saber* (Spring 1977), 13–17; "The Pea That Duty Locks: Lesbian and Feminist-Heterosexual Readings of Emily Dickinson's Poetry,"*Lesbian Texts and Contexts: Radical Revisions*, ed. Karla Jay and Joanne Glasgow (New York: New York University Press, 1990). John Cody, *After Great Pain: The Inner Life of Emily Dickinson* (Cambridge: Harvard University Press, 1971). Lillian Faderman, "Emily Dickinson's Letters to Sue Gilbert," *Massachusetts Review*, XVIII:2 (Summer 1977), pp. 197–225; Lillian Faderman, "Emily Dickinson's Homoerotic Poetry," *Higginson Journal*, 18 (first half, 1978), 19–27. Ellen Louise Hart, "The Encoding of Homoerotic Desire: Emily Dickinson's Letters and Poems to Sue Gilbert, 1850–1886," *Tulsa Studies in Women's Literature*, 9: 2 (Fall 1990), 251–72. Rebecca Patterson, *The Riddle of Emily Dickinson* (Boston: Houghton Mifflin, 1951). Martha Nell Smith, *Rowing in Eden: Rereading Emily Dickinson* (Austin: University of Texas Press, 1992).

From *The Letters of Emily Dickinson*

To Abial Root, March 14, 1847

We have a delightful school this term under the instruction of our former principals, & Miss R. Woodbridge—daughter of Rev. Dr. W. of Hadley, for preceptress. We all love her very much. Perhaps a slight description of her might be interesting to my dear A.—She is tall & rather slender, but finely proportioned, has a most witching pair of blue eyes—rich brown hair—delicate complexion—cheeks which vie with the opening rose bud—teeth like pearls—dimples which come & go like the ripples in yonder little merry brook—& then she is so affectionate & lovely. Forgive my glowing description, for you know I am always in love with my teachers.

To Emily Fowler, Early 1850?

I cannot wait to be with you—Oh ugly time, and space, and uglier snow-storm than all! Were you happy in Northampton? I was very lonely without you, and wanted to write you a letter *many* times, but Kate was there too, and I was afraid you would both laugh. I should be stronger if I could see you oftener—I am very puny alone.

You make me so happy, and glad, life seems worth living for, no matter for all the trials. When I see you I shall tell you more, for I know you are busy this morning.

That is'nt an *empty* blank where I began—it is so full of affection that you cant see any—that's all. Will you love, and remember, *me* when you have time from worthier ones? God keep you till I have seen you again!

Very earnestly yrs—

Emily

To Emily Fowler, about 1851

I'm so afraid you'll forget me dear Emily—through these cold winter days, when I cannot come to see you, that I cannot forbear writing the least little bit of a note—to put you in mind of me; perhaps it will make you laugh—it may be foolish in me but I love you so well sometimes—not that I do not *always*—but more dearly sometimes—and with such a desire to see you that I find myself addressing you almost ere I'm aware. When I am as old as you and have had so many friends, perhaps they wont seem so precious, and then I shant write any more little "billet doux" like these, but you will forgive me *now,* because I cant find many so dear to me as you—then I know I cant have you always—some day a "brave dragoon" will be stealing you away and I will have farther to go to discover you *at all*—so I shall recollect all these sweet opportunities and feel so sorry if I did'nt improve them.

To Susan Gilbert, about February 6, 1852

Will you let me come dear Susie—looking just as I do, my dress soiled and worn, my grand old apron, and my hair—Oh Susie, time would fail me to enumerate my appearance, yet I love you just as dearly as if I was e'er so fine, so you wont care, will you? I am so glad dear Susie—that our hearts are always clean, and always neat and lovely, so not to be ashamed. I have been hard at work this morning, and I ought to be working now— but I cannot deny myself the luxury of a minute or two with you.

The dishes may wait dear Susie—and the uncleared table stand, *them* I have always with me, but you, I have "not always"—*why* Susie, Christ hath saints *manie*—and I have *few,* but thee—the angels shant have Susie—no—no no! . . .

Oh my darling one, how long you wander from me, how weary I grow of waiting and looking, and calling for you; sometimes I shut my eyes, and shut my heart towards you, and try hard to forget you because you grieve me so, but you'll never go away, Oh you never will—say, Susie, promise me again, and I will smile faintly—and take up my little cross again of sad—*sad* separation. How vain it seems to *write,* when one knows how to feel—how much more near and dear to sit beside you, talk with you, hear the tones of your voice; so hard to "deny thyself, and take up thy cross, and follow me"—give me strength, Susie, write me of hope and love, and of hearts that *endured,* and great was their reward of "Our Father who art in Heaven." I dont know how I shall bear it, when the gentle spring comes; if she should come and see me and talk to me of you, Oh it would surely kill me! While the frost clings to the windows, and the World is stern and drear; this absence is easier; the *Earth* mourns too, for all her little birds; but when they all come back again, and she sings and is so merry—pray, what will become of me? Susie, forgive me, forget all what I say, get some sweet little scholar to read a gentle hymn, about Bethleem and Mary, and you will sleep on sweetly and have as peaceful dreams, as if I had never written you all these ugly things. Never mind the letter Susie, I wont be angry with you if you dont give me any at all—for I know how busy you are, and how little of that dear strength remains when it is evening, with which to think and write. Only *want* to write me, only sometimes sigh that you are far from me, and that will do, Susie! Dont you think we are good and patient, to let you go so long; and dont we think you're a darling, a real beautiful hero, to toil for people, and teach them, and leave your own dear home? Because we pine and repine, dont think we forget the precious patriot at war in other lands! Never be mournful, Susie—be happy and have cheer, for how many of the long days have gone away since I wrote you—and it is almost noon, and soon the night will come, and then there is one less day of the long pilgrimage. Mattie is very smart, talks of you *much,* my darling; I must leave you now—"one little hour of Heaven," thank who did give it me, and will he also grant me one longer and *more* when it shall please his love—bring Susie home, ie! Love always, and ever, and true!

                                                                    Emily—

To Susan Gilbert, about February 1852

It's a sorrowful morning Susie—the wind blows and it rains; "into each life some rain must fall," and I hardly know which falls fastest, the rain without, or within—Oh Susie, I would nestle close to your warm heart, and never hear the wind blow, or the storm beat, again. Is there any room there for me, or shall I wander away all homeless and alone? Thank you for loving me, darling, and *will* you "love me more if ever you come home"?—it is enough, dear Susie, I know I shall be satisfied. But what can I do towards you?—*dearer* you *cannot* be, for I love you so already, that it almost breaks my heart—perhaps I can love you *anew,* every day of my life, every morning and evening—Oh if you will let me, how happy I shall be!

The precious billet, Susie, I am wearing the paper out, reading it over and o'er, but the dear *thoughts* cant wear out if they try, Thanks to Our

Father, Susie! Vinnie and I talked of you all last evening long, and went to sleep mourning for you, and pretty soon I waked up saying "Precious treasure, thou art mine," and there you were all right, my Susie, and I hardly dared to sleep lest some one steal you away. Never mind the letter, Susie; you have so much to do; just write me every week *one line,* and let it be, "Emily, I love you," and I will be satisfied!

Your own Emily

To Susan Gilbert, late April 1852

So sweet and still, and Thee, Oh Susie, what need I more, to make my heaven whole?

Sweet Hour, blessed Hour, to carry me to you, and to bring you back to me, long enough to snatch one kiss, and whisper Good bye, again.

I have thought of it all day, Susie, and I fear of but little else, and when I was gone to meeting it filled my mind so full, I could not find a *chink* to put the worthy pastor; when he said "Our Heavenly Father," I said "Oh Darling Sue"; when he read the 100th Psalm, I kept saying your precious letter all over to myself, and Susie, when they sang—it would have made you laugh to hear one little voice, piping to the departed. I made up words and kept singing how I loved you, and you had gone, while all the rest of the choir were singing Hallelujahs. I presume nobody heard me, because I sang *so small,* but it was a kind of a comfort to think I might put them out, singing of you. I a'nt there this afternoon, tho', because I am here, writing a little letter to my dear Sue, and I am very happy. I think of ten weeks—Dear One, and I think of love, and you, and my heart grows full and warm, and my breath stands still. The sun does'nt shine at all, but I can feel a sunshine stealing into my soul and making it all summer, and every thorn, a *rose.* And I pray that such summer's sun shine on my Absent One, and cause her bird to sing!

You have been happy, Susie, and now are sad—and the whole world seems lone; but it wont be so always, "some days *must* be dark and dreary"! You wont cry any more, will you, Susie, for my father will be your father, and my home will be your home, and where you go, I will go, and we will lie side by side in the kirkyard.

To Susan Gilbert, June 11, 1852

I have but one thought, Susie, this afternoon of June, and *that* of you, and I have one prayer, only; dear Susie, *that* is *for* you. That you and I in *hand* as we e'en *do* in heart, might ramble away as children, among the woods and fields, and forget these many years, and these sorrowing cares, and each become a child again—I would it were so, Susie, and when I look around me and find myself alone, I sigh for you again; little sigh, and vain sigh, which will not bring you home.

I need you more and more, and the great world grows wider, and dear ones fewer and fewer, every day that you stay away—I miss my biggest heart; my own goes wandering round, and calls for Susie—Friends are too dear to sunder, Oh they are far too few, and how soon they will go away where you and I cannot find them, *dont* let us forget these things, for their remembrance *now* will save us many an anguish when it is *too late* to love them! Susie, forgive me Darling, for every word I say—my heart is full of you, none other than you in my thoughts, yet when I seek to say to you something not for the world, words fail me. If you were here—and Oh that you were, my Susie, we need not talk at all, our eyes would whisper for us, and your hand fast in mine, we would not ask for language—I try to bring you nearer, I chase the weeks away till they are quite departed, and fancy you have come, and I am on my way through the green lane to meet you, and my heart goes scampering so, that I have much ado to bring it back again, and learn it to be patient, till that dear Susie comes. Three weeks—they cant last always, for surely they must go with their little brothers and sisters to their long home in the west!

I shall grow more and more impatient until that dear day comes, for till now, I have only *mourned* for you; now I begin to *hope* for you.

Dear Susie, I have tried hard to think what you would love, of something I might send you—I at last saw my little Violets, they begged me to let *them* go, so here they are—and with them as Instructor, a bit of knightly grass, who also begged the favor to accompany them—they are but small, Susie, and I fear not fragrant now, but they will speak to you of warm hearts at home, and of the something faithful which "never slumbers nor sleeps"—Keep them 'neath your pillow, Susie, they will make you dream of blue-skies, and home, and the "blessed countrie"! You and I will have an hour with "Edward" and "Ellen Middleton," sometime when you get home—we must find out if some things contained therein are true, and if they are, what you and me are coming to!

Now, farewell, Susie, and Vinnie sends her love, and mother her's, and I add a kiss, shyly, lest there is somebody there! Dont let them see, *will* you Susie?

—Emilie

Why cant *I* be a Delegate to the great Whig Convention?—dont I know all about Daniel Webster, and the Tariff, and the Law? Then, Susie I could see you, during a pause in the session—but I dont like this country at all, and I shant stay here any longer! "Delenda est" America, Massachusetts and all!

open me carefully

To Susan Gilbert, June 27, 1852

My Susie's last request; yes, darling, I grant it, tho' few, and fleet the days which separate us now—but six more weary days, but six more twilight evens, and my lone little fireside, my *silent* fireside is once more full.

"We are seven, and one in heaven," we are *three* next Saturday, if *I* have *mine* and heaven has none.

Do not mistake, my Susie, and rather than the car, ride on the golden wings where you will ne'er come back again—do not forget the lane, and the little cot that stands by it, when people from the clouds will beckon you, and smile at you, to have you go with them—Oh Susie, my child, I sit here by my window, and look each little while down towards that golden gateway beneath the western trees, and I fancy I see you coming, you trip upon the green grass, and I hear the crackling leaf under your little shoe; I hide behind the chair, I think I will surprise you, I grow too eager to see you, I hasten to the door, and start to find me that you are not there. And very, very often when I have waked from sleep, *not quite* waked, I have been sure I saw you, and your dark eye beamed on me with such a look of tenderness that I could only weep, and bless God for you.

Susie, will you indeed come home next Saturday, and be my own again, and kiss me as you used to? Shall I indeed behold you, not "darkly, but face to face" or am I *fancying* so, and dreaming blessed dreams from which the day will wake me? I hope for you so much, and feel so eager for you, feel that I *cannot* wait, feel that *now* I must have you—that the expectation once more to see your face again, makes me feel hot and feverish, and my heart beats so fast—I go to sleep at night, and the first thing I know, I am sitting there wide awake, and clasping my hands tightly, and thinking of next Saturday, and "never a bit" of you.

Sometimes I must have Saturday before tomorrow comes, and I wonder if it w'd make any difference with God, to give it to me *today,* and I'd let him have Monday, to make him a Saturday; and then I feel so funnily, and wish the precious day would'nt come quite so soon, till I could know how to feel, and get my thoughts ready for it.

Why, Susie, it seems to me as if my absent Lover was coming home so soon—and my heart must be so busy, making ready for him.

While the minister this morning was giving an account of the Roman Catholic system, and announcing several facts which were usually startling, I was trying to make up my mind wh' of the two was prettiest to go and welcome *you* in, my fawn colored dress, or my blue dress. Just as I had decided by all means to wear the blue, down came the minister's fist with a terrible rap on the counter, and Susie, it scared me so, I hav'nt got over it yet, but I'm glad I reached a conclusion! I walked home from meeting with Mattie, and *incidentally* quite, something was said of you, and I think one of us remarked that you would be here next Sunday; well—Susie— what it was *I* dont presume to know, but my gaiters seemed to leave me, and I seemed to move on wings—and I move on wings now, Susie, on wings as white as snow, and as bright as the summer sunshine—because I am with you, and so few short days, you are with me at home. Be patient then, my Sister, for the hours will haste away, and Oh *so* soon! Susie, I write most hastily, and very carelessly too, for it is time for me to get the supper, and my mother is gone and besides, my darling, so near I seem to you, that I *disdain* this pen, and wait for a *warmer* language. With Vinnie's love, and my love, I am once more

Your Emilie—

To Susan Gilbert, late August 1854

Susie—

I have been very busy since you went away, but that is'nt the reason I've not written to you, and we've had a great deal of company too, but *that* is not the reason—I was foolish eno' to be vexed at a little thing, and I hope God will forgive me, as he'll have to many times, if he lives long enough.

Thro' Austin, I've known of you, and nobody in this world except Vinnie and Austin, know that in all the while, I have not heard from you. Many have asked me for you, and I have answered promptly that you had reached there safely, and were better every day, and Susie, do you think, H. Hinsdale came to our house several days ago; came just to ask for you, and went away supposing I'd heard from you quite often. Not that I told her so, but spoke of you so naturally, in such a daily way, she never guessed the fact that I'd not written to you, nor had you thus to me.

Never think of it, Susie—never mention it—I trust your truth for that, but when you meet, and I meet—we'll try and forgive each other. There has not been a day, Child, that I've not thought of you, nor have I shut my eyes upon a summer night, without your sweet remembrance, and tho' full much of sorrow has gathered at your name, that ought but peace was 'tween us, yet I remembered on, and bye and bye the day came. I do not miss you Susie—of course I do not miss you—I only sit and stare at nothing from my window, and know that all is gone—Dont *feel* it—no—any more than the stone feels, that it is very cold, or the block, that it is silent, where once 'twas warm and green, and birds danced in it's branches.

I rise, because the sun shines, and sleep has done with me, and I brush my hair, and dress me, and wonder what I am and who has made me so, and then I wash the dishes, and anon, wash them again, and then 'tis afternoon, and Ladies call, and evening, and some members of another sex come in to spend the hour, and then that day is done. And, prithee, what is Life?

To Susan Gilbert, about 1854

Sue—you can go or stay—There is but one alternative—We differ often lately, and this must be the last.

You need not fear to leave me lest I should be alone, for I often part with things I fancy I have loved,—sometimes to the grave, and sometimes to an oblivion rather bitterer than death—thus my heart bleeds so frequently that I shant mind the hemorrhage, and I only add an agony to several previous ones, and at the end of day remark—a bubble burst!

Such incidents would grieve me when I was but a child, and perhaps I could have wept when little feet hard by mine, stood still in the coffin, but eyes grow dry sometimes, and hearts get crisp and cinder, and had as lief burn.

Sue—I have lived by this. It is the lingering emblem of the Heaven I once dreamed, and though if this is taken, I shall remain alone, and though in that last day, the Jesus Christ you love, remark he does not know me— there is a darker spirit will not disown it's child.

Few have been given me, and if I love them so, that for *idolatry,* they are removed from me—I simply murmur *gone,* and the billow dies away into the boundless blue, and no one knows but me, that one went down today. We have walked very pleasantly—Perhaps this is the point at which our paths diverge—then pass on singing Sue, and up the distant hill I journey on.

I have a Bird in spring
Which for myself doth sing—
The spring decoys.
And as the summer nears—
And as the Rose appears,
Robin is gone.

Yet do I not repine
Knowing that Bird of mine
Though flown—
Learneth beyond the sea
Melody new for me
And will return.
Fast in a safer hand

Held in a truer Land
Are mine—
And though they now depart,
Tell I my doubting heart
They're thine.

In a serener Bright,
In a more golden light
I see
Each little doubt and fear,
Each little discord here
Removed.

Then will I not repine,
Knowing that Bird of mine
Though flown
Shall in a distant tree
Bright melody for me
Return.

E—

To Catherine Scott Turner (Anthon), about March 1859

I never missed a Kate before,—Two Sues—Eliza and a Martha, comprehend my girls.

Sweet at my door this March night another Candidate—Go Home! We don't like Katies here!—Stay! My heart votes for you, and what am I indeed to dispute her ballot—?—What are your qualifications? Dare you dwell in the *East* where we dwell? Are you afraid of the Sun?—When you hear the new violet sucking her way among the sods, shall you be *resolute?* All *we* are *strangers*—dear—The world is not acquainted with us, because we are not acquainted with her. And Pilgrims!—Do you hesitate? and *Soldiers* oft—some of us victors, but those I do not *see* tonight owing to the smoke.—We are hungry, and thirsty, sometimes—We are barefoot—and cold—

Will you still come? *Then* bright I record you! *Kate* gathered in March!

It is a small bouquet, dear—but what it lacks in size, it gains in fadelessness,—Many can boast a hollyhock, but few can bear a *rose!* And should new flower smile at limited associates, pray her remember, were there *many* they were not worn upon the breast—but tilled in the pasture! So I rise, wearing her—so I sleep, holding,—Sleep at last with her fast in my hand and wake bearing my flower.—

Emilie—

Sent with a pair of garters that Emily knitted for Kate late 1859?

To Catherine Scott Turner (Anthon)

When Katie walks, this simple pair accompany her side,
When Katie runs unwearied they follow on the road,
When Katie kneels, their loving hands still clasp her pious knee—
Ah! Katie! Smile at Fortune, with *two* so *knit to thee!*

Emilie

To Catherine Scott Turner (Anthon), summer 1860?

. . . Kate, Distinctly sweet your face stands in its phantom niche—I touch your hand—my cheek your cheek—I stroke your vanished hair, Why did you enter, sister, since you must depart? Had not its heart been torn enough but *you* must send your shred? Oh! our Condor Kate! Come from your crags again! Oh: Dew upon the bloom fall yet again a summer's night. Of such have been the friends which have vanquished faces—sown plant by plant the churchyard plats and occasioned angels.—There is a subject dear—on which we never touch, Ignorance of its pageantries does not deter me—I, too went out to meet the "Dust" early in the morning, I, too in Daisy mounds possess hid treasure—therefore I guard you more—You did not tell me you had once been a "Millionaire." Did my sister think that opulence could be mistaken?—Some trinket will remain—some babbling plate or jewel!—I write you from the summer. The murmuring leaves fill up the chinks thro' which the winter red shone, when Kate was here, and Frank was here—and "Frogs" sincerer than our own splash in their Maker's pools—Its but a little past—dear—and yet how far from here it seems—fled with the snow! So through the snow go many loving feet parted by "Alps" how brief from Vineyards and the Sun!—Parents and Vinnie request love to be given Girl—

Emilie—

From *The Poems of Emily Dickinson*

Her breast is fit for pearls,
But I was not a "Diver"—
Her brow is fit for thrones
But I have not a crest.

Her heart is fit for *home*—
I—a Sparrow—build there
Sweet of twigs and twine
My perennial nest.

The Lady feeds Her little Bird
At rarer intervals—
The little Bird would not dissent
But meekly recognize

The Gulf between the Hand and Her
And crumbless and afar
And fainting, on Her yellow Knee
Fall softly, and adore—

I showed her Hights she never saw—
"Would'st Climb," I said?
She said—"Not so"—
"With *me*—" I said—With *me*?
I showed her Secrets—Morning's Nest—
The Rope the Nights were put across—
And *now*—"Would'st have me for a Guest?"
She could not find her Yes—
And then, I brake my life—And Lo,
A Light, for her, did solemn glow,
The larger, as her face withdrew—
And *could* she, further, "No"?

&.

You love me—you are sure—
I shall not fear mistake—
I shall not *cheated* wake—
Some grinning morn—
To find the Sunrise left—
And Orchards—unbereft—
And Dollie*—gone!

I need not start—you're sure—
That night will never be—
When frightened—home to Thee I run—
To find the windows dark—
And no more Dollie—mark—
Quite none?

Be sure you're sure—you know—
I'll bear it better now—
If you'll just tell me so—
Than when—a little dull Balm grown—
Over this pain of mine—
You sting—again!

&.

Like Eyes that looked on Wastes—
Incredulous of Ought
But Blank—and steady Wilderness—
Diversified by Night—

Just Infinites of Nought—
As far as it could see—
So looked the face I looked upon—
So looked itself—on Me—

I offered it no Help—
Because the Cause was Mine—
The Misery a Compact
As hopeless—as divine—

* "Dollie" was Emily's pet name for Sue Gilbert.

Neither—would be absolved—
Neither would be a Queen
Without the Other—Therefore—
We perish—tho' We reign—

❦

Ourselves were wed one summer—dear—
Your Vision—was in June—
And when Your little Lifetime failed,
I wearied—too—of mine—

And overtaken in the Dark—
Where You had put me down—
By Some one carrying a Light—
I—too—received the Sign.

'Tis true—Our Futures different lay—
Your Cottage—faced the sun—
While Oceans—and the North must be—
On every side of mine

'Tis true, Your Garden led the Bloom,
For mine—in Frosts—was sown—
And yet, one Summer, we were Queens—
But You—were crowned in June—

❦

Be Mine the Doom—
Sufficient Fame—
To perish in Her Hand!

❦

Now I knew I lost her—
Not that she was gone—
But Remoteness travelled
On her Face and Tongue.

Alien, though adjoining
As a Foreign Race—
Traversed she though pausing
Latitudeless Place.

Elements Unaltered—
Universe the same
But Love's transmigration—
Somehow this had come—

Henceforth to remember
Nature took the Day
I had paid so much for—
His is Penury
Not who toils for Freedom
Or for Family
But the Restitution
Of Idolatry.

Her sweet Weight on my Heart a Night
Had scarcely deigned to lie—
When, stirring, for Belief's delight,
My Bride had slipped away—

If 'twas a Dream—made solid—just
The Heaven to confirm—
Or if Myself were dreamed of Her—
The power to presume—

With Him remain—who unto Me—
Gave—even as to All—
A Fiction superseding Faith—
By so much—as 'twas real—

Frigid and sweet Her parting Face—
Frigid and fleet my Feet—
Alien and vain whatever Clime
Acrid whatever Fate.

Given to me without the Suit
Riches and Name and Realm—
Who was She to withhold from me
Penury and Home?

*

That she forgot me was the least
I felt it second pain
That I was worthy to forget
Was most I thought upon

Faithful was all that I could boast
But Constancy became
To her, by her innominate
A something like a shame

*

To see her is a picture
To hear [her] is a Tune
To know her an intemperance
As innocent as June
By which to be undone
Is dearer than Redemption—
Which never to receive
Makes mockery of melody
It might have been to live

Christina Rossetti
(1830–94)

Like the American poet Emily Dickinson, who was born in the same year, the British poet Christina Rossetti was a recluse who lived most of her life with her family. Also like Dickinson, she was not obliged to work in order to support herself or to care for a husband and children (no easy tasks for middle-class women in nineteenth-century Europe and America). That meant she could devote all the time she desired to writing poetry. And, finally, like Dickinson, Rossetti is an enigma about whose emotional life much has been speculated but little has been determined for certain. Rossetti seems to have enjoyed being enigmatic, as one of her poems playfully suggests:

I tell my secret? No, indeed, not I:
Perhaps some day, who knows?

But not today; it froze, and blows, and snows,
And you're too curious: fie!
Only my secret's mine, and I won't tell. . . .

Perhaps some languid summer day,
When drowsy birds sing less and less,
And golden fruit is ripening to excess,
If there's not too much sun nor too much cloud,
And the warm wind is neither still nor loud,
Perhaps my secret I may say,
Or you may guess.

When only seventeen years old, she was engaged to James Collinson, a poet and painter who was a member of the Pre-Raphaelite Brotherhood, a group of English artists with revolutionary aesthetic ideals, which was headed by her brother, Dante Gabriel Rossetti. However, she broke her engagement to Collinson when she was twenty, ostensibly because he converted to Roman Catholicism and she was a staunch Anglican. Biographers have claimed one or two other heterosexual relationships for her, but no permanent heterosexual commitment.

Severe social restrictions on the middle-class Victorian woman's mobility prevented Christina from exploring the world as did her brother Dante, who led the carefree life of a bohemian. Her resentment of the limitations imposed on women is suggested in several poems of her youth, such as "From the Antique," written when she was twenty-four: "It's a weary life, it is, she said:—/ Doubly blank is a woman's lot:/ I wish and I wish I were a man." But her fear of breaking taboos and taking male privilege is also suggested in these early poems, such as "The World," a sonnet that is additionally interesting because its central personification hints at her libidinal fascination with (and terror of) other females:

By day she wooes me, soft, exceeding fair:
    But all night as the moon so changeth she;
    Loathsome and foul with hideous leprosy
And subtle serpents gliding in her hair.
By day she wooes me to the outer air,
    Ripe fruits, sweet flowers, and full satiety:
    But thro' the night, a beast she grins at me,
A very monster void of love and prayer.
By day she stands a lie: by night she stands
    In all the naked horror of the truth
With pushing horns and clawed and clutching hands.

> Is this a friend indeed, that I should sell
> My soul to her, give her my life and youth,
> Till my feet, cloven too, take hold on hell?

William Rossetti, another brother, who wrote the family memoirs in the early twentieth century, established the emphasis, which pervades subsequent biographies, on Christina's heterosexual interests. Little is known of her relationships with women, but biographers do mention a "much-loved" female cousin. And certain lines from her poems are enticing, such as the poem about an Italian woman friend, "Enrica, 1865": "She came among us from the South/ And made the North her home awhile;/ Our dimness brightened in her smile,/ Our tongue [i.e., language] grew sweeter in her mouth."

But the most provocative of Rossetti's poems is "Goblin Market," whose images impute evil to male sensuality and value the sensuality that is possible between two women. Rossetti seems to have been depicting salvation through romantic friendship in this poem, but it is interesting that many of the illustrators of "Goblin Market," even in the late nineteenth century, hinted at lesbian sexuality in their drawings.

FURTHER READING: *The Complete Poems of Christina Rossetti*, vol. I (variorum edition), ed. Rebecca Crump (Baton Rouge: Louisiana State University, 1979). *The Poetical Works of Christina Rossetti*, ed. William Michael Rossetti (1904; London: Macmillan, 1911). Margaret Homans, "Syllables of Velvet: Dickinson, Rossetti, and the Rhetorics of Sexuality," *Feminist Studies*, 11: 3 (Fall 1989), 569–93. Jeannette Foster, *Sex Variant Women in Literature* (1956; reprint, Tallahassee, FL: Naiad Press, 1985), pp. 74–76.

GOBLIN MARKET

> Morning and evening
> Maids heard the goblins cry:
> "Come buy our orchard fruits,
> Come buy, come buy:
> Apples and quinces,
> Lemons and oranges,
> Plump unpecked cherries,
> Melons and raspberries,
> Bloom-down-cheeked peaches,
> Swart-headed mulberries,
> Wild free-born cranberries,
> Crab-apples, dewberries,

Pine-apples, blackberries,
Apricots, strawberries;—
All ripe together
In summer weather,—
Morns that pass by,
Fair eves that fly;
Come buy, come buy:
Our grapes fresh from the vine,
Pomegranates full and fine,
Dates and sharp bullaces,
Rare pears and greengages,
Damsons and bilberries,
Taste them and try:
Currants and gooseberries,
Bright-fire-like barberries,
Figs to fill your mouth,
Citrons from the South,
Sweet to tongue and sound to eye;
Come buy, come buy."

Evening by evening
Among the brookside rushes,
Laura bowed her head to hear,
Lizzie veiled her blushes:
Crouching close together
In the cooling weather,
With clasping arms and cautioning lips,
With tingling cheeks and fingertips.
"Lie close," Laura said,
Pricking up her golden head:
"We must not look at goblin men,
We must not buy their fruits:
Who knows upon what soil they fed
Their hungry thirsty roots?"

"Come buy," call the goblins
Hobbling down the glen.
"Oh," cried Lizzie, "Laura, Laura,
You should not peep at goblin men."
Lizzie covered up her eyes,
Covered close lest they should look;
Laura reared her glossy head,
And whispered like the restless brook:

"Look, Lizzie, look, Lizzie,
Down the glen tramp little men.
One hauls a basket,
One bears a plate,
One lugs a golden dish
Of many pounds' weight.
How fair the vine must grow
Whose grapes are so luscious;
How warm the wind must blow
Through those fruit bushes."
"No," said Lizzie: "No, no, no;
Their offers should not charm us,
Their evil gifts would harm us."
She thrust a dimpled finger
In each ear, shut eyes and ran:
Curious Laura chose to linger
Wondering at each merchant man.
One had a cat's face,
One whisked a tail,
One tramped at a rat's pace,
One crawled like a snail,
One like a wombat prowled obtuse and furry,
One like a ratel tumbled hurry skurry.
She heard a voice like voice of doves
Cooing all together:
They sounded kind and full of loves
In the pleasant weather.

Laura stretched her gleaming neck
Like a rush-imbedded swan,
Like a lily from the beck,
Like a moonlit poplar branch,
Like a vessel at the launch
When its last restraint is gone.

Backwards up the mossy glen
Turned and trooped the goblin men,
With their shrill repeated cry,
"Come buy, come buy."
When they reached where Laura was
They stood stock still upon the moss,
Leering at each other,
Brother with queer brother;

Signalling each other,
Brother with sly brother.
One set his basket down,
One reared his plate;
One began to weave a crown
Of tendrils, leaves, and rough nuts brown
(Men sell not such in any town);
One heaved the golden weight
Of dish and fruit to offer her:
"Come buy, come buy," was still their cry.
Laura stared but did not stir,
Longed but had no money.
The whisk-tailed merchant bade her taste
In tones as smooth as honey,
The cat-faced purr'd,
The rat-paced spoke a word
Of welcome, and the snail-paced even was heard;
One parrot-voiced and jolly
Cried "Pretty Goblin" still for "Pretty Polly";
One whistled like a bird.

But sweet-tooth Laura spoke in haste:
"Good Folk, I have no coin;
To take were to purloin:
I have no copper in my purse,
I have no silver either,
And all my gold is on the furze
That shakes in windy weather
Above the rusty heather."
"You have much gold upon your head,"
They answered all together:
"Buy from us with a golden curl."
She clipped a precious golden lock.
She dropped a tear more rare than pearl,
Then sucked their fruit globes fair or red.
Sweeter than honey from the rock,
Stronger than man-rejoicing wine,
Clearer than water flowed that juice;
She never tasted such before,
How should it cloy with length of use?
She sucked and sucked and sucked the more
Fruits which that unknown orchard bore;

She sucked until her lips were sore;
Then flung the emptied rinds away
But gathered up one kernel stone,
And knew not was it night or day
As she turned home alone.

Lizzie met her at the gate
Full of wise upbraidings:
"Dear, you should not stay so late,
Twilight is not good for maidens;
Should not loiter in the glen
In the haunts of goblin men.
Do you not remember Jeanie,
How she met them in the moonlight,
Took their gifts both choice and many,
Ate their fruits and wore their flowers
Plucked from bowers
Where summer ripens at all hours?
But ever in the moonlight
She pined and pined away;
Sought them by night and day,
Found them no more, but dwindled and grew grey;
Then fell with the first snow,
While to this day no grass will grow
Where she lies low:
I planted daisies there a year ago
That never blow.
You should not loiter so."
"Nay, hush," said Laura:
"Nay, hush, my sister:
I ate and ate my fill,
Yet my mouth waters still:
To-morrow night I will
Buy more"; and kissed her.
"Have done with sorrow;
I'll bring you plums to-morrow
Fresh on their mother twigs,
Cherries worth getting;
You cannot think what figs
My teeth have met in,
What melons icy-cold
Piled on a dish of gold

Too huge for me to hold,
What peaches with a velvet nap,
Pellucid grapes without one seed:
Odorous indeed must be the mead
Whereon they grow, and pure the wave they drink
With lilies at the brink,
And sugar-sweet their sap."

Golden head by golden head,
Like two pigeons in one nest
Folded in each other's wings,
They lay down in their curtained bed:
Like two blossoms on one stem,
Like two flakes of new-fall'n snow,
Like two wands of ivory
Tipped with gold for awful kings.
Moon and stars gazed in at them,
Wind sang to them lullaby,
Lumbering owls forbore to fly,
Not a bat flapped to and fro
Round their nest:
Cheek to cheek and breast to breast
Locked together in one nest.

Early in the morning
When the first cock crowed his warning,
Neat like bees, as sweet and busy,
Laura rose with Lizzie:
Fetched in honey, milked the cows,
Aired and set to rights the house,
Kneaded cakes of whitest wheat,
Cakes for dainty mouths to eat,
Next churned butter, whipped up cream,
Fed their poultry, sat and sewed;
Talked as modest maidens should:
Lizzie with an open heart,
Laura in an absent dream,
One content, one sick in part;
One warbling for the mere bright day's delight,
One longing for the night.

At length slow evening came:
They went with pitchers to the reedy brook;

Lizzie most placid in her look,
Laura most like a leaping flame.
They drew the gurgling water from its deep.
Lizzie plucked purple and rich golden flags,
Then turning homeward said: "The sunset flushes
Those furthest loftiest crags;
Come, Laura, not another maiden lags.
No wilful squirrel wags,
The beasts and birds are fast asleep."
But Laura loitered still among the rushes,
And said the bank was steep.

And said the hour was early still,
The dew not fall'n, the wind not chill;
Listening ever, but not catching
The customary cry,
"Come buy, come buy,"
With its iterated jingle
Of sugar-baited words:
Not for all her watching
Once discerning even one goblin
Racing, whisking, tumbling, hobbling—
Let alone the herds
That used to tramp along the glen,
In groups or single,
Of brisk fruit-merchant men.

Till Lizzie urged, "O Laura, come;
I hear the fruit-call, but I dare not look:
You should not loiter longer at this brook:
Come with me home.
The stars rise, the moon bends her arc,
Each glow-worm winks her spark,
Let us get home before the night grows dark:
For clouds may gather
Though this is summer weather,
Put out the lights and drench us through;
Then if we lost our way what should we do?"

Laura turned cold as stone
To find her sister heard that cry alone,
That goblin cry,
"Come buy our fruits, come buy."

Must she then buy no more such dainty fruit?
Must she no more such succous pasture find,
Gone deaf and blind?
Her tree of life drooped from the root:
She said not one word in her heart's sore ache:
But peering thro' the dimness, nought discerning,
Trudged home, her pitcher dripping all the way;
So crept to bed, and lay
Silent till Lizzie slept;
Then sat up in a passionate yearning,
And gnashed her teeth for baulked desire, and wept
As if her heart would break.

Day after day, night after night,
Laura kept watch in vain
In sullen silence of exceeding pain.
She never caught again the goblin cry,
"Come buy, come buy;"—
She never spied the goblin men
Hawking their fruits along the glen:
But when the noon waxed bright
Her hair grew thin and grey;
She dwindled, as the fair full moon doth turn
To swift decay and burn
Her fire away.

One day remembering her kernel-stone
She set it by a wall that faced the south;
Dewed it with tears, hoped for a root,
Watched for a waxing shoot,
But there came none.
It never saw the sun,
It never felt the trickling moisture run:
While with sunk eyes and faded mouth
She dreamed of melons, as a traveller sees
False waves in desert drouth
With shade of leaf-crowned trees,
And burns the thirstier in the sandful breeze.

She no more swept the house,
Tended the fowls or cows,
Fetched honey, kneaded cakes of wheat,
Brought water from the brook:

But sat down listless in the chimney-nook
And would not eat.

Tender Lizzie could not bear
To watch her sister's cankerous care,
Yet not to share.
She night and morning
Caught the goblins' cry:
"Come buy our orchard fruits,
Come buy, come buy:"—
Beside the brook, along the glen,
She heard the tramp of goblin men,
The voice and stir
Poor Laura could not hear;
Longed to buy fruit to comfort her,
But feared to pay too dear.
She thought of Jeanie in her grave,
Who should have been a bride;
But who for joys brides hope to have
Fell sick and died
In her gay prime,
In earliest winter time,
With the first glazing rime,
With the first snow-fall of crisp winter time.

Till Laura dwindling
Seemed knocking at Death's door.
Then Lizzie weighed no more
Better and worse;
But put a silver penny in her purse,
Kissed Laura, crossed the heath with clumps of furze
At twilight, halted by the brook:
And for the first time in her life
Began to listen and look.

Laughed every goblin
When they spied her peeping:
Came towards her hobbling,
Flying, running, leaping,
Puffing and blowing,
Chuckling, clapping, crowing,
Clucking and gobbling,
Mopping and mowing,

Full of airs and graces,
Pulling wry faces,
Demure grimaces,
Cat-like and rat-like,
Ratel- and wombat-like,
Snail-paced in a hurry,
Parrot-voiced and whistler,
Helter skelter, hurry skurry,
Chattering like magpies,
Fluttering like pigeons,
Gliding like fishes,—
Hugged her and kissed her:
Squeezed and caressed her:
Stretched up their dishes,
Panniers, and plates:
"Look at our apples
Russet and dun,
Bob at our cherries,
Bite at our peaches,
Citrons and dates,
Grapes for the asking,
Pears red with basking
Out in the sun,
Plums on their twigs;
Pluck them and suck them,—
Pomegranates, figs."

"Good folk," said Lizzie,
Mindful of Jeanie:
"Give me much and many:"
Held out her apron,
Tossed them her penny.
"Nay, take a seat with us,
Honour and eat with us,"
They answered grinning:
"Our feast is but beginning.
Night yet is early,
Warm and dew-pearly,
Wakeful and starry:
Such fruits as these
No man can carry;
Half their bloom would fly,

Half their dew would dry,
Half their flavour would pass by.
Sit down and feast with us,
Be welcome guest with us,
Cheer you and rest with us."—

"Thank you," said Lizzie: "But one waits
At home alone for me:
So without further parleying,
If you will not sell me any
Of your fruits though much and many,
Give me back my silver penny
I tossed you for a fee."—
They began to scratch their pates,
No longer wagging, purring,
But visibly demurring,
Grunting and snarling.
One called her proud,
Cross-grained, uncivil;
Their tones waxed loud,
Their looks were evil.
Lashing their tails
They trod and hustled her,
Elbowed and jostled her,
Clawed with their nails,
Barking, mewing, hissing, mocking,
Tore her gown and soiled her stocking,
Twitched her hair out by the roots,
Stamped upon her tender feet,
Held her hands and squeezed their fruits
Against her mouth to make her eat.

White and golden Lizzie stood,
Like a lily in a flood,—
Like a rock of blue-veined stone
Lashed by tides obstreperously,—
Like a beacon left alone
In a hoary roaring sea,
Sending up a golden fire,—
Like a fruit-crowned orange-tree
White with blossoms honey-sweet
Sore beset by wasp and bee,—
Like a royal virgin town

Topped with gilded dome and spire
Close beleaguered by a fleet
Mad to tug her standard down.

One may lead a horse to water,
Twenty cannot make him drink.
Though the goblins cuffed and caught her,
Coaxed and fought her,
Bullied and besought her,
Scratched her, pinched her black as ink,
Kicked and knocked her,
Mauled and mocked her,
Lizzie uttered not a word;
Would not open lip from lip
Lest they should cram a mouthful in:
But laughed in heart to feel the drip
Of juice that syruped all her face,
And lodged in dimples of her chin,
And streaked her neck which quaked like curd.
At last the evil people,
Worn out by her resistance,
Flung back her penny, kicked their fruit
Along whichever road they took,
Not leaving root or stone or shoot;
Some writhed into the ground,
Some dived into the brook
With ring and ripple,
Some scudded on the gale without a sound,
Some vanished in the distance.

In a smart, ache, tingle,
Lizzie went her way;
Knew not was it night or day;
Sprang up the bank, tore thro' the furze,
Threaded copse and dingle,
And heard her penny jingle
Bouncing in her purse,—
Its bounce was music to her ear.
She ran and ran
As if she feared some goblin man
Dogged her with gibe or curse
Or something worse:
But not one goblin skurried after,

Nor was she pricked by fear;
The kind heart made her windy-paced
That urged her home quite out of breath with haste
And inward laughter.
She cried, "Laura," up the garden,
"Did you miss me?
Come and kiss me.
Never mind my bruises,
Hug me, kiss me, suck my juices
Squeezed from goblin fruits for you,
Goblin pulp and goblin dew.
Eat me, drink me, love me;
Laura, make much of me;
For your sake I have braved the glen
And had to do with goblin merchant men."

Laura started from her chair,
Flung her arms up in the air,
Clutched her hair:
"Lizzie, Lizzie, have you tasted
For my sake the fruit forbidden?
Must your light like mine be hidden,
Your young life like mine be wasted,
Undone in mine undoing,
And ruined in my ruin,
Thirsty, cankered, goblin-ridden?"—
She clung about her sister,
Kissed and kissed and kissed her:
Tears once again
Refreshed her shrunken eyes,
Dropping like rain
After long sultry drouth;
Shaking with aguish fear, and pain,
She kissed and kissed her with a hungry mouth.

Her lips began to scorch,
That juice was wormwood to her tongue,
She loathed the feast:
Writhing as one possessed she leaped and sung,
Rent all her robe, and wrung
Her hands in lamentable haste,
And beat her breast.
Her locks streamed like the torch

Borne by a racer at full speed,
Or like the mane of horses in their flight,
Or like an eagle when she stems the light
Straight toward the sun,
Or like a caged thing freed,
Or like a flying flag when armies run.

Swift fire spread through her veins, knocked at her
heart,
Met the fire smouldering there
And overbore its lesser flame;
She gorged on bitterness without a name:
Ah fool, to choose such part
Of soul-consuming care!
Sense failed in the mortal strife:
Like the watch-tower of a town
Which an earthquake shatters down,
Like a lightning-stricken mast,
Like a wind-uprooted tree
Spun about,
Like a foam-topped waterspout
Cast down headlong in the sea,
She fell at last;
Pleasure past and anguish past,
Is it death or is it life?

Life out of death.
That night long Lizzie watched by her,
Counted her pulse's flagging stir,
Felt for her breath,
Held water to her lips, and cooled her face
With tears and fanning leaves.
But when the first birds chirped about their eaves,
And early reapers plodded to the place
Of golden sheaves,
And dew-wet grass
Bowed in the morning winds so brisk to pass,
And new buds with new day
Opened of cup-like lilies on the stream,
Laura awoke as from a dream,
Laughed in the innocent old way,
Hugged Lizzie but not twice or thrice;
Her gleaming locks showed not one thread of grey,

Her breath was sweet as May,
And light danced in her eyes.

Days, weeks, months, years
Afterwards, when both were wives
With children of their own;
Their mother-hearts beset with fears,
Their lives bound up in tender lives;
Laura would call the little ones
And tell them of her early prime,
Those pleasant days long gone
Of not-returning time:
Would talk about the haunted glen,
The wicked quaint fruit-merchant men,
Their fruits like honey to the throat
But poison in the blood
(Men sell not such in any town):
Would tell them how her sister stood
In deadly peril to do her good,
And win the fiery antidote:
Then joining hands to little hands
Would bid them cling together,—
"For there is no friend like a sister
In calm or stormy weather;
To cheer one on the tedious way,
To fetch one if one goes astray,
To lift one if one totters down,
To strengthen whilst one stands."

Mary E. Wilkins (Freeman)
(1852–1930)
(See also headnote on p. 372)

Many of Mary E. Wilkins's short stories were about New England "spinsters," women who often had a choice to marry but preferred to remain
single or to live in Boston marriages with other women (as she did until
she was forty-nine years old). At the age of seven, she became friends with
a schoolmate, Mary Wales. Like the female couple in "Two Friends," the
pair remained inseparable even as adults.

Wilkins lived with her family until the death of both her parents. When, at the age of thirty-one, she no longer had family responsibilities, she moved into Mary Wales's residence, and the two women made a home together for almost two decades. Among their friends were other literary women who were coupled in Boston marriages, such as Sarah Orne Jewett and Annie Fields. During those years Wilkins produced what has generally been recognized as her best work, including *A Humble Romance and Other Stories* (1887) and *A New England Nun and Other Stories* (1891). Mary Wales managed their home and left Wilkins free to write.

However, in 1902 their household broke up and Wilkins married Dr. Charles Freeman, after several years of painful vacillation in which she repeatedly accepted his proposal and then changed her mind. We can do no more than speculate about the nature of the conflict that beset her. The marriage was apparently smooth for a few years, and Freeman encouraged his wife's writing, but he was increasingly troubled by alcoholism and was several times hospitalized. Between hospitalizations he left his wife and took up residence with a young man, to whom he tried to leave his fortune. Mary Wilkins Freeman obtained a legal separation and was successful in overturning Freeman's will, so that at his death she was left a wealthy widow.

In 1887, at the time that "Two Friends" was published in *Harper's Bazar*, Mary Wilkins and Mary Wales were at the height of domestic tranquillity, as are the two central characters in the story. Her later story, "The Long Arm" (see p. 373), may be reflective of the disintegration of their relationship. In any case, neither character in the Boston marriage depicted in "Two Friends" sees any need in her life for a more conventional kind of union. Mary Wilkins Freeman's biographers have often suggested that when she was a young woman she fell in love with a man whom she could not marry and she pined for him throughout the years. The following story provides on interesting commentary on such speculations.

FURTHER READING: *Infant Sphinx: Collected Letters of Mary E. Wilkins Freeman*, ed. Brent L. Kendrick (Metuchen, NJ: Scarecrow Press, 1985). Alice G. Brand, "Mary Wilkins Freeman: Misanthropy as Propaganda," *New England Quarterly*, 50 (1977). Edward Foster, *Mary E. Wilkins Freeman* (New York: Hendricks House, 1956).

Two Friends

"I wish you'd jest look down the road again, Mis' Dunbar, an' see if you see anything of Abby comin'."

"I don't see a sign of her. It's a real trial for you to be so short-sighted, ain't it, Sarah?"

"I guess it is. Why, you wouldn't believe it, but I can't see anybody out in the road to tell who 'tis. I can see somethin' movin', an' that's all, unless there's somethin' peculiar about 'em that I can tell 'em by. I can always tell old Mr. Whitcomb—he's got a kind of a hitch when he walks, you know; an' Mis' Addison White always carries a parasol, an' I can tell her. I can see somethin' bobbin' overhead, an' I know who 'tis."

"Queer, ain't it, how she always carries that parasol? Why, I've seen her with it in the dead of winter, when the sun was shinin', an' 'twas freezin' cold; no more need of a parasol—"

"She has to carry it to keep off the sun an' wind, 'cause her eyes are weak, I s'pose."

"Why, I never knew that."

"Abby said she told her so. Abby giggled right in her face one day when she met her with it."

"She didn't!"

"She did—laughed right out. She said she couldn't help it nohow: you know Abby laughs terrible easy. There was Mis' White sailin' along with her parasol h'isted, she said, as fine as a fiddle. You know Mis' White always walks kind of nippin' anyhow, an' she's pretty dressy. An' then it was an awful cold, cloudy day, Abby said. The sun didn't shine, an' it didn't storm, an' there wa'n't no earthly use for a parasol anyway, that she could see. So she kind of snickered. I s'pose it struck her funny all of a sudden. Mis' White took it jest as quick, Abby said, an' told her kind of short that her eyes were terrible weak, an' she had to keep 'em shaded all the time she was outdoors; the doctor had give her orders to. Abby felt pretty streaked about it. You don't see her comin' yet, do you?"

"No, I don't. I thought I see somebody then, but it ain't her. It's the Patch boy, I guess. Yes, 'tis him. What do you think of Abby, Sarah?"

"Think of Abby! What do you mean, Mis' Dunbar?"

"Why, I mean, how do you think she is? Do you think her cough is as bad as 'twas?"

Sarah Arnold, who was a little light woman of fifty, thin-necked and round-backed, with blue protruding eyes in her tiny pale face, pursed up her mouth and went on with her work. She was sewing some red roses on to a black lace bonnet.

"I never thought her cough was very bad anyhow, as far as I was concerned," said she, finally.

"Why, you didn't? I thought it sounded pretty bad. I've been feelin' kind of worried about her."

"Tain't nothin' in the world but a throat cough. Her mother before her used to cough jest the same way. It sounds kind of hard, but 'tain't the kind of cough that kills folks. Why, I cough myself half the time."

Sarah hacked a little as she spoke.

"Old Mis' Vane died of consumption, didn't she?"

"Consumption! Jest about as much consumption as I've got. Mis' Vane died of liver complaint. I guess I know. I was livin' right in the house."

"Well, of course you'd be likely to know. I was thinkin' that was what I'd heard, that was all."

"Some folks did call it consumption, but it wa'n't. See anything of Abby?"

"No, I don't. You ain't worried about her, are you?"

"Worried?—no. I ain't got no reason to be worried that I know of. She's old enough to take care of herself. All is, the supper table's been settin' an hour, an' I don't see where she is. She jest went down to the store to git some coffee."

"It's kind of damp to-night."

" 'Taint damp enough to hurt her, I guess, well as she is."

"Mebbe not. That's a pretty bonnet you're makin'."

"Well, I think it's goin' to look pretty well. I didn't know as 'twould. I didn't have much to do with."

"I s'pose it's Abby's."

"Course it's Abby's. I guess you wouldn't see me comin' out in no such bonnet as this."

"Why, you ain't any older than Abby, Sarah."

"I'm different-lookin'," said Sarah, with a look which might have meant pride.

The two women were sitting on a little piazza at the side of the story-and-a-half white house.

Before the house was a small green yard with two cherry-trees in it. Then came the road, then some flat green meadow-lands where the frogs were singing. The grass on these meadows was a wet green, and there were some clumps of blue lilies which showed a long way off in it. Beyond the meadows was the southwest sky, which looked low and red and clear, and had birds in it. It was seven o'clock of a summer evening.

Mrs. Dunbar, tall and straight, with a dark, leathery face whose features were gracefully cut, sat primly in a wooden chair, which was higher than Sarah's little rocker.

"I know Abby looks well in 'most everything," said she.

"I never saw her try on anything that she didn't look well in. There's good-lookin' women, but there ain't many like Abby. Most folks are a little dependent on their bonnets, but she wa'n't, never. Sky blue or grass green, 'twas jest made for her. See anything of her comin'?"

"I can see her," said Sarah, joyfully, in a minute.

"Abby Vane, where have you been?" she called out.

The approaching woman looked up and laughed. "Did you think you'd lost me?" she said, as she came up the piazza step. "I went into Mis' Parson's, an' I staid longer'n I meant to. Agnes was there—she'd jest got home—an'—" She began to cough violently.

"You hadn't ought to give way to that ticklin' in your throat, Abby," said Sarah, sharply.

"She'd better go into the house out of this damp air," said Mrs. Dunbar.

"Land! the air won't hurt her none. But mebbe you had better come in, Abby. I want to try on this bonnet. I wish you'd come too, Mis' Dunbar. I want you to see if you think it's deep enough in the back."

"There!" said Sarah, after the three women had entered, and she had tied the bonnet on to Abby's head, picking the bows out daintily.

"It's real handsome on her," said Mrs. Dunbar.

"Red roses on a woman of my age!" laughed Abby. "Sarah's bound to rig me up like a young girl."

Abby stood in the little sitting room before the glass. The blinds were wide open to let the evening light in. Abby was a large, well-formed woman. She held her bonneted head up, and drew her chin back with an air of arch pride. The red roses bloomed meetly enough above her candid, womanly forehead.

"If you can't wear red roses, I don't know who can," said Sarah, looking up at her with pride and resentment. "You could wear a white dress to meetin' an' look as well as any of 'em."

"Look here, where did you git the lace for this bonnet?" asked Abby, suddenly. She had taken it off and was examining it closely.

"Oh, 'twas some I had."

"See here, you tell the truth now, Sarah Arnold. Didn't you take this off your black silk dress?"

"It don't make no odds where I took it from."

"You did. What made you do it?"

" 'Taint worth talkin' 'bout. I always despised it on the dress."

"Why, Sarah Arnold! That's jest the way she does," said Abby to Mrs. Dunbar. "If I didn't watch her, she wouldn't leave herself a thing to put on."

After Mrs. Dunbar had gone, Abby sat down in a large covered rocking chair and leaned her head back. Her eyes were parted a little, and her teeth showed. She looked ghastly all at once.

"What ails you?" said Sarah.

"Nothin'. I'm a little tired, that's all."

"What are you holdin' on to your side for?"

"Oh, nothin'. It ached a little, that's all."

"Mine's been achin' all the afternoon. I should think you'd better come out an' have somethin' to eat; the table's been settin' an hour an' a half."

Abby rose meekly and followed Sarah into the kitchen with a sort of weak stateliness. She had always had a queenly way of walking. If Abby Vane should fall a victim to consumption some day, no one could say that she had brought it upon herself by non-observance of hygienic rules. Long miles of country road had she traversed with her fine swinging step, her shoulders thrown well back, her head erect, in her day. She had had the whole care of their vegetable garden, she had weeded and hoed and dug, she had chopped wood and raked hay, and picked apples and cherries.

There had always been a settled and amicable division of labor between the two women. Abby did the rough work, the man's work of the establishment, and Sarah, with her little, slim, nervous frame, the woman's work. All the dress-making and millinery was Sarah's department, all the cooking, all the tidying and furbishing of the house. Abby rose first in the morning and made the fire, and she pumped the water and brought the tubs for the washing. Abby carried the purse, too. The two had literally one between them—one worn black leather wallet. When they went to the village store, if Sarah made the purchase, Abby drew forth the money to pay the bill.

The house belonged to Abby; she had inherited it from her mother. Sarah had some shares in the village bank, which kept them in food and clothes.

Nearly all the new clothes bought would be for Abby, though Sarah had to employ many a subterfuge to bring it about. She alone could have unravelled the subtlety of that diplomacy by which the new cashmere was made for Abby instead of herself, by which the new mantle was fitted to Abby's full, shapely shoulders instead of her own lean, stooping ones.

If Abby had been a barbarous empress, who exacted her cook's head as a penalty for a failure, she could have found no more faithful and anxious artist than Sarah. All the homely New England recipes which Abby loved shone out to Sarah as if written in letters of gold. That nicety of adjustment through which the appetite should neither be cloyed by frequency nor tantalized by desire was a constant study with her. "I've found out just how many times a week Abby likes mince-pie," she told Mrs. Dunbar, triumphantly, once. "I've been studyin' it out. She likes mince pie jest about twice to really relish it. She eats it other times, but she don't really hanker after it. I've been keepin' count about six weeks now, an' I can tell pretty well."

Sarah had not eaten her own supper tonight, so she sat down with

Abby at the little square table against the kitchen wall. Abby could not eat much, though she tried. Sarah watched her, scarcely taking a mouthful herself. She had a trick of swallowing convulsively every time Abby did, whether she was eating herself or not.

"Ain't goin' to have any custard pie?" said Sarah. "Why not? I went to work an' made it on purpose."

Abby began to laugh. "Well, I'll tell you what 'tis, Sarah," said she, "near's I can put it: I've got jest about as much feelin' about takin' vittles as a pillow-tick has about bein' stuffed with feathers."

"Ain't you been eatin' nothin' this afternoon?"

"Nothin' but them few cherries before I went out."

"That was jest enough to take your appetite off. I never can taste a thing between meals without feelin' it."

"Well, I dare say that was it. Any of them cherries in the house now?"

"Yes; there's some in the cupboard. Want some?"

"I'll git 'em."

Sarah jumped up and got a plate of beautiful red cherries and set them on the table.

"Let me see, these came off the Sarah-tree," said Abby, meditatively. "There wa'n't any on the Abby one this year."

"No," said Sarah, shortly.

"Kind of queer, wa'n't it? It's always bore, ever since I can remember."

"I don't see nothin' very queer about it. It was frost-bit that cold spell last spring; that's all that ails it."

"Why, the other one wa'n't."

"This one's more exposed."

The two round, symmetrical cherry-trees in the front yard had been called Abby and Sarah ever since the two women could remember. The fancy had originated somehow far back in their childhood, and ever since it had been the "Abby-tree" and the "Sarah-tree." Both had borne plentifully until this season, when the Abby-tree displayed only her fine green leaves in fruit-time, and the Sarah-tree alone was rosy with cherries. Sarah had picked some that evening standing primly on a chair under the branches, a little basket on her arm, poking her pale inquisitive face into the perennial beauties of her woody namesake. Abby had been used to picking cherries after a more vigorous fashion, with a ladder, but she had not offered to this season.

"I couldn't git many—couldn't reach nothin' but the lowest branches," said Sarah to-night, watching Abby eat the cherries. "I guess you'd better take the ladder out there to-morrow. They're dead ripe, an' the birds are gittin' 'em. I scared off a whole flock to-day."

"Well, I will if I can," said Abby.

"Will if you can! Why, there ain't no reason why you can't, is there?"

"No, not that I know of."

The next morning Abby painfully dragged the long ladder around the house to the tree, and did her appointed task. Sarah came to the door to watch her once, and Abby was coughing distressingly up amongst the green boughs.

"Don't give up to that ticklin' in your throat, for pity's sake, Abby," she called out.

Abby's laugh floated back in answer, like a brave song, from the tree.

Presently Mrs. Dunbar came up the path; she lived alone herself, and was a constant visitor. She stood under the tree, tall and lank and vigorous in her straight-skirted brown cotton gown.

"For the land sake, Abby! you don't mean to say you're pickin' cherries?" she called out. "Are you crazy?"

"Hush!" whispered Abby, between the leaves.

"I don't see why she's crazy," spoke up Sarah; "she always picks 'em."

"You don't catch me givin' up pickin' cherries till I'm a hundred," said Abby, loudly. "I'm a regular cherry bird."

Sarah went into the house soon, and directly Abby crawled down the ladder. She was dripping with perspiration, and trembling.

"Abby Vane, I'm all out of patience," said Mrs. Dunbar.

Abby sank down on the ground, "It's this cherry bird's last season," said she, with a pathetic twinkle in her eyes.

"There ain't no sense in your doin' so."

"Well, I've picked enough for a while, I guess."

"Give me that other basket," said Mrs. Dunbar, harshly, "an' I'll go up an' pick."

"You can pick some for yourself," coughed Abby.

"I don't like 'em," said Mrs. Dunbar, jerking herself up the ladder. "Git up off the ground, an' go in."

Abby obeyed without further words. She sat down in the sitting-room rocker, and leaned her head back. Sarah was stepping about in the kitchen, and did not come in, and she was glad.

In the course of a few months this old-fashioned chair, with its green cushion, held Abby from morning till night. She did not go out any more. She had kept about as long as she could. Every summer Sunday she had sat smartly beside Sarah in church, with those brave red roses on her head. But when the cold weather came her enemy's arrows were too sharp even for her strong mail of love and resolution.

Sarah's behavior seemed inexplicable. Even now that Abby was undeniably helpless, she was constantly goading her to her old tasks. She refused to admit that she was ill. She rebelled when the doctor was called. "No more need of a doctor than nothin' at all," she said.

Affairs went on so till the middle of the winter. Abby grew weaker and weaker, but Sarah seemed to ignore it. One day she went over to Mrs. Dunbar's. One of the other neighbors was sitting with Abby. Sarah walked in suddenly. The outer door opened directly in Mrs. Dunbar's living-room, and a whiff of icy air came in with her.

"How's Abby?" asked Mrs. Dunbar.

" 'Bout the same." Sarah stood upright, staring. She had a blue plaid shawl over her head, and she clutched it together with her red bony fingers. "I've got something on my mind," said she, "an' I've got to tell somebody. I'm goin' crazy."

"What do you mean?"

"Abby's goin' to die, an' I've got something on my mind. I ain't treated her right."

"Sarah Arnold, do, for pity's sake, sit down, an' keep calm!"

"I'm calm enough. Oh, what shall I do?"

Mrs. Dunbar forced Sarah into a chair and took her shawl. "You mustn't feel so," said she. "You've been just devoted to Abby all your life, an' everybody knows it. I know when folks die we're very apt to feel as if we hadn't done right by 'em, but there ain't no sense in your feelin' so."

"I know what I'm talkin' about. I've got something awful on my mind. I've got to tell somebody."

"Sarah Arnold, what do you mean?"

"I've got to tell."

There was a puzzled look on the other woman's thin, strong face. "Well, if you've got anything you want to tell, you can tell it, but I can't think what you're drivin' at."

Sarah fixed her eyes on the wall at the right of Mrs. Dunbar. "It begins 'way back when we was girls. You know I went to live with Abby an' her mother after my folks died. Abby an' me had always been together. You remember that John Marshall that used to keep store where Simmons is, about thirty year ago. When Abby was about twenty, he begun waitin' on her. He was a good-lookin' fellar, an' I guess he was smart, though I never took a fancy to him.

"He was crazy after Abby; but her mother didn't like him. She talked again' him from the very first of it, and wouldn't take no notice of him. She declared she shouldn't have him. Abby didn't say much. She'd laugh an' tell her mother not to fret, but she'd treat him pretty well when he came.

"I s'pose she liked him. I used to watch her, an' think she did. An' he kep' comin' an' comin'. All the fellars were crazy 'bout her anyhow. She was the handsomest girl that was ever seen, about. She'd laugh an' talk with all of 'em, but I s'pose Marshall was the one.

"Well, finally Mis' Vane made such a fuss that he stopped comin'. 'Twas along about a year before she died. I never knew, but I s'pose Abby told him. He went right off to Mexico. Abby didn't say a word, but I knew she felt bad. She didn't seem to care much about goin' into company, an' didn't act jest like herself.

"Well, old Mis' Vane died sudden, you know. She'd had the consumption for years, coughed ever since I could remember, but she went real quick at last, an' Abby was away. She'd gone over to her Aunt Abby's in Cole-brook to stay a couple of days. Her aunt wa'n't well neither, an' wanted to see her, an' her mother seemed comfortable so she thought she could go. We sent for her jest as soon as Mis' Vane was took worse, but she couldn't git home in time.

"So I was with Mis' Vane when she died. She had her senses, and she left word for Abby. She said to tell her she'd give her consent to her mar-ryin' John Marshall."

Sarah stopped. Mrs. Dunbar waited, staring.

"I ain't told her from that day to this."

"What!"

"I ain't never told what her mother said."

"Why, Sarah Arnold, why not?"

"Oh, I couldn't have it nohow—I couldn't—I couldn't, Mis' Dunbar. Seemed as if it would kill me to think of it. I couldn't have her likin' anybody else, an' gittin' married. You don't know what I'd been through. All my own folks had died before I was sixteen years old, an' Mis' Vane was gone, an' she'd been jest like a mother to me. I didn't have nobody in the world but Abby. I couldn't have it so—I couldn't—I couldn't."

"Sarah Arnold, you've been livin' with her all these years, an' been such friends, an' had this shut up in your mind. What are you made of?"

"Oh, I've done everything I could for Abby—everything."

"You couldn't make it up to her in such a way as that."

"I know it. Oh, Mis' Dunbar, have I got to tell her? Have I?"

Mrs. Dunbar, with her intent, ascetic face, confronted Sarah like an embodied conscience.

"Tell her? Sarah Arnold, don't you let another sun go down over your head before you tell her."

"Oh, it don't seem as if I could."

"Don't you wait another minute. You go right home now an' tell her, if you ever want any more peace in this world."

Sarah stood gazing at her a minute, trembling. Then she pulled her shawl up over her head and turned toward the door.

"Well, I'll see," said she.

"Don't you wait a minute!" Mrs. Dunbar called after her again. Then she stood watching the lean, pitiful figure slink down the street. She wondered a good many times afterward if Sarah had told; she suspected that she had not.

Sarah avoided her, and never alluded to the matter again. She fell back on her old philosophy. "'Tain't nothin' but Abby's goin' to git over," she told people. "'Tain't on her lungs. She'll git up as soon as it comes warmer weather."

She treated Abby now with the greatest tenderness. She toiled for her day and night. Every delicacy which the sick woman had ever fancied stood waiting on the pantry shelves. Sarah went without shoes and flannels to purchase them, though the chance that they would be tasted was small.

Every spare moment which she could get she sewed for Abby, and folded and hung away new garments which would never be worn. If Abby ventured to remonstrate, Sarah was indignant, and sewed the more; sitting up through long winter nights, she stitched and hemmed with fierce zeal. She ransacked her own wardrobe for material, and hardly left herself a whole article to wear.

Toward spring, when her little dividends came in, she bought stuff for a new dress for Abby—soft cashmere of a beautiful blue. She got patterns, and cut and fitted and pleated with the best of her poor country skill.

"There," said she, when it was completed, "you've got a decent dress to put on, Abby, when you get out again."

"It's real handsome, Sarah," said Abby, smiling.

Abby did not die till the last of May. She sat in her chair by the window, and watched feebly the young grass springing up and the green film spreading over the tree boughs. Way over across in a neighbor's garden was a little peach-tree. Abby could just see it.

"Jest see that peach-tree over there," she whispered to Sarah one evening. It was all rosy with bloom. "It's the first tree I've seen blowed out this year. S'pose the Abby-tree's goin' to blossom?"

"I guess so," said Sarah; "it's leavin' out."

Abby seemed to dwell on the blossoming of the Abby-tree. She kept talking about it. One morning she saw some cherry-trees in the next yard had blossomed, and she called Sarah eagerly.

"Sarah, have you looked to see if the Abby-tree's blossomed?"

"Of course it has. What's to hinder?"

Abby's face was radiant. "Oh, Sarah, I want to see it."

"Well, you wait till afternoon," said Sarah, with a tremble in her voice.

"I'll draw you round to the front-room door after dinner, an' you can look through at it."

People passing that morning stared to see Sarah Arnold doing some curious work in the front yard. Not one blossom was there on the Abby-tree, but the Sarah-tree was white. Its delicate garlanded boughs stirred softly, and gave out a sweet smell. Bees murmured through them. Sarah had a ladder plunged into the roadward side of all this bloom and sweetness, and she was sawing and hacking at the white boughs. Then she would stagger across to the other tree with her arms full of them. They trailed on the green turf, they lay over her shoulders like white bayonets. All the air around her was full of flying petals. She looked like some homely Spring Angel. Then she bound these fair branches and twigs into the houseward side of the Abby-tree. She worked hard and fast. That afternoon one looking at the tree from the house would have been misled. That side of the Abby-tree was brave with bloom.

Sarah drew Abby in her chair a little way into the front room. "There!" said she.

"Oh! ain't it beautiful?" cried Abby.

The white branches waved before the window. Abby sat looking at it with a peaceful smile on her face.

When she was back in her old place in the sitting-room, she gave a bright look up at Sarah.

"It ain't any use to worry," said she, "the Abby-tree is bound to blossom."

Sarah cried out suddenly, "Oh, Abby! Abby! Abby! what shall I do! oh, what shall I do!" She flung herself down by Abby's chair, and put her face on her thin knees. "Oh, Abby! Abby!"

"I ain't gon' to," said Sarah, in a minute. She stood up, and wiped her eyes. "I know you're better, Abby, an' you'll be out pretty soon. All is, you've been sick pretty long, an' it's kind of wore on me, an' it come over me all of a sudden."

"Sarah," said Abby, solemnly, "what's got to come has got to. You've got to look at things reasonable. There's two of us, an' one would have to go before the other one; we've always known it. It ain't goin' to be so bad as you think. Mis' Dunbar is comin' here to live with you. I've got it all fixed with her. She's real strong, an' she can make up the fires, an' git the water an' the tubs. You're fifty years old, an' you're goin' to have some more years to live. But it's just goin' to be gittin' up one day after another an' goin' to bed at night, an' they'll be gone. It can be got through with. There's roads trod out through everything, an' there's folks ahead with lanterns, as it were. You—"

"Oh, Abby! Abby! stop!" Sarah broke in. "If you knew all there was to it. You don't know—you don't know! I ain't treated you right, Abby, I ain't. I've been keepin' something from you."

"What have you been keepin', Sarah?"

Then Abby listened. Sarah told. There had always been an arch curve to Abby's handsome mouth—a look of sweet amusement at life. It showed forth plainly toward the close of Sarah's tale. Then it deepened suddenly. The poor sick woman laughed out, with a charming, gleeful ring.

A look of joyful wonder flashed over Sarah's despairing face. She stood staring.

"Sarah," said Abby, "I wouldn't have had John Marshall if he'd come on his knees after me all the way from Mexico!"

"Michael Field"
[Katharine Bradley (1846–1914)]
[Edith Cooper (1862–1913)]

"Michael Field" was the pseudonym of British writers Katharine Bradley and Edith Cooper, a niece and aunt who lived together from the time Edith was a small child to her death at the age of fifty-one. Their first joint writing venture, a book of poems, was published in 1881, when Edith was nineteen and Katharine was thirty-five. They went on to write almost three dozen volumes of historical dramas and verse together. As their journals and poetry suggest, they were not only literary collaborators and relatives but were also intensely involved romantic friends (and perhaps lesbian lovers), although each had brief—and by comparison insignificant—heterosexual interests.

They formulated ideas together, did research for their historical plays together, and wrote pages, speeches, and even single lines together. They claimed that after a work was written they could not themselves distinguish their individual contributions. Their collaboration was for them a manifestation of their female marriage. Even the romance of Elizabeth Barrett and Robert Browning paled by comparison, as they observed in their journal: "Those two poets, man and wife, wrote alone; each wrote, but did not bless or quicken one another at their work; *we are closer married* [italics are theirs]."

They wrote during the era when the sexologists were setting love between women apart from the normal and presenting lesbianism as a morbidity. In the midst of this transitional period Cooper and Bradley championed same-sex love in the guise of romantic friendship in much of their work. In their verse drama, *The Tragedy of Pardon*, written in the early twentieth century, they declare:

> There is love
> Of woman unto woman, in its fibre
> Stronger than knits a mother to her child.
> There is no lack in it, and no defect.
> It looks nor up nor down.
> But loves from plenitude to plenitude.
> With level eyes, as in the Trinity
> God looks across and worships.

However, while their love poetry is often in the tradition of romantic friendship, some poems seem to display an erotic awareness that suggests that Michael Field's writing may be seen as a bridge between the literature of a less self-consciously sexual era and our own day. Their lives, like their work, present an interesting problem of interpretation. For example, is it significant in this respect that their closest friends were a male homosexual couple, the artists Charles Ricketts and Charles Shannon, of whom they wrote, "[they are] very much like us"? Were there reasons apart from their liberalism why Katharine and Edith identified with Oscar Wilde when he was tried for sodomy—and convicted at least partly because of his aesthete depictions of male beauty in his writing? Katharine wrote to a literary friend that Wilde's trial was a personal threat to all "who sing the praise of youth and beauty and all those things that from the beginning of the world have been priceless to every artist." Edith wrote in her journal during the trial of having dreamt that she was dining in a hotel restaurant when she heard someone whisper that all of Michael Field's writing derived from Satan.

Their journal during an 1891 trip to Germany, where Edith was hospitalized with scarlet fever, suggests their distinct awareness of erotic possibilities between women. Katharine, who demanded that she be permitted to live in the hospital room with Edith, jealously observed in her journal a nurse's sexual advances toward Edith: "Sister kisses her with a kiss that plunges down among the wraps . . . O Eros! . . . a fatal kiss." In another journal entry written at the same time, Edith described herself in a fever, imagining that she was Mars (she had been writing an essay on Botticelli's "Venus and Mars" before she left England) as she "look[ed] across at [Katharine's] little bed. I realise that she is a goddess, hidden in her hair— Venus. Yet I cannot reach her. . . . I grow wilder for pleasure and madder against the ugly Mädchen [the hospital attendant who restrains Edith]."

Sexual imagery abounds in many of their poems, but it alternates with images that are much less erotically charged and more characteristic of the literature of romantic friendship. In some poems Cooper and Bradley even consciously reject chthonic sexuality in their valorization of a lighter and sweeter form of loving. For example:

> Ah, Eros does not always smite
>   With cruel, shining dart,
> Whose bitter point with sudden might
>   Rends the unhappy heart—
> Not thus forever purple-stained
>   And sore with steely touch,
> Else were its living fountain drained
>   Too oft and over much.
> O'er it sometimes the boy will deign
>   Sweep the shaft's feathered end;
> And friendship rises without pain
>   Where the white plumes descend.

But their very rejection of the chthonic in this poem suggests a troubled awareness of its power and raises provocative questions about the meaning of the poem. What kinds of different relationships is the poem contrasting? Homosexual *vs.* heterosexual? Romantic friendship *vs.* lesbian? Or is it contrasting different stages within a single relationship? The image of Cupid's "white plumes" here is contradicted by those of the "thousand vermilion-beads" and the "harvest-secret [that] is burning red" in what appears to be a lesbian love poem, "Unbosoming" (see below).

Whether they conceived of themselves as romantic friends or lesbian lovers, or perhaps both at various times in their many years together, what is clear from their poetry and their journals is their total commitment to each other. In 1907 they joined the Roman Catholic church, as did many of their fellow aesthete writers. Their religious devotion did not lessen their devotion to each other. Edith became ill with cancer in 1912. Katharine nursed her until she died in 1913 and survived her by only six months.

FURTHER READING: Michael Field, *Underneath the Bow* (London: George Bell and Company, 1893); *The Wattlefold: Unpublished Poems by Michael Field* (Oxford: Basil Blackwell, 1930). *Works and Days: From the Journal of Michael Field*, eds. T. and D. C. Sturge Moore (London: John Murray, 1933). Henri Locard, "Works and Days: The Journals of Michael Field," *Journal of the Eighteen Nineties Society*, vol. 10, 1979. Mary Sturgeon, *Michael Field* (London: George Harrap and Company, 1922). Chris White, "Poets and Lovers Ever More: The Poetry and Journals of Michael Field," *Sexual Sameness: Textual Difference in Gay and Lesbian Writing*, ed. Joseph Bristow (New York: Routledge, 1992), pp. 26–43.

PROLOGUE

It was deep April, and the morn
Shakespeare was born;
The world was on us, pressing sore;
My Love and I took hands and swore,
Against the world, to be
Poets and lovers ever more,
To laugh and dream on Lethe's shore,
To sing to Charon in his boat,
Heartening the timid souls afloat;
Of judgment never to take heed,
But to those fast-locked souls to speed,
Who never from Apollo fled,
Who spent no hour among the dead;
Continually
With them to dwell,
Indifferent to heaven and hell.

CONSTANCY

I love her with the seasons, with the winds,
As the stars worship, as anemones
Shudder in secret for the sun, as bees
Buzz round an open flower: in all kinds
My love is perfect, and in each she finds
Herself the goal: then why, intent to teaze
And rob her delicate spirit of its ease,
Hastes she to range me with inconstant minds?
If she should die, if I were left at large
On earth without her—I, on earth, the same
Quick mortal with a thousand cries, her spell
She fears would break. And I confront the charge
As sorrowing, and as careless of my fame
As Christ intact before the infidel.

A GRAY MOB-CAP

A gray mob-cap and a girl's
  Soft circle of sprouting curls,
That proclaim she has had the fever:

How dear the days when the child was nurst!
I can but pray she may die the first,
  That I may not leave her!

Her head on my knee laid down,
That *duvet* so warm, so brown,
I fondle, I dote on its springing.
"Thou must never grow lonesome or old,
Leave me rather to darkness and cold,
  O my Life, my Singing!"

A GIRL

A girl,
Her soul a deep-wave pearl,
Dim, lucent of all lovely mysteries;
A face flowered for heart's ease,
A brow's grace soft as seas
Seen through faint forest trees:
A mouth, the lips apart,
Like aspen-leaflets trembling in the breeze
From her tempestuous heart.
Such: and our souls so knit,
I leave a page half-writ—
The work begun
Will be to heaven's conception done,
If she come to it.

UNBOSOMING

The love that breeds
In my heart for thee!
As the iris is full, brimful of seeds,
And all that it flowered for among the reeds
Is packed in a thousand vermilion-beads
That push, and riot, and squeeze, and clip,
Till they burst the sides of the silver scrip,
And at last we see
What the bloom, with its tremulous, bowery fold
Of zephyr-petal at heart did hold:
So my breast is rent

With the burthen and strain of its great content;
For the summer of fragrance and sighs is dead,
The harvest-secret is burning red,
And I would give thee, after my kind,
The final issues of heart and mind.

MY LADY HAS A LOVELY RITE

My lady has a lovely rite:
When I am gone
No prayer she saith
As one in fear:
For orison,
Pressing her pillows white
With kisses, just the sacred number,
She turns to slumber;
Adding sometimes thereto a tear
And a quick breath.

MY DARLING

Tò μέλημα τοὐμόν.
Atthis, my darling, thou did'st stray
A few feet to the rushy bed,
When a great fear and passion shook
My heart lest haply thou wert dead;
It grew so still about the brook,
As if a soul were drawn away.

My darling! Nay, our very breath
Nor light nor darkness shall divide;
Queen Dawn shall find us on one bed,
Nor must thou flutter from my side
An instant, lest I feel the dread,
At this, the immanence of death.

METHINKS MY LOVE TO THEE DOTH GROW

Methinks my love to thee doth grow
And this the sign:

I see the Spirit claim thee,
And do not blame thee,
Nor break intrusive on the Holy Ground
Where thou of God art found.

I watch the fire
Leap up, and do not bring
Fresh water from the spring
To keep it from up-flaming higher
Than my chilled hands require
For cherishing.

I see thy soul turn to her hidden grot,
And follow not;
Content thou shouldst prefer
To be with her,
The heavenly Muse, than ever find in me
Best company.

So brave my love is grown,
I joy to find thee sought
By some great thought;
And am content alone
To eat life's common fare,
While thou prepare
To be my royal moment's guest:
Live to the Best!

BELOVED, NOW I LOVE GOD FIRST

Beloved, now I love God first
There is for thee such summer burst
Where it was stirring spring before,
Lo, for thy feet a blossom-floor!

Patience! A little while to wait
Till I possess my new estate,
Then to assume thy glorious part
In my enriched and feasting heart.

LOVERS

Lovers, fresh plighting lovers in our age
Lovers in Christ—so tender at the heart
The pull about the strings as they engage—
One thing is plain:—that we can never part.
O Child, thou hauntest me in every room;
Not for an instant can we separate;
And thou or I, if absent in a tomb
Must keep unqualified our soul's debate.
Death came to me but just twelve months ago
Threatening thy life; I counted thee as dead—
Christ by thy bier took pity of my woe
And lifted thee and on my bosom spread;
And did not then retire and leave us twain:
Together for a little while we stood
And looked on Him, and chronicled His pain,
The wounds for us that started in their blood—
We, with one care, our common days shall spend,
As on that noble sorrow we attend.

BELOVED, MY GLORY IN THEE IS NOT CEASED

Beloved, my glory in thee is not ceased,
Whereas, as thou art waning, forests wane:
Unmoved, as by the victim is the priest,
I pass the world's great altitudes of pain.
But when the stars are gathered for a feast,
Or shadows threaten on a radiant plain,
Or many golden cornfields wave amain,
Oh then, as one from a filled shuttle weaves,
   My spirit grieves.

SHE IS SINGING TO THEE, *DOMINE!*

She is singing to Thee, *Domine!*
   Dost hear her now?
She is singing to Thee from a burning throat,
And melancholy as the owl's love-note;
She is singing to Thee from the utmost bough
   Of the tree of Golgotha, where it is bare,

And the fruit torn from it that fruited there;
She is singing. . . . Canst Thou stop the strain,
　　The homage of such pain?
Domine, stoop down to her again!

CAPUT TUUM UT CARMELUS

I watch the arch of her head,
As she turns away from me. . . .
I would I were with the dead,
Drowned with the dead at sea,
All the waves rocking over me!

As St. Peter turned and fled
From the Lord, because of sin,
I look on that lovely head;
And its majesty doth win
Grief in my heart as for sin.

Oh, what can Death have to do
With a curve that is drawn so fine,
With a curve that is drawn as true
As the mountain's crescent line? . . .
Let me be hid where the dust falls fine!

Sarah Orne Jewett
(1849–1909)

As a young woman, Sarah Orne Jewett had a number of romantic friendships, which she recorded in her diaries and poems. Of Kate Birckhead, for
example, Jewett wrote in her diary in 1871, "When I heard her voice on
the stairs . . . it gave me the queerest feeling. I have longed to see her, to
be with her, for so many months that I could not believe it was real. My
dear dear darling Kate!" In an 1880 poem, "Love and Friendship," whose
recipient was probably Cora Lee Rice, Jewett asked:

　　Do you remember, my darling
　　　A year ago today
　　When we gave ourselves to each other
　　　Before you went away . . . ?

How little we knew, my darling,
　All that the year would bring!
Did I think of the wretched mornings
　When I should kiss my ring
And long with all my heart to see
The girl who gave the ring to me?

But the most important relationship of her life was her Boston marriage with Annie Fields, which began around 1880 and lasted for almost three decades, until Jewett's death in 1909. Jewett commemorated their first anniversary in an 1881 letter: "Oh my darling, I had forgotten that we loved each other so much a year ago, for it all seems so new to me everyday. There 's so much for us to remember already—But a year ago last winter seems a great way off for us to have loved so much since."

Jewett's most assiduous biographers have been unable to find any trace of a heterosexual love interest in her life. When her poet friend John Greenleaf Whittier asked her, "Sarah, was thee ever in love?" she replied, blushing, "No! Whatever made you think that?" and explained to him that she had more need in her life of a wife than a husband. In a clever story about role reversal, "Tom's Husband," she shows that heterosexual marriage can be destructive to women because they risk losing their identity in their husband and dropping out of all aspects of life not related to domesticity. In her 1884 novel, *A Country Doctor*, she argued that as society "becomes more intelligent" it will recognize the unfitness of some women for marriage and will promote their pursuit of occupations that are more appropriate for them. She clearly believed that for herself romantic friendship or Boston marriage was far more suitable than heterosexual marriage.

Her "marriage" to Annie Fields, a society woman and writer, was for Jewett the perfect relationship. For several months each year Jewett retreated to her family estate in South Berwick, Maine, where she wrote her novels and stories in isolation. During the rest of the year she lived with Annie in Boston. Their correspondence suggests not only that Jewett made good use of her time alone in Maine to work at her profession, but also that her knowledge that Annie was lovingly waiting for her in Boston helped to sustain her. For example, she wrote to Annie from South Berwick in October 1882:

Here I am at the desk again, all as natural as can be and writing a first letter to you with so much love, and remembering that this is the first morning in more than seven months that I haven't waked up to hear your dear voice and see your dear face. I do miss it very much, but I look forward to no long separation, which is a comfort.

And in 1883 she wrote:

> I shall be with you tomorrow, your dear birthday. How I am
> looking forward to Thursday evening. I don't care whether there is
> starlight or a fog. Yes, dear, I will bring the last sketch and give it
> its last touches if you think that I had better spend any more time
> on it. I am tired of writing things. I want now to paint things, and
> drive things, and *kiss* things [the italics are Jewett's]. . . . Good
> night, and God bless you, dear love.

"Martha's Lady" is not a story of Boston marriage as Jewett lived it.
The central characters are of different classes, and Boston marriages generally involved women of the same class, both with economic wherewithal.
However, the story shows Jewett's views of the redemptive power of
female-female love. It presents a romantic friendship that is lived out primarily in fantasy but can nevertheless nurture and sustain.

FURTHER READING: Sarah Orne Jewett, *A Country Doctor* (Boston: Houghton Mif-
flin, 1884); *Deephaven* (1877); New Haven, CT: College and University Press, 1966).
The Letters of Sarah Orne Jewett, ed. Annie Fields (Boston: Houghton Mifflin, 1911).
Josephine Donovan, *Sarah Orne Jewett* (New York: Ungar, 1981); "The Unpublished
Love Poems of Sarah Orne Jewett," *Frontiers: A Journal of Women's Studies*, III (Fall
1979), pp. 26–31. Judith Fetterley, "Reading *Deephaven* as a Lesbian Text," in *Sexual
Practice, Textual Theory: Lesbian Cultural Criticism*, eds. Susan J. Wolfe and Julia Pe-
nelope (Cambridge, MA: Blackwell, 1993). Glenda Hobbs, "Pure and Passionate: Female
Friendship in Sarah Orne Jewett's 'Martha's Lady,' " *Studies in Short Fiction*, 17 (1980),
pp. 21–29. Judith A. Roman, *Annie Adams Fields: The Spirit of Charles Street* (Bloomington: Indiana University Press, 1990). Sarah Way Sherman, *Sarah Orne Jewett: An
American Persephone* (Hanover, NH: University Press of New England, 1988).

TOGETHER

I wonder if you really send
   These dreams of you that come and go!
I like to say, "She thought of me,
   And I have known it." Is it so?

Though other friends are by your side,
   Yet sometimes it must surely be
They wonder where your thoughts have gone—
   Because I have you here with me.

And when the busy day is done,
   When work is ended, voices cease,

And everyone has said good-night
  In fading twilight, then, in peace,

Idly I rest; you come to me,
  Your dear love holds me close to you.
If I could see you face to face,
  It would not be more sweet and true.

And now across the weary miles
  Light from my star shines. Is it, dear,
You never really went away—
  I said farewell, and—kept you here?

Martha's Lady

I

One day, many years ago, the old Judge Pyne house wore an unwonted look of gayety and youthfulness. The high-fenced green garden was bright with June flowers. Under the elms in the large shady front yard you might see some chairs placed near together, as they often used to be when the family were all at home and life was going on gayly with eager talk and pleasure-making; when the elder judge, the grandfather, used to quote that great author, Dr. Johnson, and say to his girls, "Be brisk, be splendid, and be public."

One of the chairs had a crimson silk shawl thrown carelessly over its straight back, and a passer-by, who looked in through the latticed gate between the tall gate-posts with their white urns, might think that this piece of shining East Indian color was a huge red lily that had suddenly bloomed against the syringa bush. There were certain windows thrown wide open that were usually shut, and their curtains were blowing free in the light wind of a summer afternoon; it looked as if a large household had returned to the old house to fill the prim best rooms and find them full of cheer.

It was evident to every one in town that Miss Harriet Pyne, to use the village phrase, had company. She was the last of her family, and was by no means old; but being the last, and wonted to live with people much older than herself, she had formed all the habits of a serious elderly person. Ladies of her age, something past thirty, often wore discreet caps in those days, especially if they were married, but being single, Miss Harriet clung to youth in this respect, making the one concession of keeping her waving chestnut hair as smooth and stiffly arranged as possible. She had been the dutiful companion of her father and mother in their latest years, all her elder brothers and sisters having married and gone, or died and gone, out of the old house. Now that she was left alone it seemed quite the best thing frankly to accept the fact of age, and to turn more resolutely than ever to the companionship of duty and serious books. She was more serious and given to routine than her elders themselves, as sometimes happened when the daughters of New England gentlefolks were brought up wholly in the society of their elders. At thirty-five she had more reluctance than her mother to face an unforeseen occasion, certainly more than her grandmother, who had preserved some cheerful inheritance of gayety and worldliness from colonial times.

There was something about the look of the crimson silk shawl in the front yard to make one suspect that the sober customs of the best house in a quiet New England village were all being set at defiance, and once when the mistress of the house came to stand in her own doorway, she wore the pleased but somewhat apprehensive look of a guest. In these days New England life held the necessity of much dignity and discretion of behavior; there was the truest hospitality and good cheer in all occasional festivities, but it was sometimes a self-conscious hospitality, followed by an inexorable return to asceticism both of diet and of behavior. Miss Harriet Pyne belonged to the very dullest days of New England, those which perhaps held the most priggishness for the learned professions, the most limited interpretation of the word "evangelical," and the pettiest indifference to large things. The outbreak of a desire for larger religious freedom caused at first a most determined reaction toward formalism, especially in small and quiet villages like Ashford, intently busy with their own concerns. It was high time for a little leaven to begin its work, in this moment when the great impulses of the war for liberty had died away and those of the coming war for patriotism and a new freedom had hardly yet begun.

The dull interior, the changed life of the old house, whose former activities seemed to have fallen sound asleep, really typified these larger conditions, and a little leaven had made its easily recognized appearance in the shape of a light-hearted girl. She was Miss Harriet's young Boston cousin, Helena Vernon, who, half-amused and half-impatient at the unnecessary sobermindedness of her hostess and of Ashford in general, had set herself to the difficult task of gayety. Cousin Harriet looked on at a succession of ingenious and, on the whole, innocent attempts at pleasure, as she might have looked on at the frolics of a kitten who easily substitutes a ball of yarn for the uncertainties of a bird or a wind-blown leaf, and who may at any moment ravel the fringe of a sacred curtain tassel in preference to either.

Helena, with her mischievous appealing eyes, with her enchanting old songs and her guitar, seemed the more delightful and even reasonable because she was so kind to everybody, and because she was a beauty. She had the gift of most charming manners. There was all the unconscious lovely ease and grace that had come with the good breeding of her city home, where many pleasant people came and went; she had no fear, one had almost said no respect, of the individual, and she did not need to think of herself. Cousin Harriet turned cold with apprehension when she saw the minister coming in at the front gate, and wondered in agony if Martha were properly attired to go to the door, and would by any chance hear the knocker; it was Helena who, delighted to have anything happen, ran to the door to welcome the Reverend Mr. Crofton as if he were a congenial friend of her own age. She could behave with more or less propriety during the stately first visit, and even contrive to lighten it with modest mirth, and to extort the confession that the guest had a tenor voice, though sadly out of practice; but when the minister departed a little flattered, and hoping that he had not expressed himself too strongly for a pastor upon the poems of Emerson, and feeling the unusual stir of gallantry in his proper heart, it was Helena who caught the honored hat of the late Judge Pyne from its last resting-place in the hall, and holding it securely in both hands, mimicked the minister's self-conscious entrance. She copied his pompous and anxious expression in the dim parlor in such delicious fashion that Miss Harriet, who could not always extinguish a ready spark of the original sin of humor, laughed aloud.

"My dear!" she exclaimed severely the next moment, "I am ashamed of your being so disrespectful!" and then laughed again, and took the affecting old hat and carried it back to its place.

"I would not have had any one else see you for the world," she said sorrowfully as she returned, feeling quite self-possessed again, to the parlor doorway; but Helena still sat in the minister's chair, with her small feet placed as his stiff boots had been, and a copy of his solemn expression before they came to speaking of Emerson and of the guitar. "I wish I had asked him if he would be so kind as to climb the cherry-tree," said Helena, unbending a little at the discovery that her cousin would consent to laugh no more. "There are all those ripe cherries on the top branches. I can climb as high as he, but I can't reach far enough from the last branch that will bear me. The minister is so long and thin"—

"I don't know what Mr. Crofton would have thought of you; he is a very serious young man," said cousin Harriet, still ashamed of her laughter. "Martha will get the cherries for you, or one of the men. I should not like to have Mr. Crofton think you were frivolous, a young lady of your opportunities"—but Helena had escaped through the hall and out at the garden door at the mention of Martha's name. Miss Harriet Pyne sighed anxiously, and then smiled, in spite of her deep convictions, as she shut the blinds and tried to make the house look solemn again.

The front door might be shut, but the garden door at the other end of the broad hall was wide open upon the large sunshiny garden, where the last of the red and white peonies and the golden lilies, and the first of the tall blue larkspurs lent their colors in generous fashion. The straight box borders were all in fresh and shining green of their new leaves, and there was a fragrance of the old garden's inmost life and soul blowing from the honeysuckle blossoms on a long trellis. It was now late in the afternoon, and the sun was low behind great apple-trees at the garden's end, which threw their shadows over the short turf of the bleaching-green. The cherry-trees stood at one side in full sunshine, and Miss Harriet, who presently came to the garden steps to watch like a hen at the water's edge, saw her cousin's pretty figure in its white dress of India muslin hurrying across the grass. She was accompanied by the tall, ungainly shape of Martha the new maid, who, dull and indifferent to every one else, showed a surprising willingness and allegiance to the young guest.

"Martha ought to be in the dining-room, already, slow as she is; it wants but half an hour of tea-time," said Miss Harriet, as she turned and went into the shaded house. It was Martha's duty to wait at table, and there had been many trying scenes and defeated efforts toward her education. Martha was certainly very clumsy, and she seemed the clumsier because she had replaced her aunt, a most skillful person, who had but lately married a thriving farm and its prosperous owner. It must be confessed that Miss Harriet was a most bewildering instructor, and that her pupil's brain was easily confused and prone to blunders. The coming of Helena had been somewhat dreaded by reason of this incompetent service, but the guest took no notice of frowns or futile gestures at the first tea-table, except to establish friendly relations with Martha on her own account by a reassuring smile. They were about the same age, and next morning, before cousin Harriet came down, Helena showed by a word and a quick touch the right way to do something that had gone wrong and been impossible to understand the night before. A moment later the anxious mistress came in without suspicion, but Martha's eyes were as affectionate as a dog's, and there was a new look of hopefulness on her face; this dreaded guest was a friend after all, and not a foe come from proud Boston to confound her ignorance and patient efforts.

The two young creatures, mistress and maid, were hurrying across the bleaching-green.

"I can't reach the ripest cherries," explained Helena politely, "and I think that Miss Pyne ought to send some to the minister. He has just made us a call. Why, Martha, you have n't been crying again!"

"Yes'm," said Martha sadly. "Miss Pyne always loves to send something to the minister," she acknowledged with interest, as if she did not wish to be asked to explain these latest tears.

"We'll arrange some of the best cherries in a pretty dish. I'll show you how, and you shall carry them over to the parsonage after tea," said Helena cheerfully, and Martha accepted the embassy with pleasure. Life was beginning to hold moments of something like delight in the last few days.

"You'll spoil your pretty dress, Miss Helena," Martha gave shy warning, and Miss Helena stood back and held up her skirts with unusual care while the country girl, in her heavy blue checked gingham, began to climb the cherry-tree like a boy.

Down came the scarlet fruit like bright rain into the green grass.

"Break some nice twigs with the cherries and leaves together; oh, you're a duck, Martha!" and Martha, flushed with delight, and looking far more like a thin and solemn blue heron, came rustling down to earth again, and gathered the spoils into her clean apron.

That night at tea, during her handmaiden's temporary absence, Miss Harriet announced, as if by way of apology, that she thought Martha was beginning to understand something about her work. "Her aunt was a treasure, she never had to be told anything twice; but Martha has been as clumsy as a calf," said the precise mistress of the house. "I have been afraid sometimes that I never could teach her anything. I was quite ashamed to have you come just now, and find me so unprepared to entertain a visitor."

"Oh, Martha will learn fast enough because she cares so much," said the visitor eagerly. "I think she is a dear good girl. I do hope that she will never go away. I think she does things better every day, cousin Harriet," added Helena pleadingly, with all her kind young heart. The china-closet door was open a little way, and Martha heard every word. From that moment, she not only knew what love was like, but she knew love's dear ambitions. To have come from a stony hill-farm and a bare small wooden house, was like a cave-dweller's coming to make a permanent home in an art museum, such had seemed the elaborateness and elegance of Miss Pyne's fashion of life; and Martha's simple brain was slow enough in its processes and recognitions. But with this sympathetic ally and defender, this exquisite Miss Helena who believed in her, all difficulties appeared to vanish.

Later that evening, no longer homesick or hopeless, Martha returned from her polite errand to the minister, and stood with a sort of triumph before the two ladies, who were sitting in the front doorway, as if they were waiting for visitors, Helena still in her white muslin and red ribbons, and Miss Harriet in a thin black silk. Being happily self-forgetful in the greatness of the moment, Martha's manners were perfect, and she looked for once almost pretty and quite as young as she was.

"The minister came to the door himself, and returned his thanks. He said that cherries were always his favorite fruit, and he was much obliged to both Miss Pyne and Miss Vernon. He kept me waiting a few minutes, while he got this book ready to send to you, Miss Helena."

"What are you saying, Martha? I have sent him nothing!" exclaimed Miss Pyne, much astonished. "What does she mean, Helena?"

"Only a few cherries," explained Helena. "I thought Mr. Crofton would like them after his afternoon of parish calls. Martha and I arranged them before tea, and I sent them with our compliments."

"Oh, I am very glad you did," said Miss Harriet, wondering, but much relieved. "I was afraid"—

"No, it was none of my mischief," answered Helena daringly. "I did not think that Martha would be ready to go so soon. I should have shown you how pretty they looked among their green leaves. We put them in one of your best white dishes with the openwork edge. Martha shall show you to-morrow; mamma always likes to have them so." Helena's fingers were busy with the hard knot of a parcel.

"See this, cousin Harriet!" she announced proudly, as Martha disappeared round the corner of the house, beaming with the pleasures of adventure and success. "Look! the minister has sent me a book: Sermons on *what?* Sermons—it is so dark that I can't quite see."

"It must be his 'Sermons on the Seriousness of Life;' they are the only ones he has printed, I believe," said Miss Harriet, with much pleasure. "They are considered very fine discourses. He pays you a great compliment, my dear. I feared that he noticed your girlish levity."

"I behaved beautifully while he stayed," insisted Helena. "Ministers are only men," but she blushed with pleasure. It was certainly something to receive a book from its author, and such a tribute made her of more value to the whole reverent household. The minister was not only a man, but a bachelor, and Helena was at the age that best loves conquest; it was at any rate comfortable to be reinstated in cousin Harriet's good graces.

"Do ask the kind gentleman to tea! He needs a little cheering up," begged the siren in India muslin, as she laid the shiny black volume of sermons on the stone doorstep with an air of approval, but as if they had quite finished their mission.

"Perhaps I shall, if Martha improves as much as she has within the last day or two," Miss Harriet promised hopefully. "It is something I always dread a little when I am all alone, but I think Mr. Crofton likes to come. He converses so elegantly."

II

These were the days of long visits, before affectionate friends thought it quite worth while to take a hundred miles' journey merely to dine or to pass a night in one another's houses. Helena lingered through the pleasant weeks of early summer, and departed unwillingly at last to join her family at the White Hills, where they had gone, like other households of high social station, to pass the month of August out of town. The happy-hearted young guest left many lamenting friends behind her, and promised each that she would come back again next year. She left the minister a rejected lover, as well as the preceptor of the academy, but with their pride un-wounded, and it may have been with wider outlooks upon the world and a less narrow sympathy both for their own work in life and for their neighbors' work and hindrances. Even Miss Harriet Pyne herself had lost some of the unnecessary provincialism and prejudice which had begun to harden a naturally good and open mind and affectionate heart. She was conscious of feeling younger and more free, and not so lonely. Nobody had ever been so gay, so fascinating, or so kind as Helena, so full of social resource, so simple and undemanding in her friendliness. The light of her young life cast no shadow on either young or old companions, her pretty clothes never seemed to make other girls look dull or out of fashion. When she went away up the street in Miss Harriet's carriage to take the slow train toward Boston and the gayeties of the new Profile House, where her mother waited impatiently with a group of Southern friends, it seemed as if there would never be any more picnics or parties in Ashford, and as if society had nothing left to do but to grow old and get ready for winter.

Martha came into Miss Helena's bedroom that last morning, and it was easy to see that she had been crying; she looked just as she did in that first sad week of homesickness and despair. All for love's sake she had been learning to do many things, and to do them exactly right; her eyes had grown quick to see the smallest chance for personal service. Nobody could be more humble and devoted; she looked years older than Helena, and wore already a touching air of caretaking.

"You spoil me, you dear Martha!" said Helena from the bed. "I don't know what they will say at home, I am so spoiled."

Martha went on opening the blinds to let in the brightness of the summer morning, but she did not speak.

"You are getting on splendidly, are n't you?" continued the little mistress. "You have tried so hard that you make me ashamed of myself. At first you crammed all the flowers together, and now you make them look beautiful. Last night cousin Harriet was so pleased when the table was so charming, and I told her that you did everything yourself, every bit. Won't you keep the flowers fresh and pretty in the house until I come back? It's so much pleasanter for Miss Pyne, and you'll feed my little sparrows, won't you? They're growing so tame."

"Oh, yes, Miss Helena!" and Martha looked almost angry for a moment, then she burst into tears and covered her face with her apron. "I could n't understand a single thing when I first came. I never had been anywhere to see anything, and Miss Pyne frightened me when she talked. It was you made me think I could ever learn. I wanted to keep the place, 'count of mother and the little boys; we're dreadful hard pushed. Hepsy has been good in the kitchen; she said she ought to have patience with me, for she was awkward herself when she first came."

Helena laughed; she looked so pretty under the tasseled white curtains.

"I dare say Hepsy tells the truth," she said. "I wish you had told me about your mother. When I come again, some day we'll drive up country, as you call it, to see her. Martha! I wish you would think of me sometimes after I go away. Won't you promise?" and the bright young face suddenly grew grave. "I have hard times myself; I don't always learn things that I ought to learn, I don't always put things straight. I wish you would n't forget me ever, and would just believe in me. I think it does help more than anything."

"I won't forget," said Martha slowly. "I shall think of you every day." She spoke almost with indifference, as if she had been asked to dust a room, but she turned aside quickly and pulled the little mat under the hot water jug quite out of its former straightness; then she hastened away down the long white entry, weeping as she went.

III

To lose out of sight the friend whom one has loved and lived to please is to lose joy out of life. But if love is true, there comes presently a higher joy of pleasing the ideal, that is to say, the perfect friend. The same old happiness is lifted to a higher level. As for Martha, the girl who stayed behind in Ashford, nobody's life could seem duller to those who could not understand; she was slow of step, and her eyes were almost always downcast as if intent upon incessant toil; but they startled you when she looked up, with their shining light. She was capable of the happiness of holding fast to a great sentiment, the ineffable satisfaction of trying to please one whom she truly loved. She never thought of trying to make other people pleased with herself; all she lived for was to do the best she could for others, and to conform to an ideal, which grew at last to be like a saint's vision, a heavenly figure painted upon the sky.

On Sunday afternoons in summer, Martha sat by the window of her chamber, a low-storied little room, which looked into the side yard and the great branches of an elm-tree. She never sat in the old wooden rocking-chair except on Sundays like this; it belonged to the day of rest and to happy meditation. She wore her plain black dress and a clean white apron, and held in her lap a little wooden box, with a brass ring on top for a handle. She was past sixty years of age and looked even older, but there was the same look on her face that it had sometimes worn in girlhood. She was the same Martha; her hands were old-looking and work-worn, but her face still shone. It seemed like yesterday that Helena Vernon had gone away, and it was more than forty years.

War and peace had brought their changes and great anxieties, the face of the earth was furrowed by floods and fire, the faces of mistress and maid were furrowed by smiles and tears, and in the sky the stars shone on as if nothing had happened. The village of Ashford added a few pages to its unexciting history, the minister preached, the people listened; now and then a funeral crept along the street, and now and then the bright face of a little child rose above the horizon of a family pew. Miss Harriet Pyne lived on in the large white house, which gained more and more distinction because it suffered no changes, save successive repaintings and a new railing about its stately roof. Miss Harriet herself had moved far beyond the uncertainties of an anxious youth. She had long ago made all her decisions, and settled all necessary questions; her scheme of life was as faultless as the miniature landscape of a Japanese garden, and as easily kept in order. The only important change she would ever be capable of making was the final change to another and a better world; and for that nature itself would gently provide, and her own innocent life.

Hardly any great social event had ruffled the easy current of life since Helena Vernon's marriage. To this Miss Pyne had gone, stately in appearance and carrying gifts of some old family silver which bore the Vernon crest, but not without some protest in her heart against the uncertainties of married life. Helena was so equal to a happy independence and even to the assistance of other lives grown strangely dependent upon her quick sympathies and instinctive decisions, that it was hard to let her sink her personality in the affairs of another. Yet a brilliant English match was not without its attractions to an old-fashioned gentlewoman like Miss Pyne, and Helena herself was amazingly happy; one day there had come a letter to Ashford, in which her very heart seemed to beat with love and self-forgetfulness, to tell cousin Harriet of such new happiness and high hope. "Tell Martha all that I say about my dear Jack," wrote the eager girl; "please show my letter to Martha, and tell her that I shall come home next summer and bring the handsomest and best man in the world to Ashford.

I have told him all about the dear house and the dear garden; there never was such a lad to reach for cherries with his six-foot-two." Miss Pyne, wondering a little, gave the letter to Martha, who took it deliberately and as if she wondered too, and went away to read it slowly by herself. Martha cried over it, and felt a strange sense of loss and pain; it hurt her heart a little to read about the cherry-picking. Her idol seemed to be less her own since she had become the idol of a stranger. She never had taken such a letter in her hands before, but love at last prevailed, since Miss Helena was happy, and she kissed the last page where her name was written, feeling overbold, and laid the envelope on Miss Pyne's secretary without a word.

The most generous love cannot but long for reassurance, and Martha had the joy of being remembered. She was not forgotten when the day of the wedding drew near, but she never knew that Miss Helena had asked if cousin Harriet would not bring Martha to town; she should like to have Martha there to see her married. "She would help about the flowers," wrote the happy girl; "I know she will like to come, and I'll ask mamma to plan to have some one take her all about Boston and make her have a pleasant time after the hurry of the great day is over."

Cousin Harriet thought it was very kind and exactly like Helena, but Martha would be out of her element; it was most imprudent and girlish to have thought of such a thing. Helena's mother would be far from wishing for any unnecessary guest just then, in the busiest part of her household, and it was best not to speak of the invitation. Some day Martha should go to Boston if she did well, but not now. Helena did not forget to ask if Martha had come, and was astonished by the indifference of the answer. It was the first thing which reminded her that she was not a fairy princess having everything her own way in that last day before the wedding. She knew that Martha would have loved to be near, for she could not help understanding in that moment of her own happiness the love that was hidden in another heart. Next day this happy young princess, the bride, cut a piece of a great cake and put it into a pretty box that had held one of her wedding presents. With eager voices calling her, and all her friends about her, and her mother's face growing more and more wistful at the thought of parting, she still lingered and ran to take one or two trifles from her dressing-table, a little mirror and some tiny scissors that Martha would remember, and one of the pretty handkerchiefs marked with her maiden name. These she put in the box too; it was half a girlish freak and fancy, but she could not help trying to share her happiness, and Martha's life was so plain and dull. She whispered a message, and put the little package into cousin Harriet's hand for Martha as she said good-by. She was very fond of cousin Harriet. She smiled with a gleam of her old fun; Martha's puzzled look and tall awkward figure seemed to stand suddenly before her eyes, as she promised to come again to Ashford. Impatient voices called to Helena, her lover was at the door, and she hurried away, leaving her old home and her girlhood gladly. If she had only known it, as she kissed cousin Harriet good-by, they were never going to see each other again until they were old women. The first step that she took out of her father's house that day, married, and full of hope and joy, was a step that led her away from the green elms of Boston Common and away from her own country and those she loved best, to a brilliant, much-varied foreign life, and to nearly all the sorrows and nearly all the joys that the heart of one woman could hold or know.

On Sunday afternoons Martha used to sit by the window in Ashford and hold the wooden box which a favorite young brother, who afterward died at sea, had made for her, and she used to take out of it the pretty little box with a gilded cover that had held the piece of wedding-cake, and the small scissors, and the blurred bit of a mirror in its silver case; as for the handkerchief with the narrow lace edge, once in two or three years she sprinkled it as if it were a flower, and spread it out in the sun on the old bleaching-green, and sat near by in the shrubbery to watch lest some bold robin or cherry-bird should seize it and fly away.

IV

Miss Harriet Pyne was often congratulated upon the good fortune of having such a helper and friend as Martha. As time went on this tall, gaunt woman, always thin, always slow, gained a dignity of behavior and simple affectionateness of look which suited the charm and dignity of the ancient house. She was unconsciously beautiful like a saint, like the picturesqueness of a lonely tree which lives to shelter unnumbered lives and to stand quietly in its place. There was such rustic homeliness and constancy belonging to her, such beautiful powers of apprehension, such reticence, such gentleness for those who were troubled or sick; all these gifts and graces Martha hid in her heart. She never joined the church because she thought she was not good enough, but life was such a passion and happiness of service that it was impossible not to be devout, and she was always in her humble place on Sundays, in the back pew next the door. She had been educated by a remembrance; Helena's young eyes forever looked at her reassuringly from a gay girlish face. Helena's sweet patience in teaching her own awkwardness could never be forgotten.

"I owe everything to Miss Helena," said Martha, half aloud, as she sat alone by the window; she had said it to herself a thousand times. When she looked in the little keepsake mirror she always hoped to see some faint reflection of Helena Vernon, but there was only her own brown old New England face to look back at her wonderingly.

Miss Pyne went less and less often to pay visits to her friends in Boston; there were very few friends left to come to Ashford and make long visits in the summer, and life grew more and more monotonous. Now and then there came news from across the sea and messages of remembrance, letters that were closely written on thin sheets of paper, and that spoke of lords and ladies, of great journeys, of the death of little children and the proud successes of boys at school, of the wedding of Helena Dysart's only daughter; but even that had happened years ago. These things seemed far away and vague, as if they belonged to a story and not to life itself; the true links with the past were quite different. There was the unvarying flock of ground-sparrows that Helena had begun to feed; every morning Martha scattered crumbs for them from the side doorsteps while Miss Pyne watched from the dining-room window, and they were counted and cherished year by year.

Miss Pyne herself had many fixed habits, but little ideality or imagination, and so at last it was Martha who took thought for her mistress, and gave freedom to her own good taste. After a while, without any one's observing the change, the every-day ways of doing things in the house came to be the stately ways that had once belonged only to the entertainment of guests. Happily both mistress and maid seized all possible chances for hospitality, yet Miss Harriet nearly always sat alone at her exquisitely served table with its fresh flowers, and the beautiful old china which Martha handled so lovingly that there was no good excuse for keeping it hidden on closet shelves. Every year when the old cherry-trees were in fruit, Martha carried the round white old English dish with a fretwork edge, full of pointed green leaves and scarlet cherries, to the minister, and his wife never quite understood why every year he blushed and looked so conscious of the pleasure, and thanked Martha as if he had received a very particular attention. There was no pretty suggestion toward the pursuit of the fine art of housekeeping in Martha's limited acquaintance with newspapers that she did not adopt; there was no refined old custom of the Pyne housekeeping that she consented to let go. And every day, as she had promised, she thought of Miss Helena,—oh, many times in every day: whether this thing would please her, or that be likely to fall in with her fancy or ideas of fitness. As far as was possible the rare news that reached Ashford through an occasional letter or the talk of guests was made part of Martha's own life, the history of her own heart. A worn old geography often stood open at the map of Europe on the light-stand in her room, and a little old-fashioned gilt button, set with a bit of glass like a ruby, that had broken and fallen from the trimming of one of Helena's dresses, was used to mark the city of her dwelling-place. In the changes of a diplomatic life Martha followed her lady all about the map. Sometimes the button was at Paris, and sometimes at Madrid; once, to her great anxiety, it remained long at St. Petersburg. For such a slow scholar Martha was not unlearned at last, since everything about life in these foreign towns was of interest to her faithful heart. She satisfied her own mind as she threw crumbs to the tame sparrows; it was all part of the same thing and for the same affectionate reasons.

V

One Sunday afternoon in early summer Miss Harriet Pyne came hurrying along the entry that led to Martha's room and called two or three times before its inhabitant could reach the door. Miss Harriet looked unusually cheerful and excited, and she held something in her hand. "Where are you, Martha?" she called again. "Come quick, I have something to tell you!"

"Here I am, Miss Pyne," said Martha, who had only stopped to put her precious box in the drawer, and to shut the geography.

"Who do you think is coming this very night at half-past six? We must have everything as nice as we can; I must see Hannah at once. Do you remember my cousin Helena who has lived abroad so long? Miss Helena Vernon,—the Honorable Mrs. Dysart, she is now."

"Yes, I remember her," answered Martha, turning a little pale.

"I knew that she was in this country, and I had written to ask her to come for a long visit," continued Miss Harriet, who did not often explain things, even to Martha, though she was always conscientious about the kind messages that were sent back by grateful guests. "She telegraphs that she means to anticipate her visit by a few days and come to me at once. The heat is beginning in town, I suppose. I daresay, having been a foreigner so long, she does not mind traveling on Sunday. Do you think Hannah will be prepared? We must have tea a little later."

"Yes, Miss Harriet," said Martha. She wondered that she could speak as usual, there was such a ringing in her ears. "I shall have time to pick some fresh strawberries; Miss Helena is so fond of our strawberries."

"Why, I had forgotten," said Miss Pyne, a little puzzled by something quite unusual in Martha's face. "We must expect to find Mrs. Dysart a good deal changed, Martha; it is a great many years since she was here; I have not seen her since her wedding, and she has had a great deal of trouble, poor girl. You had better open the parlor chamber, and make it ready before you go down."

"It is all ready," said Martha. "I can carry some of those little sweet-brier roses upstairs before she comes."

"Yes, you are always thoughtful," said Miss Pyne, with unwonted feeling.

Martha did not answer. She glanced at the telegram wistfully. She had never really suspected before that Miss Pyne knew nothing of the love that had been in her heart all these years; it was half a pain and half a golden joy to keep such a secret; she could hardly bear this moment of surprise.

Presently the news gave wings to her willing feet. When Hannah, the cook, who never had known Miss Helena, went to the parlor an hour later on some errand to her old mistress, she discovered that this stranger guest must be a very important person. She had never seen the tea-table look exactly as it did that night, and in the parlor itself there were fresh blossoming boughs in the old East India jars, and lilies in the paneled hall, and flowers everywhere, as if there were some high festivity.

Miss Pyne sat by the window watching, in her best dress, looking stately and calm; she seldom went out now, and it was almost time for the carriage. Martha was just coming in from the garden with the strawberries, and with more flowers in her apron. It was a bright cool evening in June, the golden robins sang in the elms, and the sun was going down behind the apple-trees at the foot of the garden. The beautiful old house stood wide open to the long-expected guest.

"I think that I shall go down to the gate," said Miss Pyne, looking at Martha for approval, and Martha nodded and they went together slowly down the broad front walk.

There was a sound of horses and wheels on the roadside turf: Martha could not see at first; she stood back inside the gate behind the white lilac-bushes as the carriage came. Miss Pyne was there; she was holding out both arms and taking a tired, bent little figure in black to her heart. "Oh, my Miss Helena is an old woman like me!" and Martha gave a pitiful sob; she had never dreamed it would be like this; this was the one thing she could not bear.

"Where are you, Martha?" called Miss Pyne. "Martha will bring these in; you have not forgotten my good Martha, Helena?" Then Mrs. Dysart looked up and smiled just as she used to smile in the old days. The young eyes were there still in the changed face, and Miss Helena had come.

That night Martha waited in her lady's room just as she used, humble and silent, and went through with the old unforgotten loving services. The long years seemed like days. At last she lingered a moment trying to think of something else that might be done, then she was going silently away, but Helena called her back. She suddenly knew the whole story and could hardly speak.

"Oh, my dear Martha!" she cried, "won't you kiss me good-night? Oh, Martha, have you remembered like this, all these long years!"

Katharine Lee Bates
(1859–1929)

Katharine Lee Bates, who is best remembered as the author of the song that almost became the United States's national anthem, "America the Beautiful," also wrote numerous poems about her love for another woman, Katharine Coman. Their romantic friendship began in the 1880s when they were both in their twenties and lasted until Coman's death twenty-five years later.

From her earliest years, Katharine Bates was a feminist and a rebel against the limited roles that were deemed legitimate for females. At the age of nine, in 1868, the precocious child wrote in her diary:

> I am happy to say [women] have become impatient under the re-
> straint men put upon them. So the great question of womens rights
> has arisen. . . . Girls are a very necessary portion of creation. They
> are full as necessary as boys. Girls (except a speches [sic] called
> tomboys) play with dolls when young. . . . Sewing is always ex-
> pected of girls. Why not of boys? Boys don't do much but outdoor
> work. Girls work is most all indoors. It isn't fair.

Like many other rebellious young middle-class females of her era, she went to a women's college, Wellesley, and took herself very seriously as a scholar. A few years after her college graduation she returned to Wellesley to teach and remained on the faculty until her retirement in 1925. It was on the Wellesley faculty that she met Katharine Coman. Bates eventually became chair of the English Department. Coman became chair of the Economics Department and Dean of the college.

A 1952 biographer described Coman as Bates's "closest and dearest friend throughout her life." The two women, who both spent the greater portion of their lives in the nineteenth century, would probably have been happy with that description. Regardless of the nature of their relationship, even if it was sexual, they would have had difficulty applying the word "lesbian" to themselves. Although the concept of romantic friendship was quickly becoming anachronistic by the time Coman died, it was an idea they would have felt comfortable with and could have availed themselves of as an explicit or implicit explanation to society of their relationship, or they might have described themselves as living in a Boston marriage.

Though the two women lived together for most of their relationship, they occasionally traveled alone. Some of the love letters that passed between them during those times are extant. For example, in 1891 Bates went to Oxford in order to study. She wrote Coman:

> I wonder if an English spring can be as beautiful as Princeton was a year ago. Do you remember the sunset sky that Sunday evening, when we strayed home from the Rock and there were two hands in one pocket? We will go to Princeton again sometime.
>
> For I am coming back to you, my Dearest, whether I come back to Wellesley or not. You are always in my heart and in my longings. I've been so homesick for you on this side of the ocean and yet so still and happy in the memory and consciousness of you. It was the living away from you that made, at first, the prospect of leaving Wellesley so heartachy. . . . It was never possible to leave Wellesley, because so many love anchors held me there, and it seemed least of all possible when I had just found the long-desired way to your dearest heart. . . . Of course I want to come to you, very much as I want to come to Heaven. . . . I'm tired of taking care of your Katharine. If I bring her back to you, will you take care of her yourself? Sweetheart, I always love you, more dearly than you know. Please take care of *my* Katharine.

Bates and Coman were part of a social group of women—such as the writers and activists Vida Scudder and Florence Converse at Wellesley, and the president and chair of the English Department at Mount Holyoke, Mary Woolley and Jeanette Marks—who lived in couples as they did, and who expressed such sentiments to each other in letters. Bates seems to have been quite without self-consciousness with regard to those sentiments. She often called Coman "Joy of Life" not only when they were alone together, but even in her published writing, such as her book about their dog, *Sigurd: Our Golden Collie.*

In 1912 Coman discovered she had cancer. Bates nursed her until her death in 1915. The poems that follow are from *Yellow Clover,* a volume of verses commemorating Bates's relationship with Coman, printed in a limited edition of 750 in 1922 and distributed to Bates's friends and colleagues as an Easter present. In 1926 Bates wrote to a friend, "So much of me died with Katharine Coman that I'm sometimes not quite sure whether I'm alive or not." Bates died three years later, at the age of seventy.

FURTHER READING: Katharine Lee Bates, *Yellow Clover: A Book of Remembrance* (New York: E. P. Dutton, 1922); *Selected Poems* (Boston: Houghton Mifflin, 1930). Dorothy Burgess, *Dream and Deed: The Story of Katharine Lee Bates* (Norman, Oklahoma: University of Oklahoma Press, 1952). Judith Schwarz, "Yellow Clover: Katharine Lee Bates and Katharine Coman," *Frontiers: A Journal of Women's Studies*, 4: 1 (Spring 1979), pp. 59–67.

IF YOU COULD COME

My love, my love, if you could come once more
   From your high place,
I would not question you for heavenly lore,
But, silent, take the comfort of your face.

I would not ask you if those golden spheres
   In love rejoice,
If only our stained star hath sin and tears,
But fill my famished hearing with your voice.

One touch of you were worth a thousand creeds.
   My wound is numb
Through toil-pressed day, but all night long it bleeds
In aching dreams, and still you cannot come.

YELLOW CLOVER

Must I, who walk alone,
Come on it still,
This Puck of plants
The wise would do away with,
The sunshine slants
To play with,
Our wee, gold-dusty flower, the yellow clover,
Which once in parting for a time
That then seemed long,
Ere time for you was over,
We sealed our own?
Do you remember yet,
O Soul beyond the stars,
Beyond the uttermost dim bars
Of space,
Dear Soul who found earth sweet,
Remember by love's grace,

In dreamy hushes of the heavenly song,
How suddenly we halted in our climb,
Lingering, reluctant, up that farthest hill,
Stooped for the blossoms closest to our feet,
And gave them as a token
Each to each,
In lieu of speech,
In lieu of words too grievous to be spoken,
Those little, gypsy, wondering blossoms wet
With a strange dew of tears?

So it began,
This vagabond, unvalued yellow clover,
To be our tenderest language. All the years
It lent a new zest to the summer hours,
As each of us went scheming to surprise
The other with our homely, laureate flowers,
Sonnets and odes,
Fringing our daily roads.
Can amaranth and asphodel
Bring merrier laughter to your eyes?
Oh, if the Blest, in their serene abodes,
Keep any wistful consciousness of earth,
Not grandeurs, but the childish ways of love,
Simplicities of mirth,
Must follow them above
With touches of vague homesickness that pass
Like shadows of swift birds across the grass.
How oft, beneath some foreign arch of sky,
The rover,
You or I,
For life oft sundered look from look,
And voice from voice, the transient dearth
Schooling my soul to brook
This distance that no messages may span,
Would chance
Upon our wilding by a lonely well,
Or drowsy watermill,
Or swaying to the chime of convent bell,
Or where the nightingales of old romance
With tragical contraltos fill
Dim solitudes of infinite desire;

And once I joyed to meet
Our peasant gadabout
A trespasser on trim, seigniorial seat,
Twinkling a saucy eye
As potentates paced by.

Our golden cord! our soft, pursuing flame
From friendship's altar fire!
How proudly we would pluck and tame
The dimpling clusters, mutinously gay!
How swiftly they were sent
Far, far away
On journeys wide
By sea and continent,
Green miles and blue leagues over,
From each of us to each,
That so our hearts might reach
And touch within the yellow clover,
Love's letter to be glad about
Like sunshine when it came!

My sorrow asks no healing; it is love;
Let love then make me brave
To bear the keen hurts of
This careless summertide,
Ay, of our own poor flower,
Changed with our fatal hour,
For all its sunshine vanished when you died.
Only white clover blossoms on your grave.

TO ONE WHO WAITS

I count the years by Junes that flush our laurel,
Our clustered bushes at the corner-wall,
And coax the crinkled buds to spread their small,
White chalices pricked out with rose and coral.
Slow are the seasons, yet I may not quarrel
With beauty. Dawns and stars, blossoms that foam
Enchanted orchards, where the orioles call,
Green leaves that flutter, golden leaves that fall,
Cloud caravans of snow will bring me home.
I count the years by Junes that flush our laurel.

What changes chronicle the life eternal?
Beyond the starry archipelagoes,
How do you calendar the stream that flows,
Forever singing, from the Throne supernal?
For as in wheat the sweetness of the kernel
Is ripened with the sunshine more and more,
Let sorrow trust, where mortal wisdom knows
Nothing, ah nothing, that the love of those
Who made earth heaven is greater than before
And watches for us in the life eternal.

If human love be but the soul's rehearsal
For that high harmony so piercing sweet
Its rhythm is pulsing in the wildest beat
Of passion, in the quietest dispersal
Of household blessings, Love the universal
Music of being, must not, Dear and True,
Our love that longs in me still yearn in you,
New-christened at the wide-winged Mercy seat
To a redeeming grace, my Paraclete,
For the divine accord my soul's rehearsal?

I count the years by Junes that flush our laurel,
And you, perchance, in some shy interspace
Of Paradise, have found a woodsy place,
A bit of wild that welcomes fern and sorrel,
Where mystery of moss and prickly moral
Of briar-rose may spring in finer bloom,
And Time's old witchery so far presume
That you, impatient for the glad embrace,
May now and then a dewy footpath trace
To see if June again has flushed the laurel.

Helen Rose Hull
(1888–1971)

Helen Hull was the author of over five dozen short stories and approximately twenty novels. Only her early works deal with love between women, although almost all of her adult life was spent in a Boston marriage. In 1912, as a young woman of twenty-four, Hull became a professor at Wellesley where she met another faculty member, Mabel Robinson. The two were soon part of a circle of women who lived in romantic dyads. In 1916, when Hull assumed a professorship at Columbia University, Mabel Robinson accompanied her, completing a dissertation there on women's colleges and then joining the Columbia faculty also. The two women remained together for fifty years, until Robinson's death in 1962.

The following story, "The Fire," is the first of five stories about Cynthia, a young feminist who rejects the conventional roles of women and seeks her own way in life. "Separation," a 1920 story, specifically focuses on the idea that Cynthia's crushes on other females are seen by the world as "unwholesome," but "The Fire," which was published three years earlier, emphasizes the constructive effects of such romantic feelings. Much of the Cynthia material was incorporated into Hull's most interesting novel, *Quest* (1922), in which the female hero, Jean, like Cynthia, is averse to marriage and sees the flaws in heterosexual unions. Jean too falls in love with older women, despite her mother's warnings that some older women "take a fancy for young girls, strong, healthy girls like you." Her mother has been influenced by the new "medical knowledge" about lesbianism. What had earlier been seen as romantic friendship was now morbid "sentimentality" or worse.

Hull's novel *Labyrinth* (1923), which followed *Quest,* presents a workable Boston marriage between two minor characters who are contrasted to the major (unhappy) heterosexual couple. One of the women in the female couple proclaims, as Hull herself might have, "I know lots of women who prefer to set up an establishment with another woman. Then you go fifty-fifty on everything. Work and feeling and all the rest, and no King waiting around for his humble servant."

Although Hull's later works were often feminist, she seldom dared broach the subject of love between women again. She realized the extent to which times had changed, and that what many people in an earlier era might have sympathetically viewed as "innocent" romantic friendship was now universally regarded as corrupt and/ or neurotic and was met with increasing hostility. Readers of "The Fire" in 1917 would surely have seen the mother as the sick character in the story. By the 1920s it is Miss Egert who would have come under suspicion. In her book *Heterodoxy* (which deals with a 1912–1940 feminist organization in Greenwich Village to which Hull belonged), Judith Schwarz quotes a letter, written to a club member, from a woman who visited a Heterodoxy meeting in 1927. The letter gives important insight into changing attitudes about feminism and "appropriate" roles and relationships in the mid-twenties, as well as Hull's emotional response to those attitudes:

One thing interested or rather bothered me terribly in that meeting.
. . . It was the woman who sat two places to the left of Doctor
Hollingworth. I think her name was Miss Hull. It seemed to me
that something awfully cruel was done to her at that meeting—and
I felt that she was going through hell all the time. . . . When Doctor
Hollingworth included in her definition of a perfect feminist a
woman happily married and with children, it shattered all Miss
Hull's defense mechanism. Did you notice how she turned to the
other psychoanalyst with white hair (Doctor Potter, wasn't it?) and
to one or two others, and hoped they would back her up—and
when they did not, did you see her face and notice that she never
spoke again?

The letter seems to record a crucial moment, when Hull realized that feminism had become heterosexualized, as it was not in earlier eras, and that
other forms of love relationships, such as the Boston marriage she lived,
had come into disfavor. Not even her comrades in Heterodoxy—many of
whom lived with other women or had long been supportive of their friends'
Boston marriages—dared come to her defense.

"The Fire" presents a transition time. Love between women by 1917
was not yet widely stigmatized, although, as Cynthia's mother's response
suggests, it was beginning to create suspicion as an "abnormality" in some
circles. Unlike writers only a few years later, however, Hull in 1917 could
present a female's love for another female and not focus on psychoanalyz-
ing or otherwise medicalizing its meaning.

Hull was apparently frustrated that she did not have that luxury in
later years. In 1953, inspired by the Kinsey report that showed that lesbianism was much more common than society had been willing to admit,
Hull fantasized in her journal about the possibility of being able to deal
positively with love between women in her writing once again. She wrote
that she was confirmed by Kinsey in "what I have always thought, that
conduct is not in any way consistent with either social code or law." She
reflected that most of the women she knew best had not conformed to the
stated mores of society, "even when they have been important through their
work and recognized positions." Hull briefly considered putting some of
her lesbian friends into a novel: "K. . . . had courage and serenity, had
groups of followers, must have had people whom she helped; E. had courage and liveliness and capacity for work and ingeniousness about developing her school. . . . She kept her sanguineness and her invincibility." Hull
realized that if she could have created characters out of those people she
might have challenged the invariable stereotypes of the lesbian as morbid
or villainous in fiction of the 1950s. But courage failed her; the price she

would have had to pay for such an unpopular stance seemed to be too dear, and she concluded: "I don't want to be associated with the subject."

FURTHER READING: Helen Rose Hull, "Separation," *Touchstone*, 6 (March 1920). Helen Rose Hull, *Quest* (1922; reprint, New York: The Feminist Press, 1990, afterword by Patricia McClelland Miller). Helen Rose Hull, *Labyrinth* (New York: Macmillan, 1923). Judith Schwarz, *Radical Feminists of Heterodoxy: Greenwich Village, 1912–1940* (Norwich, VT: New Victoria, 1986).

The Fire by Helen Rose Hull

Cynthia blotted the entry in the old ledger and scowled across the empty office at the door. Mrs. Moriety had left it ajar when she departed with her receipt for the weekly fifty cents on her "lot." If you supplied the missing gilt letters, you could read the sign on the glass of the upper half: "H.P. Bates. Real Estate. Notary Public." Through the door at Cynthia's elbow came the rumbling voice of old Fleming, the lawyer down the hall; he had come in for his Saturday night game of chess with her father.

Cynthia pushed the ledger away from her, and with her elbows on the spotted, green felt of the desk, her fingers burrowing into her cheeks, waited for two minutes by the nickel clock; then, with a quick, awkward movement, she pushed back her chair and plunged to the doorway, her young face twisted in a sort of fluttering resolution.

"Father—"

Her father jerked his head toward her, his fingers poised over a pawn. Old Fleming did not look up.

"Father, I don't think anybody else will be in."

"Well, go on home, then." Her father bent again over the squares, the light shining strongly on the thin places about his temples.

"Father, please,"—Cynthia spoke hurriedly—"you aren't going for a while? I want to go down to Miss Egert's for a minute."

"Eh? What's that?" He leaned back in his chair now, and Mr. Fleming lifted his severe, black beard to look at this intruder. "What for? You can't take any more painting lessons. Your mother doesn't want you going there any more."

"I just want to get some things I left there. I can get Jack to go home with you."

"But your mother said she didn't like your hanging around down there in an empty house with an old maid. What did she tell you about it?"

"Couldn't I just get my sketches, Father, and tell Miss Egert I'm not coming any more? She would think it was awfully funny if I didn't. I won't stay. But she—she's been good to me—"

"What set your mother against her, then? What you been doing down there?"

Cynthia twisted her hands together, her eyes running from Fleming's amused stare to her father's indecision. Only an accumulated determination could have carried her on into speech.

"I've just gone down once a week for a lesson. I want to get my things. If I'm not going, I ought to tell her."

"Why didn't you tell her that last week?"

"I kept hoping I could go on."

"Um." Her father's glance wavered toward his game. "Isn't it too late?"

"Just eight, Father." She stepped near her father, color flooding her cheeks. "If you'll give me ten cents, I can take the car—"

"Well—" He dug into his pocket, nodding at Fleming's grunt, "The women always want cash, eh, Bates?"

Then Cynthia, the dime pressed into her palm, tiptoed across to the nail where her hat and sweater hung, seized them, and still on tiptoe, lest she disturb the game again, ran out to the head of the stairs.

She was trembling as she pulled on her sweater; as she ran down the dark steps to the street the tremble changed to a quiver of excitement. Suppose her father had known just what her mother *had* said! That she could not see Miss Egert again; could never go hurrying down to the cluttered room they called the studio for more of those strange hours of eagerness and pain when she bent over the drawing-board, struggling with the mysteries of color. That last sketch—the little, purpling mint-leaves from the garden—Miss Egert had liked that. And they thought she could leave those sketches there! Leave Miss Egert, too, wondering why she never came again! She hurried to the corner, past the bright store windows. In thought she could see Miss Egert setting out the jar of brushes, the dishes of water, pushing back the litter of magazines and books to make room for the drawing-board, waiting for her to come. Oh, she had to go once more, black as her disobedience was!

The half-past-eight car was just swinging round the curve. She settled herself behind two German housewives, shawls over their heads, market-baskets beside them. They lived out at the end of the street; one of them sometimes came to the office with payments on her son's lot. Cynthia pressed against the dirty window, fearful lest she miss the corner. There it was, the new street light shining on the sedate old house! She ran to the platform, pushing against the arm the conductor extended.

"Wait a minute, there!" He released her as the car stopped, and she fled across the street.

In front of the house she could not see a light, upstairs or down, except staring reflections in the windows from the white arc light. She walked past the dark line of box which led to the front door. At the side of the old square dwelling jutted a new, low wing; and there in two windows were soft slits of light along the curtain-edges. Cynthia walked along a little dirt path to a door at the side of the wing. Standing on the door-step, she felt in the shadow for the knocker. As she let it fall, from the garden behind her came a voice:

"I'm out here. Who is it?" There was a noise of feet hurrying through dead leaves, and as Cynthia turned to answer, out of the shadow moved a blur of face and white blouse.

"Cynthia! How nice!" The woman touched Cynthia's shoulder as she pushed open the door. "There, come in."

The candles on the table bent their flames in the draft; Cynthia followed Miss Egert into the room.

"You're busy?" Miss Egert had stood up by the door an old wooden-toothed rake. "I don't want to bother you." Cynthia's solemn, young eyes implored the woman and turned hastily away. The intensity of defiance which had brought her at such an hour left her confused.

"Bother? I was afraid I had to have my grand bonfire alone. Now we can have it a party. You'd like to?"

Miss Egert darted across to straighten one of the candles. The light caught in the folds of her crumpled blouse, in the soft, drab hair blown out around her face.

"I can't stay very long." Cynthia stared about the room, struggling to hide her turmoil under ordinary casualness. "You had the carpenter fix the bookshelves, didn't you?"

"Isn't it nice now! All white and gray and restful—just a spark of life in that mad rug. A good place to sit in and grow old."

Cynthia looked at the rug, a bit of scarlet Indian weaving. She wouldn't see it again! The thought poked a derisive finger into her heart.

"Shall we sit down just a minute and then go have the fire?"

Cynthia dropped into the wicker chair, wrenching her fingers through one another.

"My brother came in tonight, his last attempt to make me see reason," said Miss Egert.

Cynthia lifted her eyes. Miss Egert wasn't wondering why she had come; she could stay without trying to explain.

Miss Egert wound her arms about her knees as she went on talking. Her slight body was wrenched a little out of symmetry, as though from straining always for something uncaptured; there was the same lack of symmetry in her face, in her eyebrows, in the line of her mobile lips. But her eyes had nothing fugitive, nothing pursuing in their soft, gray depth. Their warm, steady eagerness shone out in her voice, too, in its swift inflections.

"I tried to show him it wasn't a bit disgraceful for me to live here in a wing of my own instead of being a sort of nurse-maid adjunct in his house." She laughed, a soft, throaty sound. "It's my house. It's all I have left to keep me a person, you see. I won't get out and be respectable in his eyes."

"He didn't mind your staying here and taking care of—them!" cried Cynthia.

"It's respectable, dear, for an old maid to care for her father and mother; but when they die she ought to be useful to some one else instead of renting her house and living on the edge of it."

"Oh,"—Cynthia leaned forward—"I should think you'd hate him! I think families are—terrible!"

"Hate him?" Miss Egert smiled. "He's nice. He just doesn't agree with me. As long as he lets the children come over—I told him I meant to have a beautiful time with them, with my real friends—with you."

Cynthia shrank into her chair, her eyes tragic again.

"Come, let's have our bonfire!" Miss Egert, with a quick movement, stood in front of Cynthia, one hand extended.

Cynthia crouched away from the hand.

"Miss Egert,"—her voice came out in a desperate little gasp—"I can't come down any more. I can't take any more painting lessons." She stopped. Miss Egert waited, her head tipped to one side. "Mother doesn't think I better. I came down—after my things."

"They're all in the workroom." Miss Egert spoke quietly. "Do you want them now?"

"Yes," Cynthia pressed her knuckles against her lips. Over her hand her eyes cried out. "Yes, I better get them," she said heavily.

Miss Egert, turning slowly, lifted a candle from the table.

"We'll have to take this. The wiring isn't done." She crossed the room, her thin fingers, not quite steady, bending around the flame.

Cynthia followed through a narrow passage. Miss Egert pushed open a door, and the musty odor of the store room floated out into a queer chord with the fresh plaster of the hall.

"Be careful of that box!" Miss Egert set the candle on a pile of trunks. "I've had to move all the truck from the attic and studio in here. Your sketches are in the portfolio, and that's—somewhere!"

Cynthia stood in the doorway, watching Miss Egert bend over a pile of canvases, throwing up a grotesque, rounded shadow on the wall. Round the girl's throat closed a ring of iron.

"Here they are, pile up—"

Cynthia edged between the boxes. Miss Egert was dragging the black portfolio from beneath a pile of books.

"And here's the book I wanted you to see." The pile slipped crashing to the floor as Miss Egert pulled out a magazine. "Never mind those. See here." She dropped into the chair from which she had knocked the books, the portfolio under one arm, the free hand running through the pages of an old art magazine. The chair swung slightly; Cynthia, peering down between the boxes, gave a startled "Oh!"

"What is it?" Miss Egert followed Cynthia's finger. "The chair?" She was silent a moment. "Do you think I keep my mother prisoner here in a wheel chair now that she is free?" She ran her hand along the worn arm. "I tried to give it to an old ladies' home, but it was too used up. They wanted more style."

"But doesn't it remind you—" Cynthia hesitated.

"It isn't fair to remember the years she had to sit here waiting to die. You didn't know her. I've been going back to the real years—" Miss Egert smiled at Cynthia's bewildered eyes. "Here, let's look at these." She turned another page. "See, Cynthia. Aren't they swift and glad? That's what I was trying to tell you the other day. See that arm, and the drapery there! Just a line—" The girl bent over the page, frowning at the details the quick finger pointed out. "Don't they catch you along with them?" She held the book out at arm's length, squinting at the figures. "Take it along. There are several more." She tucked the book into the portfolio and rose. "Come on; we'll have our fire."

"But, Miss Egert,"—Cynthia's voice hardened as she was swept back into her own misery—"I can't take it. I can't come any more."

"To return a book?" Miss Egert lowered her eyelids as if she were again sizing up a composition. "You needn't come just for lessons."

Cynthia shook her head.

"Mother thinks—" She fell into silence. She couldn't say what her mother thought—dreadful things. If she could only swallow the hot pressure in her throat!

"Oh. I hadn't understood." Miss Egert's fingers paused for a swift touch on Cynthia's arm, and then reached for the candle. "You can go on working by yourself."

"It isn't that—" Cynthia struggled an instant, and dropped into silence again. She couldn't say out loud any of the things she was feeling. There were too many walls between feeling and speech: loyalty to her mother, embarrassment that feelings should come so near words, a fear of hurting Miss Egert.

"Don't mind so much, Cynthia." Miss Egert led the way back to the livingroom. "You can stay for the bonfire? That will be better than sitting here. Run into the kitchen and bring the matches and marshmallows—in a dish in the cupboard."

Cynthia, in the doorway, stared at Miss Egert. Didn't she care at all! Then the dumb ache in her throat stopped throbbing as Miss Egert's gray eyes held her steadily a moment. She did care! She did! She was just helping her. Cynthia took the candle and went back through the passageway to the kitchen, down at the very end.

She made a place on the table in the litter of dishes and milk bottles for the candle. The matches had been spilled on the shelf of the stove and into the sink. Cynthia gathered a handful of the driest. Shiftlessness was one of her mother's counts against Miss Egert. Cynthia flushed as she recalled her stumbling defense: Miss Egert had more important things to do; dishes were kept in their proper place; and her mother's: "Important! Mooning about!"

"Find them, Cynthia?" The clear, low voice came down the hall, and Cynthia hurried back.

Out in the garden it was quite black. As they came to the far end, the old stone wall made a dark bank against the sky, with a sharp star over its edge. Miss Egert knelt; almost with the scratch of the match the garden leaped into yellow, with fantastic moving shadows from the trees and in the corner of the wall. She raked leaves over the blaze, pulled the great mound into firmer shape, and then drew Cynthia back under the wall to watch. The light ran over her face; the delighted gestures of her hands were like quick shadows.

"See the old apple-tree dance! He's too old to move fast."

Cynthia crouched by the wall, brushing away from her face the scratchy leaves of the dead hollyhocks. Excitement tingled through her; she felt the red and yellow flames seizing her, burning out the heavy rebellion, the choking weight. Miss Egert leaned back against the wall, her hands spread so that her thin fingers were fire-edged.

"See the smoke curl up through those branches! Isn't it lovely, Cynthia?" She darted around the pile to push more leaves into the flames.

Cynthia strained forward, hugging her arms to her body. Never had there been such a fire! It burned through her awkwardness, her self-consciousness. It ate into the thick, murky veils which hung always between her and the things she struggled to find out. She took a long breath, and the crisp scent of smoke from the dead leaves tingled down through her body.

Miss Egert was at her side again. Cynthia looked up; the slight, asymmetrical figure was like the apple tree, still, yet dancing!

"Why don't you paint it?" demanded Cynthia, abruptly, and then was frightened as Miss Egert's body stiffened, lost its suggestion of motion.

"I can't." The woman dropped to the ground beside Cynthia, crumpling a handful of leaves. "It's too late." She looked straight at the fire. "I must be content to see it." She blew the pieces of leaves from the palm of her hand and smiled at Cynthia. "Perhaps some day you'll paint it—or write it."

"I can't paint." Cynthia's voice quivered. "I want to do something. I can't even see things except what you point out. And now—"

Miss Egert laid one hand over Cynthia's clenched fingers. The girl trembled at the cold touch.

"You must go on looking." The glow, as the flames died lower, flushed her face. "Cynthia, you're just beginning. You mustn't stop just because you aren't to come here any more. I don't know whether you can say things with your brush; but you must find them out. You mustn't shut your eyes again."

"It's hard alone."

"That doesn't matter."

Cynthia's fingers unclasped, and one hand closed desperately around Miss Egert's. Her heart fluttered in her temples, her throat, her breast. She clung to the fingers, pulling herself slowly up from an inarticulate abyss.

"Miss Egert,"—she stumbled into words—"I can't bear it, not coming here! Nobody else cares except about sensible things. You do, beautiful, wonderful things."

"You'd have to find them for yourself, Cynthia." Miss Egert's fingers moved under the girl's grasp. Then she bent toward Cynthia, and kissed her with soft, pale lips that trembled against the girl's mouth. "Cynthia, don't let any one stop you! Keep searching!" She drew back, poised for a moment in the shadow before she rose. Through Cynthia ran the swift feet of white ecstasy. She was pledging herself to some tremendous mystery, which trembled all about her.

"Come, Cynthia, we're wasting our coals."

Miss Egert held out her hands. Cynthia, laying hers in them, was drawn to her feet. As she stood there, inarticulate, full of a strange, excited, shouting hope, behind them the path crunched. Miss Egert turned, and Cynthia shrank back.

Her mother stood in the path, making no response to Miss Egert's "Good evening, Mrs. Bates."

The fire had burned too low to lift the shadow from the mother's face. Cynthia could see the hem of her skirt swaying where it dipped up in front. Above that two rigid hands in gray cotton gloves; above that the suggestion of a white, strained face.

Cynthia took a little step toward her.

"I came to get my sketches," she implored her. Her throat was dry.

What if her mother began to say cruel things—the things she had already said at home.

"I hope I haven't kept Cynthia too late," Miss Egert said. "We were going to toast marshmallows. Won't you have one, Mrs. Bates?" She pushed the glowing leaf-ashes together. The little spurt of flame showed Cynthia her mother's eyes, hard, angry, resting an instant on Miss Egert and then assailing her.

"Cynthia knows she should not be here. She is not permitted to run about the streets alone at night."

"Oh, I'm sorry." Miss Egert made a deprecating little gesture. "But no harm has come to her."

"She has disobeyed me."

At the tone of her mother's voice Cynthia felt something within her breast curl up like a leaf caught in flame.

"I'll get the things I came for." She started toward the house, running past her mother. She must hurry, before her mother said anything to hurt Miss Egert.

She stumbled on the door-step, and flung herself against the door. The portfolio was across the room, on the little, old piano. The candle beside it had guttered down over the cover. Cynthia pressed out the wobbly flame, and hugging the portfolio, ran back across the room. On the threshold she turned for a last glimpse. The row of Botticelli details over the bookcases were blurred into gray in the light of the one remaining candle; the Indian rug had a wavering glow. Then she heard Miss Egert just outside.

"I'm sorry Cynthia isn't to come any more," she was saying.

Cynthia stepped forward. The two women stood in the dim light, her mother's thickened, settled body stiff and hostile, Miss Egert's slight figure swaying toward her gently.

"Cynthia has a good deal to do," her mother answered. "We can't afford to give her painting lessons, especially—" Cynthia moved down between the women—"especially," her mother continued, "as she doesn't seem to get much of anywhere. You'd think she'd have some picture to show after so many lessons."

"Perhaps I'm not a good teacher. Of course she's just beginning."

"She'd better put her time on her studies."

"I'll miss her. We've had some pleasant times together."

Cynthia held out her hand toward Miss Egert, with a fearful little glance at her mother.

"Good-by, Miss Egert."

Miss Egert's cold fingers pressed it an instant.

"Good night, Cynthia," she said slowly.

Then Cynthia followed her mother's silent figure along the path; she turned her head as they reached the sidewalk. Back in the garden winked the red eye of the fire.

They waited under the arc light for the car, Cynthia stealing fleeting glances at her mother's averted face. On the car she drooped against the window edge, away from her mother's heavy silence. She was frightened now, a panicky child caught in disobedience. Once, as the car turned at the corner below her father's office, she spoke:

"Father will expect me—"

"He knows I went after you," was her mother's grim answer.

Cynthia followed her mother into the house. Her small brother was in the sitting-room, reading. He looked up from his book with wide, knowing eyes. Rebellious humiliation washed over Cynthia; setting her lips against their quivering, she pulled off her sweater.

"Go on to bed, Robert," called her mother from the entry, where she was hanging her coat. "You've sat up too late as it is."

He yawned, and dragged his feet with provoking slowness past Cynthia.

"Was she down there, Mama?" He stopped on the bottom step to grin at his sister.

"Go on, Robert. Start your bath. Mother'll be up in a minute."

"Aw, it's too late for a bath." He leaned over the rail.

"It's Saturday. I couldn't get back sooner."

Cynthia swung away from the round, grinning face. Her mother went past her into the dining room. Robert shuffled upstairs; she heard the water splashing into the tub.

Her mother was very angry with her. Presently she would come back, would begin to speak. Cynthia shivered. The familiar room seemed full of hostile, accusing silence, like that of her mother. If only she had come straight home from the office, she would be sitting by the table in the old Morris chair, reading, with her mother across from her sewing, or glancing through the evening paper. She gazed about the room at the neat scrolls of the brown wall paper, at a picture above the couch, cows by a stream. The dull, ordinary comfort of life there hung about her, a reproaching shadow, within which she felt the heavy, silent discomfort her transgression dragged after it. It would be much easier to go on just as she was expected to do. Easier. The girl straightened her drooping body. That things were hard didn't matter. Miss Egert had insisted upon that. She was forgetting the pledge she had given. The humiliation slipped away, and a cold exaltation trembled through her, a remote echo of the hope that had shouted within her back there in the garden. Here it was difficult to know what she had promised, to what she had pledged herself—something that the familiar, comfortable room had no part in.

She glanced toward the dining room, and her breath quickened. Between the faded green portieres stood her mother, watching her with hard, bright eyes. Cynthia's glance faltered; she looked desperately about the room as if hurrying her thoughts to some shelter. Beside her on the couch lay the portfolio. She took a little step toward it, stopping at her mother's voice.

"Well, Cynthia, have you anything to say?"

Cynthia lifted her eyes.

"Don't you think I have trouble enough with your brothers? You, a grown girl, defying me! I can't understand it."

"I went down for this." Cynthia touched the black case.

"Put that down! I don't want to see it!" The mother's voice rose, breaking down the terrifying silences. "You disobeyed me. I told you you weren't to go there again. And then I telephoned your father to ask you to do an errand for me, and find you there—with that woman!"

"I'm not going again." Cynthia twisted her hands together. "I had to go a last time. She was a friend. I could not tell her I wasn't coming—"

"A friend! A sentimental old maid; older than your mother! Is that a friend for a young girl? What were you doing when I found you? Holding hands! Is that the right thing for you? She's turned your head. You aren't the same Cynthia, running off to her, complaining of your mother."

"Oh, no!" Cynthia flung out her hand. "We were just talking." Her misery confused her.

"Talking? About what?"

"About—" The recollection rushed through Cynthia—"about beauty." She winced, a flush sweeping up to the edge of her fair hair, at her mother's laugh.

"Beauty! You disobey your mother, hurt her, to talk about beauty at night with an old maid!"

There was a hot beating in Cynthia's throat; she drew back against the couch.

"Pretending to be an artist," her mother drove on, "to get young girls who are foolish enough to listen to her sentimentalizing."

"She was an artist," pleaded Cynthia. "She gave it up to take care of her father and mother. I told you all about that—"

"Talking about beauty doesn't make artists."

Cynthia stared at her mother. She had stepped near the table, and the light through the green shade of the reading-lamp made queer pools of color about her eyes, in the waves of her dark hair. She didn't look real. Cynthia threw one hand up against her lips. She was sucked down and down in an eddy of despair. Her mother's voice dragged her again to the surface.

"We let you go there because you wanted to paint, and you maunder and say things you'd be ashamed to have your mother hear. I've spent my life working for you, planning for you, and you go running off—" Her voice broke into a new note, a trembling, grieved tone. "I've always trusted you, depended on you; now I can't even trust you."

"I won't go there again. I had to explain."

"I can't believe you. You don't care how you make me feel."

Cynthia was whirled again down the sides of the eddy.

"I can't believe you care anything for me, your own mother."

Cynthia plucked at the braid on her cuff.

"I didn't do it to make you sorry," she whispered. "I—it was—" The eddy closed about her, and with a little gasp she dropped down on the couch, burying her head in the sharp angle of her elbows.

The mother took another step toward the girl; her hand hovered above the bent head and then dropped.

"You know mother wants just what is best for you, don't you? I can't let you drift away from us, your head full of silly notions."

Cynthia's shoulders jerked. From the head of the stairs came Robert's shout:

"Mama, tub's full!"

"Yes; I'm coming."

Cynthia looked up. She was not crying. About her eyes and nostrils strained the white intensity of hunger.

"You don't think—" She stopped struggling with her habit of inarticulateness. "There might be things—not silly—you might not see what—"

"Cynthia!" The softness snapped out of the mother's voice.

Cynthia stumbled up to her feet; she was as tall as her mother. For an instant they faced each other, and then the mother turned away, her eyes tear-brightened. Cynthia put out an awkward hand.

"Mother," she said piteously, "I'd like to tell you—I'm sorry—"

"You'll have to show me you are by what you do." The woman started wearily up the stairs. "Go to bed. It's late."

Cynthia waited until the bath room door closed upon Robert's splashings. She climbed the stairs slowly, and shut herself into her room. She laid the portfolio in the bottom drawer of her white bureau; then she stood by her window. Outside, the big elm-tree, in fine, leafless dignity, showed dimly against the sky, a few stars caught in the arch of its branches.

A swift, tearing current of rebellion swept away her unhappiness, her confused misery; they were bits of refuse in this new flood. She saw, with a fierce, young finality that she was pledged to a conflict as well as to a search. As she knelt by the window and pressed her cheek on the cool glass, she felt the house about her, with its pressure of useful, homely things, as a very prison. No more journeyings down to Miss Egert's for glimpses of escape. She must find her own ways. Keep searching! At the phrase, excitement again glowed within her; she saw the last red wink of the fire in the garden.

Part II

A Man Trapped in a Woman's Body: The Literature of Sexual Inversion

INTRODUCTION

Romantic friends of previous centuries generally did not come under social scrutiny for illicit sexual behavior because in class-conscious and patriarchal eras it was difficult for men to believe that "good," that is, well-brought-up, women had an autonomous sexual drive on which they could or would act. That incredulity was sometimes challenged, however, by masculine women who claimed male prerogatives. There are, in fact, numerous cases of women, even into the eighteenth century in Western Europe, who were executed because they dressed in men's clothing and used "illicit inventions" to "supplement the shortcomings of their sex," as did Catharina Linck, a German woman who in male guise had served in several armies and married a woman. She was sentenced to death in 1721 upon discovery of her real sex.

The 1746 case of Mary Hamilton, who was described by the eighteenth-century novelist and judge Henry Fielding as "the Female Husband," provides a clear view of eighteenth-century attitudes about such women (and an interesting contrast to nineteenth-century medical views on the subject). Fielding considers Hamilton, who had sex with women, using a dildo, as belonging not to a separate category from the majority of humanity, as doctors in the next century would have presented her, but as committing immoral acts such as any wrong-headed person might commit. Fielding observes, "If once our carnal appetites are let loose, without those prudent and secure guides [of virtue and religion], there is no excess of disorder which they are not liable to commit." To Fielding, Mary Hamilton's behavior is not explained as being a result of congenital defects or childhood trauma but of keeping bad company. Such behavior was seen as a moral problem from which decent women were saved by their virtue and religion.

As socially troublesome as women's attempt to steal the male sexual prerogative of penetration may have been, however, there is also abundant evidence to suggest that women of other centuries could dress or comport themselves in a masculine fashion and still not be suspected of improper sexual behavior as long as they were not caught "with the goods," that is, a dildo, which alone might signify to men the commission of a sexual act with another woman. Women of wealth or position were usually above suspicion. For example, Charlotte Charke, the eighteenth-century actress and daughter of the famous playwright Colly Cibber, passed as Mr. Brown for a period of time and traveled everywhere with a Mrs. Brown, but appears never to have been accused of illicit sexual behavior and was unmolested by society or the law for her transvestism.

Ann Lister, a wealthy woman of the early nineteenth century, whose diaries reveal not only her masculine identification but also her numerous sexual relationships with other women, was likewise unmolested, perhaps because she was shielded by convictions about the innocence of women of her class. There is some evidence that in late-eighteenth-century London a few upper-class women came under suspicion of being "tommies," a term that appears to have described masculine women who had sex with other women. But that term was not in widespread usage, and probably such suspicions were rare. Masculine women were sometimes the butt of satire in the eighteenth and nineteenth centuries in works such as Maria Edgeworth's *Belinda* (1801), yet what was satirized most often was not their sexual predilection but their "inappropriate" gender behavior, manifested especially by intellectual or athletic ability or by their pioneering feminism.

Several decades later, such women were looked on in a different light. While our era of post–Second Wave feminism often derides notions of appropriate gender behavior, the latter half of the nineteenth century held those notions sacrosanct. It was at that time that European medical men, influenced by a new passion of the science community to classify everything, turned their attention to sexuality and began to categorize normal and abnormal sexual behavior. Their classifications most often did not escape from the prejudices of their gender, class, and religious affiliations, their claim to scientific objectivity notwithstanding. Therefore, for example, they were most likely to see and accept the notion of "abnormal behavior" among those who were socioeconomically different from them, the lower and the aristocratic classes. It is significant that many of the cases they cited of female "sexual inversion" were either poor or titled women, from the scullery maid Karl Westphal observed in 1869 to the Countess Sarolta, whom Krafft-Ebing observed in the 1890s.

What their Judeo-Christian background had taught the medical men to consider *immoral* now often became, in their writings, *abnormal,* though their moralism shone through their scientific statements. For example, Krafft-Ebing says of a female sexual invert who learned to eschew sexual expression, "She became a decent, sexually at least, neutral person." Moreover, these sexologists' strong Victorian convictions about appropriate gender behavior frequently led them to conflate sex-role behavior, gender identification, and sexual-object choice. For example, they believed that a female with a predilection for wearing pants not only saw herself as a man but also had erotic desires for women.

In fact, in other eras women's motives for what had been considered masculine self-presentation were undoubtedly complex. Some women were transvestites for the sake of convenience: it was far easier to travel alone and even to get a better-paying working-class job if one looked like a man. Many female transvestites were actually heterosexual but dressed as men in order to be able to accompany their male lovers more easily than they could have as unmarried women. Others may have suffered from a gender dysphoria. Such gender dysphoria sometimes included (and sometimes did not include) a sexual interest in other females in which the dysphoric woman would play what has traditionally been a male role. Others may have been transvestites for the sheer adventure involved. The sexologists, however, generally associated cross-dressing or any other form of "masculine" behavior in a woman with congenital inversion and categorized her as a member of the "third sex."

With the successes of the first feminist movement in the late nineteenth century, many more middle-class women began to exhibit "masculine" behavior. They agitated for and received the privilege of higher education. They wanted and often got jobs that would allow them to be socially and financially independent. They wore tailored clothing to work in the new careers that had recently opened to them. If, together with their masculine sex-role behavior, they exhibited feelings of romantic friendship for other females, they might now have come under suspicion for sexual abnormality, which would not have been attributed to them earlier. In fact, many of the sexologists who wrote about female sexual inversion began to connect it to feminism by the turn of the century. Havelock Ellis, for example, complained (in apparent contradiction to his theory about inversion as hereditary), that the women's movement has "involved an increase in feminine criminality and in feminine insanity. . . . In connection with these we can scarcely be surprised to find an increase in homosexuality, which has always been regarded as belonging to an allied, if not the same group of phenomena." He went on to explain his apparent contradiction by saying that the woman who comes to lesbianism through feminism may be only a "spurious imitation" of the real invert, or feminism might bring out the "germs" of inversion that is latent in a particular woman by "promot[ing] her] hereditary neurosis."

Many of the women who comprised the case histories of these sexologists had feelings for other females that were no different from those that numerous romantic friends of other eras recorded in their letters and journals. Often their "inverted" relationships were not sexual. Ellis, for example, identifies as a congenital invert a Miss M. whom he quotes as saying, "I love few people . . . but in those instances when I have permitted my heart to go out to a friend I have always experienced most exalted feelings, and have been made better by them morally, mentally, and spiritually. Love is with me a religion. The very nature of my affections for my friends precludes the possibility of any element entering into it which is not absolutely sacred." Krafft-Ebing wrote of one of his female "sexual inverts": "The patient is not aware of her inclination to persons of the same sex being of a sexual character." And Freud, in his study of a young female "homosexual" observed: "With none of the subjects of her adoration had the patient enjoyed anything beyond a few kisses and embraces; her genital chastity . . . had remained intact." Freud also admitted that the young woman "kept insisting on the purity of her love and her physical repulsion against the idea of any sexual intercourse." So what distinguished all these women from earlier romantic friends other than the scientists' categorizations, which in some cases had operated to make the women see themselves as different from other women?

It was this perception of a woman's masculinity that most often identified her as a sexual invert in the writings of the sexologists. But in their insistence on conflating gender identification, sex-role behavior, and sexual-object choice, the sexologists offered some ludicrous examples of the masculinity of women who loved other women. Havelock Ellis, for instance, spoke of an Italian lesbian who was very hirsute, as though most Mediterranean women are not, and he quoted an American doctor who observed that inverted women have "the tendency to growth of hair on the legs," as though most women who didn't shave wouldn't have hairy legs. The sexologists examined head size, foot size, genital size, anything for telltale signs of the masculinity that betrays inversion. Even when, as Freud did, they attempted to deny the necessary connection between masculinity and lesbianism, their observations hinted that they believed otherwise. Freud began by claiming that his lesbian patient was feminine, but he soon insisted on her masculinity, which revealed itself through her *intellect*: those "male" qualities of "acuteness of comprehension" and "lucid objectivity."

Such views had a significant effect on twentieth-century literary representations of the lesbian. Some contemporary critics are suggesting that literature that appears to take seriously the sexological view of the lesbian as a man trapped in a woman's body really laughs at orthodox theories of gender behavior and demonstrates that gender is nothing but performance, that a female can play at being a man just as well as a male can—and that both butch female and male are merely "performing gender." Such a theory is an appealing one for our day, but to what extent does it ignore the seriousness with which other generations invested the concept of gender?

The sexologists such as Karl von Westphal, Paul Moreau, and Cesare Lombroso, as well as Krafft-Ebing and Ellis, attributed other characteristics to their congenital inverts, which were then reflected in twentieth-century literature. To the nineteenth-century sexologists especially, homosexuality was associated with hereditary taint. One was born a lesbian, and it was generally a manifestation of a diseased family background. The Countess Sarolta's insane family of hysterics, obsessive-compulsives, and paranoids is typical. When, in 1892, an American woman, Alice Mitchell, cut the throat of Freda Ward, her woman lover, sexologists took her as an example of, in Havelock Ellis's description, "a typical invert." (Ellis followed his description of her case with two other cases of lesbian murder and attempted murder, and then stated: "Homosexual relationships are also a cause of suicide among women"—with the apparent implication that heterosexual relationships never are.)

The image of the violent female sexual invert had considerable appeal to the Euro-American literary imagination at this time. Soon after the Mitchell case made front-page headlines in the Western world, a number of novels and short stories appeared about masculine women who killed or attempted to kill their women lovers or their rivals. In 1895 alone Mary Wilkins Freeman published "The Long Arm," Mary Hatch published *The Strange Disappearance of Eugene Comstocks,* and John Carhart published *Norma Trist . . . : A Story of the Inversion of the Sexes,* all fictional accounts of lesbian murderers or would-be murderers. Thanks primarily to the sexologists, the literary image of love between women was undergoing profound changes as it became associated not only with masculinity but also with violence, congenital defects (especially insanity), and other kinds of medical problems.

During the first half of the twentieth century, the depiction of the lesbian as a man trapped in a woman's body, a member of the third sex, was a predominant image in literature that dealt with women's relationships. This was not because most twentieth-century authors of lesbian novels were familiar with the writings of the sexologists, but rather because of the tremendous success of Radclyffe Hall's novel of sexual inversion, *The Well of Loneliness* (1928). Hall very consciously incorporated into her depiction of Stephen Gordon many of the theories about the third sex that were promulgated by the sexologists. She had Havelock Ellis write a preface to her novel, and she even placed in the mouth of Stephen Gordon, her inverted woman hero, lines borrowed from the Countess Sarolta's exhortation to God as presented by Krafft-Ebing. Thus it was Stephen Gordon, who virtually stepped out of the pages of sexological writing, who became a literary prototype for the lesbian in British and American literature for many decades.

Another literary model became the young woman presented by Sigmund Freud in his "Psychogenesis of a Case of Homosexuality in a Woman." While not daring to dismiss entirely the possibility that his patient inherited her predisposition to homosexuality, he posits its genesis in environmental factors and especially penis envy. (Freud's subject may not wear a dildo as does Krafft-Ebing's countess, but she carries one around with her in her subconscious.) Her subconscious desire for her father's baby, her guilt-provoking sexual competition with her mother, and her terrible ambivalence about femininity, also help to explain her lesbian drives. The Freudian influence on lesbian literary depictions may be seen in writers such as Henry Handel [Ethel] Richardson, whose female characters love other women because of the various childhood traumas they endured.

As dismal as the medicalized depiction of love between women was, it found many champions among females who identified as lesbians. For some the pronouncements of the sexologists permitted them to explain themselves to others and to take themselves and their life choices much more seriously. Here was an official medical reason that would help them argue, for example, that because of their congenital inversion their love for another woman was not "a rehearsal in girlhood for the great drama" of their lives but the great drama itself. The sexologists also served such women by informing them that they were a "type"—which meant there were others like them. The lesbian society described by Colette, for example, which self-consciously identified itself as inverted, was aided in its conceptions of itself by sexological pronouncements. The sexologists may have been observing some existing specimens of "inverts," but their observations in turn assisted in the growth of a community by providing a category that many more women could claim as their own and seek to experience with others who claimed that category.

Autobiographical writings of the first half of the twentieth century suggest how useful the sexologists' pronouncements were to lesbians in identifying their differentness, explaining their sexual drives, and denying moral culpability for who they were and what they did. The sexologists' work gave them ammunition to argue against moralists who condemned lesbian sexuality. If lesbians were born men trapped in women's bodies then they could not help their sexual urges, and they had as much right to sexual expression as men fortunate enough to be born into the right bodies. The image of the innocent man trapped in a woman's body, a member of the third sex, persisted into the pulp novels of the 1950s and '60s, such as Ann Bannon's *Beebo Brinker* series. While the sexologists were responsible for making love between women a medical problem rather than a ubiquitous experience, as was romantic friendship, the literature that was influenced by sexological writing reveals that lesbians often learned to use the sexologists for their own political and personal ends.

MEN'S WRITING ON

A MAN TRAPPED IN A

WOMAN'S BODY

The Female Husband by Henry Fielding

That propense inclination which is for very wise purposes implanted in the one sex for the other, is not only necessary for the continuance of the human species; but is, at the same time, when govern'd and directed by virtue and religion, productive not only of corporeal delight, but of the most rational felicity.

But if once our carnal appetites are let loose, without those prudent and secure guides, there is no excess and disorder which they are not liable to commit, even while they pursue their natural satisfaction; and, which may seem still more strange, there is nothing monstrous and unnatural, which they are not capable of inventing, nothing so brutal and shocking which they have not actually committed.

Of these unnatural lusts, all ages and countries have afforded us too many instances; but none I think more surprising than what will be found in the history of Mrs. *Mary,* otherwise Mr. *George Hamilton.*

This heroine in iniquity was born in the Isle of *Man,* on the 16th Day of *August,* 1721. Her father was formerly a serjeant of grenadiers in the Foot-Guards, who having the good fortune to marry a widow of some estate in that island, purchased his discharge from the army, and retired thither with his wife.

He had not been long arrived there before he died, and left his wife with child of this *Mary;* but her mother, tho' she had not two months to reckon, could not stay till she was delivered, before she took a third husband.

As her mother, tho' she had three husbands, never had any other child, she always express'd an extraordinary affection for this daughter, to whom she gave as good an education as the island afforded; and tho' she used her with much tenderness, yet was the girl brought up in the strictest principles of virtue and religion; nor did she in her younger years discover the least proneness to any kind of vice, much less give cause of suspicion that she would one day disgrace her sex by the most abominable and unnatural pollutions. And indeed she hath often declared from her conscience, that no irregular passion ever had any place in her mind, till she was first seduced by one *Anne Johnson,* a neighbour of hers, with whom she had been acquainted from her childhood; but not with such intimacy as afterwards grew between them.

This *Anne Johnson* going on some business to *Bristol,* which detained her there near half a year, became acquainted with some of the people called *Methodists,* and was by them persuaded to embrace their sect.

At her return to the Isle of *Man,* she soon made an easy convert of *Molly Hamilton,* the warmth of whose disposition rendered her susceptible enough of Enthusiasm, and ready to receive all those impressions which her friend the *Methodist* endeavoured to make on her mind.

These two young women became now inseparable companions, and at length bed-fellows: For *Molly Hamilton* was prevail'd on to leave her mother's house, and to reside entirely with Mrs. *Johnson,* whose fortune was not thought inconsiderable in that cheap country.

Young Mrs. *Hamilton* began to conceive a very great affection for her friend, which perhaps was not returned with equal faith by the other. However, Mrs. *Hamilton* declares her love, or rather friendship, was totally innocent, till the temptations of *Johnson* first led her astray. This latter was, it seems, no novice in impurity, which, as she confess'd, she had learnt and often practiced at *Bristol* with her methodistical sisters.

As *Molly Hamilton* was extremely warm in her inclinations, and as those inclinations were so violently attached to Mrs. *Johnson,* it would not have been difficult for a less artful woman, in the most private hours, to turn the ardour of enthusiastic devotion into a different kind of flame.

Their conversation, therefore, soon became in the highest manner criminal, and transactions not fit to be mention'd past between them.

They had not long carried on this wicked crime before Mrs. *Johnson* was again called by her affairs to visit *Bristol,* and her friend was prevail'd on to accompany her thither.

Here when they arrived, they took up their lodgings together, and live in the same detestable manner as before; till an end was put to their vile amours, by the means of one *Rogers,* a young fellow, who by his extraordinary devotion (for he was a very zealous *Methodist*) or by some other charms, (for he was very jolly and handsome) gained the heart of Mrs. *Johnson,* and married her.

This amour, which was not of any long continuance before it was brought to a conclusion, was kept an entire secret from Mrs. *Hamilton;* but she was no sooner informed of it, than she became almost frantic, she tore her hair, beat her breasts, and behaved in as outrageous a manner as the fondest husband could, who had unexpectedly discovered the infidelity of a beloved wife.

In the midst of these agonies she received a letter from Mrs. *Johnson,* in the following words, or as near them as she can possibly remember. "DEAR MOLLY,

"I know you will condemn what I have now done; but I condemn myself much more for what I have done formerly: For I take the whole shame and guilt of what hath passed between us on myself. I was indeed the first seducer of your innocence, for which I ask GOD's pardon and yours. All the amends I can make you, is earnestly to beseech you, in the name of the Lord, to forsake all such evil courses, and to follow my example now, as you before did my temptation, and enter as soon as you can into that holy state into which I was yesterday called. In which, tho' I am yet but a novice, believe me, there are delights infinitely surpassing the faint endearments we have experienc'd together. I shall always pray for you, and continue your friend."

This letter rather increased than abated her rage, and she resolved to go immediately and upbraid her false friend; but while she was taking this resolution, she was informed that Mr. *Rogers* and his bride were departed from *Bristol* by a messenger, who brought her a second short note, and a bill for some money from Mrs. *Rogers.*

As soon as the first violence of her passion subsided, she began to consult what course to take, when the strangest thought imaginable suggested itself to her fancy. This was to dress herself in mens cloaths, to embarque for *Ireland,* and commence Methodist teacher.

Nothing remarkable happened to her during the rest of her stay at *Bristol,* which adverse winds occasioned to be a whole week, after she had provided herself with her dress; but at last having procured a passage, and the wind becoming favourable, she set sail for *Dublin.*

As she was a very pretty woman, she now appeared a most beautiful youth. A circumstance which had its consequences aboard the ship, and had like to have discovered her, in the very beginning of her adventures.

There happened to be in the same vessel with this adventurer, a Methodist, who was bound to the same place, on the same design with herself.

These two being alone in the cabin together, and both at their devotions, the man in the extasy of his enthusiasm, thrust one of his hands into the other's bosom. Upon which, in her surprize, she gave so effeminate a squawl, that it reached the Captain's ears, as he was smoaking his pipe upon deck. Hey day, says he, what have we a woman in the ship! and immediately descended into the cabbin, where he found the two Methodists on their knees.

Pox on't, says the Captain, I thought you had had a woman with you here; I could have sworn I had heard one cry out as if she had been ravishing, and yet the Devil must have been in you, if you could convey her in here without my knowledge.

I defy the Devil and all his works, answered the He Methodist. He has no power but over the wicked; and if he be in the ship, thy oaths must have brought him hither: for I have heard thee pronounce more than twenty since I came on board; and we should have been at the bottom before this, had not my prayers prevented it.

Don't abuse my vessel, cried the Captain, she is as safe a vessel, and as good a sailer as ever floated, and if you had been afraid of going to the bottom, you might have stay'd on shore and been damn'd.

The Methodist made no answer, but fell a groaning, and that so loud, that the Captain giving him a hearty curse or two, quitted the cabbin, and resumed his pipe.

He was no sooner gone, than the Methodist gave farther tokens of brotherly love to his companion, which soon became so importunate and troublesome to her, that after having gently rejected his hands several times, she at last recollected the sex she had assumed, and gave him so violent a blow in the nostrils, that the blood issued from them with great Impetuosity.

Whether fighting be opposite to the tenets of this sect (for I have not the honour to be deeply read in their doctrines) or from what other motive it proceeded, I will not determine; but the Methodist made no other return to this rough treatment, than by many groans, and prayed heartily to be delivered soon from the conversation of the wicked; which prayers were at length so successful, that, together with a very brisk gale, they brought the vessel into *Dublin* harbour.

Here our adventurer took a lodging in a back-street near *St. Stephen's Green,* at which place she intended to preach the next day; but had got a cold in the voyage, which occasioned such a hoarseness that made it impossible to put that design in practice.

There lodged in the same house with her, a brisk widow of near 40 Years of age, who had buried two husbands, and seemed by her behaviour to be far from having determined against a third expedition to the land of matrimony.

To this widow our adventurer began presently to make addresses, and as he at present wanted tongue to express the ardency of his flame, he was obliged to make use of actions of endearment, such as squeezing, kissing, toying, etc.

These were received in such a manner by the fair widow, that her lover thought he had sufficient encouragement to proceed to a formal declaration of his passion. And this she chose to do by letter, as her voice still continued too hoarse for uttering the soft accents of love.

A letter therefore was penned accordingly in the usual stile, which, to prevent any miscarriages, Mrs. *Hamilton* thought proper to deliver with her own hands; and immediately retired to give the adored lady an opportunity of digesting the contents alone, little doubting of an answer agreeable to her wishes, or at least such a one as the coyness of the sex generally dictates in the beginning of an amour, and which lovers, by long experience, know pretty well how to interpret.

But what was the gallant's surprize, when in return to an amorous epistle, she read the following sarcasms, which it was impossible for the most sanguine temper to misunderstand, or construe favourably.

"SIR,

I Was greatly astonished at what you put into my hands. Indeed I thought, when I took it, it might have been an Opera song, and which for certain reasons I should think, when your cold is gone, you might sing as well as *Farinelli,* from the great resemblance there is between your persons. I know not what you mean by encouragement to your hopes; if I could have conceived my innocent freedoms could have been so misrepresented, I should have been more upon my guard: but you have taught me how to watch my actions for the future, and to preserve myself even from any suspicion of forfeiting the regard I owe to the memory of the best of men, by any future choice. The remembrance of that dear person makes me incapable of proceeding farther."

And so firm was this resolution, that she would never afterwards admit of the least familiarity with the despairing Mrs. *Hamilton;* but perhaps that destiny which is remarked to interpose in all matrimonial things, had taken the widow into her protection: for in a few days afterwards, she was married to one *Jack Strong,* a cadet in an *Irish* regiment.

Our adventurer being thus disappointed in her love, and what is worse, her money drawing towards an end, began to have some thoughts of returning home, when fortune seemed inclined to make her amends for the tricks she had hitherto played her, and accordingly now threw another Mistress in her way, whose fortune was much superior to the former widow, and who received Mrs. *Hamilton's* addresses with all the complaisance she could wish.

This Lady, whose name was *Rushford,* was the widow of a rich cheese-monger, who left her all he had, and only one great grand-child to take care of, whom, at her death, he recommended to be her Heir; but wholly at her own power and discretion.

She was now in the sixty eighth year of her age, and had not, it seems, entirely abandoned all thoughts of the pleasures of this world: for she was no sooner acquainted with Mrs. *Hamilton,* but, taking her for a beautiful lad of about eighteen, she cast the eyes of affection on her, and having pretty well outlived the bashfulness of her youth, made little scruple of giving hints of her passion of her own accord.

It has been observed that women know more of one another than the wisest men (if ever such have been employed in the study) have with all their art been capable of discovering. It is therefore no wonder that these hints were quickly perceived and understood by the female gallant, who animadverting on the conveniency which the old gentlewoman's fortune would produce in her present situation, very gladly embraced the opportunity, and advancing with great warmth of love to the attack, in which she was received almost with open arms, by the tottering citadel, which presently offered to throw open the gates, and surrender at discretion.

In her amour with the former widow, Mrs. *Hamilton* had never had any other design than of gaining the lady's affection, and then discovering herself to her, hoping to have had the same success which Mrs. *Johnson* had found with her: but with this old lady, whose fortune only she was desirous to possess, such views would have afforded very little gratification. After some reflection, therefore, a device entered into her head, as strange and surprizing, as it was wicked and vile; and this was actually to marry the old woman, and to deceive her, by means which decency forbids me even to mention.

The wedding was accordingly celebrated in the most public manner, and with all kind of gaiety, the old woman greatly triumphing in her shame, and instead of hiding her own head for fear of infamy, was actually proud of the beauty of her new husband, for whose sake she intended to disinherit her poor great-grandson, tho' she had derived her riches from her husband's family, who had always intended this boy as his heir. Nay, what may seem very remarkable, she insisted on the parson's not omitting the prayer in the matrimonial service for fruitfulness; drest herself as airy as a girl of eighteen, concealed twenty years of her age, and laughed and promoted all the jokes which are usual at weddings; but she was not so well pleased with a repartee of her great-grandson, a pretty and a smart lad, who, when somebody jested on the bridegroom because he had no beard, answered smartly: There should never be a beard on both-sides: For indeed the old lady's chin was pretty well stocked with bristles.

Nor was this bride contented with displaying her shame by a public wedding dinner, she would have the whole ceremony compleated, and the stocking was accordingly thrown with the usual sport and merriment.

During the three first days of the marriage, the bride expressed herself so well satisfied with her choice, that being in company with another old lady, she exulted so much in her happiness, that her friend began to envy her, and could not forbear inveighing against effeminacy in men; upon which a discourse arose between the two ladies, not proper to be repeated, if I knew every particular; but ended at the last, in the unmarried lady's declaring to the bride, that she thought her husband looked more like a woman than a man. To which the other replied in triumph, he was the best man in *Ireland*.

This and the rest which past, was faithfully recounted to Mrs. *Hamilton* by her wife, at their next meeting, and occasioned our young bridegroom to blush, which the old lady perceiving and regarding as an effect of youth, fell upon her in a rage of love like a tygress, and almost murdered her with kisses.

One of our English Poets remarks in the case of a more able husband than Mrs. *Hamilton* was, when his wife grew amorous in an unseasonable time.

> *The doctor understood the call,*
> *But had not always wherewithal.*

So it happened to our poor bridegroom, who having not at that time *the wherewithal* about her, was obliged to remain meerly passive, under all this torrent of kindness of his wife, but this did not discourage her, who was an experienced woman, and thought she had a cure for this coldness in her husband, the efficacy of which, she might perhaps have essayed formerly. Saying therefore with a tender smile to her husband, I believe you are a woman, her hands began to move in such direction, that the discovery would absolutely have been made, had not the arrival of dinner, at that very instant, prevented it.

However, as there is but one way of laying the spirit of curiosity, when once raised in a woman, *viz.* by satisfying it, so that discovery, though delayed, could not now be long prevented. And accordingly the very next night, the husband and wife had not been long in bed together, before a storm arose, as if drums, guns, wind and thunder were all roaring together. Villain, rogue, whore, beast, cheat, all resounded at the same instant, and were followed by curses, imprecations and threats, which soon waked the poor great-grandson in the garret; who immediately ran down stairs into his great-grandmother's room. He found her in the midst of it in her shift, with a handful of shirt in one hand, and handful of hair in the other, stamping and crying, I am undone, cheated, abused, ruined, robbed by a vile jade, impostor, whore. . . . What is the matter, dear Madam, answered the youth; O child, replied she, undone! I am married to one who is no man. My husband? a woman, a woman, a woman. Ay, said the grandson, where is she? . . . Run away, gone, said the great-grandmother, and indeed so she was: For no sooner was the fatal discovery made than the poor female bridegroom, whipt on her breeches, in the pockets of which, she had stowed all the money she could, and slipping on her shoes, with her coat, waiste-coat and stockings in her hands, had made the best of her way into the street, leaving almost one half of her shirt behind, which the enraged wife had tore from her back.

As Mrs. *Hamilton* well knew that an adventure of that kind would soon fill all *Dublin*, and that it was impossible for her to remain there undiscovered, she hastened away to the Key, where by good fortune, she met with a ship just bound to *Dartmouth*, on board of which she immediately went, and sailed out of the harbour, before her pursuers could find out or overtake her.

She was a full fortnight in her passage, during which time, no adventure occurred worthy remembrance. At length she landed at *Dartmouth*, where she soon provided herself with linnen, and thence went to Totness, where she assumed the title of a doctor of physic, and took lodgings in the house of one Mrs. *Baytree.*

Here she soon became acquainted with a young girl, the daughter of one Mr. *Ivythorn*, who had the green sickness; a distemper which the doctor gave out he could cure by an infallible *nostrum.*

The doctor had not been long intrusted with the care of this young patient before he began to make love to her: for though her complexion was somewhat faded with her distemper, she was otherwise extremely pretty.

This Girl became an easy conquest to the doctor, and the day of their marriage was appointed, without the knowledge, or even suspicion of her father, or of an old aunt who was very fond of her, and would neither of them have easily given their consent to the match, had the doctor been as good a Man as the niece thought him.

At the day appointed, the doctor and his mistress found means to escape very early in the morning from *Totness*, and went to a town called *Ashburton* in *Devonshire*, where they were married by a regular Licence which the doctor had previously obtained.

Here they staid two days at a public house, during which time the Doctor so well acted his part, that his bride had not the least suspicion of the legality of her marriage, or that she had not got a husband for life. The third day they returned to *Totness,* where they both threw themselves at Mr. *Ivythorn's* feet, who was highly rejoic'd at finding his daughter restor'd to him, and that she was not debauched, as he had suspected of her. And being a very worthy goodnatur'd man, and regarding the true interest and happiness of his daughter more than the satisfying his own pride, ambition or obstinacy, he was prevailed on to forgive her, and to receive her and her husband into his house, as his children, notwithstanding the opposition of the old aunt, who declared she would never forgive the wanton slut, and immediately quitted the house, as soon as the young couple were admitted into it.

The Doctor and his wife lived together above a fortnight, without the least doubt conceived either by the wife, or by any other person of the Doctor's being what he appeared; till one evening the Doctor having drank a little too much punch, slept somewhat longer than usual, and when he waked, he found his wife in tears, who asked her husband, amidst many sobs, how he could be so barbarous to have taken such advantage of her ignorance and innocence, and to ruin her in such a manner? The Doctor being surprized and scarce awake, asked her what he had done. Done, says she, have you not married me a poor young girl, when you know, you have not . . . you have not . . . what you ought to have. I always thought indeed your shape was something odd, and have often wondered that you had not the least bit of beard; but I thought you had been a man for all that, or I am sure I would not have been so wicked to marry you for the world. The Doctor endeavoured to pacify her, by every kind of promise, and telling her she would have all the pleasures of marriage without the inconveniences. No, no, said she, you shall not persuade me to that, nor will I be guilty of so much wickedness on any account. I will tell my Papa of you as soon as I am up; for you are no husband of mine, nor will I ever have any thing more to say to you. Which resolution the Doctor finding himself unable to alter, she put on her cloaths with all the haste she could, and taking a horse, which she had bought a few days before, hastened instantly out of the town, and made the best of her way, thro' bye-roads and across country, into *Somersetshire,* missing *Exeter,* and every other great town which lay in the road.

And well it was for her, that she used both this haste and precaution: For Mr. *Ivythorn* having heard his daughter's story, immediately obtained a warrant from a justice of peace, with which he presently dispatch'd the proper officers; and not only so, but set forward himself to *Exeter,* in order to try if he could learn any news of his son-in-law, or apprehend her there; till after much search being unable to hear any tidings of her, he was obliged to set down contented with his misfortune, as was his poor daughter to submit to all the ill-natured sneers of her own sex, who were often witty at her expence, and at the expence of their own decency.

The Doctor having escaped, arrived safe at *Wells* in *Somersetshire,* where thinking herself at a safe distance from her pursuers, she again sat herself down in quest of new adventures.

She had not been long in this city, before she became acquainted with one *Mary Price,* a girl of about eighteen years of age, and of extraordinary beauty. With this girl, hath this wicked woman since her confinement declared, she was really much in love, as it was possible for a man ever to be with one of her own sex.

The first opportunity our Doctor obtain'd of conversing closely with this new mistress, was at a dancing among the inferior sort of people, in contriving which the Doctor had herself the principal share. At that meeting the two lovers had an occasion of dancing all night together; and the Doctor lost no opportunity of shewing his fondness, as well by his tongue as by his hands, whispering many soft things in her ears, and squeezing as many soft things into her hands, which, together with a good number of kisses, &c. so pleased and warmed this poor girl, who never before had felt any of those tender sensations which we call love, that she retired from the dancing in a flutter of spirits, which her youth and ignorance could not well account for; but which did not suffer her to close her eyes, either that morning or the next night.

The Day after that the Doctor sent her the following letter.

"*My Dearest Molly,*

"Excuse the fondness of that expression; for I assure you, my angel, all I write to you proceeds only from my heart, which you have so entirely conquered, and made your own, that nothing else has any share in it; and, my angel, could you know what I feel when I am writing to you, nay even at every thought of my *Molly,* I know I should gain your pity if not your love; if I am so happy to have already succeeded in raising the former, do let me have once more an opportunity of seeing you, and that soon, that I may breathe forth my soul at those dear feet, where I would willingly die, if I am not suffer'd to lie there and live. My sweetest creature, give me leave to subscribe myself

"*Your fond, doating,*

"*Undone* SLAVE."

This letter added much to the disquietude which before began to torment poor *Molly*'s breast. She read it over twenty times, and, at last, having carefully survey'd every part of the room, that no body was present, she kissed it eagerly. However, as she was perfectly modest, and afraid of appearing too forward, she resolved not to answer this first letter; and if she met the Doctor, to behave with great coldness towards him.

Her mother being ill, prevented her going out that day; and the next morning she received a second letter from the Doctor, in terms more warm and endearing than before, and which made so absolute a conquest over the unexperience'd and tender heart of this poor girl, that she suffered herself to be prevailed on, by the intreaties of her lover, to write an answer, which nevertheless she determin'd should be so distant and cool, that the woman of the strictest virtue and modesty in *England* might have no reason to be asham'd of having writ it; of which letter the reader hath here an exact copy:

"SUR,

"I Haf recevd boath your too litters, and sur I ham much surprise hat the loafe you priten to have for so pur a garl as mee. I kan nut beleef you wul desgrace yourself by marring sutch a yf as mee, and Sur I wool nut be thee hore of the gratest man in the kuntry. For thof mi vartu his all I haf, yit hit is a potion I ham rissolv to kare to mi housband, soe noe moor at present, from your umble savant to cummand."

The Doctor received this letter with all the ecstasies any lover could be inspired with, and, as Mr. *Congreve* says in his *Old Batchelor,* Thought there was more eloquence in the false spellings, with which it abounded, than in all *Aristotle.* She now resolved to be no longer contented with this distant kind of conversation, but to meet her mistress face to face. Accordingly that very afternoon she went to her mother's house, and enquired for her poor *Molly,* who no sooner heard her lover's voice than she fell a trembling in the most violent manner. Her sister who opened the door informed the Doctor she was at home, and let the impostor in; but *Molly* being then in dishabille, would not see him till she had put on clean linnen, and was arrayed from head to foot in as neat, tho' not so fine a manner, as the highest court lady in the kingdom could attire herself in, to receive her embroider'd lover.

Very tender and delicate was the interview of this pair, and if any corner of *Molly*'s heart remain'd untaken, it was now totally subdued. She would willingly have postponed the match somewhat longer, from her strict regard to decency; but the earnestness and ardour of her lover would not suffer her, and she was at last obliged to consent to be married within two days.

Her sister, who was older than herself, and had over-heard all that had past, no sooner perceiv'd the Doctor gone, than she came to her, and wishing her joy with a sneer, said much good may it do her with such a husband; for that, for her own part, she would almost as willingly be married to one of her own sex, and made some remarks not so proper to be here inserted. This was resented by the other with much warmth. She said she had chosen for herself only, and that if she was pleased, it did not become people to trouble their heads with what was none of their business. She was indeed so extremely enamoured, that I question whether she would have exchanged the Doctor for the greatest and richest match in the world.

And had not her affections been fixed in this strong manner, it is possible that an accident which happened the very next night might have altered her mind: for being at another dancing with her lover, a quarrel arose between the Doctor and a man there present, upon which the mother [*sic*] seizing the former violently by the collar, tore open her wastecoat, and rent her shirt, so that all her breast was discovered, which, tho' beyond expression beautiful in a woman, were of so different a kind from the bosom of a man, that the married women there set up a great titter; and tho' it did not bring the Doctor's sex into an absolute suspicion, yet caused some whispers, which might have spoiled the match with a less innocent and less enamoured virgin.

It had however no such effect on poor *Molly*. As her fond heart was free from any deceit, so was it entirely free from suspicion; and accordingly, at the fixed time she met the Doctor, and their nuptials were celebrated in the usual form.

The mother was extremely pleased at this preferment (as she thought it) of her daughter. The joy of it did indeed contribute to restore her perfectly to health, and nothing but mirth and happiness appeared in the faces of the whole family.

The new married couple not only continued, but greatly increased the fondness which they had conceived for each other, and poor *Molly,* from some stories she told among her acquaintances, the other young married women of the town, was received as a great fibber, and was at last universally laughed at as such among them all.

Three months past in this manner, when the Doctor was sent for to *Glastonbury* to a patient (for the fame of our adventurer's knowledge in physic began now to spread) when a person of *Totness* being accidentally present, happened to see and know her, and having heard upon enquiry, that the Doctor was married at *Wells,* as we have above mentioned, related the whole story of Mr. *Ivythorn*'s daughter, and the whole adventure at *Totness.*

News of this kind seldom wants wings; it reached *Wells,* and the ears of the Doctor's mother [-in-law] before her return from *Glastonbury.* Upon this the old woman immediately sent for her daughter, and very strictly examined her, telling her the great sin she would be guilty of, if she concealed a fact of this kind, and the great disgrace she would bring on her own family, and even on her whole sex, by living quietly and contentedly with a husband who was in any degree less a man than the rest of his neighbours.

Molly assured her mother of the falsehood of this report; and as it is usual for persons who are too eager in any cause, to prove too much, she asserted some things which staggered her mother's belief, and made her cry out, O child, there is no such thing in human nature.

Such was the progress this story had made in *Wells,* that before the Doctor arrived there, it was in every body's mouth; and as the Doctor rode through the streets, the mob, especially the women, all paid their compliments of congratulation. Some laughed at her, others threw dirt at her, and others made use of terms of reproach not fit to be commemorated. When she came to her own house, she found her wife in tears, and having asked her the cause, was informed of the dialogue which had past between her and her mother. Upon which the Doctor, tho' he knew not yet by what means the discovery had been made, yet too well knowing the truth, began to think of using the same method, which she had heard before put in practice, of delivering herself from any impertinence; for as to danger, she was not sufficiently versed in the laws to apprehend any.

In the mean time the mother, at the solicitation of some of her relations, who, notwithstanding the stout denial of the wife, had given credit to the story, had applied herself to a magistrate, before whom the *Totness* man appeared, and gave evidence as is before mentioned. Upon this a warrant was granted to apprehend the Doctor, with which the constable arrived at her house, just as she was meditating her escape.

The husband was no sooner seized, but the wife threw herself into the greatest agonies of rage and grief, vowing that he was injured, and that the information was false and malicious, and that she was resolved to attend her husband wherever they conveyed him.

And now they all proceeded before the Justice, where a strict examination being made into the affair, the whole happened to be true, to the great shock and astonishment of every body; but more especially of the poor wife, who fell into fits, out of which she was with great difficulty recovered.

The whole truth having been disclosed before the Justice, and something of too vile, wicked and scandalous a nature, which was found in the Doctor's trunk, having been produced in evidence against her, she was committed to *Bridewell,* and Mr. *Gold,* an eminent and learned counsellor at law, who lives in those parts, was consulted with upon the occasion, who gave his advice that she should be prosecuted at the next sessions, on a clause in the vagrant act, *for having by false and deceitful practices endeavoured to impose on some of his Majesty's subjects.*

As the Doctor was conveyed to *Bridewell,* she was attended by many insults from the mob; but what was more unjustifiable, was the cruel treatment which the poor innocent wife received from her own sex, upon the extraordinary accounts which she had formerly given of her husband.

Accordingly at the ensuing sessions of the peace for the county of *Somerset,* the Doctor was indicted for the abovementioned diabolical fact, and after a fair trial convicted, to the entire satisfaction of the whole court.

At the trial the said *Mary Price* the wife, was produced as a witness, and being asked by the council, whether she had ever any suspicion of the Doctor's sex during the whole time of the courtship, she answered positively in the negative. She was then asked how long they had been married, to which she answered three months; and whether they had cohabited the whole time together? to which her reply was in the affirmative. Then the council asked her, whether during the time of this cohabitation, she imagined the Doctor had behaved to her as a husband ought to his wife? Her modesty confounded her a little at this question; but she at last answered she did imagine so. Lastly, she was asked when it was that she first harboured any suspicion of her being imposed upon? To which she answered, she had not the least suspicion till her husband was carried before a magistrate, and there discovered, as hath been said above.

The prisoner having been convicted of this base and scandalous crime, was by the court sentenced to be publickly and severely whipt four several times, in four market towns within the county of *Somerset,* to wit, once in each market town, and to be imprisoned, &c.

These whippings she has accordingly undergone, and very severely have they been inflicted, insomuch, that those persons who have more regard to beauty than to justice, could not refrain from exerting some pity toward her, when they saw so lovely a skin scarified with rods, in such a manner that her back was almost flead; yet so little effect had the smart or shame of this punishment on the person who underwent it, that the very evening she had suffered the first whipping, she offered the goaler money, to procure her a young girl to satisfy her most monstrous and unnatural desires.

But it is to be hoped that this example will be sufficient to deter all others from the commission of any such foul and unnatural crimes: for which, if they should escape the shame and ruin which they so well deserve in this world, they will be most certain of meeting with their full punishment in the next: for unnatural affections are equally vicious and equally detestable in both sexes, nay, if modesty be the peculiar characterstick of the fair sex, it is in them most shocking and odious to prostitute and debase it.

In order to caution therefore that lovely sex, which, while they preserve their natural innocence and purity, will still look most lovely in the eyes of men, the above pages have been written, which, that they might be worthy of their perusal, such strict regard hath been had to the utmost decency, that notwithstanding the subject of this narrative be of a nature so difficult to be handled inoffensively, not a single word occurs through the whole, which might shock the most delicate ear, or give offence to the purest chastity.

From *Psychopathia Sexualis* by Richard von Krafft-Ebing

Case 166. *Gynandry.* History: On 4th November, 1889, the father-in-law of a certain Countess V., complained that the latter had swindled him out of 800f., under the pretence of requiring a bond as secretary of a stock company. It was ascertained that Sandor had entered into matrimonial contracts and escaped from the nuptials in the spring of 1889; and, more than this, that this ostensible Count Sandor was no man at all, but a woman in male attire—Sarolta (Charlotte), Countess V.

S. was arrested, and, on account of deception and forgery of public documents, brought to examination. At the first hearing S. confessed that she was born on the 6th Sept., 1866; that she was a female, Catholic, single, and worked as an authoress under the name of Count Sandor V.

From the autobiography of this man-woman I have gleaned the following remarkable facts that have been independently confirmed:—

S. came of an ancient, noble and highly respected family of Hungary, in which there had been eccentricity and family peculiarities. A sister of the maternal grandmother was hysterical, a somnambulist, and lay seventeen years in bed, on account of fancied paralysis. A second great-aunt spent seven years in bed, on account of a fancied fatal illness, and at the same time gave balls. A third had the whim that a certain table in her *salon* was bewitched. When anything was laid on this table, she would become greatly excited and cry, "Bewitched! bewitched!" and run with the object into a room which she called the "Black Chamber," and the key of which she never let out of her hands. After the death of this lady, there were found in this chamber a number of shawls, ornaments, bank-notes, etc. A fourth great-aunt during two years did not leave her room, and neither washed herself nor combed her hair; then she again made her appearance. All these ladies were, nevertheless, intellectual, finely educated and amiable.

S.'s mother was nervous, and could not bear the light of the moon.

She inherited many of the peculiarities of her father's family. One line of the family gave itself up almost entirely to spiritualism. Two blood re-lations on the father's side shot themselves. The majority of her male rel-atives were unusually talented; the females were decidedly narrow-minded and domesticated. S.'s father had a high position, which, however, on ac-count of his eccentricity and extravagance (he wasted over a million and a half), he lost.

Among many foolish things that her father encouraged in her was the fact that he brought her up as a boy, called her Sandor, allowed her to ride, drive and hunt, admiring her muscular energy.

On the other hand, this foolish father allowed his second son to go about in female attire, and had him brought up as a girl. This farce ceased when the son was sent to a higher school at the age of fifteen.

Sarolta-Sandor remained under her father's influence till her twelfth year, and then came under the care of her eccentric maternal grandmother in Dresden, by whom, when the masculine play became too obvious, she was placed in an institute and made to wear female attire.

At thirteen she had a love-relation with an English girl, to whom she represented herself as a boy, and ran away with her.

Sarolta returned to her mother, who, however, could do nothing, and was compelled to allow her daughter to again become Sandor, wear male clothes, and, at least once a year, to fall in love with persons of her own sex.

At the same time S. received a careful education and made long journeys with her father, of course always as a young gentleman. She early became independent and visited *cafés*, even those of doubtful character, and, in-deed, boasted one day that in a brothel she had had a girl sitting on each knee. S. was often intoxicated, had a passion for masculine sports and was a very skilful fencer.

She felt herself drawn particularly toward actresses, or others of similar position, and, if possible, toward those who were not very young. She asserted that she never had any inclination for a young man, and that she had felt, from year to year, an increasing dislike for young men.

"I preferred to go into the society of ladies with ugly, ill-favoured men, so that none of them could put me in the shade. If I noticed that any of the men awakened the sympathies of the ladies, I felt jealous. I preferred ladies who were bright and pretty; I could not endure them if they were fat or much inclined toward men. It delighted me if the passion of a lady was disclosed under a poetic veil. All immodesty in a woman was disgusting to me. I had an indescribable aversion for female attire,—indeed, for ev-erything feminine, but only in as far as it concerned me; for, on the other hand, I was all enthusiasm for the beautiful sex."

During the last ten years S. had lived almost constantly away from her relatives, in the guise of a man. She had had many *liaisons* with ladies, travelled much, spent much, and made debts.

At the same time she carried on literary work, and was a valued collaborator on two noted journals of the capital.

Her passion for ladies was very changeable; constancy in love was entirely wanting.

Only once did such a *liaison* last three years. It was years before that S., at Castle G., made the acquaintance of Emma E., who was ten years older than herself. She fell in love with her, made a marriage contract with her, and they lived together as man and wife for three years at the capital.

A new love, which proved fatal to S., caused her to sever her matrimonial relations with E. The latter would not have it so. Only with the greatest sacrifice was S. able to purchase her freedom from E., who still looked upon herself as a divorced wife, and regarded herself as the Countess V.! That S. also had the power to excite passion in other women was shown by the fact that when she (before her marriage with E.) had grown tired of a Miss D., after having spent thousands of guldens on her, she was threatened with shooting by D. if she should become untrue.

It was in the summer of 1887, while at a watering-place, that S. made the acquaintance of a distinguished official's family. Immediately she fell in love with the daughter, Marie, and her love was returned.

Her mother and cousin tried in vain to break up this affair. During the winter the lovers corresponded zealously. In April, 1888, Count S. paid her a visit, and in May, 1889, attained her wish; in that Marie—who, in the meantime, had given up a position as teacher—became her bride in the presence of a friend of her lover, the ceremony being performed in an arbour, by a pseudo-priest, in Hungary. S., with her friend, forged the marriage certificate. The pair lived happily, and, without the interference of the father-in-law, this false marriage, probably, would have lasted much longer. It is remarkable that, during the comparatively long existence of the relation, S. was able to deceive completely the family of her bride with regard to her true sex.

S. was a passionate smoker, and in all respects her tastes and passions were masculine. Her letters and even legal documents reached her under the address of "Count S." She often spoke of having to drill. From remarks of the father-in-law it seems that S. (and she afterward confessed it) knew how to imitate a scrotum with handkerchiefs or gloves stuffed in the trousers. The father-in-law also, on one occasion, noticed something like an erected member on his future son-in-law (probably a priapus). She also occasionally remarked that she was obliged to wear a suspensory bandage while riding. The fact is, S. wore a bandage around the body possibly as a means of retaining a priapus.

Though S. often had herself shaved *pro forma,* the servants in the hotel where she lived were convinced that she was a woman, because the chambermaids found traces of menstrual blood on her linen (which S. explained, however, as hæmorrhoidal); and, on the occasion of a bath which S. was accustomed to take, they claimed to have convinced themselves of her real sex by looking through the key-hole.

The family of Marie make it seem probable that she for a long time was deceived with regard to the true sex of her false bridegroom. The following passage in a letter from Marie to S., 26th August, 1889, speaks in favour of the incredible simplicity and innocence of this unfortunate girl: "I don't like children any more, but if I had a little Bezerl or Patscherl by my Sandi—ah, what happiness, Sandi mine!"

A large number of manuscripts allow conclusions to be drawn concerning S.'s mental individuality. The chirography possesses the character of firmness and certainty. The characters are genuinely masculine. The same peculiarities repeat themselves everywhere in their contents—wild, unbridled passion; hatred and resistance to all that opposes the heart thirsting for love; poetical love, which is not marred by one ignoble blot, enthusiasm for the beautiful and noble; appreciation of science and the arts.

Her writings betray a wonderfully wide range of reading in classics of all languages, in citations from poets and prose writers of all lands. The evidence of those qualified to judge literary work shows that S.'s poetical and literary ability was by no means small. The letters and writings concerning the relation with Marie are psychologically worthy of notice.

S. speaks of the happiness there was for her when by M.'s side, and expresses boundless longing to see her beloved, if only for a moment. After such a happiness she could have but one wish—to exchange her cell for the grave. The bitterest thing was the knowledge that now Marie, too, hated her. Hot tears, enough to drown herself in, she had shed over her lost happiness. Whole quires of paper are given up to the apotheosis of this love, and reminiscences of the time of the first love and acquaintance.

S. complained of her heart, that would allow no reason to direct it; she expressed emotions which were such as only could be felt—not simulated. Then, again, there were outbreaks of most silly passion, with the declaration that she could not live without Marie. "Thy dear, sweet voice; the voice whose tone perchance would raise me from the dead; that has been for me like the warm breath of Paradise! Thy presence alone were enough to alleviate my mental and moral anguish. It was a magnetic stream; it was a peculiar power your being exercised over mine, which I cannot quite define; and, therefore, I cling to that ever-true definition: I love you because I love you. In the night of sorrow I had but one star—the star of Marie's love. That star has lost its light; now there remains but its shimmer—the sweet, sad memory which even lights with its soft ray the deepening night of death—a ray of hope."

This writing ends with the apostrophe: "Gentlemen, you learned in the law, psychologists and pathologists, do me justice! Love led me to take the step I took; all my deeds were conditioned by it. God put it in my heart.

"If he created me so, and not otherwise, am I then guilty; or is it the eternal, incomprehensible way of fate? I relied on God, that one day my emancipation would come; for my thought was only love itself, which is the foundation, the guiding principle, of His teaching and His kingdom.

"O God, Thou All-pitying, Almighty One! Thou seest my distress; Thou knowest how I suffer. Incline Thyself to me; extend Thy helping hand to me, deserted by all the world. Only God is just. How beautifully does Victor Hugo describe this in his 'Legendes du Siècle'! How sad do Mendelssohn's words sound to me: 'Nightly in dreams I see thee'!"

Though S. knew that none of her writings reached her lover, she did not grow tired writing of her pain and delight in love, in page after page of deification of Marie. And to induce one more pure flood of tears, on one still, clear summer evening, when the lake was aglow with the setting sun like molten gold, and the bells of St. Anna and Maria-Wörth, blending in harmonious melancholy, gave tidings of rest and peace, she wrote: "For that poor soul, for this poor heart that beats for thee till the last breath."

Personal examination: The first meeting which the experts had with S. was in a measure, a time of embarrassment to both sides; for them, because perhaps S.'s somewhat dazzling and forced masculine carriage impressed them; for her, because she thought she was to be marked with the stigma of moral insanity. She had a pleasant and intelligent face, which, in spite of a certain delicacy of features and diminutiveness of all its parts, gave a decidedly masculine impression, had it not been for the absence of a moustache. It was even difficult for the experts to realise that they were concerned with a woman, despite the fact of female attire and constant association; while, on the other hand, intercourse with the man Sandor was much more free, natural, and apparently correct. The accused also felt this. She immediately became more open, more communicative, more free, as soon as she was treated like a man.

In spite of her inclination for the female sex, which had been present from her earliest years, she asserted that in her thirteenth year she first felt a trace of sexual feeling, which expressed itself in kisses, embraces, and caresses, with sexual pleasure, and this on the occasion of her elopement with the red-haired English girl from the Dresden institute. At that time feminine forms exclusively appeared to her in dream-pictures, and ever since, in sensual dreams, she felt herself in the situation of a man, and occasionally, also, at such times, experienced ejaculation.

She knew nothing of solitary or mutual onanism. Such a thing seemed very disgusting to her, and not conducive to manliness. She had, also, never allowed herself to be touched *ad genitalia* by others, because it would have revealed her great secret. The menses began at seventeen, but were always scanty and without pain. It was plain to be seen that S. had a horror of speaking of menstruation; that it was a thing repugnant to her masculine consciousness and feeling. She recognised the abnormality of her sexual inclinations, but had no desire to have them changed, since in this perverse feeling she felt both well and happy. The idea of sexual intercourse with men disgusted her, and she also thought it would be impossible.

Her modesty was so great that she would prefer to sleep among men rather than among women. Thus, when it was necessary for her to answer the calls of nature or to change her linen, it was necessary for her to ask her companion in the cell to turn her face to the window, that she might not see her.

When occasionally S. came in contact with this companion,—a woman from the lower walks of life,—she experienced a sexual excitement that made her blush. Indeed, without being asked, S. related that she was overcome with actual fear when, in her cell, she was compelled to force herself into the unusual female attire. Her only comfort was that she was at least allowed to keep a shirt. Remarkable, and what also speaks for the significance of olfactory sensations in her *vita sexualis,* is her statement that, on the occasions of Marie's absence, she had sought those places on which Marie's head was accustomed to repose, and smelled them, in order to experience the delight of inhaling the odour of her hair. Among women, those who were beautiful, or voluptuous, or quite young, did not particularly interest her. The physical charms of women she made subordinate. As by magnetic attraction, she felt herself drawn to those between twenty-four and thirty. She found her sexual satisfaction exclusively in *corpore feminæ* (never in her own person), in the form of manustupration of the beloved woman, or cunnilingus. Occasionally she availed herself of a stocking stuffed with oakum as a priapus. These admissions were made only unwillingly by S., and with apparent shame; just as in her writings immodesty or cynicism are never found.

She was religious, had a lively interest in all that is noble and beautiful,—men excepted,—and was very sensitive to the opinion others entertained of her morality.

She deeply regretted that in her passion she made Marie unhappy, and regarded her sexual feelings as perverse, and such a love of one woman for another, among normal individuals, as morally reprehensible. She had great literary talent and an extraordinary memory. Her only weakness was her great frivolity and her incapability to manage money and property reasonably. But she was conscious of this weakness, and did not care to talk about it.

She was 153 centimetres tall, of delicate build, thin, but remarkably muscular on the breast and thighs. Her gait in female attire was awkward. Her movements were powerful, not unpleasing, though they were somewhat masculine and lacking in grace. She greeted one with a firm pressure of the hand. Her whole carriage was decided, firm and somewhat self-conscious. Her glance was intelligent; mien somewhat diffident. Feet and hands remarkably small, having remained in an infantile stage of development. Extensor surfaces of the extremities remarkably well covered with hair, while there was not the slightest trace of beard, in spite of all shaving experiments. The hips did not correspond in any way with those of a female. Waist wanting. Pelvis so slim and so little prominent, that a line drawn from the axilla to the corresponding knee was straight—not curved inward by a waist or outward by the pelvis. The skull slightly oxycephalic, and in all its measurements below the average of the female skull by at least one centimetre.

Circumference of the head 52 centimetres; occipital half circumference, 24 centimetres; line from ear to ear, over the vertex, 23 centimetres; anterior half-circumference, 28.5 centimetres; line from glabella to occiput, 30 centimetres; ear-chin line, 26.5 centimetres; long diameter, 17 centimetres; greatest lateral diameter, 13 centimetres; diameter at auditory meati, 12 centimetres; zygomatic diameter, 11.2 centimetres. Upper jaw strikingly projecting, its alveolar process projecting beyond the under jaw about 0.5 centimetre. Position of the teeth not fully normal; right upper canine not developed. Mouth remarkably small; ears prominent; lobes not differentiated, passing over into the skin of the cheek. Hard palate, narrow and high; voice rough and deep; mammæ fairly developed, soft and without secretion. Mons veneris covered with thick, dark hair. Genitals completely feminine, without trace of hermaphroditic appearance, but at the stage of development of those of a ten-year-old girl. The labia majora touching each other almost completely; labia minora having a cock's-comb-like form, and projecting under the labia majora. Clitoris small and very sensitive. Frenulum delicate; perineum very narrow; introitus vaginæ narrow; mucous membrane normal. Hymen wanting (probably congenitally); likewise the carunculæ myrtiformes. Vagina so narrow that the insertion of a membrum virile would be impossible, also very sensitive; certainly coitus had not taken place. Uterus felt, through the rectum, to be about the size of a walnut, immovable and retroflected.

Pelvis generally narrowed (dwarf-pelvis), and of decidedly masculine type. Distance between anterior superior spines 22.5 centimetres (instead of 26.3 centimetres). Distance between the crests of the ilii, 26.5 centimetres (instead of 29.3 centimetres); between the trochanters, 27.7 centimetres (31); the external conjugate diameter, 17.2 centimetres (19 to 20); therefore, the internal conjugate, presumably, 7.7 centimetres (10.8). On account of narrowness of the pelvis, the direction of the thighs not convergent, as in a woman, but straight.

The opinion given showed that in S. there was a congenitally abnormal inversion of the sexual instinct, which, indeed, expressed itself, anthropologically, in anomalies of development of the body, depending upon great hereditary taint; further, that the criminal acts of S. had their foundation in her abnormal and irresistible sexuality.

S.'s characteristic expressions—"God put love in my heart. If He created me so, and not otherwise, am I, then, guilty; or is it the eternal, incomprehensible way of fate?"—are really justified.

The court granted pardon. The "countess in male attire," as she was called in the newspapers, returned to her home, and again gave herself out as Count Sandor. Her only distress was her lost happiness with her beloved Marie.

From *The Psychogenesis of a Case of Homosexuality in a Woman* by Sigmund Freud

I

Homosexuality in women, which is certainly not less common than in men, although much less glaring, has not only been ignored by the law, but has also been neglected by psychoanalytic research. The narration of a single case, not too pronounced in type, in which it was possible to trace its origin and development in the mind with complete certainty and almost without a gap may, therefore, have a certain claim to attention. If this presentation of it furnishes only the most general outlines of the various events concerned and of the conclusions reached from a study of the case, while suppressing all the characteristic details on which the interpretation is founded, this limitation is easily to be explained by the medical discretion necessary in discussing a recent case.

A beautiful and clever girl of eighteen, belonging to a family of good standing, had aroused displeasure and concern in her parents by the devoted adoration with which she pursued a certain "society lady" who was about ten years older than herself. The parents asserted that, in spite of her distinguished name, this lady was nothing but a *cocotte*. It was well known, they said, that she lived with a friend, a married woman, and had intimate relations with her, while at the same time she carried on promiscuous affairs with a number of men. The girl did not contradict these evil reports, but neither did she allow them to interfere with her worship of the lady, although she herself was by no means lacking in a sense of decency and propriety. No prohibitions and no supervision hindered the girl from seizing every one of her rare opportunities of being together with her beloved, of ascertaining all her habits, of waiting for her for hours outside her door or at a tram-halt, of sending her gifts of flowers, and so on. It was evident that this one interest had swallowed up all others in the girl's mind. She did not trouble herself any further with educational studies, thought nothing of social functions or girlish pleasures, and kept up relations only with a few girl friends who could help her in the matter or serve as confidantes. The parents could not say to what lengths their daughter had gone in her relations with the questionable lady, whether the limits of devoted admiration had already been exceeded or not. They had never remarked in their daughter any interest in young men, nor pleasure in their attentions, while, on the other hand, they were sure that her present attachment to a woman was only a continuation, in a more marked degree, of a feeling she had displayed of recent years for other members of her own sex which had already aroused her father's suspicion and anger.

There were two details of her behaviour, in apparent contrast with each other, that most especially vexed her parents. On the one hand, she did not scruple to appear in the most frequented streets in the company of her undesirable friend, being thus quite neglectful of her own reputation; while, on the other hand, she disdained no means of deception, no excuses and no lies that would make meetings with her possible and cover them. She thus showed herself too open in one respect and full of deceitfulness in the other. One day it happened, indeed, as was sooner or later inevitable in the circumstances, that the father met his daughter in the company of the lady, about whom he had come to know. He passed them by with an angry glance which boded no good. Immediately afterwards the girl rushed off and flung herself over a wall down the side of a cutting on to the suburban railway line which ran close by. She paid for this undoubtedly serious attempt at suicide with a considerable time on her back in bed, though fortunately little permanent damage was done. After her recovery she found it easier to get her own way than before. The parents did not dare to oppose her with so much determination, and the lady, who up till then had received her advances coldly, was moved by such an unmistakable proof of serious passion and began to treat her in a more friendly manner.

About six months after this episode the parents sought medical advice and entrusted the physician with the task of bringing their daughter back to a normal state of mind. The girl's attempted suicide had evidently shown

them that strong disciplinary measures at home were powerless to overcome her disorder. Before going further, however, it will be desirable to
deal separately with the attitudes of her father and of her mother to the
matter. The father was an earnest, worthy man, at bottom very tender-
hearted, but he had to some extent estranged his children by the sternness
he had adopted towards them. His treatment of his only daughter was too
much influenced by consideration for his wife. When he first came to know
of his daughter's homosexual tendencies he flew into a rage and tried to
suppress them by threats. At that time perhaps he hesitated between different, though equally distressing, views—regarding her either as vicious,
as degenerate, or as mentally afflicted. Even after the attempted suicide he
did not achieve the lofty resignation shown by one of our medical colleagues who remarked of a similar irregularity in his own family: "Well,
it's just a misfortune like any other." There was something about his
daughter's homosexuality that aroused the deepest bitterness in him, and
he was determined to combat it with all the means in his power. The low
estimation in which psychoanalysis is so generally held in Vienna did not
prevent him from turning to it for help. If this way failed he still had in
reserve his strongest counter-measure: a speedy marriage was to awaken
the natural instincts of the girl and stifle her unnatural tendencies.

The mother's attitude towards the girl was not so easy to grasp. She
was still a youngish woman, who was evidently unwilling to give up her
own claims to attractiveness. All that was clear was that she did not take
her daughter's infatuation so tragically as did the father, nor was she so
incensed at it. She had even for some time enjoyed her daughter's confidence concerning her passion. Her opposition to it seemed to have been
aroused mainly by the harmful publicity with which the girl displayed her
feelings. She had herself suffered for some years from neurotic troubles and
enjoyed a great deal of consideration from her husband; she treated her
children in quite different ways, being decidedly harsh towards her daughter and overindulgent to her three sons, the youngest of whom had been
born after a long interval and was then not yet three years old. It was not
easy to ascertain anything more definite about her character, for, owing to
motives that will only later become intelligible, the patient was always reserved in what she said about her mother, whereas in regard to her father
there was no question of this. . . .

I had made [a] prognosis partly dependent on how far the girl had
succeeded in satisfying her passion. The information I obtained during the
analysis seemed favourable in this respect. With none of the objects of her
adoration had the patient enjoyed anything beyond a few kisses and embraces; her genital chastity, if one may use such a phrase, had remained
intact. As for the *demi-mondaine* who had roused her most recent and by

far her strongest emotions, she had always been treated coldly by her and never been allowed any greater favour than to kiss her hand. She was probably making a virtue of necessity when she kept insisting on the purity of her love and her physical repulsion against the idea of any sexual intercourse. But perhaps she was not altogether wrong when she boasted of her wonderful beloved that, being of good birth as she was, and forced into her present position only by adverse family circumstances, she had preserved, in spite of her situation, much nobility of character. For the lady used to recommend the girl every time they met to withdraw her affection from herself and from women in general, and she had persistently rejected the girl's advances up to the time of the attempted suicide.

A second point, which I at once tried to investigate, concerned any possible motives in the girl herself which might serve as a support for psycho-analytic treatment. She did not try to deceive me by saying that she felt any urgent need to be freed from her homosexuality. On the contrary, she said she could not conceive of any other way of being in love, but she added that for her parents' sake she would honestly help in the therapeutic attempt, for it pained her very much to be the cause of so much grief to them. To begin with, I could not but take this, too, as a propitious sign; for I could not guess the unconscious affective attitude that lay concealed behind it. What came to light later in this connection decisively influenced the course taken by the analysis and determined its premature conclusion.

Readers unversed in psycho-analysis will long have been awaiting an answer to two other questions. Did this homosexual girl show physical characteristics plainly belonging to the opposite sex, and did the case prove to be one of congenital or acquired (later-developed) homosexuality?

I am aware of the importance attaching to the first of these questions. But one should not exaggerate it and allow it to overshadow the fact that sporadic secondary characteristics of the opposite sex are very often present in normal individuals, and that well-marked physical characteristics of the opposite sex may be found in persons whose choice of object has undergone no change in the direction of inversion; in other words, that in both sexes *the degree of physical hermaphroditism is to a great extent independent of psychical hermaphroditism.* In modification of these statements it must be added that this independence is more evident in men than women, where bodily and mental traits belonging to the opposite sex are apt to coincide. Still I am not in a position to give a satisfactory answer to the first of our questions about my patient. The psycho-analyst customarily forgoes a thorough physical examination of his patients in certain cases. Certainly there was no obvious deviation from the feminine physical type, nor any menstrual disturbance. The beautiful and well-made girl had, it is true, her father's tall figure, and her facial features were sharp rather than soft and girlish, traits which might be regarded as indicating a physical masculinity. Some of her intellectual attributes also could be connected with masculinity: for instance, her acuteness of comprehension and her lucid objectivity, in so far as she was not dominated by her passion. But these distinctions are conventional rather than scientific. What is certainly of greater importance is that in her behaviour towards her love-object she had throughout assumed the masculine part: that is to say, she displayed the humility and the sublime overvaluation of the sexual object so characteristic of the male lover, the renunciation of all narcissistic satisfaction, and the preference for being the lover rather than the beloved. She had thus not only chosen a feminine love-object, but had also developed a masculine attitude towards that object.

The second question, whether this was a case of congenital or acquired homosexuality, will be answered by the whole history of the patient's abnormality and its development. The study of this will show how far this question is a fruitless and inapposite one.

II

After this highly discursive introduction I am only able to present a very concise summary of the sexual history of the case under consideration. In childhood the girl had passed through the normal attitude characteristic of the feminine Oedipus complex in a way that was not at all remarkable, and had later also begun to substitute for her father a brother slightly older than herself. She did not remember any sexual traumas in early life, nor were any discovered by the analysis. Comparison of her brother's genital organs and her own, which took place about the beginning of the latency period (at five years old or perhaps a little earlier), left a strong impression on her and had far-reaching after-effects. There were very few signs pointing to infantile masturbation, or else the analysis did not go far enough to throw light on this point. The birth of a second brother when she was between five and six years old exercised no special influence upon her development. During the prepubertal years at school she gradually became acquainted with the facts of sex, and she received this knowledge with mixed feelings of lasciviousness and frightened aversion, in a way which may be called normal and was not exaggerated in degree. This amount of information about her seems meagre enough, nor can I guarantee that it is complete. It may be that the history of her youth was much richer in experiences; I do not know. As I have already said, the analysis was broken off after a short time, and therefore yielded an anamnesis not much more reliable than the other anamneses of homosexuals, which there is good cause to question. Further, the girl had never been neurotic, and came to the analysis without even one hysterical symptom, so that opportunities for investigating the history of her childhood did not present themselves so readily as usual.

At the age of thirteen to fourteen she displayed a tender and, according to general opinion, exaggeratedly strong affection for a small boy, not quite three years old, whom she used to see regularly in a children's playground. She took to the child so warmly that in consequence a lasting friendship grew up between herself and his parents. One may infer from this episode that at that time she was possessed of a strong desire to be a mother herself and to have a child. However, after a short time she grew indifferent to the boy, and began to take an interest in mature, but still youthful, women. The manifestations of this interest soon brought upon her a severe chastisement at the hands of her father.

It was established beyond all doubt that this change occurred simultaneously with a certain event in the family, and one may therefore look to this for some explanation of the change. Before it happened, her libido was concentrated on a maternal attitude, while afterwards she became a homosexual attracted to mature women, and remained so ever since. The event which is so significant for our understanding of the case was a new pregnancy of her mother's, and the birth of a third brother when she was about sixteen.

The position of affairs which I shall now proceed to lay bare is not a product of my inventive powers; it is based on such trustworthy analytic evidence that I can claim objective validity for it. It was in particular a series of dreams, interrelated and easy to interpret, that decided me in favour of its reality.

The analysis revealed beyond all shadow of doubt that the lady-love was a substitute for—her mother. It is true that the lady herself was not a mother, but then she was not the girl's first love. The first objects of her affection after the birth of her youngest brother were really mothers, women between thirty and thirty-five whom she had met with their children during summer holidays or in the family circle of acquaintances in town. Motherhood as a *sine qua non* in her love-object was later on given up, because that precondition was difficult to combine in real life with another one, which grew more and more important. The specially intense bond with her latest love had still another basis which the girl discovered quite easily one day. Her lady's slender figure, severe beauty, and downright manner reminded her of the brother who was a little older than herself. Her latest choice corresponded, therefore, not only to her feminine but also to her masculine ideal; it combined satisfaction of the homosexual tendency with that of the heterosexual one. It is well known that analysis of male homosexuals has in numerous cases revealed the same combination, which should warn us not to form too simple a conception of the nature and genesis of inversion, and to keep in mind the universal bisexuality of human beings.

But how are we to understand the fact that it was precisely the birth of a child who came late in the family (at a time when the girl herself was already mature and had strong wishes of her own) that moved her to bestow her passionate tenderness upon the woman who gave birth to this child, i.e. her own mother, and to express that feeling towards a substitute for her mother? From all that we know we should have expected just the opposite. In such circumstances mothers with daughters of nearly a marriageable age usually feel embarrassed in regard to them, while the daughters are apt to feel for their mothers a mixture of compassion, contempt and envy which does nothing to increase their tenderness for them. The girl we are considering had in any case altogether little cause to feel affection for her mother. The latter, still youthful herself, saw in her rapidly developing daughter an inconvenient competitor; she favoured the sons at her expense, limited her independence as much as possible, and kept an especially strict watch against any close relation between the girl and her father. A yearning from the beginning for a kinder mother would, therefore, have been quite intelligible, but why it should have flared up just then, and in the form of a consuming passion, is hard to understand.

The explanation is as follows. It was just when the girl was experiencing the revival of her infantile Oedipus complex at puberty that she suffered her great disappointment. She became keenly conscious of the wish to have a child, and a male one; that what she desired was her *father's* child and an image of *him,* her consciousness was not allowed to know. And what happened next? It was not *she* who bore the child, but her unconsciously hated rival, her mother. Furiously resentful and embittered, she turned away from her father and from men altogether. After this first great reverse she forswore her womanhood and sought another goal for her libido.

In doing so she behaved just as many men do who after a first distressing experience turn their backs for ever upon the faithless female sex and become woman-haters. It is related of one of the most attractive and unfortunate princely figures of our time that he became a homosexual because the lady he was engaged to marry betrayed him with another man. I do not know whether this is true historically, but an element of psychological truth lies behind the rumour. In all of us, throughout life, the libido normally oscillates between male and female objects; the bachelor gives up his men friends when he marries, and returns to club-life when married life has lost its savour. Naturally, when the swing-over is fundamental and final, we suspect the presence of some special factor which definitely favours one side or the other, and which perhaps has only waited for the appropriate moment in order to turn the choice of object in its direction.

After her disappointment, therefore, this girl had entirely repudiated her wish for a child, her love of men, and the feminine role in general. It is evident that at this point a number of very different things might have happened. What actually happened was the most extreme case. She changed into a man and took her mother in place of her father as the object of her love. Her relation to her mother had certainly been ambivalent from the beginning, and it proved easy to revive her earlier love for her mother and with its help to bring about an overcompensation for her current hostility towards her. Since there was little to be done with the real mother, there arose from this transformation of feeling the search for a substitute mother to whom she could become passionately attached.

There was, in addition, a practical motive for this change, derived from her real relations with her mother, which served as a [secondary] gain from her illness. The mother herself still attached great value to the attentions and the admiration of men. If, then, the girl became homosexual and left men to her mother (in other words, "retired in favour of" her mother), she would remove something which had hitherto been partly responsible for her mother's dislike. . . .

III

Linear presentation is not a very adequate means of describing complicated mental processes going on in different layers of the mind. I am therefore obliged to pause in the discussion of the case and treat more fully and deeply some of the points brought forward above.

I mentioned the fact that in her behaviour to her adored lady the girl had adopted the characteristic masculine type of love. Her humility and her tender lack of pretensions, *"che poco spera e nulla chiede,"*[1] her bliss when she was allowed to accompany the lady a little way and to kiss her hand on parting, her joy when she heard her praised as beautiful (while any recognition of her own beauty by another person meant nothing at all to her), her pilgrimages to places once visited by the loved one, the silence of all more sensual wishes—all these little traits in her resembled the first passionate adoration of a youth for a celebrated actress whom he regards as far above him, to whom he scarcely dares lift his bashful eyes. The correspondence with "a special type of choice of object made by men" that I have described elsewhere whose special features I traced to attachment to the mother, held good even to the smallest details. It may seem remarkable that she was not in the least repelled by the bad reputation of her beloved,

---

[1] "Hoping little and asking for nothing."

although her own observations sufficiently confirmed the truth of such rumours. She was after all a well-brought-up and modest girl, who had avoided sexual adventures for herself, and who regarded coarsely sensual satisfactions as unaesthetic. But already her first passions had been for women who were not celebrated for specially strict propriety. The first protest her father made against her love-choice had been evoked by the pertinacity with which she sought the company of a film actress at a summer resort. Moreover, in all these affairs it had never been a question of women who had any reputation for homosexuality, and who might, therefore, have offered her some prospect of homosexual satisfaction; on the contrary, she illogically courted women who were coquettes in the ordinary sense of the word, and she rejected without hesitation the willing advances made by a homosexual friend of her own age. For her, the bad reputation of her "lady," however, was positively a "necessary condition for love." All that is enigmatic in this attitude vanishes when we remember that in the case too of the *masculine* type of object-choice derived from the mother it is a necessary condition that the loved object should be in some way or other "of bad repute" sexually—someone who really may be called a *cocotte*. When the girl learnt later how far her adored lady deserved this description and that she lived simply by giving her bodily favours, her reaction took the form of great compassion and of phantasies and plans for "rescuing" her beloved from these ignoble circumstances. We were struck by the same urge to "rescue" in the men of the type referred to above, and in my description of it I have tried to give the analytic derivation of this urge.

We are led into quite another realm of explanation by the analysis of the attempt at suicide, which I must regard as seriously intended, and which, incidentally, considerably improved her position both with her parents and with the lady she loved. She went for a walk with her one day in a part of the town and at an hour at which she was not unlikely to meet her father on his way from his office. So it turned out. Her father passed them in the street and cast a furious look at her and her companion, about whom he had by that time come to know. A few moments later she flung herself into the railway cutting. The explanation she gave of the immediate reasons determining her decision sounded quite plausible. She had confessed to the lady that the man who had given them such an irate glance was her father, and that he had absolutely forbidden their friendship. The lady became incensed at this and ordered the girl to leave her then and there, and never again to wait for her or to address her—the affair must now come to an end. In her despair at having thus lost her loved one for ever, she wanted to put an end to herself. The analysis, however, was able to disclose another and deeper interpretation behind the one she gave, which was confirmed by the evidence of her own dreams. The attempted suicide was, as might have been expected, determined by two other motives besides the one she gave: it was the fulfilment of a punishment (self-punishment), and the fulfilment of a wish. As the latter it meant the attainment of the very wish which, when frustrated, had driven her into homosexuality—namely, the wish to have a child by her father, for now she "fell" through her father's fault. The fact that at that moment the lady had spoken in just the same terms as her father, and had uttered the same prohibition, forms the connecting link between this deep interpretation and the superficial one of which the girl herself was conscious. From the point of view of self-punishment the girl's action shows us that she had developed in her unconscious strong death-wishes against one or other of her parents—perhaps against her father, out of revenge for impeding her love, but more probably against her mother too, when she was pregnant with the little brother. For analysis has explained the enigma of suicide in the following way: probably no one finds the mental energy required to kill himself unless, in the first place, in doing so he is at the same time killing an object with whom he has identified himself, and, in the second place, is turning against himself a death-wish which had been directed against someone else. Nor need the regular discovery of these unconscious death-wishes in those who have attempted suicide surprise us (any more than it ought to make us think that it confirms our deductions), since the unconscious of all human beings is full enough of such death-wishes, even against those they love. Since the girl identified herself with her mother, who should have died at the birth of the child denied to herself, this punishment-fulfilment itself was once again a wish-fulfilment. Finally, the discovery that several quite different motives, all of great strength, must have co-operated to make such a deed possible is only in accordance with what we should expect.

In the girl's account of her conscious motives the father did not figure at all; there was not even any mention of fear of his anger. In the motives laid bare by the analysis, on the other hand, he played the principal part. Her relation to her father had the same decisive importance for the course and outcome of the analytic treatment, or rather, analytic exploration. Behind her pretended consideration for her parents, for whose sake she had been willing to make the attempt to be transformed, lay concealed her attitude of defiance and revenge against her father which held her fast to her homosexuality. Secure under this cover, the resistance set a considerable region free to analytic investigation. The analysis went forward almost without any signs of resistance, the patient participating actively with her intellect, though absolutely tranquil emotionally.

In the case of our patient, it was not doubt but the affective factor of revenge against her father that made her cool reserve possible, that divided the analysis into two distinct phases, and rendered the results of the first phase so complete and perspicuous. It seemed, further, as though nothing resembling a transference to the physician had been effected. That, however, is of course absurd, or, at least, is a loose way of expressing things. For some kind of relation to the analyst must come into being, and this relation is almost always transferred from an infantile one. In reality she transferred to me the sweeping repudiation of men which had dominated her ever since the disappointment she had suffered from her father. Bitterness against men is as a rule easy to gratify upon the physician; it need not evoke any violent emotional manifestations, it simply expresses itself by rendering futile all his endeavours and by clinging to the illness. I know from experience how difficult it is to make a patient understand just precisely this mute kind of symptomatic behaviour and to make him aware of this latent, and often exceedingly strong, hostility without endangering the treatment. As soon, therefore, as I recognized the girl's attitude to her father, I broke off the treatment and advised her parents that if they set store by the therapeutic procedure it should be continued by a woman doctor. The girl had in the meanwhile promised her father that at any rate she would give up seeing the "lady," and I do not know whether my advice, the reasons for which are obvious, will be followed.

There was a single piece of material in the course of this analysis which I could regard as a positive transference, as a greatly weakened revival of the girl's original passionate love for her father. Even this manifestation was not quite free from other motives, but I mention it because it brings up, in another direction, an interesting problem of analytic technique. At a certain period, not long after the treatment had begun, the girl brought a series of dreams which, distorted according to rule and couched in the usual dream-language, could nevertheless be easily translated with certainty. Their content, when interpreted, was, however, remarkable. They anticipated the cure of the inversion through the treatment, expressed her joy over the prospects in life that would then be opened before her, confessed her longing for a man's love and for children, and so might have been welcomed as a gratifying preparation for the desired change. The contradiction between them and the girl's utterances in waking life at the time was very great. She did not conceal from me that she meant to marry, but only in order to escape from her father's tyranny and to follow her true inclinations undisturbed. As for the husband, she remarked rather contemptuously, she would easily deal with him, and besides, one could have sexual relations with a man and a woman at one and the same time, as the example of the adored lady showed. Warned through some slight impression or other, I told her one day that I did not believe these dreams, that I regarded them as false or hypocritical, and that she intended to deceive me just as she habitually deceived her father. I was right; after I had made this clear, this kind of dream ceased. But I still believe that, besides the intention to mislead me, the dreams partly expressed the wish to win my favour; they were also an attempt to gain my interest and my good opinion—perhaps in order to disappoint me all the more thoroughly later on. . . .

IV

I now come back, after this digression, to the consideration of my patient's case. We have made a survey of the forces which led the girl's libido from the normal Oedipus attitude into that of homosexuality, and of the psychical paths traversed by it in the process. Most important in this respect was the impression made by the birth of her little brother, and we might from this be inclined to classify the case as one of late-acquired inversion.

But at this point we become aware of a state of things which also confronts us in many other instances in which light has been thrown by psycho-analysis on a mental process. So long as we trace the development from its final outcome backwards, the chain of events appears continuous, and we feel we have gained an insight which is completely satisfactory or even exhaustive. But if we proceed the reverse way, if we start from the premises inferred from the analysis and try to follow these up to the final result, then we no longer get the impression of an inevitable sequence of events which could not have been otherwise determined. We notice at once that there might have been another result, and that we might have been just as well able to understand and explain the latter. The synthesis is thus not so satisfactory as the analysis; in other words, from a knowledge of the premises we could not have foretold the nature of the result.

It is very easy to account for this disturbing state of affairs. Even supposing that we have a complete knowledge of the aetiological factors that decide a given result, nevertheless what we know about them is only their quality, and not their relative strength. Some of them are suppressed by others because they are too weak, and they therefore do not affect the final result. But we never know beforehand which of the determining factors will prove the weaker or the stronger. We only say at the end that those which succeeded must have been the stronger. Hence the chain of causation can always be recognized with certainty if we follow the line of analysis, whereas to predict it along the line of synthesis is impossible.

We do not, therefore, mean to maintain that every girl who experiences a disappointment such as this of the longing for love that springs from the Oedipus attitude at puberty will necessarily on that account fall a victim to homosexuality. On the contrary, other kinds of reaction to this trauma are undoubtedly commoner. If so, however, there must have been present in this girl special factors that turned the scale, factors outside the trauma, probably of an internal nature. Nor is there any difficulty in pointing them out.

It is well known that even in a normal person it takes a certain time before the decision in regard to the sex of the love-object is finally made. Homosexual enthusiasms, exaggeratedly strong friendships tinged with sensuality, are common enough in both sexes during the first years after puberty. This was also so with our patient, but in her these tendencies undoubtedly showed themselves to be stronger, and lasted longer, than with others. In addition, these presages of later homosexuality had always occupied her *conscious* life, while the attitude arising from the Oedipus complex had remained *unconscious* and had appeared only in such signs as her tender behaviour to the little boy. As a school-girl she had been for a long time in love with a strict and unapproachable mistress, obviously a substitute mother. She had taken a specially lively interest in a number of young mothers long before her brother's birth and therefore all the more certainly long before the first reprimand from her father. From very early years, therefore, her libido had flowed in two currents, the one on the surface being one that we may unhesitatingly designate as homosexual. This latter was probably a direct and unchanged continuation of an infantile fixation on her mother. Possibly the analysis described here actually revealed nothing more than the process by which, on an appropriate occasion, the deeper heterosexual current of libido, too, was deflected into the manifest homosexual one.

The analysis showed, further, that the girl had brought along with her from her childhood a strongly marked "masculinity complex." A spirited girl, always ready for romping and fighting, she was not at all prepared to be second to her slightly older brother; after inspecting his genital organs she had developed a pronounced envy for the penis, and the thoughts derived from this envy still continued to fill her mind. She was in fact a feminist; she felt it to be unjust that girls should not enjoy the same freedom as boys, and rebelled against the lot of woman in general. At the time of the analysis the idea of pregnancy and child-birth was disagreeable to her, partly, I surmise, on account of the bodily disfigurement connected with them. Her girlish narcissism had fallen back on this defence, and ceased to express itself as pride in her good looks. Various clues indicated that she must formerly have had strong exhibitionist and scopophilic tendencies. Anyone who is anxious that the claims of acquired as opposed to hereditary factors should not be under-estimated in aetiology will call attention to the fact that the girl's behaviour, as described above, was exactly what would follow from the combined effect in a person with a strong mother-fixation of the two influences of her mother's neglect and her comparison of her genital organs with her brother's. It is possible here to attribute to the impress of the operation of external influence in early life something which one would have liked to regard as a constitutional peculiarity. On the other hand, a part even of this acquired disposition (if it *was* really acquired) has to be ascribed to inborn constitution. So we see in practice a continual mingling and blending of what in theory we should try to separate into a pair of opposites—namely, inherited and acquired characters.

If the analysis had come to an earlier, still more premature end, it might have led to the view that this was a case of late-acquired homosexuality, but as it is, a consideration of the material impels us to conclude that it is rather a case of congenital homosexuality which, as usual, became fixed and unmistakably manifest only in the period following puberty. Each of these classifications does justice only to one part of the state of affairs ascertainable by observation, but neglects the other. It would be best not to attach too much value to this way of stating the problem.

The literature of homosexuality usually fails to distinguish clearly enough between the questions of the choice of object on the one hand, and of the sexual characteristics and sexual attitude of the subject on the other, as though the answer to the former necessarily involved the answers to the latter. Experience, however, proves the contrary: a man with predominantly male characteristics and also masculine in his erotic life may still be inverted in respect to his object, loving only men instead of women. A man in whose character feminine attributes obviously predominate, who may, indeed, behave in love like a woman, might be expected, from this feminine attitude, to choose a man for his love-object; but he may nevertheless be heterosexual, and show no more inversion in respect to his object than an average normal man. The same is true of women; here also mental sexual character and object-choice do not necessarily coincide. The mystery of homosexuality is therefore by no means so simple as it is commonly depicted in popular expositions—"a feminine mind, bound therefore to love a man, but unhappily attached to a masculine body; a masculine mind, irresistibly attracted by women, but, alas! imprisoned in a feminine body." It is instead a question of three sets of characteristics, namely—

Physical sexual characters
(physical hermaphroditism)

Mental sexual characters
(masculine or feminine attitude)

Kind of object-choice

which, up to a certain point, vary independently of one another, and are met with in different individuals in manifold permutations. Tendentious literature has obscured our view of this interrelationship by putting into the foreground, for practical reasons, the third feature (the kind of object-choice), which is the only one that strikes the layman, and in addition by exaggerating the closeness of the association between this and the first feature. Moreover, it blocks the way to a deeper insight into all that is uniformly designated as homosexuality, by rejecting two fundamental facts which have been revealed by psycho-analytic investigation. The first of these is that homosexual men have experienced a specially strong fixation on their mother; the second, that, in addition to their manifest heterosexuality, a very considerable measure of latent or unconscious homosexuality can be detected in all normal people. If these findings are taken into account, then, clearly, the supposition that nature in a freakish mood created a "third sex" falls to the ground.

It is not for psycho-analysis to solve the problem of homosexuality. It must rest content with disclosing the psychical mechanisms that resulted in determining the object-choice, and with tracing back the paths from them to the instinctual dispositions. There its work ends, and it leaves the rest to biological research, which has recently brought to light, through Steinach's experiments, such very important results concerning the influence exerted by the first set of characteristics mentioned above upon the second and third. Psycho-analysis has a common basis with biology, in that it presupposes an original bisexuality in human beings (as in animals). But psycho-analysis cannot elucidate the intrinsic nature of what in conventional or in biological phraseology is termed "masculine" and "feminine"; it simply takes over the two concepts and makes them the foundation of its work.

WOMEN'S WRITING ON
A MAN TRAPPED IN A
WOMAN'S BODY

Charlotte Cibber Charke
(1713–60)

Charlotte Cibber Charke was the tenth child of the popular eighteenth-century British dramatist and poet laureate Colly Cibber. Her preference for men's clothes and occupations such as riding, hunting, and playing male roles on stage made her a likely subject for exploration in Havelock Ellis's studies of sexual inversion, but Ellis dismissed the possibility that she was "sexually inverted" since she was twice married to men, had a daughter, and did not write about sexual relations with other women in her autobiography, *A Narrative of the Life of Mrs. Charlotte Charke* (1755).

Some more recent biographers of Charke, who appear to be uncomfortable with the subject of homosexuality, also dismiss the possibility that she was a lesbian and are quick to explain her transvestism as being merely practical: It permitted her to travel without male protection. It permitted her a disguise in which to escape the bailiffs who often sought her because of her debts. It permitted her to audition more convincingly for male theatrical roles, and so on. Other biographers, largely on the basis of Charke's admission of transvestism and an interest in masculine pursuits, have called her *Narrative* "a document in the history of sexual deviance" and have observed, "The probability is that her sexual tastes were exclusively lesbian."

Of course, it is impossible to know whether Charke actually had sexual relations with other women. But the fact that she was married and had a child or that she does not discuss having had lesbian sexual relations in her autobiography obviously cannot obviate the possibility that she did have such relations. As the following excerpts indicate, women often fell in love with her when she was in male guise, and at least one woman, "Mrs. Brown," with whom she lived as "Mr. Brown," followed her through good times and bad. On the other hand, such evidence is hardly conclusive. It was undoubtedly convenient for two women to appear to the world like a heterosexual married couple, since it meant that they would not be molested by unwelcome advances, and one of them could provide an income working in male guise that was far better than what they could have received had both worked in the usual jobs available to women. But on the basis of the available evidence we will never know whether Charke's relationship with Mrs. Brown was what the eighteenth century would have called romantic friendship, or what our era would call lesbian.

Charke herself gives little help in such an analysis. Her novel, *The History of Henry Dumont Esq.; and Miss Charlotte Evelyn* (1756), serves to obfuscate the subject even further. She presents a male transvestite who has sexual relations with other men, and she observes about people like him, "No punishment was sufficiently severe for such unnatural monsters." How are we to read such a statement? Was she mocking and teasing her readers with irony? Was she throwing them off track with regard to herself by appearing to despise a behavior in which she indulged? Had she internalized her society's views about inappropriate gender behavior and therefore made such a statement as an expression of her self-loathing? And how are we to read Charlotte Charke's naming her character "Charlotte"?

Charke's writing and subsequent interpretations of it are interesting as demonstrations of the difficulty in analyzing lives that were lived in a social context different from that of our own. They also demonstrate the extent to which transvestism and traditionally masculine pursuits have become in our culture a signal for lesbianism, which then challenges the historian to either disprove or assume the subject's homosexuality.

FURTHER READING: Charlotte Charke, *A Narrative of the Life of Mrs. Charlotte Charke, Youngest Daughter of Colly Cibber*, 2nd ed. (1755; Gainesville, FL: Scholars' Facsimiles and Reprints, 1969). R. H. Baker, *Mr. Cibber of Drury Lane* (1939; reprint, New York: AMS Press, 1966). Lynne Friedli, "Passing Women: A Study of Gender Boundaries in the Eighteenth Century," in *Sexual Underworlds of the Enlightenment*, eds. G. S. Rousseau and Roy Porter (Chapel Hill: University of North Carolina Press, 1988). Fidelis Morgan, *The Well-Known Troublemaker: A Life of Charlotte Charke* (London: Faber and Faber, 1988). *Everyman Companion to the Theatre*, eds. Peter Thomson and Gamini Salgado (London: J. M. Dent, 1985).

From *A Narrative of the Life of Mrs. Charlotte Charke*

I confess, I believe I came not only an unexpected, but an unwelcome Guest into the Family, (exclusive of my Parents,) as my Mother had borne no Children for some few Years before; so that I was rather regarded as an impertinent Intruder, than one who had a natural Right to make up the circular Number of my Father's Fireside: Yet, be it as it may, the Jealousy of me, from her other Children, laid no Restraint on her Fondness for me, which my Father and she both testified in their tender Care of my Education. His paternal Love omitted nothing that could improve any natural Talents Heaven had been pleas'd to endow me with; the Mention of which, I hope, won't be imputed to me as a vain Self-conceit, of knowing more, or thinking better, than any other of my Sister Females. No! far be it from me; for as all Advantages from Nature are the favourable Gifts of the Power Divine, consequently no Praise can be arrogated to ourselves, for that which is not in ourselves POSSIBLE TO BESTOW.

I should not have made this Remark, but, as 'tis likely my Works may fall into the Hands of People of disproportion'd Understandings, I was willing to prevent an Error a weak Judgment might have run into, by inconsiderately throwing an Odium upon me, I could not possibly deserve— For, ALAS! ALL CANNOT JUDGE ALIKE.

As I have instanc'd, that my Education was not only a genteel, but in Fact a liberal one, and such indeed as might have been sufficient for a Son instead of a Daughter; I must beg Leave to add, that I was never made much acquainted with that necessary Utensil which forms the houswifery Part of a young Lady's Education, call'd a Needle; which I handle with the same clumsey Awkwardness a Monkey does a Kitten, and am equally capable of using the one, as Pug is of nursing the other.

This is not much to be wonder'd at, as my Education consisted chiefly in Studies of various Kinds, and gave me a different Turn of Mind than what I might have had, if my Time had been employ'd in ornamenting a Piece of Canvas with Beasts, Birds and the Alphabet; the latter of which I understood in *French,* rather before I was able to speak *English.*

As I have promis'd to conceal nothing that might raise a Laugh, I shall begin with a small Specimen of my former Madness, when I was but four Years of Age. Having, even then, a passionate Fondness for a Perriwig, I crawl'd out of Bed one Summer's Morning at *Twickenham,* where my Father had Part of a House and Gardens for the Season and, taking it into my small Pate, that by Dint of a Wig and a Waistcoat I should be the perfect Representative of my Sire, I crept softly into the Servants-Hall, where I had the Night before espied all Things in Order, to perpetrate the happy Design I had framed for the next Morning's Expedition. Accordingly I paddled down Stairs, taking with me my Shoes, Stockings, and little Dimity Coat; which I artfully contrived to pin up, as well as I could, to supply the Want of a Pair of Breeches. By the Help of a long Broom, I took down a Waistcoat of my Brother's, and an enormous bushy Tie-wig of my Father's, which entirely enclos'd my Head and Body, with the Knots of the Ties thumping my little Heels as I march'd along, with slow and solemn Pace. The Covert of Hair in which I was conceal'd, with the Weight of a monstrous Belt and large Silver-hilted Sword, that I could scarce drag along, was a vast Impediment in my Procession: And, what still added to the other Inconveniences I labour'd under, was whelming myself under one of my Father's large Beaver-hats, laden with Lace, as thick and broad as a Brickbat.

Being thus accoutred, I began to consider that 'twould be impossible for me to pass for Mr. *Cibber* in Girl's Shoes, therefore took an opportunity to slip out of Doors after the Gardener, who went to his Work, and roll'd into a dry Ditch, which was as deep as I was high; and, in this Grotesque Pigmy-State, walk'd up and down the Ditch bowing to all who came by. But, behold, the Oddity of my Appearance soon assembled a Croud about me; which yielded me no small Joy, as I conceiv'd their Risibility on this Occasion to be Marks of Approbation, and walk'd myself into a Fever, in the happy Thought of being taken for the 'Squire.

When the Family arose, 'till which Time I had employ'd myself in this regular March in my Ditch, I was the first Thing enquir'd after, and miss'd; 'till *Mrs. Heron,* the Mother of the late celebrated Actress of that Name, happily espied me, and directly call'd forth the whole Family to be Witness of my State and Dignity.

The Drollery of my Figure render'd it impossible, assisted by the Fondness of both Father and Mother, to be angry with me; but, alas! I was borne off on the Footman's Shoulders, to my Shame and Disgrace, and forc'd into my proper Habiliments. . . .

[Despite her masculine tastes, Charlotte, when a young woman, falls in love with a man]:

After six Months Acquaintance I was, by Consent, espoused at St. *Martin's* Church to Mr. *Charke,* and thought at that Time the Measure of my Happiness was full, and of an ever-during Nature: But, alas! I soon found myself deceiv'd in that fond Conceit; for we were both so young and indiscreet, we ought rather to have been sent to School than to Church, in Regard to any Qualifications on either Side, towards rendering the Marriage-State comfortable to one another. To be sure, I thought it gave me an Air of more Consequence to be call'd Mrs. *Charke,* than Miss *Charlotte;* and my Spouse, on his Part, I believe, thought it a fine Feather in his Cap, to be Mr. *Cibber's* Son-in-Law: Which indeed it would have proved, had he been skilful enough to have managed his Cards rightly, as my Father was greatly inclined to be his Friend, and endeavoured to promote his Interest extreamly amongst People of Quality and Fashion. His Merit, as a Proficient in Musick, I believe is incontestible; and, being tolerably agreeable in his Person, both concurr'd to render him the general Admiration of those Sort of Ladies, who, regardless of their Reputations, make 'em the unhappy Sacrifices to every pleasing Object: Which, *entre nous,* was a most horrible Bar in my Eschutcheon of content; insomuch that married Miss was, the first Twelvemonth of her connubial State, industriously employed in the Pursuit of fresh Sorrow, by tracing her Spouse from Morn to Eve through the Hundreds of *Drury.*

I had, indeed, too often very shocking Confirmations of my Suspicions, which made me at last grow quite indifferent; nor can I avoid confessing, that Indifference was strongly attended with contempt. I was in Hopes that my being blest with a Child would, in some Degree, have surmounted that unconquerable Fondness for Variety, but 'twas all one; and, I firmly believe, nothing but the Age of *Methuselah,* could have made the least Alteration in his Disposition.

This loose and unkind Behaviour, consequently made me extravagant and wild in my Imagination; and, finding that we were in the same Circumstances, in Regard to each other, that Mr. *Sullen* and his Wife were, we agreed to part. Accordingly I made our Infant my Care, nor did the Father's Neglect render me careless of my Child; for I really was so fond of it, I thought myself more than amply made Amends for his Follies, in the Possession of her.

When Mr. *Charke* thought proper he paid us a Visit, and I received him with the same good Nature and Civility I might an old, decay'd Acquaintance, that I was certain came to ask me a Favour; which was often the Case, for I seldom had the Honour of his Company but when Cash run low, and I as constantly supplied his Wants; and have got from my Father many an auxiliary Guinea, I am certain, to purchase myself a new Pair of Horns.

[She goes on stage to support herself and often plays "pant roles," continuing to wear men's clothes offstage as well.]

It happened, not long after, that I was applied to by a strange, unaccountable Mortal, call'd *Jocky Adams;* famous for dancing the *Jockey Dance,* to the Tune of *Horse to New-Market.* As I was gaping for a Crust, I readily snap'd at the first that offered, and went with this Person to a

Town within four Miles of *London,* where a very extraordinary Occurrence happened; and which, had I been really what I represented, might have rid in my own Coach, in the Rear of six Horses.

Notwithstanding my Distresses, the Want of Cloaths was not amongst the Number. I appeared as Mr. *Brown* . . . in a very genteel Manner; and, not making the least Discovery of my Sex by my Behaviour, ever endeavouring to keep up to the well-bred Gentleman, I became, as I may most properly term it, the unhappy Object of Love in a young Lady, whose Fortune was beyond all earthly Power to deprive her of, had it been possible for me to have been, what she designed me, nothing less than her Husband. She was an Orphan Heiress, and under Age; but so near it, that, at the Expiration of eight Months, her Guardian resigned his Trust, and I might have been at once possessed of the Lady, and forty thousand Pounds in the Bank of *England;* Besides Effects in the Indies, that were worth about twenty Thousand more.

This was a most horrible Disappointment on both Sides; the Lady of the Husband, and I of the Money; which would have been thought an excellent Remedy for Ills, by those less surrounded with Misery than I was. I, who was the Principal in this Tragedy, was the last acquainted with it: but it got Wind from the Servants, to some of the Players; who, as *Hamlet* says, *Can't keep a Secret,* and they immediately communicated it to me.

Contrary to their Expectation, I received the Information with infinite Concern; not more in regard to myself, than from the poor Lady's Misfortune, in placing her Affection on an improper Object; and whom, by Letters I afterwards received, confirmed me, *"She was too fond of her mistaken Bargain."*

The Means by which I came by her Letters, was through the Perswasion of her Maid; who, like most Persons of her Function, are too often ready to carry on Intrigues. 'Twas no difficult Matter to perswade an amorous Heart to follow its own Inclination; and accordingly a Letter came to invite me to drink Tea, at a Place a little distant from the House where she lived.

The Reason given for this Interview was, the Desire some young Ladies of her Acquaintance had to hear me sing; and, as they never went to Plays in the Country, 'twould be a great Obligation to her if I would oblige her Friends, by complying with her Request.

The Maid who brought this Epistle, inform'd me of the real Occasion of its being wrote; and told me, if I pleased, I might be happiest Man in the Kingdom, before I was eight and forty Hours older. This frank Declaration from the Servant, gave me but an odd Opinion of the Mistress; and I sometimes conceived, being conscious how unfit I was to embrace so favourable an Opportunity, that it was all a Joke.

However, be it as it might, I resolved to go and know the Reality. The

Maid too insisted that I should, and protested her Lady had suffered much on my Account, from the first Hour she saw me; and, but for her, the Secret had never been disclosed. She farther added, I was the first Person who had ever made that Impression on her Mind. I own I felt a tender Concern, and resolved within myself to wait on her; and, by honestly confessing who I was, kill or cure her Hopes of me for ever.

In Obedience to the Lady's Command I waited on her, and found her with two more much of her own Age, who were her Confidents, and entrusted to contrive a Method to bring this Business to an End, by a private Marriage. When I went into the Room I made a general Bow to all, and was for seating myself nearest the Door; but was soon lugg'd out of my Chair by a young Mad-cap of Fashion; and, to both the Lady's Confusion and mine, awkwardly seated by her.

We were exactly in the Condition of Lord *Hardy* and Lady *Charlotte*, in *The Funeral;* and I sat with as much Fear in my Countenance, as if I had stole her Watch from her Side. She, on her Part, often attempted to speak, but had such a Tremor on her Voice, she ended only in broken Sentences. 'Tis true, I have undergone the dreadful Apprehensions of a Bomb-Bailiff; but I should have thought one at that Time a seasonable Relief, and without repining have gone with him.

The before-mention'd Mad-cap, after putting us more out of Countenance by bursting into a violent Fit of Laughing, took the other by the Sleeve and withdrew, as she thought, to give me a favourable Opportunity of paying my Addresses; but she was deceived, for, when we were alone, I was ten thousand Times in worse Plight than before: And what added to my Confusion was, seeing the poor Soul dissolve into Tears, which she endeavoured to conceal.

This gave me Freedom of Speech, by a gentle Enquiry into the Cause; and, by tenderly trying to soothe her into a Calm, I unhappily encreased rather than asswaged the dreadful Conflict of Love and Shame which labour'd in her Bosom.

With much Difficulty, I mustered up Courage sufficient to open a Discourse, by which I began to make a Discovery of my Name and Family, which struck the poor Creature into Astonishment; but how much greater was her Surprise, when I positively assured her that I was actually the youngest Daughter of Mr. *Cibber,* and not the Person she conceived me! She was absolutely struck speechless for some little Time; but, when she regained the Power of Utterance, entreated me not to urge a Falshood of that Nature, which she looked upon only as an Evasion, occasioned, she supposed, through a Dislike of her Person. Adding, that her Maid had plainly told her I was no Stranger to her miserable Fate, as she was pleased to term it; and, indeed, as I really thought it.

I still insisted on the Truth of my Assertion; and desired her to consider, whether 'twas likely an indigent young Fellow must not have thought it an unbounded Happiness, to possess at once so agreeable a Lady and immense a Fortune, both which many a Nobleman in this Kingdom would have thought it worth while to take Pains to atchieve.

Notwithstanding all my Arguments, she was hard to be brought into a Belief of what I told her; and conceived that I had taken a Dislike to her, from her too readily consenting to her Servant's making that Declaration of her Passion for me; and, for that Reason, she supposed I had but a light Opinion of her. I assured her of the contrary, and that I was sorry for us both, that Providence had not ordained me to be the happy Person she designed me; that I was much obliged for the Honour she conferr'd on me, and sincerely grieved it was not in my Power to make a suitable Return.

With many Sighs and Tears on her Side, we took a melancholly Leave; and, in a few Days, the Lady retir'd into the Country, where I have never heard from, or of her since; but hope she is made happy in some worthy Husband, that might deserve her.

She was not the most Beautiful I have beheld, but quite the Agreeable; sung finely, and play'd the Harpsichord as well; understood Languages, and was a Woman of real good Sense: But she was, poor Thing! an Instance, in regard to me, *that the Wisest may sometimes err.*

On my Return Home, the Itinerant-Troop all assembled round me, to hear what had passed between the Lady and me—when we were to celebrate the Nuptials?—Besides many other impertinent, stupid Questions; some offering, agreeable to their villainous Dispositions, as the Marriage they suppos'd would be a Secret, to supply my Place in the Dark, to conceal the Fraud: Upon which I look'd at them very sternly, and, with the Contempt they deserved, demanded to know what Action of my Life had been so very monstrous, to excite them to think me capable of one so cruel and infamous?

For the Lady's sake, whose Name I would not for the Universe have had banded about by the Mouths of low Scurrility, I not only told them I had revealed to her who I was, but made it no longer a Secret in the Town; that, in Case it was spoke of, it might be regarded as an Impossibility, or, at worst, a trump'd-up Tale by some ridiculous Blockhead, who was fond of hearing himself prate, as there are indeed too many such. . . .

[Charlotte, under the name of Mr. Brown, later roams around England with another woman, who calls herself Mrs. Brown.]

Perhaps the Reader may think, that the repeated Rebuffs of Fortune might have brought me to some Degree of Reflection, which might have regulated the Actions of my Life; but, that I may not impose upon the Opinions of the good-natured Part of the World, who might charitably bestow a favourable Thought on me in that Point, I must inform them, that the Aversion I had conceived for Vagabondizing (for such I shall ever esteem it) and the good Nature of my Friends in *Chepstow,* put it strongly in my Head to settle there, to which End I determined to turn Pastry-Cook and Farmer.

. . . With the necessary Utensils for the Pastry-Cook's Shop, and the friendly Assistance of some of our good Friends, we took Leave, and set out for a little Place called *Pill,* a Sort of Harbour for Ships, five Miles of this Side of *Bristol.*

. . . I took a little Shop, and because I was resolved to set off my Matters as grand as possible, I had a Board put over my Door, with this Inscription,

BROWN, PASTRY-COOK, FROM LONDON.

At which Place I can't charge myself with ever having, in the Course of my Life, attempted to spoil the Ingredients necessary in the Composition of a Tart. But that did not signify, as long as I was a *Londoner,* to be sure my Pastry must be good.

While the Ships were coming in from *Ireland* (which is in the Months of *June, July,* and *August*) I had a good running Trade; but, alas! the Winter was most terrible, and if an Uncle of my Friend's (who died while we were there) had not left her a Legacy, we must inevitably have perished.

About the Time the News came of her Money, we were involved to the Amount of about Four or Five and Thirty Shillings; and, if a Shilling would have saved us from total Destruction, we did not know where to raise it.

On the Receipt of the Letter I showed it to the Landlord, hoping he would lend me a Guinea to bear my Charges to Mrs. *Brown's* Aunt, who lives in *Oxfordshire,* where I was to go to receive her Legacy, which was a genteel one, and I should have left her as a Hostage 'till my Return.

But the incredulous Blockhead conceived the Letter to be forged; and, as he himself was capable of such a Fraud, imagined we had artfully contrived to get a Guinea out of him, and reward him by running away in his Debt. But he was quite mistaken, as he was afterwards convinced, and made a Thousand aukward Excuses for his Unkindness when we received the Money, and had discharged his trifling Demands.

I consulted on my Pillow what was best to be done, and communicated my Thoughts to my Friend; upon which we concluded, without speaking a Word to any Body, both to set out and fetch the Money, according to Order, from her Relation's, though there was two very great Bars to such Progress, in the Eye of Reason, but I stepped over both.

One was, having no more than a single Groat in the World between us: And the other, my having been obliged to pledge my Hat at *Bristol* a

Fortnight before for Half a Crown, to carry on the anatomical Business, we haplessly pursued.

Yet notwithstanding these terrible Disasters I was resolved, at all Events, to go the Journey. I took my Fellow-Sufferer with me, who was lost in Wonder at so daring an Enterprize, to set out, without either Hat or Money, fourscore Miles on Foot. But I soon eased the Anxiety of Mind she laboured under, by assuring her, that when we got to *Bristol* I would apply to a Friend, who would furnish me with a small Matter to carry us on to *Bath*.

This pacified the poor Soul, who could scarce see her Way for Tears, before I told her my Design; which never entered my Imagination, 'till we had got two Miles beyond the detested Place we lived in. Our Circumstances were then so desperate, I thought

> "*Whatever World we next were thrown upon,*
> *Cou'd not be worse than* Pill."

As we were on our March, we were met by some of our unneighbourly Neighbours, who took Notice of my being in full Career, without a Hat; and of Mrs. *Brown*, with a Bundle in her Hand, which contained only a Change of Linnen for us, on our Travel.

They soon alarmed our Landlord with the Interview, with many Conjectures of our being gone off; and concluded, my being bare-headed was intended as a Blind for our Excursion: But let their Thoughts be what they would, we were safe in *Bristol* by the Time they got Home to make their political Report; and I obtained, at the first Word, the timely Assistance our Necessities required to procure a Supper and Bed that Night, besides what served to bear our Charges to *Bath* next Morning.

The only Distress I had to overcome, was to procure a Covering for my unthinking Head; but Providence kindly directed us to a House where there was a young Journeyman, a Sort of a *Jemmy-Smart,* who dress'd entirely in Taste, that lodged where we lay that Night. As I appeared, barring the want of a Hat, as smart as himself in Dress, he entered into conversation with me; and, finding him a good-natured Man, ventured (as I was urged by downright Necessity) to beg the Favour of him to lend me a Hat, which, by being very dusty, I was well assured had not been worn some Time, from which I conceived he would not be in a violent Hurry to have it restored; and, framing an Excuse of having sent my own to be dress'd, easily obtained the Boon.

Next Morning, at the Hour of Five, we set out, and staid at *Bath* 'till the Morning following: Though I remember I was obliged to give the Landlady my Waistcoat for the Payment of my Lodging before we went to Bed, which I had the Comfort of redeeming, by the Help of Mr. *Kennedy* and Company, and set forwards on my Journey with the Favour they were pleased to bestow on me. . . .

As soon as I was empowered, by the Help of a little Cash, we set out from *Bath* to *Oxfordshire;* and, in three Days, arrived at the happy Spot, where we were furnished with that Opiate for Grief, the want of which had many tedious Nights kept us waking.

Our Journey Home was expedited by taking a Double-Horse from *Whitney* to *Cirencester;* and now and then, for the rest of the Way, mounting up into a Hay-Cart, or a timely Waggon.

When we returned to *Bristol,* we met with several of the *Pill* Gentry, who were surprized to see us, and informed us how terribly we had been exploded, as being Cheats and Run-aways; and though they themselves, in our Absence, were as inveterate as the rest of the vulgar Crew, were the first to condemn others for a Fault they were equally guilty of.

I returned the borrowed Hat, and went Home triumphant in my own —Paid my Landlord, and, as long as the Money lasted, was the worthiest Gentleman in the Country; but when our Stock was exhausted, and we were reduced to a second Necessity of contracting a fresh Score, I was as much disregarded as a dead Cat, without the Remembrance of a single Virtue I was Master of, while I had a remaining Guinea in my Pocket.

Business daily decreasing, from the want of Shipping coming in, and the Winter growing fast upon us, we had no Prospect before us, but of dying by Inches with Cold and Hunger; and, what aggravated my own Distress, was having unfortunately drawn in my Friend to be a melancholly Partaker of my Sufferings.

This Reflection naturally rouzed me into an honourable Spirit of Resolution, not to let her perish through my unhappy and mistaken Conduct, which I meant all for the best, though it unfortunately proved otherwise; and, that I might not stay at *Pill* 'till we were past the Power of getting away, I sat down and wrote a little Tale, which filled up the first and second Columns of a News-Paper, and got a Friend to introduce me to Mr. W——d, Printer, on the *T*——y; who engaged me, at a small Pittance *per* Week, to write, and correct the Press, when Business was in a Hurry; which indeed it generally was, as he is a Man of Reputation, and greatly respected.

I believe, if he had been perfectly assured who I was, and had known how much I had it in my Power to have been useful to him, as well as myself, it had been much better for us both: However, it was kind in him to employ a distressed Person, and a Stranger, to whom he could not possibly be under the least Obligation.

Having secured something to piddle on, for I can call it no better, I ran back to *Pill,* to bless my Friend with the glad Tydings; and, as it was a long and dirty Walk from thence to *Bristol,* and infinitely dangerous over *Leigh-Down,* which is full three Miles in Length, besides two miserable Miles before that to trudge, we thought it better to give up what we had to the Landlord, to whom we were but Eighteen Shillings indebted, though we left him as much as fairly stood us in Five Pounds ready Money; but, if we had offered to have made a Sale of it, I knew their Consciences would have given us Six-pence for that which might be worth a Crown or Ten Shillings: So we even locked up the Shop, and went with the Key in my Pocket to *Bristol;* and, in two Days Time, I sent it back with a Note, to let him know what we had left was entirely his own, for that we should never more return.

In Truth I have been as good as my Word, and shall continue so; for if Business or Inclination should ever excite me to take a Trip to *Ireland,* I would go *Chester* Way: And if Travellers knew as much as I do of that horrid Seat of Cruelty and Extortion, they would all come into the same Determination.

Having thus comfortably withdrawn ourselves from this hated Place, we took a Lodging at Two Shillings *per* Week; and, if I had not had the good Fortune to be kindly accepted on by a few Friends who were constantly inviting me, the remaining Part of my Wages would not have been sufficient to have afforded us, with other Expences, above two good Meals in a Week.

But Thanks to my Friend, who empower'd me to consign it all to the Use of one, to whom I should have thought, on this Occasion, if every Shilling had been a Guinea, I had made but a reasonable Acknowledgement, after having immers'd her in Difficulties which nothing but real Friendship and a tender Regard to my Health (which, through repeated Grievances, was much impaired) could have made her blindly inconsistent with her own Interest to give into, and so patiently endure.

Maria Edgeworth
(1767–1849)

Maria Edgeworth was the second of the twenty-one children of Richard Edgeworth. When Maria's mother died in 1773 her father married a succession of women, who were stepmothers to Maria, including Honora Sneyd, the lost beloved of bluestocking Anna Seward (see p. 37). Under her father's tutelage, Maria too, ironically perhaps, became something of a bluestocking, publishing novels, translations, and light philosophical discourses. She claimed that she began writing and continued writing simply to please her father, whose own philosophy informed her work and who played an active role as editor of what she published. Although she survived him by about thirty years, she wrote only two more books after his death, a novel and a completion of his memoirs.

Maria Edgeworth never married, and she is known to have turned down at least one credible proposal, but her novels often extolled marriage and motherhood. That aspect of her fiction illustrates the alienation from themselves that many women authors reflected in their writing. They were often allowed to achieve recognition as writers in their day as long as they confirmed certain stereotypes about females that promoted the reigning social prejudices.

Belinda: Early Lessons and Moral Tales (1801), from which the following selection is taken, is typical of Maria Edgeworth's work in its didactic and conservative message. *Belinda* was written more than a half-century before the first sexologists began describing the female sexual invert. However, its overt moral outrage and vast discomfort with inappropriate gender behavior reveal something of the nineteenth-century social attitudes that led to the formulation by the sexologists of the "scientific" category of the female congenital invert.

Mrs. Freke (the "Mrs." is, of course, an honorific) is a "freak" because she eschews all aspects of what was considered appropriate female gender behavior. There is no hint that she has sexual relations with women (though she does express an "inappropriate" appreciation for female pulchritude and is flirtatious with Belinda); but she is socially culpable specifically because she lacks all the refinements necessary for nineteenth-century womanhood, most especially modesty and passivity. She dashes instead of glides. She is boisterous and calls attention to herself. She relishes her own strength and wants other women to be strong. She meets men on their own terms. She is totally lacking in softness, grace, and delicacy. In short, she is one of the social outlaws—the strong women, the independent women, the feminists—who, later in the century, became medicalized into a "third sex." Mrs. Freke is the forerunner of those females who came to be depicted as "congenitally burdened" by "anomalies" that were socially constructed to be anomalous.

FURTHER READING: Maria Edgeworth, *Belinda: Early Lessons and Moral Tales* (1801; London: Pandora Press, 1986); *Letters for Literary Ladies* (1795; reprint, New York: Garland Press, 1974); *The Education of the Heart: The Correspondence of Rachel Mordecai Lazarus and Maria Edgeworth*, ed. Edgar E. MacDonald (Chapel Hill: University of North Carolina Press, 1977).

From *Belinda*: "Rights of Woman"

Belinda was alone, and reading, when Mrs. Freke dashed into the room.

"How do, dear creature?" cried she, stepping up to her, and shaking hands with her boisterously—"How do?—Glad to see you, faith!—Been long here?—Tremendously hot to-day!"

She flung herself upon the sofa beside Belinda, threw her hat upon the table, and then continued speaking.

"And how d'ye go on here, poor child?—Gad! I'm glad you're alone —expected to find you encompassed by a whole host of the righteous. Give me credit for my courage in coming to deliver you out of their hands. Luttridge and I had such compassion upon you, when we heard you were close prisoner here! I swore to set the distressed damsel free, in spite of all the dragons in Christendom; so let me carry you off in triumph in my unicorn, and leave these good people to stare when they come home from their sober walk, and find you gone. There's nothing I like so much as to make good people stare—I hope you're of my way o' thinking—you don't look as if you were, though; but I never mind young ladies' looks—always give the lie to their thoughts. Now we talk o' looks—never saw you look so well in my life—as handsome as an angel! And so much the better for me. Do you know, I've a bet of twenty guineas on your head—on your face, I mean. There's a young bride at Harrowgate, Lady H——, they're all mad about her; the men swear she's the handsomest woman in England, and I swear I know one ten times as handsome. They've dared me to make good my word, and I've pledged myself to produce my beauty at the next ball, and to pit her against their belle for any money. Most votes carry it. I'm willing to double my bet since I've seen you again. Come, had not we best be off? Now don't refuse me and make speeches—you know that's all nonsense—I'll take all the blame upon myself."

Belinda, who had not been suffered to utter a word whilst Mrs. Freke ran on in this strange manner, looked in unfeigned astonishment; but when she found herself seized and dragged towards the door, she drew back with a degree of gentle firmness that astonished Mrs. Freke. With a smiling countenance, but a steady tone, she said, "that she was sorry Mrs. Freke's knight-errantry should not be exerted in a better cause, for that she was neither a prisoner, nor a distressed damsel."

"And will you make me lose my bet?" cried Mrs. Freke. "O, at all events, you must come to the ball!—I'm down for it. But I'll not press it now, because you're frightened out of your poor little wits, I see, at the bare thoughts of doing anything considered out of rule by these good peo- ple. Well, well! it shall be managed for you—leave that to me: I'm used to managing for cowards. Pray tell me—You and Lady Delacour are off, I understand?—Give ye joy!—She and I were once great friends; that is to say, I had over her 'that power which strong minds have over weak ones,' but she was too weak for me—one of those people that have neither courage to be good, nor to be bad."

"The courage to be bad," said Belinda, "I believe, indeed, she does not possess."

Mrs. Freke stared. "Why, I heard you had quarrelled with her!"

"If I had," said Belinda, "I hope that I should still do justice to her merits. It is said that people are apt to suffer more by their friends than their enemies. I hope that will never be the case with Lady Delacour, as I confess that I have been one of her friends."

" 'Gad, I like your spirit—you don't want courage, I see, to fight even for your enemies. You are just the kind of girl I admire. I see you have been prejudiced against me by Lady Delacour; but whatever stories she may have trumped up, the truth of the matter is this, there's no living with her, she's so jealous—so ridiculously jealous—of that lord of hers, for whom all the time she has the impudence to pretend not to care more than I do for the sole of my boot," said Mrs. Freke, striking it with her whip; "but she hasn't the courage to give him tit for tat: now this is what I call weakness. Pray, how do she and Clarence Hervey go on together?—Are they out o' the hornbook of platonics yet?"

"Mr. Hervey was not in town when I left it," said Belinda.

"Was not he?—Ho! ho!—He's off then!—Ay, so I prophesied; she's not the thing for him: he has some strength of mind—some soul—above vulgar prejudices; so must a woman be to hold him. He was caught at first by her grace and beauty, and that sort of stuff; but I knew it could not last—knew she'd dilly dally with Clary, till he would turn upon his heel and leave her there."

"I fancy that you are entirely mistaken both with respect to Mr. Hervey and Lady Delacour," Belinda very seriously began to say. But Mrs. Freke interrupted her, and ran on—"No! no! no! I'm not mistaken; Clarence has found her out. She's a *very* woman—*that* he could forgive her, and so could I; but she's a *mere* woman—and that he can't forgive—no more can I."

There was a kind of drollery about Mrs. Freke, which, with some people, made the odd things she said pass for wit. Humour she really possessed; and when she chose it, she could be diverting to those who like buffoonery in women. She had set her heart upon winning Belinda over to her party. She began by flattery of her beauty; but as she saw that this had no effect, she next tried what could be done by insinuating that she had a high opinion of her understanding, by talking to her as an esprit fort.

"For my part," said she, "I own I should like a strong devil better than a weak angel."

"You forget," said Belinda, "that it is not Milton, but Satan, who says—

'Fallen spirit, to be weak is to be miserable.' "

"You read, I see!—I did not know you were a reading girl. So was I once; but I never read now. Books only spoil the originality of genius; very well for those who can't think for themselves—but when one has made up one's opinions, there is no use in reading."

"But to *make* them up," replied Belinda, "may it not be useful?"

"Of no use upon earth to minds of a certain class. You, who can think for yourself, should never read."

"But I read that I may think for myself."

"Only ruin your understanding, trust me. Books are full of trash—nonsense; conversation is worth all the books in the world."

"And is there never any nonsense in conversation?"

"What have you here?" continued Mrs. Freke, who did not choose to attend to this question; exclaiming, as she reviewed each of the books on the table in their turns, in the summary language of presumptuous ignorance, "Smith's Theory of Moral Sentiments—milk and water! Moore's Travels—hasty pudding! La Bruyere—nettle porridge! This is what you were at when I came in, was it not?" said she, taking up a book in which she saw Belinda's mark: "Essay on the Inconsistency of Human Wishes. Poor thing! who bored you with this task?"

"Mr. Percival recommended it to me, as one of the best essays in the English language."

"The devil! they seem to have put you in a course of the bitters—a course of the woods might do your business better. Do you ever hunt?—Let me take you out with me some morning—you'd be quite an angel on horseback; or let me drive you out some day in my unicorn."

Belinda declined this invitation, and Mrs. Freke strode away to the window to conceal her mortification, threw up the sash, and called out to her groom, "Walk those horses about, blockhead!"

Mr. Percival and Mr. Vincent at this instant came into the room.

"Hail, fellow! well met!" cried Mrs. Freke, stretching out her hand to Mr. Vincent.

It has been remarked, that an antipathy subsists between creatures, who, without being the same, have yet a strong external resemblance. Mr. Percival saw this instinct rising in Mr. Vincent, and smiled.

"Hail, fellow! well met! I say. Shake hands and be friends, man!

Though I'm not in the habit of making apologies, if it will be any satisfaction to you, I beg your pardon for frightening your poor devil of a black."

Then turning towards Mr. Percival, she measured him with her eye, as a person whom she longed to attack. She thought, that if Belinda's opinion of the understanding of *these Percivals* could be lowered, she should rise in her esteem: accordingly, she determined to draw Mr. Percival into an argument.

"I've been talking treason, I believe, to Miss Portman," cried she; "for I've been opposing some of your opinions, Mr. Percival."

"If you opposed them all, madam," said Mr. Percival, "I should not think it treason."

"Vastly polite!—But I think all our politeness hypocrisy: what d'ye say to that?"

"You know that best, madam!"

"Then I'll go a step farther; for I'm determined you shall contradict me: I think all virtue is hypocrisy."

"I need not contradict you, madam," said Mr. Percival, "for the terms which you make use of contradict themselves."

"It is my system," pursued Mrs. Freke, "that shame is always the cause of the vices of women."

"It is sometimes the effect," said Mr. Percival; "and, as cause and effect are reciprocal, perhaps you may, in some instances, be right."

"O! I hate qualifying arguers—plump assertion or plump denial for me: you shan't get off so. I say shame is the cause of all women's vices."

"False shame, I suppose you mean?" said Mr. Percival.

"Mere play upon words! All shame is false shame—we should be a great deal better without it. What say you, Miss Portman?—Silent, hey? Silence that speaks."

"Miss Portman's blushes," said Mr. Vincent, "speak *for* her."

"*Against* her," said Mrs. Freke: "women blush because they understand."

"And you would have them understand without blushing?" said Mr. Percival. "I grant you that nothing can be more different than innocence and ignorance. Female delicacy—"

"This is just the way you men spoil women," cried Mrs. Freke, "by talking to them of the *delicacy of their sex,* and such stuff. This *delicacy* enslaves the pretty delicate dears."

"No; it enslaves us," said Mr. Vincent.

"I hate slavery! Vive la liberté!" cried Mrs. Freke. "I'm a champion for the Rights of Women."

"I am an advocate for their happiness," said Mr. Percival, "and for their delicacy, as I think it conduces to their happiness."

"I'm an enemy to their delicacy, as I am sure it conduces to their misery."

"You speak from experience?" said Mr. Percival.

"No, from observation. Your most delicate women are always the greatest hypocrites; and, in my opinion, no hypocrite can or ought to be happy."

"But you have not proved the hypocrisy," said Belinda. "Delicacy is not, I hope, an indisputable proof of it? If you mean *false* delicacy—"

"To cut the matter short at once," cried Mrs. Freke, "why, when a woman likes a man, does not she go and tell him so honestly?"

Belinda, surprised by this question from a woman, was too much abashed instantly to answer.

"Because she's a hypocrite. That is and must be the answer."

"No," said Mr. Percival, "because, if she be a woman of sense, she knows that by such a step she would disgust the object of her affection."

"Cunning!—cunning!—cunning!—the arms of the weakest."

"Prudence! prudence!—the arms of the strongest. Taking the best means to secure our own happiness without injuring that of others is the best proof of sense and strength of mind, whether in man or woman. Fortunately for society, the same conduct in ladies which best secures their happiness most increases ours."

Mrs. Freke beat the devil's tattoo for some moments, and then exclaimed, "You may say what you will, but the present system of society is radically wrong:—whatever is, is wrong."

"How would you improve the state of society?" asked Mr. Percival calmly.

"I'm not tinker-general to the world," said she.

"I am glad of it," said Mr. Percival; "for I have heard that tinkers often spoil more than they mend."

"But if you want to know," said Mrs. Freke, "what I would do to improve the world, I'll tell you: I'd have both sexes call things by their right names."

"This would doubtless be a great improvement," said Mr. Percival; "but you would not overturn society to attain it, would you? Should we find things much improved by tearing away what has been called the decent drapery of life?"

"Drapery, if you ask me my opinion," cried Mrs. Freke, "drapery, whether wet or dry, is the most confoundedly indecent thing in the world."

"That depends on *public* opinion, I allow," said Mr. Percival. "The Lacedaemonian ladies, who were veiled only by public opinion, were better covered from profane eyes than some English ladies are in wet drapery."

"I know nothing of the Lacedaemonian ladies: I took my leave of them when I was a schoolboy—girl, I should say. But pray, what o'clock is it by you? I've sat till I'm cramped all over," cried Mrs. Freke, getting up and stretching herself so violently that some part of her habiliments gave way. "Honi soit qui mal y pense!" said she, bursting into a horse laugh.

Without sharing in any degree that confusion which Belinda felt for her, she strode out of the room, saying, "Miss Portman, you understand these things better than I do; come and set me to rights."

When she was in Belinda's room, she threw herself into an arm-chair, and laughed immoderately.

"How I have trimmed Percival this morning!" said she.

"I am glad you think so," said Belinda; "for I really was afraid he had been too severe upon you."

"I only wish," continued Mrs. Freke, "I only wish his wife had been by. Why the devil did not she make her appearance? I suppose the prude was afraid of my demolishing and unrigging her."

"There seems to have been more danger of that for you than for anybody else," said Belinda, as she assisted to set Mrs. Freke's *rigging,* as she called it, to rights.

"I do of all things delight in hauling good people's opinions out of their musty drawers, and seeing how they look when they're all pulled to pieces before their faces! Pray, are those Lady Anne's drawers or yours?" said Mrs. Freke, pointing to a chest of drawers.

"Mine."

"I'm sorry for it; for if they were hers, to punish her for *shirking* me, by the Lord, I'd have every rag she has in the world out in the middle of the floor in ten minutes! You don't know me—I'm a terrible person when provoked—stop at nothing!"

As Mrs. Freke saw no other chance left of gaining her point with Belinda, she tried what intimidating her would do.

"I stop at nothing," repeated she, fixing her eyes upon Miss Portman, to fascinate her by terror. "Friend or foe! peace or war! Take your choice. Come to the ball at Harrowgate, I win my bet, and I'm your sworn friend. Stay away, I lose my bet, and am your sworn enemy."

"It is not in my power, madam," said Belinda calmly, "to comply with your request."

"Then you'll take the consequences," cried Mrs. Freke. She rushed past her, hurried downstairs, and called out, "Bid my blockhead bring my unicorn."

She, her unicorn, and her blockhead, were out of sight in a few minutes.

Anne Lister
(1791–1840)

Unlike most early-nineteenth-century British females of the middle class, Anne Lister was a woman of independent means. Although she had four brothers, they all died young and it was she who became heir to the comfortable family estate. Most importantly for her, her inheritance permitted her to escape marriage and to pursue a life she designed for herself. Clearly her experiences were not those of most early-nineteenth-century women who loved other women but were usually constrained to marry men for economic reasons if no other.

Lister spent her life studying Greek, Latin, mathematics, and history, traveling, playing the flute, riding, hunting, and pursuing women in search of a mate. Her love affairs with other women are chronicled "in a cipher of her own devising," according to Helena Whitbread, the editor of Lister's journals, who has deciphered Lister's code to reveal a very rare record by an early-nineteenth-century woman of her explicitly sexual interest in other women.

Lister apparently saw herself as a great anomaly. In her journal she quotes from the *Confessions* of Rousseau, applying his self-description to herself: "I know my own heart and understand my fellow man. But I am made unlike anyone I have ever met. I dare to say that I am like no one in the whole world."

The sexologists, who did not begin their observations until thirty years after Lister's death, formulated a category of "sexual inversion" in which Lister would have recognized herself and hence understood herself to be not the unique individual she describes in her journal entry. Her masculine appearance and behavior were much like what the sexologists posited as being most characteristic of the female congenital invert.

It is impossible to judge, of course, to what extent her "inversion" was congenital, and to what extent its apparent manifestations were based on her freedom to eschew the inevitable female subservience of her era and to claim her right to what had been considered male prerogatives. Like the later sexologists, however, she seems often to have conflated gender identification and sexual orientation. Loving women was, for her, part of her masculinity.

But Lister also had sentiments and ambitions that we would identify as feminist in our era. Whitbread describes her as a "trail-blazer for the emancipation of women from the mores of her day." She was actively interested in schools and the spread of education. She managed her own estates, dealing with the business of farming, supervising workmen, developing coal mining on her land, and even tackling various physical jobs herself. She became known in her community as "Gentleman Jack," but it is doubtful that her neighbors who called her that usually assumed a connection between the gender role she played and her sexuality.

However, her diary, as Whitbread has deciphered it, leaves no doubts. She was erotically interested in a number of women, had affairs with several of them, and finally settled in a domestic life with Ann Walker, another woman of independent means.

FURTHER READING: *I Know My Own Heart: The Diaries of Anne Lister, 1791–1840,* ed. Helena Whitbread (1988; reprint, New York: New York University Press, 1992). *No Priest But Love: The Journals of Anne Lister, from 1824–1826,* ed. Helena Whitbread (New York: New York University Press, 1992). Terry Castle, "The Diaries of Anne Lister," in *The Apparitional Lesbian: Female Homosexuality and Modern Culture* (New York: Columbia University Press, 1993).

From *The Journal of Anne Lister*

1820

Wednesday 9 February [York]
M—— & Eli & I stayed at home . . . Just before Harriet [Milne, née Belcombe] went, happening to talk a little to her in the complimentary style, M—— & Eli remonstrated. M—— & I talked about an hour after we got into bed. A very little would make M—— desperately jealous. Speaking of my manners, she owned they were not masculine but such was my form, voice & style of conversation, such a peculiar flattery & attention did I shew, that if this sort of thing was not carried off by my talents & cleverness, I should be disgusting. I took all in good part. Vowed over & over, constantly, etc., & M—— gave me a good kiss.

Thursday 17 February [York]
In the evening . . . would not have the girls in our room & had a comfortable, cosy conversation. M—— loves me. Certainly her heart is wholly mine. If I could have allowed her twenty or thirty pounds a year in addition to what she had, she certainly would not have married. But what could she do on her allowance of only thirty pounds a year? Passed an affectionate hour or two.

Saturday 18 March [York]
Slept with M—— in Anne's room upstairs over the drawing-room . . .
Little tiff with Tib . . . Said taking snuff & lying in bed did not suit me &
she knew it. Answer; I never found fault with M——, & proceeded to it.
It was a pity I let her marry. M—— advised me last night to tell Tib every
now & then she did not suit me & not to let her dwell so on the idea of
our living together . . . Told Louisa I should not like to be long in the same
house with M—— & Tib. Lou is sure I like M—— the best.

Wednesday 22 March [York]
Mrs. Simpson came unexpectedly at 9. . . . [She] told M——this morning
she could not bear me, that I was the only woman she was ever afraid of.
Wondered how anyone ever got acquainted with me. Mentioned my deep-
toned voice as very singular. The girls said they were afraid of me but could
like me because M—— did.

Thursday 23 March [York]
Someone who did not know me said to Mrs. John Raper of me, "One must
not speak to her. She is a bluestocking." "I don't know," replied Mrs.
Raper, "but she is very agreeable."
    On 30 March, Anne returned to Halifax taking M—— with her.
M—— stayed at Shibden until 14 April.

Sunday 2 April [Halifax]
Wet morning, sun, rain & wind. Had a chaise & my aunt & M—— & I
went to morning church. . . . Miss Browne at church. M—— rather nervous, I suppose at seeing her. At least, we talked about her on our return.
M—— said she did not like the thing & shewed her fondness for me by
her care & quiet tears about it. I will not doubt her love any more.

Monday 3 April [Halifax]
M—— said, very sweetly & with tears at the bare thought, she could never
bear me to do anything wrong with . . . anyone in my own rank of life.
She could bear it better with an inferior, where the danger of her being
supplanted could not be so great. But to get into any scrape would make
her pine away. She thought she could not bear it. I never before believed
she loved me so dearly & fondly. She has more romance than I could have
thought & I am satisfied . . . I thought of its being my birthday, but let it
pass without notice. How time steals away! What will the next year bring
to pass? May I improve it more than the last!

Tuesday 4 April [Halifax]

After coming up, M—— was to look over some of our old letters. In getting them, happened to stumble on some memoranda I made in 1817 on her conduct, her selfishness in marrying, the waste & distraction of my love, etc. Began reading these & went on thoughtlessly till I heard a book fall from her hands &, turning round, saw her motionless & speechless, in tears. Tried very soothing & affectionate means. She had never before known how I loved her or half what her marriage had cost me. Had she known, she could not have done it & it was evident that repentance now pressed heavily. I endeavoured, & successfully, to prove it to have been done for the best. She said she had never deserved some of the remarks made, but it was quite natural in me to make them. She grieved over what I had suffered & would never doubt me again. I am indeed persuaded & satisfied of her love.

Wednesday 5 April [Halifax]

Came upstairs at 10½. Sat up talking about my manners being too attentive; having too much of the civility of a well-bred gentleman, that I unintentionally spoilt people. Shewed her Emma Saltmarshe's last note before my leaving. She said it proved that I gave rise to an interest which people did not understand, or why they felt [as they did]. I promised to make my manners less attentive. She convinced me that my society was no advantage to Miss Browne as it might unfit her for that of others. M—— said, after we got into bed, that if she did [not] believe me bound to her in heart as much as any promise could bind me, she should not think it right & certainly would not kiss me.

Monday 10 April [Halifax (Haugh-end)]

In the evening Captain & Mrs. Priestly & Lou [who was staying at Haugh-end together with Anne & M——] went to a dance & sandwiches at Mrs. Rawson's (Hope Hall) & got back at 4. Mrs. Rawson had, thro' the medium of a note, to Mrs. Edwards, invited M—— & me, also, in spite of the awkwardness between us, but we were delighted to have a snug evening to ourselves. I was on the amoroso till M—— made me read aloud the first 126pp., vol. 2, of Sir Walter Scott's (he has just been made a baronet) last novel *The Monastery,* in 3 vols., 12 mo. Stupid enough. Tea at 7½. Went upstairs at 11. Sat up lovemaking, she conjuring me to be faithful, to consider myself as married, & always to act to other women as if I was M——'s husband.

Thursday 13 April [Halifax (Haugh-end)]

Walked (we 4) by Brockwell to Sowerby church . . . & as we returned, just went into the public school for the children of the lower classes . . . Walked

& sauntered about after dinner. All four went up & saw a cow calve in a field, several people being present, men, women, & children. After supper, read aloud (took me 40 minutes) Canning's speech to his constituents at Liverpool on his election for this present parliament. Fine day. Went upstairs at 11.20. M—— & I had a good deal of talk. She again conjured me to be faithful & let the rule of my conduct to ladies be—what would a married man do? . . . She was very low after we came upstairs. As soon as Watson went & even while Lou was lolling on the bed, she cried a good deal & seemed very miserable at the thought of leaving. I said & did everything that was kind. Told her I believed she loved me most fondly & faithfully & I loved her better & had more confidence now than ever before. I said I would do or promise anything, but that she needed no further promise than my heart, at that moment, gave her. (I made no promises.) I am indeed satisfied of her regard & I shall now begin to think & act as if she were indeed my wife.

Thursday 20 April [Halifax]

Miss Browne met me at their farther gate, turned down "Callista Lane" on to the moor . . . Parted after about an hour & a half. Behaved kindly. Said nothing about ever seeing her in the future, but bade her to think that, if I should not see her of twenty years, I should be equally interested in her welfare. . . . Just after getting thro' Skircoat Green, she asked me if my watch riband was worn out. I shewed it her & she said it was not. I told her I guessed her intention & she hoped I would do her the honour to accept one she had made for me, tho' it was very ugly & she was much dissatisfied with it. She meant it to be purple but it was scarlet. Certainly I would not wear the thing but admired it & thanked her very prettily & excused my not wearing it by saying I should value it too highly & would put it by with several other presents that I thought too valuable to wear. She seemed pleased . . . How different my feelings now & formerly. I felt rather ashamed of being seen with her. Felt sorry for myself. Would be glad to see her no more & regretted that she would have to return [to Halifax before her marriage]. I said I was sorry at her going several times over & I think she believed me. Yet I was only anxious not to seem inconsistent or less kind than usual & to appear as I wished, or rather as I thought proper, was an effort to me. We met Miss Maria Brown & Mr. Higham, one of the officers of the Sixth Foot, & Mrs. Lees & Miss Tipping & Mrs. Louis Alexander. I was sorry for myself & ashamed of my company. Poor girl. How little she thought this. I rejoiced she could not know, she could not think it. I am indeed glad she is going. Told my uncle & aunt she was going to be married. Very good match, I said, & we were all glad . . . Yet I believe she likes me very much & feels grateful for all my attention. This has its effect on me. Her heart is unvitiated by the world. I would gladly do anything in the world to serve or give her pleasure.

Wednesday 3 May [Halifax]
Musing on the subject of being my own master. Of going to Buxton in my own carriage with a man & a maidservant. Meeting with an elegant girl of family & fortune; paying her attention; taking her to see Castleton; staying all night; having a double bedroom; gaining her affections, etc. Mused on all this but did not let it lead to anything worse.

Friday 5 May [Halifax]
In stopping a moment or two, as I often do, to look down the valley from the top of our lane, a carter overtook me, accosted me by name & asked civilly, which I answered, some questions about how the Walkers' carriage was overturned. I had wished him goodnight & had not gone more than 2 or three yards before he called out, "Young woman, do you want a sweetheart?" "What!" said I angrily, "I never listen to such impertinence but I shall know you again, & mind you never speak to me again." He muttered something, I know not what. Did the man mean to be impertinent, or was he encouraged by my talking to him? It will be a lesson to me to take care whom I talk to in future. One can hardly carry oneself too high or keep people at too great a distance.

1821

Monday 29 January [Halifax]
Cutting curl papers half an hour . . . Arranging & putting away my last year's letters. Looked over & burnt several very old ones from indifferent people . . . Burnt . . . Mr. Montagu's farewell verses that no trace of any man's admiration may remain. It is not meet for me. I love, & only love, the fairer sex & thus beloved by them in turn, my heart revolts from any other love than theirs.

Thursday 8 February [Halifax]
Came upstairs at 11 a.m. Spent my time from then till 3, writing to M——very affectionately, more so than I remember to have done for long . . . Wrote the following crypt, "I can live upon hope, forget that we grow older, & love you as warmly as ever. Yes, Mary, you cannot doubt the love of one who has waited for you so long & patiently. You can give me all of happiness I care for &, prest to the heart which I believe my own,

caressed & treasured there, I will indeed be constant & never, from that moment, feel a wish or thought for any other than my wife. You shall have every smile & every breath of tenderness. 'One shall our union & our interests be' & every wish that love inspires & every kiss & every dear feeling of delight shall only make me more securely & entirely yours." Then, after hoping to see her in York next winter & at Steph's before the end of the summer, I further wrote in crypt as follows, "I do not like to be too long estranged from you sometimes, for, Mary, there is a nameless tie in that soft intercourse which blends us into one & makes me feel that you are mine. There is no feeling like it. There is no pledge which gives such sweet possession."

Monday 12 February [Halifax]
Letter . . . from Anne Belcombe (Petergate, York) . . . nothing but news & concluded, "from your ever sincere, affectionate, Anne Belcombe." The seal, Cupid in a boat guided by a star. "Si je te perds, je suis perdu." Such letters as these will keep up much love on my part. I shall not think much about her but get out of the scrape as well as I can, sorry & remorseful to have been in it at all. Heaven forgive me, & may M—— never know it.

Wednesday 14 February [Halifax]
From 1 to 3, read the first 100pp. vol. 3 *Leontine de Blondheim* . . . It is altogether a very interesting thing & I have read it with a sort of melancholy feeling, the very germ of which I thought had died for ever. I cried a good deal over the second & more over the third this morning, & as soon as I was alone during supper. Arlhofe reminds me of C——, Leontine of M——, & Wallerstein of myself. I find my former feelings are too soon awakened & I have, still, more romance than can let me bear the stimulus, the fearful rousing, of novel reading. I must not indulge in it. I must keep to graver things & strongly occupy myself with other thoughts & perpetual exertions. I am not happy. I get into what I have been led with . . . Anne. Oh, that I were more virtuous & quiet. Reflection distracts me & now I could cry like a child but will not, must not give way.

Sunday 18 February [Halifax]
George took to the post office, this morning, my letter to Anne Belcombe (Petergate, York). There was the following observation on the 2nd page . . . "You know I am not always happy; it is my misfortune to be singular in sentiment, & there lies the source of all that I lament in practice or in thought, & thence the deadly shaft that poisons my tranquillity. 'But, mortal pleasure, what art thou in truth! The torrent's smoothness ere it dash below!'" Mary, Mary, if thou were with me, I think I should be happy.

Monday 7 May [Halifax]
Foolish fancying about Caroline Greenwood, meeting her on Skircoat
Moor, taking her into a shed there is there & being connected with her.
Supposing myself in men's clothes & having a penis, tho' nothing more.
All this is very bad. Let me try to make a great exertion & get the better
of this lazyness [*sic*] in a morning—the root of all evil. . . . Now I will try
& turn over a new leaf & waste no more time in bed or any way else that
I can help. May God's help attend this resolution.

Monday 14 May [Halifax]
Went straight by North Parade to Mrs. Stansfield Rawson's. Found them
sitting down to tea . . . Talked away famously about one thing or other,
society, etc, without reserve. I fancy they thought me amusing & agreeable.
At least, they were as civil as possible. They asked me about my studies.
Said how I had neglected them for several years &, in fact, had only begun
to read regularly about 2 or 3 years ago, much the greater part of which
time I had wasted in bad management by gaping after too many things at
once e.g. mathematics before breakfast, French, Hebrew, Latin & Greek
during the rest of the morning . . . Expressed my particular wish that all
this should not be mentioned for that I should not like to have it known
& should not have told it at all had not she, Mrs. Rawson, asked me so
particularly. I do not think Catherine will make much out as a scholar. She
seems better suited to be made a beauty of. With good manners & fashionable accompaniments, she might have been much admired. These would
have served her better, I think, than Latin & Greek.

Tuesday 22 May [Halifax]
Sat near an hour with Mrs. Waterhouse. Very civil & very glad to see me
& a thoroughly good woman, but I am out of my element here & must
have other society in days to come.

Sunday 27 May [Halifax]
All went to the old church. . . . Noticed Miss Alexander, Dr. Gervase's
eldest daughter, at church. Paris seems to have improved her exceedingly.
She appeared a fine-looking girl. I stared upwards towards her so often that
I think she observed it; in coming out of church, too & I thought of her
all the while. I could soon admire her, I fancy, from seeing her this morning,
but it would be great imprudence to think of such a thing. She is, or ought
to be, quite out of my reach.

Tuesday 12 June [Halifax]
At 10¾, Miss Rawson (Catherine) & Miss Crackenthorpe . . . called &
staid ½ hour, Miss Rawson to say that, as it was Whitsuntide week, her

father & mother did not like her to be out & hoped we should excuse her coming this evening . . . In the afternoon, at 5¼, walked along the new road & got past Pump when Miss Ann Walker of Crownest overtook me, having run herself almost out of breath. Walked with her as far as the Lidget entrance to their own grounds & got home at 6.40. Made myself, as I fancied, very agreeable & was particularly civil & attentive in my manner. I really think the girl is flattered by it & likes me. She wished me to drink tea with them. I hoped for another walk to Giles House & the readiness she expressed shewed that my proposition was by no means unwelcome. She has certainly no aversion to my conversation & company. After parting I could not help smiling to myself & saying the flirting with this girl has done me good. It is heavy work to live without women's society & I would far rather while away an hour with this girl, who has nothing in the world to boast but good humour, than not flirt at all. If I had M—— I should be very different. She has my heart & I should want no more than her, but now I am solitary & dull.

Wednesday 13 June [Halifax]
Finished my letter to M—— . . . I have not exactly given her a promise in a set form of words but I have done nearly, in fact, the same thing, so that I cannot now retract with honour. Well, I am satisfied to have done. I love her & her heart is mine in return. Liberty & wavering made us both wretched & why throw away our happiness so foolishly? She is my wife in honour & in love & why not acknowledge her such openly & at once? I am satisfied to have her mind, & my own, at ease. The chain is golden & shared with M——. I love it better than any liberty.

Friday 22 June [Halifax]
I owe a good deal to this journal. By unburdening my mind on paper I feel, as it were, in some degree to get rid of it; it seems made over to a friend that hears it patiently, keeps it faithfully, and by never forgetting anything, is always ready to compare the past & present & thus to cheer & edify the future.

Constance Fenimore Woolson
(1840–94)

Constance Fenimore Woolson achieved great popular and critical success as a writer in the decades following the Civil War and then lapsed into obscurity until some recent feminist attempts to revive an interest in her work. She has been mentioned most often in literary histories as a close friend of the novelist Henry James. Predictably, and despite what is now common knowledge of James's erotic interest in young men, even recent biographers have attempted to create a love affair between Woolson and James. With more naïveté than humor, one even asks (with regard to James's being Woolson's lover), "But what of his obscure hurt, the injury that exempted him from serving in the Civil War?"

"Felipa" was published in 1876, only a few years after the earliest of the sexologists, Karl Ulrichs and Karl Von Westphal, began writing about "the third sex" and "contrary sexual feeling." It is not known whether Woolson was familiar with these early writings, but "Felipa" may be seen to demonstrate in a complex manner how the specter of sexual inversion might have loomed as a threat at this time to a woman who engaged in a romantic friendship.

The conflicts that comprise the drama in "Felipa" are somewhat illuminated by the little that is known of Woolson's emotional life and by her other fiction. Heterosexual love in her stories is usually presented as robbing a woman of her full personhood. There is no convincing record of Woolson's own amorous interest in a male at any time during her adult years. She was friends with several female couples, including Henry James's sister Alice and her romantic friend Katherine Loring, as well as Sarah Orne Jewett and Annie Fields. Though not much is known of her own intimate relations with other women, what has come to light is revealing. When her close friend Arabella Carter was about to marry, Woolson wrote her to explain why she might now seem more distant: "I have felt such a conviction that you would someday lose your interest in me, and also all outside things, that I thought best to prepare for the worst. . . . I don't mean to say that you will ever come actually to dislike me, but you will probably take a middle course." A review she wrote for *Atlantic* in 1878 of a novel by Alice Perry, *Esther Pennefather,* provides an interesting gloss to this earlier letter. She speaks in the review of "the singular power one woman sometimes has over another," until one of them marries, and then they can only look from a distance at "the old adoration which was so intense and so pure, so self-sacrificing and so far away."

Although Woolson's photographs do not suggest an androgynous appearance such as she attributes to young Felipa, she does seem to have had ambivalences with regard to what her era considered appropriate gender behavior. She was uninterested in domestic affairs, a feminist with radical views about women's education, and possessed of a "rebellious streak" and an adventurous spirit. Woolson was the grandniece of the writer James Fenimore Cooper and preferred to be called by the androgynous name "Fenimore" rather than "Constance."

"Felipa" may be seen as a subtle meditation on the connection between romantic friendship and sexual inversion. Recent critics have attempted to associate Felipa's androgyny with the refusal of the artist to limit herself to socially defined roles. But obviously the perceptive grandfather at the end of the story is worrying not about the difficulties in store for his granddaughter as a young artist but rather those in store for his granddaughter who has now unmistakably demonstrated what he senses is the dangerous, ineluctable pattern of sexual inversion.

Felipa is a kind of alter ego to the narrator Catherine. Among their many similarities is their admiration for Christine. Catherine, whose feeling is not without ambivalence, sees Christine as self-absorbed and capable of cruelty; nevertheless, she admires the beauty of the woman she describes as a "tall, lissome maid," and she admits, "I kissed her fondly—I never could help loving her now and then." In the context of the era's encouragement of romantic friendship, such love is quite safe. But when it is expressed in the "sexual inversion" of Felipa it leads to danger. Although Catherine may have felt wild jealousy at Christine's engagement (as Woolson herself might have at Arabella's engagement), the conventions of romantic friendship would have forced her to repress it. "Sexual inversion" had no such conventions. Sexual inversion may have represented to Woolson the unbridled forces of the subconscious that could turn romantic friendship into frightening passion.

FURTHER READING: Rayburn S. Moore, *Constance Fenimore Woolson* (New York: Twayne, 1963). Cheryl B. Torsney, *Constance Fenimore Woolson: The Grief of Artistry* (Athens: University of Georgia Press, 1989). Joan Myers Weimer, introduction, *Women Artists, Women Exiles: "Miss Grief" and Other Stories* by Constance Fenimore Woolson (New Brunswick: Rutgers University Press, 1988).

Felipa

Glooms of the live-oaks, beautiful-braided and woven
With intricate shades of the vines that, myriad cloven,
Clamber the forks of the multiform boughs.
>   . . . Green colonnades
Of the dim sweet woods, of the dear dark woods,
Of the heavenly woods and glades,
That run to the radiant marginal sand-beach within
>   The wide sea-marches of Glynn.
>   . . . Free
By a world of marsh that borders a world of sea.
Sinuous southward and sinuous northward the shimmering band
Of the sand-beach fastens the fringe of the marsh to the folds of the land.

Inward and outward to northward and southward the beach-lines linger
>   and curl
As a silver-wrought garment that clings to and follows the firm, sweet
>   limbs of a girl. . . .
A league and a league of marsh-grass, waist-high, broad in the blade,
Green, and all of a height, and unflecked with a light or a shade.
>   *Sidney Lanier*, "The Marshes of Glynn"

Christine and I found her there. She was a small, dark-skinned, yellow-eyed child, the offspring of the ocean and the heats, tawny, lithe and wild, shy yet fearless—not unlike one of the little brown deer that bounded through the open reaches of the pine-barren behind the house. She did not come to us—we came to her; we loomed into her life like genii from another world, and she was partly afraid and partly proud of us. For were we not her guests? proud thought! and, better still, were we not women? "I have only seen three women in all my life," said Felipa, inspecting us gravely, "and I like women. I am a woman too, although these clothes of the son of Pedro make me appear as a boy; I wear them on account of the boat and the hauling in of the fish. The son of Pedro being dead at a convenient age, and his clothes fitting me, what would you have? It was a chance not to be despised. But when I am grown I shall wear robes long and beautiful like the señora's." The little creature was dressed in a boy's suit of dark-blue linen, much the worse for wear, and torn.

"If you are a girl, why do you not mend your clothes?" I said.

"Do you mend, señora?"

"Certainly: all women sew and mend."

"The other lady?"

Christine laughed as she lay at ease upon the brown carpet of pine-needles, warm and aromatic after the tropic day's sunshine. "The child has divined me already, Catherine," she said.

Christine was a tall, lissome maid, with an unusually long stretch of arm, long sloping shoulders, and a long fair throat; her straight hair fell to her knees when unbound, and its clear flaxen hue had not one shade of gold, as her clear gray eyes had not one shade of blue. Her small, straight, rose-leaf lips parted over small, dazzlingly white teeth, and the outline of her face in profile reminded you of an etching in its distinctness, although it was by no means perfect according to the rules of art. Still, what a comfort it was, after the blurred outlines and smudged profiles many of us possess—seen to best advantage, I think, in church on Sundays, crowned with flower-decked bonnets, listening calmly serene to favorite ministers, unconscious of noses! When Christine had finished her laugh—and she never hurried anything—she stretched out her arm carelessly and patted Felipa's curly head. The child caught the descending hand and kissed the long white fingers.

It was a wild place where we were, yet not new or crude—the coast of Florida, that old-new land, with its deserted plantations, its skies of Paradise, and its broad wastes open to the changeless sunshine. The old house stood on the edge of the dry land, where the pine-barren ended and the salt-marsh began; in front curved the tide-water river that seemed ever trying to come up close to the barren and make its acquaintance, but could not quite succeed, since it must always turn and flee at a fixed hour, like Cinderella at the ball, leaving not a silver slipper behind, but purple driftwood and bright seaweeds, brought in from the Gulf Stream outside. A planked platform ran out into the marsh from the edge of the barren, and at its end the boats were moored; for, although at high tide the river was at our feet, at low tide it was far away out in the green waste somewhere, and if we wanted it we must go and seek it. We did not want it, however; we let it glide up to us twice a day with its fresh salt odors and flotsam of the ocean, and the rest of the time we wandered over the barrens or lay under the trees looking up into the wonderful blue above, listening to the windows as they rushed across from sea to sea. I was an artist, poor and painstaking. Christine was my kind friend. She had brought me South because my cough was troublesome, and here because Edward Bowne recommended the place. He and three fellow sportsmen were down at the Madre Lagoon, farther south; I thought it probable we should see him, without his three fellow sportsmen, before very long.

"Who were the three women you have seen, Felipa?" said Christine.

"The grandmother, an Indian woman of the Seminoles who comes sometimes with baskets, and the wife of Miguel of the island. But they are all old, and their skins are curled: I like better the silver skin of the señora."

Poor little Felipa lived on the edge of the great salt-marsh alone with her grandparents, for her mother was dead. The yellow old couple were slow-witted Minorcans, part pagan, part Catholic, and wholly ignorant; their minds rarely rose above the level of their orange-trees and their fish-nets. Felipa's father was a Spanish sailor, and, as he had died only the year before, the child's Spanish was fairly correct, and we could converse with her readily, although we were slow to comprehend the patois of the old people, which seemed to borrow as much from the Italian tongue and the Greek as from its mother Spanish. "I know a great deal," Felipa remarked confidently, "for my father taught me. He had sailed on the ocean out of sight of land, and he knew many things. These he taught to me. Do the gracious ladies think there is anything else to know?"

One of the gracious ladies thought not, decidedly. In answer to my remonstrance, expressed in English, she said, "Teach a child like that, and you ruin her."

"Ruin her?"

"Ruin her happiness—the same thing."

Felipa had a dog, a second self—a great gaunt yellow creature of un-known breed, with crooked legs, big feet, and the name Drollo. What Drollo meant, or whether it was an abbreviation, we never knew; but there was a certain satisfaction in it, for the dog was droll: the fact that the Minorcan title, whatever it was, meant nothing of that sort, made it all the better. We never saw Felipa without Drollo. "They look a good deal alike," observed Christine—"the same coloring."

"For shame!" I said.

But it was true. The child's bronzed yellow skin and soft eyes were not unlike the dog's, but her head was crowned with a mass of short black curls, while Drollo had only his two great flapping ears and his low smooth head. Give him an inch or two more of skull, and what a creature a dog would be! For love and faithfulness even now what man can match him? But, although ugly, Felipa was a picturesque little object always, whether attired in boy's clothes or in her own forlorn bodice and skirt. Olive-hued and meager-faced, lithe and thin, she flew over the pine-barrens like a crea-ture of air, laughing to feel her short curls toss and her thin childish arms buoyed up on the breeze as she ran, with Drollo barking behind. For she loved the winds, and always knew when they were coming—whether down from the north, in from the ocean, or across from the Gulf of Mexico: she watched for them, sitting in the doorway, where she could feel their first breath, and she taught us the signs of the clouds. She was a queer little thing: we used to find her sometimes dancing alone out on the barren in a circle she had marked out with pine-cones, and once she confided to us that she talked to the trees. "They hear," she said in a whisper; "you should see how knowing they look, and how their leaves listen."

Once we came upon her most secret lair in a dense thicket of thorn-myrtle and wild smilax—a little bower she had made, where was hidden a horrible-looking image formed of the rough pieces of saw-palmetto grubbed up by old Bartolo from his garden. She must have dragged these fragments thither one by one, and with infinite pains bound them to-gether with her rude withes of strong marsh-grass, until at last she had formed a rough trunk with crooked arms and a sort of a head, the red hairy surface of the palmetto looking not unlike the skin of some beast, and making the creature all the more grotesque. This fetich was kept crowned with flowers, and after this we often saw the child stealing away with Drollo to carry to it portions of her meals or a new-found treasure—a sea-shell, a broken saucer, or a fragment of ribbon. The food always mysteriously disappeared, and my suspicion is that Drollo used to go back secretly in the night and devour it, asking no questions and telling no lies: it fitted in nicely, however, Drollo merely performing the ancient part of the priests of Jupiter, men who have been much admired. "What a little pagan she is!" I said.

"Oh, no, it is only her doll," replied Christine.

I tried several times to paint Felipa during these first weeks, but those eyes of hers always evaded me. They were, as I have said before, yellow—that is, they were brown with yellow lights—and they stared at you with the most inflexible openness. The child had the full-curved, half-open mouth of the tropics, and a low Greek forehead. "Why isn't she pretty?" I said.

"She is hideous," replied Christine; "look at her elbows."

Now Felipa's arms *were* unpleasant: They were brown and lean, scratched and stained, and they terminated in a pair of determined little paws that could hold on like grim Death. I shall never forget coming upon a tableau one day out on the barren—a little Florida cow and Felipa, she holding on by the horns, and the beast with its small fore feet stubbornly set in the sand; girl pulling one way, cow the other; both silent and deter-mined. It was a hard contest, but the girl won.

"And if you pass over her elbows, there are her feet," continued Chris-tine languidly. For she was a sybaritic lover of the fine linens of life, that friend of mine—a pre-Raphaelite lady with clinging draperies and a me-diaeval clasp on her belt. Her whole being rebelled against ugliness, and the mere sight of a sharp-nosed, light-eyed woman on a cold day made her uncomfortable.

"Have we not feet too?" I replied sharply.

But I knew what she meant. Bare feet are not pleasant to the eye now-adays, whatever they may have been in the days of the ancient Greeks; and Felipa's little brown insteps were half the time torn or bruised by the thorns of the chaparral. Besides, there was always the disagreeable idea that she might step upon something cold and squirming when she prowled through the thickets knee-deep in the matted grasses. Snakes abounded, although we never saw them; but Felipa went up to their very doors, as it were, and rang the bell defiantly.

One day old Grandfather Bartolo took the child with him down to the coast: she was always wild to go to the beach, where she could gather shells and sea-beans, and chase the little ocean-birds that ran along close to the waves with that swift gliding motion of theirs, and where she could listen to the roar of the breakers. We were several miles up the salt-marsh, and to go down to the ocean was quite a voyage to Felipa. She bade us good-by joyously; then ran back to hug Christine a second time, then to the boat again; then back.

"I thought you wanted to go, child?" I said, a little impatiently; for I was reading aloud, and these small irruptions were disturbing.

"Yes," said Felipa, "I want to go; and still— Perhaps if the gracious señora would kiss me again—"

Christine only patted her cheek and told her to run away: she obeyed, but there was a wistful look in her eyes, and, even after the boat had started, her face, watching us from the stern, haunted me.

"Now that the little monkey has gone, I may be able at last to catch and fix a likeness of her," I said; "in this case a recollection is better than the changing quicksilver reality."

"You take it as a study of ugliness?"

"Do not be hard upon the child, Christine."

"Hard? Why, she adores me," said my friend, going off to her hammock under the tree.

Several days passed, and the boat returned not. I accomplished a fine amount of work, and Christine a fine amount of swinging in the hammock and dreaming. At length one afternoon I gave my final touch, and carried my sketch over to the pre-Raphaelite lady for criticism. "What do you see?" I said.

"I see a wild-looking child with yellow eyes, a mat of curly black hair, a lank little bodice, her two thin brown arms embracing a gaunt old dog with crooked legs, big feet, and turned-in toes."

"Is that all?"

"All."

"You do not see latent beauty, courage, and a possible great gulf of love in that poor wild little face?"

"Nothing of the kind," replied Christine decidedly. "I see an ugly little girl; that is all."

The next day the boat returned, and brought back five persons, the old grandfather, Felipa, Drollo, Miguel of the island, and—Edward Bowne.

"Already?" I said.

"Tired of the Madre, Kitty; thought I would come up here and see you for a while. I knew you must be pining for me."

"Certainly," I replied; "do you not see how I have wasted away?"

He drew my arm through his and raced me down the plank-walk toward the shore, where I arrived laughing and out of breath.

"Where is Christine?" he asked.

I came back into the traces at once. "Over there in the hammock. You wish to go to the house first, I suppose?"

"Of course not."

"But she did not come to meet you, Edward, although she knew you had landed."

"Of course not, also."

"I do not understand you two."

"And of course not, a third time," said Edward, looking down at me with a smile. "What do peaceful little artists know about war?"

"Is it war?"

"Something very like it, Kitty. What is that you are carrying?"

"Oh! my new sketch. What do you think of it?"

"Good, very good. Some little girl about here, I suppose?"

"Why, it is Felipa!"

"And who is Felipa? Seems to me I have seen that old dog, though."

"Of course you have; he was in the boat with you, and so was Felipa; but she was dressed in boy's clothes, and that gives her a different look."

"Oh! that boy? I remember him. His name is Philip. He is a funny little fellow," said Edward calmly.

"Her name is Felipa, and she is not a boy or a funny little fellow at all," I replied.

"Isn't she? I thought she was both," replied Ned carelessly; and then he went off toward the hammock. I turned away, after noting Christine's cool greeting, and went back to the boat.

Felipa came bounding to meet me. "What is his name?" she demanded.

"Bowne."

"Buon—Buona; I can not say it."

"Bowne, child—Edward Bowne."

"Oh! Eduardo; I know that. Eduardo—Eduardo—a name of honey."

She flew off singing the name, followed by Drollo carrying his mistress's palmetto basket in his big patient mouth; but when I passed the house a few moments afterward she was singing, or rather talking volubly of, another name—"Miguel," and "the wife of Miguel," who were apparently important personages on the canvas of her life. As it happened, I never really saw that wife of Miguel, who seemingly had no name of her own; but I imagined her. She lived on a sand-bar in the ocean not far from the mouth of our salt-marsh; she drove pelicans like ducks with a long switch, and she had a tame eagle; she had an old horse also, who dragged the driftwood across the sand on a sledge, and this old horse seemed like a giant horse always, outlined as he was against the flat bar and the sky. She went out at dawn, and she went out at sunset, but during the middle of the burning day she sat at home and polished sea-beans, for which she obtained untold sums; she was very tall, she was very yellow, and she had but one eye. These items, one by one, had been dropped by Felipa at various times, and it was with curiosity that I gazed upon the original Miguel, the possessor of this remarkable spouse. He was a grave-eyed, yellow man, who said little and thought less, applying *cui bono?* to mental much as the city man applies it to bodily exertion, and therefore achieving, I think, a finer degree of inanition. The tame eagle, the pelicans, were nothing to him; and, when I saw his lethargic, gentle countenance, my own curiosity about them seemed to die away in haze, as though I had breathed in an invisible opiate. He came, he went, and that was all; exit Miguel.

Felipa was constantly with us now. She and Drollo followed the three of us wherever we went—followed the two also whenever I staid behind to sketch, as I often staid, for in those days I was trying to catch the secret of the salt-marsh; a hopeless effort—I know it now. "Stay with me, Felipa," I said; for it was natural to suppose that the lovers might like to be alone. (I call them lovers for want of a better name, but they were more like haters; however, in such cases it is nearly the same thing.) And then Christine, hearing this, would immediately call "Felipa!" and the child would dart after them, happy as a bird. She wore her boy's suit now all the time, because the señora had said she "looked well in it." What the señora really said was, that in boy's clothes she looked less like a grasshopper. But this had been translated as above by Edward Bowne when Felipa suddenly descended upon him one day and demanded to be instantly told what the gracious lady was saying about her; for she seemed to know by intuition when we spoke of her, although we talked in English and mentioned no names. When told, her small face beamed, and she kissed Christine's hand joyfully and bounded away. Christine took out her handkerchief and wiped the spot.

"Christine," I said, "do you remember the fate of the proud girl who walked upon bread?"

"You think that I may starve for kisses some time?" said my friend, going on with the wiping.

"Not while I am alive," called out Edward from behind. His style of courtship *was* of the sledge-hammer sort sometimes. But he did not get much for it on that day; only lofty tolerance, which seemed to amuse him greatly.

Edward played with Felipa very much as if she was a rubber toy or a little trapeze performer. He held her out at arm's length in mid-air, he poised her on his shoulder, he tossed her up into the low myrtle-trees, and dangled her by her little belt over the claret-colored pools on the barren; but he could not frighten her; she only laughed and grew wilder and wilder, like a squirrel. "She has muscles and nerves of steel," he said admiringly.

"Do put her down; she is too excitable for such games," I said in French, for Felipa seemed to divine our English now. "See the color she has."

For there was a trail of dark red over the child's thin oval cheeks which made her look unlike herself. As she caught our eyes fixed upon her, she suddenly stopped her climbing and came and sat at Christine's feet. "Some day I shall wear robes like the señora's," she said, passing her hand over the soft fabric; "and I think," she added after some slow consideration, "that my face will be like the señora's too."

Edward burst out laughing. The little creature stopped abruptly and scanned his face.

"Do not tease her," I said.

Quick as a flash she veered around upon me. "He does not tease me," she said angrily in Spanish; "and, besides, what if he does? I like it." She looked at me with gleaming eyes and stamped her foot.

"What a little tempest!" said Christine.

Then Edward, man-like, began to explain. "You could not look much like this lady, Felipa," he said, "because you are so dark, you know."

"Am I dark?"

"Very dark; but many people are dark, of course; and for my part I always liked dark eyes," said this mendacious person.

"Do you like my eyes?" asked Felipa anxiously.

"Indeed I do: they are like the eyes of a dear little calf I once owned when I was a boy."

The child was satisfied, and went back to her place beside Christine. "Yes, I shall wear robes like this," she said dreamily, drawing the flowing drapery over her knees clad in the little linen trousers, and scanning the effect; "they would trail behind me—so." Her bare feet peeped out below the hem, and again we all laughed, the little brown toes looked so comical coming out from the silk and the snowy embroideries. She came down to reality again, looked at us, looked at herself, and for the first time seemed to comprehend the difference. Then suddenly she threw herself down on the ground like a little animal, and buried her head in her arms. She would not speak, she would not look up: she only relaxed one arm a little to take in Drollo, and then lay motionless. Drollo looked at us out of one eye solemnly from his uncomfortable position, as much as to say: "No use; leave her to me." So after a while we went away and left them there.

That evening I heard a low knock at my door. "Come in," I said, and Felipa entered. I hardly knew her. She was dressed in a flowered muslin gown which had probably belonged to her mother, and she wore her grand-mother's stockings and large baggy slippers; on her mat of curly hair was perched a high-crowned, stiff white cap adorned with a ribbon streamer; and her lank little neck, coming out of the big gown, was decked with a chain of large sea-beans, like exaggerated lockets. She carried a Cuban fan in her hand which was as large as a parasol, and Drollo, walking behind, fairly clanked with the chain of sea-shells which she had wound around him from head to tail. The droll tableau and the supreme pride on Felipa's countenance overcame me, and I laughed aloud. A sudden cloud of rage and disappointment came over the poor child's face: she threw her cap on the floor and stamped on it; she tore off her necklace and writhed herself out of her big flowered gown, and, running to Drollo, nearly strangled him in her fierce efforts to drag off his shell chains. Then, a half-dressed, wild little phantom, she seized me by the skirts and dragged me toward the looking-glass. "You are not pretty either," she cried. "Look at yourself! Look at yourself!"

"I did not mean to laugh at you, Felipa," I said gently; "I would not laugh at any one; and it is true I am not pretty, as you say. I can never be pretty, child; but, if you will try to be more gentle, I could teach you how to dress yourself so that no one would laugh at you again. I could make you a little bright-barred skirt and a scarlet bodice: you could help, and that would teach you to sew. But a little girl who wants all this done for her must be quiet and good."

"I am good," said Felipa; "as good as everything."

The tears still stood in her eyes, but her anger was forgotten: she improvised a sort of dance around my room, followed by Drollo dragging his twisted chain, stepping on it with his big feet, and finally winding himself up into a knot around the chair-legs.

"Couldn't we make Drollo something too? dear old Drollo!" said Felipa, going to him and squeezing him in an enthusiastic embrace. I used to wonder how his poor ribs stood it: Felipa used him as a safety-valve for her impetuous feelings.

She kissed me good night, and then asked for "the other lady."

"Go to bed, child," I said; "I will give her your good night."

"But I want to kiss her too," said Felipa.

She lingered at the door and would not go; she played with the latch, and made me nervous with its clicking; at last I ordered her out. But on opening my door half an hour afterward there she was sitting on the floor outside in the darkness, she and Drollo, patiently waiting. Annoyed, but unable to reprove her, I wrapped the child in my shawl and carried her out into the moonlight, where Christine and Edward were strolling to and fro under the pines. "She will not go to bed, Christine, without kissing you," I explained.

"Funny little monkey!" said my friend, passively allowing the embrace.

"Me too," said Edward, bending down. Then I carried my bundle back satisfied.

The next day Felipa and I in secret began our labors; hers consisted in worrying me out of my life and spoiling material—mine in keeping my temper and trying to sew. The result, however, was satisfactory, never mind how we got there. I led Christine out one afternoon: Edward followed. "Do you like tableaux?" I said. "There is one I have arranged for you."

Felipa sat on the edge of the low, square-curbed Spanish well, and Drollo stood behind her, his great yellow body and solemn head serving as a background. She wore a brown petticoat barred with bright colors, and a little scarlet bodice fitting her slender waist closely; a chemisette of soft cream-color with loose sleeves covered her neck and arms, and set off the dark hues of her cheeks and eyes; and around her curly hair a red scarf was twisted, its fringed edges forming a drapery at the back of the head, which, more than anything else, seemed to bring out the latent character of her face. Brown moccasins, red stockings, and a quantity of bright beads completed her costume.

"By Jove!" cried Edward, "the little thing is almost pretty."

Felipa understood this, and a great light came into her face: forgetting her pose, she bounded forward to Christine's side. "I am pretty, then?" she said with exultation; "I *am* pretty, then, after all? For now you yourself have said it—have said it."

"No, Felipa," I interposed, "the gentleman said it." For the child had a curious habit of confounding the two identities which puzzled me then as now. But this afternoon, this happy afternoon, she was content, for she was allowed to sit at Christine's feet and look up into her fair face unmolested. I was forgotten, as usual.

"It is always so," I said to myself. But cynicism, as Mr. Aldrich says, is a small brass field-piece that eventually bursts and kills the artilleryman. I knew this, having been blown up myself more than once; so I went back to my painting and forgot the world. Our world down there on the edge of the salt-marsh, however, was a small one: when two persons went out of it there was a vacuum.

One morning Felipa came sadly to my side. "They have gone away," she said.

"Yes, child."

"Down to the beach to spend all the day."

"Yes, I know it."

"And without me!"

This was the climax. I looked up. Her eyes were dry, but there was a hollow look of disappointment in her face that made her seem old; it was as though for an instant you caught what her old-woman face would be half a century on.

"Why did they not take me?" she said. "I am pretty now: she herself said it."

"They can not always take you, Felipa," I replied, giving up the point as to who had said it.

"Why not? I am pretty now: she herself said it," persisted the child. "In these clothes, you know: she herself said it. The clothes of the son of Pedro you will never see more: they are burned."

"Burned?"

"Yes, burned," replied Felipa composedly. "I carried them out on the barren and burned them. Drollo singed his paw. They burned quite nicely. But they are gone, and I am pretty now, and yet they did not take me! What shall I do?"

"Take these colors and make me a picture," I suggested. Generally, this was a prized privilege, but to-day it did not attract; she turned away, and a few moments after I saw her going down to the end of the plank-walk, where she stood gazing wistfully toward the ocean. There she staid all day, going into camp with Drollo, and refusing to come to dinner in spite of old Dominga's calls and beckonings. At last the patient old grandmother went down herself to the end of the long walk where they were, with some bread and venison on a plate. Felipa ate but little, but Drollo, after waiting politely until she had finished, devoured everything that was left in his calmly hungry way, and then sat back on his haunches with one paw on the plate, as though for the sake of memory. Drollo's hunger was of the chronic kind; it seemed impossible either to assuage it or to fill him. There was a gaunt leanness about him which I am satisfied no amount of food could ever fatten. I think he knew it too, and that accounted for his resignation. At length, just before sunset, the boat returned, floating up the marsh with the tide, old Bartolo steering and managing the brown sails.

Felipa sprang up joyfully; I thought she would spring into the boat in her eagerness. What did she receive for her long vigil? A short word or two; that was all. Christine and Edward had quarreled.

How do lovers quarrel ordinarily? But I should not ask that, for these were no ordinary lovers: they were extraordinary.

"You should not submit to her caprices so readily," I said the next day while strolling on the barren with Edward. (He was not so much cast down, however, as he might have been.)

"I adore the very ground her foot touches, Kitty."

"I know it. But how will it end?"

"I will tell you: some of these days I shall win her, and then—she will adore me."

Here Felipa came running after us, and Edward immediately challenged her to a race: a game of romps began. If Christine had been looking from her window she might have thought he was not especially disconsolate over her absence; but she was not looking. She was never looking out of anything or for anybody. She was always serenely content where she was. Edward and Felipa strayed off among the pine-trees, and gradually I lost sight of them. But as I sat sketching an hour afterward Edward came into view, carrying the child in his arms. I hurried to meet them.

"I shall never forgive myself," he said; "the little thing has fallen and injured her foot badly, I fear."

"I do not care at all," said Felipa; "I like to have it hurt. It is *my* foot, isn't it?"

These remarks she threw at me defiantly, as though I had laid claim to the member in question. I could not help laughing.

"The other lady will not laugh," said the child proudly. And in truth Christine, most unexpectedly, took up the *rôle* of nurse. She carried Felipa to her own room—for we each had a little cell opening out of the main apartment—and as white-robed Charity she shone with new radiance, "Shone" is the proper word; for through the open door of the dim cell, with the dark little face of Felipa on her shoulder, her white robe and skin seemed fairly to shine, as white lilies shine on a dark night. The old grandmother left the child in our care and watched our proceedings wistfully, very much as a dog watches the human hands that extract the thorn from the swollen foot of her puppy. She was grateful and asked no questions; in fact, thought was not one of her mental processes. She did not think much; she felt. As for Felipa, the child lived in rapture during those days in spite of her suffering. She scarcely slept at all—she was too happy: I heard her voice rippling on through the night, and Christine's low replies. She adored her beautiful nurse.

The fourth day came: Edward Bowne walked into the cell. "Go out and breathe the fresh air for an hour or two," he said in the tone more of a command than a request.

"The child will never consent," replied Christine sweetly.

"Oh, yes, she will; I will stay with her," said the young man, lifting the feverish little head on his arm and passing his hand softly over the bright eyes.

"Felipa, do you not want me?" said Christine, bending down.

"He stays; it is all the same," murmured the child.

"So it is.—Go, Christine," said Edward with a little smile of triumph.

Without a word Christine left the cell. But she did not go to walk; she came to my room, and, throwing herself on my bed, fell in a moment into a deep sleep, the reaction after her three nights of wakefulness. When she awoke it was long after dark, and I had relieved Edward in his watch.

"You will have to give it up," he said as our lily came forth at last with sleep-flushed cheeks and starry eyes shielded from the light. "The spell is broken; we have all been taking care of Felipa, and she likes one as well as the other."

Which was not true, in my case at least, since Felipa had openly derided my small strength when I lifted her, and beat off the sponge with which I attempted to bathe her hot face, "They" used no sponges, she said, only their nice cool hands; and she wished "they" would come and take care of her again. But Christine had resigned *in toto*. If Felipa did not prefer her to all others, then Felipa should not have her; she was not a common nurse. And indeed she was not. Her fair face, ideal grace, cooing voice, and the strength of her long arms and flexible hands, were like magic to the sick, and—distraction to the well; the well in this case being Edward Bowne looking in at the door.

"You love them very much, do you not, Felipa?" I said one day when the child was sitting up for the first time in a cushioned chair.

"Ah, yes; it is so strong when they carry me," she replied. But it was Edward who carried her.

"He is very strong," I said.

"Yes; and their long soft hair, with the smell of roses in it too," said Felipa dreamily. But the hair was Christine's.

"I shall love them for ever, and they will love me for ever," continued the child. "Drollo too." She patted the dog's head as she spoke, and then concluded to kiss him on his little inch of forehead; next she offered him all her medicines and lotions in turn, and he smelled at them grimly. "He likes to know what I am taking," she explained.

I went on: "You love them, Felipa, and they are fond of you. They will always remember you, no doubt."

"Remember!" cried Felipa, starting up from her cushions like a Jack-in-a-box. "They are not going away? Never! never!"

"But of course they must go some time, for—"

But Felipa was gone. Before I could divine her intent she had flung herself out of her chair down on the floor, and was crawling on her hands and knees toward the outer room. I ran after her, but she reached the door before me, and, dragging her bandaged foot behind her, drew herself toward Christine. "You are *not* going away! You are not! you are not!" she sobbed, clinging to her skirts.

Christine was reading tranquilly; Edward stood at the outer door mending his fishing-tackle. The coolness between them remained, unwarmed by so much as a breath. "Run away, child; you disturb me," said Christine, turning over a leaf. She did not even look at the pathetic little bundle at her feet. Pathetic little bundles must be taught some time what ingratitude deserves.

"How can she run, lame as she is?" said Edward from the doorway.

"You are not going away, are you? Tell me you are not," sobbed Felipa in a passion of tears, beating on the floor with one hand, and with the other clinging to Christine.

"I am not going," said Edward. "Do not sob so, you poor little thing!"

She crawled to him, and he took her up in his arms and soothed her into stillness again; then he carried her out on the barren for a breath of fresh air.

"It is a most extraordinary thing how that child confounds you two," I said. "It is a case of color-blindness, as it were—supposing you two were colors."

"Which we are not," replied Christine carelessly. "Do not stray off into mysticism, Catherine."

"It is not mysticism; it is a study of character—"

"Where there is no character," replied my friend.

I gave it up, but I said to myself: "Fate, in the next world make me one of those long, lithe, light-haired women, will you? I want to see how it feels."

Felipa's foot was well again, and spring had come. Soon we must leave our lodge on the edge of the pine-barren, our outlook over the salt-marsh, with the river sweeping up twice a day, bringing in the briny odors of the ocean; soon we should see no more the eagles far above us or hear the night-cry of the great owls, and we must go without the little fairy flowers of the barren, so small that a hundred of them scarcely made a tangible bouquet, yet what beauty! what sweetness! In my portfolio were sketches and studies of the salt-marsh, and in my heart were hopes. Somebody says somewhere: "Hope is more than a blessing; it is a duty and a virtue." But

I fail to appreciate preserved hope—hope put up in cans and served out in seasons of depression. I like it fresh from the tree. And so when I hope it *is* hope, and not that well-dried, monotonous cheerfulness which makes one long to throw the persistent smilers out of the window. Felipa danced no more on the barrens; her illness had toned her down; she seemed content to sit at our feet while we talked, looking up dreamily into our faces, but no longer eagerly endeavoring to comprehend. We were there; that was enough.

"She is growing like a reed," I said; "her illness has left her weak."

"Minded," suggested Christine.

At this moment Felipa stroked the lady's white hand tenderly and laid her brown cheek against it.

"Do you not feel reproached?" I said.

"Why? Must we give our love to whoever loves us? A fine parcel of paupers we should all be, wasting our inheritance in pitiful small change! Shall I give a thousand beggars a half hour's happiness, or shall I make one soul rich his whole life long?"

"The latter," remarked Edward, who had come up unobserved.

They gazed at each other unflinchingly. They had come to open battle during those last days, and I knew that the end was near. Their words had been cold as ice, cutting as steel, and I said to myself, "At any moment." There would be a deadly struggle, and then Christine would yield. Even I comprehended something of what that yielding would be.

"Why do they hate each other so?" Felipa said to me sadly.

"Do they hate each other?"

"Yes, for I feel it here," she answered, touching her breast with a dramatic little gesture.

"Nonsense! Go and play with your doll, child." For I had made her a respectable, orderly doll to take the place of the ungainly fetich out on the barren.

Felipa gave me a look and walked away. A moment afterward she brought the doll out of the house before my very eyes, and, going down to the end of the dock, deliberately threw it into the water; the tide was flowing out, and away went my toy-woman out of sight, out to sea.

"Well!" I said to myself. "What next?"

I had not told Felipa we were going; I thought it best to let it take her by surprise. I had various small articles of finery ready as farewell gifts, which should act as sponges to absorb her tears. But Fate took the whole matter out of my hands. This is how it happened: One evening in the jasmine arbor, in the fragrant darkness of the warm spring night, the end came; Christine was won. She glided in like a wraith, and I, divining at once what had happened, followed her into her little room, where I found her lying on her bed, her hands clasped on her breast, her eyes open and veiled in soft shadows, her white robe drenched with dew. I kissed her fondly—I never could help loving her then or now—and next I went out to find Edward. He had been kind to me all my poor gray life; should I not go to him now? He was still in the arbor, and I sat down by his side quietly; I knew that the words would come in time. They came; what a flood! English was not enough for him. He poured forth his love in the rich-voweled Spanish tongue also; it has sounded doubly sweet to me ever since.

> "Have you felt the wool of the beaver?
> Or swan's down ever?
> Or have smelt the bud o' the brier?
> Or the nard in the fire?
> Or ha' tasted the bag o' the bee?
> Oh so white, oh so soft, oh so sweet is she!"

said the young lover; and I, listening there in the dark fragrant night, with the dew heavy upon me, felt glad that the old simple-hearted love was not entirely gone from our tired metallic world.

It was late when we returned to the house. After reaching my room I found that I had left my cloak in the arbor. It was a strong fabric; the dew could not hurt it, but it could hurt my sketching materials and various trifles in the wide inside pockets—*objets de luxe* to me, souvenirs of happy times, little artistic properties that I hang on the walls of my poor studio when in the city. I went softly out into the darkness again and sought the arbor; groping on the ground I found, not the cloak, but—Felipa! She was crouched under the foliage, face downward; she would not move or answer.

"What is the matter, child?" I said, but she would not speak. I tried to draw her from her lair, but she tangled herself stubbornly still farther among the thorny vines, and I could not move her. I touched her neck; it was cold. Frightened, I ran back to the house for a candle.

"Go away," she said in a low hoarse voice when I flashed the light over her. "I know all, and I am going to die. I have eaten the poison things in your box, and just now a snake came on my neck and I let him. He has bitten me, and I am glad. Go away; I am going to die."

I looked around; there was my color-case rifled and empty, and the other articles were scattered on the ground. "Good Heavens, child!" I cried, "what have you eaten?"

"Enough," replied Felipa gloomily, "I knew they were poisons; you told me so. And I let the snake stay."

By this time the household, aroused by my hurried exit with the candle, came toward the arbor. The moment Edward appeared Felipa rolled herself up like a hedgehog again and refused to speak. But the old grandmother knelt down and drew the little crouching figure into her arms with gentle tenderness, smoothing its hair and murmuring loving words in her soft dialect.

"What is it?" said Edward; but even then his eyes were devouring Christine, who stood in the dark vine-wreathed doorway like a picture in a frame. I explained.

Christine smiled. "Jealousy," she said in a low voice. "I am not surprised."

But at the first sound of her voice Felipa had started up, and, wrenching herself free from old Dominga's arms, threw herself at Christine's feet. "Look at *me* so," she cried—"me too; do not look at him. He has forgotten poor Felipa; he does not love her any more. But *you* do not forget, señora; *you* love me—*you* love me. Say you do, or I shall die!"

We were all shocked by the pallor and the wild, hungry look of her uplifted face. Edward bent down and tried to lift her in his arms; but when she saw him a sudden fierceness came into her eyes; they shot out yellow light and seemed to narrow to a point of flame. Before we knew it she had turned, seized something, and plunged it into his encircling arm. It was my little Venetian dagger.

We sprang forward; our dresses were spotted with the fast-flowing blood; but Edward did not relax his hold on the writhing, wild little body he held until it lay exhausted in his arms. "I am glad I did it," said the child, looking up into his face with her inflexible eyes. "Put me down— put me down, I say, by the gracious señora, that I may die with the trailing of her white robe over me." And the old grandmother with trembling hands received her and laid her down mutely at Christine's feet.

AH, WELL! Felipa did not die. The poisons racked but did not kill her, and the snake must have spared the little thin brown neck so despairingly offered to him. We went away; there was nothing for us to do but to go away as quickly as possible and leave her to her kind. To the silent old grandfather I said: "It will pass; she is but a child."

"She is nearly twelve, señora. Her mother was married at thirteen."

"But she loved them both alike, Bartolo. It is nothing; she does not know."

"You are right, lady; she does not know," replied the old man slowly; "but *I* know. It was two loves, and the stronger thrust the knife."

[Sidonie Gabrielle] Colette
(1873–1954)

Although Colette was married to three men during her life, she was intrigued by lesbianism. She often created lesbian characters in her fiction, and she experienced several lesbian relationships. Had she lived in our day she would perhaps have called herself a bisexual. In her era she saw herself as merely adventurous, with a desire to indulge in all manner of love and sex. Her *belle époque* daring, however, did not always transcend the received wisdom of her day. The lesbian characters in her work are often men trapped in women's bodies, or they are budding or blooming carnivorous flowers (see Part III).

Colette began writing at the age of twenty-seven, having been urged to literary production by her first husband, Willy (Henri Gauthier-Villars), a music critic and writer of light fiction who often signed his own name to work he paid other authors to write. In 1900 Willy asked Colette to produce for him her memories of herself as a fifteen-year-old schoolgirl, including her lesbian relationships at school. Willy, like Claudine's husband in a later novel, *Claudine Is Married,* seems to have had a voyeuristic interest in lesbianism, as well as in female transvestism, even encouraging Colette to dress in men's clothing. The description of Claudine's urbane, *belle époque* husband, who promoted his wife's lesbian experimentations and who "posed as immoral and modern," was perhaps modeled on Willy.

In any case, Willy laid claim to Colette's first literary effort, which was published as *Claudine at School.* The work was so popular that Colette wrote four sequels in the next seven years, three of them coming out under Willy's name. Each of these works includes the subject of love between women to a greater or lesser extent, although in each novel lesbian relationships are generally seen as far less significant than the heterosexual relationships that Claudine experiences.

It is difficult to tell exactly to what extent Colette shared the views and experiences of Claudine, but her marriage to Willy was followed by a love affair with a famous silent-screen actress of her day, Marguerite Moreno, and another one with the actress Polaire, who played Claudine on stage. Her most important lesbian relationship was with the Marquise de Belbeuf—great-granddaughter of the Empress Josephine and the niece of Napoleon III—a very masculine woman who was known as Missy.

Colette lived with Missy in Brittany for more than five years, in a villa that Missy bought for her. During that period Colette was said to have worn a bracelet with the inscription "I belong to Missy." At one point the two women appeared together in a mime ballet, *Rêve d'Égypte,* in which the Marquise, dressed in drag, exchanged a long kiss with Colette that led to a near riot instigated by the Marquise's abandoned husband, who was in the audience. When the relationship with Missy was over, Colette married Henry de Jouvenel, with whom she had a daughter. Colette's third and last husband was a man fifteen years her junior, who served as a kind of wife to his famous spouse. Despite her various marriages she continued to have friendships with lesbians, including Natalie Barney, the Princess de Polignac, Countess Elisabeth de Gramont, Radclyffe Hall, and Violet Trefusis.

Masculinity is frequently associated with lesbianism in Colette's work, just as effeminacy is associated with male homosexuality. When Claudine pursues relationships with other females the reader is reminded that she is athletic, independent, and desirous of conquest and domination—all traits that the early twentieth century connected to masculinity (though those aspects of Claudine disappear when she relates to men, by whom she wants to be mastered). Colette's later writing also frequently connects lesbianism and masculinity, at least for one of the pair in a lesbian couple, as in her short story "Habit," which depicts a butch-femme dyad.

The following selection is from *The Pure and the Impure,* a collection of reminiscences from Colette's life. La Chevalière is Missy, the Marquise de Belbeuf. It is interesting to note that the society that Colette depicts here, which she knew firsthand during her years with Missy, is made up largely of masculine upper-class women and feminine lower-class women. Such a social configuration was not uncommon in Europe but was rare in the United States where, historically, lesbians have seldom class-mixed, and butch-femme-type relationships have been much more common in the working-class lesbian community than among middle- or upper-class lesbians.

FURTHER READING: Colette, *The Pure and the Impure* (1930; reprint, New York: Farrar, Straus and Giroux, 1966). Elaine Marks, "Lesbian Intertextuality," in *Homosexualities and French Literature,* ed. Elaine Marks and George Stambolian (Ithaca, NY: Cornell University Press, 1979), pp. 353–77. Yvonne Mitchell, *Colette: A Taste for Life* (New York: Harcourt, Brace, 1975). Joanna Richardson, *Colette* (London: Methuen, 1983). Michele Sarde, *Collette: Free and Fettered,* trans. Richard Miller (New York: Morrow, 1980). Jane Rule, *Lesbian Images* (Garden City, NY: Doubleday, 1975).

From *The Pure and the Impure*

How timid I was, at that period when I was trying to look like a boy, and how feminine I was beneath my disguise of cropped hair. "Who would take us to be women? Why, women." They alone were not fooled. With such distinguishing marks as pleated shirt front, hard collar, sometimes a waistcoat, and always a silk pocket handkerchief, I frequented a society perishing on the margin of all societies. Although morals, good and bad, have not changed during the past twenty-five or thirty years, class consciousness, in destroying itself, has gradually undermined and debilitated the clique I am referring to, which tried, trembling with fear, to live without hypocrisy, the breathable air of society. This clique, or sect, claimed the right of "personal freedom" and equality with homosexuality, that imperturbable establishment. And they scoffed, if in whispers, at "Papa" Lépine, the Prefect of Police, who never could take lightly the question of women in men's clothes. The adherents of this clique of women exacted secrecy for their parties, where they appeared dressed in long trousers and dinner jackets and behaved with unsurpassed propriety. They tried to reserve for themselves certain bars and restaurants and to enjoy there the guilty pleasures of backgammon and bezique. Then they gave up the struggle, and the sect's most stubborn proselytes never crossed the street or left their carriage without putting on, heart pounding, a long plain cloak which gave them an excessively respectable look and effectively concealed their masculine attire.

At the home of the best-known woman among them—the best known and the most misunderstood—fine wines, long cigars, photographs of a smartly turned-out horseman, one or two languorous portraits of very pretty women, bespoke the sensual and rakish life of a bachelor. But the lady of the house, in dark masculine attire, belied any idea of gaiety or bravado. Pale, without blemish or blush, pale like certain antique Roman marbles that seem steeped in light, the sound of her voice muffled and sweet, she had all the ease and good manners of a man, the restrained gestures, the virile poise of a man. Her married name, when I knew her, was still disturbing. Her friends, as well as her enemies, never referred to her except by her title and a charming Christian name, title and name alike clashing with her stocky masculine physique and reserved, almost shy manner. From the highest strata of society, La Chevalière, as we shall call her, was having her fling, sowing her wild oats like a prince. And like a prince, she had her counterparts. Napoleon III gave us Georges Ville, who survived him for a long time. La Chevalière could not prevent this man-woman, deathly pale, powdered, self-assertive, from exhibiting herself and signing the same initials as her model.

Where could I find, nowadays, messmates like those who, gathered around La Chevalière, emptied her wine cellar and her purse? Baronesses of the Empire, canonesses, lady cousins of Czars, illegitimate daughters of grand-dukes, exquisites of the Parisian bourgeoisie, and also some aged horsewomen of the Austrian aristocracy, hand and eye of steel . . . Some of these ladies fondly kept in their protective and jealous shadow women younger than they, clever young actresses, the next to the last authentic demimondaine of the epoch, a music-hall star . . . You heard them in whispered conversation, but to the great disappointment of the curious ear, the dialogue was banal. "How did your lesson go? Do you have it now, your Chopin waltz?" "Take your furs off here, you will get hot and won't be in voice this evening. Yes, you know better than I do, of course. But I studied with Nilsson, please remember that, my dear. . . ." "Tut, tut, my sweet, one doesn't cut a baba with a knife. . . . Take a small fork. . . ." "You have no idea of time, and if I didn't think for you, my pet . . . What do you mean by putting your husband into a bad humor by going home late every time?"

Among these women, free yet timorous, addicted to late hours, darkened rooms, gambling, and indolence, I almost never detected a trace of cynicism. Sparing of words, all they needed was an allusion. I heard one of them, one only—a German princess with the fresh chubby face of a butcher boy—introduce her *petite amie* one day as "my spouse," whereupon my blunt gentlemen in skirts wrinkled their noses in distaste and pretended not to hear. "It's not that I conceal anything," briefly commented the Vicomtesse de X. "It's simply that I don't like showing off."

It was otherwise with their protégées, who were, more often than not, rather rude young creatures, insinuating and grasping. Not surprising, this, for these ladies in male attire had, by birth and from infancy, a taste for below-stairs accomplices and comrades-in-livery—and, as a consequence, an incurable timidity, which they dissimulated as best they could. Pride in giving pleasure relieved them of the need for any other dignity; they tolerated being addressed familiarly by these young creatures and found again, beneath the insult, the tremulous and secret pleasure of their childhood when dining at the servants' table.

In the servants' quarters, from their first toddling steps, they had found their allies and their tormentors, whom they and their brothers equally feared and loved. It is quite necessary for a child to love. The women of whom I am speaking were considerably older than I, they had grown up in an epoch when the aristocracy, even more than the rich bourgeoisie, handed over their progeny to the domestic staff. It is a question who was worth more to the children, the paid tormentor or the depraved ally. My narrators did not judge them. They did not bother to embroider their tales but calmly described the orgies in the pantry, when strong liquor was poured out for the dazed children, or told how those underlings would one day stuff the babies with food and next day forget to feed them at all. . . . They did not speak in the maudlin tone of cheap journalism; none of these women claimed the grade of infant martyr, not even the daughter of the Duke de X, who said that from six to fifteen she had never worn a pair of new shoes, that her shoes had all been hand-me-downs from her elder brother or sister, and with holes in the soles. Blandly, and at times rather mockingly, she described incidents of her childhood.

"In the corridor outside our nursery," she related, "was a small antique lady's desk in rosewood, incrusted with a large medallion in Sèvres porcelain, with the monogram of a queen and her crown glittering in diamonds. My mother did not like that small piece of furniture and had sentenced it to exile in the corridor, where it stood between two doors. Well, to please my mother, when we dressed for dinner we always set our muddy shoes on the top of that *bonheur-du-jour,* right on the Sèvres medallion and its diamonds. . . ."

Married to a man she hated, my narrator had not dared to confess her despair when she fancied she was pregnant, except to an old footman, an ancient corrupter of princelings, a valet she feared.

"He brought me a concoction to drink," she said, touched at the recollection. "He, and he alone in the world, pitied me. . . . What he gave me to drink was pretty horrible . . . I remember that I wept. . . ."

"With grief?"

"No. I cried because, while I swallowed that horror, the old fellow tried to hearten me by calling me *niña* and *pobrecita,* just as he had when I was a child."

These women who had been dispossessed of their rightful childhoods and who, as girls, had been more than orphans, were now in their maturity the fond instructors of a younger generation. They never seemed ridiculous to me. Yet some of them wore a monocle, a white carnation in the buttonhole, took the name of God in vain, and discussed horses competently. These mannish women I am calling to mind were, indeed, almost as fond of the horse, that warm, enigmatic, stubborn, and sensitive creature, as they were of their young protégées. With their strong slender hands they were able to break in and subjugate a horse, and when age and hard times deprived them of the whip and the hunting crop, they lost their final scepter. A garage, no matter how elegant, can never equal the smartness of a stable. The motorcar cannot be mounted; a mechanical carriage bestows no psychological glamour on its driver. But the dust of the bridle paths in the Bois still haloes, in countless memories, those equestriennes who did not need to ride astride to assert their ambiguity.

Seated on the handsome back of a lean thoroughbred, mounted on the twin pedestal of a chestnut crupper, where shimmered two ellipses of unctuous light, they were freed of the awkward, toed-out stance of the ballet dancer that marred their walk. The thing women in men's clothes imitate worst is a man's stride. "They raise their knees too high, they don't tuck in their bottoms as they should," was the severe pronouncement of La Chevalière. The exciting scent of horses, that so masculine odor, never quite left these women, but lingered on after the ride. I saw and hailed the decline of these women. They tried to describe and explain their vanished charm. They tried to render intelligible for us their success with women and their defiant taste for women. The astonishing thing is that they managed to do so. I am not referring here to La Chevalière, who by character as well as physique was above them. Restless and uncertain in her pursuit of love, she searched with her anxious eyes, so dark they were almost black beneath a low, white forehead, for what she never found: a settled and sentimental attachment. For more than forty years, this woman with the bearing of a handsome boy endured the pride and punishment of never being able to establish a real and lasting affair with a woman. It was not for lack of trying, because she asked nothing better or worse. But the salacious expectations of women shocked her very natural platonic tendencies, which resembled more the suppressed excitement, the diffuse emotion of an adolescent, than a woman's explicit need. Twenty years ago she tried, with bitterness, to explain herself to me. "I do not know anything about completeness in love," she said, "except the *idea* I have of it. But they, the women, have never allowed me to stop at that point. . . ."

"Without exception?"

"Without exception."

"Why?"

"I'm sure I don't know."

La Chevalière shrugged. The expression that appeared on her face recalled for a minute Damien's expression when he had assured me that "women go too far. . . ." Like Damien, she seemed to be recalling something rather sad, rather repellent, and she was about to say more, but like him she contained herself.

"I'm sure I don't know," she repeated.

"But what in heaven's name do they hope for, by going further? Do they give so much credit to the physical act, the idea of the paroxysm of pleasure?"

"No doubt," she said, uncertainly.

"They must at least have an opinion on that special pleasure? Do they fling themselves upon it as upon a panacea, do they see in it a kind of consecration? Do they demand it, or accept it, more simply, as a proof of mutual trust?"

La Chevalière averted her eyes, flicked off the long ash on her cigar, waved her hand as a discreet man might do.

"This is beyond me," she said. "It does not even concern me."

"And yet . . ."

She repeated her gesture and smiled to dissuade me from persisting.

"I'm of the opinion," she said, "that in the ancient Nativities the portrait of the 'donor' occupies far too much space in the picture. . . ."

La Chevalière always had, still has wit, a quick sense of repartee. The years have made little change in her and have let her keep her smile, which is so difficult to depict, so difficult to forget. That smile of the "donor" who despises his gifts did not, however, discourage me from questioning her. But she was shy and rejected this subject of conversation, to which, however, I will add a remark she let fall one day when an ugly young woman was being described in detail in her hearing.

"That girl, if she didn't have her two eyes . . ."

"What more does a woman need besides her two eyes?" asked La Chevalière.

In effect, I knew she was mad about blue-green eyes, and when I told her she shared with Jean Lorrain the obsession of "green" eyes, she was annoyed.

"Oh," she said, "but it's not the same thing at all! Jean Lorrain takes off from green eyes to go . . . you know where. He's a man for whom 'the deep calleth to deep.' . . ."

The remark is worth more than her epoch and the literature of the turn of the century, swollen with masks and voodoo, black Masses, blissful decapitated women whose heads float among narcissi and blue toads. For a timid soul, exalted in silence and perpetually adolescent, what more seductive depths could one plunge into than the eyes of the loved one, and descend in thought and blissfully lose one's life between the seaweed and the star?

The seduction emanating from a person of uncertain or dissimulated sex is powerful. Those who have never experienced it liken it to the banal attraction of the love that evicts the male element. This is a gross misconception. Anxious and veiled, never exposed to the light of day, the androgynous creature wanders, wonders, and implores in a whisper. . . . Its half equal, man, is soon scared and flees. There remains its half equal, a woman. There especially remains for the androgynous creature the right, even the obligation, never to be happy. If jovial, the androgynous creature is a monster. But it trails irrevocably among us its seraphic suffering, its glimmering tears. It goes from a tender inclination to maternal adoption. . . . As I write this, I am thinking of La Chevalière. It was she who most often bruised herself in a collision with a woman—a woman, that whispering guide, presumptuous, strangely explicit, who took her by the hand and said, "Come, I will help you find yourself. . . ."

"I am neither that nor anything else, alas," said La Chevalière, dropping the vicious little hand. "What I lack cannot be found by searching for it."

She is the person who has no counterpart anywhere. At one time she believed that she had her counterpart in the features of a young woman, and again in the features of a handsome young man—yes, of a young man, why not?—so handsome that love seemed to despair of him, and who, moreover, clung to no one. He gave to La Chevalière a name that made her blush with joy and gratitude: he called her "my father." But she soon saw that again she had been mistaken, that one can adopt only the child one has begotten. . . .

"All the same," the solitary woman sighs at times, "I must not complain, I shall have been a mirage. . . ."

Around her, beneath her, a quarrelsome and timid life gravitated. She served as the ideal, as the target, and ignored the fact. She was praised, she was slandered, her name was repeated in the midst of a subdued and almost subterranean tumult, was heard especially in the friendly little dives, the tiny, neighborhood cinemas frequented by groups of her women friends— basement rooms arranged as restaurants, dim, and blue with tobacco smoke. There was also a cellar in Montmartre that welcomed these uneasy women, haunted by their own solitude, who felt safe within the low- ceilinged room beneath the eye of a frank proprietress who shared their predilections, while an unctuous and authentic cheese fondue sputtered and the loud contralto of an artiste, one of their familiars, sang to them the romantic ballads of Augusta Holmès. . . . The same need for a refuge, warmth, and darkness, the same fear of intruders and sightseers assembled here these women whose faces, if not their names, soon became familiar to me. Literature and the makers of literature were absent from these gath- erings and I delighted in that absence, along with the empty gaiety of the chatter and the diverting and challenging exchange of glances, the cryptic reference to certain treasons, comprehended at once, and the sudden out- bursts of ferocity. I reveled in the admirable quickness of their half-spoken language, the exchange of threats, of promises, as if, once the slow-thinking male had been banished, every message from woman to woman became clear and overwhelming, restricted to a small but infallible number of signs. . . .

All amours tend to create a dead-end atmosphere. "There! It's finished, we've arrived, and beyond us two there is nothing now, not even an opening for escape," murmurs one woman to her protégée, using the language of a lover. And as a proof, she indicates the low ceiling, the dim light, the women who are their counterparts, making her listen to the masculine rumble of the outside world and hear how it is reduced to the booming of a distant danger.

Willa Cather
(1873–1947)

At the age of fifteen Willa Cather was cutting her hair "shorter than most boys." She often dressed in men's clothes, signed her name "William Cather, Jr.," and later liked to be called "Dr. Will." She enjoyed participating in community theater productions, where she insisted on taking male roles. Her fellow students at the University of Nebraska recalled a first meeting of a Greek class at which she opened the door and peeped in. When Cather inquired if she was in the right classroom, only the upper part of her was showing. The other students assumed from the boyish voice, the short hair, and the tailored jacket that a male was about to enter. When she stepped in and they saw her skirt the class broke up in shocked and hysterical laughter.

Later, as a famous writer, she toned down her masculine presentation, although she continued to favor the "tailored" look. There is little concrete evidence to indicate to us how Cather interpreted her masculinity—whether she actually saw herself in medicalized terms as a man trapped in a woman's body—because she became very secret about her life, even destroying many letters that would undoubtedly have been revealing, and forbidding quotation from other letters that are extant.

Nevertheless, it is clear that her significant relationships were all with other women. She lived in Pittsburgh with Isabelle McClung and Isabelle's parents on and off from 1901 to 1915. When Isabelle's father protested Cather's presence in the beginning, Isabelle threatened to leave home unless her father welcomed Cather into the household. Cather later declared that Isabelle was her muse and that all her novels were written to Isabelle. They remained close even after they no longer lived together.

Cather's early journalism career often took her to New York, even during her Pittsburgh years, and there she met Edith Lewis. When the relationship with Isabelle came to an end and Isabelle married a man, in 1915, Cather set up a household in New York with Lewis, which lasted until Cather's death, more than forty years later. Although Lewis had a career of her own, she also functioned as Cather's Alice B. Toklas, Una Troubridge, or Ada Russell. She encouraged Cather's writing, accompanied her on trips, entertained with and for her, and even proofread her manuscripts. Lewis wrote the first biography of Cather.

None of Cather's works deal specifically with lesbian relationships, though many critics have pointed out that her male characters are often women in drag, and that novels such as *My Ántonia* (1918) and *One of Ours* (1922) can be read as lightly encoded lesbian stories. The narrator of *My Ántonia,* for example, is nominally a heterosexual male, but his interests, experiences, haunts, and attitudes have generally been associated with femaleness, and thus the character can easily be read as lesbian.

Cather long used such a device of gender switching in her work. Her mentor and friend Sarah Orne Jewett pointed out in 1908, when Cather sent her a new story, "On the Gulls' Road," that the male lover did not ring true. His characterization, which really suggested to Jewett a female, could only be seen as "something of a masquerade," she said. But perhaps these "masquerades" were for Cather a perfectly workable device. If she could not feel free to deal openly with lesbian material and, at the same time, if the lesbian really was to her a man trapped in a woman's body, she might have felt that nothing is lost and everything is gained by presenting as male those female characters she had anyway conceived as having a masculine identification.

The following short story, "Tommy, the Unsentimental," was published in *Home Monthly* in 1896. It too may be seen as a kind of masquerade, not one in which a female plays a male, but rather one in which a lesbian plays a heterosexual woman. The masculine businesswoman in this story appears in other fiction by Cather—she is, for example, Frances Harling in *My Ántonia.* But Cather generally avoids recognition of the sexual implications of her "inverted" characters. In "Tommy, the Unsentimental" homosexuality is hinted at when the men of Tommy's town think it "the worst sign in the world" for a "rebellious girl like Tommy" to be "sweet and gentle to one of her own sex." But Cather attempts to turn aside the suspicions, which are certainly shared by the reader as well, with her tacked-on ending that suggests Tommy's interest in the opposite sex. It is tempting to speculate that Cather was writing two stories in a work like "Tommy, the Unsentimental" one for the general reader of *Home Monthly,* who would not have been happy with a story about sexual inversion, particularly one that does not focus on the medical aspects of the phenomenon; and another story for the reader who was herself a "sexual invert" and would not be fooled by perfunctory heterosexual masquerade.

FURTHER READING: Willa Cather, *My Ántonia* (1918; reprinted Boston: Houghton Mifflin, 1988). Timothy Dow Adams, "My Gay Ántonia: The Politics of Willa Cather's Lesbianism," in *Historical, Literary and Erotic Aspects of Lesbianism*, ed. Monika Kehoe (New York: Haworth Press, 1986), pp. 89–98. Judith Fetterley, "My Ántonia, Jim Burden, and the Dilemma of the Lesbian Writer," *Lesbian Texts and Contexts: Radical Revisions*, eds. Karla Jay and Joanne Glasgow (New York: New York University Press, 1990). Edith Lewis, *Willa Cather Living* (New York: Knopf, 1953). Sharon O'Brien, *Willa Cather: The Emerging Voice* (New York: Oxford University Press, 1987). Joanna Russ, "To Write Like a Woman: Transformations of Identity in the Work of Willa Cather," *Historical, Literary and Erotic Aspects of Lesbianism*, ed. Monika Kehoe (New York: Haworth Press, 1986), pp. 77–87. James Woodress, *Willa Cather: Her Life and Art* (Lincoln: Nebraska University Press, 1970).

Tommy, the Unsentimental

"Your father says he has no business tact at all, and of course that's dreadfully unfortunate."

"Business," replied Tommy, "he's a baby in business; he's good for nothing on earth but to keep his hair parted straight and wear that white carnation in his buttonhole. He has 'em sent down from Hastings twice a week as regularly as the mail comes, but the drafts he cashes lie in his safe until they are lost, or somebody finds them. I go up occasionally and send a package away for him myself. He'll answer your notes promptly enough, but his business letters—I believe he destroys them unopened to shake the responsibility of answering them."

"I am at a loss to see how you can have such patience with him, Tommy, in so many ways he is thoroughly reprehensible."

"Well, a man's likeableness don't depend at all on his virtues or acquirements, nor a woman's either, unfortunately. You like them or you don't like them, and that's all there is to it. For the why of it you must appeal to a higher oracle than I. Jay is a likeable fellow, and that's his only and sole acquirement, but after all it's a rather happy one."

"Yes, he certainly is that," replied Miss Jessica, as she deliberately turned off the gas jet and proceeded to arrange her toilet articles. Tommy watched her closely and then turned away with a baffled expression.

Needless to say, Tommy was not a boy, although her keen gray eyes and wide forehead were scarcely girlish, and she had the lank figure of an active half grown lad. Her real name was Theodosia, but during Thomas Shirley's frequent absences from the bank she had attended to his business and correspondence signing herself "T. Shirley," until everyone in Southdown called her "Tommy." That blunt sort of familiarity is not unfrequent in the West, and is meant well enough. People rather expect some business ability in a girl there, and they respect it immensely. That, Tommy undoubtedly had, and if she had not, things would have gone at sixes and sevens in the Southdown National. For Thomas Shirley had big land interests in Wyoming that called him constantly away from home, and his cashier, little Jay Ellington Harper, was, in the local phrase, a weak brother in the bank. He was the son of a friend of old Shirley's, whose papa had sent him West, because he had made a sad mess of his college career, and had spent too much money and gone at too giddy a pace down East. Conditions changed the young gentleman's life, for it was simply impossible to live either prodigally or rapidly in Southdown, but they could not materially affect his mental habits or inclinations. He was made cashier of Shirley's bank because his father bought in half the stock, but Tommy did his work for him.

The relation between these two young people was peculiar; Harper was, in his way, very grateful to her for keeping him out of disgrace with her father, and showed it by a hundred little attentions which were new to her and much more agreeable than the work she did for him was irksome. Tommy knew that she was immensely fond of him, and she knew at the same time that she was thoroughly foolish for being so. As she expressed it, she was not of his sort, and never would be. She did not often take pains to think, but when she did she saw matters pretty clearly, and she was of a peculiarly unfeminine mind that could not escape meeting and acknowledging a logical conclusion. But she went on liking Jay Ellington Harper, just the same. Now Harper was the only foolish man of Tommy's acquaintance. She knew plenty of active young business men and sturdy ranchers, such as one meets about live western towns, and took no particular interest in them, probably just because they were practical and sensible and thoroughly of her own kind. She knew almost no women, because in those days there were few women in Southdown who were in any sense interesting, or interested in anything but babies and salads. Her best friends were her father's old business friends, elderly men who had seen a good deal of the world, and who were very proud and fond of Tommy. They recognized a sort of squareness and honesty of spirit in the girl that Jay Ellington Harper never discovered, or, if he did, knew too little of its rareness to value highly. Those old speculators and men of business had always felt a sort of responsibility for Tom Shirley's little girl, and had rather taken her mother's place, and been her advisers on many points upon which men seldom feel at liberty to address a girl.

She was just one of them; she played whist and billiards with them, and made their cocktails for them, not scorning to take one herself occasionally. Indeed, Tommy's cocktails were things of fame in Southdown, and the professional compounders of drinks always bowed respectfully to her as though acknowledging a powerful rival.

Now all these things displeased and puzzled Jay Ellington Harper, and Tommy knew it full well, but clung to her old manner of living with a stubborn pertinacity, feeling somehow that to change would be both foolish and disloyal to the Old Boys. And as things went on, the seven Old Boys made greater demands upon her time than ever, for they were shrewd men, most of them, and had not lived fifty years in this world without learning a few things and unlearning many more. And while Tommy lived on in the blissful delusion that her role of indifference was perfectly played and without a flaw, they suspected how things were going and were perplexed as to the outcome. Still, their confidence was by no means shaken, and as Joe Elsworth said to Joe Sawyer one evening at billiards, "I think we can pretty nearly depend on Tommy's good sense."

They were too wise to say anything to Tommy, but they said just a word or two to Thomas Shirley, Sr., and combined to make things very unpleasant for Mr. Jay Ellington Harper.

At length their relations with Harper became so strained that the young man felt it would be better for him to leave town, so his father started him in a little bank of his own up in Red Willow. Red Willow, however, was scarcely a safe distance, being only some twenty-five miles north, upon the Divide, and Tommy occasionally found excuse to run up on her wheel to straighten out the young man's business for him. So when she suddenly decided to go East to school for a year, Thomas, Sr., drew a sigh of great relief. But the seven Old Boys shook their heads; they did not like to see her gravitating toward the East; it was a sign of weakening, they said, and showed an inclination to experiment with another kind of life, Jay Ellington Harper's kind.

But to school Tommy went, and from all reports conducted herself in a most seemly manner; made no more cocktails, played no more billiards. She took rather her own way with the curriculum, but she distinguished herself in athletics, which in Southdown counted for vastly more than erudition.

Her evident joy on getting back to Southdown was appreciated by everyone. She went about shaking hands with everybody, her shrewd face, that was so like a clever wholesome boy's, held high with happiness. As she said to old Joe Elsworth one morning, when they were driving behind his stud through a little thicket of cottonwood scattered along the sun-parched bluffs, "It's all very fine down East there, and the hills are great, but one gets mighty homesick for this sky, the old intense blue of it, you know. Down there the skies are all pale and smoky. And this wind, this

hateful, dear, old everlasting wind that comes down like the sweep of cav-
alry and is never tamed or broken, O Joe, I used to get hungry for this
wind! I couldn't sleep in that lifeless stillness down there."

"How about the people, Tom?"

"O, they are fine enough folk, but we're not their sort, Joe, and never
can be."

"You realize that, do you, fully?"

"Quite fully enough, thank you, Joe." She laughed rather dismally, and
Joe cut his horse with the whip.

The only unsatisfactory thing about Tommy's return was that she
brought with her a girl she had grown fond of at school, a dainty, white,
languid bit of a thing, who used violet perfumes and carried a sunshade.
The Old Boys said it was a bad sign when a rebellious girl like Tommy
took to being sweet and gentle to one of her own sex, the worst sign in
the world.

The new girl was no sooner in town than a new complication came
about. There was no doubt of the impression she made on Jay Ellington
Harper. She indisputably had all those little evidences of good breeding
that were about the only things which could touch the timid, harassed
young man who was so much out of his element. It was a very plain case
on his part, and the souls of the seven were troubled within them. Said Joe
Elsworth to the other Joe, "The heart of the cad is gone out to the little
muff, as is right and proper and in accordance with the eternal fitness of
things. But there's the other girl who has the blindness that may not be
cured, and she gets all the rub of it. It's no use, I can't help her, and I am
going to run down to Kansas City for awhile. I can't stay here and see the
abominable suffering of it." He didn't go, however.

There was just one other person who understood the hopelessness of
the situation quite as well as Joe, and that was Tommy. That is, she understood Harper's attitude. As to Miss Jessica's she was not quite so certain,
for Miss Jessica, though pale and languid and addicted to sunshades, was
a maiden most discreet. Conversations on the subject usually ended without
any further information as to Miss Jessica's feelings, and Tommy sometimes
wondered if she were capable of having any at all.

At last the calamity which Tommy had long foretold descended upon
Jay Ellington Harper. One morning she received a telegram from him begging her to intercede with her father; there was a run on his bank and he
must have help before noon. It was then ten thirty, and the one sleepy little
train that ran up to Red Willow daily had crawled out of the station an
hour before. Thomas Shirley, Sr., was not at home.

"And it's a good thing for Jay Ellington he's not, he might be more
stony hearted than I," remarked Tommy, as she closed the ledger and

turned to the terrified Miss Jessica. "Of course we're his only chance, no one else would turn their hand over to help him. The train went an hour ago and he says it must be there by noon. It's the only bank in the town, so nothing can be done by telegraph. There is nothing left but to wheel for it. I may make it, and I may not. Jess, you scamper up to the house and get my wheel out, the tire may need a little attention. I will be along in a minute."

"O, Theodosia, can't I go with you? I must go!"

"You go! O, yes, of course, if you want to. You know what you are getting into, though. It's twenty-five miles uppish grade and hilly, and only an hour and a quarter to do it in."

"O, Theodosia, I can do anything now!" cried Miss Jessica, as she put up her sunshade and fled precipitately. Tommy smiled as she began cramming bank notes into a canvas bag. "May be you can, my dear, and may be you can't."

The road from Southdown to Red Willow is not by any means a favorite bicycle road; it is rough, hilly and climbs from the river bottoms up to the big Divide by a steady up grade, running white and hot through the scorched corn fields and grazing lands where the long-horned Texan cattle browse about in the old buffalo wallows. Miss Jessica soon found that with the pedaling that had to be done there was little time left for emotion of any sort, or little sensibility for anything but the throbbing, dazzling heat that had to be endured. Down there in the valley the distant bluffs were vibrating and dancing with the heat, the cattle, completely overcome by it, had hidden under the shelving banks of the "draws" and the prairie dogs had fled to the bottom of their holes that are said to reach to water. The whirr of the seventeen-year locust was the only thing that spoke of animation, and that ground on as if only animated and enlivened by the sickening, destroying heat. The sun was like hot brass, and the wind that blew up from the south was hotter still. But Tommy knew that wind was their only chance. Miss Jessica began to feel that unless she could stop and get some water she was not much longer for this vale of tears. She suggested this possibility to Tommy, but Tommy only shook her head, "Take too much time," and bent over her handle bars, never lifting her eyes from the road in front of her. It flashed upon Miss Jessica that Tommy was not only very unkind, but that she sat very badly on her wheel and looked aggressively masculine and professional when she bent her shoulders and pumped like that. But just then Miss Jessica found it harder than ever to breathe, and the bluffs across the river began doing serpentines and skirt dances, and more important and personal considerations occupied the young lady.

When they were fairly over the first half of the road, Tommy took out her watch. "Have to hurry up, Jess, I can't wait for you."

"O, Tommy, I can't," panted Miss Jessica, dismounting and sitting down in a little heap by the roadside. "You go on, Tommy, and tell him —tell him I hope it won't fail, and I'd do anything to save him."

By this time the discreet Miss Jessica was reduced to tears, and Tommy nodded as she disappeared over the hill laughing to herself. "Poor Jess, anything but the one thing he needs. Well, your kind have the best of it generally, but in little affairs of this sort my kind come out rather strongly. We're rather better at them than at dancing. It's only fair, one side shouldn't have all."

Just at twelve o'clock, when Jay Ellington Harper, his collar crushed and wet about his throat, his eyeglass dimmed with perspiration, his hair hanging damp over his forehead, and even the ends of his moustache dripping with moisture, was attempting to reason with a score of angry Bohemians, Tommy came quietly through the door, grip in hand. She went straight behind the grating, and standing screened by the bookkeeper's desk, handed the bag to Harper and turned to the spokesman of the Bohemians.

"What's all this business mean, Anton? Do you all come to bank at once nowadays?"

"We want 'a money, want 'a our money, he no got it, no give it," bawled the big beery Bohemian.

"O, don't chaff 'em any longer, give 'em their money and get rid of 'em, I want to see you," said Tommy carelessly, as she went into the consulting room.

When Harper entered half an hour later, after the rush was over, all that was left of his usual immaculate appearance was his eyeglass and the white flower in his buttonhole.

"This has been terrible!" he gasped. "Miss Theodosia, I can never thank you."

"No," interrupted Tommy. "You never can, and I don't want any thanks. It was rather a tight place, though, wasn't it? You looked like a ghost when I came in. What started them?"

"How should I know? They just came down like the wolf on the fold. It sounded like the approach of a ghost dance."

"And of course you had no reserve? O, I always told you this would come, it was inevitable with your charming methods. By the way, Jess sends her regrets and says she would do anything to save you. She started out with me, but she has fallen by the wayside. O, don't be alarmed, she is not hurt, just winded. I left her all bunched up by the road like a little white rabbit. I think the lack of romance in the escapade did her up about as much as anything; she is essentially romantic. If we had been on fiery steeds bespattered with foam I think she would have made it, but a wheel hurt her dignity. I'll tend bank; you'd better get your wheel and go and look her up and comfort her. And as soon as it is convenient, Jay, I wish you'd marry her and be done with it, I want to get this thing off my mind."

Jay Ellington Harper dropped into a chair and turned a shade whiter.

"Theodosia, what do you mean? Don't you remember what I said to you last fall, the night before you went to school? Don't you remember what I wrote you—"

Tommy sat down on the table beside him and looked seriously and frankly into his eyes.

"Now, see here, Jay Ellington, we have been playing a nice little game, and now it's time to quit. One must grow up sometime. You are horribly wrought up over Jess, and why deny it? She's your kind, and clean daft about you, so there is only one thing to do. That's all."

Jay Ellington wiped his brow, and felt unequal to the situation. Perhaps he really came nearer to being moved down to his stolid little depths than he ever had before. His voice shook a good deal and was very low as he answered her.

"You have been very good to me, I didn't believe any woman could be at once so kind and clever. You almost made a man of even me."

"Well, I certainly didn't succeed. As to being good to you, that's rather a break, you know; I am amiable, but I am only flesh and blood after all. Since I have known you I have not been at all good, in any sense of the word, and I suspect I have been anything but clever. Now, take mercy upon Jess—and me—and go. Go on, that ride is beginning to tell on me. Such things strain one's nerve. . . . Thank Heaven he's gone at last and had sense enough not to say anything more. It was growing rather critical. As I told him I am not at all superhuman."

After Jay Ellington Harper had bowed himself out, when Tommy sat alone in the darkened office, watching the flapping blinds, with the bank books before her, she noticed a white flower on the floor. It was the one Jay Ellington Harper had worn in his coat and had dropped in his nervous agitation. She picked it up and stood holding it a moment, biting her lip. Then she dropped it into the grate and turned away, shrugging her thin shoulders.

"They are awful idiots, half of them, and never think of anything beyond their dinner. But O, how we do like 'em!"

Henry Handel Richardson
[Ethel Florence Lindesay Richardson]
(1870–1946)

Like many women writers of the nineteenth and early twentieth centuries, such as Currer, Ellis, and Acton Bell (the Brontës), George Eliot (Mary Ann Evans), and Ralph Iron (Olive Schreiner), Richardson was a woman who wrote under a man's name. Her choice of middle name, Handel, reflects her serious interest in classical music. When Richardson left Australia in 1887 she went to Leipzig to study for a career as a concert pianist. Discovering she was ill-suited for such a profession, she married John George Robertson, a professor of Germanic literature, who, much like Virginia Woolf's husband, Leonard, nurtured her career as a writer. Robertson and Richardson (she refused to take his name) lived in Germany until 1903 and then moved to London. Though Richardson became an expatriate by the time she was seventeen, most of her fiction looks back to the memories of her Australian youth (she is considered one of the leading Australian authors). Richardson can be compared to writers such as Willa Cather and James Joyce, who set their most important works in places from which they had fled when young.

In 1919, when Richardson was forty-nine years old, she met Olga Roncoroni, a much younger woman, who moved into the Robertson-Richardson household in London and became, as biographers generally describe such relationships, Richardson's "lifelong companion." After Richardson's husband's death in 1933, the two women lived together until Richardson's death in 1946. More about Richardson's personal life will be known when her letters to an old school friend, Mary Kernot, written between 1911 and 1946, are opened to scholars in 1996.

Love between females is an important theme in Richardson's writing. *The Getting of Wisdom* (1910), which can be read as Richardson's own "Portrait of the Artist as a Young Woman," focuses on the intense affectional relationships between females at a boarding school (much like the Melbourne school Richardson attended), a subject that has interested writers who dealt with lesbian subject matter from the very beginning of the century, starting with Colette's *Claudine at School* (1900), and continuing through the century with Clemence Dane's *Regiment of Women,* Christa Winsloe's *The Child Manuela,* Dorothy Bussy's *Olivia,* Violette Leduc's *Therese and Isabelle.* Unlike some of these works, however, in Richardson's novel the love between the girls, while very passionate, is not specifically sexual. It might easily have passed for romantic friendship, even by 1910.

In later work, such as stories collected in *The End of Childhood* (1934), Richardson's image of love between women suggests a far greater sophistication about sexuality and what the psychoanalysts were positing as the genesis or etiology of female homosexuality. Her female characters in several of these stories are sexually traumatized at the height of their innocence and therefore sent along the lesbian path, as the Freudians were insisting. In the following story from *The End of Childhood*, "Two Hanged Women," the influence of the Freudians is apparent not only in the depiction of the girl's fear and disgust regarding male sexuality, but especially in her ambivalence about her overbearing mother and her confused need to retreat to the womb as an escape from the threat imposed by the phallus.

The title of the story, however, suggests an influence apart from that of the sexologists. The term "hanged" can be used as a meaningless expletive among the British, as the young man apparently does at the beginning of the story. But it has an added force in the story because it is associated, in the young man's vehemence, with "damned." And, in fact, there is little to separate "hanged" and "damned" in Richardson's depiction: These "hanged women" of the story are "damned" women, connecting them with women of Baudelaire's lesbian poem "Femmes Damnées" (see p. 299).

FURTHER READING: Henry Handel Richardson, *The Getting of Wisdom* (New York: Duffield, 1910); *The End of Childhood* (London: Heinemann, 1934). Eva Jarring Corones, *The Portrayal of Women in the Fiction of Henry Handel Richardson* (Uppsala: Lund, 1983). Leonie Kramer, *Myself When Laura: Fact and Fiction in Henry Handel Richardson's School Career* (Melbourne: Heinemann, 1967). G. A. Wilkes, "Henry Handel Richardson: Some Associations," *Southerly: The Magazine of the Australian English Association*, 47: 2 (June 1987), 207–13.

Two Hanged Women

Hand in hand the youthful lovers sauntered along the esplanade. It was a night in midsummer; a wispy moon had set, and the stars glittered. The dark mass of the sea, at flood, lay tranquil, slothfully lapping the shingle.

"Come on, let's make for the usual," said the boy.

But on nearing their favourite seat they found it occupied. In the velvety shade of the overhanging sea-wall, the outlines of two figures were visible.

"Oh, blast!" said the lad. "That's torn it. What now, Baby?"

"Why, let's stop here, Pincher, right close up, till we frighten 'em off."

And very soon loud, smacking kisses, amatory pinches and ticklings, and skittish squeals of pleasure did their work. Silently the intruders rose and moved away.

But the boy stood gaping after them, open-mouthed.

"Well, I'm *damned!* If it wasn't just two hanged women!"

Retreating before a salvo of derisive laughter, the elder of the girls said: "We'll go out on the breakwater." She was tall and thin, and walked with a long stride.

Her companion, shorter than she by a bobbed head of straight flaxen hair, was hard put to it to keep pace. As she pegged along she said doubtfully, as if in self-excuse: "Though I really ought to go home. It's getting late. Mother will be angry."

They walked with finger-tips lightly in contact; and at her words she felt what was like an attempt to get free, on the part of the fingers crooked in hers. But she was prepared for this, and held fast, gradually working her own up till she had a good half of the other hand in her grip.

For a moment neither spoke. Then, in a low, muffled voice, came the question: "Was she angry last night, too?"

The little fair girl's reply had an unlooked-for vehemence. "You know she wasn't!" And, mildly despairing: "But you never *will* understand. Oh, what's the good of . . . of anything!"

And on sitting down she let the prisoned hand go, even putting it from her with a kind of push. There it lay, palm upwards, the fingers still curved from her hold, looking like a thing with a separate life of its own; but a life that was ebbing.

On this remote seat, with their backs turned on lovers, lights, the town, the two girls sat and gazed wordlessly at the dark sea, over which great Jupiter was flinging a thin gold line. There was no sound but the lapping, sucking, sighing, of the ripples at the edge of the breakwater, and the occasional screech of an owl in the tall trees on the hillside.

But after a time, having stolen more than one side glance at her companion, the younger seemed to take heart of grace. With a childish toss of the head that set her loose hair swaying, she said, in a tone of meaning emphasis: "I like Fred."

The only answer was a faint, contemptuous shrug.

"I tell you I *like* him!"

"Fred? Rats!"

"No it isn't . . . that's just where you're wrong, Betty. But you think you're so wise. Always."

"I know what I know."

"Or imagine you do! But it doesn't matter. Nothing you can say makes any difference. I like him and always shall. In heaps of ways. He's so big and strong, for one thing: it gives you such a safe sort of feeling to be with him . . . as if nothing could happen while you were. Yes, it's . . . it's . . . well, I can't help it, Betty, there's something *comfy* in having a boy to go about with—like other girls do. One they'd eat their hats to get, too! I can see it in their eyes when we pass; Fred with his great long legs and broad shoulders—I don't nearly come up to them—and his blue eyes with the black lashes, and his shiny black hair. And I like his tweeds, the Harris smell of them, and his dirty old pipe, and the way he shows his teeth—he's got *topping* teeth—when he laughs and says *'rather!'* And other people, when they see us, look . . . well I don't quite know how to say it, but they look sort of pleased; and they make room for us and let us into the dark corner-seats at the pictures, just as if we'd a right to them. And they never laugh. (Oh, I can't *stick* being laughed at!—and that's the truth.) Yes, it's so comfy, Betty darling . . . such a warm cosy comfy feeling. Oh, *won't* you understand?"

"Gawd! why not make a song of it?" But a moment later, very fiercely: "And who is it's taught you to think all this? Who's hinted it and suggested it till you've come to believe it? . . . believe it's what you really feel."

"She hasn't! Mother's never said a word . . . about Fred."

"Words?—why waste words? . . . when she can do it with a cock of the eye. For your Fred, that!" and the girl called Betty held her fingers aloft and snapped them viciously. "But your mother's a different proposition."

"I think you're simply horrid."

To this there was no reply.

"*Why* have you such a down on her? What's she ever done to you? . . . except not get ratty when I stay out late with Fred. And I don't see how you can expect . . . being what she is . . . and with nobody but me—after all she *is* my mother . . . you can't alter that. I know very well —and you know, too—I'm not *too* putrid-looking. But"—beseechingly— "I'm *nearly* twenty-five now, Betty. And other girls . . . well, she sees them, every one of them, with a boy of their own, even though they're ugly, or fat, or have legs like sausages—they've only got to ogle them a bit—the girls, I mean . . . and there they are. And Fred's a good sort—he is, really!—and he dances well, and doesn't drink, and so . . . so why *shouldn't* I like him? . . . and off my own bat . . . without it having to be all Mother's fault, and me nothing but a parrot, and without any will of my own?"

"Why? Because I know her too well, my child! I can read her as you'd never dare to . . . even if you could. She's sly, your mother is, so sly there's no coming to grips with her . . . one might as well try to fill one's hand with cobwebs. But she's got a hold on you, a stranglehold, that nothing'll loosen. Oh! mothers aren't fair—I mean it's not fair of nature to weigh us down with them and yet expect us to be our own true selves. The handicap's too great. All those months, when the same blood's running through two sets of veins—there's no getting away from that, ever after. Take yours.

As I say, does she need to open her mouth? Not she! She's only got to let it hang at the corners, and you reek, you drip with guilt."

Something in these words seemed to sting the younger girl. She hit back. "I know what it is, you're jealous, that's what you are! . . . and you've no other way of letting it out. But I tell you this. If ever I marry—yes, *marry!*—it'll be to please myself, and nobody else. Can you imagine me doing it to oblige her?"

Again silence.

"If I only think what it would be like to be fixed up and settled, and able to live in peace, without this eternal dragging two ways . . . just as if I was being torn in half. And see Mother smiling and happy again, like she used to be. Between the two of you I'm nothing but a punch-ball. Oh, I'm fed up with it! . . . fed up to the neck. As for you . . . And yet you can sit there as if you were made of stone! Why don't you *say* something? *Betty!* Why won't you speak?"

But no words came.

"I can *feel* you sneering. And when you sneer I hate you more than any one on earth. If only I'd never seen you!"

"Marry your Fred, and you'll never need to again."

"I will, too! I'll marry him, and have a proper wedding like other girls, with a veil and bridesmaids and bushels of flowers. And I'll live in a house of my own, where I can do as I like, and be left in peace, and there'll be no one to badger and bully me—Fred wouldn't . . . ever! Besides, he'll be away all day. And when he came back at night, he'd . . . I'd . . . I mean I'd—" But here the flying words gave out; there came a stormy breath and a cry of: "Oh, Betty, Betty! . . . I couldn't, no, I couldn't! It's when I think of *that* . . . Yes, it's quite true! I like him all right, I do indeed, but only as long as he doesn't come too near. If he even sits too close, I have to screw myself up to bear it"—and flinging herself down over her companion's lap, she hid her face. "And if he tries to touch me, Betty, or even takes my arm or puts his round me . . . And then his face . . . when it looks like it does sometimes . . . all wrong . . . as if it had gone all wrong—oh! then I feel I shall have to scream—out loud. I'm afraid of him . . . when he looks like that. Once . . . when he kissed me . . . I could have died with the horror of it. His breath . . . his breath . . . and his mouth— like fruit pulp—and the black hairs on his wrists . . . and the way he looked—and . . . and everything! No, I can't, I can't . . . nothing will make me . . . I'd rather die twice over. But what am I to do? Mother'll *never* understand. Oh, why has it got to be like this? I want to be happy, like other girls, and to make her happy, too . . . and everything's all wrong. You tell me, Betty darling, you help me, you're older . . . you *know* . . .

and you can help me, if you will . . . if you only will!" And locking her arms round her friend she drove her face deeper into the warmth and darkness, as if, from the very fervour of her clasp, she could draw the aid and strength she needed.

Betty had sat silent, unyielding, her sole movement being to loosen her own arms from her sides and point her elbows outwards, to hinder them touching the arms that lay round her. But at this last appeal she melted; and gathering the young girl to her breast, she held her fast—And so for long she continued to sit, her chin resting lightly on the fair hair, that was silky and downy as an infant's, and gazing with sombre eyes over the stealthily heaving sea.

1934

Radclyffe Hall
(1880–1943)

Radclyffe Hall was born Marguerite Radclyffe Hall, but she recalled wanting to be known as Peter or John from her youth. Biographical evidence suggests some revisionism in her view of her early history—even to the extent of altering as an adult a very feminine picture of herself as a child by blacking out her long hair and thus making herself appear incontrovertibly masculine from her earliest years, like Stephen Gordon, her inverted female hero of *The Well of Loneliness*. (In fact, until she was forty, Hall allowed her hair to grow waist-length and wore it in a chignon.) But regardless of when she actually assumed her totally masculine identification, Hall presented herself, especially after the publication of *The Well of Loneliness*, as a true congenital invert, a man trapped in a woman's body. She was very impressed with the theories of the nineteenth-century sexologists who identified people like her as members of the third sex, and she even requested that Havelock Ellis, the most famous living sexologist of her day, write a preface for *The Well of Loneliness*.

In 1901, at twenty-one years of age, she inherited a fortune from her father, who had divorced her mother when Hall was a young child. Thus being freed of the economic need to marry, she was able to eschew traditionally feminine pursuits and indulge her love of hunting, fast horses, and fast cars. She had numerous love affairs with young women, and she dabbled in poetry. In 1906 she published a volume of verse, *'Twixt Earth and Stars*. The following year, when Hall was twenty-seven, she met Mabel Veronica Batten, a famous beauty of her day, a woman of style and sophistication, who was then fifty years old. Batten, called "Ladye" by her friends, was a patron of music and an amateur lieder singer of considerable repute. According to Hall, it was Ladye who civilized her, turning her away from her rougher pursuits, giving her the patina of sophistication that she had lacked, making her take herself seriously as a writer. Under Ladye's tutelage and encouragement, Hall went on to publish four more books of poetry.

Even in the five volumes of verse that she published from 1906 to 1915, before she turned to fiction, lesbian themes are broached or at least encoded. In some poems she offers a double discourse, one for the heterosexual reader and another for the lesbian reader. For example, in "Ode to Sappho," which appeared in her 1908 volume, *A Sheaf of Verses,* she begins with an epigram from Ovid that presents Sappho as being in love with a young man, Phaon. But the epigram is contradicted in the middle of the poem by hints of Sappho's interest in another kind of love. The lesbian reader of 1908, steeped in nineteenth-century French writers such as Baudelaire and Verlaine, who delighted in shocking readers with verse about lesbian ecstasy and pain (see p. 299) would have recognized through Hall's tone, language, and imagery that it was not heterosexual love to which she was referring:

> Once thou didst seek the solace of thy kind,
>   The madness of a kiss was more to thee
> Than Heaven or Hell, the greatness of thy mind
>   Could not conceive more potent ecstasy!
>
> Life was thy slave, and gave thee of her store
>   Rich gifts and many, yet with all the pain
> Of hopeless longing made thy spirit sore,
>   E'en *thou* didst yearn, and couldest not attain.
>
> Oh! Sappho, sister, by that agony
>   Of soul and body hast thou gained a place
> Within each age that shines majestic'ly
>   Across the world from out the dusk of space.
>
> Not thy deep pleasures, nor thy swiftest joys,
>   Have made thee thus, immortal and yet dear
> To mortal hearts, but that which naught destroys,
>   The sacred image of thy falling tear.
>
> Beloved Lesbian! we would dare to claim
>   By that same tear fond union with thy lot;

Yet 'tis enough, if when we breathe thy name
Thy soul but listens, and forgets us not.

In 1913 Mabel Batten began urging her young lover to turn to prose. She introduced Hall to her friend, the publisher William Heinemann, who was encouraging when Hall presented him with some of her short stories but said he would prefer to publish a novel by her. It was more than ten years, however, before Hall produced her first novels. In 1924 she published *The Forge* and *The Unlit Lamp*. *The Forge*, a comic novel, barely hints at lesbianism in the guise of a married woman's brief infatuation with a female artist who inspires her to want to try her hand at art. The married woman ends, however, by giving up her unrealistic ambitions and returning to her far-from-perfect marriage. *The Unlit Lamp*, which is arguably Hall's best novel, goes much further, describing a love relationship between two women that is ultimately frustrated by one of the women's lack of courage to leave her mother's home and claim her right to her own life. The heterosexual reader, or any reader familiar with the literature of romantic friendship, might easily miss the point that the relationship being depicted was lesbian. Hall avoids using explicit terms, does not describe the relationship in the medical language that was already being used with regard to love between women, and never suggests that the women are sexual together. But undoubtedly many lesbian readers understood well enough what Hall was intending.

The idyllic relationship between Hall and Ladye had been disrupted by 1915 when Hall met Una Troubridge, an artist and wife of a naval officer. After some months Ladye discovered the seriousness of the affair between Hall and Una, and she had a stroke that killed her. Hall, distraught at Ladye's death, attempted to end the relationship with Una, whose persistence dissuaded her. In 1918 Una got a legal separation from her husband, and the two women remained together until Hall's death in 1943. Una and Hall became involved in spiritualism (a fad of their day) in order to contact Ladye's ghost and ask for forgiveness.

Una, like Ladye, was extremely supportive of Hall's endeavors as an author. She encouraged Hall to write *The Well of Loneliness*, although she realized its publication would expose her, along with Hall, as a lesbian during unsympathetic times. Both of them saw the novel as a political piece of literature whose goal was to encourage tolerance for love between women. It is directly addressed not to Hall's lesbian readers but to heterosexuals, of whom she begs understanding and sympathy. Hall reasoned that the best way to promote tolerance was to argue that homosexuals could not help being as they were, that they were born with their "condition." To assist her in her argument she called on what she believed to be medical knowledge, even eliciting the help of Havelock Ellis, who, in response to her plea, wrote a preface for the novel, vouching that *The Well of Loneliness* was indeed a genuine depiction of female congenital inversion. For her pains, the book was banned in England on the charge that it was obscene, despite attempts by leading writers of the day such as Virginia Woolf and E. M. Forster to argue in its favor. But, perhaps because of the ban, *The Well of Loneliness* became the most famous novel about love between women ever to be written. It reflected and further promoted the stereotype of the lesbian as a man trapped in a woman's body.

When *The Well of Loneliness* was under trial for obscenity, Una stood staunchly by her in public, as Hall says in one of the letters in this section. Theirs was a solid relationship. In 1934, however, Hall, then a woman of fifty-four who had achieved fame not only as a novelist but as the primary spokesperson for the female invert, met Evguenia Souline, a Russian émigrée nurse in her thirties, who had been hired to take care of Una during an illness. Souline, as Hall preferred to call her, became Hall's mistress, though Hall continued to live with Una. Long after the passion was over Hall took some financial responsibility for Souline and continued to be solicitous of her welfare.

Hall seems to have seen herself in the relationship with Souline much as she depicted Stephen Gordon in her relationship with Mary. It was Hall who was the congenital invert here, and Souline who was a very feminine woman. But, as Hall says of Stephen and Mary in *The Well of Loneliness,* the relationship took on other dimensions as well: Stephen is "all things to Mary; father, mother, friend and lover, all things, and Mary is all things to her—the child, the friend, the beloved, all things."

FURTHER READING: Michael Baker, *Our Three Selves: The Life of Radclyffe Hall* (New York: William Morrow, 1985). Lillian Faderman and Ann Williams, "Radclyffe Hall and the Lesbian Image," *Conditions*, I: 1 (April 1977), 31–41. Claudia Stillman Franks, *Beyond the Well of Loneliness: The Fiction of Radclyffe Hall* (London: Avebury, 1982). Rebecca O'Rourke, *Reflecting on The Well of Loneliness* (London: Routledge, 1989). Sonja Ruehl, "Inverts and Experts: Radclyffe Hall and the Lesbian Identity," in *Feminism, Culture and Politics*, eds. Rosalind Brunt and Caroline Rowan (London: Lawrence and Wishart, 1982. Una Troubridge, *The Life of Radclyffe Hall* (New York: Citadel Press, 1961). Gillian Whitlock, " 'Everything is Out of Place': Radclyffe Hall and the Lesbian Literary Tradition," *Feminist Studies*, 13:3 (Fall 1987), 555–82.

Letters

July 20, 1934

My very dear. Your *darling stiff* little letter came yesterday. I wish that I could write French as well as you write English—only in one place did your English go wrong: in my country one would not—in the circumstances—have begun: "My dear Miss Hall"! Try to get it into your head that never again can I be "Miss Hall" to you. Call me anything or nothing, as you will, but not that except when you are speaking of me to strangers.

And now about our plans for the 26th. I want to change them. What I want you to do on that day is this: meet me at Lapeyroure (you know, Quai des Grands Augustines) at 12.30 and we will lunch there alone together, just you and I. After lunch we will go back to my hotel where I shall have a sitting room and there (if you are willing) we will spend the afternoon. We shall be quite alone and able to talk undisturbed.

. . . I am counting on this meeting in Paris as I have counted on few things in my life.

July 24, 1934

Darling. Thank you for your little note of welcome. Yes, I am here in Paris, and it seems so strange that only a few weeks ago I did not know that Paris meant you. I want to come to you—its [sic] red hell to be here and not to be able to see you until the day after tomorrow and then only for a few hours. But I cannot come nor am I going to ring you up, even though I long to hear your voice speaking to me in your darling broken English. Please, Soulina, never learn to speak English quite properly, will you? No, you can't do anything for me except to think of me a very great deal until we meet on Thursday, yes, and after. One other thing you can do also, and that is to take a taxi on Thursday. I insist upon this, and you will pocket your pride and let me pay for the taxi too. I am not going to rush forward and pay the man myself that would be to [sic] obvious. You will pay him and I will pay you later—that is how it will be done, says John.

Bless you. There is so much I want to say but my pen won't write it.

Yours, John

July 27, 1934

It was as though you had taken my strength away with you, leaving an empty tank behind, and last night I slept from sheer exhaustion. I slept, Souline, as once before in my life I slept as the result of fearful grief. . . .

But now I am awake, very terribly awake. I woke up almost before it was light with those last words of yours hammering on my heart. "I can't believe that this is the last time I shall see you." And this is going to be a day of deep pain—and there will be many days of such deep pain, and I am tormented because of you, and this torment is now only partly of the senses—but is now an even more enduring thing and more impossible to cure—any more, because it is a torment of tenderness, of yearning over you, of longing to help you—of longing to take you into my arms and comfort you indefinitely and most sweetly as I would comfort a little child, whispering to you all sorts of foolish words of love that has nothing to do with nobody. And then I would want you to fall asleep with your head on my breast for a while, Souline, and then I want you to wake up again and feel glad because I was lying beside you, and because you were touching this flesh of mine that is so consumed by reason of your flesh, yet so suffocated and crushed by my pity, that the whole of me would gladly melt into tears, becomming [sic] a cup of cold water for your drinking. And if this is wrong than [sic] there is no God, but only some cruel and hateful fiend who creates such a one as I am for the pleasure that he will gain from my ultimate destruction. But there is a God, make no mistake, and I have my rightful place in his creation, and if you are as I am you share that place, and our God is more merciful than the world, and since He made us is understanding. And He knows very well what the end will be, seeing what you and I cannot see, knowing why you and I have been forced to meet. And why this great hassle has come upon us. Souline, I implore you to cling to this belief, because without faith our souls will be undone at this time of unendurable suffering.

I am haunted by the thought of your loneliness, by the knowledge that I am leaving you alone, by my terror that you will fret or get ill, and perhaps do something reckless and most foolish, for me you seem even younger than your age, and then you have no one to whom you can talk or go to for advice and help in your need, and this thought make [sic] me feel that I must go mad. But I shall not go mad, but will keep very sane for your sake, so that I can always help you.

Oh, I know what you are enduring this day—every mile of the road I am there beside you, and your hand is in mine, and your heart is in mine, and your pain is my pain, and your need is my need, and I cannot, no, I cannot see the light but just shuffle along beside you in the darkness, and yet I know that the light exists, and this is faith, to realize the light even if only painfully and dimly. . . . I have got to make you also realize the light is no less bright because I may fail to submerge the flesh entirely in the spirit.

. . . While we are both in this world there is hope—and surely, surely we shall meet again. It is as though I struck the rock with the staff of my love and at last the spring gushed out, out of your heart into mine, beloved.

. . . For you are not made out of ice and this I well know, my little virgin, and I agonized to take your virginity and to bind you to me with the Chains of the flesh, because I had and have so vast a need that my wretched body has become tormented, but through it all my spirit cries out to you, Souline, and it tells you that love is never a sin, that the flesh may be weak but the spirit is strong—yesterday it was my spirit that saved you. Must I always save you? I do not know. I cannot see far beyond this pain—this pain that I feared would come with the morning.

This is a very terrible day, for we are so near, and I long to come to you and make you forget everything but me—God help me, I ought not to write like this for our time is not yet. . . . But I love you, I love you.

If you also love me you will not fail to write, will take care of yourself in everyway, and will not quite shut me out of your life—that would break me completely, utterly, and I do not feel that you ought to break me. But you will not Soulina, because you love me.

Lady Troubridge has been very wonderful, she sends you her love and asks me to tell you that she will write to you from Sirmione.

I cannot, I dare not write anymore, and since you have your living to earn and I a marked woman, as I told you, I beg you to lock up this letter of mine together with the other letters. Souline, I do love you too terribly.
    John

July 31, 1934
    My beloved.
    . . . I had been counting on this—I had thought "I shall see her once more before I go back and take up the burdens of my everyday life—perhaps I shall see her several times even"; it was something that Una said that made me dare to hope. And then in Paris she seemed so merciful. You remember that she sent you her love and said that she would write to you, then yesterday she did actually write to you. Last evening I got your letter in answer to mine written on the Friday before I left for Italy, and your letter made me long so much to see you and touch you and hear you speak if only once again, and I said: "I shall try to see Souline on my way home, I shall go and see her." And some how, God knows why, I thought Una would consent, for she knows how it is with me, with us, and she knows something that I have not told you: she knows that I am ill with misery—not seriously ill, nothing for you to worry about, but all is not very well with me, which in the circumstances is natural. Then I found that she means to keep us apart. I dare not blame her, I do not blame her. She and I have been together 18 years. When all the world seemed to be against me at the

time of the "Well of Loneliness" persecutions, Una stood shoulder to shoulder with me, fighting every inch of the terrific battle. She has given me all of her interest and indeed all of her life ever since we made common cause, therefore she has a right to do what she is doing and she will not ceed [*sic*] this right, but insists on it with all her strength which lies—as she well knows—in her physical weakness.

. . . She endlessly hurled herself onto the floor and behaved as though she were going demented. I think that it may very well be that her operation has made her excitable—women are like that after those operations. Then she has reminded me over and over again until I have nearly gone mad, that I have always stood for fidelity in the case of inverted unions, that the eyes of the inverted all over the world are turned towards me, that they have respected me because for years my union has been faithful and open. And when she says that I can find no answer, because she is only telling the truth—I have tried to help my own poor lot by setting an example, especially of courage, and thousands have turned to me for help and found it, if I may believe their letters, and she says that I want to betray my inverts who look upon me almost as their leader. Oh, but what's the use of telling you any more of the hell that I went through last night and this morning —I have a debt of honour to pay, I am under a terrific obligation, and can I shirk the intolerable load? It is less whether I can shirk my load than whether I have the strength to bear it. But one small comfort would Una concede, she agrees that we shall write to each other—I think she knows that there comes a stage when human nature can no longer endure, and then simply I cannot endure never hearing from you—that would kill me, I should die, Soulina. . . .

July 31, 1934 (second letter of the day)

I am haunted by these words in your letter of the 28th: "But can't love be only spiritual?" They seem to me to be a kind of appeal—as though something in you, your virginity, your blessed innocence, your youth (and like all your people you are young and rather undeveloped for your age in spite of being so fine in your profession and so clever in a thousand other respects—yes, in matters of sex you are still very young) was asking for mercy and pity in my hands, was still asking this as you asked it in Paris, so that I scourged myself but spared you—for remember this is my favor, beloved, remember it always when thinking of John—I spare you because I love you so intensely. And if it is love of the spirit that you crave from me, that only, and nothing less exhalted [*sic*], then for your sake I give you that love. With the whole of me I desire to know this—I offer it to you beloved, on my knees, I say: "Take it—here is the love of my spirit. And if it were possible for us to be together, even living together day to night, even sleeping clasped in each others arms as I have so often pictured our sleeping—I think—I think that if you desired it I could put my body in chains, for although my body is terribly strong, having needs for you that are intensely urgent, yet the love of my spirit is intensely strong too, and its great need of you is equally urgent.

. . . Souline if you will promise to be careful, and to take care of yourself for my miserable sake, then I shall have still greater cause to bless you.

Always yours
John

August 4, 1934

. . . When the post arrives bringing nothing from you I get panic stricken, feeling that I have lost touch with you.

. . . When I get back to Paris we will have a long talk about your future plans—this course you want to take—you remember you told me something about it—perhaps I shall be able to help you over that—pay the fees whatever they are.

August 7, 1934

Is it foolish to wish to help someone one loves, someone whom one cannot really protect from hardship and strain and the buffets of the world because she is not free to protect them? . . . If all this is foolish then I am your Fool and as such you will have to take me, Souline. But you also say that you "love me to [sic] much." That is utterly false, you don't love me enough—perfect love knows neither doubting nor has false pride, it knows only that while it would give all things it would also gladly accept all things, my Souline. . . . These are the thoughts of perfect love, and I beg you to let your dear love for me think them and thus become free from the smallest blemish. Accept the miserable £100 and by doing so make me eternally your debtor.

. . . You say that you will not write unless I *insist that you shall do so.* I do insist, let there be no mistake. I insist upon this in sheer self-preservation. If I lose sight of you utterly and entirely as I must do if you will not write to me, then I shall most surely lose sight of myself—I shall lose myself in a wilderness of doubt, anxiety and complete desolation. Is it for this that you came into my life, in order that you might destroy my life and destroy what is left of my inspirations?

. . . But adoring you as I do I could make it—for the physical aspect is so much less than the other and spiritual side of my love—I suppose you would call it: "The love of the Spirit."

August 11, 1934

. . . P.S. About your clothes. Don't laugh, but I often think about your clothes. . . . I don't want you to look like the Russian Ballet, but unless you remember your type you look wrong. . . . The next time you are getting yourself new clothes remember what I say and dress to your type, it should not cost anymore money to do so.

August 13, 1934

Darling . . .

. . . How strange it is how little I know about you the woman I have come to love and how little that woman knows about me—we know that we love each other intensely and this is all that matters, my Souline; and yet, just because I do love you so much there are thousands of less important things that I am longing to know about you, and this is not curiosity but the need to feel, to creep very close, to creep into your every day life and thoughts—even foolish and trivial things become dear when they are a part of the creature one loves—Don't you feel this about me too? Yes you must; and letters are so unsatisfactory—though without them where should I be these days? . . . Well, now, what do I know about you, sweetheart?

I know a name—Evguenia Souline; perhaps it is your true name perhaps not—but to me you will never be anything but Soulina, because by that name I first loved you. I know that you are afraid of life. This I think I knew the moment I met you—I told you that you were afraid of the life at Bagnoles. I know that you are a little afraid of love though now your fear cannot help you; *love you must,* so better make friends with love. I know that you have suffered very deeply, so deeply that you have become very silent and reserved, have put on a kind of armor, defending yourself against the world, or is it perhaps against yourself? I am not yet quite sure, but one day you will tell me. I know that you brood, you brood a great deal—remembering things that I can only guess at, but I think they are things that cause you regret, that sometimes make you hate your present position, and make you not only hate it, Souline, but resent it with everything in you—very bitterly indeed I feel that you resent your position. And one other thing I feel that I know—some one once gave you an emmotional [*sic*] shock—who was it, I wonder—a man or a woman? And did you love them as much as you love me? I don't want to think too much about this because I am now so far away, and I can't hear your voice, or see your dear face, or feel your arms round me—Did you love them as much? Listen, they can't have loved you as much as I do—I know from my soul they can't. I love you more than you have ever been loved or will ever be as long as you live—so forget about them *in me,* Souline. And remember this oh, you beloved of my heart: the circumstances that have made you what you are—lonely and homeless and none too rich, are the circumstances that have brought us together. But for all that has happened we might never have met, for you might well have still been in Russia. Could you have done without meeting me? I say that now you have met me, you could not—and so it all had to be as it was, the resentment, the pain, the years of suffering all because I was waiting for you in the world —I, who have so little to offer as I realized with my own bitterness, for the bitterness is not *all* yours, beloved, but I who can and do offer you my love, the love of my body, my mind and my spirit. . . . But because we are human I want to protect you, to do for you little simple humble things— put you to bed early when you feel tired, take care of *you* whose whole life is spent in taking such care of other people. I want to discuss what clothes you buy, and to find out what is your favourite sweet, even what things you like to eat. And then I want to order those things and sit and watch you while you eat them! I want your bathroom to be very nice, your bedroom to be very large and sunny. I want you to have everything on this earth that I can possibly afford to buy you. This is my particular bitterness, that your life must be made apart from mine. But at least my devotion is mine to give, and at least you can let me help you a little—that I demand in return for my love—that you let me help you, my obediant [sic] servant. I am wondering whether you are going away; but of course you will let me know in good time. Meanwhile remember that the world is not so large and that we are going to meet in Paris.

August 14, 1934

Beloved . . . Yesterday came no letter from you and again there is none this morning.

. . . Surely a letter will come very soon if only because I need it. . . . I am doing my best to enjoy myself here as you told me I must for the sake of our love, but you have set me a difficult task—this place of all others cries out for fulfillment—this place in my present stress is hell, were you here instead of me you would understand; when we meet I will tell you about it. Darling I think that you have bewitched me—there are times when I feel you so intensely, as though you were dragging my heart out of me, as though you were calling me—Do you feel this? Do you feel as though I were calling you, as though you must leave everything and come to me? It comes over me in waves, and when this happens I wonder if it is happening to you also. Yesterday it began at lunch time; it ceased for a little in the afternoon but began again more violently . . . in the evening, so that for most of the night I lay awake thinking about you, and wondering about you, and longing to have your body in my arms, close, very close against my own body, and to hear you speak words of love. Yes, even if you must lie innocently (like a child) in my arms—I could even let you lie innocently for the blessid [sic] relief of feeling your pressure. What are you, who are you who have done this thing to me? If I knew that I would not see you again then I swear to you that I would not go on living. Beside you all the rest of my life seems nothing. And the way in which it has struck me down, so swiftly, like an evergreen blown in the dark. And with you, you have told me, this thing came swiftly—I think that you knew this. Yet for so many years we lived in the same world—were we always waiting, [while] we lived, for our meeting? What does it mean? I am older than you, I am possibly therefore wiser than you, and yet I am like a leaf tossed by the wind, because of my love I have no resistance. I believe that some women enjoy a sense of power—but no, that is not like you at all. Forgive me, I don't know what I am writing, beloved. And little things now get the upper hand of me—last night I worried because I imagined that you might resent what I wrote about your clothes, might think I had been impertinent even. Darling, you didn't mind what I wrote? Its only because I adore you so completely that I keep on thinking of first this then that in connection with every detail of you.

Well, Souline, what ever has gone before in your life, you know now and will always know one thing as long as you live, and it is this: You have taken me body and soul into your hands; all that I am, all that I have become through years of God alone knows what struggle, what fighting for a right to recognition, what hours and months and years of hard work—all that I have become because of those things is now in those very white hands of yours—be gentle and merciful to it, beloved. Your hands must have hurried many back to life, must have eased so many when they were in pain, and surely they will be no less merciful to me—I trust myself in your hands absolutely. I love you so much. I am going to stop writing because sometimes you say that I frighten you and this is a poor return for your love. You do love me with the whole of you, don't you, Souline? Are you *perfectly certain* that you love me like that? Suppose you could never see me again, never hear from me again—suppose it were to you as though I were dead? Ask yourself what you would do and what you would feel in those conditions? The answer will tell you whether I mean as much to you as you mean to me; and I want you to be very sure of this answer.

Yours, John

September 6, 1934

. . . I'm sorry if she's a very sick woman, but I'm not going to have you be anyone's slave. If your [sic] anyone's slave your [sic] going to be mine, only I'd hate to have you my slave—I prefer to have the other way round. Well, dearest, do what you know to be best to ensure perfect peace while I'm in Paris.

... I am starving for you, that's God's truth, Soulina. Be kind to me in Paris my little child—please take me into your arms and be very kind, please tell me that you want me as I want you, and then kiss me the way I taught you to kiss. . . .

September 7, 1934

No, you won't be frightened when you see me—I hope you will be too happy to think, and when one can't think one can't be frightened, for fear is the result of your imagination. But you don't know quite what you think, do you Sweetheart.

... There is so much beauty in being in love, in giving oneself completely to another as I have given myself to you, so that I have no real life at all except the life I am living through you, and now all that I see I seem to see through you. . . .

... Do they make you feel so shy to write them? That's foolish, sweetheart; and another thing, I should never think that your efforts were childish—nor would I laugh. I might want to cry because you are still so innocent somehow, and that touches all that is pitiful in me; so then I am torn in half—one side of me longs to destroy that innocence and put a more vital state in its place, one side of me clamours to make a woman of you, so then whatever happens in your life you will at least have known the meaning of passion—not in "theory," but in practice, beloved, and believe me a mighty big gulf is between them; the other side of me longs to take you in my arms and let you quietly sleep like a baby.

September 8, 1934

Are you really afraid my little child? Are you truly afraid of John? Sweetheart then I am afraid of you. . . . Oh, foolish and pathetic creature you are.

... Sweetheart, you want to be in my arms—you want to feel me close, very close, and you want to feel my kisses, beloved.

... Your (sic) not the only woman who has ever been desired in this world. And you certainly won't be the last, but no woman could have possibly been more desired than you are.

September 13, 1934

My own little Chink—do take care of yourself—must you sit up until eleven at night when you have to get up at 6. every morning? And please don't forget to buy those flowers for your room, and to have your photograph taken, and to go on loving me more and more, so when I come and take you in my arms you won't be able to speak for love, or to breathe either when I've kissed you.

September 22, 1934

Soulina, be at peace—I am not going to force you to do anything that you don't want to do. Dearest, one does not force a woman's love. You are your own to give or to withhold.

. . . God bless you my darling—my poor, poor child—now, stop being scared—I insist upon that, because by being so scared you insult me.

Your friend,
John

October 4, 1934

My beloved. Since we have slept in each other's arms, beloved seems such an inadequate word—but then there can't be any word in any language that can possibly express what I feel about you.

Soulina, take care of your precious self—you who no longer belong to yourself, you who belong to me and my life, to me, darling, who couldn't go on living without you.

October 9, 1934

I can't see anything but your room in Paris, I can't feel anything but your arms and your lips—and yet the room is far away, and your arms and your lips are not against my body—Soulina, I am mad for you today—I am ill with longing for you and only you can cure me.

October 21, 1934

. . . You see, my dear, I had thought that your coming would fill you with happiness—was I wrong? Moreover I have done many foolish little things, the things that are done very often by lovers. I have sent my sitting room curtains to be cleaned, have ordered a new suit and some new shirts, have been planning about having flowers in the flat and also in our appartment [sic] at Folkestone—have been thinking about what wine you would like the first night at dinner, and telling myself that on the first night there should be no love-making because you would feel tired after the journey and the crossing.

. . . Soulina, I am giving you all I have to give of love and desire and thought and care. I am giving you so much more than my body—I am giving you my mind and my spirit, Soulina. I have not played my cards with precautions and skill as I have often done in the past—as many a man will do with a woman; no, I have let you see into my heart, I have let you see just how much you mean to me.

. . . I have thought that you did certain things against your will, that you gave yourself to me in order to please me. I have thought that you turned like a poor trapped creature first this way then that, when suddenly confronted with having to come and be with me in England, and this is why your letter was full of such trivial worries about nothing. . . .

. . . I will not accept half a loaf from you—give me a whole loaf as I give it to you, love me utterly or leave me, Soulina.

October 22, 1934

About money, I hope you have enough. Of course, I *insist* on paying your fare, don't argue. About this there is simply *no question,* but if you've got enough for the moment I'd rather settle the paying part in England. And when you are in my arms you won't mind letting me talk to you about money.

October 23, 1934

. . . Darling. I don't very much like your Princess—she sounds mad and to me not awfully attractive, nor do I think she sounds good for your health. You know what I told you about drinking spirits—however I suppose I am not your keeper. If you want to get drunk what am I to say? Spirits are the most fatal things for T.B., the most ignorant fool on Earth knows this, and you know it who have had a medical training. You are healed but you should not run any risks. Is there nothing in this life for you to keep well for? Do you want your lungs to go wrong again—do I count for nothing? Am I less than a cocktail? I am not angry only terribly worried.

. . . Darling, Darling, do stop drinking, please. You can't think how worried and wretched I am—just utterly wretched.

October 29, 1934

Instructions!!!!

1) Take a *return* ("back and forth") ticket as far as Folkestone only, *providing* the "back and forth" ticket is good for one month. If it is not good for one month, then take a single (one way) ticket to Folkestone.

Cloths [sic]

1) For Gods sake bring your fur coat, here it has turned abominably cold. Also a fur coat may be needed for the evening.

2) Bring a coat and skirt or two—I liked you in the one you wore the day I left.

3) Bring an evening dress if you happen to have one—it may never be needed but better be on the safe side. If you have not

got one don't go and buy one in Paris, wait 'till you get here so that I can choose it.

4) Bring Soulina, otherwise John will soon require a gravestone.

November 20, 1934 [wire]

AM WITH YOU ALWAY TO THE END AND BEYOND—JOHN

November 24, 1934

. . . I cannot judge yet, but this I want you *clearly to understand, you are to do nothing of any kind without first consulting me.* You are not to get impulsive, not to act on the advice of any one until you have heard my advice. You belong exclusively to me now and I shall look after you, but I can only do this if you consult me before doing anything of a serious nature. *No acting on impulse please, my heart.* Impulse in your case must be curbed at the moment.

November 27, 1934

. . . Soulina, you are not a beautiful woman. I suppose I was right when I thought you were ugly—but while I thought this I fell madly in love, and now I can see no face but yours, no face seems beautiful to me but yours —your queer little ugly, alian [sic] Chink face. And no voice seems beautiful to me but yours—your queer, alian [sic] voice speaking broken English. . . .

December 4, 1934

. . . When we are together we will talk and talk of "we three" as you call it—that is if you wish to. My beloved what do you mean by being "privileged"? I am not, and I have not been for years, the least bit in love with Una. I feel a deep gratitude towards her, a deep respect and a very deep affection—also an enormously strong sense of duty, all this for reasons that I have told you. For you I feel what? A consuming need that is not the need of our bodies only, and this you well know, as if you don't, well, if circumstances made it impossible for us to be lovers (which Heaven forbid!) I would be prepared to prove this to you. I feel for you the strong, vital love—the combative love, the protective love, the anxious, yearning, restless love—and very often the selfless love of the very young.

. . . Feel loved and protected and "priviledged [sic]" my own—surely sitting beside the fire in my heart is a priviledge [sic], isn't it beloved?

December 10, 1934

I say no & no & no to your doing floor duty. Firstly it is much to [sic] straining for you physically and secondly it would entirely spoil our time together in Paris. Don't please even think of it—I won't have it for you. Beloved child, you will get a job eventually and whenever you're out of work you simply must let me help you. Do you want me to go mad with worrying about you? You don't? Very well then stop being "rebellious," end this at once; if you don't then I'll take away the smart collars and put on a shabby old one, on which will be engraved: "This is Chink-face-please beat it!"

. . . Darling, how much is an orchestra seat at your Paris theatres? Let me know this and I will send you the price of 2 seats every now and then—you can take Liza or anyone you like. This will give *me* pleasure— a great deal of pleasure.

These are my question [sic] quick please answer:

1) What is price of theatre seat?
2) Have you found care of your ring?
3) Do you know of a really first class hair specialist who could treat your hair?

. . . Again I say no to floor duty—no, no—your health is to [sic] precious—I will not consent to any work that is so overtiring.

December 10, 1934 (second letter of the day)

. . . But darling you have me, and I forbid you to worry. I can't give you as much as I should like—but I can send the £10 a month until you can get work—I wish it could be more. You are *not* to get depressed and worried this only reacts on me and then I get worried and depressed and my work goes to pot.

. . . Oh, my dearest—if only I could protect you more—do more for you. Love you more I could not. I am thinking how cold your room must be at 6 a.m.—I want you to find another room—you and I are going to look for one together.

. . . Are you getting enough to eat? Soulina—I am worried in case you are not. Please eat nourishing food, my darling.

December 18, 1934 (third letter of the day)

. . . Soulina, sweetheart—my love & my joy—I can't find words to express my devotion, my love, my tenderness, my respect—the whole thing is almost too big for my heart, my heart is just bursting out of my body. Oh, if only I had you here in my arms—I think I would rock you very quietly, like a baby. I think I'd rather like you to cry, to cry very hard so that I could comfort—yes, I'm sure that I rather like you to cry. Cry for me, darling, when I'm with you in Paris!

December 29, 1934

. . . What is it? Try to tell me my darling. I am rocking you in my arms like a baby—I am saying: "There—there—it's all right my darling, Johnnie's here—you're quite safe in Johnnie's arms." That's what I'm saying, beloved.

December 30, 1934

. . . I was torn in half by desire and pity. Do you remember how I fed you that night? I fed you from my plate as though you were a baby. I can see you now, sitting hunched up at the table, all broken and sorrowful and terribly anxious, and you spoiling everything through nerves and through being so terribly excited yet apprehensive—a most fatal combination. I have had many women, as you know, in my life, but no one quite like you, and I adore you. Darling, I am all on fire for you this morning—I keep thinking of the joy I have in your body—my own body is thoroughly unruly this morning. If I had you here, and we two alone, I would show you whether I had ceased to love you. . . .

. . . Darling I simply *must* get down to work. "For men must work and women must weap [*sic*]." At best this unhappy invert must work, but Soulina *must not weap* [*sic*]. *I won't have it.*

April 4, 1935 [Telegram from London]

HAVE YOUR LETTER OF TWENTY THIRD THESE ARE MY ABSOLUTE ORDERS EAT WELL TAKE TAXIS KEEP ROOM WELL HEATED TIP CONSIERGE [SIC] TO LOOK AFTER FIRE AND STOVE DO NOT NEGLECT TREATMENTS KEEP AWAY FROM CINIMAS [SIC] AND SO ON FOR THE MOMENT WEAR FUR COAT ABOVE ALL SLEEP WITH YOUR HEAD AWAY FROM WINDOW DEVOTEDLY—JOHN

May 25, 1935

On the one side of the scales is Johnnie with all Johnnie's drawbacks of disposition and circumstances and so on. On the other side of the scales is life without Johnnie—never to see me any more, never again to hear my voice scold a little—life as it was before we found each other—no, not quite, because now you know another life—the life we are having as lovers. Beloved—when you feel angry and blue because Earth cannot turn into Heaven—when you wish that I were a man and could marry you & give you more protection—when all the black thoughts leap into your mind and wound you until you must turn and wound me—when this happens, weigh me up—weigh our love on the scales against what life would be without it. . . . Oh, I understand all that you feel—yes I do—and I want to put my arms around you and comfort you as I write this. Comfort you for being a little white Russian who must bear with so many ridiculous restrictions. Comfort you for having had to go through ill health & anxiety all alone. . . . Comfort you for every sorrow and pain.

May 31, 1935 (Written after sending a wire with the same message)
How dare you have accepted a contagious case? Oh, Soulina you are my despair—you are that! Thank God you have been taken off the case. I forbid you to take a contagious case again and have wired you to that effect. Also I do not wish you to take *any other* case before coming here. If you do so I am going to be angry. I am serious—I mean what I say.
. . . Someone has got to be the master, my child, and I am going to be that person. There is only one will and that is John's will, and that will is for your own good being prompted by love and devotion.

May 31, 1935 (Third letter of the day)
. . . And I can't help wondering why you were so pig-headed. But I don't want to nag, for you've done it now; but I do want you to answer the following questions. . . .

1) What risk of contagion precisely did you run?
2) Was it a very serious risk?
3) How long before we shall know that you are safe—how long is the incubation period?

. . . And what I forbid is your taking any other case of any kind before your holiday. Have I made this clear? I *will not* have it, Soulina. . . . I am not to be disobeyed about this. I've had quite enough of giving in to you.
. . . no more going against my judgement—no more of it. My judgement is sound and wise, whereas you have no judgement.

July 18, 1937
. . . As long as I know that you are happy and taking care of yourself I think I can work. Of course, I worry about you—wondering if you are getting wet, wondering if you are catching cold—oh, you know, wondering all manner of things; but I must trust you, I do trust you. For my sake, beloved, keep that Heart which is my Heart, beating.
. . . I have no words in which to express my love & my desire, but also

my little, little child—the child that through some unkind trick of fate—
you cannot give me [*sic*]. And since you cannot give me a child you must
sometimes become one in order to pacify me. Oh, I know that you are big
and independent and all that, but I demand of our love that you sometimes
become as the little child for who I so much long—the little Chink child
—our child, our most precious spoiled and naughty little Chink. Say you
are also my little, little Chink, if you do not say this I will beat you!

September 18, 1938
. . . Darling, *are* you taking care of my Piggie? Wire, good Piggie Hall (that
is suggestion!) wire, good and careful Piggie Hall who puts on warm coats,
and keeps its hoofs dry, and never goes out without an enormous Pig umbrella! Also, who goes to bed nice and early. And only drinks milk and
soda water—a wonderful pig who is nearly a saint—and oh, so good tem-
pered, gentle and loving.

February 9, 1939
Never think, never delude yourself into thinking that I am resigned to the
idea of your spending the winter in Paris. I am not so resigned and never
shall be. But since you insisted, I thought the matter over from every angle
and came to the conclusion that if in addition to all the other risks, I let
you remain in Paris without money, the risks would be doubled, and I
could not bear it.

. . . but alas, Piggie promises mean very little.

Well, Evguenia, I am your home remember, I am your family, your
refuge and your home, your hope in the present and in the future. I am
indeed all you have, so far, in the world and without me my Pig would be
very much along and Pigs hate it when they feel deserted and lonely.

You have come to a turning point in your life when you have just *got*
to have a sense of values.

March 3, 1939
. . . And so there must never be anything between us ever again unless you
desire me. I must never be tempted to debase you, Evguenia, or myself even
would you let me. At one time, perhaps for only a short time, you and I
had a perfect physical relation. Could it ever come again, could we ever
recapture the blessed harmony of our bodies, the blessed sense of peace
that came after? Maybe, I do not know, Evguenia. Well my dear, my very
dear "friend." . . .

March 9, 1939
. . . And, yes, you did want me first as just a friend, and maybe it was there that I went wrong, maybe I ought never have let you know that I had fallen so terribly in love, and then asked you to take me as your lover.

Vita Sackville-West
(1892–1962)

Vita Sackville-West suffered a hard penalty for not having been born male. Knole, her beloved family estate, the largest remaining private residence in England, had belonged to her ancestors for hundreds of years and would have been hers if she had not been a woman. But Knole was inherited instead by a male relative who could have had no claim to the property had Vita's parents produced a male heir. Her gender discontent manifested itself early, perhaps because she was aware early of the inevitable loss of Knole. She recalled that at Knole, where she lived until she was twenty-one, she "made a great deal of being hardy and as much like a boy as possible." She was further penalized for having been born female by being denied the university education she would have loved to have, and, as a woman of the upper class, was urged only to marry appropriately. It is no wonder that in her fantasy life she sometimes saw herself as a man.

The sexologists who so simplistically defined the lesbian in congenital terms as a man trapped in a woman's body often failed to take into account reasons that women such as Vita Sackville-West had for envying masculinity and wanting to claim it for themselves. The sexologists failed to understand female anger at the rules of male privilege—anger that would cause women to want to violate men's prerogatives through their own belligerent claims to masculinity. Vita's insight into her hostility toward the authorities that neatly segregated what was appropriate to men from what was appropriate to women is revealing. As she observed in her journal about her own experience in passing as a man: "I never appreciated anything so much as living like that with my tongue perpetually in my cheek, and in defiance of every policeman that I passed." But a further complexity in Vita Sackville-West's gender identification and sexual orientation is that sometimes she unquestioningly internalized the sexologists' definition of the lesbian as a man trapped in a woman's body, just as she (contradictorily) internalized the notions of Decadent literature that characterized the lesbian impulse as evil.

During girlhood and young womanhood Vita had several romantic friendships as well as a lesbian relationship. When she was eighteen she became platonic friends with Harold Nicolson, a gay man who was a career diplomat. Three years later they were engaged, but Vita continued a love affair with Rosamund Grovesnor, a very feminine woman of Vita's own class, with whom she said she "was very much in love," despite her description of Rosamund as "quite stupid."

Once Vita married Harold the relationship with Rosamund came to an end. Vita and Harold managed to produce two sons and then apparently terminated their sexual attachment. Their son Nigel, in his book about his parents, *Portrait of a Marriage*, says that Vita and Harold truly loved one another, but their love was largely platonic. Several years after the birth of Vita's sons, Violet Trefusis, a girlhood romantic friend, reappeared in Vita's life and unlocked the masculine persona that Vita had been repressing. As part of the sexual and social dynamic between them, she encouraged Vita to see herself as "Julian," while she would be Julian's woman. Violet wrote to Vita:

> You could do anything with me—or rather Julian could. I love Julian overwhelmingly, possessively, exorbitantly. For me he stands for all emancipation, for all liberty, for youth, for ambition, for attainment. He is my ideal. There is nothing he can't do. I am his slave, body and soul.

Vita's journal, in which she records her affairs with Rosamund and Violet, is reproduced in her son's book because, he claims, he knows his mother preserved the journal to share with posterity. The journal suggests a great struggle over her attraction to women, made more difficult because of her ambivalence and confusion about her masculine identification, which she associates with the dark side of her nature. Her masculinity also appears sometimes as an amusing masquerade and sometimes as a self-consciously romantic stance: she is Heathcliff out of *Wuthering Heights*, she is a male Gypsy out of nineteenth-century romantic poetry, she is a young soldier wounded in the Great War—all interesting, daring roles that were denied to women. As Vita suggests in her journal, she was acquainted with the theories of the sexologists, and they resonated with her, but it is not always easy for the reader to determine to what extent she had true conviction about her masculinity and to what extent it was a nose-thumbing and/or drama-loving pose.

After her affair with Violet came to an end, Vita was involved with a number of other women. Her sexual relationship with Virginia Woolf lasted for about a year, although they remained good friends for many more years, until Woolf's death. Woolf wrote for Vita what Nigel Nicolson describes as "the longest and most charming love letter in literature," a fanciful novel, *Orlando*, which questions accepted concepts about gender by taking the character of Vita through four centuries and permitting her to alternate between being a man and being a woman while always remaining the same person. By the time Vita was involved with Virginia Woolf her lesbian persona had apparently taken on dimensions beyond Julian. Woolf describes her as being very maternal and observes that Vita is "in short (what I have never been), a real woman."

In Vita's novel *Challenge,* written during her affair with Violet (though not published until several years later), she depicts herself as a young man—called Julian, of course—a Byronic hero who is in love with Eve, a thinly veiled characterization of Violet. In her only novel to present love between women in clear terms, *The Dark Island,* written almost fifteen years later, neither of the women is masculine and gender identity is not seen as integral to lesbian identity.

FURTHER READING: Vita Sackville-West, *Challenge* (New York: George H. Doran, 1924); *The Dark Island* (New York: Doubleday, 1934). Louise A. DeSalvo, "Lighting the Cave: The Relationship Between Vita Sackville-West and Virginia Woolf," *Signs*, 8: 2 (Winter 1982), 195–214. Nigel Nicolson, *Portrait of a Marriage* (New York: Atheneum, 1973). Joanne Trautman, *The Jessamy Brides: The Friendship of Virginia Woolf and V. Sackville-West* (University Park: Pennsylvania State University Press, 1973). Virginia Woolf, *Orlando* (London: Hogarth Press, 1928).

From *Journals*

August 1, 1920

I hate writing this, but I must, I must. When I began this I swore I would shirk nothing, and no more I will. So here is the truth: I was never so much in love with Rosamund as during those weeks in Italy and the months that followed. It may seem that I should have missed Harold more. I admit everything, to my shame, but I have never pretended to have anything other than a base and despicable character. I seem to be incapable of fidelity, as much then as now. But, as a sole justification, I separate my loves into two halves: Harold, who is unalterable, perennial, and *best;* there has never been anything but absolute purity in my love for Harold, just as there has never been anything but absolute bright purity in his nature. And on the other hand stands my perverted nature, which loved and tyrannized over Rosamund and ended by deserting her without one heart-pang, and which now is linked irremediably with Violet. I have here a scrap of paper on which Violet, intuitive psychologist, has scribbled, "The upper half of

your face is so pure and grave—almost childlike. And the lower half is so
domineering, sensual, almost brutal—it is the most absurd contrast, and
extraordinarily symbolical of your Dr. Jekyll and Mr. Hyde personality."
That is the whole crux of the matter, and I see now that my whole curse
has been a duality with which I was too weak and too self-indulgent to
struggle.

I really worshipped Rosamund then. We motored all over Italy, and I
think it was our happiest time. . . . I didn't go to Italy [in the spring of
1913], I went instead to Spain, which I looked on as partially my own
country, and where in three weeks I picked up Spanish with comparative
fluency. I loved Spain. I would give my soul to go there with Violet—Violet!
Violet! How bloodless the Rosamund affair appears now under the glare
of my affinity with Violet; how seraphic and childlike my years of marriage
with Harold, when that side of me was completely submerged! I am so
frightened of that side sometimes—it's so brutal and hard and savage, and
Harold knows nothing of it; it would drive over his soul like an armoured
chariot. He has blundered upon it once or twice, but he doesn't
understand—he could no more understand it than Ben could understand
algebra.

Things began to rush, after I came back from Spain. The delay over
my engagement began to irritate me, and one day I wrote to Harold saying
we had perhaps better give up the idea. He sent me a despairing telegram
in reply, and then I scarcely know what happened inside my heart: something snapped, and I loved Harold from that day on; I think his energy in
sending me a telegram impressed me, just as I was impressed when he came
after me in an aeroplane when I ran away. Anyway, I wired back that
everything was as before, and the letter which followed the telegram
touched me greatly, for I saw by it how much he truly cared. But I continued my liaison with Rosamund. I say this with deep shame.

September 27, 1920

In April [1918], when we were back in the country, Violet wrote to
ask whether she could come and stay with me for a fortnight. I was bored
by the idea, as I wanted to work, and I did not know how to entertain her;
but I could scarcely refuse. So she came. We were both bored. My serenity
got on her nerves, and her restlessness got on mine. She went up to London
for the day as often as she could, but she came back in the evenings because
the air-raids frightened her. She had been here [Long Barn] I think about
a week when everything changed suddenly—changed far more than I fore-
saw at the time; changed my life. It was the 18th of April. An absurd
circumstance gave rise to the whole thing; I had just got clothes like the
women-on-the-land were wearing, and in the unaccustomed freedom of

breeches and gaiters I went into wild spirits; I ran, I shouted, I jumped, I climbed, I vaulted over gates, I felt like a schoolboy let out on a holiday; and Violet followed me across fields and woods with a new meekness, saying very little, but never taking her eyes off me, and in the midst of my exuberance I knew that all the old under-current had come back stronger than ever and that my old domination over her had never been diminished. I remember that wild irresponsible day. It was one of the most vibrant days of my life. As it happened, Harold was not coming down that night. Violet and I dined alone together, and then, after dinner, we went into my sitting-room, and for some time made conversation, but that broke down, and from ten o'clock until two in the morning—for four hours, or perhaps more—we talked.

Violet had struck the secret of my duality; she attacked me about it, and I made no attempt to conceal it from her or from myself. I talked myself out, until I could hear my own voice getting hoarse, and the fire went out, and all the servants had long since gone to bed, and there was not a soul in the house except Violet and me, and I talked out the whole of myself with absolute sincerity and pain, and Violet only listened—which was skilful of her. She made no comments and no suggestions until I had finished—until, that is, I had dug into every corner and brought its contents out to the light. I had been vouchsafed insight, as one sometimes is. Then, when I had finished, when I had told her how all the gentleness and all the femininity of me was called out by Harold alone, but how towards everyone else my attitude was completely otherwise—then, still with her infinite skill, she brought me round to my attitude towards herself, as it had always been ever since we were children, and then she told me how she had loved me always, and reminded me of incidents running through years, which I couldn't pretend to have forgotten. She was far more skilful than I. I might have been a boy of eighteen, and she a woman of thirty-five. She was infinitely clever—she didn't scare me, she didn't rush me, she didn't allow me to see where I was going; it was all conscious on her part, but on mine it was simply the drunkenness of liberation—the liberation of half my personality. She opened up to me a new sphere. And for her, of course, it meant the supreme effort to conquer the love of the person she had always wanted, who had always repulsed her (when things seemed to be going too far), out of a sort of fear, and of whom she was madly jealous —a fact I had not realized so adept was she at concealment, and so obtuse was I at her psychology.

She lay on the sofa, I sat plunged in the armchair; she took my hands, and parted my fingers to count the points as she told me why she loved me. I hadn't dreamt of such an art of love. Such things had been direct for me always; I had known no love possessed of that Latin artistry (whether instinctive or acquired). I was infinitely troubled by the softness of her touch and the murmur of her lovely voice. She appealed to my unawakened senses; she wore, I remember, a dress of red velvet, that was exactly the colour of a red rose, and that made of her, with her white skin and the tawny hair, the most seductive being. She pulled me down until I kissed her—I had not done so for many years. Then she was wise enough to get up and go to bed; but I kissed her again in the dark after I had blown out our solitary lamp. She let herself go entirely limp and passive in my arms. (I shudder to think of the experience that lay behind her abandonment.) I can't think I slept at all that night—not that much of the night was left.

I don't know how to go on; I keep thinking that Harold, if he ever reads this, will suffer so, but I ask him to remember that he is reading about a *different person* from the one he knew. Also I am not writing this for fun, but for several reasons which I will explain. (1) As I started by saying, because I want to tell the *entire* truth. (2) Because I know of no truthful record of such a connection—one that is written, I mean, with no desire to appeal to a vicious taste in any possible readers; and (3) because I hold the conviction that as centuries go on, and the sexes become more nearly merged on account of their increasing resemblances, I hold the conviction that such connections will to a very large extent cease to be regarded as merely unnatural, and will be understood far better, at least in their *intellectual* if not in their physical aspect. (Such is already the case in Russia.) I believe that then the psychology of people like myself will be a matter of interest, and I believe it will be recognized that many more people of my type do exist than under the present-day system of hypocrisy is commonly admitted. I am not saying that such personalities, and the connections which result from them, will not be deplored as they are now; but I do believe that their greater prevalence, and the spirit of candour which one hopes will spread with the progress of the world, will lead to their recognition, if only as an inevitable evil. The first step in the direction of such candour must be taken by the general admission of normal but illicit relations, and the facilitation of divorce, or possibly even the reconstruction of the system of marriage. Such advance must necessarily come from the more educated and liberal classes. Since "unnatural" means "removed from nature," only the most civilized, because the least natural, class of society can be expected to tolerate such a product of civilization.

I advance, therefore, the perfectly accepted theory that cases of dual personality do exist, in which the feminine and the masculine elements alternately preponderate. I advance this in an impersonal and scientific spirit, and claim that I am qualified to speak with the intimacy a professional scientist could acquire only after years of study and indirect information, because I have the object of study always to hand, in my own heart, and can gauge the exact truthfulness of what my own experience tells me. However frank, people would always keep back something. I can't keep back anything from myself.

September 29th [1920]

I think Violet stayed on for about five days after that. All the time I was in fantastic spirits; and, not realizing how different she was from me in many ways, I made her follow me on wild courses all over the country, and, because she knew she had me only lightly hooked, she obeyed without remonstrance. There was very little between us during those days, only an immense excitement and a growing wish to go away somewhere alone together. This wish was carried out, by arranging to go down to Cornwall for the inside of a week; it was the first time I had ever been away from Harold, and he obviously minded my going.

We went. We met again in London, lunched at a restaurant, and filled with a spirit of adventure took the train for Exeter. On the way there we decided to go on to Plymouth. We arrived at Plymouth to find our luggage had of course been put out at Exeter. We had only an assortment of French poetry with us. We didn't care. We went to the nearest hotel, exultant to feel that nobody in the world knew where we were; at the booking office we were told there was only one room. It seemed like fate. We engaged it. We went and had supper—cider and ham—over which we talked fast and tremulously; she was frightened of me by then.

The next day we went on to Cornwall, where we spent five blissful days; I felt like a person translated, or re-born; it was like beginning one's life again in a different capacity. We were very miserable to come away, but we were constantly together during the whole of the summer months following. Once we went down to Cornwall again for a fortnight. It was a lovely summer. She was radiant. But I never thought it would last; I thought of it as an adventure, an escapade. I kept telling myself she was fickle, that I was the latest toy; she used to assure me of the contrary. She did this with such gravity that sometimes I was almost convinced; but now the years have convinced me thoroughly.

She no longer flirted, and got rid of the last person she had been engaged to, when we went to Cornwall. But there was a man out in France, who used to write to her; she hardly knew him, and I wasn't jealous. He was called Denzil [Denys Trefusis]. She described him to me as fiery—hair like gold wire, blue eyes starting out of his head, and winged nostrils. I listened, not very much interested. I now hate him more than I have ever hated anyone in this life, or am likely to; and there is no injury I would not do him with the utmost pleasure.

Well, the whole of that summer she was mine—a mad and irresponsible summer of moonlight nights, and infinite escapades, and passionate letters, and music, and poetry. Things were not tragic for us then, because although we cared passionately we didn't care deeply—not like now, though it was deepening all the time; no, things weren't tragic, they were rapturous and new, and one side of my life was opened to me, and, to hide nothing, I found things out about my own temperament that I had never been sure of before. Of course I wish now that I had never made those discoveries. One doesn't miss what one doesn't know, and now life is made wretched for me by privations. I often long for ignorance and innocence. I think that if anything happened to bring my friendship with Violet to an end, I might have the strength of mind to blot all that entirely out of my life.

At the end of that summer Denys came home on leave, and I met him. He was very tall and slender, and had the winged look that she had described—I could compare him to many things, to a race-horse, to a Crusader, to a greyhound, to an ascetic in search of the Holy Grail. I liked him then (oh irony!), and he liked me. I could afford to like him, because I was accustomed to Violet's amusements. Even now I see his good points, and they are many; but I see them only by translating myself into an impersonal spectator, and I see them, above all, when Violet makes him suffer. I see that he is a rare, sensitive, proud idealist, and I recognize that through me he has undergone months of suffering, and that his profound love for Violet has been thwarted of its fulfilment. And I am sorry enough for him, at moments, just sorry enough to wish vaguely that he could have cared for someone other than Violet. I see his tragedy—for he is a tragic person. But none of this softens my hatred of him, which is certainly the most violent feeling I have ever experienced. I only hope he returns it in full measure; he has a hundred times more cause to hate me than I to hate him.

He was in London for about ten days. It was already arranged that Violet and I were to go abroad together that winter for a month. There were scenes connected with our going. Violet and I had a row over something; I refused to go abroad; she came round to my house and we made friends again; then I had a dreadful scene with Mother, who was furious at my going; however to make a long story short we left for Paris at the end of November [1918]. I was to be away until Christmas!

Oct. 5th [1920]

Paris . . . We were there for about a week, living in a flat that was lent us in the Palais Royal. Even now the intoxication of some of those hours in Paris makes me see confusedly; other hours were, I admit, wretched, because Denys came (the war being just over), and I wanted Violet to myself. But the evenings were ours. I have never told a soul of what I did. I hesitate to write it here, but I must; shirking the truth here would be like cheating oneself playing patience. I dressed as a boy. It was easy, because I could put a khaki bandage round my head, which in those days was so common that it attracted no attention at all. I browned my face and hands. It must have been successful, because no one looked at me at all curiously or suspiciously—never once, out of the many times I did it. My height of course was my great advantage. I looked like a rather untidy young man, a sort of undergraduate, of about nineteen. It was marvellous fun, all the more so because there was always the risk of being found out. Of course it was easy in the Palais Royal because I could let myself in and out by a latchkey; in hotels it was more difficult. I had done it once already in England; that was one of the boldest things I ever did. I will tell about it: I changed in my own house in London late one evening (the darkened streets made me bold), and drove with Violet in a taxi as far as Hyde Park Corner. There I got out. I never felt so free as when I stepped off the kerb, down Piccadilly, alone, and knowing that if I met my own mother face to face she would take no notice of me. I walked along, smoking a cigarette, buying a newspaper off a little boy who called me "sir," and being accosted now and then by women. In this way I strolled from Hyde Park Corner to Bond Street, where I met Violet and took her in a taxi to Charing Cross. (The extraordinary thing was, how natural it all was for me.) Nobody, even in the glare of the station, glanced at me twice. I had wondered about my voice, but found I could sink it sufficiently. Well, I took Violet as far as Orpington by train, and there we found a lodging house where we could get a room. The landlady was very benevolent and I said Violet was my wife. Next day of course I had to put on the same clothes, although I was a little anxious about the daylight, but again nobody took the slightest notice. We went to Knole!, which was, I think, brave. Here I slipped into the stables, and emerged as myself.

Well, this discovery was too good to be wasted, and in Paris I practically lived in that role. Violet used to call me Julian. We dined together every evening in cafés and restaurants, and went to all the theatres. I shall never forget the evenings when we walked back slowly to our flat through the streets of Paris. I, personally, had never felt so free in my life. Perhaps we have never been so happy since. When we got back to the flat, the windows all used to be open onto the courtyard of the Palais Royal, and the fountains splashed below. It was all incredible—like a fairy-tale.

It couldn't go on for ever, and at the end of the week we left for Monte Carlo, stopping on the way at St. Raphael. The weather was perfect, Monte Carlo was perfect, Violet was perfect. Again as Julian, I took her to a dance there, and had a success with a French family, who asked me to come and play bridge with them, and, I think, had an eye on me for their daughter, a plain girl whose head I tried to turn with compliments. They said "*On voit que monsieur est valseur,*" and their son, a French officer, asked me about my "*blessure,*" and we exchanged war reminiscences.

I didn't go back at Christmas. I didn't go back till nearly the end of March, and everybody was very angry with me, and I felt like suicide after those four wild and radiant months. The whole of that time is dreadful, a nightmare. Harold was in Paris, and I was alone with Mother and Dada, who were both very angry, and wanted me to give Violet up. (There had been a lot of scandal, by then.) On the other hand, Denys had been in England a month, and was agitating to announce his engagement to Violet. Violet was like a hunted creature. I could have prevented the engagement by very few words, but I thought that would be too outrageously selfish; there was Violet's mother, a demon of a woman, longing to get her safely married, and having told all London that she was going to marry Denys. She had already so bad a reputation for breaking engagements that this would have been the last straw. Besides, we both thought she would gain more liberty by marrying, and Denys was prepared to marry her on her own terms—that is, of merely brotherly relations.

I was absolutely miserable. I went to Brighton, alone, in a great empty dust-sheeted house, and all night I used to lie awake, and all day I used to wonder whether I wouldn't throw myself over the cliffs. Everyone questioned me as to why I looked so ill. On the fifth day Violet's engagement was announced in the papers; I bought the paper at Brighton station and nearly fainted as I read it, although I had expected to find it there. Not very long after that I went to Paris, to join Harold, who by that time knew the whole truth of the affair. I was terribly unhappy in Paris. When I came back to London, Violet began to declare that nothing would induce her to go through with the thing, and that I must save her from it by taking her away; in fact I believe she used Denys very largely as a lever to get me to do so. Living permanently with me had become an obsession in her mind. I don't absolutely remember the process in detail, but I know that I ended by consenting. After that we were both less unhappy; I could afford to see her ostensibly engaged to Denys when I knew that instead of marrying him she was coming away with me. I really intended to take her; we had every plan made. We were to go the day before her wedding—not sooner, because we thought we should be overtaken and brought back. It was of course only this looking-forward which enabled me to endure the period of her engagement.

Then about five days before her wedding I suddenly got by the same post three miserable letters from Harold, who had scented danger, because, in order to break it to him more or less gently (and also because I was in a dreadful state of mind myself during all that time), I had been writing him letters full of hints. When I read those letters something snapped in my mind. I saw Harold, all sweet and gentle and dependent upon me. Violet was there. She was terrified. I remember saying, "It's no good, I can't take you away." She implored me by everything she could think of, but I was obdurate. We went up to London together, Violet nearly off her head, and me repeating to myself phrases out of Harold's letters to give myself strength. I telegraphed to him to say I was coming to Paris; I had only one idea, to fly as quickly as I could and to put distance between me and temptation. I saw Violet twice more; once in my own house in London; she looked ill and changed; and once in the early morning at her mother's house, where I went to say goodbye to her on my way to the station. There was a dreary slut scrubbing the doorstep, for it was very early, and I stepped in over the soapy pail, and saw Violet in the morning-room. Then I went to Paris, alone. That is one of the worst days I remember. While I was in the train going to Folkestone I still felt I could change my mind and go back if I wanted to, for she had told me she would wait for me up to the very last minute, and would come straightaway if I appeared, or telephoned for her. At Folkestone I felt it becoming more irrevocable, and tried to get off the boat again, but they were moving the gangway and pushed me back. I had Harold's letters with me, and kept reading them until they almost lost all sense. The journey had never seemed so slow; it remains with me simply as a nightmare. I couldn't eat, and tears kept running down my face. Harold met me at the Gare du Nord. I said I wanted to go straight back, but he said, "No, no," and took me out to Versailles in a motor. The next day was Sunday, and he stayed with me all day. By then I had got such a reaction that I was feverishly cheerful, and he might have thought nothing was the matter. I gave him the book I was writing [*Challenge*], because I knew Violet would hate me to do that, as it was all about her. I was awake nearly all that night. Next day was Monday, 16th June [1919]; Harold had to go into Paris, and I sat quite dazed in my room holding my watch in my hand and watching the hands tick past the hour of Violet's wedding. All that time, I knew, she was expecting a prearranged message from me, which I never sent.

I was so stunned by all this at the time that I could not even think; it is only since then that I have realized how every minute has burnt itself into me.

On Tuesday night Violet and Denys came to Paris. On Wednesday I went to see her, at the Ritz. She was wearing clothes I had never seen before, but no wedding ring. I can't describe how terrible it all was—that meeting, and everything. It makes me physically ill to write about it and think about it, and my cheeks are burning. It was dreadful, dreadful. By then I had left Versailles, and was living alone in a small hotel. I took her there, I treated her savagely, I made love to her, I had her, I didn't care, I only wanted to hurt Denys, even though he didn't know of it. I make no excuse, except that I had suffered too much during the past week and was really scarcely responsible. The next day I saw Denys at an awful interview. Violet told him she had meant to run away with me instead of marrying him; she told him she didn't care for him. He got very white, and I thought he was going to faint. I restrained myself from saying much more. I wanted to say, "Don't you know, you stupid fool, that she is mine in every sense of the word?" but I was afraid that he would kill her if I did that. That night I dined at the Ritz, and from the open window of her room Violet watched me, and Denys sobbed in the room behind her. That day seems to have made a great impression upon him, as he constantly referred to it in his letters to her afterwards.

After that they went away to St. Jean de Luz, and I went to Switzerland with Harold, and then back to England alone. After three weeks Violet came back. Things were not quite so bad then. She had a house in Sussex, and Denys only came there for the weekends, and I spent all the rest of the week there. He and I never met, because in Paris he had said to me it must be war or peace. We met once, when he arrived earlier than was expected; I was just leaving, and Violet threw some things into a bag and came with me. I never saw anyone look so angry as he did. He was dead white and his lips were shaking. I tried to make Violet go back, because I thought it was really humiliating the man too much, but she wouldn't. On the whole, however, she was on friendly terms with him, and I am bound to say that he was friendly as an angel to her, and above all he kept the promises he had made, which I think few men would have done. I think on the whole that that was the period when Violet liked him best.

Oct. 21st [1920]

But she was incessantly trying to get me to come away with her. For a very long time I wouldn't, because I thought she had played me a mean trick over her marriage, and I wouldn't sacrifice Harold to someone whom I thought unworthy. I thought she had played Denys a worse than mean trick too, marrying him like that and accepting his devotion, and deceiving him all the time, and I held myself in almost equal contempt for being a party to the deception, and altogether I was pretty miserable and sickened of the whole thing. My only consolation was that Harold knew all about it; and so did Mother, for I had told her the whole truth about myself the evening I came back from Paris; and if Violet didn't choose to be as frank as I had been, it wasn't really my business. It wasn't my business to look after Denys and see that he wasn't deceived. So I tried to argue, but without bringing myself much satisfaction.

It was not till the end of August that I agreed to go away with Violet.

Harold was still in Paris, and I could leave Ben and Nigel at Knole, so it was comparatively easy. We were to go to Greece, because my book was about Greece, and that provided a reason; and there wasn't much opposition except from Mother at the last minute, but I went in spite of that. We started in October—not a very propitious departure, because Violet was so ill that we had to spend the night at Folkestone. Once we got to Paris it was different, and we led the same life as the year before, of cafés, theatres, and "Julian." There was no abatement, rather the reverse, in our caring for one another; there was no abatement either in my passion for the freedom of that life. I used to stroll about the boulevards as I had strolled down Piccadilly, I used to sit in cafés drinking coffee, and watching people go by; sometimes I saw people I knew, and wondered what they would think if they knew the truth about the slouching boy with the bandaged head and the rather *voyou* appearance, and if they would recognize the silent and rather scornful woman they had perhaps met at a dinner-party or a dance?

I never appreciated anything so much as living like that with my tongue perpetually in my cheek, and in defiance of every policeman I passed.

We didn't stay very long in Paris, but went on to Monte Carlo en route for Greece. It was divine, returning to Monte Carlo where we had been so happy, and we stood at the open window of our old rooms looking out over the lights and the night and the sea, and really it was one of those moments when one can hardly believe one is alive for sheer happiness. For complicated and merely practical reasons we never went to Greece after all, and although I was disappointed I wasn't heartbroken, because it was delicious at Monte Carlo and Violet so loved being there. A complication arose over Denys announcing his arrival at Cannes. Violet didn't want to go; she wanted to make off, but I thought that if he arrived at Cannes confidently expecting her and then found she had bolted, he might do anything in a fit of despair. So I took her to Cannes, and went on myself to Paris; she was to tell Denys and I Harold. We hated leaving one another, even for (as we thought) a few days. We had then been together two months. But when I got to Paris I found Harold with an abscess in the knee, and he had to be operated, and had a great deal of pain, so of course I dismissed every idea of letting him know anything was amiss. I stayed with him a fortnight (Mother was there too), and then went to England to see after Ben and Nigel. Violet came back to England a day or two later, and Harold was to follow. In the meantime Violet, Denys and I met at a grotesque interview in London, when he asked me how much money I should have to keep Violet and myself on if we went away, so that I felt like a young man wanting to marry Violet and being interviewed by her father. Denys, who had come to see me by his own request, was very quiet and businesslike, and looked like death. We did not shake hands. He turned to Violet and asked her if she wished to renounce everything and live with me. She was frightened, and asked for a week. We both agreed to that, and to abide by her decision, and he went away.

On the day that Harold came home Violet tried to rush things. She telephoned to me and told me Denys had said we must be gone by the following evening or not at all. Like a fool I believed her. This entailed telling Harold the moment he arrived. I met him at Victoria; he was very lame and on two sticks; the recollection of him goes through me like a stab even now. We dined at his parents' house, and after dinner I went upstairs to his room and told him I was leaving England with Violet next day. He broke down and cried. Then his mother came in, and I told her what I was going to do, and why; and of course she implored me not to; she had taken off her false hair, and although she didn't realize it a bit, was one of the most pathetic and sincere figures at that moment I have ever beheld. I felt so alien from the whole kindly, law-abiding house; I felt like a pariah, and his mother's tolerance only increased my shame; she didn't push me away, but put both her arms round me and said that nothing I could do was wrong but only mistaken. I felt blackened, and I was so unhappy, and felt my alienation from them and my affinity with Violet so keenly that I only wanted to fly where I would not pollute their purity any longer. I went away to a little hotel, where I had got a bedroom already, and sat up half the night writing letters. The room was full of white lilac that Violet had sent me. Next day I went round to see Harold. He pleaded his illness, and asked me at least to spend the fortnight of his sick leave with him. In order to arrange that, I went to find Violet. I was harsh to her as I never have been to Harold; I absolutely refused to go with her that day. After luncheon I took Harold to see her. He told her that at the end of the fortnight he would let me go with her if I still wanted to. Then he and I went to Knole, and the subject was not renewed between us. I don't know what he thought about during all that fortnight—I don't even know whether he took the danger of my leaving him at all seriously. There were he and I, Ben, Nigel, and Dada; because I am so preoccupied with my own affairs that I forgot to say that in the May of the previous year Mother had left Dada and Knole, and had never returned. So there were only us five, and to me at least it was pretty fantastic, and not the least fantastic part was the fact that Harold never made any allusion to my going.

On the very last day (it was January), I went up to London with him and still he wouldn't talk about it except when I forced him to. He went back to Paris, and I to Knole, wondering when, if ever, I should see him again. At Knole I made every arrangement, and next day went up to London with my luggage. Violet behaved in an extraordinary fashion, which I have never been able to explain. She said she must have that evening in which to talk business with Denys, but I then discovered that she had arranged to go to a play with him. However we agreed to go the next day. I would go back to Knole for the night. Violet came to the station with me, with her luggage, wanting to come away then and there; but she had given her word of honour to Denys that she would be at home that evening, and I said she must wait until next day. She implored me not to make her go back, and I almost had to push her out of my train, where she had forced her way into my carriage. As soon as I got to Knole she rang me up from a hotel in Trafalgar Square, saying that nothing would induce her to return to Denys, but as I couldn't bear to think of her alone in goodness knows what *bouge* of an hotel I persuaded her to go back. She wanted to come to the inn at Sevenoaks. I understood nothing then, and understand no more of it now; but I ought in justice to her always to remember that she tried desperately to get to me that night, and that she had told me for days that she was terrified of Denys breaking his promise.

Next day I called for her in a taxi in London, and we left for Lincoln.

It was bitterly cold, but we were happy in Lincoln. I took her with me to the fen country, which I was writing a book about; that was the object of going to Lincoln. Then we came back to London to the Liverpool Street hotel, and she telephoned for Denys, who came, and she told him she was leaving England next day. I was not present, but I saw him. As we were waiting for a taxi with our luggage in the hall of the hotel next morning, he came in again. He asked her to go and speak to him, but I don't know what he said. He gave her a long letter he had written her, and she gave it to me to read in the taxi on the way to Victoria, and having read it I did the only thing I am in the very least proud of: I said I would give her up if she would go back to him. She refused vehemently and said nothing would induce her to, not even my leaving her. I urged her—I really did urge her; he had written her a letter that really touched me. I travelled down to Dover with her, and all the way I tried to persuade her. But she was adamant. The only concession she would make was to start for France by herself, because she seemed to think he would mind that less. So I saw her off, absolutely firm in her resolution, but childishly terrified of the journey on the boat, and I was to join her at Amiens the next day.

I remained alone at Dover, watching her boat out of sight, and then I went to a lodging house and got myself a room for the night. I lunched, and feeling very disconsolate I walked down to the station and stood staring out over the sea, when turning round I saw Denys coming towards me. He looked very anxious, and wore big motor gloves. He said, "Where's Violet?" and I answered that she had gone. He wanted to follow her. I took him back to my lodging house, and he paced up and down my bedroom there for the rest of the afternoon. At first I would not tell him where she had gone, but as he threatened to stay with me until I left Dover, saying that he knew I was going to join her, I told him I was leaving next day. He promised not to steal a march on me, and we said we would go together and give her the choice between us. I did not hate him in the least then; I was only very sorry. We stalked out together to the post office, and sent telegrams to Violet's family and to mine, and then parted with extreme grimness. During the evening I got a panic-stricken telegram from Violet, which I telephoned through to Denys.

During the night a gale got up, and as I lay in bed I could feel the whole house—which was old and probably frail—shaking under me. I couldn't sleep. I lay in a sort of waking nightmare; at one moment I was convinced that the house would catch fire, that the wind would blow it instantly into a roar of flame, and that as my bedroom was at the top of the house I would stand no chance of escape. I got up, and went to peer over the well of the staircase; gas-jets burnt on every landing, flickering in the draught, and I thought nothing more likely than that the fire should be started by one of them. I took some aspirin, went back to bed, and presently slept; I dreamt horribly, and woke once with the tears running down my face. I woke constantly, until the dawn began to show behind the blinds, and I got up and dressed.

It poured with rain, and the wind seemed stronger than ever; I went out, and was blown clean across the road. The sea was mud-coloured, and very rough; even the ships in the harbour rocked violently, and outside the harbour the waves flung showers of spray over the piers. I never remember such a gale. I went to the boat to get a cabin, and there encountered Denys on the same errand. The sight of us both bribing for cabins in the purser's office was so comic that it made us less grim to one another. I don't know what Denys thought, but personally I was rather exhilarated at the prospect of steaming out into that storm and insecurity after the nervous and in-active hours I had lived through. Once out there, there could be no weak-ness or turning back; one might pray for a respite but one would pray in vain; one wouldn't be let off or eased for a minute; one would have to fight one's way to the other side before one could find peace. Very salutary to one who, like me, had been fighting with human affairs that could be shelved or postponed when one felt one's strength failing one! Out there one was given no time to breathe or recover; the ship ran again right down under the grey valleys of waves; water broke all over her, running blackly off her decks; everything was wet, uncomfortable, and quite remorseless; the wind buffeted one, shook and raged at one, noise and tumult bewil-dered one; one had to think primarily of keeping one's feet and fighting for one's balance; all the hair-splitting niceties that assailed one on dry land, were, thank heaven, in this good rough world of elements, entirely out of the question.

Anyhow, that symbolic crossing beat cordiality into Denys and into me, and we joked about sea-sick remedies, and he dared me to smoke, and by the time we drew alongside at Calais he was asking me to lunch with him in the buffet. He then said he would look after my luggage if I would go on and get a table. I went into the buffet, and there Violet rushed up to me, white and shaking and nearly hysterical. I said, "Good God, why aren't you at Amiens? Denys is with me," and she said she must get away at once, but at that moment he came in. We realized at once that she was ill and starving (she had had nothing to eat since twenty-four hours or more), so we made her sit down and eat chicken and drink champagne. She said she had left all her possessions at Amiens, but there was no question of taking her there that day, or of anything except putting her to bed and getting a doctor. We all three trundled across Calais in a shut cab, found a hotel, and started putting her to bed; but it was so dirty that we took her to another one. She was completely docile in our hands, and we were too busy getting her hot-water bottles, sponges, soup, and a doctor, to realize the absurdity of the whole thing. What made it more ridiculous, was that Denys and I were given communicating rooms, while she was a little way off. When we had got her safely to bed, we both sat in her room and beamed at her with relief. She had recovered then, and amused us by telling us stories of her adventures on the way to Amiens. We had both been anxious about her, and were conscious of nothing but delight in merely having her safe; at least I know that was what *I* felt, and I am sure from Denys's manner that he felt the same. The immense problem that the three of us had got to solve, and all the agony and heartburning its solution must entail for one of us—all that was set aside by triple consent. We were all gay, we were even light-hearted, not negatively, but positively; it was as though time were suspended, and all human relations suspended too, except Denys's and my common love for Violet. We had no hostility I think, towards one another. We were foes who, while our enmity was in abeyance, were prepared to like one another. Our enmity was an extrinsic, not an intrinsic thing. We argued and discussed upon all the detached topics that were as dear to Denys as they were to me; we discussed music, poetry, and immortality, and all the while Violet lay like a princess propped up by a pillow in an enormous bed and listened to us with a *narquois* expression of amazed amusement, and frank relish at the farcical turn affairs had taken. This was after dinner. We had all three dined in her bedroom, and Denys and I had, in turn, waited upon her. She was altogether charming and amusing that evening. At the beginning of dinner our lips were twitching with the temptation to *fou rire,* and Violet alone saved the situation.

After dinner, as I have said, it was Denys and I who talked. I saw that evening how intelligent he was, how absorbed in un-sordid things; I even saw with regret what good friends we might have been under other circumstances; and above all I was touched by his very naive joy at having Violet safe, and present; I was touched by this, because I shared and could understand it.

Next morning Violet was better, and we three breakfasted together, and afterwards got a motor to go across to Boulogne. Still the essential subject had not been raised, except as a joke on the previous evening by Denys, who suggested that we should go to Jamaica and grow sugar. We were both grimmer again now, realizing that the discussion could not much longer be put off. The motor drive was a dreary business. It was a black day, and the road lay across bleak country, hedgeless, monotonous country, and once we nearly got smashed up, and Denys said to me, "Perhaps that would be the best solution after all." We lunched at Boulogne, then took the train to Amiens. We had agreed to discuss it at Amiens, but in the train in the midst of writing limericks and jokes, Denys wrote on a piece of paper that he knew Violet's mind was made up, and that he would leave us at Amiens and go on himself to Paris, never to see Violet again. Everything was tragic again in an instant. I was tongue-tied, and could say nothing. We were then about two hours distant from Amiens, and feeling that the journey would really be too painful, I went away and sat in the compartment next door. Denys cried the whole way to Amiens, and at Amiens Violet and I got out, and so did he, as he had to get into another train; he looked awful as he went away, and Violet and I were alone.

That was a bad two hours.

We went to the Hôtel du Rhin, where Violet's things already were. I think I was more sorry for Denys than she was. If he had not made up his mind like that in the train I had meant to urge her again to go with him, although I knew it would be quite useless. I could not understand her indifference towards him, for even I was oppressed by the thought of what he must be suffering, and of what he would suffer next day on his way through from Paris to London, when he passed through Amiens knowing that Violet was still there with me. I was so much disturbed by all this, that I telephoned myself to Paris to find out if he was all right, and was told that he had already left for London.

We spent that day looking at the devastations of Amiens, and at the very lovely cathedral. I telegraphed to Harold where I was in case he should be anxious. (I did not know that he had had no letters or telegrams from me at all, as he was by then looking for me in England, having crossed in the same gale, only in the opposite direction.) Violet and I meant to motor past Paris (I couldn't bear to go actually into Paris where I thought Harold was), and then to get a train and go to Sicily. If she had been well we should probably have done this the same day, but she was still ill from the effects of her fright and starvation, so we stayed in Amiens. After dinner that night her father [Colonel George Keppel] arrived at our hotel. He was pompous, theatrical, and unimpressive. He stormed at us, and it was all we could do to keep from laughing. The tiresome part was that he had wired for Denys, and refused to leave us lest we should slip away.

Now comes the worst part. Denys and Harold arrived together by aeroplane early in the morning [February 14, 1920]. I was very much astonished, because of course I had thought Harold was in Paris all this time, getting letters more or less all the time from me. He came up to my room, hard on Violet's heels, and told me to pack. Then there was an unpleasant scene. I sat on the window-sill, and Violet stood near me, and we defied first Harold and then Denys, and then both together. This sounds absurd and childish, and so I dare say it was. Denys was the most silent of all; he just looked at Violet while she abused him. The upshot of it was that we refused to leave each other, and Harold said we should be starved out by having someone always with us till we gave way—it was all undignified and noisy to a degree, and I hated it, and was rude to Harold, and he said a lot of silly things that showed him in a wrong light to Violet, and I was sorry about that too. Then Violet and I went together and met Denys in a passage, and he leaned against the wall looking like a stained-glass window saint, very pale and frail, and quite golden-haired, while she said she loathed him, and never to my dying day shall I forget the look on his face. He said nothing at all, but again only stared at her, and if he had slipped down and died at our feet I should scarcely have been surprised.

Then I went upstairs again, to where Harold was sitting in my room, and he tried to talk to me sensibly, and I was less rude, but firm. Then he said a thing which made all the room spin round my head. He said, "Are you sure Violet is as faithful to you as she makes you believe? Because Denys has told your mother quite a different story." I thought I should go mad when he said that. I rushed downstairs, and at the foot of the stairs I met Denys. I stopped him and said, "I am very sorry, but I must ask you the most terribly indiscreet question: have you ever been really married to Violet?" He answered, "I refuse to tell you; that is a matter which lies entirely between Violet and myself." (I can remember every single one of the words we all spoke at that time.) I caught his sleeve; I kept him; I insisted. I said, "If you tell me you have, I swear to you I will never set eyes on Violet again." He hesitated a little at that, and then said again, "I can't answer."

I let him go; I went into the restaurant where Violet was sitting at a little table waiting for her breakfast. I went straight up to her and said (as though the words were being put into my lips), "Why have you not told me you have deceived me with Denys?" I never saw such absolute terror leap into anyone's face. She stammered something, I don't know what. I said, "You have belonged to him." She said "Yes." I said "When?" and she said, "The night before we went to Lincoln." Yet I knew she was a virgin.

I don't know what I said then, I only know that I broke away from her as she tried to hold me, and said quite wildly that I was going away from her. She followed me, and we got into the sitting-room; somehow the doors and woodwork of the sitting-room were pocked with bullet marks. Denys was there too, and she kept saying all kinds of wild things, like, "Let me explain," or, "Tell her it isn't true," and I kept saying only that I wanted to go. I was half mad with pain and not understanding. She was crying, and held me so strongly that I couldn't get away till Denys helped me. Then I rushed upstairs while he held her in the sitting-room, and I packed my things, blind with passion and pain, not able to think or speak, but only thinking that I must get away at all costs. I went downstairs, and found that Harold was with her. Denys was guarding the door. I had just enough sense left to beg him not to leave her for a moment. When Harold came out I went in, although they tried to prevent me. I kissed Violet. Then I went away as quickly as I could, in a motor, with Harold. We had to get his bag out of the aeroplane, and we waited a long time on the aerodrome. That was awful, as Amiens was so near, and we had to drive through Amiens again to get to the station, but I heard Harold tell the chauffeur to avoid the street where the hotel was, and we went by slums. There was no train for Paris for about an hour.

Oct. 22nd [1920]

Harold had lunch in the buffet, but I couldn't eat anything. I saw Violet's father also going to Paris by the same train, so I knew she was alone with Denys, and I hated him then as I never had before. But I couldn't think of anything clearly at all. Harold took me to his hotel in Paris; I didn't care where I went, or what became of me. I couldn't cry. I don't remember when we got to Paris, or what I did until it was time for dinner. I had not swallowed a mouthful of food all day, and I was beginning to feel slightly light-headed, so I went down to the restaurant and had some soup. I began to get the usual reaction after one has gone through too much strain, and in consequence I started talking to Harold and making jokes, and all the time a hammer in my head went, "Violet! Violet!" and it was rather like the day before her wedding, when I was at Versailles with Harold.

We hadn't been in the restaurant long when I saw Violet come in. I dropped my knife and fork, and went to her; it was like warmth rushing back when one has been deadly cold, because for the first second I forgot that something much worse than mere distance had parted us. Harold told me to take her upstairs, and I was shut into the sitting-room alone with her. I got behind a chair so that she shouldn't come near me; I was shivering all over. I don't remember our conversation very distinctly; I remember saying over and over again, "You mustn't ask me to think; I've been stunned and I haven't recovered." She was very urgent and desperate, and said that if I cast her off altogether she would throw herself into the river, and I am sure this was true. She also said that things had not been quite as I had first believed. She had never belonged to Denys, although matters had gone halfway in that direction. I still kept shivering and saying that I couldn't think. At that moment Harold and Denys came in. She asked Harold to go out, and asked Denys to corroborate what she had just told me. He walked up and down the room and seemed to be struggling with himself. Then he said, "This must never go further than this room: I promise you that there has never been anything of that kind between Violet and me." I could have cried with relief, but still it was bad enough that she should have deceived me even to a certain extent—especially on the very night when I was innocently making every disposition to give up everything in the world for her next day. That was what hurt me most bitterly. When I was again alone with her I said I could not bear to see her for at least two months.

Next day she left Paris by motor for the south of France, and every day she used to telephone to me from the various provincial towns where they stopped for the night; and every day her voice was fainter as the distances increased. It must have been a nightmare journey—Denys collapsed and fell ill, but she urged on the motor as though she had been driven by a demon, and it was on that journey, I think, that Denys finally lost what slight hope he still had that she might come to care for him.

I won't say what I went through during the six weeks that passed before I saw her again. I seemed to know every variety of torment—that of longing and aching miserably for someone in whom I had lost faith, that of loving to desperation someone in whose worth I no longer believed. Before, I had always buoyed myself with the thought that although she might hold no other moral precept, at least she was whole-hearted and true where she did love. To this day I don't understand what prompted her to give in, even so little. I think it was a mixture of pity and remorse because she knew she was intending to leave him for good the next day, and she had certainly told me for weeks that he was increasingly importunate. Anyhow I don't want to speculate, it's too painful.

I stayed in Paris for some time, then came back to England. Violet was at Bordighera, living in a villa, while he lived in an hotel. In March I went out to join her at Avignon. I hadn't seen her for six weeks, and I travelled straight through. It ought to have been a good meeting, but it wasn't. Three hours after my arrival we were already quarrelling because she had apparently thought she could persuade me to stay with her for good, and was angry when she found she couldn't. We motored from Avignon to Bordighera, and quarrelled the whole time, and I was acutely wretched. Then at San Remo I lost my head and said I would stay, and for a few days we were happy. We went on to Venice, but I don't really look back on that journey with much pleasure. She was ill, with a touch of jaundice, a most unromantic complaint, and I could do nothing with her, especially after I had gone back on what I had said at San Remo. I admit that I behaved badly over that. One ought not to allow oneself the luxury of losing one's head.

Part III

Carnivorous Flowers: The Literature of Exotic and Evil Lesbians

INTRODUCTION

Before the nineteenth century there existed a sizable body of porno-graphic and satirical literature by men that depicted sexual relations be-tween women. Hard-core and soft-core pornography, such as Brantôme's sixteenth-century *Lives of Fair and Gallant Ladies* or Cleland's eighteenth-century *Memoirs of a Woman of Pleasure,* were generally morally neutral but showed sex between females to be merely *faute de mieux.* As Brantôme says with good-natured optimism of women who have sex with other women, "If they but find a chance and opportunity free from scandal [they will] straight quit their comrades and go throw their arms around some good man's neck." Satirical writings that focused on sex between women, such as Mairobert's *L'Espion Anglois* or William King's *The Toast,* two eighteenth-century works, were not morally neutral. They evinced outrage ostensibly over women's ability to satisfy each other sexually, but their actual agenda was most often to shame a particular woman or group of women for breaches committed against appropriate gender behavior. The women were, for example, too socially independent or they were too ag-gressive (or skillful) in business dealings with the author of the satire. Therefore, they were more like men than women, the author implied, and thus their sexuality must be transgressive.

The nineteenth century, however, saw the birth of different kinds of images of female-female sexuality. One such image was, of course, the re-sult of the sexologists' depiction of the sexual invert, the female who was really a man trapped in a woman's body. But a second nineteenth-century image, which antedated the German and English sexologists, appeared orig inally in works that were primarily French: the image of the fascinatingly unorthodox, dark, and mysterious female who purposefully sought means to transgress societal propriety in ways that intrigued the (male) artist even as they made him uncomfortable and furious. The first such work was Henri LaTouche's 1829 novel, *Fragoletta,* about a beautiful young woman who pretends to have a twin brother, in whose guise she seduces another woman. *Fragoletta* influenced two 1835 novels, Théophile Gautier's *Mademoiselle de Maupin* and Honoré de Balzac's *The Girl with the Golden Eyes.* In their turn, Gautier's and Balzac's novels had great influence in establishing literary prototypes of lesbians for years to come. Gautier's work presented sex between women from a voyeuristic stance and imbued it with a delicious exoticism. Balzac was no less aroused, but he overlaid the exotic lesbian sexuality he presented with moralism, depicting it as destructive and evil.

Some historians have suggested that it was the astounding figure of the notorious George Sand going about Paris in men's clothing that triggered such works at this time. Others have theorized that the catalyst was the threat of an emerging feminist movement. But both Gautier and Balzac articulated other motives for their literary creations. In his preface to *Mademoiselle de Maupin,* Gautier, an early "bohemian," expressed his artistic disgust at the "rehabilitation of virtue undertaken by all the journals" in the France of his day, which was ruled by Louis Philippe, the Bourgeois King. Gautier believed that the artist needed to stand apart or his art would be destroyed by the boring, unimaginative "fashion now to be Christian and Virtuous." Gautier's response to what he regarded as the dull ideals of his era was to *épater le bourgeois* by the most shocking and simultaneously gorgeous images he could fabricate, images that would convey his own antibourgeois aesthetic and Decadent ideals. Two beautiful women making love together, such as he presents in *Mademoiselle de Maupin,* constituted for him the perfect reification of his artistic values.

Balzac claimed not to have found the French too virtuous and Christian, but on the contrary, too "universally tolerant." He complained that anything was acceptable in France of the 1830s and hence corruption flourished. Like Gautier, he sought an image that would be compelling and shocking to his readers, but unlike Gautier, his avowed purpose was to jar them out of their moral complacency by demonstrating an apogee of the corruption he claimed to see everywhere. The artistic device, however, by which he intended to demand their attention, betrayed his own voyeuristic fascination with female-female sexuality. *The Girl with the Golden Eyes* presents the Marquise de St. Réal, a disturbingly beautiful, androgynous woman, who buys the eponymous character when she is twelve years old from her mother. In a few years the Marquise takes her adorable chattel to Paris and holds her prisoner in a room "built for love," that is, soundproofed so that the Marquise can avariciously guard the "accents and music" of their orgies *à deux*. But the climax of the novel comes when the voluptuous, sexy Marquise brutally murders the voluptuous, sexy girl with the golden eyes in graphic detail after discovering that she has managed to be unfaithful with a man. Despite his professed intentions, Balzac intended his readers to be not only repelled but also turned on by his depiction of transgressive sexuality. Like many subsequent writers on the subject, Balzac's expression of disapproval of lesbianism became blurred by his eroticized and prurient interests.

Under the express influence of these two novels, images of lesbian exoticism and evil abounded in France and then England for much of the century. The very exoticism of the lesbian could render her evil and monstrous, and thus a subject for sensationalistic literature that was often overlaid with moralism. As the romantic critic Mario Praz has pointed out, "Of all the monstrosities which pullulate in the [literature] of this period, Lesbians are among the most popular."

Charles Baudelaire, for example, who dedicated his 1857 book of poetry *Les Fleurs du Mal* to Gautier, but whose moralizing aligned him with Balzac as well, was entranced by the beautiful, decadent lesbian, whom he admired but also (slave to his Catholic baptism) condemned to hell. The lesbian was to him the perfect embodiment of a flower of evil. In fact, in 1846, Baudelaire's publisher announced a forthcoming volume by him to be called *Les Lesbiennes,* which was probably an earlier draft of the book that was finally published eleven years later. *Les Fleurs du Mal* contains three poems that are explicitly lesbian, in which the lovers are presented as women who are damned: engaging in sterile ecstasy and frenzied mirth combined with dark despair. Like Gautier he admires his lesbians' "daring hearts" but like Balzac he also associates lesbian sexuality with destruction: lesbian charms are "death-pale," and "screams of torment" arise from Lesbos in the night. Lesbians are beasts that mark their victims with their teeth and then gloat at leisure on their hapless prize. They are wild-eyed sadists and pallid prey. In his depiction of the lesbian as a fascinating monster who drains the lifeblood of her victim, Baudelaire creates one of the earliest images of lesbian as vampire, which continued to be emulated well into the twentieth century.

Arguably the first such image was produced by the British writer Samuel Taylor Coleridge in "Christabel," a poem that he began in 1798 and never completed, though it was published during his lifetime, in 1816. Coleridge's nineteenth-century English critics, who were much more reluctant than the French to dwell on the possibilities of autonomous female sexuality, sometimes suggested that the evil Geraldine, who gains access to Christabel's bed, is really a man in disguise. But the British author Sheridan Le Fanu, who wrote the lesbian vampire story *Carmilla* in 1872, clearly read and was influenced by "Christabel" as a lesbian tale. The similarities between the two works, though superficial, are nevertheless striking. Both Christabel and Le Fanu's Laura come from ancient noble families and live on grand estates; the "vampire" characters in both works claim some connection to the heroine's family, and both gain entrance into their victims' homes by claiming to be dazed and in dire straits; the heroine's father in each case takes responsibility for the "vampire," and the heroine's dead mother tries to come to her defense from the other world. These similarities, as nonsubstantive as they are, may provide further evidence of a long history of literary influences in the depiction of the lesbian.

When the lesbian was not being depicted in subsequent decades as a man trapped in a woman's body, she was often portrayed both literally and metaphorically as a vampire. To a world in which love between women in the form of romantic friendship was ubiquitous but sex between (decent) women was virtually inconceivable, the lesbian, and more particularly lesbian eroticism, represented the passing strange, the unknown, the frightening, the uncontrollable, the ungodly. Without the sexologists' explanation of sexual inversion as a trick of nature, female-female sexuality was inexplicable. It was nonprocreative, and if something as powerful and stirring as sex was not associated with life, it could easily be associated with death, with vampirism. The lesbian cunnilingual act (unlike the emulation of heterosexual intercourse that a man trapped in a woman's body was supposed to have favored) could even look like sucking blood. The woman who *chose* lesbian sexuality was not nature's sport but more likely a spawn of dark, supernatural forces. Well into the twentieth century, lesbian evil was frequently described in vampire terms, as Dorothy Sayers does, for example, in her 1927 novel *Unnatural Death,* in which the lesbian villain is depicted as a "beastly, blood-sucking woman."

As frightening as this dark image of the lesbian was, it was undoubtedly sexually arousing to many men and to those women who had managed to break through nineteenth- and early-twentieth-century inner censors that mandated self-repression of chthonic appetites in females. But such inner liberation must have been difficult to come by for females in socially repressive eras. Queer theorists of the 1990s have reclaimed the image of the vampire as being the epitome of queer and therefore a hero of transgressive sexuality in literature. But this valorization is, of course, revisionist, a product of our own *fin de siècle.* (For an example of this revisionism in contemporary lesbian fiction see p. 426.) The last *fin de siècle* and the decades that followed evinced an equivalent fascination with vampires and related monsters but were much less eager to attribute heroic virtues to them.

Although the earliest literary images of lesbian exoticism and evil were created by men, many women writers, even those who were lesbians, soon adopted those same images into their own work, illustrating perhaps the appeal of the chthonic for some women but also the extent to which literature is much less a reflection of real experiences than of other literature. A direct line of literary descent may be traced, for example, from Baudelaire to Pierre Louÿs, author of *Songs of Bilitis* (1894), to the German poet Marie-Madeleine (the Baroness von Puttkamer) and the Anglo-American poet who wrote in French, Renée Vivien. The Baroness's volume *On Cypress*, which appeared the year after *Songs of Bilitis* was translated into German, abounds with images of exotic lesbian beauty as well as those of lesbians marked by sinful kisses that glow on their white flesh like purple wounds. Renée Vivien, who declared that Louÿs was her mentor and brought her poems to him for criticism, depicted the lesbian as fatally gorgeous, mysterious, accomplished in the "delicate art of . . . vice," a thing of subtle, disturbing, and generally unhappy artifice. Perfume, intoxicating perversity, and destruction pervade Vivien's lesbian poems.

Fiction of the first half of the twentieth century often employed images of the exotic and evil lesbian. With few exceptions, the lesbian in such fiction is beautiful—which often accounts for her powers of destruction. Frequently she is the direct or indirect perpetrator of murder, whether in fiction by male authors such as Sinclair Lewis (*Ann Vickers*), or by purportedly heterosexual female authors such as Dorothy Sayers (*Unnatural Death*), bisexuals such as Dorothy Bussy (*Olivia*), or lesbian authors such as Clemence Dane (*Regiment of Women*.) In the words of Arthur Koestler in his novel *Arrival and Departure* (1943), the lesbian is a "carnivorous flower" in whose seductive embrace "the victim" is gleefully destroyed.

Inevitably, the lesbian's wicked ways destroy not only others but herself also. She may survive physically but her soul is blasted and she is doomed to loneliness and despair. Her exotic evil is the stuff of which many of the lesbian pulp novels of the 1950s was comprised. But even in autobiographical works with serious intent, such as Djuna Barnes's *Nightwood* and Anaïs Nin's novels and diaries, the literary legacy of the tormenting and tormented lesbian is apparent.

In the words of Barnes's contemporary Thomas Purdy, who reviewed *Nightwood* for the *Saturday Review* in 1937, the novel reproduces an atmosphere of decay that "stems from the *fin de siècle* Frenchmen." The love of woman for woman in *Nightwood* is described by Barnes as "insane passion for unmitigated anguish," and the main character says of her lesbianism, "There's something evil in me that loves evil and degradation." Anaïs Nin's depiction of lesbian evil and exoticism was inherited directly from Djuna Barnes, who was, Nin said, her literary hero and role model. In Nin's work lesbianism is compelling in its beauty, but it represents danger, the dark side, the chthonic, or, as she describes it in *Ladders to Fire*

(1946), it is "the negative pole, the pole of confused and twisted nature." Like many lesbian and bisexual authors of the first part of the twentieth century, whatever their own experiences of lesbianism may have been, Barnes and Nin adopted the attitudes and the language of literary conventions that had been established by the aesthete and Decadent writers of the nineteenth century to describe female-female erotic relations.

MEN'S WRITING ON
THE "CARNIVOROUS FLOWER"

From *Les Fleurs du Mal* by Charles Baudelaire

FEMMES DAMNÉES

Under the sickly cressets' languid beams,
on the deep cushions steeped in strange incense
Hippolyta of fierce caresses dreams
which raised the veil of her young innocence.

In her simplicity she sought with eyes
stirred by the tempest something far away,
as a traveler turns his head toward the skies
lost in horizons passed at early day.

In her deadened eyes the stupor, idle tears,
her broken air, the dulled voluptuousness,
her vanquished arms, cast down like futile spears,
all served as part of her frail loveliness.

Stretched at her feet, calmly Delphine lay,
joyous, watching with hot eyes, short breath,
as a strong animal regards its prey,
having already marked it with his teeth.

Strong beauty kneeling before beauty frail,
superb, now she begins to move toward

the girl, already drinking of the pale
wine of triumph, for the sweet reward.

She seeks deep in her pallid victim's eye
to find the silent song that sings of pleasure,
of gratitude sublime and without measure
which leaves the eyelid as with a long sigh:

"Hippolyta, dear heart, come, be advised:
Do you know burnt offerings need not be made
of your first roses as a sacrifice
to violent breaths that ripen them to fade?

"My kiss is light as in the evening air
the touch of May-flies on the limpid lake;
but those grooved ruts that your brisk lovers make
are like those cut by chariot or plowshare.

"They will ride over you with the heavy pace
of spans of horses, oxen with cruel hoof . . .
Hippolyta, my sister, turn your face
to me, my soul and heart, my dearer half,

"turn to me those eyes filled with stars and azure!
For one of those charming glances, divine balm,
I will lift the veil of the most mysterious pleasure,
and give you sleep with dreams of endless calm!"

Hippolyta then, raising her young head:
"I'm not ungrateful, I don't repent in the least,
Delphine, but I often toss restlessly in bed
and suffer as after a heavy midnight feast.

"I feel the terrors swoop with heavy loads
on me, and scattered phantoms in black battalions
are trying to lure me onto shifting roads
toward a bloody, tightly closed horizon.

"Have we done anything we should not do?
Explain, if you can, my terror and my trouble:
when you call me 'Angel' it makes me tremble,
and yet I feel my mouth moving toward you.

"My heart's-ease, do not look at me that way!
I love you forever, sister of my election,

even though you be an ambush to waylay,
even though you be the beginning of my perdition!"

Then Delphine, shaking out her tragic fell,
as if stamping by the iron tripod, her eyes
fatal, in a tyrant's voice replies:
"Who before love shall dare to speak of hell?

"Accursèd be the futile dreamer forever,
the first who wished, in his stupidity,
loving a sterile problem which can never
be solved, to mingle love and honesty!

"Who would in mystical accord enmesh
day with night, the shadow with the flame,
shall never excite his paralytic flesh
with this red sun—love is its common name.

"Go hunt a stupid husband if you wish;
run offer a virgin heart to his cruel kisses;
and, filled with remorse and horror, pale as ash,
you will come to me, your breasts covered with bruises. . . .

"Woman here below serves but one master!"
But the young girl, whose grief was infinite,
cried out: "I feel my being grows a vaster
yawning abyss; and my heart is this pit!

"flaming volcano, deep as oblivion's flood;
nothing can glut this monster's stridencies,
nor cool the thirst of the Eumenides
who, torch in hand, burn him to the blood.

"When the drawn curtain shuts us in our room,
and lassitude is leading us to rest,
I want to lose myself in your deep breast
and find in your heart the coolness of the tomb!"

—Lamentable victims, down, go down,
go down the pathway to eternal hell!
Plunge in the deepest gulf where the crimes yell,
whipped by a wind the sky has never known,

boiling pell-mell, with the crash of storm.
Mad shades, run to the goal of your desires;

never will you glut your lust and ire;
from your delights your punishments are born.

Never will a cool ray light your caverns;
feverish poisons through the chinks will come
and, catching fire, as if they were lanterns,
pervade your flesh with hideous perfume.

The harsh sterility of your tired passions
excites your thirst and toughens up your skin,
and the furious wind of concupiscence
whips your flesh like an old flag, worn thin.

Far from living people, condemned and strayed,
run off into the desert, like the wolves;
dissolute spirits, follow the doom you made,
and flee the infinite borne in yourselves.

Like cattle ruminating on the sand,
they gaze at the horizon of the seas;
feet search for other feet, hands grope for hands,
with bitter shudders and soft ecstasies.

Some, with their hearts charmed by long confessions,
in the deep thickets where the streams are prattling,
spell out with young timidity their passion
and carve the green wood of the tender saplings.

Others, more like sisters, grave and slow,
walk among the rocks of apparitions
where holy Anthony saw like lava flow
the naked purple breasts of his temptations.

Some, in the gleam of crumbling resin, deep
in silent clefts of ancient heathen caves,
call on your succor as their fevers rave,
O Bacchus! who lulls old remorse to sleep!

And others, whose throats love the scapulary,
who hide the whip beneath long, sober vestments,
mingle in somber woods and solitary
nights the foam of pleasure and tears of torment.

O virgins, demons, O monsters and martyrs,
great souls contemptuous of realities,

seeking the infinite, devotees and satyrs,
so full of tears and so full of cries,

you whom my soul has followed into your hell,
poor sisters, I love you because I feel the hurt
of your dull griefs, your thirsts insatiable,
and for the great urns of your love-brimmed hearts!

Carmilla by Sheridan Le Fanu

PROLOGUE

Upon a paper attached to the Narrative which follows, Doctor Hesselius
has written a rather elaborate note, which he accompanies with a reference
to his Essay on the strange subject which the MS. illuminates.

This mysterious subject he treats, in that Essay, with his usual learning
and acumen, and with remarkable directness and condensation. It will form
but one volume of the series of that extraordinary man's collected papers.

As I publish the case, in this volume, simply to interest the "laity," I
shall forestall the intelligent lady, who relates it, in nothing; and, after due
consideration, I have determined, therefore, to abstain from presenting any
précis of the learned Doctor's reasoning, or extract from his statement on
a subject which he describes as "involving, not improbably, some of the
profoundest arcana of our dual existence, and its intermediates."

I was anxious, on discovering this paper, to reopen the correspondence
commenced by Doctor Hesselius, so many years before, with a person so
clever and careful as his informant seems to have been. Much to my regret,
however, I found that she had died in the interval.

She, probably, could have added little to the Narrative which she com-
municates in the following pages, with, so far as I can pronounce, such a
conscientious particularity.

I
AN EARLY FRIGHT

In Styria, we, though by no means magnificent people, inhabit a castle, or
schloss. A small income, in that part of the world, goes a great way. Eight
or nine hundred a year does wonders. Scantily enough ours would have
answered among wealthy people at home. My father is English, and I bear
an English name, although I never saw England. But here, in this lonely

and primitive place, where everything is so marvellously cheap, I really don't see how ever so much more money would at all materially add to our comforts, or even luxuries.

My father was in the Austrian service, and retired upon a pension and his patrimony, and purchased this feudal residence, and the small estate on which it stands, a bargain.

Nothing can be more picturesque or solitary. It stands on a slight eminence in a forest. The road, very old and narrow, passes in front of its drawbridge, never raised in my time, and its moat, stocked with perch, and sailed over by many swans, and floating on its surface white fleets of water-lilies.

Over all this the schloss shows its many-windowed front; its towers, and its Gothic chapel.

The forest opens in an irregular and very picturesque glade before its gate, and at the right a steep Gothic bridge carries the road over a stream that winds in deep shadow through the wood.

I have said that this is a very lonely place. Judge whether I say truth. Looking from the hall door towards the road, the forest in which our castle stands extends fifteen miles to the right, and twelve to the left. The nearest inhabited village is about seven of your English miles to the left. The nearest inhabited schloss of any historic associations, is that of old General Spielsdorf, nearly twenty miles away to the right.

I have said "the nearest *inhabited* village," because there is, only three miles westward, that is to say in the direction of General Spielsdorf's schloss, a ruined village, with its quaint little church, now roofless, in the aisle of which are the mouldering tombs of the proud family of Karnstein, now extinct, who once owned the equally-desolate château which, in the thick of the forest, overlooks the silent ruins of the town.

Respecting the cause of the desertion of this striking and melancholy spot, there is a legend which I shall relate to you another time.

I must tell you now, how very small is the party who constitute the inhabitants of our castle. I don't include servants, or those dependants who occupy rooms in the buildings attached to the schloss. Listen, and wonder! My father, who is the kindest man on earth, but growing old; and I, at the date of my story, only nineteen. Eight years have passed since then. I and my father constituted the family at the schloss. My mother, a Styrian lady, died in my infancy, but I had a good-natured governess, who had been with me from, I might almost say, my infancy. I could not remember the time when her fat, benignant face was not a familiar picture in my memory. This was Madame Perrodon, a native of Berne, whose care and good nature in part supplied to me the loss of my mother, whom I do not even remember, so early I lost her. She made a third at our little dinner party. There was a fourth, Mademoiselle De Lafontaine, a lady such as you term, I believe, a "finishing governess." She spoke French and German, Madame Perrodon French and broken English, to which my father and I added English, which, partly to prevent its becoming a lost language among us, and partly from patriotic motives, we spoke every day. The consequence was a Babel, at which strangers used to laugh, and which I shall make no attempt to reproduce in this narrative. And there were two or three young lady friends besides, pretty nearly of my own age, who were occasional visitors, for longer or shorter terms; and these visits I sometimes returned.

These were our regular social resources; but of course there were chance visits from "neighbours" of only five or six leagues' distance. My life was, notwithstanding, rather a solitary one, I can assure you.

My gouvernantes had just so much control over me as you might conjecture such sage persons would have in the case of a rather spoiled girl, whose only parent allowed her pretty nearly her own way in everything.

The first occurrence in my existence, which produced a terrible impression upon my mind, which, in fact, never has been effaced, was one of the very earliest incidents of my life which I can recollect. Some people will think it so trifling that it should not be recorded here. You will see, however, by-and-by, why I mention it. The nursery, as it was called, though I had it all to myself, was a large room in the upper story of the castle, with a steep oak roof. I can't have been more than six years old, when one night I awoke, and looking round the room from my bed, failed to see the nursery-maid. Neither was my nurse there; and I thought myself alone. I was not frightened, for I was one of those happy children who are studiously kept in ignorance of ghost stories, of fairy tales, and of all such lore as makes us cover up our heads when the door creaks suddenly, or the flicker of an expiring candle makes the shadow of a bed-post dance upon the wall, nearer to our faces. I was vexed and insulted at finding myself, as I conceived, neglected, and I began to whimper, preparatory to a hearty bout of roaring; when to my surprise, I saw a solemn, but very pretty face looking at me from the side of the bed. It was that of a young lady who was kneeling, with her hands under the coverlet. I looked at her with a kind of pleased wonder, and ceased whimpering. She caressed me with her hands, and lay down beside me on the bed, and drew me towards her, smiling; I felt immediately delightfully soothed, and fell asleep again. I was wakened by a sensation as if two needles ran into my breast very deep at the same moment, and I cried loudly. The lady started back, with her eyes fixed on me, and then slipped down upon the floor, and, as I thought, hid herself under the bed.

I was now for the first time frightened, and I yelled with all my might and main. Nurse, nursery-maid, housekeeper, all came running in, and hearing my story, they made light of it, soothing me all they could mean-while. But, child as I was, I could perceive that their faces were pale with an unwonted look of anxiety, and I saw them look under the bed, and about the room, and peep under tables and pluck open cupboards; and the housekeeper whispered to the nurse: "Lay your hand along that hollow in the bed; some one *did* lie there, so sure as you did not; the place is still warm."

I remember the nursery-maid petting me, and all three examining my chest, where I told them I felt the puncture, and pronouncing that there was no sign visible that any such thing had happened to me.

The housekeeper and the two other servants who were in charge of the nursery, remained sitting up all night; and from that time a servant always sat up in the nursery until I was about fourteen.

I was very nervous for a long time after this. A doctor was called in, he was pallid and elderly. How well I remember his long saturnine face, slightly pitted with small-pox, and his chestnut wig. For a good while, every second day, he came and gave me medicine, which of course I hated.

The morning after I saw this apparition I was in a state of terror, and could not bear to be left alone, daylight though it was, for a moment.

I remember my father coming up and standing at the bedside, and talk-ing cheerfully, and asking the nurse a number of questions, and laughing very heartily at one of the answers; and patting me on the shoulder, and kissing me, and telling me not to be frightened, that it was nothing but a dream and could not hurt me.

But I was not comforted, for I knew the visit of the strange woman was *not* a dream; and I was *awfully* frightened.

I was a little consoled by the nursery-maid's assuring me that it was she who had come and looked at me, and lain down beside me in the bed and that I must have been half-dreaming not to have known her face. But this, though supported by the nurse, did not quite satisfy me.

I remember, in the course of that day, a venerable old man, in a black cassock, coming into the room with the nurse and housekeeper, and talking a little to them, and very kindly to me; his face was very sweet and gentle, and he told me they were going to pray, and joined my hands together, and desired me to say, softly, while they were praying, "Lord, hear all good prayers for us, for Jesus' sake." I think these were the very words, for I often repeated them to myself, and my nurse used for years to make me say them in my prayers.

I remember so well the thoughtful sweet face of that white-haired old man, in his black cassock, as he stood in that rude, lofty, brown room, with the clumsy furniture of a fashion three hundred years old, about him, and the scanty light entering its shadowy atmosphere through the small lattice. He kneeled, and the three women with him, and he prayed aloud with an earnest quavering voice for, what appeared to me, a long time. I forget all my life preceding that event, and for some time after it is all obscure also; but the scenes I have just described stand out vivid as the isolated pictures of the phantasmagoria surrounded by darkness.

II
A GUEST

I am now going to tell you something so strange that it will require all your faith in my veracity to believe my story. It is not only true, nevertheless, but truth of which I have been an eye-witness.

It was a sweet summer evening, and my father asked me, as he sometimes did, to take a little ramble with him along that beautiful forest vista which I have mentioned as lying in front of the schloss.

"General Spielsdorf cannot come to us so soon as I had hoped," said my father, as we pursued our walk.

He was to have paid us a visit of some weeks, and we had expected his arrival next day. He was to have brought with him a young lady, his niece and ward, Mademoiselle Rheinfeldt, whom I had never seen, but whom I had heard described as a very charming girl, and in whose society I had promised myself many happy days. I was more disappointed than a young lady living in a town, or a bustling neighbourhood can possibly imagine. This visit, and the new acquaintance it promised, had furnished my day dream for many weeks.

"And how soon does he come?" I asked.

"Not till autumn. Not for two months, I dare say," he answered. "And I am very glad now, dear, that you never knew Mademoiselle Rheinfeldt."

"And why?" I asked, both mortified and curious.

"Because the poor young lady is dead," he replied. "I quite forgot I had not told you, but you were not in the room when I received the General's letter this evening."

I was very much shocked. General Spielsdorf had mentioned in his first letter, six or seven weeks before, that she was not so well as he would wish her, but there was nothing to suggest the remotest suspicion of danger.

"Here is the General's letter," he said, handing it to me. "I am afraid he is in great affliction; the letter appears to me to have been written very nearly in distraction."

We sat down on a rude bench, under a group of magnificent lime trees. The sun was setting with all its melancholy splendour behind the sylvan horizon, and the stream that flows beside our home, and passes under the steep old bridge I have mentioned, wound through many a group of noble trees, almost at our feet, reflecting in its current the fading crimson of the sky. General Spielsdorf's letter was so extraordinary, so vehement, and in some places so self-contradictory, that I read it twice over—the second time aloud to my father—and was still unable to account for it, except by supposing that grief had unsettled his mind.

It said, "I have lost my darling daughter, for as such I loved her. During the last days of dear Bertha's illness I was not able to write to you. Before then I had no idea of her danger. I have lost her, and now learn *all,* too late. She died in the peace of innocence, and in the glorious hope of a blessed futurity. The fiend who betrayed our infatuated hospitality has done it all. I thought I was receiving into my house innocence, gaiety, a charming companion for my lost Bertha. Heavens! what a fool have I been! I thank God my child died without a suspicion of the cause of her sufferings. She is gone without so much as conjecturing the nature of her illness, and the accursed passion of the agent of all this misery. I devote my remaining days to tracking and extinguishing a monster. I am told I may hope to accomplish my righteous and merciful purpose. At present there is scarcely a gleam of light to guide me. I curse my conceited incredulity, my despicable affectation of superiority, my blindness, my obstinacy—all—too late. I cannot write or talk collectedly now. I am distracted. So soon as I shall have a little recovered, I mean to devote myself for a time to enquiry, which may possibly lead me as far as Vienna. Some time in the autumn, two months hence, or earlier if I live, I will see you—that is, if you permit me; I will then tell you all that I scarce dare put upon paper now. Farewell. Pray for me, dear friend."

In these terms ended this strange letter. Though I had never seen Bertha Rheinfeldt, my eyes filled with tears at the sudden intelligence; I was startled, as well as profoundly disappointed.

The sun had now set, and it was twilight by the time I had returned the General's letter to my father.

It was a soft clear evening, and we loitered, speculating upon the possible meanings of the violent and incoherent sentences which I had just been reading. We had nearly a mile to walk before reaching the road that passes the schloss in front, and by that time the moon was shining brilliantly. At the drawbridge we met Madame Perrodon and Mademoiselle De Lafontaine, who had come out, without their bonnets, to enjoy the exquisite moonlight.

We heard their voices gabbling in animated dialogue as we approached. We joined them at the drawbridge, and turned about to admire with them the beautiful scene.

The glade through which we had just walked lay before us. At our left the narrow road wound away under clumps of lordly trees, and was lost to sight amid the thickening forest. At the right the same road crosses the steep and picturesque bridge, near which stands a ruined tower, which once guarded that pass; and beyond the bridge an abrupt eminence rises, covered with trees, and showing in the shadow some grey ivy-clustered rocks.

Over the sward and low grounds, a thin film of mist was stealing, like smoke, marking the distances with a transparent veil; and here and there we could see the river faintly flashing in the moonlight.

No softer, sweeter scene could be imagined. The news I had just heard made it melancholy; but nothing could disturb its character of profound serenity, and the enchanted glory and vagueness of the prospect.

My father, who enjoyed the picturesque, and I, stood looking in silence over the expanse beneath us. The two good governesses, standing a little way behind us, discoursed upon the scene, and were eloquent upon the moon.

Madame Perrodon was fat, middle-aged, and romantic, and talked and sighed poetically. Mademoiselle De Lafontaine—in right of her father, who was a German, assumed to be psychological, metaphysical, and something of a mystic—now declared that when the moon shone with a light so intense it was well known that it indicated a special spiritual activity. The effect of the full moon in such a state of brilliancy was manifold. It acted on dreams, it acted on lunacy, it acted on nervous people; it had marvellous physical influences connected with life. Mademoiselle related that her cousin, who was mate of a merchant ship, having taken a nap on deck on such a night, lying on his back, with his face full in the light of the moon, had wakened, after a dream of an old woman clawing him by the cheek, with his features horribly drawn to one side; and his countenance had never quite recovered its equilibrium.

"The moon, this night," she said, "is full of odylic and magnetic influence—and see, when you look behind you at the front of the schloss, how all its windows flash and twinkle with that silvery splendour, as if unseen hands had lighted up the rooms to receive fairy guests."

There are indolent states of the spirits in which, indisposed to talk ourselves, the talk of others is pleasant to our listless ears; and I gazed on, pleased with the tinkle of the ladies' conversation.

"I have got into one of my moping moods to-night," said my father, after a silence, and quoting Shakespeare, whom, by way of keeping up our English, he used to read aloud, he said:—

> " 'In truth I know not why I am so sad:
>   It wearies me; you say it wearies you;
>   But how I got it—came by it.'

"I forget the rest. But I feel as if some great misfortune were hanging over us. I suppose the poor General's afflicted letter has had something to do with it."

At this moment the unwonted sound of carriage wheels and many hoofs upon the road, arrested our attention.

They seemed to be approaching from the high ground overlooking the bridge, and very soon the equipage emerged from that point. Two horsemen first crossed the bridge, then came a carriage drawn by four horses, and two men rode behind.

It seemed to be a travelling carriage of a person of rank; and we were all immediately absorbed in watching that very unusual spectacle. It became, in a few moments, greatly more interesting, for just as the carriage had passed the summit of the steep bridge, one of the leaders, taking fright, communicated his panic to the rest, and, after a plunge or two, the whole team broke into a wild gallop together, and dashing between the horsemen who rode in front, came thundering along the road towards us with the speed of a hurricane.

The excitement of the scene was made more painful by the clear, long-drawn screams of a female voice from the carriage window.

We all advanced in curiosity and horror; my father in silence, the rest with various ejaculations of terror.

Our suspense did not last long. Just before you reach the castle draw-bridge, on the route they were coming, there stands by the roadside a magnificent lime tree, on the other stands an ancient stone cross, at sight of which the horses, now going at a pace that was perfectly frightful, swerved so as to bring the wheel over the projecting roots of the tree.

I knew what was coming. I covered my eyes, unable to see it out, and turned my head away; at the same moment I heard a cry from my lady-friends, who had gone on a little.

Curiosity opened my eyes, and I saw a scene of utter confusion. Two of the horses were on the ground, the carriage lay upon its side, with two wheels in the air; the men were busy removing the traces, and a lady, with a commanding air and figure had got out, and stood with clasped hands, raising the handkerchief that was in them every now and then to her eyes. Through the carriage door was now lifted a young lady, who appeared to be lifeless. My dear old father was already beside the elder lady, with his hat in his hand, evidently tendering his aid and the resources of his schloss. The lady did not appear to hear him, or to have eyes for anything but the slender girl who was being placed against the slope of the bank.

I approached; the young lady was apparently stunned, but she was certainly not dead. My father, who piqued himself on being something of a physician, had just had his fingers to her wrist and assured the lady, who declared herself her mother, that her pulse, though faint and irregular, was undoubtedly still distinguishable. The lady clasped her hands and looked upward, as if in a momentary transport of gratitude; but immediately she broke out again in that theatrical way which is, I believe, natural to some people.

She was what is called a fine-looking woman for her time of life, and must have been handsome; she was tall, but not thin, and dressed in black velvet, and looked rather pale, but with a proud and commanding countenance, though now agitated strangely.

"Was ever being so born to calamity?" I heard her say, with clasped hands, as I came up. "Here am I, on a journey of life and death, in prosecuting which to lose an hour is possibly to lose all. My child will not have recovered sufficiently to resume her route for who can say how long. I must leave her; I cannot, dare not, delay. How far on, sir, can you tell, is the nearest village? I must leave her there; and shall not see my darling, or even hear of her till my return, three months hence."

I plucked my father by the coat, and whispered earnestly in his ear, "Oh! papa, pray ask her to let her stay with us—it would be so delightful. Do, pray."

"If Madame will entrust her child to the care of my daughter, and of her good gouvernante, Madame Perrodon, and permit her to remain as our guest, under my charge, until her return, it will confer a distinction and an obligation upon us, and we shall treat her with all the care and devotion which so sacred a trust deserves."

"I cannot do that, sir, it would be to task your kindness and chivalry too cruelly," said the lady, distractedly.

"It would, on the contrary, be to confer on us a very great kindness at the moment when we most need it. My daughter has just been disappointed by a cruel misfortune, in a visit from which she had long anticipated a great deal of happiness. If you confide this young lady to our care it will be her best consolation. The nearest village on your route is distant, and affords no such inn as you think of placing your daughter at; you cannot allow her to continue her journey for any considerable distance without danger. If, as you say, you cannot suspend your journey, you must part with her to-night, and nowhere could you do so with more honest assurances of care and tenderness than here."

There was something in this lady's air and appearance so distinguished, and even imposing, and in her manner so engaging, as to impress one, quite apart from the dignity of her equipage, with a conviction that she was a person of consequence.

By this time the carriage was replaced in its upright position, and the horses, quite tractable, in the traces again.

The lady threw on her daughter a glance which I fancied was not quite so affectionate as one might have anticipated from the beginning of the scene; then she beckoned slightly to my father, and withdrew two or three steps with him out of hearing; and talked to him with a fixed and stern countenance, not at all like that with which she had hitherto spoken.

I was filled with wonder that my father did not seem to perceive the change, and also unspeakably curious to learn what it could be that she was speaking, almost in his ear, with so much earnestness and rapidity.

Two or three minutes at most, I think, she remained thus employed, then she turned, and a few steps brought her to where her daughter lay, supported by Madame Perrodon. She kneeled beside her for a moment and whispered, as Madame supposed, a little benediction in her ear; then hastily kissing her, she stepped into her carriage, the door was closed, the footmen in stately liveries jumped up behind, the outriders spurred on, the postilions cracked their whips, the horses plunged and broke suddenly into a furious canter that threatened soon again to become a gallop, and the carriage whirled away, followed at the same rapid pace by the two horsemen in the rear.

III
WE COMPARE NOTES

We followed the *cortège* with our eyes until it was swiftly lost to sight in the misty wood; and the very sound of the hoofs and wheels died away in the silent night air.

Nothing remained to assure us that the adventure had not been an illusion of a moment but the young lady, who just at that moment opened her eyes. I could not see, for her face was turned from me, but she raised her head, evidently looking about her, and I heard a very sweet voice ask complainingly, "Where is mamma?"

Our good Madame Perrodon answered tenderly, and added some comfortable assurances.

I then heard her ask:

"Where am I? What is this place?" and after that she said, "I don't see the carriage; and Matska, where is she?"

Madame answered all her questions in so far as she understood them; and gradually the young lady remembered how the misadventure came about, and was glad to hear that no one in, or in attendance on, the carriage was hurt; and on learning that her mama had left her here, till her return in about three months, she wept.

I was going to add my consolations to those of Madame Perrodon when Mademoiselle De Lafontaine placed her hand upon my arm, saying:

"Don't approach, one at a time is as much as she can at present converse with; a very little excitement would possibly overpower her now."

As soon as she is comfortably in bed, I thought, I will run up to her room and see her.

My father in the meantime had sent a servant on horseback for the physician, who lived about two leagues away; and a bedroom was being prepared for the young lady's reception.

The stranger now rose, and leaning on Madame's arm, walked slowly over the drawbridge and into the castle gate.

In the hall, servants waited to receive her, and she was conducted forthwith to her room.

The room we usually sat in as our drawing-room is long, having four windows, that looked over the moat and drawbridge, upon the forest scene I have just described.

It is furnished in old carved oak, with large carved cabinets, and the chairs are cushioned with crimson Utrecht velvet. The walls are covered with tapestry, and surrounded with great gold frames, the figures being as large as life, in ancient and very curious costume, and the subjects represented are hunting, hawking and generally festive. It is not too stately to be extremely comfortable; and here we had our tea, for with his usual patriotic leanings he insisted that the national beverage should make its appearance regularly with our coffee and chocolate.

We sat here this night, and with candles lighted, were talking over the adventure of the evening.

Madame Perrodon and Mademoiselle De Lafontaine were both of our party. The young stranger had hardly lain down in her bed when she sank into a deep sleep; and those ladies had left her in the care of a servant.

"How do you like our guest?" I asked, as soon as Madame entered. "Tell me all about her?"

"I like her extremely," answered Madame, "she is, I almost think the prettiest creature I ever saw; about your age, and so gentle and nice."

"She is absolutely beautiful," threw in Mademoiselle, who had peeped for a moment into the stranger's room.

"And such a sweet voice!" added Madame Perrodon.

"Did you remark a woman in the carriage, after it was set up again, who did not get out," inquired Mademoiselle, "but only looked from the window?"

No, we had not seen her.

Then she described a hideous black woman, with a sort of coloured turban on her head, who was gazing all the time from the carriage window, nodding and grinning derisively towards the ladies, with gleaming eyes and large white eye-balls, and her teeth set as if in fury.

"Did you remark what an ill-looking pack of men the servants were?" asked Madame.

"Yes," said my father, who had just come in, "ugly, hang-dog looking fellows, as ever I beheld in my life. I hope they mayn't rob the poor lady in the forest. They are clever rogues, however; they got everything to rights in a minute."

"I dare say they are worn out with too long travelling," said Madame. "Besides looking wicked, their faces were so strangely lean, and dark, and sullen. I am very curious, I own; but I dare say the young lady will tell us about it to-morrow, if she is sufficiently recovered."

"I don't think she will," said my father, with a mysterious smile, and a little nod of his head, as if he knew more about it than he cared to tell us.

This made me all the more inquisitive as to what had passed between him and the lady in the black velvet, in the brief but earnest interview that had immediately preceded her departure.

We were scarcely alone, when I entreated him to tell me. He did not need much pressing.

"There is no particular reason why I should not tell you. She expressed a reluctance to trouble us with the care of her daughter, saying she was in delicate health, and nervous, but not subject to any kind of seizure—she volunteered that—nor to any illusion; being, in fact, perfectly sane."

"How very odd to say all that!" I interpolated. "It was so unnecessary."

"At all events it *was* said," he laughed, "and as you wish to know all that passed, which was indeed very little, I tell you. She then said, 'I am making a long journey of *vital* importance'—she emphasized the word— 'rapid and secret; I shall return for my child in three months; in the mean-time, she will be silent as to who we are, whence we come, and whither we are travelling.' That is all she said. She spoke very pure French. When she said the word 'secret,' she paused for a few seconds, looking sternly, her eyes fixed on mine. I fancy she makes a great point of that. You saw how quickly she was gone. I hope I have not done a very foolish thing, in taking charge of the young lady."

For my part, I was delighted. I was longing to see and talk to her; and only waiting till the doctor should give me leave. You, who live in towns, can have no idea how great an event the introduction of a new friend is, in such a solitude as surrounded us.

The doctor did not arrive till nearly one o'clock; but I could no more have gone to my bed and slept, than I could have overtaken, on foot, the carriage in which the princess in black velvet had driven away.

When the physician came down to the drawing-room, it was to report very favourably upon his patient. She was now sitting up, her pulse quite regular, apparently perfectly well. She had sustained no injury, and the little shock to her nerves had passed away quite harmlessly. There could be no harm certainly in my seeing her, if we both wished it; and, with this permission, I sent, forthwith, to know whether she would allow me to visit her for a few minutes in her room.

The servant returned immediately to say that she desired nothing more.

You may be sure I was not long in availing myself of this permission.

Our visitor lay in one of the handsomest rooms in the schloss. It was, perhaps a little stately. There was a sombre piece of tapestry opposite the foot of the bed, representing Cleopatra with the asps to her bosom; and other solemn classic scenes were displayed, a little faded, upon the other walls. But there was gold carving, and rich and varied colour enough in the other decorations of the room, to more than redeem the gloom of the old tapestry.

There were candles at the bed side. She was sitting up; her slender pretty figure enveloped in the soft silk dressing-gown, embroidered with flowers, and lined with thick quilted silk, which her mother had thrown over her feet as she lay upon the ground.

What was it that, as I reached the bed side and had just begun my little greeting, struck me dumb in a moment, and made me recoil a step or two from before her? I will tell you.

I saw the very face which had visited me in my childhood at night, which remained so fixed in my memory, and on which I had for so many years so often ruminated with horror, when no one suspected of what I was thinking.

It was pretty, even beautiful; and when I first beheld it, wore the same melancholy expression.

But this almost instantly lighted into a strange fixed smile of recognition.

There was a silence of fully a minute, and then at length *she* spoke; *I* could not.

"How wonderful!" she exclaimed. "Twelve years ago, I saw your face in a dream, and it has haunted me ever since."

"Wonderful indeed!" I repeated, overcoming with an effort the horror that had for a time suspended my utterances. "Twelve years ago, in vision or reality, *I* certainly saw you. I could not forget your face. It has remained before my eyes ever since."

Her smile had softened. Whatever I had fancied strange in it, was gone, and it and her dimpling cheeks were now delightfully pretty and intelligent.

I felt reassured, and continued more in the vein which hospitality in-

dicated, to bid her welcome, and to tell her how much pleasure her accidental arrival had given us all, and especially what a happiness it was
to me.

I took her hand as I spoke. I was a little shy, as lonely people are, but
the situation made me eloquent, and even bold. She pressed my hand, she
laid hers upon it, and her eyes glowed, as, looking hastily into mine, she
smiled again, and blushed.

She answered my welcome very prettily. I sat down beside her, still
wondering; and she said:

"I must tell you my vision about you; it is so very strange that you and
I should have had, each of the other so vivid a dream, that each should
have seen, I you and you me, looking as we do now, when of course we
both were mere children. I was a child, about six years old, and I awoke
from a confused and troubled dream, and found myself in a room, unlike
my nursery, wainscoted clumsily in some dark wood, and with cupboards
and bedsteads, and chairs, and benches placed about it. The beds were, I
thought, all empty, and the room itself without any one but myself in it;
and I, after looking about me for some time, and admiring especially an
iron candlestick, with two branches, which I should certainly know again,
crept under one of the beds to reach the window; but as I got from under
the bed, I heard some one crying; and looking up, while I was still upon
my knees, I saw *you*—most assuredly you—as I see you now; a beautiful
young lady, with golden hair and large blue eyes, and lips—your lips—
you, as you are here. Your looks won me; I climbed on the bed and put
my arms about you, and I think we both fell asleep. I was aroused by a
scream; you were sitting up screaming. I was frightened, and slipped down
upon the ground, and, it seemed to me, lost consciousness for a moment;
and when I came to myself, I was again in my nursery at home. Your face
I have never forgotten since. I could not be misled by mere resemblance.
You *are* the lady whom I then saw."

It was now my turn to relate my corresponding vision, which I did, to
the undisguised wonder of my new acquaintance.

"I don't know which should be most afraid of the other," she said,
again smiling. "If you were less pretty I think I should be very much afraid
of you, but being as you are, and you and I both so young, I feel only that
I have made your acquaintance twelve years ago, and have already a right
to your intimacy; at all events, it does seem as if we were destined, from
our earliest childhood, to be friends. I wonder whether you feel as strangely
drawn towards me as I do to you; I have never had a friend—shall I find
one now?" She sighed, and her fine dark eyes gazed passionately on me.

Now the truth is, I felt rather unaccountably towards the beautiful
stranger. I did feel, as she said, "drawn towards her," but there was also

something of repulsion. In this ambiguous feeling, however, the sense of attraction immensely prevailed. She interested and won me, she was so beautiful and so indescribably engaging.

I perceived now something of languor and exhaustion stealing over her, and hastened to bid her good-night.

"The doctor thinks," I added, "that you ought to have a maid to sit up with you to-night; one of ours is waiting, and you will find her a very useful and quiet creature."

"How kind of you, but I could not sleep, I never could with an attendant in the room. I shan't require any assistance—and, shall I confess my weakness, I am haunted with a terror of robbers. Our house was robbed once, and two servants murdered, so I always lock my door. It has become a habit—and you look so kind I know you will forgive me. I see there is a key in the lock."

She held me close in her pretty arms for a moment and whispered in my ear, "Good-night, darling, it is very hard to part with you, but good-night; to-morrow, but not early, I shall see you again."

She sank back on the pillow with a sigh, and her fine eyes followed me with a fond and melancholy gaze, and she murmured again "Good-night, dear friend."

Young people like, and even love, on impulse. I was flattered by the evident, though as yet undeserved, fondness she showed me. I liked the confidence with which she at once received me. She was determined that we should be very dear friends.

Next day came and we met again. I was delighted with my companion; that is to say, in many respects.

Her looks lost nothing in daylight—she was certainly the most beautiful creature I had ever seen, and the unpleasant remembrance of the face presented in my early dream, had lost the effect of the first unexpected recognition.

She confessed that she had experienced a similar shock on seeing me, and precisely the same faint antipathy that had mingled with my admiration of her. We now laughed together over our momentary horrors.

IV

Her Habits—A Saunter

I told you that I was charmed with her in most particulars.

There were some that did not please me so well.

She was above the middle height of women. I shall begin by describing her. She was slender, and wonderfully graceful. Except that her movements were languid—*very* languid—indeed, there was nothing in her appearance to indicate an invalid. Her complexion was rich and brilliant; her features were small and beautifully formed; her eyes large, dark, and lustrous; her hair was quite wonderful, I never saw hair so magnificently thick and long when it was down about her shoulders; I have often placed my hands under it, and laughed with wonder at its weight. It was exquisitely fine and soft, and in colour a rich very dark brown, with something of gold. I loved to let it down, tumbling with its own weight, as, in her room, she lay back in her chair talking in her sweet low voice, I used to fold and braid it, and spread it out and play with it. Heavens! If I had but known all!

I said there were particulars which did not please me. I have told you that her confidence won me the first night I saw her; but I found that she exercised with respect to herself, her mother, her history, everything in fact connected with her life, plans, and people, an ever-wakeful reserve. I dare say I was unreasonable, perhaps I was wrong; I dare say I ought to have respected the solemn injunction laid upon my father by the stately lady in black velvet. But curiosity is a restless and unscrupulous passion, and no one girl can endure, with patience, that hers should be baffled by another. What harm could it do anyone to tell me what I so ardently desired to know? Had she no trust in my good sense or honour? Why would she not believe me when I assured her, so solemnly, that I would not divulge one syllable of what she told me to any mortal breathing.

There was a coldness, it seemed to me, beyond her years, in her smiling melancholy persistent refusal to afford me the least ray of light.

I cannot say we quarrelled upon this point, for she would not quarrel upon any. It was, of course, very unfair of me to press her, very ill-bred, but I really could not help it; and I might just as well have let it alone.

What she did tell me amounted, in my unconscionable estimation—to nothing.

It was all summed up in three very vague disclosures:

First.—Her name was Carmilla.

Second.—Her family was very ancient and noble.

Third.—Her home lay in the direction of the west.

She would not tell me the name of her family, nor their armorial bearings, nor the name of their estate, nor even that of the country they lived in.

You are not to suppose that I worried her incessantly on these subjects. I watched opportunity, and rather insinuated than urged my inquiries. Once or twice, indeed, I did attack her more directly. But no matter what my tactics, utter failure was invariably the result. Reproaches and caresses were all lost upon her. But I must add this, that her evasion was conducted with so pretty a melancholy and deprecation, with so many, and even passionate declarations of her liking for me, and trust in my honour, and with so many promises that I should at last know all, that I could not find it in my heart long to be offended with her.

She used to place her pretty arms about my neck, draw me to her, and laying her cheek to mine, murmur with her lips near my ear, "Dearest, your little heart is wounded; think me not cruel because I obey the irresistible law of my strength and weakness; if your dear heart is wounded, my wild heart bleeds with yours. In the rapture of my enormous humiliation I live in your warm life, and you shall die—die, sweetly die—into mine. I cannot help it; as I draw near to you, you, in your turn, will draw near to others, and learn the rapture of that cruelty, which yet is love; so, for a while, seek to know no more of me and mine, but trust me with all your loving spirit."

And when she had spoken such a rhapsody, she would press me more closely in her trembling embrace, and her lips in soft kisses gently glow upon my cheek.

Her agitations and her language were unintelligible to me.

From these foolish embraces, which were not of very frequent occurrence, I must allow, I used to wish to extricate myself; but my energies seemed to fail me. Her murmured words sounded like a lullaby in my ear, and soothed my resistance into a trance, from which I only seemed to recover myself when she withdrew her arms.

In these mysterious moods I did not like her. I experienced a strange tumultuous excitement that was pleasurable, ever and anon, mingled with a vague sense of fear and disgust. I had no distinct thoughts about her while such scenes lasted, but I was conscious of a love growing into adoration, and also of abhorrence. This I know is paradox, but I can make no other attempt to explain the feeling.

I now write, after an interval of more than ten years, with a trembling hand, with a confused and horrible recollection of certain occurrences and situations, in the ordeal through which I was unconsciously passing; though with a vivid and very sharp remembrance of the main current of my story. But, I suspect, in all lives there are certain emotional scenes, those in which our passions have been most wildly and terribly roused, that are of all others the most vaguely and dimly remembered.

Sometimes after an hour of apathy, my strange and beautiful companion would take my hand and hold it with a fond pressure, renewed again and again; blushing softly, gazing in my face with languid and burning eyes, and breathing so fast that her dress rose and fell with the tumultuous respiration. It was like the ardour of a lover; it embarrassed me; it was hateful and yet overpowering; and with gloating eyes she drew me to her, and her hot lips travelled along my cheek in kisses; and she would whisper, almost in sobs, "You are mine, you *shall* be mine, and you and I are one for ever." Then she has thrown herself back in her chair, with her small hands over her eyes, leaving me trembling.

"Are we related," I used to ask; "what can you mean by all this? I remind you perhaps of some one whom you love; but you must not, I hate it; I don't know you—I don't know myself when you look so and talk so."

She used to sigh at my vehemence, then turn away and drop my hand.

Respecting these very extraordinary manifestations I strove in vain to form any satisfactory theory—I could not refer them to affectation or trick. It was unmistakably the momentary breaking out of suppressed instinct and emotion. Was she, notwithstanding her mother's volunteered denial, subject to brief visitations of insanity; or was there here a disguise and a romance? I had read in old story books of such things. What if a boyish lover had found his way into the house, and sought to prosecute his suit in masquerade, with the assistance of a clever old adventuress. But there were many things against this hypothesis, highly interesting as it was to my vanity.

I could boast of no little attentions such as masculine gallantry delights to offer. Between these passionate moments there were long intervals of common-place, of gaiety, of brooding melancholy, during which, except that I detected her eyes so full of melancholy fire, following me, at times I might have been as nothing to her. Except in these brief periods of mysterious excitement her ways were girlish; and there was always a languor about her, quite incompatible with a masculine system in a state of health.

In some respects her habits were odd. Perhaps not so singular in the opinion of a town lady like you, as they appeared to us rustic people. She used to come down very late, generally not till one o'clock, she would then take a cup of chocolate, but eat nothing; we then went out for a walk, which was a mere saunter, and she seemed, almost immediately, exhausted, and either returned to the schloss or sat on one of the benches that were placed, here and there, among the trees. This was a bodily languor in which her mind did not sympathise. She was always an animated talker, and very intelligent.

She sometimes alluded for a moment to her own home, or mentioned an adventure or situation, or an early recollection, which indicated a people of strange manners, and described customs of which we knew nothing. I gathered from these chance hints that her native country was much more remote than I had at first fancied.

As we sat thus one afternoon under the trees a funeral passed us by. It was that of a pretty young girl, whom I had often seen, the daughter of one of the rangers of the forest. The poor man was walking behind the coffin of his darling; she was his only child, and he looked quite heartbroken. Peasants walking two-and-two came behind, they were singing a funeral hymn.

I rose to mark my respect as they passed, and joined in the hymn they were very sweetly singing.

My companion shook me a little roughly, and I turned surprised.

She said brusquely, "Don't you perceive how discordant that is?"

"I think it very sweet, on the contrary," I answered, vexed at the interruption, and very uncomfortable, lest the people who composed the little procession should observe and resent what was passing.

I resumed, therefore, instantly, and was again interrupted. "You pierce my ears," said Carmilla, almost angrily, and stopping her ears with her tiny fingers. "Besides, how can you tell that your religion and mine are the same; your forms wound me, and I hate funerals. What a fuss! Why, *you* must die—*everyone* must die; and all are happier when they do. Come home."

"My father has gone on with the clergyman to the churchyard. I thought you knew she was to be buried to-day."

"*She?* I don't trouble my head about peasants. I don't know who she is," answered Carmilla, with a flash from her fine eyes.

"She is the poor girl who fancied she saw a ghost a fortnight ago, and has been dying ever since, till yesterday, when she expired."

"Tell me nothing about ghosts. I shan't sleep to-night if you do."

"I hope there is no plague or fever coming; all this looks very like it," I continued. "The swineherd's young wife died only a week ago, and she thought something seized her by the throat as she lay in her bed, and nearly strangled her. Papa says such horrible fancies do accompany some forms of fever. She was quite well the day before. She sank afterwards, and died before a week."

"Well, *her* funeral is over, I hope, and *her* hymn sung; and our ears shan't be tortured with that discord and jargon. It has made me nervous. Sit down here, beside me; sit close; hold my hand; press it hard—hard—harder."

We had moved a little back, and had come to another seat.

She sat down. Her face underwent a change that alarmed and even terrified me for a moment. It darkened, and became horribly livid; her teeth and hands were clenched, and she frowned and compressed her lips, while she stared down upon the ground at her feet, and trembled all over with a continued shudder as irrepressible as ague. All her energies seemed strained to suppress a fit, with which she was then breathlessly tugging; and at length a low convulsive cry of suffering broke from her, and gradually the hysteria subsided. "There! That comes of strangling people with hymns!" she said at last. "Hold me, hold me still. It is passing away."

And so gradually it did; and perhaps to dissipate the sombre impression which the spectacle had left upon me, she became unusually animated and chatty; and so we got home.

This was the first time I had seen her exhibit any definable symptoms of that delicacy of health which her mother had spoken of. It was the first time, also, I had seen her exhibit anything like temper.

Both passed away like a summer cloud; and never but once afterwards did I witness on her part a momentary sign of anger. I will tell you how it happened.

She and I were looking out of one of the long drawing-room windows, when there entered the court-yard, over the drawbridge, a figure of a wanderer whom I knew very well. He used to visit the schloss generally twice a year.

It was the figure of a hunchback, with the sharp lean features that generally accompany deformity. He wore a pointed black beard, and he was smiling from ear to ear, showing his white fangs. He was dressed in buff, black, and scarlet, and crossed with more straps and belts than I could count, from which hung all manner of things. Behind, he carried a magic-lantern, and two boxes, which I well knew, in one of which was a sala-mander, and in the other a mandrake. These monsters used to make my father laugh. They were compounded of parts of monkeys, parrots, squir-rels, fish, and hedgehogs, dried and stitched together with great neatness and startling effect. He had a fiddle, a box of conjuring apparatus, a pair of foils and masks attached to his belt, several other mysterious cases dan-gling about him, and a black staff with copper ferrules in his hand. His companion was a rough spare dog, that followed at his heels, but stopped short, suspiciously at the drawbridge, and in a little while began to howl dismally.

In the meantime, the mountebank, standing in the midst of the court-yard, raised his grotesque hat, and made us a very ceremonious bow, pay-ing his compliments very volubly in execrable French, and German not much better. Then, disengaging his fiddle, he began to scrape a lively air, to which he sang with a merry discord, dancing with ludicrous airs and activity, that made me laugh, in spite of the dog's howling.

Then he advanced to the window with many smiles and salutations, and his hat in his left hand, his fiddle under his arm, and with a fluency that never took breath, he grabbed a long advertisement of all his accom-plishments, and the resources of the various arts which he placed at our service, and the curiosities and entertainments which it was in his power, at our bidding to display.

"Will your ladyships be pleased to buy an amulet against the oupire, which is going like the wolf, I hear, through these woods," he said, dropping his hat on the pavement. "They are dying of it right and left, and here is a charm that never fails; only pinned to the pillow, and you may laugh in his face."

These charms consisted of oblong slips of vellum, with cabalistic ciphers and diagrams upon them.

Carmilla instantly purchased one, and so did I.

He was looking up, and we were smiling down upon him, amused; at least, I can answer for myself. His piercing black eye, as he looked up in our faces, seemed to detect something that fixed for a moment his curiosity.

In an instant he unrolled a leather case, full of all manner of odd little steel instruments.

"See here, my lady," he said, displaying it, and addressing me, "I profess, among other things less useful, the art of dentistry. Plague take the dog!" he interpolated. "Silence, beast! He howls so that your ladyships can scarcely hear a word. Your noble friend; the young lady at your right, has the sharpest tooth—long, thin, pointed, like an awl, like a needle; ha, ha! With my sharp and long sight, as I look up, I have seen it distinctly; now if it happens to hurt the young lady, and I think it must, here am I, here are my file, my punch, my nippers; I will make it round and blunt, if her ladyship pleases; no longer the tooth of a fish, but of a beautiful young lady as she is. Hey? Is the young lady displeased? Have I been too bold? Have I offended her?"

The young lady, indeed, looked very angry as she drew back from the window.

"How dares that mountebank insult us so? Where is your father? I shall demand redress from him. My father would have had the wretch tied up to the pump, and flogged with a cart-whip, and burnt to the bones with the castle brand!"

She retired from the window a step or two, and sat down, and had hardly lost sight of the offender, when her wrath subsided as suddenly as it had risen, and she gradually recovered her usual tone, and seemed to forget the little hunchback and his follies.

My father was out of spirits that evening. On coming in he told us that there had been another case very similar to the two fatal ones which had lately occurred. The sister of a young peasant on his estate, only a mile away, was very ill, had been, as she described it, attacked very nearly in the same way, and was now slowly but steadily sinking.

"All this," said my father, "is strictly referable to natural causes. These poor people infect one another with their superstitions, and so repeat in imagination the images of terror that have infested their neighbours."

"But that very circumstance frightens one horribly," said Carmilla.

"How so?" inquired my father.

"I am so afraid of fancying I see such things; I think it would be as bad as reality."

"We are in God's hands; nothing can happen without His permission, and all will end well for those who love Him. He is our faithful creator; He has made us all, and will take care of us."

"Creator! *Nature!*" said the young lady in answer to my gentle father. "And this disease that invades the country is natural. Nature. All things spring from Nature—don't they? All things in the heaven, in the earth, and under the earth, act and live as Nature ordains? I think so."

"The doctor said he would come here to-day," said my father, after a silence. "I want to know what he thinks about it, and what he thinks we had better do."

"Doctors never did me any good," said Carmilla.

"Then you have been ill?" I asked.

"More ill than ever you were," she answered.

"Long ago?"

"Yes, a long time. I suffered from this very illness; but I forget all but my pain and weakness, and they were not so bad as are suffered in other diseases."

"You were very young then?"

"I dare say; let us talk no more of it. You would not wound a friend?" She looked languidly in my eyes, and passed her arm round my waist lovingly, and led me out of the room. My father was busy over some papers near the window.

"Why does your papa like to frighten us?" said the pretty girl, with a sigh and a little shudder.

"He doesn't, dear Carmilla, it is the very furthest thing from his mind."

"Are you afraid, dearest?"

"I should be very much if I fancied there was any real danger of my being attacked as those poor people were."

"You are afraid to die?"

"Yes, every one is."

"But to die as lovers may—to die together, so that they may live together. Girls are caterpillars while they live in the world, to be finally butterflies when the summer comes; but in the meantime there are grubs and larvae, don't you see—each with their peculiar propensities, necessities and structure. So says Monsieur Buffon, in his big book, in the next room."

Later in the day the doctor came, and was closeted with papa for some time. He was a skilful man, of sixty and upwards, he wore powder, and shaved his pale face as smooth as a pumpkin. He and papa emerged from the room together, and I heard papa laugh, and say as they came out:

"Well, I do wonder at a wise man like you. What do you say to hippogriffs and dragons?"

The doctor was smiling, and made answer, shaking his head—

"Nevertheless, life and death are mysterious states, and we know little of the resources of either."

And so they walked on, and I heard no more. I did not then know what the doctor had been broaching, but I think I guess it now.

V

A WONDERFUL LIKENESS

This evening there arrived from Gratz the grave, dark-faced son of the picture-cleaner, with a horse and cart laden with two large packing-cases, having many pictures in each. It was a journey of ten leagues, and whenever a messenger arrived at the schloss from our little capital of Gratz, we used to crowd about him in the hall, to hear the news.

This arrival created in our secluded quarters quite a sensation. The cases remained in the hall, and the messenger was taken charge of by the servants till he had eaten his supper. Then with assistants, and armed with hammer, ripping chisel, and turnscrew, he met us in the hall, where we had assembled to witness the unpacking of the cases.

Carmilla sat looking listlessly on, while one after the other the old pictures, nearly all portraits, which had undergone the process of renovation, were brought to light. My mother was of an old Hungarian family, and most of these pictures, which were about to be restored to their places, had come to us through her.

My father had a list in his hand, from which he read, as the artist rummaged out the corresponding numbers. I don't know that the pictures were very good, but they were undoubtedly very old, and some of them very curious also. They had, for the most part, the merit of being now seen by me, I may say, for the first time; for the smoke and dust of time had all but obliterated them.

"There is a picture that I have not seen yet," said my father. "In one corner, at the top of it, is the name, as well as I could read, 'Marcia Karnstein,' and the date '1698'; and I am curious to see how it has turned out."

I remembered it; it was a small picture, about a foot and a half high, and nearly square, without a frame; but it was so blackened by age that I could not make it out.

The artist now produced it, with evident pride. It was quite beautiful; it was startling; it seemed to live. It was the effigy of Carmilla!

"Carmilla, dear, here is an absolute miracle. Here you are, living, smiling, ready to speak, in this picture. Isn't it beautiful, papa? And see, even the little mole on her throat."

My father laughed, and said, "Certainly it is a wonderful likeness," but he looked away, and to my surprise seemed but little struck by it, went on talking to the picture-cleaner; who was also something of an artist, and discoursed with intelligence about the portraits or other works, which his art had just brought into light and colour, while I was more and more lost in wonder the more I looked at the picture.

"Will you let me hang this picture in my room, papa?" I asked.

"Certainly, dear," said he, smiling, "I'm very glad you think it so like. It must be prettier even than I thought it, if it is."

The young lady did not acknowledge this pretty speech, did not seem to hear it. She was leaning back in her seat, her fine eyes under their long lashes gazing on me in contemplation, and she smiled in a kind of rapture.

"And now you can read quite plainly the name that is written in the corner. It is not Marcia; it looks as if it was done in gold. The name is Mircalla, Countess Karnstein, and this is a little coronet over it, and underneath A.D. 1698. I am descended from the Karnsteins; that is, mamma was."

"Ah!" said the lady, languidly, "so am I, I think, a very long descent, very ancient. Are there any Karnsteins living now?"

"None who bear the name, I believe. The family were ruined, I believe, in some civil wars, long ago, but the ruins of the castle are only about three miles away."

"How interesting!" she said, languidly. "But see what beautiful moonlight!" She glanced through the hall door, which stood a little open. "Suppose you take a little ramble round the court, and look down at the road and river."

"It is so like the night you came to us," I said.

She sighed, smiling.

She rose, and each with her arm about the other's waist, we walked out upon the pavement.

In silence, slowly we walked down to the drawbridge, where the beautiful landscape opened before us.

"And so you were thinking of the night I came here?" she almost whispered. "Are you glad I came?"

"Delighted, dear Carmilla," I answered.

"And you ask for the picture you think like me, to hang in your room," she murmured with a sigh, as she drew her arm closer about my waist, and let her pretty head sink upon my shoulder.

"How romantic you are, Carmilla," I said. "Whenever you tell me your story, it will be made up chiefly of some one great romance."

She kissed me silently.

"I am sure, Carmilla, you have been in love; that there is, at this moment, an affair of the heart going on."

"I have been in love with no one, and never shall," she whispered, "unless it should be with you."

How beautiful she looked in the moonlight!

Shy and strange was the look with which she quickly hid her face in my neck and hair, with tumultuous sighs, that seemed almost to sob, and pressed in mine a hand that trembled.

Her soft cheek was glowing against mine. "Darling, darling," she murmured, "I live in you; and you would die for me, I love you so."

I started from her.

She was gazing on me with eyes from which all fire, all meaning had flown, and a face colourless and apathetic.

"Is there a chill in the air, dear?" she said drowsily. "I almost shiver; have I been dreaming? Let us come in. Come, come; come in."

"You look ill, Carmilla; a little faint. You certainly must take some wine," I said.

"Yes, I will. I'm better now. I shall be quite well in a few minutes. Yes, do give me a little wine," answered Carmilla, as we approached the door. "Let us look again for a moment; it is the last time, perhaps, I shall see the moonlight with you."

"How do you feel now, dear Carmilla? Are you really better?" I asked.

I was beginning to take alarm, lest she should have been stricken with the strange epidemic that they said had invaded the country about us.

"Papa would be grieved beyond measure," I added, "if he thought you were ever so little ill, without immediately letting us know. We have a very skilful doctor near this, the physician who was with papa to-day."

"I'm sure he is. I know how kind you all are; but, dear child, I am quite well again. There is nothing ever wrong with me, but a little weakness. People say I am languid; I am incapable of exertion; I can scarcely walk as far as a child of three years old; and every now and then the little strength I have falters, and I become as you have just seen me. But after all I am very easily set up again; in a moment I am perfectly myself. See how I have recovered."

So, indeed, she had; and she and I talked a great deal, and very animated she was; and the remainder of that evening passed without any recurrence of what I called her infatuations. I mean her crazy talk and looks, which embarrassed, and even frightened me.

But there occurred that night an event which gave my thoughts quite a new turn, and seemed to startle even Carmilla's languid nature into momentary energy.

VI
A VERY STRANGE AGONY

When we got into the drawing-room, and had sat down to our coffee and chocolate, although Carmilla did not take any, she seemed quite herself again and Madame, and Mademoiselle De Lafontaine, joined us, and made a little card party, in the course of which papa came in for what he called his "dish of tea."

When the game was over he sat down beside Carmilla on the sofa, and asked her, a little anxiously, whether she had heard from her mother since her arrival.

She answered "No."

He then asked her whether she knew where a letter would reach her at present.

"I cannot tell," she answered, ambiguously, "but I have been thinking of leaving you; you have been already too hospitable and too kind to me. I have given you an infinity of trouble, and I should wish to take a carriage to-morrow, and post in pursuit of her; I know where I shall ultimately find her, although I dare not tell you."

"But you must not dream of any such thing," exclaimed my father, to my great relief. "We can't afford to lose you so, and I won't consent to your leaving us, except under the care of your mother, who was so good as to consent to your remaining with us till she should herself return. I should be quite happy if I knew that you heard from her; but this evening the accounts of the progress of the mysterious disease that has invaded our neighbourhood, grow even more alarming; and my beautiful guest, I do feel the responsibility, unaided by advice from your mother, very much. But I shall do my best; and one thing is certain, that you must not think of leaving us without her distinct direction to that effect. We should suffer too much in parting from you to consent to it easily."

"Thank you, sir, a thousand times for your hospitality," she answered, smiling bashfully. "You have all been too kind to me; I have seldom been so happy in all my life before, as in your beautiful château, under your care, and in the society of your dear daughter."

So he gallantly, in his old-fashioned way, kissed her hand, smiling, and pleased at her little speech.

I accompanied Carmilla as usual to her room, and sat and chatted with her while she was preparing for bed.

"Do you think," I said, at length, "that you will ever confide fully in me?"

She turned round smiling, but made no answer, only continued to smile on me.

"You won't answer that?" I said. "You can't answer pleasantly; I ought not to have asked you."

"You were quite right to ask me that, or anything. You do not know how dear you are to me, or you could not think any confidence too great to look for. But I am under vows, no nun half so awfully, and I dare not tell my story yet, even to you. The time is very near when you shall know everything. You will think me cruel, very selfish, but love is always selfish; the more ardent the more selfish. How jealous I am you cannot know. You must come with me, loving me, to death; or else hate me, and still come with me, and *hating* me through death and after. There is no such word as indifference in my apathetic nature."

"Now, Carmilla, you are going to talk your wild nonsense again," I said hastily.

"Not I, silly little fool as I am, and full of whims and fancies; for your sake I'll talk like a sage. Were you ever at a ball?"

"No; how you do run on. What is it like? How charming it must be."

"I almost forget, it is years ago."

I laughed.

"You are not so old. Your first ball can hardly be forgotten yet."

"I remember everything about it—with an effort. I see it all, as divers see what is going on above them, through a medium, dense, rippling, but transparent. There occurred that night what has confused the picture, and made its colours faint. I was all but assassinated in my bed, wounded *here*," she touched her breast, "and never was the same since."

"Were you near dying?"

"Yes, very—a cruel love—strange love, that would have taken my life. Love will have its sacrifices. No sacrifice without blood. Let us go to sleep now; I feel so lazy. How can I get up just now and lock my door?"

She was lying with her tiny hands buried in her rich wavy hair, under her cheek, her little head upon the pillow, and her glittering eyes followed me wherever I moved, with a kind of shy smile that I could not decipher.

I bid her good-night, and crept from the room with an uncomfortable sensation.

I often wondered whether our pretty guest ever said her prayers. I certainly had never seen her upon her knees. In the morning she never came down until long after our family prayers were over, and at night she never left the drawing-room to attend our brief evening prayers in the hall.

If it had not been that it had casually come out in one of our careless talks that she had been baptised, I should have doubted her being a Christian. Religion was a subject on which I had never heard her speak a word. If I had known the world better, this particular neglect or antipathy would not have so much surprised me.

The precautions of nervous people are infectious, and persons of a like temperament are pretty sure, after a time, to imitate them. I had adopted Carmilla's habit of locking her bed-room door, having taken into my head all her whimsical alarms about midnight invaders, and prowling assassins. I had also adopted her precaution of making a brief search through her room, to satisfy herself that no lurking assassin or robber was "ensconced."

These wise measures taken, I got into my bed and fell asleep. A light was burning in my room. This was an old habit, of very early date, and which nothing could have tempted me to dispense with.

Thus fortified I might take my rest in peace. But dreams come through stone walls, light up dark rooms, or darken light ones, and their persons make their exits and their entrances as they please, and laugh at locksmiths.

I had a dream that night that was the beginning of a very strange agony.

I cannot call it a nightmare, for I was quite conscious of being asleep. But I was equally conscious of being in my room, and lying in bed, precisely as I actually was. I saw, or fancied I saw, the room and its furniture just as I had seen it last, except that it was very dark, and I saw something moving round the foot of the bed, which at first I could not accurately distinguish. But I soon saw that it was a sooty-black animal that resembled a monstrous cat. It appeared to me about four or five feet long, for it measured fully the length of the hearth-rug as it passed over it; and it continued to-ing and fro-ing with the lithe sinister restlessness of a beast in a cage. I could not cry out, although as you may suppose, I was terrified. Its pace was growing faster, and the room rapidly darker and darker, and at length so dark that I could no longer see anything of it but its eyes. I felt it spring lightly on the bed. The two broad eyes approached my face, and suddenly I felt a stinging pain as if two large needles darted, an inch or two apart, deep into my breast. I waked with a scream. The room was lighted by the candle that burnt there all through the night, and I saw a female figure standing at the foot of the bed, a little at the right side. It was in a dark loose dress, and its hair was down and covered its shoulders. A block of stone could not have been more still. There was not the slightest stir of respiration. As I stared at it, the figure appeared to have changed its place, and was now nearer the door; then, close to it, the door opened, and it passed out.

I was now relieved, and able to breathe and move. My first thought was that Carmilla had been playing me a trick, and that I had forgotten to secure my door. I hastened to it, and found it locked as usual on the inside. I was afraid to open it—I was horrified. I sprang into my bed and covered my head up in the bed-clothes, and lay there more dead than alive till morning.

VII
DESCENDING

It would be vain my attempting to tell you the horror with which, even now, I recall the occurrence of that night. It was no such transitory terror as a dream leaves behind it. It seemed to deepen by time, and communicated itself to the room and the very furniture that had encompassed the apparition.

I could not bear next day to be alone for a moment. I should have told papa, but for two opposite reasons. At one time I thought he would laugh at my story, and I could not bear its being treated as a jest; and at another, I thought he might fancy that I had been attacked by the mysterious complaint which had invaded our neighbourhood. I had myself no misgivings of the kind, and as he had been rather an invalid for some time, I was afraid of alarming him.

I was comfortable enough with my good-natured companions, Madame Perrodon, and the vivacious Mademoiselle Lafontaine. They both perceived that I was out of spirits and nervous, and at length I told them what lay so heavy at my heart.

Mademoiselle laughed, but I fancied that Madame Perrodon looked anxious.

"By-the-by," said Mademoiselle, laughing, "the long lime tree walk, behind Carmilla's bedroom window, is haunted!"

"Nonsense!" exclaimed Madame, who probably thought the theme rather inopportune, "and who tells that story, my dear?"

"Martin says that he came up twice, when the old yard-gate was being repaired before sunrise, and twice saw the same female figure walking down the lime tree avenue."

"So he well might, as long as there are cows to milk in the river fields," said Madame.

"I daresay; but Martin chooses to be frightened, and never did I see fool *more* frightened."

"You must not say a word about it to Carmilla, because she can see down that walk from her room window," I interposed, "and she is, if possible, a greater coward than I."

Carmilla came down rather later than usual that day.

"I was so frightened last night," she said, so soon as we were together, "and I am sure I should have seen something dreadful if it had not been for that charm I bought from the poor little hunchback whom I called such hard names. I had a dream of something black coming round my bed, and I awoke in a perfect horror, and I really thought, for some seconds, I saw a dark figure near the chimney piece, but I felt under my pillow for my charm, and the moment my fingers touched it, the figure disappeared, and I felt quite certain, only that I had it by me, that something frightful would have made its appearance, and, perhaps, throttled me, as it did those poor people we heard of."

"Well, listen to me," I began, and recounted my adventure, at the recital of which she appeared horrified.

"And had you the charm near you?" she asked earnestly.

"No, I had dropped it into a china vase in the drawing-room, but I shall certainly take it with me to-night, as you have so much faith in it."

At this distance of time I cannot tell you, or even understand, how I overcame my horror so effectually as to lie alone in my room that night. I remember distinctly that I pinned the charm to my pillow. I fell asleep almost immediately, and slept even more soundly than usual all night.

Next night I passed as well. My sleep was delightfully deep and dreamless. But I wakened with a sense of lassitude and melancholy, which, however, did not exceed a degree that was almost luxurious.

"Well, I told you so," said Carmilla, when I described my quiet sleep, "I had such delightful sleep myself last night; I pinned the charm to the breast of my nightdress. It was too far away the night before. I am quite sure it was all fancy, except the dreams. I used to think that evil spirits made dreams, but our doctor told me it is no such thing. Only a fever passing by, or some other malady, as they often do, he said, knocks at the door, and not being able to get in, passes on, with that alarm."

"And what do you think the charm is?" said I.

"It has been fumigated or immersed in some drug, and is an antidote against the malaria," she answered.

"Then it acts only on the body?"

"Certainly; you don't suppose that evil spirits are frightened by bits of ribbon, or the perfumes of a druggist's shop? No, these complaints, wandering in the air, begin by trying the nerves, and so infect the brain; but before they can seize upon you, the antidote repels them. That I am sure is what the charm has done for us. It is nothing magical, it is simply natural."

I should have been happier if I could quite have agreed with Carmilla, but I did my best, and the impression was a little losing its force.

For some nights I slept profoundly; but still every morning I felt the same lassitude, and a languor weighed upon me all day. I felt myself a changed girl. A strange melancholy was stealing over me, a melancholy that I would not have interrupted. Dim thoughts of death began to open, and an idea that I was slowly sinking took gentle, and, somehow, not unwelcome possession of me. If it was sad, the tone of mind which this induced was also sweet. Whatever it might be, my soul acquiesced in it.

I would not admit that I was ill, I would not consent to tell my papa, or to have the doctor sent for.

Carmilla became more devoted to me than ever, and her strange paroxysms of languid adoration more frequent. She used to gloat on me with increasing ardour the more my strength and spirits waned. This always shocked me like a momentary glare of insanity.

Without knowing it, I was now in a pretty advanced stage of the strangest illness under which mortal ever suffered. There was an unaccountable fascination in its earlier symptoms that more than reconciled me to the incapacitating effect of that stage of the malady. This fascination increased for a time, until it reached a certain point, when gradually a sense of the horrible mingled itself with it, deepening as you shall hear, until it discoloured and perverted the whole state of my life.

The first change I experienced was rather agreeable. It was very near the turning point from which began the descent of Avernus.

Certain vague and strange sensations visited me in my sleep. The prevailing one was of that pleasant, peculiar cold thrill which we feel in bathing, when we move against the current of a river. This was soon accompanied by dreams that seemed interminable, and were so vague that I could never recollect their scenery and persons, or any one connected portion of their action. But they left an awful impression, and a sense of exhaustion, as if I had passed through a long period of great mental exertion and danger. After all these dreams there remained on waking a remembrance of having been in a place very nearly dark, and of having spoken to people whom I could not see; and especially of one clear voice, of a female's, very deep, that spoke as if at a distance, slowly, and producing always the same sensation of indescribable solemnity and fear. Sometimes there came a sensation as if a hand was drawn softly along my cheek and neck. Sometimes it was as if warm lips kissed me, and longer and more lovingly as they reached my throat, but there the caress fixed itself. My heart beat faster, my breathing rose and fell rapidly and full drawn; a sobbing, that rose into a sense of strangulation, supervened, and turned into a dreadful convulsion, in which my senses left me, and I became unconscious.

It was now three weeks since the commencement of this unaccountable state. My sufferings had, during the last week, told upon my appearance. I had grown pale, my eyes were dilated and darkened underneath, and the languor which I had long felt began to display itself in my countenance.

My father asked me often whether I was ill; but, with an obstinacy which now seems to me unaccountable, I persisted in assuring him that I was quite well.

In a sense this was true. I had no pain, I could complain of no bodily derangement. My complaint seemed to be one of the imagination, or the nerves, and, horrible as my sufferings were, I kept them, with a morbid reserve, very nearly to myself.

It could not be that terrible complaint which the peasants call the oupire, for I had now been suffering for three weeks, and they were seldom ill for much more than three days, when death put an end to their miseries.

Carmilla complained of dreams and feverish sensations, but by no means of so alarming a kind as mine. I say that mine were extremely alarming. Had I been capable of comprehending my condition, I would have invoked aid and advice on my knees. The narcotic of an unsuspected influence was acting upon me, and my perceptions were benumbed.

I am going to tell you now of a dream that led immediately to an odd discovery.

One night, instead of the voice I was accustomed to hear in the dark, I heard one, sweet and tender, and at the same time terrible, which said, "Your mother warns you to beware of the assassin." At the same time a light unexpectedly sprang up, and I saw Carmilla, standing near the foot of my bed, in her white nightdress, bathed, from her chin to her feet, in one great stain of blood.

I wakened with a shriek, possessed with the one idea that Carmilla was being murdered. I remember springing from my bed, and my next recollection is that of standing on the lobby, crying for help.

Madame and Mademoiselle came scurrying out of their rooms in alarm; a lamp burned always on the lobby, and seeing me, they soon learned the cause of my terror.

I insisted on our knocking at Carmilla's door. Our knocking was unanswered. It soon became a pounding and an uproar. We shrieked her name, but all was vain.

We all grew frightened, for the door was locked. We hurried back, in panic, to my room. There we rang the bell long and furiously. If my father's room had been at that side of the house, we would have called him up at once to our aid. But, alas! he was quite out of hearing, and to reach him involved an excursion for which we none of us had courage.

Servants, however, soon came running up the stairs; I had got on my dressing-gown and slippers meanwhile, and my companions were already similarly furnished. Recognizing the voices of the servants on the lobby, we sallied out together; and having renewed, as fruitlessly, our summons at Carmilla's door, I ordered the men to force the lock. They did so, and we stood, holding our lights aloft, in the doorway, and so stared into the room.

We called her by name; but there was still no reply. We looked round the room. Everything was undisturbed. It was exactly in the state in which I left it on bidding her good night. But Carmilla was gone.

VIII
SEARCH

At sight of the room, perfectly undisturbed except for our violent entrance, we began to cool a little, and soon recovered our senses sufficiently to dismiss the men. It had struck Mademoiselle that possibly Carmilla had been wakened by the uproar at her door, and in her first panic had jumped from her bed, and hid herself in a press, or behind a curtain, from which she could not, of course, emerge until the majordomo and his myrmidons had withdrawn. We now recommenced our search, and began to call her by name again.

It was all to no purpose. Our perplexity and agitation increased. We examined the windows, but they were secured. I implored of Carmilla, if she had concealed herself, to play this cruel trick no longer—to come out, and to end our anxieties. It was all useless. I was by this time convinced that she was not in the room, nor in the dressing-room, the door of which was still locked on this side. She could not have passed it. I was utterly puzzled. Had Carmilla discovered one of those secret passages which the old housekeeper said were known to exist in the schloss, although the tradition of their exact situation had been lost. A little time would, no doubt, explain all—utterly perplexed as, for the present, we were.

It was past four o'clock, and I preferred passing the remaining hours of darkness in Madame's room. Daylight brought no solution of the difficulty.

The whole household, with my father at its head, was in a state of agitation next morning. Every part of the château was searched. The grounds were explored. Not a trace of the missing lady could be discovered. The stream was about to be dragged; my father was in distraction; what a tale to have to tell the poor girl's mother on her return. I, too, was almost beside myself, though my grief was quite of a different kind.

The morning was passed in alarm and excitement. It was now one o'clock, and still no tidings. I ran up to Carmilla's room, and found her standing at her dressing-table. I was astounded. I could not believe my eyes. She beckoned me to her with her pretty finger, in silence. Her face expressed extreme fear.

I ran to her in an ecstasy of joy; I kissed and embraced her again and again. I ran to the bell and rang it vehemently, to bring others to the spot, who might at once relieve my father's anxiety.

"Dear Carmilla, what has become of you all this time? We have been in agonies of anxiety about you," I exclaimed. "Where have you been? How did you come back?"

"Last night has been a night of wonders," she said.

"For mercy's sake, explain all you can."

"It was past two last night," she said, "when I went to sleep as usual in my bed, with my doors locked, that of the dressing-room, and that opening upon the gallery. My sleep was uninterrupted, and, so far as I know, dreamless; but I awoke just now on the sofa in the dressing-room there, and I found the door between the rooms open, and the other door forced. How could all this have happened without my being wakened? It must have been accompanied with a great deal of noise, and I am particularly easily wakened; and how could I have been carried out of my bed without my sleep having been interrupted, I whom the slightest stir startles?"

By this time, Madame, Mademoiselle, my father, and a number of the servants were in the room. Carmilla was, of course, overwhelmed with inquiries, congratulations, and welcomes. She had but one story to tell, and seemed the least able of all the party to suggest any way of accounting for what had happened.

My father took a turn up and down the room, thinking. I saw Carmilla's eye follow him for a moment with a sly, dark glance.

When my father had sent the servants away, Mademoiselle having gone in search of a little bottle of valerian and sal-volatile, and there being no one now in the room with Carmilla except my father, Madame, and myself, he came to her thoughtfully, took her hand very kindly, led her to the sofa, and sat down beside her.

"Will you forgive me, my dear, if I risk a conjecture, and ask a question?"

"Who can have a better right?" she said. "Ask what you please, and I will tell you everything. But my story is simply one of bewilderment and darkness. I know absolutely nothing. Put any question you please. But you know, of course, the limitations mamma has placed me under."

"Perfectly, my dear child. I need not approach the topics on which she desires our silence. Now, the marvel of last night consists in your having been removed from your bed and your room without being wakened, and this removal having occurred apparently while the windows were still secured, and the two doors locked upon the inside. I will tell you my theory, and first ask you a question."

Carmilla was leaning on her hand dejectedly; Madame and I were listening breathlessly.

"Now, my question is this. Have you ever been suspected of walking in your sleep?"

"Never since I was very young indeed."

"But you did walk in your sleep when you were young?"

"Yes; I know I did. I have been told so often by my old nurse."

My father smiled and nodded.

"Well, what has happened is this. You got up in your sleep, unlocked the door, not leaving the key, as usual, in the lock, but taking it out and locking it on the outside; you again took the key out, and carried it away with you to some one of the five-and-twenty rooms on this floor, or perhaps upstairs or downstairs. There are so many rooms and closets so much heavy furniture, and such accumulations of lumber, that it would require a week to search this old house thoroughly. Do you see, now, what I mean?"

"I do, but not all," she answered.

"And how, papa, do you account for her finding herself on the sofa in the dressing-room, which we had searched so carefully?"

"She came there after you had searched it, still in her sleep, and at last awoke spontaneously, and was as much surprised to find herself where she was as any one else. I wish all mysteries were as easily and innocently explained as yours, Carmilla," he said, laughing. "And so we may congratulate ourselves on the certainty that the most natural explanation of the occurrence is one that involves no drugging, no tampering with locks, no burglars, or poisoners, or witches—nothing that need alarm Carmilla, or any one else, for our safety."

Carmilla was looking charmingly. Nothing could be more beautiful than her tints. Her beauty was, I think, enhanced by that graceful languor that was peculiar to her. I think my father was silently contrasting her looks with mine, for he said:—

"I wish my poor Laura was looking more like herself," and he sighed.

So our alarms were happily ended, and Carmilla restored to her friends.

IX
THE DOCTOR

As Carmilla would not hear of an attendant sleeping in her room, my father arranged that a servant should sleep outside her door, so that she could not attempt to make another such excursion without being arrested at her own door.

That night passed quietly; and next morning early, the doctor, whom my father had sent for without telling me a word about it, arrived to see me.

Madame accompanied me to the library; and there the grave little doctor, with white hair and spectacles, whom I mentioned before, was waiting to receive me.

I told him my story, and as I proceeded he grew graver and graver.

We were standing, he and I, in the recess of one of the windows, facing one another. When my statement was over, he leaned with his shoulders against the wall, and with his eyes fixed on me earnestly, with an interest in which was a dash of horror.

After a minute's reflection, he asked Madame if he could see my father.

He was sent for accordingly, and as he entered, smiling, he said:

"I dare say, doctor, you are going to tell me that I am an old fool for having brought you here; I hope I am."

But his smile faded into shadow as the doctor, with a very grave face, beckoned him to him.

He and the doctor talked for some time in the same recess where I had just conferred with the physician. It seemed an earnest and argumentative conversation. The room is very large, and I and Madame stood together, burning with curiosity, at the further end. Not a word could we hear, however, for they spoke in a very low tone, and the deep recess of the window quite concealed the doctor from view, and very nearly my father, whose foot, arm, and shoulder only could we see; and the voices were, I suppose, all the less audible for the sort of closet which the thick wall and window formed.

After a time my father's face looked into the room; it was pale, thoughtful, and, I fancied, agitated.

"Laura, dear, come here for a moment. Madame, we shan't trouble you, the doctor says, at present."

Accordingly I approached, for the first time a little alarmed; for, although I felt very weak, I did not feel ill; and strength, one always fancies, is a thing that may be picked up when we please.

My father held out his hand to me as I drew near, but he was looking at the doctor, and he said:

"It certainly *is* very odd; I don't understand it quite. Laura, come here, dear; now attend to Doctor Spielsberg, and recollect yourself."

"You mentioned a sensation like that of two needles piercing the skin, somewhere about your neck, on the night when you experienced your first horrible dream. Is there still any soreness?"

"None at all," I answered.

"Can you indicate with your finger about the point at which you think this occurred?"

"Very little below my throat—*here,*" I answered.

I wore a morning dress, which covered the place I pointed to.

"Now you can satisfy yourself," said the doctor. "You won't mind your papa's lowering your dress a very little. It is necessary, to detect a symptom of the complaint under which you have been suffering."

I acquiesced. It was only an inch or two below the edge of my collar.

"God bless me!—so it is," exclaimed my father, growing pale.

"You see it now with your own eyes," said the doctor, with a gloomy triumph.

"What is it?" I exclaimed, beginning to be frightened.

"Nothing, my dear young lady, but a small blue spot, about the size of the tip of your little finger; and now," he continued, turning to papa, "the question is what is best to be done?"

"Is there any danger?" I urged, in great trepidation.

"I trust not, my dear," answered the doctor. "I don't see why you should not recover. I don't see why you should not begin *immediately* to get better. That is the point at which the sense of strangulation begins?"

"Yes," I answered.

"And—recollect as well as you can—the same point was a kind of centre of that thrill which you described just now, like the current of a cold stream running against you?"

"It may have been; I think it was."

"Ay, you see?" he added, turning to my father. "Shall I say a word to Madame?"

"Certainly," said my father.

He called Madame to him, and said:

"I find my young friend here far from well. It won't be of any great consequence, I hope; but it will be necessary that some steps be taken, which I will explain by-and-by; but in the meantime, Madame, you will be so good as not to let Miss Laura be alone for one moment. That is the only direction I need give for the present. It is indispensable."

"We may rely upon your kindness, Madame, I know," added my father.

Madame satisfied him eagerly.

"And you, dear Laura, I know you will observe the doctor's direction."

"I shall have to ask your opinion upon another patient, whose symptoms slightly resemble those of my daughter, that have just been detailed to you—very much milder in degree, but I believe quite of the same sort. She is a young lady—our guest; but as you say you will be passing this way again this evening, you can't do better than take your supper here, and you can then see her. She does not come down till the afternoon."

"I thank you," said the doctor. "I shall be with you, then, at about seven this evening."

And then they repeated their directions to me and to Madame, and with this parting charge my father left us, and walked out with the doctor; and I saw them pacing together up and down between the road and the moat, on the grassy platform in front of the castle, evidently absorbed in earnest conversation.

The doctor did not return. I saw him mount his horse there, take his leave, and ride away eastward through the forest. Nearly at the same time I saw the man arrive from Dranfeld with the letters, and dismount and hand the bag to my father.

In the meantime, Madame and I were both busy, lost in conjecture as to the reasons of the singular and earnest direction which the doctor and my father had concurred in imposing. Madame, as she afterwards told me, was afraid the doctor apprehended a sudden seizure, and that, without prompt assistance, I might either lose my life in a fit, or at least be seriously hurt.

This interpretation did not strike me; and I fancied, perhaps luckily for my nerves, that the arrangement was prescribed simply to secure a companion, who would prevent my taking too much exercise, or eating unripe fruit, or doing any of the fifty foolish things to which young people are supposed to be prone.

About half-an-hour after my father came in—he had a letter in his hand—and said:

"This letter had been delayed; it is from General Spielsdorf. He might have been here yesterday, he may not come till to-morrow, or he may be here to-day."

He put the open letter into my hand; but he did not look pleased, as he used when a guest, especially one so much loved as the General, was coming. On the contrary, he looked as if he wished him at the bottom of the Red Sea. There was plainly something on his mind which he did not choose to divulge.

"Papa, darling, will you tell me this?" said I, suddenly laying my hand on his arm, and looking, I am sure, imploringly in his face.

"Perhaps," he answered, smoothing my hair caressingly over my eyes.

"Does the doctor think me very ill?"

"No, dear; he thinks, if right steps are taken, you will be quite well again, at least on the high road to a complete recovery, in a day or two," he answered, a little drily. "I wish our good friend, the General, had chosen any other time; that is, I wish you had been perfectly well to receive him."

"But do tell me, papa," I insisted, "*what* does he think is the matter with me?"

"Nothing; you must not plague me with questions," he answered, with more irritation than I ever remember him to have displayed before; and seeing that I looked wounded, I suppose, he kissed me, and added, "You shall know all about it in a day or two; that is, all that *I* know. In the meantime, you are not to trouble your head about it."

He turned and left the room, but came back before I had done wondering and puzzling over the oddity of all this; it was merely to say that he was going to Karnstein, and had ordered the carriage to be ready at twelve, and that I and Madame should accompany him; he was going to see the priest who lived near those picturesque grounds upon business, and as Carmilla had never seen them, she could follow, when she came down, with Mademoiselle, who would bring materials for what you call a pic-nic, which might be laid for us in the ruined castle.

At twelve o'clock, accordingly, I was ready, and not long after, my father, Madame and I set out upon our projected drive. Passing the drawbridge we turn to the right, and follow the road over the steep Gothic bridge, westward, to reach the deserted village and ruined castle of Karnstein.

No sylvan drive can be fancied prettier. The ground breaks into gentle hills and hollows, all clothed with beautiful wood, totally destitute of the comparative formality which artificial planting and early culture and pruning impart.

The irregularities of the ground often lead the road out of its course, and cause it to wind beautifully round the sides of broken hollows and the steeper sides of the hills, among varieties of ground almost inexhaustible.

Turning one of these points, we suddenly encountered our old friend, the General, riding towards us, attended by a mounted servant. His portmanteaus were following in a hired waggon, such as we term a cart.

The General dismounted as we pulled up, and, after the usual greetings, was easily persuaded to accept the vacant seat in the carriage, and sent his horse on with his servant to the schloss.

X
BEREAVED

It was about ten months since we had last seen him; but that time had sufficed to make an alteration of years in his appearance. He had grown thinner; something of gloom and anxiety had taken the place of that cordial serenity which used to characterise his features. His dark blue eyes, always penetrating, now gleamed with a sterner light from under his shaggy grey eyebrows. It was not such a change as grief alone usually induces, and angrier passions seemed to have had their share in bringing it about.

We had not long resumed our drive, when the General began to talk, with his usual soldierly directness, of the bereavement, as he termed it, which he had sustained in the death of his beloved niece and ward; and he then broke out in a tone of intense bitterness and fury, inveighing against the "hellish arts" to which she had fallen a victim, and expressing, with more exasperation than piety, his wonder that Heaven should tolerate so monstrous an indulgence of the lusts and malignity of hell.

My father, who saw at once that something very extraordinary had befallen, asked him, if not too painful to him, to retail the circumstances which he thought justified the strong terms in which he expressed himself.

"I should tell you all with pleasure," said the General, "but you would not believe me."

"Why should I not?" he asked.

"Because," he answered testily, "you believe in nothing but what consists with your own prejudices and illusions. I remember when I was like you, but I have learned better."

"Try me," said my father; "I am not such a dogmatist as you suppose. Besides which, I very well know that you generally require proof for what you believe, and am, therefore, very strongly predisposed to respect your conclusions."

"You are right in supposing that I have not been led lightly into a belief in the marvellous—for what I have experienced *is* marvellous—and I have been forced by extraordinary evidence to credit that which ran counter, diametrically, to all my theories. I have been made the dupe of a preternatural conspiracy."

Notwithstanding his professions of confidence in the General's penetration, I saw my father, at this point, glance at the General, with, as I thought, a marked suspicion of his sanity.

The General did not see it, luckily. He was looking gloomily and curiously into the glades and vistas of the woods that were opening before us.

"You are going to the Ruins of Karnstein?" he said. "Yes, it is a lucky coincidence; do you know I was going to ask you to bring me there to inspect them. I have a special object in exploring. There is a ruined chapel, ain't there, with a great many tombs of that extinct family?"

"So there are—highly interesting," said my father. "I hope you are thinking of claiming the title and estates?"

My father said this gaily, but the General did not recollect the laugh, or even the smile, which courtesy exacts for a friend's joke; on the contrary, he looked grave and even fierce, ruminating on a matter that stirred his anger and horror.

"Something very different," he said, gruffly. "I mean to unearth some of those fine people. I hope, by God's blessing, to accomplish a pious sacrilege here, which will relieve our earth of certain monsters, and enable honest people to sleep in their beds without being assailed by murderers. I have strange things to tell you, my dear friend, such as I myself would have scouted as incredible a few months since."

My father looked at him again, but this time not with a glance of suspicion—with an eye, rather, of keen intelligence and alarm.

"The house of Karnstein," he said, "has been long extinct: a hundred years at least. My dear wife was maternally descended from the Karnsteins. But the name and title have long ceased to exist. The castle is a ruin; the very village is deserted; it is fifty years since the smoke of a chimney was seen there; not a roof left."

"Quite true. I have heard a great deal about that since I last saw you; a great deal that will astonish you. But I had better relate everything in the order in which it occurred," said the General. "You saw my dear ward— my child, I may call her. No creature could have been more beautiful, and only three months ago none more blooming."

"Yes, poor thing! when I saw her last she certainly was quite lovely," said my father. "I was grieved and shocked more than I can tell you, my dear friend; I knew what a blow it was to you."

He took the General's hand, and they exchanged a kind pressure. Tears gathered in the old soldier's eyes. He did not seek to conceal them. He said:

"We have been very old friends; I knew you would feel for me, childless as I am. She had become an object of very dear interest to me, and repaid my care by an affection that cheered my home and made my life happy. That is all gone. The years that remain to me on earth may not be very long; but by God's mercy I hope to accomplish a service to mankind before I die, and to subserve the vengeance of Heaven upon the fiends who have murdered my poor child in the spring of her hopes and beauty!"

"You said, just now, that you intended relating everything as it oc-curred," said my father. "Pray do; I assure you that it is not mere curiosity that prompts me."

By this time we had reached the point at which the Drunstall road, by which the General had come, diverges from the road which we were trav-elling to Karnstein.

"How far is it to the ruins?" inquired the General, looking anxiously forward.

"About half a league," answered my father. "Pray let us hear the story you were so good as to promise."

XI
THE STORY

"With all my heart," said the General, with an effort; and after a short pause in which to arrange his subject, he commenced one of the strangest narratives I ever heard.

"My dear child was looking forward with great pleasure to the visit you had been so good as to arrange for her to your charming daughter." Here he made me a gallant but melancholy bow. "In the meantime we had an invitation to my old friend the Count Carlsfeld, whose schloss is about six leagues to the other side of Karnstein. It was to attend the series of fêtes which, you remember, were given by him in honour of his illustrious visitor, the Grand Duke Charles."

"Yes; and very splendid, I believe, they were," said my father.

"Princely! But then his hospitalities are quite regal. He has Aladdin's lamp. The night from which my sorrow dates was devoted to a magnificent masquerade. The grounds were thrown open, the trees hung with coloured lamps. There was such a display of fireworks as Paris itself had never witnessed. And such music—music, you know, is my weakness—such ravishing music! The finest instrumental band, perhaps, in the world, and the finest singers who could be collected from all the great operas in Europe. As you wandered through these fantastically illuminated grounds, the moon-lighted château throwing a rosy light from its long rows of windows, you would suddenly hear these ravishing voices stealing from the silence of some grove, or rising from boats upon the lake. I felt myself, as I looked and listened, carried back into the romance and poetry of my early youth. "When the fireworks were ended, and the ball beginning, we returned to the noble suite of rooms that were thrown open to the dancers. A masked ball, you know, is a beautiful sight; but so brilliant a spectacle of the kind I never saw before.

"It was a very aristocratic assembly. I was myself almost the only 'nobody' present.

"My dear child was looking quite beautiful. She wore no mask. Her excitement and delight added an unspeakable charm to her features, always lovely. I remarked a young lady, dressed magnificently, but wearing a mask, who appeared to me to be observing my ward with extraordinary interest. I had seen her, earlier in the evening, in the great hall, and again, for a few minutes, walking near us, on the terrace under the castle windows, similarly employed. A lady, also masked, richly and gravely dressed, and with a stately air, like a person of rank, accompanied her as a chaperon. Had the young lady not worn a mask, I could, of course, have been much more certain upon the question whether she was really watching my poor darling. I am now well assured that she was.

"We were now in one of the *salons*. My poor dear child had been dancing, and was resting a little in one of the chairs near the door; I was standing near. The two ladies I have mentioned had approached, and the younger took the chair next my ward; while her companion stood beside me, and for a little time addressed herself, in a low tone, to her charge.

"Availing herself of the privilege of her mask, she turned to me, and in the tone of an old friend, and calling me by my name, opened a conversation with me, which piqued my curiosity a good deal. She referred to many scenes where she had met me—at Court, and at distinguished houses. She alluded to little incidents which I had long ceased to think of, but which, I found, had only lain in abeyance in my memory, for they instantly started into life at her touch.

"I became more and more curious to ascertain who she was, every moment. She parried my attempts to discover very adroitly and pleasantly. The knowledge she showed of many passages in my life seemed to me all but unaccountable; and she appeared to take a not unnatural pleasure in foiling my curiosity, and in seeing me flounder in my eager perplexity, from one conjecture to another.

"In the meantime the young lady, whom her mother called by the odd name of Millarca, when she once or twice addressed her, had, with the same ease and grace, got into conversation with my ward.

"She introduced herself by saying that her mother was a very old acquaintant of mine. She spoke of the agreeable audacity which a mask rendered practicable; she talked like a friend; she admired her dress, and insinuated very prettily her admiration of her beauty. She amused her with laughing criticisms upon the people who crowded the ballroom, and laughed at my poor child's fun. She was very witty and lively when she pleased, and after a time they had grown very good friends, and the young stranger lowered her mask, displaying a remarkably beautiful face. I had never seen it before, neither had my dear child. But though it was new to us, the features were so engaging, as well as lovely, that it was impossible not to feel the attraction powerfully. My poor girl did so. I never saw anyone more taken with another at first sight, unless, indeed, it was the stranger herself, who seemed quite to have lost her heart to her.

"In the meantime, availing myself of the licence of a masquerade, I put not a few questions to the elder lady.

" 'You have puzzled me utterly,' I said, laughing. 'Is that not enough? won't you, now, consent to stand on equal terms, and do me the kindness to remove your mask?'

" 'Can any request be more unreasonable?' she replied. 'Ask a lady to yield an advantage! Beside, how do you know you should recognize me? Years make changes.'

" 'As you see,' I said, with a bow, and, I suppose, a rather melancholy little laugh.

" 'As philosophers tell us,' she said; 'and how do you know that a sight of my face would help you?'

" 'I should take chance for that,' I answered. 'It is vain trying to make yourself out an old woman; your figure betrays you.'

" 'Years, nevertheless, have passed since I saw you, rather since you saw me, for that is what I am considering. Millarca, there, is my daughter; I cannot then be young, even in the opinion of people whom time has taught to be indulgent, and I may not like to be compared with what you remember me. You have no mask to remove. You can offer me nothing in exchange.'

" 'My petition is to your pity, to remove it.'

" 'And mine to yours, to let it stay where it is,' she replied.

" 'Well, then, at least you will tell me whether you are French or German; you speak both languages so perfectly.'

" 'I don't think I shall tell you that, General; you intend a surprise, and are meditating the particular point of attack.'

" 'At all events, you won't deny this,' I said, 'that being honoured by your permission to converse, I ought to know how to address you. Shall I say Madame la Comtesse?'

"She laughed, and she would, no doubt, have met me with another evasion—if, indeed, I can treat any occurrence in an interview every circumstance of which was pre-arranged, as I now believe, with the profoundest cunning, as liable to be modified by accident.

" 'As to that,' she began; but she was interrupted, almost as she opened her lips, by a gentleman, dressed in black, who looked particularly elegant and distinguished, with this drawback, that his face was the most deadly pale I ever saw, except in death. He was in no masquerade—in the plain evening dress of a gentleman; and he said without a smile, but with a courtly and unusually low bow:—

" 'Will Madame la Comtesse permit me to say a very few words which may interest her?'

"The lady turned quickly to him, and touched her lip in token of silence; she then said to me, 'Keep my place for me, General; I shall return when I have said a few words.'

"And with this injunction, playfully given, she walked a little aside with the gentleman in black, and talked for some minutes, apparently very earnestly. They then walked away slowly together in the crowd, and I lost them for some minutes.

"I spent the interval in cudgelling my brains for conjecture as to the identity of the lady who seemed to remember me so kindly, and I was thinking of turning about and joining in the conversation between my pretty ward and the Countess's daughter, and trying whether, by the time she returned, I might not have a surprise in store for her, by having her name, title, chateau, and estates at my fingers' ends. But at this moment she returned, accompanied by the pale man in black, who said:

" 'I shall return and inform Madame la Comtesse when her carriage is at the door.'

"He withdrew with a bow."

XII
A Petition

" 'Then we are to lose Madame la Comtesse, but I hope only for a few hours,' I said, with a low bow.

" 'It may be that only, or it may be a few weeks. It was very unlucky his speaking to me just now as he did. Do you now know me?"

"I assured her I did not.

" 'You shall know me,' she said, 'but not at present. We are older and better friends than, perhaps, you suspect. I cannot yet declare myself. I shall in three weeks pass your beautiful schloss about which I have been making enquiries. I shall then look in upon you for an hour or two, and renew a friendship which I never think of without a thousand pleasant recollections. This moment a piece of news has reached me like a thunderbolt. I must set out now, and travel by a devious route, nearly a hundred miles, with all the dispatch I can possibly make. My perplexities multiply. I am only deterred by the compulsory reserve I practise as to my name from making a very singular request of you. My poor child has not quite recovered her strength. Her horse fell with her, at a hunt which she had ridden out to witness, her nerves have not yet recovered the shock, and our physician says that she must on no account exert herself for some time to come. We came here, in consequence, by very easy stages—hardly six leagues a day. I must now travel day and night, on a mission of life and death—a mission the critical and momentous nature of which I shall be able to explain to you when we meet, as I hope we shall, in a few weeks, without the necessity of any concealment.'

"She went on to make her petition, and it was in the tone of a person from whom such a request amounted to conferring, rather than seeking a favour. This was only in manner, and, as it seemed, quite unconsciously. Than the terms in which it was expressed, nothing could be more deprecatory. It was simply that I would consent to take charge of her daughter during her absence.

"This was, all things considered, a strange, not to say, an audacious request. She in some sort disarmed me, by stating and admitting everything that could be urged against it, and throwing herself entirely upon my chivalry. At the same moment, by a fatality that seems to have predetermined all that happened, my poor child came to my side, and, in an undertone, besought me to invite her new friend, Millarca, to pay us a visit. She had just been sounding her, and thought, if her mamma would allow her, she would like it extremely.

"At another time I should have told her to wait a little, until, at least, we knew who they were. But I had not a moment to think in. The two ladies assailed me together, and I must confess the refined and beautiful face of the young lady, about which there was something extremely engaging, as well as the elegance and fire of high birth, determined me; and quite overpowered, I submitted, and undertook too easily, the care of the young lady, whom her mother called Millarca.

"The Countess beckoned to her daughter, who listened with grave attention while she told her, in general terms, how suddenly and peremptorily she had been summoned, and also of the arrangement she had made for her under my care, adding that I was one of her earliest and most valued friends.

"I made, of course, such speeches as the case seemed to call for, and found myself, on reflection, in a position which I did not half like.

"The gentleman in black returned, and very ceremoniously conducted the lady from the room.

"The demeanour of this gentleman was such as to impress me with the conviction that the Countess was a lady of very much more importance than her modest title alone might have led me to assume.

"Her last charge to me was that no attempt was to be made to learn more about her than I might have already guessed, until her return. Our distinguished host, whose guest she was, knew her reasons.

" 'But here,' she said, 'neither I nor my daughter could safely remain for more than a day. I removed my mask imprudently for a moment, about an hour ago, and, too late, I fancied you saw me. So I resolved to seek an opportunity of talking a little to you. Had I found that you *had* seen me, I should have thrown myself on your high sense of honour to keep my secret for some weeks. As it is, I am satisfied that you did not see me; but if you now *suspect,* or, on reflection, *should* suspect, who I am, I commit myself, in like manner, entirely to your honour. My daughter will observe the same secrecy, and I well know that you will, from time to time, remind her, lest she should thoughtlessly disclose it.'

"She whispered a few words to her daughter, kissed her hurriedly twice, and went away, accompanied by the pale gentleman in black, and disappeared in the crowd.

" 'In the next room,' said Millarca, 'there is a window that looks upon the hall door. I should like to see the last of mamma, and to kiss my hand to her.'

"We assented, of course, and accompanied her to the window. We looked out, and saw a handsome old-fashioned carriage, with a troop of couriers and footmen. We saw the slim figure of the pale gentleman in black, as he held a thick velvet cloak, and placed it about her shoulders and threw the hood over her head. She nodded to him, and just touched his hand with hers. He bowed low repeatedly as the door closed, and the carriage began to move.

" 'She is gone,' said Millarca, with a sigh.

" 'She is gone,' I repeated to myself, for the first time—in the hurried moments that had elapsed since my consent—reflecting upon the folly of my act.

" 'She did not look up,' said the young lady, plaintively.

" 'The Countess had taken off her mask, perhaps, and did not care to show her face,' I said; 'and she could not know that you were in the window.'

"She sighed and looked in my face. She was so beautiful that I relented. I was sorry I had for a moment repented of my hospitality, and I determined to make her amends for the unavowed churlishness of my reception.

"The young lady, replacing her mask, joined my ward in persuading me to return to the grounds, where the concert was soon to be renewed. We did so, and walked up and down the terrace that lies under the castle windows. Millarca became very intimate with us, and amused us with lively descriptions and stories of most of the great people whom we saw upon the terrace. I liked her more and more every minute. Her gossip, without being ill-natured, was extremely diverting to me, who had been so long out of the great world. I thought what life she would give to our sometimes lonely evenings at home.

"This ball was not over until the morning sun had almost reached the horizon. It pleased the Grand Duke to dance till then, so loyal people could not go away, or think of bed.

"We had just got through a crowded saloon, when my ward asked me what had become of Millarca. I thought she had been by her side, and she fancied she was by mine. The fact was, we had lost her.

"All my efforts to find her were vain. I feared that she had mistaken, in the confusion of a momentary separation from us, other people for her new friends, and had, possibly, pursued and lost them in the extensive grounds which were thrown open to us.

"Now, in its full force, I recognized a new folly in my having undertaken the charge of a young lady without so much as knowing her name; and fettered as I was by promises, of the reasons for imposing which I knew nothing, I could not even point my inquiries by saying that the missing young lady was the daughter of the Countess who had taken her departure a few hours before.

"Morning broke. It was clear daylight before I gave up my search. It was not till near two o'clock next day that we heard anything of my missing charge.

"At about that time a servant knocked at my niece's door, to say that he had been earnestly requested by a young lady, who appeared to be in great distress, to make out where she could find the General Baron Spielsdorf and the young lady, his daughter, in whose charge she had been left by her mother.

"There could be no doubt, notwithstanding the slight inaccuracy, that our young friend had turned up; and so she had. Would to Heaven we had lost her!

"She told my poor child a story to account for her having failed to recover us for so long. Very late, she said, she had got into the housekeeper's bedroom in despair of finding us, and had then fallen into a deep sleep which, long as it was, had hardly sufficed to recruit her strength after the fatigues of the ball.

"That day Millarca came home with us. I was only too happy, after all, to have secured so charming a companion for my dear girl.

XIII
THE WOOD-MAN

"There soon, however, appeared some drawbacks. In the first place, Millarca complained of extreme languor—the weakness that remained after her late illness—and she never emerged from her room till the afternoon was pretty far advanced. In the next place, it was accidentally discovered, although she always locked her door on the inside, and never disturbed the key from its place, till she admitted the maid to assist at her toilet, that she was undoubtedly sometimes absent from her room in the very early morning, and at various times later in the day, before she wished it to be understood that she was stirring. She was repeatedly seen from the windows of the schloss, in the first faint grey of the morning, walking through the trees, in an easterly direction, and looking like a person in a trance. This convinced me that she walked in her sleep. But this hypothesis did not solve the puzzle. How did she pass out from her room, leaving the door locked on the inside. How did she escape from the house without unbarring door or window?

"In the midst of my perplexities, an anxiety of a far more urgent kind presented itself.

"My dear child began to lose her looks and health, and that in a manner so mysterious, and even horrible, that I became thoroughly frightened.

"She was at first visited by appalling dreams; then, as she fancied, by a spectre, sometimes resembling Millarca, sometimes in the shape of a beast, indistinctly seen, walking round the foot of her bed, from side to side. Lastly came sensations. One, not unpleasant, but very peculiar, she said, resembled the flow of an icy stream against her breast. At a later time, she felt something like a pair of large needles pierce her, a little below the throat, with a very sharp pain. A few nights after, followed a gradual and convulsive sense of strangulation; then came unconsciousness."

I could hear distinctly every word the kind old General was saying, because by this time we were driving upon the short grass that spreads on either side of the road as you approach the roofless village which had not shown the smoke of a chimney for more than half a century.

You may guess how strangely I felt as I heard my own symptoms so exactly described in those which had been experienced by the poor girl who, but for the catastrophe which followed, would have been at that moment a visitor at my father's château. You may suppose, also, how I felt as I heard him detail habits and mysterious peculiarities which were, in fact, those of our beautiful guest, Carmilla!

A vista opened in the forest; we were on a sudden under the chimneys and gables of the ruined village, and the towers and battlements of the dismantled castle, round which gigantic trees are grouped, overhung us from a slight eminence.

In a frightened dream I got down from the carriage, and in silence, for we had each abundant matter for thinking; we soon mounted the ascent, and were among the spacious chambers, winding stairs, and dark corridors of the castle.

"And this was once the palatial residence of the Karnsteins!" said the old General at length, as from a great window he looked out across the village, and saw the wide, undulating expanse of forest. "It was a bad family, and here its blood-stained annals were written," he continued. "It is hard that they should, after death, continue to plague the human race with their atrocious lusts. That is the chapel of the Karnsteins, down there."

He pointed down to the grey walls of the Gothic building, partly visible through the foliage, a little way down the steep. "And I hear the axe of a woodman," he added, "busy among the trees that surround it; he possibly may give us the information of which I am in search, and point out the grave of Mircalla, Countess of Karnstein. These rustics preserve the local traditions of great families, whose stories die out among the rich and titled so soon as the families themselves become extinct."

"We have a portrait, at home, of Mircalla, the Countess Karnstein; should you like to see it?" asked my father.

"Time enough, dear friend," replied the General. "I believe that I have seen the original; and one motive which has led me to you earlier than I at first intended, was to explore the chapel which we are now approaching."

"What! see the Countess Mircalla," exclaimed my father; "why, she has been dead more than a century!"

"Not so dead as you fancy, I am told," answered the General.

"I confess, General, you puzzle me utterly," replied my father, looking at him, I fancied, for a moment with a return of the suspicion I detected before. But although there was anger and detestation, at times, in the old General's manner, there was nothing flighty.

"There remains to me," he said, as we passed under the heavy arch of the Gothic church—for its dimensions would have justified its being so styled—"but one object which can interest me during the few years that remain to me on earth, and that is to wreak on her the vengeance which, I thank God, may still be accomplished by a mortal arm."

"What vengeance can you mean?" asked my father, in increasing amazement.

"I mean, to decapitate the monster," he answered, with a fierce flush, and a stamp that echoed mournfully through the hollow ruin, and his clenched hand was at the same moment raised, as if it grasped the handle of an axe, while he shook it ferociously in the air.

"What!" exclaimed my father, more than ever bewildered.

"To strike her head off."

"Cut her head off?"

"Aye, with a hatchet, with a spade, or with anything that can cleave through her murderous throat. You shall hear," he answered, trembling with rage. And hurrying forward he said:

"That beam will answer for a seat; your dear child is fatigued; let her be seated, and I will, in a few sentences, close my dreadful story."

The squared block of wood, which lay on the grass-grown pavement of the chapel, formed a bench on which I was very glad to seat myself, and in the meantime the General called to the woodman, who had been removing some boughs which leaned upon the old walls; and, axe in hand, the hardy old fellow stood before us.

He could not tell us anything of these monuments; but there was an old man, he said, a ranger of this forest, at present sojourning in the house of the priest, about two miles away, who could point out every monument of the old Karnstein family; and, for a trifle, he undertook to bring him back with him, if we would lend him one of our horses, in little more than half-an-hour.

"Have you been long employed about this forest?" asked my father of the old man.

"I have been a woodman here," he answered in his *patois,* "under the forester, all my days; so has my father before me, and so on, as many generations as I can count up. I could show you the very house in the village here, in which my ancestors lived."

"How came the village to be deserted?" asked the General.

"It was troubled by *revenants,* sir; several were tracked to their graves, there detected by the usual tests, and extinguished in the usual way, by decapitation, by the stake, and by burning; but not until many of the villagers were killed.

"But after all these proceedings according to law," he continued—"so many graves opened, and so many vampires deprived of their horrible animation—the village was not relieved. But a Moravian nobleman, who happened to be travelling this way, heard how matters were, and being skilled—as many people are in his country—in such affairs, he offered to deliver the village from its tormentor. He did so thus: There being a bright moon that night, he ascended, shortly after sunset, the tower of the chapel here, from whence he could distinctly see the churchyard beneath him; you can see it from that window. From this point he watched until he saw the vampire come out of his grave, and place near it the linen clothes in which he had been folded, and glide away towards the village to plague its inhabitants.

"The stranger, having seen all this, came down from the steeple, took the linen wrappings of the vampire, and carried them up to the top of the tower, which he again mounted. When the vampire returned from his prowlings and missed his clothes, he cried furiously to the Moravian, whom he saw at the summit of the tower, and who, in reply, beckoned him to ascend and take them. Whereupon the vampire, accepting his invitation, began to climb the steeple, and so soon as he had reached the battlements, the Moravian, with a stroke of his sword, clove his skull in twain, hurling him down to the churchyard, whither, descending by the winding stairs, the stranger followed and cut his head off, and next day delivered it and the body to the villagers, who duly impaled and burnt them.

"This Moravian nobleman had authority from the then head of the family to remove the tomb of Mircalla, Countess Karnstein, which he did effectually, so that in a little while its site was quite forgotten."

"Can you point out where it stood?" asked the General, eagerly.

The forester shook his head and smiled.

"Not a soul living could tell you that now," he said; "besides, they say her body was removed; but no one is sure of that either."

Having thus spoken, as time pressed, he dropped his axe and departed, leaving us to hear the remainder of the General's strange story.

XIV
The Meeting

"My beloved child," he resumed, "was now growing rapidly worse. The physician who attended her had failed to produce the slightest impression upon her disease, for such I then supposed it to be. He saw my alarm, and suggested a consultation. I called in an abler physician, from Gratz. Several days elapsed before he arrived. He was a good and pious, as well as a learned man. Having seen my poor ward together, they withdrew to my library to confer and discuss. I, from the adjoining room, where I waited their summons, heard these two gentlemen's voices raised in something sharper than a strictly philosophical discussion. I knocked at the door and entered. I found the old physician from Gratz maintaining his theory. His rival was combating it with undisguised ridicule, accompanied with bursts of laughter. This unseemly manifestation subsided and the altercation ended on my entrance.

" 'Sir,' said my first physician, 'my learned brother seems to think that you want a conjuror, and not a doctor.'

" 'Pardon me,' said the old physician from Gratz, looking displeased, 'I shall state my own view of the case in my own way another time. I grieve, Monsieur le General, that by my skill and science I can be of no use. Before I go I shall do myself the honour to suggest something to you.'

"He seemed thoughtful, and sat down at a table, and began to write. Profoundly disappointed, I made my bow, and as I turned to go, the other doctor pointed over his shoulder to his companion who was writing, and then, with a shrug, significantly touched his forehead.

"This consultation, then, left me precisely where I was. I walked out into the grounds, all but distracted. The doctor from Gratz, in ten or fifteen minutes, overtook me. He apologised for having followed me, but said that he could not conscientiously take his leave without a few words more. He told me that he could not be mistaken; no natural disease exhibited the same symptoms; and that death was already very near. There remained, however, a day, or possibly two, of life. If the fatal seizure were at once arrested, with great care and skill her strength might possibly return. But all hung now upon the confines of the irrevocable. One more assault might extinguish the last spark of vitality which is, every moment, ready to die.

" 'And what is the nature of the seizure you speak of?' I entreated.

" 'I have stated all fully in this note, which I place in your hands, upon the distinct condition that you send for the nearest clergyman, and open my letter in his presence, and on no account read it till he is with you; you would despise it else, and it is a matter of life and death. Should the priest fail you, then, indeed, you may read it.'

"He asked me, before taking his leave finally, whether I would wish to see a man curiously learned upon the very subject, which, after I had read his letter, would probably interest me above all others, and he urged me earnestly to invite him to visit him there; and so took his leave.

"The ecclesiastic was absent, and I read the letter by myself. At another time, or in another case, it might have excited my ridicule. But into what quackeries will not people rush for a last chance, where all accustomed means have failed, and the life of a beloved object is at stake?

"Nothing, you will say, could be more absurd than the learned man's letter. It was monstrous enough to have consigned him to a madhouse. He said that the patient was suffering from the visits of a vampire! The punctures which she described as having occurred near the throat were, he insisted, the insertion of those two long, thin, and sharp teeth which, it is well known, are peculiar to vampires; and there could be no doubt, he added, as to the well-defined presence of the small livid mark which all concurred in describing as that induced by the demon's lips, and every symptom described by the sufferer was in exact conformity with those recorded in every case of similar visitation.

"Being myself wholly sceptical as to the existence of any such portent as the vampire, the supernatural theory of the good doctor furnished, in my opinion, but another instance of learning and intelligence oddly associated with some one hallucination. I was so miserable, however, that, rather than try nothing, I acted upon the instructions of the letter.

"I concealed myself in the dark dressing-room, that opened upon the poor patient's room, in which a candle was burning, and watched there till she was fast asleep. I stood at the door, peeping through the small crevice, my sword laid on the table beside me, as my directions prescribed, until, a little after one, I saw a large black object, very ill-defined, crawl, as it seemed to me, over the foot of the bed, and swiftly spread itself up to the poor girl's throat, where it swelled, in a moment, into a great, palpitating mass.

"For a few moments I had stood petrified. I now sprang forward, with my sword in my hand. The black creature suddenly contracted toward the front of the bed, glided over it, and, standing on the floor about a yard below the foot of the bed, with a glare of skulking ferocity and horror fixed on me, I saw Millarca. Speculating I know not what, I struck at her instantly with my sword; but I saw her standing near the door, unscathed. Horrified, I pursued, and struck again. She was gone! and my sword flew to shivers against the door.

"I can't describe to you all that passed on that horrible night. The whole house was up and stirring. The spectre Millarca was gone. But her victim was sinking fast, and before the morning dawned, she died."

The old General was agitated. We did not speak to him. My father walked to some little distance, and began reading the inscriptions on the tombstones; and thus occupied, he strolled into the door of a side chapel to prosecute his researches. The General leaned against the wall, dried his eyes, and sighed heavily. I was relieved on hearing the voices of Carmilla and Madame, who were at that moment approaching. The voices died away.

In this solitude, having just listened to so strange a story, connected, as it was, with the great and titled dead, whose monuments were mouldering among the dust and ivy round us, and every incident of which bore so awfully upon my own mysterious case—in this haunted spot, darkened by the towering foliage that rose on every side, dense and high above its noiseless walls—a horror began to steal over me, and my heart sank as I thought that my friends were, after all, not about to enter and disturb this triste and ominous scene.

The old General's eyes were fixed on the ground, as he leaned with his hand upon the basement of a shattered monument.

Under a narrow, arched doorway, surmounted by one of those demoniacal grotesques in which the cynical and ghastly fancy of old Gothic carving delights, I saw very gladly the beautiful face and figure of Carmilla enter the shadowy chapel.

I was just about to rise and speak, and nodded smiling, in answer to her peculiarly engaging smile; when with a cry, the old man by my side caught up the woodman's hatchet, and started forward. On seeing him a brutalised change came over her features. It was an instantaneous and horrible transformation, as she made a crouching step backwards. Before I could utter a scream, he struck at her with all his force, but she dived under his blow, and unscathed, caught him in her tiny grasp by the wrist. He struggled for a moment to release his arm, but his hand opened, the axe fell to the ground, and the girl was gone.

He staggered against the wall. His grey hair stood upon his head, a moisture shone over his face, as if he were at the point of death.

The frightful scene had passed in a moment. The first thing I recollect after, is Madame standing before me, and impatiently repeating again and again, the question, "Where is Mademoiselle Carmilla?"

I answered at length, "I don't know—I can't tell—she went there," and I pointed to the door through which Madame had just entered; "only a minute or two since."

"But I have been standing there, in the passage, ever since Mademoiselle Carmilla entered; and she did not return."

She then began to call "Carmilla" through every door and passage and from the windows, but no answer came.

"She called herself Carmilla?" asked the General, still agitated.

"Carmilla, yes," I answered.

"Aye," he said; "that is Millarca. That is the same person who long ago was called Mircalla, Countess Karnstein. Depart from this accursed ground, my poor child, as quickly as you can. Drive to the clergyman's house, and stay there till we come. Begone! May you never behold Carmilla more; you will not find her here."

XV
ORDEAL AND EXECUTION

As he spoke one of the strangest-looking men I ever beheld, entered the chapel at the door through which Carmilla had made her entrance and her exit. He was tall, narrow-chested, stooping, with high shoulders, and dressed in black. His face was brown and dried in with deep furrows; he wore an oddly-shaped hat with a broad leaf. His hair, long and grizzled, hung on his shoulders. He wore a pair of gold spectacles, and walked slowly, with an odd shambling gait, with his face sometimes turned up to the sky, and sometimes bowed down toward the ground, seemed to wear a perpetual smile; his long thin arms were swinging, and his lank hands, in old black gloves ever so much too wide for them, waving and gesticulating in utter abstraction.

"The very man!" exclaimed the General, advancing with manifest delight. "My dear Baron, how happy I am to see you, I had no hope of meeting you so soon." He signed to my father, who had by this time returned, and leading the fantastic old gentleman, whom he called the Baron, to meet him. He introduced him formally, and they at once entered into earnest conversation. The stranger took a roll of paper from his pocket, and spread it on the worn surface of a tomb that stood by. He had a pencil case in his fingers, with which he traced imaginary lines from point to point on the paper, which from their often glancing from it, together, at certain points of the building, I concluded to be a plan of the chapel. He accompanied, what I may term his lecture, with occasional readings from a dirty little book, whose yellow leaves were closely written over.

They sauntered together down the side aisle, opposite to the spot where I was standing, conversing as they went; then they begun measuring distances by paces, and finally they all stood together, facing a piece of the side-wall, which they began to examine with great minuteness; pulling off the ivy that clung over it, and rapping the plaster with the ends of their sticks, scraping here, and knocking there. At length they ascertained the existence of a broad marble tablet, with letters carved in relief upon it.

With the assistance of the woodman, who soon returned, a monumental inscription, and carved escutcheon, were disclosed. They proved to be those of the long lost monument of Mircalla, Countess Karnstein.

The old General, though not I fear given to the praying mood, raised his hands and eyes to heaven, in mute thanksgiving for some moments.

"To-morrow," I heard him say; "the commissioner will be here, and the Inquisition will be held according to law."

Then turning to the old man with the gold spectacles, whom I have described, he shook him warmly by both hands and said:

"Baron, how can I thank you? How can we all thank you? You will have delivered this region from a plague that has scourged its inhabitants for more than a century. The horrible enemy, thank God, is at last tracked."

My father led the stranger aside, and the General followed. I knew that he had led them out of hearing, that he might relate my case, and I saw them glance often quickly at me, as the discussion proceeded.

My father came to me, kissed me again and again, and leading me from the chapel said:

"It is time to return, but before we go home, we must add to our party the good priest, who lives but a little way from this; and persuade him to accompany us to the schloss."

In this quest we were successful: and I was glad, being unspeakably fatigued when we reached home. But my satisfaction was changed to dismay, on discovering that there were no tidings of Carmilla. Of the scene that had occurred in the ruined chapel, no explanation was offered to me, and it was clear that it was a secret which my father for the present determined to keep from me.

The sinister absence of Carmilla made the remembrance of the scene more horrible to me. The arrangements for that night were singular. Two servants and Madame were to sit up in my room that night; and the ecclesiastic with my father kept watch in the adjoining dressing-room.

The priest had performed certain solemn rites that night, the purport of which I did not understand any more than I comprehended the reason of this extraordinary precaution taken for my safety during sleep.

I saw all clearly a few days later.

The disappearance of Carmilla was followed by the discontinuance of my nightly sufferings.

You have heard, no doubt, of the appalling superstition that prevails in Upper and Lower Styria, in Moravia, Silesia, in Turkish Servia, in Poland, even in Russia; the superstition, so we must call it, of the vampire.

If human testimony, taken with every care and solemnity, judicially, before commissions innumerable, each consisting of many members, all chosen for integrity and intelligence, and constituting reports more voluminous perhaps than exist upon any one other class of cases, is worth anything, it is difficult to deny, or even to doubt the existence of such a phenomenon as the vampire.

For my part I have heard no theory by which to explain what I myself have witnessed and experienced, other than that supplied by the ancient and well-attested belief of the country.

The next day the formal proceedings took place in the Chapel of Karnstein. The grave of the Countess Mircalla was opened; and the General and my father recognized each his perfidious and beautiful guest, in the face now disclosed to view. The features, though a hundred and fifty years had passed since her funeral, were tinted with the warmth of life. Her eyes were open; no cadaverous smell exhaled from the coffin. The two medical men, one officially present, the other on the part of the promotor of the inquiry, attested the marvellous fact, that there was a faint but appreciable respiration, and a corresponding action of the heart. The limbs were perfectly flexible, the flesh elastic; and the leaden coffin floated with blood, in which to a depth of seven inches, the body lay immersed. Here then, were all the admitted signs and proofs of vampirism. The body, therefore, in accordance with the ancient practice, was raised, and a sharp stake driven through the heart of the vampire, who uttered a piercing shriek at the moment, in all respects such as might escape from a living person in the last agony. Then the head was struck off, and a torrent of blood flowed from the severed neck. The body and head were next placed on a pile of wood, and reduced to ashes, which were thrown upon the river and borne away, and that territory has never since been plagued by the visits of a vampire.

My father has a copy of the report of the Imperial Commission, with the signatures of all who were present at these proceedings, attached in verification of the statement. It is from this official paper that I have summarized my account of this last shocking scene.

XVI
Conclusion

I write all this you suppose with composure. But far from it; I cannot think of it without agitation. Nothing but your earnest desire so repeatedly expressed, could have induced me to sit down to a task that has unstrung my nerves for months to come, and reinduced a shadow of the unspeakable horror which years after my deliverance continued to make my days and nights dreadful, and solitude insupportably terrific.

Let me add a word or two about that quaint Baron Vordenburg, to whose curious lore we were indebted for the discovery of the Countess Mircalla's grave.

He had taken up his abode in Gratz, where, living upon a mere pittance, which was all that remained to him of the once princely estates of his family, in Upper Styria, he devoted himself to the minute and laborious investigation of the marvellously authenticated tradition of vampirism. He had at his fingers' ends all the great and little works upon the subject. "Magia Posthuma," "Phlegon de Mirabilibus," "Augustinus de curâ pro Mortuis," "Philosophicae et Christinae Cogitationes de Vampiris," by John Christofer Herenberg; and a thousand others, among which I remember only a few of those which he lent to my father. He had a voluminous digest of all the judicial cases, from which he had extracted a system of principles that appear to govern—some always, and others occasionally only—the condition of the vampire. I may mention, in passing, that the deadly pallor attributed to that sort of *revenants,* is a mere melodramatic fiction. They present, in the grave, and when they show themselves in human society, the appearance of healthy life. When disclosed to light in their coffins, they exhibit all the symptoms that are enumerated as those which proved the vampire-life of the long-dead Countess Karnstein.

How they escape from their graves and return to them for certain hours every day, without displacing the clay or leaving any trace of disturbance in the state of the coffin or the cerements, has always been admitted to be utterly inexplicable. The amphibious existence of the vampire is sustained by daily renewed slumber in the grave. Its horrible lust for living blood supplies the vigour of its waking existence. The vampire is prone to be fascinated with engrossing vehemence, resembling the passion of love, by particular persons. In pursuit of these it will exercise inexhaustible patience and stratagem, for access to a particular object may be obstructed in a hundred ways. It will never desist until it has satiated its passion, and drained the very life of its coveted victim. But it will, in these cases, husband and protract its murderous enjoyment with the refinement of an epicure, and heighten it by the gradual approaches of an artful courtship. In these cases it seems to yearn for something like sympathy and consent. In ordinary ones it goes direct to its object, overpowers with violence, and strangles and exhausts often at a single feast.

The vampire is, apparently, subject, in certain situations, to special conditions. In the particular instance of which I have given you a relation, Mircalla seemed to be limited to a name which, if not her real one, should at least reproduce, without the omission or addition of a single letter, those, as we say, anagrammatically, which compose it. *Carmilla* did this; so did *Millarca*.

My father related to the Baron Vordenburg, who remained with us for two or three weeks after the expulsion of Carmilla, the story about the Moravian nobleman and the vampire at Karnstein churchyard, and then he asked the Baron how he had discovered the exact position of the long-concealed tomb of the Countess Millarca? The Baron's grotesque features puckered up into a mysterious smile; he looked down, still smiling on his worn spectacle-case and fumbled with it. Then looking up, he said:

"I have many journals, and other papers, written by that remarkable man; the most curious among them is one treating of the visit of which you speak, to Karnstein. The tradition, of course, discolours and distorts a little. He might have been termed a Moravian nobleman, for he had changed his abode to that territory, and was, beside, a noble. But he was, in truth, a native of Upper Styria. It is enough to say that in very early youth he had been a passionate and favoured lover of the beautiful Mircalla, Countess Karnstein. Her early death plunged him into inconsolable grief. It is the nature of vampires to increase and multiply, but according to an ascertained and ghostly law.

"Assume, at starting, a territory perfectly free from that pest. How does it begin, and how does it multiply itself? I will tell you. A person, more or less wicked, puts an end to himself. A suicide, under certain circumstances, becomes a vampire. That spectre visits living people in their slumbers; *they* die, and almost invariably, in the grave, develop into vampires. This happened in the case of the beautiful Mircalla, who was haunted by one of those demons. My ancestor, Vordenburg, whose title I still bear, soon discovered this, and in the course of the studies to which he devoted himself, learned a great deal more.

"Among other things, he concluded that suspicion of vampirism would probably fall, sooner or later, upon the dead Countess, who in life had been his idol. He conceived a horror, be she what she might, of her remains being profaned by the outrage of a posthumous execution. He has left a curious paper to prove that the vampire, on its expulsion from its amphibious existence, is projected into a far more horrible life; and he resolved to save his once beloved Mircalla from this.

"He adopted the stratagem of a journey here, a pretended removal of her remains, and a real obliteration of her monument. When age had stolen upon him, and from the vale of years he looked back on the scenes he was leaving, he considered, in a different spirit, what he had done, and a horror took possession of him. He made the tracings and notes which have guided me to the very spot, and drew up a confession of the deception that he had practised. If he had intended any further action in this manner, death prevented him; and the hand of a remote descendant has, too late for many, directed the pursuit to the lair of the beast."

We talked a little more, and among other things he said was this:

"One sign of the vampire is the power of the hand. The slender hand of Mircalla closed like a vice of steel on the General's wrist when he raised the hatchet to strike. But its power is not confined to its grasp; it leaves a numbness in the limb it seizes, which is slowly, if ever, recovered from."

The following Spring my father took me a tour through Italy. We remained away for more than a year. It was long before the terror of recent events subsided; and to this hour the image of Carmilla returns to memory with ambiguous alternations—sometimes the playful, languid, beautiful girl; sometimes the writhing fiend I saw in the ruined church; and often from a reverie I have started, fancying I heard the light step of Carmilla at the drawing-room door.

WOMEN'S WRITING ON
THE "CARNIVOROUS FLOWER"

Marie-Madeleine,
Baroness von Puttkamer
(late nineteenth century)

Writing in the 1930s, Jethro Bithell, the German literary historian, divided German women writers of the preceding decades into "two armies of naughty girls and good girls." Marie-Madeleine was at the top of his "naughty girl" list. Bithell identifies her as one of the troop of late-nineteenth-century feminists who demanded "unrestricted liberty in [women's] sexual functions, even if perverse." His view of her, however, bespeaks his own extreme discomfort with her subject matter. He does not seem to notice her very ambivalent attitudes toward sexuality in general and lesbianism in particular.

If the poems in her 1895 volume *On Cypress* are an indication, Marie-Madeleine was probably bisexual. The preponderance of the poems in that volume are heterosexual, though many of them deal clearly with homosexuality. But her lesbian poems appear to derive from literary influence at least as much as from actual experience. In fact, a rather direct line of influence may be discerned in those poems from Baudelaire to Pierre Louÿs, whose 1894 volume *Songs of Bilitis* had been translated into German by the famous German writer Richard Dehmel the year before *On Cypress* appeared.

Marie-Madeleine has the distinction of being the first woman poet who depicted lesbianism through "carnivorous flower" imagery. The line of influence may even have continued through her to Renée Vivien, who may have been encouraged by Marie-Madeleine's exotic poems about lesbianism to write similar ones. In any case, Vivien was an accomplished reader of German and was probably familiar with *On Cypress,* though she also knew *Songs of Bilitis* well and specifically acknowledged the influence of Pierre Louÿs on her work.

Marie-Madeleine's lesbian poems reveal a fascination with "sweet sin" at least as much as a fascination with love between women. Her lesbians are invariably, like Baudelaire's, *femmes damnées,* who ignite in each other "mad fires" while destroying purity and innocence. Their sexual debauchery turns them into social outcasts, although they often appear to relish their suffering and revel in emotional sadomasochism. From a contemporary perspective we might guess that Marie-Madeleine had an erotic appreciation for the deliciousness of the psychosexual torment of her lesbian figures. But if we consider her as a product of her time, it is just as possible that in her ambivalence she would not have disagreed with Jethro Bithell's puritanical characterization of the "shocking" lesbian content of her poems as "disgusting revelations of inner urges."

FURTHER READING: Marie-Madeleine [Baroness von Puttkamer], *Auf Kypros* (Berlin: Vita, 1895). Jethro Bithell, *Modern German Literature: 1880–1938* (London: Methuen, 1939). Jeannette Foster, *Sex Variant Women in Literature* (1956; reprint, Tallahassee, FL: Naiad Press, 1985).

WORDS OF OLD AGE*

I cannot sleep at night. I cannot.
When my tired eyes
have barely closed, youth
appears to me in dreams.

A naked, regal, blonde woman,
wild lust bright in her glances:
So like springtime her body blossoms,
her white breasts, so like god!

She stares at me with a mad laugh,
a bawdy, echoing peal.
I hear her laughter everywhere; so sweet
and so full of scorn.

* I would like to acknowledge the assistance of Brigitte Eriksson and Frankie Hucklenbroich in rendering these poems into English.

Oh, how wildly she mocks me!
Her body blossoms so like springtime,
a young, young, young woman . . .
I cannot sleep at night.

CRUCIFIXA

I saw you tortured on a stake,
high on a dark cross I saw you tied.
The marks of my sinful kisses
glowed on your white flesh like purple wounds.

How slender your young limbs are,
and how childish your budlike breasts!
But in your eyes, my blonde child,
burn the torches of wild lust.

And yet, you were cool, white velvet,
stainless as a sharpened sword,
when your young innocence enflamed me
and I desired you so boundlessly.

I gave you of my own poison,
and I gave you my poison's strength.
And now that you are fully ablaze
my soul shudders at what I have done.

I want to kneel before the altars
my own wanton daring destroyed . . .
Madonna with a whore's eyes
I myself crucified you!

SAPPHO

Gently, the ocean waves
sing their eternal dirge
and softly the humid spring night
enfolds me. My soul
searches for you.

Oh, come, sweet flocks of girls!
I want to drink of your beauty.
Give your wild hair to the wind,

and drop your raiments
silently.

My pale child, give me your mouth, and feed
my own mad fires. How cool
your red lips are. You haven't learned how love
feels yet.

And you, with your thick mane of red-gold curls
flowing almost to your heels,
like waves of flame,
show me the fires that glitter and flicker
from your eyes. You must not ever leave me,
for you are as beautiful
as the glowing sun.

And you two shy and slender sisters
are pale as moonlight,
with your quiet heartache
and your silent pangs of love.

With your limbs' marble splendor
shining white as the waves' glimmering foam,
and your hair the night,
you are more silent
than a dream.

Oh, bouquet of blossoms! Oh, flock of girls!
I want to drink of your beauty.
Give your wild hair to the wind,
and drop your raiments
silently.

VAGABONDS

You will leave house
and hearth
for the sake of my eyes' dark glow.
You will be despised
and dishonored,
like a beggar.
And you will throw your happiness and your fame
into the dusty street. I will be
your only possession!

At night when the streetlamps, with their flame-red stars,
peer tiredly through the fog,
we will wander through the streets, work
and sweet sin
surging noisily around us,
and lust and hunger, like the sea!

On and on we will wander,
listening reverently to the wild waltz-melodies
and to what the silken dresses rustle, and to what
the lace shirts whisper, and what the sweet, wild,
curling, long hair of girls
crackles.

Then, the fever-roses
will bloom brightly on our cheeks
and all our senses will open,
though our longing won't die!
Grinning, we will drink the cup of life
that brims with pain . . .

And hate and mockery surrounding us,
and everyone condemning us, and all the preachers
threatening us with punishment
and hell-fire, we are
forever damned! And yet, you will leave
house and hearth
for my eyes' weariness. . . .

Renée Vivien (Pauline Tarn)
(1877–1909)

Pauline Tarn, an Anglo-American, took the name Renée Vivien (which suggests rebirth and life) when she decided, after an unhappy youth in London,
to return to France, where she had gone to school as a child, and devote
the rest of her life to becoming a poet. Vivien had from her early years
been in love with a girlfriend, Violet Shilleto. As impassioned as their relationship was, however, the two young women conducted it as a romantic
friendship. Despite the fact that they were not sexual together, the violet
became a symbol of deep female same-sex feeling in the iconography of
Vivien's writing, which may figure as the root of the widespread association

of lesbianism with that flower and even with the color lavender in the 1920s and '30s (see, for example, Mary Casal's lesbian autobiography *The Stone Wall* and Édouard Bourdet's play *The Captive*, in which violets are a symbol of lesbian love). Shilleto's early death left Vivien distraught.

It was in Paris that Vivien dared to explore lesbian sexuality. Having settled there with the help of a considerable inheritance, in 1899 she met the young American heiress Natalie Barney, and the two attractive and literary women became lovers. The relationship was fraught with difficulties because of serious temperamental differences between them, as Vivien recorded in her 1904 novel, *A Woman Appeared to Me*. But the two women had great dreams of "reestablishing" a fictive Lesbos of women writers and intellectuals. To that end, they rented adjoining villas on Sappho's isle of Mytilene, although again temperamental differences prevented them from realizing their plan. Years after Vivien's death Barney did, however, establish an "Academy of Women," a salon that encouraged women writers and may have been modeled in part on their common dream.

A few of Vivien's poems were militantly feminist, an impulse she explains in *A Woman Appeared to Me,* when she has San Giovanni, an autobiographical character, say that she discovered both feminism and the love of women at the age of seventeen when "a great passion for justice seized me. I was aroused on behalf of women, so misunderstood, so made use of by male tyranny. I began to hate the male for the base cruelty of his laws and the impunity of his morals. I considered his works and judged them evil." Her consideration leads San Giovanni to open her eyes to female suffering, courage, and beauty.

While Vivien's novel and some of her poems are based on such real-life epiphanies, the preponderance of her poetry, particularly as it deals with the subject of lesbianism, betrays the power of literary influences. The lyrics of Sappho figured heavily in several of Vivien's poems that celebrate lesbian love. Equally important in its impact on Vivien was Pierre Louÿs's *Songs of Bilitis,* which pretended to be a reconstruction of the lesbian poems of a contemporary of Sappho's but were, in fact, his original efforts. Louÿs poems, and subsequently Vivien's, were far more heavily influenced by the images of lesbianism that appeared in Decadent poetry, such as that of Baudelaire, Swinburne, and Verlaine, than by Sappho's work. One critic, Clarissa Cooper, has accused Vivien of having a "Baudelairean preoccupation with vice," but it would seem that Vivien's preoccupation was rather with the only literary examples she knew of how to render the image of the lesbian. Although occasionally the lesbian in her poetry lives in the Golden Age of Greece, more often she is a modern European social outcast who is condemned to suffer love's torments whenever she seeks love's delights.

A more recent critic, Karla Jay, has convincingly explained that Vivien was daring as a woman poet in even broaching her subject matter, and that it would be unreasonable to expect stylistic originality of her as well. Vivien learned from her male predecessors to penetrate areas of sensibility where earlier, pre-Decadent and pre-Symbolist writers dared not go. And she simply did not foresee that, in adapting the imagery of male Decadent and Symbolist poetry to her own purposes, she would also adopt the attitudes that underlie it, "attitudes which were embedded in a male-centered, even misogynist, world-view."

FURTHER READING: *The Muse of the Violets: Poems by Renée Vivien*, trans. Margaret Porter and Catherine Kroger (Bates City, Mo.: Naiad Press, 1977). Renée Vivien, *A Woman Appeared to Me* (1904), trans. Jeannette Foster (Reno, Nev.: Naiad Press, 1976). Pamela J. Annas, " 'Drunk With Chastity': The Poetry of Renée Vivien," *Women's Studies*, 13: 1/2 (1986), 11–22. Elyse Blankley, "Return to Mytilene: Renée Vivien and the City of Women," in *Women Writers and the City: Essays in Feminist Literary Criticism*, ed. Susan Merrill Squier (Knoxville, Tenn.: University of Tennessee Press, 1984), pp. 45–67. Clarissa Burnham Cooper, *Women Poets of the Twentieth Century in France* (New York: King's Crown Press, 1943). Karla Jay, *The Amazon and the Page: Natalie Clifford Barney and Renée Vivien* (Bloomington: Indiana University Press, 1988).

CHANSON

The pomp of jewels, the vanity of curled tresses
Mix the polish of art with your perverse charm.
Even the gardenias which winter cannot harm
Die in your hands of your impure caresses.

Your delicately delineated mouth expresses
The artifice, the inflections of poetry.
Your breasts blossom in pale luxury
Under the cleverly half-open folds of your dresses.

The reflection of sapphires darkens in the somber night
Of your eyes. Your undulous body that troubles my sight
Makes a gleaming furrow of gold in the middle of the night.

When you pass, holding a subtle smile for me,
Blonde pastel surcharged with gems and perfumery,
I dream of the splendor of your body naked and free.

UNDINE

Your laughter is light, your caress deep,
Your cold kisses love the harm they do;
Your eyes—blue lotus waves
And the water lilies are less pure than your face.

You flee, a fluid parting,
Your hair falls in gentle tangles;
Your voice—a treacherous tide;
Your arms—supple reeds,

Long river reeds, their embrace
Enlaces, chokes, strangles savagely,
Deep in the waves, an agony
Extinguished in a night drift.

YOUR STRANGE HAIR

Your strange hair, cold light,
Has pale glows and blond dullness;
Your gaze has the blue of ether and waves;
Your gown has the chill of the breeze and the woods.

I burn the whiteness of your fingers with kisses.
The night air spreads the dust from many worlds.
Still I don't know anymore, in the heart of those deep nights,
How to see you with the passion of yesterday.

The moon grazed you with a slanted glow . . .
It was terrible, like prophetic lightning
Revealing the hideous below your beauty.

I saw—as one sees a flower fade—
On your mouth, like summer auroras,
The withered smile of an old whore.

SAD WORDS

What sadness now, after our pleasure, dearest,
Our last kiss, like a sob,
Falls from your pale mouth
And sad and slow, no words,
You walk away, heavy, Oh my love!

The sadness of our weary love-making, nights,
Comes like the pain of parting
Comes like the poems that don't move us anymore
Passes like the black imperial march,
The dark sound of torches towards evening . . .

And I know you feel cheated and I feel distant. . . .
We stay together, with the eyes of exile,
And a thin, gold string holds us,
With weary eyes, we follow our flown dream. . . .
Gone already, you smile, far away.

ROSES RISING

My brunette with the golden eyes, your ivory body, your amber
Has left bright reflections in the room
    Above the garden.

The clear midnight sky, under my closed lids,
Still shines. . . . I am drunk from so many roses
    Redder than wine.

Leaving their garden, the roses have followed me. . . .
I drink their brief breath, I breathe their life.
    All of them are here.

It's a miracle. . . . The stars have risen,
Hastily, across the wide windows
    Where the melted gold pours.

Now, among the roses and the stars,
You, here in my room, loosening your robe,
    And your nakedness glistens.

Your unspeakable gaze rests on my eyes. . . .
Without stars and without flowers, I dream the impossible
    In the cold night.

Mary E. Wilkins Freeman
(See also headnote on p. 76)

Mary E. Wilkins Freeman's 1887 story about a happy romantic friendship, "Two Friends" (see p. 77), provides a revealing contrast to her 1895 story, "The Long Arm," demonstrating that in a very brief period of time the image of romantic friendship began to change to one of lesbian evil in the popular media. In the later story she uses characters very similar to those in "Two Friends," but her focus is on the unhealthiness of female-female relationships. Refashioning her earlier material, in "The Long Arm" the author presents one woman attempting to maintain possession of another by violently interfering with her heterosexual aspirations.

"The Long Arm" was written late in the relationship between Mary Wilkins and Mary Wales, which spanned more than forty years and was broken up by Wilkins's unhappy middle-aged heterosexual marriage. The story may reflect something of the real-life conflicts between the two women in the last years of their relationship. But it is also likely that Mary Wilkins's depiction of the murderous Phoebe had its source in the 1892 Alice Mitchell case (see p. 139), which stimulated a spate of sensationalistic stories about murderous lesbians in the popular media.

"The Long Arm" is also interesting because its language and metaphors indicate some influence of earlier French and English depictions of the lesbian vampire. Phoebe is described as being deathly pale, and Sarah even concludes that she is demoniacally possessed. There are other touches as well that suggest the influence of the myths of the terrifying lesbian. Phoebe is overbearing and all the women are intimidated by her. She is diabolical in her ability to manipulate others. Before the reader is given an explanation, the murder she commits even suggests vampirish abilities. Not only is the door of entry to the victim locked from within so that it seems that, as in *Carmilla*, it was a supernatural creature who penetrated the murdered person's abode, but blood figures heavily in the appearance of the crime. The supernatural elements are finally undercut by the rational, but Phoebe remains a desperate figure of lesbian evil, a hypocritical, sick, self-absorbed carnivorous flower.

The Long Arm

I
THE TRAGEDY

(From notes written by Miss Sarah Fairbanks immediately
after the report of the Grand Jury.)

As I take my pen to write this, I have a feeling that I am in the witness-box—for, or against myself, which? The place of the criminal in the dock I will not voluntarily take. I will affirm neither my innocence nor my guilt. I will present the facts of the case as impartially and as coolly as if I had nothing at stake. I will let all who read this judge me as they will.

This I am bound to do, since I am condemned to something infinitely worse than the life-cell or the gallows. I will try my own self in lieu of judge and jury; my guilt or my innocence I will prove to you all, if it be in mortal power. In my despair I am tempted to say, I care not which it may be, so something be proved. Open condemnation could not overwhelm me like universal suspicion.

Now, first, as I have heard is the custom in the courts of law, I will present the case. I am Sarah Fairbanks, a country school teacher, twenty-nine years of age. My mother died when I was twenty-three. Since then, while I have been teaching at Digby, a cousin of my father's, Rufus Bennett, and his wife have lived with my father. During the long summer vacation they returned to their little farm in Vermont, and I kept house for my father.

For five years I have been engaged to be married to Henry Ellis, a young man whom I met in Digby. My father was very much opposed to the match, and has told me repeatedly that if I insisted upon marrying him in his lifetime he would disinherit me. On this account Henry never visited me at my own home; while I could not bring myself to break off my engagement. Finally, I wished to avoid an open rupture with my father. He was quite an old man, and I was the only one he had left of a large family.

I believe that parents should honor their children, as well as children their parents; but I had arrived at this conclusion: in nine-tenths of the cases wherein children marry against their parents' wishes, even when the parents have no just grounds for opposition, the marriages are unhappy.

I sometimes felt that I was unjust to Henry, and resolved that, if ever I suspected that his fancy turned toward any other girl, I would not hinder it, especially as I was getting older and, I thought, losing my good looks.

A little while ago, a young pretty girl came to Digby to teach the school in the south district. She boarded in the same house with Henry. I heard that he was somewhat attentive to her, and I made up my mind I would not interfere. At the same time it seemed to me that my heart was breaking. I heard her people had money, too, and she was an only child. I had always felt that Henry ought to marry a wife with money, because he had nothing himself, and was not very strong.

School closed five weeks ago, and I came home for the summer vacation. The night before I left, Henry came to see me, and urged me to marry him. I refused again; but I never before had felt that my father was so hard and cruel as I did that night. Henry said that he should certainly see me during the vacation, and when I replied that he must not come, he was angry, and said—but such foolish things are not worth repeating. Henry has really a very sweet temper, and would not hurt a fly.

The very night of my return home Rufus Bennett and my father had words about some maple sugar which Rufus made on his Vermont farm and sold to father, who made a good trade for it to some people in Boston. That was father's business. He had once kept a store, but had given it up, and sold a few articles that he could make a large profit on here and there at wholesale. He used to send to New Hampshire and Vermont for butter, eggs, and cheese. Cousin Rufus thought father did not allow him enough profit on the maple sugar, and in the dispute father lost his temper, and said that Rufus had given him under weight. At that, Rufus swore an oath, and seized father by the throat. Rufus's wife screamed. "Oh, don't! don't! oh, he'll kill him!"

I went up to Rufus and took hold of his arm.

"Rufus Bennett," said I, "you let go my father!"

But Rufus's eyes glared like a madman's, and he would not let go. Then I went to the desk-drawer where father had kept a pistol since some houses in the village were broken into; I got out the pistol, laid hold of Rufus again, and held the muzzle against his forehead.

"You let go of my father," said I, "or I'll fire!"

Then Rufus let go, and father dropped like a log. He was purple in the face. Rufus's wife and I worked a long time over him to bring him to.

"Rufus Bennett," said I, "go to the well and get a pitcher of water." He went, but when father had revived and got up, Rufus gave him a look that showed he was not over his rage.

"I'll get even with you yet, Martin Fairbanks, old man as you are!" he shouted out, and went into the outer room.

We got father to bed soon. He slept in the bedroom downstairs, out of the sitting-room. Rufus and his wife had the north chamber, and I had the south one. I left my door open that night, and did not sleep. I listened; no one stirred in the night. Rufus and his wife were up very early in the morning, and before nine o'clock left for Vermont. They had a day's journey, and would reach home about nine in the evening. Rufus's wife bade father good-bye, crying, while Rufus was getting their trunk downstairs, but Rufus did not go near father nor me. He ate no breakfast; his very back looked ugly when he went out of the yard.

That very day about seven in the evening, after tea, I had just washed the dishes and put them away, and went out on the north doorstep, where father was sitting, and sat down on the lowest step. There was a cool breeze there; it had been a very hot day.

"I want to know if that Ellis fellow has been to see you any lately?" said father all at once.

"Not a great deal," I answered.

"Did he come to see you the last night you were there?" said father.

"Yes, sir," said I, "he did come."

"If you ever have another word to say to that fellow while I live, I'll kick you out of the house like a dog, daughter of mine though you be," said he. Then he swore a great oath and called God to witness. "Speak to that fellow again, if you dare, while I live!" said he.

I did not say a word; I just looked up at him as I sat there. Father turned pale and shrank back, and put his hand to his throat, where Rufus had clutched him. There were some purple finger-marks there.

"I suppose you would have been glad if he had killed me," father cried out.

"I saved your life," said I.

"What did you do with that pistol?" he asked.

"I put it back in the desk-drawer."

I got up and went around and sat on the west doorstep, which is the front one. As I sat there, the bell rang for the Tuesday evening meeting, and Phoebe Dole and Maria Woods, two old maiden ladies, dressmakers, our next-door neighbors, went past on their way to the meeting. Phoebe stopped and asked if Rufus and his wife were gone. Maria went around the house. Very soon they went on, and several other people passed. When they had all gone, it was as still as death.

I sat alone a long time, until I could see by the shadows that the full moon had risen. Then I went to my room and went to bed.

I lay awake a long time, crying. It seemed to me that all hope of marriage between Henry and me was over. I could not expect him to wait for me. I thought of that other girl; I could see her pretty face wherever I looked. But at last I cried myself to sleep.

At about five o'clock I awoke and got up. Father always wanted his breakfast at six o'clock, and I had to prepare it now.

When father and I were alone, he always built the fire in the kitchen stove, but that morning I did not hear him stirring as usual, and I fancied that he must be so out of temper with me, that he would not build the fire.

I went to my closet for a dark blue calico dress which I wore to do housework in. It had hung there during all the school term.

As I took it off the hook, my attention was caught by something strange about the dress I had worn the night before. This dress was made of thin summer silk; it was green in color, sprinkled over with white rings. It had been my best dress for two summers, but now I was wearing it on hot afternoons at home, for it was the coolest dress I had. The night before, too, I had thought of the possibility of Henry's driving over from Digby and passing the house. He had done this sometimes during the last summer vacation, and I wished to look my best if he did.

As I took down the calico dress I saw what seemed to be a stain on the green silk. I threw on the calico hastily, and then took the green silk and carried it over to the window. It was covered with spots—horrible great splashes and streaks down the front. The right sleeve, too, was stained, and all the stains were wet.

"What have I got on my dress?" said I.

It looked like blood. Then I smelled of it, and it was sickening in my nostrils, but I was not sure what the smell of blood was like. I thought I must have got the stains by some accident the night before.

"If that is blood on my dress," I said, "I must do something to get it off at once, or the dress will be ruined."

It came to my mind that I had been told that bloodstains had been removed from cloth by an application of flour paste on the wrong side. I took my green silk, and ran down the back stairs, which lead—having a door at the foot—directly into the kitchen.

There was no fire in the kitchen stove, as I had thought. Everything was very solitary and still, except for the ticking of the clock on the shelf. When I crossed the kitchen to the pantry, however, the cat mewed to be let in from the shed. She had a little door of her own by which she could enter or leave the shed at will, an aperture just large enough for her Maltese body to pass at ease beside the shed door. It had a little 'lid, too, hung upon a leathern hinge. On my way I let the cat in; then I went into the pantry and got a bowl of flour. This I mixed with water into a stiff paste, and applied to the under surface of the stains on my dress. I then hung the dress up to dry in the dark end of a closet leading out of the kitchen, which contained some old clothes of father's.

Then I made up the fire in the kitchen stove. I made coffee, baked biscuits, and poached some eggs for breakfast.

Then I opened the door into the sitting-room and called, "Father, breakfast is ready." Suddenly I started. There was a red stain on the inside of the sitting-room door. My heart began to beat in my ears. "Father!" I called out—"father!"

There was no answer.

"Father!" I called again, as loud as I could scream. "Why don't you speak? What is the matter?"

The door of his bedroom stood open. I had a feeling that I saw a red reflection in there. I gathered myself together and went across the sitting-room to father's bedroom door. His little looking-glass hung over his bureau opposite his bed, which was reflected in it.

That was the first thing I saw, when I reached the door. I could see father in the looking-glass and the bed. Father was dead there; he had been murdered in the night.

II

The Knot of Ribbon

I think I must have fainted away, for presently I found myself on the floor, and for a minute I could not remember what had happened. Then I remembered, and an awful, unreasoning terror seized me. "I must lock all the doors quick," I thought; "quick, or the murderer will come back."

I tried to get up, but I could not stand. I sank down again. I had to crawl out of the room on my hands and knees.

I went first to the front door; it was locked with a key and a bolt. I went next to the north door, and that was locked with a key and bolt. I went to the north shed door, and that was bolted. Then I went to the little-used east door in the shed, beside which the cat had her little passage-way, and that was fastened with an iron hook. It has no latch.

The whole house was fastened on the inside. The thought struck me like an icy hand, "The murderer is in this house!" I rose to my feet then; I unhooked that door, and ran out of the house, and out of the yard, as for my life.

I took the road to the village. The first house, where Phoebe Dole and Maria Woods live, is across a wide field from ours. I did not intend to stop there, for they were only women, and could do nothing; but seeing Phoebe looking out of the window, I ran into the yard.

She opened the window.

"What is it?" said she. "What is the matter, Sarah Fairbanks?"

Maria Woods came and leaned over her shoulder. Her face looked almost as white as her hair, and her blue eyes were dilated. My face must have frightened her.

"Father—father is murdered in his bed!" I said.

There was a scream, and Maria Woods's face disappeared from over Phoebe Dole's shoulder—she had fainted. I do not know whether Phoebe looked paler—she is always very pale—but I saw in her black eyes a look which I shall never forget. I think she began to suspect me at that moment.

Phoebe glanced back at Maria, but she asked me another question.

"Has he had words with anybody?" said she.

"Only with Rufus," I said; "but Rufus is gone."

Phoebe turned away from the window to attend to Maria, and I ran on to the village.

A hundred people can testify what I did next—can tell how I called for the doctor and the deputy-sheriff; how I went back to my own home with the horror-stricken crowd; how they flocked in and looked at poor father; but only the doctor touched him, very carefully, to see if he were quite dead; how the coroner came, and all the rest.

The pistol was in the bed beside father, but it had not been fired; the charge was still in the barrel. It was blood-stained, and there was one bruise on father's head which might have been inflicted by the pistol, used as a club. But the wound which caused his death was in his breast, and made evidently by some cutting instrument, though the cut was not a clean one; the weapon must have been dull.

They searched the house, lest the murderer should be hidden away. I heard Rufus Bennett's name whispered by one and another. Everybody seemed to know that he and father had had words the night before; I could not understand how, because I had told nobody except Phoebe Dole, who had had no time to spread the news, and I was sure that no one else had spoken of it.

They looked in the closet where my green silk dress hung, and pushed it aside to be sure nobody was concealed behind it, but they did not notice anything wrong about it. It was dark in the closet, and besides, they did not look for anything like that until later.

All these people—the deputy-sheriff, and afterwards the high sheriff, and other out-of-town officers, for whom they had telegraphed, and the neighbors—all hunted their own suspicion, and that was Rufus Bennett. All believed he had come back, and killed my father. They fitted all the facts to that belief. They made him do the deed with a long, slender screwdriver, which he had recently borrowed from one of the neighbors and had not returned. They made his finger-marks, which were still on my father's throat, fit the red prints of the sitting-room door. They made sure that he had returned and stolen into the house by the east door shed, while father and I sat on the doorsteps the evening before; that he had hidden himself away, perhaps in that very closet where my dress hung, and afterwards stolen out and killed my father, and then escaped.

They were not shaken when I told them that every door was bolted and barred that morning. They themselves found all the windows fastened down, except a few which were open on account of the heat, and even these last were raised only the width of the sash, and fastened with sticks, so that they could be raised no higher. Father was very cautious about fastening the house, for he sometimes had considerable sums of money by him. The officers saw all these difficulties in the way, but they fitted them somehow to their theory, and two deputy-sheriffs were at once sent to apprehend Rufus.

They had not begun to suspect me then, and not the slightest watch was kept on my movements. The neighbors were very kind, and did everything to help me, relieving me altogether of all those last offices—in this case so much sadder than usual.

An inquest was held, and I told freely all I knew, except about the blood-stains on my dress. I hardly knew why I kept that back. I had no feeling that I might have done the deed myself, and I could not bear to convict myself, if I was innocent.

Two of the neighbors, Mrs. Holmes and Mrs. Adams, remained with me all that day. Towards evening, when there were very few in the house, they went into the parlor to put it in order for the funeral, and I sat down alone in the kitchen. As I sat there by the window I thought of my green silk dress, and wondered if the stains were out. I went to the closet and brought the dress out to the light. The spots and streaks had almost disappeared. I took the dress out into the shed, and scraped off the flour paste, which was quite dry; I swept up the paste, burned it in the stove, took the dress upstairs to my own closet, and hung it in its old place. Neighbors remained with me all night.

At three o'clock in the afternoon of the next day, which was Thursday, I went over to Phoebe Dole's to see about a black dress to wear at the funeral. The neighbors had urged me to have my black silk dress altered a little, and trimmed with crape.

I found only Maria Woods at home. When she saw me she gave a little scream, and began to cry. She looked as if she had already been weeping for hours. Her blue eyes were bloodshot.

"Phoebe's gone over to—Mrs. Whitney's to—try on her dress," she sobbed.

"I want to get my black silk dress fixed a little," said I.

"She'll be home—pretty soon," said Maria.

I laid my dress on the sofa and sat down. Nobody ever consults Maria about a dress. She sews well, but Phoebe does all the planning.

Maria Woods continued to sob like a child, holding her little soaked handkerchief over her face. Her shoulders heaved. As for me, I felt like a stone; I could not weep.

"Oh," she gasped out finally, "I knew—I knew! I told Phoebe—I knew just how it would be, I—knew!"

I roused myself at that.

"What do you mean?" said I.

"When Phoebe came home Tuesday night and said she heard your father and Rufus Bennett having words, I knew how it would be," she choked out. "I knew he had a dreadful temper."

"Did Phoebe Dole know Tuesday night that father and Rufus Bennett had words?" said I.

"Yes," said Maria Woods.

"How did she know?"

"She was going through your yard, the short cut to Mrs. Ormsby's, to carry her brown alpaca dress home. She came right home and told me; and she overheard them."

"Have you spoken of it to anybody but me?" said I.

Maria said she didn't know; she might have done so. Then she remembered hearing Phoebe herself speak of it to Harriet Sargent when she came in to try on her dress. It was easy to see how people knew about it.

I did not say any more, but I thought it was strange that Phoebe Dole had asked me if father had had words with anybody when she knew it all the time.

Phoebe came in before long. I tried on my dress, and she made her plan about the alterations, and the trimming. I made no suggestions. I did not care how it was done, but if I had cared it would have made no difference. Phoebe always does things her own way. All the women in the village are in a manner under Phoebe Dole's thumb. The garments are visible proofs of her force of will.

While she was taking up my black silk on the shoulder seams, Phoebe Dole said—

"Let me see—you had a green silk made at Digby three summers ago, didn't you?"

"Yes," I said.

"Well," said she, "why don't you have it dyed black? those thin silks dye quite nice. It would make you a good dress."

I scarcely replied, and then she offered to dye it for me herself. She had a recipe which she used with great success. I thought it was very kind of her, but did not say whether I would accept her offer or not. I could not fix my mind upon anything but the awful trouble I was in.

"I'll come over and get it to-morrow morning," said Phoebe.

I thanked her. I thought of the stains, and then my mind seemed to wander again to the one subject. All the time Maria Woods sat weeping. Finally Phoebe turned to her with impatience.

"If you can't keep calmer, you'd better go upstairs, Maria," said she. "You'll make Sarah sick. Look at her! she doesn't give way—and think of the reason she's got."

"I've got reason, too," Maria broke out; then, with a piteous shriek, "Oh, I've got reason."

"Maria Woods, go out of the room!" said Phoebe. Her sharpness made me jump, half dazed as I was.

Maria got up without a word, and went out of the room, bending almost double with convulsive sobs.

"She's been dreadfully worked up over your father's death," said Phoebe calmly, going on with the fitting. "She's terribly nervous. Sometimes I have to be real sharp with her, for her own good."

I nodded. Maria Woods has always been considered a sweet, weakly, dependent woman, and Phoebe Dole is undoubtedly very fond of her. She has seemed to shield her, and take care of her nearly all her life. The two have lived together since they were young girls.

Phoebe is tall, and very pale and thin; but she never had a day's illness. She is plain, yet there is a kind of severe goodness and faithfulness about her colorless face, with the smooth bands of white hair over her ears.

I went home as soon as my dress was fitted. That evening Henry Ellis came over to see me. I do not need to go into details concerning that visit. It seemed enough to say that he tendered the fullest sympathy and protection, and I accepted them. I cried a little for the first time, and he soothed and comforted me.

Henry had driven over from Digby and tied his horse in the yard. At ten o'clock he bade me good night on the doorstep, and was just turning his buggy around, when Mrs. Adams came running to the door.

"Is this yours?" said she, and she held out a knot of yellow ribbon.

"Why, that's the ribbon you have around your whip, Henry," said I. He looked at it.

"So it is," he said. "I must have dropped it." He put it into his pocket and drove away.

"He didn't drop that ribbon to-night!" said Mrs. Adams. "I found it Wednesday morning out in the yard. I thought I remembered seeing him have a yellow ribbon on his whip."

III
SUSPICION IS NOT PROOF

When Mrs. Adams told me she had picked up Henry's whip-ribbon Wednesday morning, I said nothing, but thought that Henry must have driven over Tuesday evening after all, and even come up into the yard, although the house was shut up, and I in bed, to get a little nearer to me. I felt conscience-stricken, because I could not help a thrill of happiness, when my father lay dead in the house.

My father was buried as privately and as quietly as we could bring it about. But it was a terrible ordeal. Meantime word came from Vermont that Rufus Bennett had been arrested on his farm. He was perfectly willing to come back with the officers, and indeed, had not the slightest trouble in proving that he was at his home in Vermont when the murder took place. He proved by several witnesses that he was out of the State long before my father and I sat on the steps together that evening, and that he proceeded directly to his home as fast as the train and stage-coach could carry him.

The screw-driver with which the deed was supposed to have been committed was found, by the neighbor from whom it had been borrowed, in his wife's bureau drawer. It had been returned, and she had used it to put a picture-hook in her chamber. Bennett was discharged and returned to Vermont.

Then Mrs. Adams told of the finding of the yellow ribbon from Henry Ellis's whip, and he was arrested, since he was held to have a motive for putting my father out of the world. Father's opposition to our marriage was well known, and Henry was suspected also of having had an eye to his money. It was found, indeed, that my father had more money than I had known myself.

Henry owned to having driven into the yard that night, and to having missed the ribbon from his whip on his return; but one of the hostlers in the livery stables in Digby, where he kept his horse and buggy, came forward and testified to finding the yellow ribbon in the carriage-room that Tuesday night before Henry returned from his drive. There were two yellow ribbons in evidence, therefore, and the one produced by the hostler seemed to fit Henry's whip-stock the more exactly.

Moreover, nearly the exact minute of the murder was claimed to be proved by the post-mortem examination; and by the testimony of the stable man as to the hour of Henry's return and the speed of his horse, he was further cleared of suspicion; for, if the opinion of the medical experts was correct, Henry must have returned to the livery stable too soon to have committed the murder.

He was discharged, at any rate, although suspicion still clung to him. Many people believe now in his guilt—those who do not, believe in mine; and some believe we were accomplices.

After Henry's discharge, I was arrested. There was no one else left to accuse. There must be a motive for the murder; I was the only person left with a motive. Unlike the others, who were discharged after preliminary examination, I was held to the grand jury and taken to Dedham, where I spent four weeks in jail, awaiting the meeting of the grand jury.

Neither at the preliminary examination, nor before the grand jury, was I allowed to make the full and frank statement that I am making here. I was told simply to answer the questions that were put to me, and to volunteer nothing and I obeyed.

I know nothing about law. I wished to do the best I could—to act in the wisest manner, for Henry's sake and my own. I said nothing about the green silk dress. They searched the house for all manner of things, at the time of my arrest, but the dress was not there—it was in Phoebe Dole's dye-kettle. She had come over after it one day when I was picking beans in the garden, and had taken it out of the closet. She brought it back herself, and told me this, after I had returned from Dedham.

"I thought I'd get it and surprise you," said she. "It's taken a beautiful black."

She gave me a strange look—half as if she would see into my very soul, in spite of me, half as if she were in terror of what she would see there, as she spoke. I do not know just what Phoebe Dole's look meant. There may have been a stain left on that dress after all, and she may have seen it.

I suppose if it had not been for that flour-paste which I had learned to make, I should have hung for the murder of my father. As it was, the grand jury found no bill against me because there was absolutely no evidence to convict me and I came home a free woman. And if people were condemned for their motives, would there be enough hangmen in the world?

They found no weapon with which I could have done the deed. They found no blood-stains on my clothes. The one thing which told against me, aside from my ever-present motive, was the fact that on the morning after the murder the doors and windows were fastened. My volunteering this information had of course weakened its force as against myself.

Then, too, some held that I might have been mistaken in my terror and excitement, and there was a theory, advanced by a few, that the murderer had meditated making me also a victim, and had locked the doors that he might not be frustrated in his designs, but had lost heart at the last, and had allowed me to escape, and then fled himself. Some held that he had intended to force me to reveal the whereabouts of father's money, but his courage had failed him.

Father had quite a sum in a hiding-place which only he and I knew. But no search for money had been made, as far as any one could see—not a bureau drawer had been disturbed, and father's gold watch was ticking peacefully under his pillow; even his wallet in his vest pocket had not been opened. There was a small roll of bank-notes in it, and some change; father never carried much money. I suppose if father's wallet and watch had been taken, I should not have been suspected at all.

I was discharged, as I have said, from lack of evidence, and have returned to my home—free, indeed, but with this awful burden of suspicion on my shoulders. That brings me up to the present day. I returned yesterday evening. This evening Henry Ellis has been over to see me; he will not come again, for I have forbidden him to do so. This is what I said to him—

"I know you are innocent, you know I am innocent. To all the world beside we are under suspicion—I more than you, but we are both under suspicion. If we are known to be together that suspicion is increased for both of us. I do not care for myself, but I do care for you. Separated from me the stigma attached to you will soon fade away, especially if you should marry elsewhere."

Then Henry interrupted me.

"I will never marry elsewhere," said he.

I could not help being glad that he said it, but I was firm.

"If you should see some good woman whom you could love, it will be better for you to marry elsewhere," said I.

"I never will!" he said again. He put his arms around me, but I had strength to push him away.

"You never need, if I succeed in what I undertake before you meet the other," said I. I began to think he had not cared for that pretty girl who boarded in the same house after all.

"What is that?" he said. "What are you going to undertake?"

"To find my father's murderer," said I.

Henry gave me a strange look; then, before I could stop him, he took me fast in his arms and kissed my forehead.

"As God is my witness, Sarah, I believe in your innocence," he said; and from that minute I have felt sustained and fully confident of my power to do what I had undertaken.

My father's murderer I will find. To-morrow I begin my search. I shall first make an exhaustive examination of the house, such as no officer in the case has yet made, in the hope of finding a clue. Every room I propose to divide into square yards, by line and measure, and every one of these square yards I will study as if it were a problem in algebra.

I have a theory that it is impossible for any human being to enter any house, and commit in it a deed of this kind, and not leave behind traces which are the known quantities in an algebraic equation to those who can use them.

There is a chance that I shall not be quite unaided. Henry has promised not to come again until I bid him, but he is to send a detective here from Boston—one whom he knows. In fact, the man is a cousin of his, or else there would be small hope of our securing him, even if I were to offer him a large price.

The man has been remarkably successful in several cases, but his health is not good; the work is a severe strain upon his nerves, and he is not driven to it from any lack of money. The physicians have forbidden him to undertake any new case, for a year at least, but Henry is confident that we may rely upon him for this.

I will now lay aside this and go to bed. To-morrow is Wednesday; my father will have been dead seven weeks. To-morrow morning I will commence the work, in which, if it be in human power, aided by a higher wisdom, I shall succeed.

IV

THE BOX OF CLUES

*(The pages which follow are from Miss Fairbanks's
journal, begun after the conclusion of the notes already given to the reader.)*

Wednesday night.—I have resolved to record carefully each day the progress I made in my examination of the house. I began to-day at the bottom—that is, with the room least likely to contain any clue, the parlor. I took a chalk-line and a yard-stick, and divided the floor into square yards, and every one of these squares I examined on my hands and knees. I found in this way literally nothing on the carpet but dust, lint, two common white pins, and three inches of blue sewing-silk.

At last I got the dustpan and brush, and yard by yard swept the floor. I took the sweepings in a white paste-board box out into the yard in the strong sunlight, and examined them. There was nothing but dust and lint and five inches of brown woollen thread—evidently a ravelling of some dress material. The blue silk and the brown thread are the only possible clues which I found to-day, and they are hardly possible. Rufus's wife can probably account for them.

Nobody has come to the house all day. I went down to the store this afternoon to get some necessary provisions, and people stopped talking when I came in. The clerk took my money as if it were poison.

Thursday night.—To-day I have searched the sitting-room, out of which my father's bedroom opens. I found two bloody footprints on the carpet which no one had noticed before—perhaps because the carpet itself is red and white. I used a microscope which I had in my school work. The footprints, which are close to the bedroom door, pointing out into the sitting-room, are both from the right foot; one is brighter than the other, but both are faint. The foot was evidently either bare or clad only in a stocking—the prints are so widely spread. They are wider than my father's shoes. I tried one in the brightest print.

I found nothing else new in the sitting-room. The blood-stains on the doors which have been already noted are still there. They had not been washed away, first by order of the sheriff, and next by mine. These stains are of two kinds; one looks as if made by a bloody garment brushing against it; the other, I should say, was made in the first place by the grasp of a bloody hand, and then brushed over with a cloth. There are none of these marks upon the door leading to the bedroom—they are on the doors leading into the front entry and the china closet. The china closet is really a pantry, although I use it only for my best dishes and preserves.

Friday night.—To-day I searched the closet. One of the shelves, which is about as high as my shoulders, was blood-stained. It looked to me as if the murderer might have caught hold of it to steady himself. Did he turn faint after his dreadful deed? Some tumblers of jelly were ranged on that shelf and they had not been disturbed. There was only that bloody clutch on the edge.

I found on this closet floor, under the shelves, as if it had been rolled there by a careless foot, a button, evidently from a man's clothing. It is an ordinary black enamelled metal trousers-button; it had evidently been worn off and clumsily sewn on again, for a quantity of stout white thread is still clinging to it. This button must have belonged either to a single man or to one with an idle wife.

If one black button had been sewn on with white thread, another is likely to be. I may be wrong, but I regard this button as a clue.

The pantry was thoroughly swept—cleaned, indeed, by Rufus's wife, the day before she left. Neither my father nor Rufus could have dropped it there, and they never had occasion to go to that closet. The murderer dropped the button.

I have a white pasteboard box which I have marked "clues." In it I have put the button.

This afternoon Phoebe Dole came in. She is very kind. She had recut the dyed silk, and she fitted it to me. Her great shears clicking in my ears made me nervous. I did not feel like stopping to think about clothes. I hope I did not appear ungrateful, for she is the only soul beside Henry who has treated me as she did before this happened.

Phoebe asked me what I found to busy myself about, and I replied, "I am searching for my father's murderer." She asked me if I thought I should find a clue, and I replied, "I think so." I had found the button then, but I did not speak of it. She said Maria was not very well.

I saw her eyeing the stains on the doors, and I said I had not washed them off, for I thought they might yet serve a purpose in detecting the murderer. She looked closely at those on the entry door—the brightest ones—and said she did not see how they could help, for there were no plain finger-marks there, and she should think they would make me nervous.

"I'm beyond being nervous," I replied.

Saturday.—To-day I have found something which I cannot understand. I have been at work in the room where my father came to his dreadful end. Of course some of the most startling evidences have been removed. The bed is clean, and the carpet washed, but the worst horror of it all clings to that room. The spirit of murder seemed to haunt it. It seemed to me at first that I could not enter that room, but in it I made a strange discovery.

My father, while he carried little money about his person, was in the habit of keeping considerable sums in the house; there is no bank within ten miles. However he was wary; he had a hiding-place which he had revealed to no one but myself. He had a small stand in his room near the end of his bed. Under this stand, or rather under the top of it, he had tacked a large leather wallet. In this he kept all his spare money. I remember how his eyes twinkled when he showed it to me.

"The average mind thinks things have either got to be in or on," said my father. "They don't consider there's ways of getting around gravitation and calculation."

In searching my father's room I called to mind that saying of his, and his peculiar system of concealment, and then I made my discovery. I have argued that in a search of this kind I ought not only to search for hidden traces of the criminal, but for everything which had been for any reason concealed. Something which my father himself had hidden, something from his past history, may furnish a motive for some one else.

The money in the wallet under the table, some five hundred dollars, had been removed and deposited in the bank. Nothing more was to be found there. I examined the bottom of the bureau, and the undersides of the chair seats. There are two chairs in the room, besides the cushioned rocker—green-painted wooden chairs, with flag seats. I found nothing under the seats.

Then I turned each of the green chairs completely over, and examined the bottoms of the legs. My heart leaped when I found a bit of leather tacked over one. I got the tack-hammer and drew the tacks. The chair-leg had been hollowed out, and for an inch the hole was packed tight with cotton. I began picking out the cotton, and soon I felt something hard. It proved to be an old-fashioned gold band, quite wide and heavy, like a wedding-ring.

I took it over to the window and found this inscription on the inside: "Let love abide for ever." There were two dates—one in August, forty years ago, and the other in August of the present year.

I think the ring had never been worn; while the first part of the inscription is perfectly clear, it looks old, and the last is evidently freshly cut.

This could not have been my mother's ring. She had only her wedding-ring, and that was buried with her. I think my father must have treasured up this ring for years; but why? What does it mean? This can hardly be a clue; this can hardly lead to the discovery of a motive, but I will put it in the box with the rest.

Sunday night.—To-day, of course, I did not pursue my search. I did not go to church. I could not face old friends that could not face me. Sometimes I think that everybody in my native village believes in my guilt. What must I have been in my general appearance and demeanor all my life? I have studied myself in the glass, and tried to discover the possibilities of evil that they must see in my face.

This afternoon about three o'clock, the hour when people here have just finished their Sunday dinner, there was a knock on the north door. I answered it, and a strange young man stood there with a large book under his arm. He was thin and cleanly shaved, with a clerical air.

"I have a work here to which I would like to call your attention," he began; and I stared at him in astonishment, for why should a book agent be peddling his wares upon the Sabbath?

His mouth twitched a little.

"It's a Biblical Cyclopaedia," said he.

"I don't think I care to take it," said I.

"You are Miss Sarah Fairbanks, I believe?"

"That is my name," I replied stiffly.

"Mr. Henry Ellis, of Digby, sent me here," he said next. "My name is Dix—Francis Dix."

Then I knew it was Henry's first cousin from Boston—the detective who had come to help me. I felt the tears coming to my eyes.

"You are very kind to come," I managed to say.

"I am selfish, not kind," he returned, "but you had better let me come in, or any chance of success in my book agency is lost, if the neighbors see me trying to sell it on a Sunday. And, Miss Fairbanks, this is a *bonâ fide* agency. I shall canvass the town."

He came in. I showed him all that I have written, and he read it carefully. When he had finished he sat still for a long time, with his face screwed up in a peculiar meditative fashion.

"We'll ferret this out in three days at the most," said he finally, with a sudden clearing of his face and a flash of his eyes at me.

"I had planned for three years, perhaps," said I.

"I tell you, we'll do it in three days," he repeated. "Where can I get board while I canvass for this remarkable and interesting book under my arm? I can't stay here, of course, and there is no hotel. Do you think the two dressmakers next door, Phoebe Dole and the other one, would take me in?"

I said they had never taken boarders.

"Well, I'll go over and inquire," said Mr. Dix; and he had gone, with his book under his arm, almost before I knew it.

Never have I seen any one act with the strange noiseless soft speed that this man does. Can he prove me innocent in three days? He must have succeeded in getting board at Phoebe Dole's, for I saw him go past to meeting with her this evening. I feel sure he will be over very early to-morrow morning.

V
The Evidence Points to One

Monday night.—The detective came as I expected. I was up as soon as it was light, and he came across the dewy fields, with his cyclopaedia under his arm. He had stolen out from Phoebe Dole's back door.

He had me bring my father's pistol; then he bade me come with him out into the back yard.

"Now, fire it," he said, thrusting the pistol into my hands. As I have said before, the charge was still in the barrel.

"I shall arouse the neighborhood," I said.

"Fire it," he ordered.

I tried; I pulled the trigger as hard as I could.

"I can't do it," I said.

"And you are a reasonably strong woman, too, aren't you?"

I said I had been considered so. Oh, how much I heard about the strength of my poor woman's arms, and their ability to strike that murderous weapon home!

Mr. Dix took the pistol himself, and drew a little at the trigger.

"I could do it," he said, "but I won't. It would arouse the neighborhood."

"This is more evidence against me," I said despairingly. "The murderer had tried to fire the pistol and failed."

"It is more evidence against the murderer," said Mr. Dix.

We went into the house, where he examined my box of clues long and carefully. Looking at the ring, he asked whether there was a jeweller in this village, and I said there was not. I told him that my father oftener went on business to Acton, ten miles away, than elsewhere.

He examined very carefully the button which I had found in the closet, and then asked to see my father's wardrobe. That was soon done. Besides the suit in which father was laid away there was one other complete one in the closet in his room. Besides that, there were in this closet two over-coats, an old black frock coat, a pair of pepper-and-salt trousers, and two black vests. Mr. Dix examined all the buttons; not one was missing.

There was still another old suit in the closet off the kitchen. This was examined, and no button found wanting.

"What did your father do for work the day before he died?" he then asked.

I reflected and said that he had unpacked some stores which had come down from Vermont, and done some work out in the garden.

"What did he wear?"

"I think he wore the pepper-and-salt trousers and the black vest. He wore no coat, while at work."

Mr. Dix went quietly back to father's room and his closet, I following. He took out the gray trousers and the black vest, and examined them closely.

"What did he wear to protect these?" he asked.

"Why, he wore overalls!" I said at once. As I spoke I remembered seeing father go around the path to the yard, with those blue overalls drawn up high under his arms.

"Where are they?"

"Weren't they in the kitchen closet?"

"No."

We looked again, however, in the kitchen closet; we searched the shed thoroughly. The cat came in through her little door, as we stood there, and brushed around our feet. Mr. Dix stooped and stroked her. Then he went quickly to the door, beside which her little entrance was arranged, un-hooked it, and stepped out. I was following him, but he motioned me back.

"None of my boarding mistress's windows command us," he said, "but she might come to the back door."

I watched him. He passed slowly around the little winding footpath, which skirted the rear of our house and extended faintly through the grassy fields to the rear of Phoebe Dole's. He stopped, searched a clump of sweet-briar, went on to an old well, and stopped there. The well had been dry many a year, and was choked up with stones and rubbish. Some boards are laid over it, and a big stone or two, to keep them in place.

Mr. Dix, glancing across at Phoebe Dole's back door, went down on his knees, rolled the stones away, then removed the boards and peered down the well. He stretched far over the brink, and reached down. He made many efforts; then he got up and came to me, and asked me to get for him an umbrella with a crooked handle, or something that he could hook into clothing.

I brought my own umbrella, the silver handle of which formed an exact hook. He went back to the well, knelt again, thrust in the umbrella and drew up, easily enough, what he had been fishing for. Then he came bringing it to me.

"Don't faint," he said, and took hold of my arm. I gasped when I saw what he had—my father's blue overalls, all stained and splotched with blood!

I looked at them, then at him.

"Don't faint," he said again. "We're on the right track. This is where the button came from—see, see!" He pointed to one of the straps of the overalls, and the button was gone. Some white thread clung to it. Another black metal button was sewed on roughly with the same white thread that I found on the button in my box of clues.

"What does it mean?" I gasped out. My brain reeled.

"You shall know soon," he said. He looked at his watch. Then he laid down the ghastly bundle he carried. "It has puzzled you to know how the murderer went in and out and yet kept the doors locked, has it not?" he said.

"Yes."

"Well, I am going out now. Hook that door after me."

He went out, still carrying my umbrella. I hooked the door. Presently I saw the lid of the cat's door lifted, and his hand and arm thrust through. He curved his arm up towards the hook, but it came short by half a foot. Then he withdrew his arm, and thrust in my silver-handled umbrella. He reached the door-hook easily enough with that.

Then he hooked it again. That was not so easy. He had to work a long time. Finally he accomplished it, unhooked the door again, and came in.

"That was how!" I said.

"No, it was not," he returned. "No human being, fresh from such a deed, could have used such patience as that to fasten the door after him. Please hang your arm down by your side."

I obeyed. He looked at my arm, then at his own.

"Have you a tape measure?" he asked.

I brought one out of my work-basket. He measured his arm, then mine, and then the distance from the cat-door to the hook.

"I have two tasks for you to-day and to-morrow," he said. "I shall come here very little. Find all your father's old letters, and read them. Find a man or woman in this town whose arm is six inches longer than yours. Now I must go home, or my boarding-mistress will get curious."

He went through the house to the front door, looked all ways to be sure no eyes were upon him, made three strides down the yard, and was pacing soberly up the street, with his cyclopaedia under his arm.

I made myself a cup of coffee, then I went about obeying his instructions. I read old letters all the forenoon; I found packages in trunks in the garret; there were quantities in father's desk. I have selected several to submit to Mr. Dix. One of them treats of an old episode in father's youth, which must have years since ceased to interest him. It was concealed after his favorite fashion—tacked under the bottom of his desk. It was written forty years ago, by Maria Woods, two years before my father's marriage —and it was a refusal of an offer to his hand. It was written in the stilted fashion of that day; it might have been copied from a "Complete Letter-writer."

My father must have loved Maria Woods as dearly as I love Henry, to keep that letter so carefully all these years. I thought he cared for my mother. He seemed as fond of her as other men of their wives, although I did use to wonder if Henry and I would ever get to be quite so much accustomed to each other.

Maria Woods must have been as beautiful as an angel when she was a girl. Mother was not pretty; she was stout, too, and awkward, and I suppose people would have called her rather slow and dull. But she was a good woman, and tried to do her duty.

Tuesday night.—This evening was my first opportunity to obey the second of Mr. Dix's orders. It seemed to me the best way to compare the average length of arms was to go to the prayer-meeting. I could not go about the town with my tape measure, and demand of people that they should hold out their arms. Nobody knows how I dreaded to go to the meeting, but I went, and I looked not at my neighbors' cold altered faces, but at their arms.

I discovered what Mr. Dix wished me to, but the discovery can avail nothing, and it is one he could have made himself. Phoebe Dole's arm is fully seven inches longer than mine. I never noticed it before, but she has an almost abnormally long arm. But why should Phoebe Dole have unhooked that door?

She made a prayer—a beautiful prayer. It comforted even me a little.

She spoke of the tenderness of God in all the troubles of life, and how it never failed us.

When we were all going out I heard several persons speak of Mr. Dix and his Biblical Cyclopaedia. They decided that he was a theological student, book-canvassing to defray the expenses of his education.

Maria Woods was not at the meeting. Several asked Phoebe how she was, and she replied, "Not very well."

It is very late. I thought Mr. Dix might be over tonight, but he has not been here.

Wednesday.—I can scarcely believe what I am about to write. Our investigations seem to point all to one person, and that person— It is incredible! I will not believe it.

Mr. Dix came as before, at dawn. He reported, and I reported. I showed Maria Woods's letter. He said he had driven to Acton, and found that the jeweller there had engraved the last date in the ring about six weeks ago.

"I don't want to seem rough, but your father was going to get married again," said Mr. Dix.

"I never knew him to go near any woman since mother died," I protested.

"Nevertheless, he had made arrangements to be married," persisted Mr. Dix.

"Who was the woman?"

He pointed at the letter in my hand.

"Maria Woods!"

He nodded.

I stood looking at him—dazed. Such a possibility had never entered my head.

He produced an envelope from his pocket, and took out a little card with blue and brown threads neatly wound upon it.

"Let me see those threads you found," he said.

I got the box and we compared them. He had a number of pieces of blue sewing-silk and brown woollen ravellings, and they matched mine exactly.

"Where did you find them?" I asked.

"In my boarding-mistress's piece-bag."

I stared at him.

"What does it mean?" I gasped out.

"What do you think?"

"It is impossible!"

VI
The Revelation

Wednesday, continued.—When Mr. Dix thus suggested to me the absurd possibility that Phoebe Dole had committed the murder, he and I were sitting in the kitchen. He was near the table; he laid a sheet of paper upon it, and began to write. The paper is before me.

"First," said Mr. Dix, and he wrote rapidly as he talked, "whose arm is of such length that it might unlock a certain door of this house from the outside?—Phoebe Dole's.

"Second, who had in her piece-bag bits of the same threads and ravellings found upon your parlor floor, where she had not by your knowledge entered?—Phoebe Dole.

"Third, who interested herself most strangely in your blood-stained green silk dress, even to dyeing it?—Phoebe Dole.

"Fourth, who was caught in a lie, while trying to force the guilt of the murder upon an innocent man?—Phoebe Dole."

Mr. Dix looked at me. I had gathered myself together.

"That proves nothing," I said. "There is no motive in her case."

"There is a motive."

"What is it?"

"Maria Woods shall tell you this afternoon."

He then wrote—

"Fifth, who was seen to throw a bundle down the old well, in the rear of Martin Fairbanks's house, at one o'clock in the morning?—Phoebe Dole."

"Was she—seen?" I gasped.

Mr. Dix nodded. Then he wrote.

"Sixth, who had a strong motive, which had been in existence many years ago?—Phoebe Dole."

Mr. Dix laid down his pen, and looked at me again.

"Well, what have you to say?" he asked.

"It is impossible!"

"Why?"

"She is a woman."

"A man could have fired that pistol, as she tried to do."

"It would have taken a man's strength to kill with the kind of weapon that was used," I said.

"No, it would not. No great strength is required for such a blow."

"But she is a woman!"

"Crime has no sex."

"But she is a good woman—a church member. I heard her pray yesterday afternoon. It is not in character."

"It is not for you, nor for me, nor for any mortal intelligence, to know what is or is not in character," said Mr. Dix.

He arose and went away. I could only stare at him in a half-dazed manner.

Maria Woods came this afternoon, taking advantage of Phoebe's absence on a dress-making errand. Maria has aged ten years in the last few weeks. Her hair is white, her cheeks are fallen in, her pretty color is gone.

"May I have the ring he gave me forty years ago?" she faltered.

I gave it to her; she kissed it and sobbed like a child.

"Phoebe took it away from me before," she said; "but she shan't this time."

Maria related with piteous sobs the story of her long subordination to Phoebe Dole. This sweet child-like woman had always been completely under the sway of the other's stronger nature. The subordination went back beyond my father's original proposal to her; she had, before he made love to her as a girl, promised Phoebe she would not marry; and it was Phoebe who, by representing to her that she was bound by this solemn promise, had led her to write a letter to my father declining his offer, and sending back the ring.

"And after all, we were going to get married, if he had not died," she said. "He was going to give me this ring again, and he had had the other date put in. I should have been so happy!"

She stopped and stared at me with horror-stricken inquiry.

"What was Phoebe Dole doing in your backyard at one o'clock that night?" she cried.

"What do you mean?" I returned.

"What was Phoebe Dole doing in your backyard at one o'clock that very night. She had a bundle in her arms. She went along the path about as far as the old well, then she stooped down, and seemed to be working at something. When she got up she didn't have the bundle. I was watching at our back door. I thought I heard her go out a little while before, and went downstairs, and found that door unlocked. I went in quick, and up to my chamber, and into my bed, when she started home across the fields. Pretty soon I heard her come in, then I heard the pump going. She slept downstairs; she went on to her bedroom. What was she doing in your backyard that night?"

"You must ask her," said I. I felt my blood running cold.

"I've been afraid to," moaned Maria Woods. "She's been dreadful strange lately. I wish that book agent was going to stay at our house."

Maria Woods went home in about an hour. I got a ribbon for her, and she has my poor father's ring concealed in her withered bosom. Again I cannot believe this.

Thursday.—It is all over, Phoebe Dole has confessed! I do not know now in exactly what way Mr. Dix brought it about—how he accused her of her crime. After breakfast I saw them coming across the fields; Phoebe came first, advancing with rapid strides like a man, Mr. Dix followed, and my father's poor old sweetheart tottered behind, with her handkerchief at her eyes. Just as I noticed them the front door bell rang; I found several people there, headed by the high sheriff. They crowded into the sitting-room just as Phoebe Dole came rushing in, with Mr. Dix and Maria Woods.

"I did it!" Phoebe cried out to me. "I am found out, and I have made up my mind to confess. She was going to marry your father—I found it out. I stopped it once before. This time I knew I couldn't unless I killed him. She's lived with me in that house for over forty years. There are other ties as strong as the marriage one, that are just as sacred. What right had he to take her away from me and break up my home?

"I overheard your father and Rufus Bennett having words. I thought folks would think he did it. I reasoned it all out. I had watched your cat go in that little door, I knew the shed door hooked, I knew how long my arm was; I thought I could undo it. I stole over here a little after midnight. I went all around the house to be sure nobody was awake. Out in the front yard I happened to think my shears were tied on my belt with a ribbon, and I untied them. I thought I put the ribbon in my pocket—it was a piece of yellow ribbon—but I suppose I didn't, because they found it afterwards, and thought it came off your young man's whip.

"I went round to the shed door, unhooked it, and went in. The moon was light enough. I got out your father's overalls from the kitchen closet; I knew where they were. I went through the sitting-room to the parlor.

"In there I slipped off my dress and skirts and put on the overalls. I put a handkerchief over my face, leaving only my eyes exposed. I crept out then into the sitting-room; there I pulled off my shoes and went into the bedroom.

"Your father was fast asleep; it was such a hot night, the clothes were thrown back and his chest was bare. The first thing I saw was that pistol on the stand beside his bed. I suppose he had had some fear of Rufus Bennett coming back, after all. Suddenly I thought I'd better shoot him. It would be surer and quicker; and if you were aroused I knew that I could get away, and everybody would suppose that he had shot himself.

"I took up the pistol and held it close to his head. I had never fired a pistol, but I knew how it was done. I pulled, but it would not go off. Your father stirred a little—I was mad with horror—I struck at his head with the pistol. He opened his eyes and cried out; then I dropped the pistol, and took these"—Phoebe Dole pointed to the great shining shears hanging at her waist—"for I am strong in my wrists. I only struck twice, over his heart.

"Then I went back into the sitting-room. I thought I heard a noise in the kitchen—I was full of terror then—and slipped into the sitting-room closet. I felt as if I were fainting, and clutched the shelf to keep from falling.

"I felt that I must go upstairs to see if you were asleep, to be sure you had not waked up when your father cried out. I thought if you had I should have to do the same by you. I crept upstairs to your chamber. You seemed sound asleep, but, as I watched, you stirred a little; but instead of striking at you I slipped into your closet. I heard nothing more from you. I felt myself wet with blood. I caught something hanging in your closet, and wiped myself over with it. I knew by the feeling it was your green silk. You kept quiet, and I saw you were asleep, so crept out of the closet, and down the stairs, got my clothes and shoes, and, out in the shed, took off the overalls and dressed myself. I rolled up the overalls, and took a board away from the old well and threw them in as I went home. I thought if they were found it would be no clue to me. The handkerchief, which was not much stained, I put to soak that night, and washed it out next morning, before Maria was up. I washed my hands and arms carefully that night, and also my shears.

"I expected Rufus Bennett would be accused of the murder, and, maybe, hung. I was prepared for that, but I did not like to think I had thrown suspicion upon you by staining your dress. I had nothing against you. I made up my mind I'd get hold of that dress—before anybody suspected you—and dye it black. I came in and got it, as you know. I was astonished not to see any more stains on it. I only found two or three little streaks that scarcely anybody would have noticed. I didn't know what to think. I suspected, of course, that you had found the stains and got them off, thinking they might bring suspicion upon you.

"I did not see how you could possibly suspect me in any case. I was glad when your young man was cleared. I had nothing against him. That is all I have to say."

I think I must have fainted away then. I cannot describe the dreadful calmness with which that woman told this—that woman with the good face, whom I had last heard praying like a saint in meeting. I believe in demoniacal possession after this.

When I came to, the neighbors were around me, putting camphor on my head, and saying soothing things to me, and the old friendly faces had returned. But I wish I could forget!

They have taken Phoebe Dole away—I only know that. I cannot bear to talk any more about it when I think there must be a trial, and I must go!

Henry has been over this evening. I suppose we shall be happy after all, when I have had a little time to get over this. He says I have nothing more to worry about. Mr. Dix has gone home. I hope Henry and I may be able to repay his kindness some day.

*   *   *   *   *   *

A month later. I have just heard that Phoebe Dole has died in prison. This is my last entry. May God help all other innocent women in hard straits as He has helped me!

Rose O'Neill
(1874–1944)

Rose O'Neill was best known as the originator of Kewpie dolls, sentimental little cupid figures that she illustrated in the pages of *Ladies' Home Journal* in 1909 and then patented and marketed in 1913. Although she became a millionaire with the success of her Kewpies, she continued to publish commercial novels and magazine stories. Before she made her fortune, O'Neill had been married to men twice, each time for five years. During the course of her first marriage (1896–1901), to Gray Latham, she signed her work "O'Neill Latham." In much of her writing O'Neill assumed a male persona.

O'Neill's most famous books were Gothic romances, such as *Garda* (1929) and *The Goblin Woman* (1930). Her volume of poetry, *The Master-Mistress* (1922) is unusual in her canon because a number of the poems deal specifically with lesbian subject matter. They often show the influence of the exotic lesbian imagery of nineteenth-century Decadent writers.

Her title, *The Master-Mistress*, is taken from Shakespeare's Sonnet 20, in which the male speaker refers to an androgynous young man as "the master mistress of my passion." The master-mistress in O'Neill's poems is an androgynous young woman. Unlike Shakespeare, however, who viewed androgyny in his sonnet sequence as concomitant with young male beauty, O'Neill, an early-twentieth-century American, views it as did the nineteenth-century French and English writers: It is enchantingly monstrous, exotic in its mystery and its potential for sorrow and danger.

But Americans were less romantic and more timid with regard to the subject of lesbianism than the Europeans. The more worldly of O'Neill's American critics in her day understood the lesbian touches in her poetry, but despite their "sophistication," they hinted that even they needed to work at suppressing their shock with regard to the subject. Clement Wood, for example, warned readers of *The Master-Mistress*, "Her poetry will lose a certain Puritan following because of her cryptic frankness on the theme of love. . . . It is here, in a few poems; those who are not offended by this note in the masters since the Greeks will not be offended by it here."

In an early poem in the collection O'Neill declares, "I strangely sing because my love is strange." Her love's "strangeness" is an encoding for lesbianism, which betrays her influence by Baudelaire and his European successors. In the title poem the narrator speaks of "A lovely monster . . . With dreadful beauty doomed." In "A Dream of Sappho," that first "Lesbian" is pale, deathless, fair, "but far more strange than fair." The speaker's connection with her is Dionysian—drunk and staggering—and their brief contact ends in pain and despair. The androgynous woman of "Lee" is associated with "golden sorrows." And "The Sister" is reminiscent of Christina Rossetti's "Goblin Market," overlaid with the forbidden erotic knowledge of Baudelaire and Renée Vivien.

FURTHER READING: Rose O'Neill, *The Master-Mistress* (New York: Knopf, 1922). Clement Wood, *Poets of America* (New York: Dutton, 1925).

THE MASTER-MISTRESS

All in the drowse of life I saw a shape,
A lovely monster reared up from the restless rock,
More secret and more loud than other beasts.
It, seeming two in one,
With dreadful beauty doomed,
Folded itself, in chanting like a flood.
I said, "Your name, O Master-mistress?"
But it, answering not,
Folded itself, in chanting like a flood.

LEE
(A Portrait)

Darkling eye and golden hair,
Velvet captive of a long despair;
Lonely heart and Yorick's tongue,
Gay and valiant, and forever young;
Soul that weaves a magic like the moon,
Soul that voyages—a vanished tune!

Mimic, dancer, cavalier,
Silky hand the proud horse loves to fear;
Sailor and adventurer;
Dark eyed peoples look and long for her,
And the Spaniard claims her for his own;
She who lingers, loves, and goes alone.
Tall as the Giralda and as fair,
Darkling eye and golden hair!

Golden hair and darkling eye,
Where the golden sorrows ever lie,
Velvet prisoners they are, and wild;
One, a woman weeping for a child,
(Her own childhood lost among the deeps,)
One, a child that for a woman weeps,
One, a wide desire that never sleeps.

Golden hair and silken knee,
It is wide, the longing for the sea!
Darkling eye and petal lips,
Wide the windy longing for the ships!
Painter's hand and poet's heart,
Wide the cloudy hunger for an Art!
Sigh that smiles and smile that is a sigh;
Golden hair and darkling eye!

A DREAM OF SAPPHO

She slowly came, I knew her by the sign,
    And fair she was, but far more strange than fair.
        I knew her by the roses in her hair,
        Pierian, and she saluted mine,
Lifting her pale hand in that gesture high
The deathless use to those that cannot die.

        (She bore a purple napkin for her lap;
        Her sandal had a fair-wrought Lydian strap.)

She touched my lyre and listened—while she seemed
    As one dimmed in some doubtful dream redreamed;
Then, ah, the voice she from those lips released,
    All birds and bees and singing in a sigh—
"Once, with a thing like this—" she said, and ceased.

And then,
  That flowery fluting fell again;
"I passed, as some far, careless queen doth pass,
  While, gem by gem, her broken necklace streams:
Perhaps one follows, finding fearful gleams,
  Long after in the pale, pale grass."

  I said, "None with more living lives
  Than those fierce fugitives!"

"But I am dead," she said, "the violet-twined
  Is dead with *that which never man can find.*"

    "Rubies enough," I weeping said,
    "And red to broider all thy bed!"

Then she, with queenhood most ineffable,
  Put by her golden throat's bereaven swell:
"Stand up, O friend," she said, "stand face to face,
  And of they hidden eyes unveil the grace!"

Then with what looks we leaned and gazed long while!
  Drunkard meets wreathèd drunkard with *that smile!*
  And what full-lyred beaker brimmèd up,
  With wet lips meeting on the honied cup!
  And as sweet drunkards, reeling, spill
  The crested waves of cups they fill,
  With lovely laughs, inside the purple vest,
So we with laughter, staggered breast to breast.

I wake, the book drops from my dreaming hand,
  As now thy palm august falls out of mine.
Oh, where is that strong singing! Where the wine!
  Prevailing lip! And leafy brow of thine!

Only the long sea and the Lesbian strand!
  Art thou but sand that blows with trodden sand?
  Where is thy burning hand. . . .

THE SISTER
Kallista

She came to show her beauties dear,
  And brought her kissing eyes.
Her breasts were like two little hills

Where the snow-drift lies.
Her hair went reaching down and down
    With little arms that hugged and slipped,
And it was gold and it was brown.
    Her little feet, they twinkled, tripped,
And sweetly, foolishly, they skipped.
    Her sister kissed her on the eyes
Where hidden angels went and came,
    She drew her hair back from her throat,
And there she did the same.
    She kissed her hair on either side,
She kissed it on the part,
    She kissed her on her wide young breast
Above her golden heart.

(And then she took her by the waist
    And laid her on her bed;
And then she said unto herself,
    "Good God, if *this* were dead!")

Clemence Đane
(Winifred Ashton)
(1888–1965)

Under the name of Clemence Dane, Winifred Ashton, a physically stunning woman who was for a time an actress on the British stage, had a literary career that spanned more than forty years. She wrote novels, magazine articles, and popular plays, including *A Bill of Divorcement*. Drama critics generally agreed that while she was skillful in creating female characters, her male characters were totally unconvincing (compare Willa Cather). She never married and appears to have had several relationships with women.

Her first attempt at fiction has been described by Jeannette Foster in *Sex Variant Women in Literature* as "the first British novel . . . devoted wholly to variance." Foster's pronouncement about *Regiment of Women* (1917) is debatable, depending of course on how one defines "variance," but the novel probably does have the sad distinction of being the first British novel by a woman who understood herself to be "variant" yet adopted into her fiction the nineteenth-century views of lesbians as vampirelike and evil "carnivorous flowers." *Regiment of Women* may be considered evidence of the internalized homophobia that some British homosexuals were suffering by World War I.

Clemence Dane numbered among her "variant" acquaintances Noël Coward (with whom she had a lifelong close friendship), Virginia Woolf, Vita Sackville-West, and Violet Trefusis. In fact, it was to Dane that Vita and Violet went for advice when they were thinking of leaving their heterosexual mates, Harold Nicolson and Denys Trefusis, for each other. According to Victoria Glendinning in her biography *Vita,* Dane "tried to persuade them to give each other up" and return to their men. Dane's "normal" character, Alwynne Durand, in *Regiment of Women* opts for heterosexuality when she finally leaves the manipulative, destructive Clare Hartill (pun intended), fleeing to the "healthy" love of a man.

The title *Regiment of Women* comes from a sixteenth-century essay by John Knox, "First Blast of the Trumpet Against the Monstrous Regiment of Women," a diatribe against the regime of Mary of England and the Queen-Regent of Scotland. The novel's title refers to the rule of women, particularly Clare Hartill, at the girls' boarding school in which the action is set. Alwynne, once "rescued" by a man, becomes aware of what she describes as the stifling, hothouse atmosphere that is created in all-female environments. Reviewers in 1917 observed that the novel's "atmosphere is heady. The reader longs for a man," and that "the story offers an argument for co-education" by showing the dangers of same-sex schools.

Dane herself taught in a girls' boarding school shortly before writing *Regiment of Women*. But the material of the novel also has its root in familiar literary images. Clare's sadism is often a focus of the plot. The narrator says of Clare that "a struggling victim pleased her." She deliberately causes the suicide of a thirteen-year-old girl who is in love with her. Even the age difference between Clare, who is thirty-five (though still wickedly seductive), and Alwynne, who is nineteen, is meant to signal the danger in their relationship: The "old maid" feeds off youth in order to sustain herself. Alwynne's aunt, in a plea to Clare to free the girl, leaves no doubt about the monstrous nature of Clare's needs. "You are doing [Alwynne] a deep injury," she says. "I tell you it's vampirism. And when she is squeezed dry and flung aside, who will your next victim be? One day you'll grow old. What will you do when your glamour's gone? I tell you, Clare Hartill, you'll die of hunger in the end."

FURTHER READING: Clemence Dane, *Regiment of Women* (London: Heinemann, 1917). Jeannette Foster, *Sex Variant Women in Literature* (1956; reprint, Tallahassee, FL: Naiad Press, 1985).

From *Regiment of Women* by Clemence Dane
[Winifred Ashton]

"I had a letter from Louise yesterday," announced Clare.

She was curled up in a saddle-bag before the roaring golden fire, and was busy with paper and pencil. Alwynne, big with her as yet unissued invitation, sat cross-legged on the white bearskin at her feet. The floor was littered with papers and book-catalogues. At Christmas-time Clare ordered books as a housewife orders groceries, and she and Alwynne had spent a luxurious evening over her lists. The vivid flames lit up Clare's thin, lazy length, and turned the hand she held up against their heat into transparent carnelian. Her face was in shadow, but there were dancing specks of light in her sombre eyes that kept time with the leaping blaze. Clare was a sybarite over her fires. She would not endure coal or gas or stove—wood, and wood only, must be used; and she would pay any price for apple-wood, ostensibly for the quality of its flame, secretly for the mere pleasure of burning fuel with so pleasant a name; for she liked beautiful words as a child likes chocolate—a sober, acquisitive liking. She had, too, though she would not own it, a delight in destruction, costly destruction; she enjoyed the sensation of reckless power that it gave her. The trait might be morbid, but there was not a trace of pose in it; she could have enjoyed a Whittington bonfire, without needing a king to gasp applause. Yet she shivered nightly as she undressed in her cold bedroom, rather than commit the extravagance of an extra fire. She never realized the comicality of her contradictoriness, or even its existence in her character, though it qualified every act and impulse of her daily life. Her soul was, indeed, a hybrid, combining the temper of a Calvinist with the tastes of a Renascence bishop.

At the moment she was in gala mood. The autumn term was but four days dead, she had not had time to tire of holidays, though, within a week, she would be bored again, and restless for the heavy work under which she affected to groan. Her chafing mind seldom allowed her indolent body much of the peace it delighted in—was ever the American in lotus-land. It was fidgeted at the moment by Alwynne's absorption in a lavishly illustrated catalogue.

"Did you hear, Alwynne? A letter from Louise."

Alwynne's "Oh?" was absent. It was in the years of the Rackham craze, and she had just discovered a reproduction of the *Midsummer* Helen.

"Any message?" Clare knew how to prod Alwynne.

The girl glanced up amused but a little indignant.

"You've answered it already? Well! And the weeks I've had to wait sometimes."

"This was such a charming letter," said Clare smoothly. "It deserved an answer. She really has the quaintest style. And Alwynne—never a blot or a flourish! It's a pleasure to read."

Alwynne laughed ruefully. She would always squirm good-humouredly under Clare's pin-pricks, with such amusement at her own discomfiture that Clare never knew whether to fling away her needle for good, or, for the mere experiment's sake, to stab hard and savagely. At that stage of their intimacy, Alwynne's guilelessness invariably charmed and disarmed her—she knew that it would take a very crude display of cruelty to make Alwynne believe that she was being hurt intentionally. Clare was amused by the novel pedestal upon which she had been placed; she was accustomed to the panoply of Minerva, or the bow of Dian Huntress, but she had never before been hailed as Bona Dea. It tickled her to be endowed with every domestic virtue, to be loved, as Alwynne loved her, with the secure and fearless affection of a daughter for a newly-discovered and adorable young mother. She appreciated Alwynne's determination of their relationship, her nice sense of the difference in age, her modesty in reserving any claim to an equality in their friendship, her frank and affectionate admiration—yet, while it pleased her, it could pique. Calm comradeship or surrendering adoration she could cope with, but the subtle admixture of such alien states of mind was puzzling. She had acquired a lover with a sense of humour and she felt that she had her hands full. Her imperious will would, in time, she knew, eliminate either the lover or the humour—it annoyed her that she was not as yet quite convinced that it would be the humour. She intended to master Alwynne, but she realized that it would be a question of time, that she would give her more trouble than the children to whom she was accustomed. Alwynne's utter unrealization of the fact that a trial of strength was in progress, was disconcerting: yet Clare, jaded and super-subtle, found her innocence endearing. Without relaxing in her purpose, she yet caught herself wondering if an ally were not better than a slave. But the desire for domination was never entirely shaken off, and Alwynne's free bearing was in itself an ever-present challenge. Clare loved her for it, but her pride was in arms. It was her misfortune not to realize that, for all her Olympian poses, she had come to love Alwynne deeply and enduringly.

Alwynne, meanwhile, laughing and pouting on the hearth, the firelight revealing every change of expression in her piquant face, was declining to be classed with Agatha Middleton; her handwriting might be bad, but it wasn't a beetle-track; anyhow, Queen Elizabeth had a vile fist—Clare admired Queen Elizabeth, didn't she? She had always so much to say to Clare, that if she stopped to bother about handwriting—! Had Clare never got into a row for untidiness in her own young days? Elsbeth had hinted . . . But of course she reserved judgment till she had heard Clare's version! She settled to attention and Clare, inveigled into reminiscences, found herself recounting quaint and forgotten incidents to her own credit and discredit, till, before the evening was over, Alwynne knew almost as much of Clare's schooldays as Clare did herself. She could never resist telling Alwynne stories, Alwynne was always so genuinely breathless with interest.

They returned to Louise at last, and Alwynne read the letter, chuckling over the odd phrases and dainty marginal drawings. She would have dearly liked to see Clare's answer. She was glad, for all her protests, that Clare had been moved to answer; she knew so well the delight it would give Louise. The child would need cheering up. For, quite resignedly and by the way, Louise had mentioned that the Denny family had developed whooping-cough, and emigrated to Torquay, and she, in quarantine, though it was hoped she had escaped infection, was preparing for a solitary Christmas.

Alwynne looked up at Clare with wrinkled brows.

"Poor child! But what can I do? I haven't had whooping-cough, and Elsbeth is always so afraid of infection; or else she could have come to us. I know Elsbeth wouldn't have minded."

"You are going to leave me to myself then? You've quite made up your mind?"

Alwynne's eyes lighted up.

"Oh, Clare, it's all right. You are coming! At least—I mean—Elsbeth sends her kindest regards, and she would be so pleased if you will come to dinner with us on Christmas Day," she finished politely.

Clare laughed.

"It's very kind of your aunt."

"Yes, isn't it?" said Alwynne, with ingenuous enthusiasm.

"I'm afraid I can't come, Alwynne."

Alwynne's face lengthened.

"Oh, Clare! Why ever not?"

Clare hesitated. She had no valid reason, save that she preferred the comfort of her own fireside and that she had intended Alwynne to come to her. Alwynne's regretful refusal when she first mooted the arrangement, she had not considered final, but this invitation upset her plans. Elsbeth's influence was opposing her. She hated opposition. Also she did not care for Elsbeth. It would not be amiss to make Elsbeth (not her dislike of Elsbeth) the reason for her refusal. It would have its effect on Alwynne sooner or later.

She considered Alwynne narrowly, as she answered—

"My dear, I had arranged to be at home, for one thing."

Alwynne looked hurt.

"Of course, if you don't care about it—" she began.

Clare rallied her.

"Be sensible, my child. It is most kind of Miss Loveday; but—wasn't it chiefly your doing, Alwynne? Imagine her dismay if I accepted. A stranger in the gate! On Christmas Day! One must make allowances for little prejudices, you know."

"She'll be awfully disappointed," cried Alwynne, so eager for Clare that she believed it.

"Will she?" Clare laughed pleasantly. "Every one doesn't wear your spectacles. What would she do with me, for a whole day?"

"We shouldn't see her much," began Alwynne. "She spends most of her time in church. I go in the morning—(yes, I'm very good!) but I've drawn the line at turning out after lunch."

"Then why shouldn't you come to me instead? It would be so much better. I shall be all alone, you know." Clare's wistful intonation was not entirely artificial.

Alwynne was distressed.

"Oh, Clare, I'd love to—you know I'd love to—but how could I? Elsbeth would be dreadfully hurt. I couldn't leave her alone on Christmas Day."

"But you can me?"

"Clare, don't put it like that. You know I shall want to be with you all the time. But Elsbeth's like my mother. It would be beastly of me. You must put relations first at Christmas-time, even if they're not first really."

She smiled at Clare, but she felt disloyal as she said it, and hated herself. Yet wasn't it true? Clare came first, though Elsbeth must never guess it. Dear old Elsbeth was pretty dense, thank goodness! Where ignorance is bliss, etcetera! Yet she, Alwynne, felt extraordinarily mean. . . .

Clare watched her jealously. She had set her heart on securing Alwynne for Christmas Day, and had thought, ten minutes since, with a secret, confident smile, that there would not be much difficulty. And here was Alwynne holding out—refusing categorically! It was incredible! Yet she could not be angry: Alwynne so obviously was longing to be with her. . . . Equally obviously prepared to risk her displeasure (a heavy penalty already, Clare guessed, to Alwynne), rather than ignore the older claim. Clare thought that an affection that could be so loyal to a tedious old maid was better worth deflecting than many a more ardent, unscrupulous enthusiasm. Alwynne was showing strength of character.

She persisted nevertheless—

"Well, it's a pity. I must eat my Christmas dinner alone, I suppose."

"Oh, Clare, you might come to us," cried Alwynne. "I can't see why you won't."

Clare shrugged her shoulders.

"If you can't see why, my dear Alwynne, there's no more to be said."

Alwynne most certainly did not see; but Clare's delicately reproachful tone convicted her, and incidentally Elsbeth, of some failure in tact. She supposed she had blundered . . . she often did. . . . But Elsbeth, at least, must be exonerated . . . she did so want Clare to think well of Elsbeth. . . . She perjured herself in hasty propitiation.

"Yes. Yes—I do see. I ought to have known, of course. Elsbeth was quite right. She said you wouldn't, all along."

"Oh?" Clare sat up. "Oh? Your aunt said that, did she?" She spoke with detachment, but inwardly she was alert, on guard. Elsbeth had suddenly become worth attention.

"Oh, yes." Alwynne's voice was rueful. "She was quite sure of it. She said I might ask you, with pleasure, if I didn't believe her—you see, she'd love you to come—but she didn't think you would."

"I wonder," said Clare, laughing naturally, "what made her say that?"

"She said she knew you better than I did," confided Alwynne, with one of her spurts of indignation. "As if—"

"Yes, it's rather unlikely, isn't it?" said Clare, with an intimate smile. "But you're not going?"

"I must. Look at the time! Elsbeth will be having fits!" Alwynne called from the hall where she was hastily slipping on her coat and hat.

Clare stood a moment—thinking.

So the duel had been with Elsbeth! So that negligible and mouse-like woman had been aware—all along . . . had prepared, with a thoroughness worthy of Clare herself, for the inevitable encounter . . . had worsted Clare completely. . . . It was amazing. . . . Clare was compelled to admiration. It was clear to her now that Elsbeth must have distrusted her from the beginning. It had been Elsbeth's doing, not hers, that their intercourse had been so slight. . . . Yet she had never restrained Alwynne; she had risked giving her her head. . . . She was subtle! This affair of the Christmas dinner for instance—Clare appreciated its cleverness. Elsbeth had not wanted her, Clare now saw clearly; had been anxious to avoid the intimacy that such an invitation would imply; equally anxious, surely, that Alwynne should not guess her uneasy jealousy: so she had risked the invitation, counting on her knowledge of Clare's character (Clare stamped with vexation—that the woman should have such a memory!) secure that Clare, unsuspicious of her motives, would, by refusing, do exactly as Elsbeth wished. It had

been the neatest of gossamer traps—and Clare had walked straight into it.
. . . She was furious. If Alwynne, maddeningly unsuspicious Alwynne, had
but enlightened her earlier in the evening! Now she was caught, committed
by her own decision of manner to the course of action she most would
have wished to avoid. . . . She could not change her mind now without
appearing foolishly vacillating. . . . It would not do. . . . She had been
bluffed, successfully, gorgeously bluffed. . . . And Elsbeth was sitting at
home enjoying the situation . . . too sure of herself and Clare even to be
curious as to the outcome of it all. She knew. Clare stamped again. Oh,
but she would pay Elsbeth for this. . . . The *casus belli* was infinitely trivial,
but the campaign should be Homeric. . . . And this preliminary engagement
could not affect the final issues. . . . She always won in the end. . . . But,
after all, Elsbeth could not be blamed, though she must be crushed; Alwynne was worth fighting for! Elsbeth was a fool. . . . If she had treated
Clare decently, Clare might—possibly—have shared Alwynne with her.
. . . She believed she would have had scruples. . . . Now they were dispelled.
. . . Alwynne, by fair means or foul, should be detached . . . should become
Clare's property . . . should be given up to no living woman or man.

She followed Alwynne into the hall and lit the staircase candle. She
would see Alwynne out. She would have liked to keep Alwynne with her
for a month. She was a delightful companion; it was extraordinary how
indispensable she made herself. Clare knew that her flat would strike her
as a dreary place to return to, when she had shut the door on Alwynne.
She would sit and read and feel restless and lonely. Yet she did not allow
herself to feel lonely as a rule; she scouted the weakness. But Alwynne
wound herself about you, thought Clare, and you never knew, till she had
gone, what a difference she made to you.

She wished she could keep Alwynne another couple of hours. . . . But
it was eleven already . . . her hold was not yet strong enough to warrant
innovations to which Elsbeth could object. . . . Her time would come later.
. . . How much later would depend on whether it were affection that
swayed Alwynne, or only a sense of duty. . . . She believed, because she
hoped, that it was duty—a sense of duty was more easily suborned than
an affection. . . . For the present, however, Alwynne must be allowed to
do as she thought right. Clare knew when she was beaten, and, with her
capacity for wry admiration of virtues that she had not the faintest intention of incorporating in her own character, she was able to applaud Alwynne heartily. Yet she did not intend to make victory easy to her.

They went down the flights of stairs silently, side by side. Alwynne
opened the entrance doors and stood a moment, fascinated.

"Look, Clare! What a night!"

The moon was full and flooded earth and sky with bright, cold light. The garden, roadway, roofs, trees and fences glittered like powdered diamonds, white with frost and moonshine. The silence was exquisite.

They stood awhile, enjoying it.

Suddenly Clare shivered. Alwynne became instantly and anxiously practical.

"Clare, what am I thinking of? Go in at once—you'll catch a dreadful cold."

With unusual passivity Clare allowed herself to be hurried in. At the staircase Alwynne said good-bye, handing her her candle, and waiting till she should have passed out of sight. On the fourth step Clare hesitated, and turned—

"Alwynne—come to me for Christmas!"

Alwynne flung out her hands.

"Clare! I mustn't."

"Alwynne—come to me for Christmas?"

"You know I mustn't! You know you'd think me a pig if I did, now wouldn't you?"

"I expect so."

"But I'll come in for a peep at you," cried Alwynne, brightening, "while Elsbeth's at afternoon service. I could do that. And to say Merry Christmas!"

"Come to dinner?"

"I can't."

"Then you needn't come at all." Clare turned away.

Alwynne caught her hand, as it leaned on the balustrade. In the other the candle shook a little.

"Lady Macbeth! Dear Lady Macbeth! Miss Hartill of the Upper Sixth, whom I'm scared to death of, really—you're behaving like a very naughty small child. Now, aren't you? Honestly? Oh, do turn round and crush me with a look for being impudent, and then tell me that I'm only doing what you really approve. I don't want to, Clare, but you know you hate selfishness."

Clare looked down at her.

"All right, Alwynne. You must do as you like."

"Say good-night to me," demanded Alwynne. "Nicely, Clare, very nicely! It's Christmas-time."

Carefully Clare deposited her candlestick on the stair above. Leaning over the banisters, she put her arms round Alwynne and kissed her passionately and repeatedly.

"Good-night, my darling," said Clare.

Then, recoiling, she caught up her candlestick, and without another word or look, hurried up the stairs.

Alwynne walked home on air.

Djuna Barnes
(1892–1982)

Djuna Barnes, one of the leading women modernist writers of the first half of the twentieth century, was a member of Natalie Barney's circle of largely expatriate lesbians in Paris. Barnes's *Ladies Almanack*, a clever and often brilliant comic depiction of the members of that circle, was published in 1928, the same year as *The Well of Loneliness*. It received far less attention than Hall's book, however, partly because it was privately printed and had a small circulation, and partly because it did not conform to any of the more familiar literary approaches to love between women (e.g., romantic friends, men trapped in women's bodies, carnivorous flowers) and thus may have puzzled its readers.

In other works dealing with lesbian themes, Barnes was somewhat more orthodox. She was fascinated by the Decadent nineteenth-century French and English writers, and especially by their depictions of lesbianism. In a 1923 poem, "Six Songs of Khalidine" (dedicated to the woman who was probably her first lesbian lover, Mary Pyne), the beloved's red hair flames and crawls and creeps. Her fallen eyelids are stained with ebony. She and the speaker are in darkness, there is a thread of fear between them, they hear a lost bird cry. The speaker exclaims, "It is not gentleness but mad despair/ That sets us kissing mouths, O Khalidine."

In her lesbian story "A Little Girl Tells a Story to a Lady" (1929), the exotic and erotically charged setting is reminiscent of that in French and English Decadent novels, as well as in those novels in which evil supernatural beings such as vampires figure prominently. For example, "The room was dark except for the moon, and two thin candles. . . . The curtains over the bed were red velvet, very Italian, with gold fringes." Literary critics have observed her "fascination with dissolution and the decadent which closely corresponds to the lure of the perverse." The lesbian in her work is almost invariably a personification of perversity.

As a young woman Barnes was an art student and lived in Greenwich Village. It was probably there that she came out as a lesbian. In 1920 she left for Europe and became involved with the sculptor Thelma Wood, who had also been the lover of Edna St. Vincent Millay for a brief period. Barnes's relationship with Wood, which lasted until 1931, has been described by Barnes's biographers, such as Andrew Field, as "tempestuous." It was one of the models for the Nora-Robin relationship in *Nightwood*. Like Nora, Barnes purchased a lavish flat for herself and Thelma in Paris. Also like Nora, "Frequently Djuna would have to go out in search of her lover, who would be totally drunk and lurching from bar to bar." Barnes began *Nightwood* (whose title incorporates Thelma Wood's name) immediately after the relationship ended.

However, while the novel may have contained many autobiographical elements, its literary influences in Decadent literature are undebatable. Its atmosphere of decay, as one 1937 reviewer observed, "stems from the fin-de-siècle Frenchmen." Nora and Robin in the novel live in a world of despair and destruction. Love between women is described as an "insane passion for unmitigated anguish." Nora says of her love for Robin, "There is something evil in me that loves evil and degradation." The melodrama of mutual destruction that is intrinsic to their relationship echoes Baudelaire as well as later French writers through whose work lesbians pullulate. "In death Robin would belong to her," Nora thinks. "Death went with them, together and alone, and with the torment and catastrophe, thoughts of resurrection, the second duel."

FURTHER READING: Carolyn J. Allen, "Sexual Narrative in the Fiction of Djuna Barnes," in *Sexual Practice, Textual Theory: Lesbian Cultural Criticism*, ed. Susan J. Wolfe and Julia Penelope (Cambridge, MA: Blackwell, 1993). Lynn DeVore, "The Background of *Nightwood*: Robin, Felix and Nora," *Journal of Modern Literature*, 10 (March 1983). Andrew Field, *Djuna: The Formidable Miss Barnes* (Austin: University of Texas Press, 1985). Louis F. Kannenstine, *The Art of Djuna Barnes: Duality and Damnation* (New York: New York University Press, 1977). Susan Lanser, "Speaking in Tongues: *Ladies Almanack* and the Language of Celebration," *Frontiers*, 4: 3 (Fall 1979). Hank O'Neal, *"Life Is Painful, Nasty and Short . . . In My Case It Has Only Been Painful and Nasty": Djuna Barnes, 1978–1981, An Informal Memoir* (New York: Paragon House, 1990).

From *Nightwood* by Djuna Barnes

Clowns in red, white and yellow, with the traditional smears on their faces, were rolling over the sawdust, as if they were in the belly of a great mother where there was yet room to play. A black horse, standing on trembling hind legs that shook in apprehension of the raised front hooves, his beautiful ribboned head pointed down and toward the trainer's whip, pranced slowly, the foreshanks flickering to the whip. Tiny dogs ran about trying to look like horses, then in came the elephants.

A girl sitting beside Nora took out a cigarette and lit it; her hands shook and Nora turned to look at her; she looked at her suddenly because the animals, going around and around the ring, all but climbed over at that point. They did not seem to see the girl, but as their dusty eyes moved past, the orbit of their light seemed to turn on her. At that moment Nora turned.

The great cage for the lions had been set up, and the lions were walking up and out of their small strong boxes into the arena. Ponderous and furred they came, their tails laid down across the floor, dragging and heavy, making the air seem full of withheld strength. Then as one powerful lioness came to the turn of the bars, exactly opposite the girl, she turned her furious great head with its yellow eyes afire and went down, her paws thrust through the bars and, as she regarded the girl, as if a river were falling behind impassable heat, her eyes flowed in tears that never reached the surface. At that the girl rose straight up. Nora took her hand. "Let's get her out of here!" the girl said, and still holding her hand Nora took her out.

In the lobby Nora said, "My name is Nora Flood," and she waited. After a pause the girl said, "I'm Robin Vote." She looked about her distractedly. "I don't want to be here." But it was all she said; she did not explain where she wished to be.

She stayed with Nora until the mid-winter. Two spirits were working in her, love and anonymity. Yet they were so "haunted" of each other that separation was impossible.

Nora closed her house. They travelled from Munich, Vienna and Budapest into Paris. Robin told only a little of her life, but she kept repeating in one way or another her wish for a home, as if she were afraid she would be lost again, as if she were aware, without conscious knowledge, that she belonged to Nora, and that if Nora did not make it permanent by her own strength, she would forget.

Nora bought an apartment in the *rue du Cherche-Midi*. Robin had chosen it. Looking from the long windows one saw a fountain figure, a tall granite woman bending forward with lifted head; one hand was held over the pelvic round as if to warn a child who goes incautiously.

In the passage of their lives together every object in the garden, every item in the house, every word they spoke, attested to their mutual love, the combining of their humours. There were circus chairs, wooden horses bought from a ring of an old merry-go-round, Venetian chandeliers from the Flea Fair, stage-drops from Munich, cherubim from Vienna, ecclesiastical hangings from Rome, a spinet from England, and a miscellaneous collection of music boxes from many countries; such was the museum of their encounter . . .

When the time came that Nora was alone most of the night and part of the day, she suffered from the personality of the house, the punishment of those who collect their lives together. Unconsciously at first, she went about disturbing nothing; then she became aware that her soft and careful movements were the outcome of an unreasoning fear—if she disarranged anything Robin might become confused—might lose the scent of home.

Love becomes the deposit of the heart, analogous in all degrees to the "findings" in a tomb. As in one will be charted the taken place of the body, the raiment, the utensils necessary to its other life, so in the heart of the lover will be traced, as an indelible shadow, that which he loves. In Nora's heart lay the fossil of Robin, intaglio of her identity, and about it for its maintenance ran Nora's blood. Thus the body of Robin could never be unloved, corrupt or put away. Robin was now beyond timely changes, except in the blood that animated her. That she could be spilled of this fixed the walking image of Robin in appalling apprehension on Nora's mind—Robin alone, crossing streets, in danger. Her mind became so trans-fixed that, by the agency of her fear, Robin seemed enormous and polar-ized, all catastrophes ran toward her, the magnetized predicament; and crying out, Nora would wake from sleep, going back through the tide of dreams into which her anxiety had thrown her, taking the body of Robin down with her into it, as the ground things take the corpse, with minute persistence, down into the earth, leaving a pattern of it on the grass, as if they stitched as they descended.

Yes now, when they were alone and happy, apart from the world in their appreciation of the world, there entered with Robin a company un-aware. Sometimes it rang clear in the songs she sang, sometimes Italian, sometimes French or German, songs of the people, debased and haunting, songs that Nora had never heard before, or that she had never heard in company with Robin. When the cadence changed, when it was repeated on a lower key, she knew that Robin was singing of a life that she herself had no part in; snatches of harmony as tell-tale as the possessions of a traveller from a foreign land! songs like a practised whore who turns away from no one but the one who loves her. Sometimes Nora would sing them after Robin, with the trepidation of a foreigner repeating words in an un-known tongue, uncertain of what they may mean. Sometimes unable to endure the melody that told so much and so little, she would interrupt Robin with a question. Yet more distressing would be the moment when, after a pause, the song would be taken up again from an inner room where Robin, unseen, gave back an echo of her unknown life more nearly tuned to its origin. Often the song would stop altogether, until unthinking, just as she was leaving the house, Robin would break out again in anticipation, changing the sound from a reminiscence to an expectation.

Yet sometimes, going about the house, in passing each other, they would fall into an agonized embrace, looking into each other's face, their two heads in their four hands, so strained together that the space that divided them seemed to be thrusting them apart. Sometimes in these moments of insurmountable grief Robin would make some movement, use a peculiar turn of phrase not habitual to her, innocent of the betrayal, by which Nora was informed that Robin had come from a world to which she would return. To keep her (in Robin there was this tragic longing to be kept, knowing herself astray) Nora knew now that there was no way but death. In death Robin would belong to her. Death went with them, together and alone; and with the torment and catastrophe, thoughts of resurrection, the second duel.

Looking out into the fading sun of the winter sky, against which a little tower rose just outside the bedroom window, Nora would tabulate by the sounds of Robin dressing the exact progress of her toilet; chimes of cosmetic bottles and cream jars; the faint perfume of hair heated under the electric curlers; seeing in her mind the changing direction taken by the curls that hung on Robin's forehead, turning back from the low crown to fall in upward curves to the nape of the neck, the flat uncurved back head that spoke of some awful silence. Half narcoticized by the sounds and the knowledge that this was in preparation for departure, Nora spoke to herself: "In the resurrection, when we come up looking backward at each other, I shall know you only of all that company. My ear shall turn in the socket of my head; my eyeballs loosened where I am the whirlwind about that cashed expense, my foot stubborn on the cast of your grave." In the doorway Robin stood. "Don't wait for me," she said.

In the years that they lived together, the departures of Robin became a slowly increasing rhythm. At first Nora went with Robin; but as time passed, realizing that a growing tension was in Robin, unable to endure the knowledge that she was in the way or forgotten, seeing Robin go from table to table, from drink to drink, from person to person, realizing that if she herself were not there Robin might return to her as the one who, out of all the turbulent night, had not been lived through, Nora stayed at home, lying awake or sleeping. Robin's absence, as the night drew on, became a physical removal, insupportable and irreparable. As an amputated hand cannot be disowned because it is experiencing a futurity, of which the victim is its forebear, so Robin was an amputation that Nora could not renounce. As the wrist longs, so her heart longed, and dressing she would go out into the night that she might be "beside herself," skirting the café in which she could catch a glimpse of Robin.

Once out in the open Robin walked in a formless meditation, her hands thrust into the sleeves of her coat, directing her steps toward that night life that was a known measure between Nora and the cafés. Her meditations, during this walk, were a part of the pleasure she expected to find when the walk came to an end. It was this exact distance that kept the two ends of her life—Nora and the cafés—from forming a monster with two heads.

Her thoughts were in themselves a form of locomotion. She walked with raised head, seeming to look at every passer-by, yet her gaze was anchored in anticipation and regret. A look of anger, intense and hurried, shadowed her face and drew her mouth down as she neared her company; yet as her eyes moved over the façades of the buildings, searching for the sculptured head that both she and Nora loved (a Greek head with shocked protruding eyeballs, for which the tragic mouth seemed to pour forth tears), a quiet joy radiated from her own eyes; for this head was a remembrance of Nora and her love, making the anticipation of the people she was to meet set and melancholy. So, without knowing she would do so, she took the turn that brought her into this particular street. If she was diverted, as was sometimes the case, by the interposition of a company of soldiers, a wedding or a funeral, then by her agitation she seemed a part of the function to the persons she stumbled against, as a moth by his very entanglement with the heat that shall be his extinction, is associated with flame as a component part of its activity. It was this characteristic that saved her from being asked too sharply "where" she was going; pedestrians who had it on the point of their tongues, seeing her rapt and confused, turned instead to look at each other.

The doctor, seeing Nora out walking alone, said to himself, as the tall black-caped figure passed ahead of him under the lamps, "There goes the dismantled—Love has fallen off her wall. A religious woman," he thought to himself, "without the joy and safety of the Catholic faith, which at a pinch covers up the spots on the wall when the family portraits take a slide; take that safety from a woman," he said to himself, quickening his step to follow her, "and love gets loose and into the rafters. She sees her everywhere," he added, glancing at Nora as she passed into the dark. "Out looking for what she's afraid to find—Robin. There goes mother of mischief, running about, trying to get the world home."

Looking at every couple as they passed, into every carriage and car, up to the lighted windows of the houses, trying to discover not Robin any longer, but traces of Robin, influences in her life (and those which were yet to be betrayed), Nora watched every moving figure for some gesture that might turn up in the movements made by Robin; avoiding the quarter where she knew her to be, where by her own movements the waiters, the people on the terraces, might know that she had a part in Robin's life.

Returning home, the interminable night would begin. Listening to the faint sounds from the street, every murmur from the garden, an unevolved and tiny hum that spoke of the progressive growth of noise that would be Robin coming home, Nora lay and beat her pillow without force, unable to cry, her legs drawn up. At times she would get up and walk, to make something in her life outside more quickly over, to bring Robin back by the very velocity of the beating of her heart. And walking in vain, suddenly she would sit down on one of the circus chairs that stood by the long window overlooking the garden, bend forward, putting her hands between her legs, and begin to cry, "Oh, God! Oh, God! Oh, God!" repeated so often that it had the effect of all words spoken in vain. She nodded and awoke again and began to cry before she opened her eyes, and went back to the bed and fell into a dream which she recognized; though in the finality of this version she knew that the dream had not been "well dreamt" before. Where the dream had been incalculable, it was now completed with the entry of Robin.

Nora dreamed that she was standing at the top of a house, that is, the last floor but one—this was her grandmother's room—an expansive, decaying splendour; yet somehow, though set with all the belongings of her grandmother, was as bereft as the nest of a bird which will not return. Portraits of the great-uncle, Llewellyn, who died in the Civil War, faded pale carpets, curtains that resembled columns from their time in stillness— a plume and an ink well—the ink faded into the quill; standing, Nora looked down into the body of the house, as if from a scaffold, where now Robin had entered the dream, lying among a company below. Nora said to herself, "The dream will not be dreamed again." A disc of light, which seemed to come from someone or thing standing behind her and which was yet a shadow, shed a faintly luminous glow upon the upturned still face of Robin, who had the smile of an "only survivor," a smile which fear had married to the bone.

From round about her in anguish Nora heard her own voice saying, "Come up, this is Grandmother's room," yet knowing it was impossible because the room was taboo. The louder she cried out the farther away went the floor below, as if Robin and she, in their extremity, were a pair of opera glasses turned to the wrong end, diminishing in their painful love; a speed that ran away with the two ends of the building, stretching her apart.

This dream that now had all its parts had still the former quality of never really having been her grandmother's room. She herself did not seem to be there in person, nor able to give an invitation. She had wanted to put her hands on something in this room to prove it; the dream had never permitted her to do so. This chamber that had never been her grandmother's, which was, on the contrary, the absolute opposite of any known room her grandmother had ever moved or lived in, was nevertheless saturated with the lost presence of her grandmother, who seemed in the continual process of leaving it. The architecture of dream had rebuilt her everlasting and continuous, flowing away in a long gown of soft folds and chin laces, the pinched gatherings that composed the train taking an upward line over the back and hips in a curve that not only bent age but fear of bent age demands.

With this figure of her grandmother who was not entirely her recalled grandmother went one of her childhood, when she had run into her at the corner of the house—the grandmother who, for some unknown reason, was dressed as a man, wearing a billy-cock and a corked moustache, ridiculous and plump in tight trousers and a red waistcoat, her arms spread saying with a leer of love, "My little sweetheart!"—her grandmother "drawn upon" as a prehistoric ruin is drawn upon, symbolizing her life out of her life, and which now appeared to Nora as something being done to Robin, Robin disfigured and eternalized by the hieroglyphics of sleep and pain.

Waking, she began to walk again, and looking out into the garden in the faint light of dawn, she saw a double shadow falling from the statue, as if it were multiplying, and thinking perhaps this was Robin, she called and was not answered. Standing motionless, straining her eyes, she saw emerge from the darkness the light of Robin's eyes, the fear in them developing their luminosity until, by the intensity of their double regard, Robin's eyes and hers met. So they gazed at each other. As if that light had power to bring what was dreaded into the zone of their catastrophe, Nora saw the body of another woman swim up into the statue's obscurity, with head hung down, that the added eyes might not augment the illumination; her arms about Robin's neck, her body pressed to Robin's, her legs slackened in the hang of the embrace.

Unable to turn her eyes away, incapable of speech, experiencing a sensation of evil, complete and dismembering, Nora fell to her knees, so that her eyes were not withdrawn by her volition, but dropped from their orbit by the falling of her body. Her chin on the sill, she knelt, thinking, "Now they will not hold together," feeling that if she turned away from what Robin was doing, the design would break and melt back into Robin alone. She closed her eyes, and at that moment she knew an awful happiness. Robin, like something dormant, was protected, moved out of death's way by the successive arms of women; but as she closed her eyes, Nora said "Ah!" with the intolerable automatism of the last "Ah!" in a body struck at the moment of its final breath.

Anaïs Nin
(1903–1977)

Anaïs Nin, who was born in Paris, traveled throughout Europe as a young child with her father, a Spanish pianist and painter. At the age of eleven she went to live in New York with her two brothers and her mother, who was by then separated from her father. It was at this time, in a fantasy attempt to communicate with her father, that Nin began the first of her voluminous diaries, which traced her life in great detail for sixty years, until 1974.

At the age of twenty Nin married a banker, Hugh Guiler, who remains a shadowy figure in her biography. In the 1930s Nin returned to France, where she met Henry Miller, who was at work on his first erotic autobiographical novel, *Tropic of Cancer*. Miller and his wife, June, both became her lovers. While the relationships with both the Millers were conflictual they were also important grist for her writer's mill. Henry Miller's work served as a model for her own explorations of the graphically erotic in her writing, and June Miller served as her muse in her literary treatment of lesbian subject matter. The first of the diaries (1931–34), published 1966, delineates the lesbian relationship between them in some detail. Nin's sexual life with both the Millers also became the subject of the film *Henry and June* (1990), which was based on the 1931–34 diary.

June Miller is the model for Sabina in the following excerpt from Nin's novel *House of Incest* (1936). The "house" of the title affirms the narcissist view of lesbianism: It is "where we only love ourselves in each other." Lesbian narcissism is a prevalent image in other writing by Nin also. In *Ladders to Fire* (1946), for example, Nin presents two women making love in autoerotic imagery: "Their bodies touched and then fell away, as if both of them had touched a mirror, their own image upon the mirror." In *House of Incest* June-Sabina is also depicted as a mirror image, the darker side of Nin, which she keeps hidden.

But June-Sabina is primarily the fatal woman, associated with death. "I will let you carry me into the fecundity of destruction," Nin says of her. Nin uses the language of lesbian vampire fiction to describe her, from her "ancient stare" to her "waxy, immobile face" to her "black cape" that hangs "half-floating around her body." Sabina draws blood from the speaker not through her bite but "with each lie." The speaker hears the "inhuman rhythm of her march."

It is not surprising to discover that Nin greatly admired the writing of Djuna Barnes and tried, unsuccessfully, to make contact with her (the admiration was not mutual). In *Ladders to Fire* Nin compartmentalized herself into three characters, naming one of them Djuna after her idol. In *Collages* (1964) she presents an autobiographical figure who says to another character that is modeled on Barnes: "I feel that, in a sense, you gave birth to me. . . . When you deny me your presence you commit spiritual murder." Regardless of Barnes's lack of interest in the fact, there was indeed a direct line of influence that can be traced from Nin back to Barnes and then further back to the nineteenth-century male writers, such as Baudelaire, who created the literary image of lesbianism as, to use Nin's language in *Ladders to Fire*, "the negative pole, the pole of confused and twisted nature."

FURTHER READING: Anaïs Nin, *House of Incest* (Paris: Siana Editions, 1936); *Ladders to Fire* (New York: E. P. Dutton, 1946). *The Diaries of Anaïs Nin: 1931–1934* (New York: Harcourt, Brace and World, 1966). Richard Centing, ed. *Under the Sign of Pisces: Anaïs Nin and Her Circle*, vols. 1–12 (1970–1981) (quarterly journal). Nancy Scholar, *Anaïs Nin* (Boston: Twayne Publishers, 1984).

From *House of Incest*

The night surrounded me, a photograph unglued from its frame. The lining of a coat ripped open like the two shells of an oyster. The day and night unglued, and I falling in between not knowing on which layer I was resting, whether it was the cold grey upper leaf of dawn, or the dark layer of night.

Sabina's face was suspended in the darkness of the garden. From the eyes a simoun wind shrivelled the leaves and turned the earth over; all things which had run a vertical course now turned in circles, round the face, around HER face. She stared with such an ancient stare, heavy luxuriant centuries flickering in deep processions. From her nacreous skin perfumes spiralled like incense. Every gesture she made quickened the rhythm of the blood and aroused a beat chant like the beat of the heart of the desert, a chant which was the sound of her feet treading down into the blood the imprint of her face.

A voice that had traversed the centuries, so heavy it broke what it touched, so heavy I feared it would ring in me with eternal resonance; a voice rusty with the sound of curses and the hoarse cries that issue from the delta in the last paroxysm of orgasm.

Her black cape hung like black hair from her shoulders, half-draped, half-floating around her body. The web of her dress moving always a moment before she moved, as if aware of her impulses, and stirring long after she was still, like waves ebbing back to the sea. Her sleeves dropped like a sigh and the hem of her dress danced round her feet.

The steel necklace on her throat flashed like summer lightning and the sound of the steel was like the clashing of swords. . . . Le pas d'acier . . . The steel of New York's skeleton buried in granite, buried standing up. Le pas d'acier . . . notes hammered on the steel-stringed guitars of the gypsies, on the steel arms of chairs dulled with her breath; steel mail curtains falling like the flail of hail, steel bars and steel barrage cracking. Her necklace thrown around the world's neck, unmeltable. She carried it like a trophy wrung of groaning machinery, to match the inhuman rhythm of her march.

The leaf fall of her words, the stained-glass hues of her moods, the rust in her voice, the smoke in her mouth, her breath on my vision like human breath blinding a mirror.

Talk—half-talk, phrases that had no need to be finished, abstractions, Chinese bells played on with cotton-tipped sticks, mock orange blossoms painted on porcelain. The muffled, close, half-talk of soft-fleshed women. The men she had embraced, and the women, all washing against the resonance of my memory. Sound within sound, scene within scene, woman within woman—like acid revealing an invisible script. One woman within another eternally, in a far-reaching procession, shattering my mind into fragments, into quarter tones which no orchestral baton can ever make whole again.

The luminous mask of her face, waxy, immobile, with eyes like sentinels. Watching my sybaritic walk, and I the sibilance of her tongue. Deep into each other we turned our harlot eyes. She was an idol in Byzance, an idol dancing with legs parted; and I wrote with pollen and honey. The soft secret yielding of woman I carved into men's brains with copper words; her image I tattooed in their eyes. They were consumed by the fever of their entrails, the indissoluble poison of legends. If the torrent failed to engulf them, or did they extricate themselves, I haunted their memory with the tale they wished to forget. All that was swift and malevolent in woman might be ruthlessly destroyed, but who would destroy the illusion on which I laid her to sleep each night? We lived in Byzance, Sabina and I, until our hearts bled from the precious stones on our foreheads, our bodies tired of the weight of brocades, our nostrils burned with the smoke of perfumes; and when we had passed into other centuries they enclosed us in copper frames. Men recognized her always: the same effulgent face, the same rust voice. And she and I, we recognized each other; I her face and she my legend.

Around my pulse she put a flat steel bracelet and my pulse beat as she willed, losing its human cadence, thumping, like a savage in orgiastic frenzy. The lamentations of flutes, the double chant of wind through our slender bones, the cracking of our bones distantly remembered when on beds of down the worship we inspired turned to lust.

As we walked along, rockets burst from the street lamps; we swallowed the asphalt road with a jungle roar and the houses with their closed eyes and geranium eyelashes; swallowed the telegraph poles trembling with messages; swallowed stray cats, trees, hills, hedges, Sabina's labyrinthian smile on the keyhole. The door moaning, opening. Her smile closed. A nightingale disleafing melliferous honeysuckle. Honey-suckled. Fluted fingers. The house opened its green gate mouth and swallowed us. The bed was floating.

The record was scratched, the crooning broken. The pieces cut our feet. It was dawn and she was lost. I put back the houses on the road, aligned the telegraph poles along the river and the stray cats jumping across the road. I put back the hills. The road came out of my mouth like a velvet ribbon—it lay there serpentine. The houses opened their eyes. The keyhole had an ironic curve, like a question mark. The woman's mouth.

I was carrying her fetiches, her marionettes, her fortune teller's cards worn at the corners like the edge of a wave. The windows of the city were stained and splintered with rainlight and the blood she drew from me with each lie, each deception. Beneath the skin of her cheeks I saw ashes: would she die before we had joined in perfidious union? The eyes, the hands, the senses that only women have.

There is no mockery between women. One lies down at peace as on one's own breast.

Sabina was no longer embracing men and women. Within the fever of her restlessness the world was losing its human shape. She was losing the human power to fit body to body in human completeness. She was delimiting the horizons, sinking into planets without axis, losing her polarity and the divine knowledge of integration, of fusion. She was spreading herself like the night over the universe and found no god to lie with. The other half belonged to the sun, and she was at war with the sun and light. She would tolerate no bars of light on open books, no orchestration of ideas knitted by a single theme; she would not be covered by the sun, and half the universe belonged to him; she was turning her serpent back to that alone which might overshadow her own stature giving her the joy of fecundation.

Come away with me, Sabina, come to my island. Come to my island of red peppers sizzling over slow braseros, Moorish earthen jars catching the gold water, palm trees, wild cats fighting, at dawn a donkey sobbing, feet on coral reefs and sea-anemones, the body covered with long seaweeds, Melisande's hair hanging over the balcony at the Opéra Comique, inexorable diamond sunlight, heavy nerveless hours in the violaceous shadows, ash-colored rocks and olive trees, lemon trees with lemons hung like lanterns at a garden party, bamboo shoots forever trembling, soft-sounding espadrilles, pomegranate spurting blood, a flute-like Moorish chant, long and insistent, of the ploughmen, trilling, swearing, trilling and cursing, dropping perspiration on the earth with the seeds.

Your beauty drowns me, drowns the core of me. When your beauty burns me I dissolve as I never dissolved before man. From all men I was different, and myself, but I see in you that part of me which is you. I feel you in me; I feel my own voice becoming heavier, as if I were drinking you in, every delicate thread of resemblance being soldered by fire and one no longer detects the fissure.

Your lies are not lies, Sabina. They are arrows flung out of your orbit by the strength of your fantasy. To nourish illusion. To destroy reality I will help you: it is I who will invent lies for you and with them we will traverse the world. But behind our lies I am dropping Ariadne's golden thread—for the greatest of all joys is to be able to retrace one's lies, to return to the source and sleep one night a year washed of all superstructures.

Sabina, you made your impression upon the world. I passed through it like a ghost. Does anyone notice the owl in the tree at night, the bat which strikes the window pane while others are talking, the eyes which reflect like water and drink like blotting paper, the pity which flickers quietly like candlelight, the understanding on which people lay themselves to sleep?

DOES ANYONE KNOW WHO I AM?

Even my voice came from other worlds. I was embalmed in my own secret vertigoes. I was suspended over the world, seeing what road I could tread without treading down even clay or grass. My step was a sentient step; the mere crepitation of gravel could arrest my walk.

When I saw you, Sabina, I chose my body.

I will let you carry me into the fecundity of destruction. I choose a body then, a face, a voice. I become you. And you become me. Silence the sensational course of your body and you will see in me, intact, your own fears, your own pities. You will see love which was excluded from the passions given you, and I will see the passions excluded from love. Step out of your role and rest yourself on the core of your true desires. Cease for a moment your violent deviations. Relinquish the furious indomitable strain.

I will take them up.

Cease trembling and shaking and gasping and cursing and find again your core which I am. Rest from twistedness, distortion, deformations. For an hour you will be me; that is, the other half of yourself. The half you lost. What you burnt, broke, and tore is still in my hands: I am the keeper of fragile things and I have kept of you what is indissoluble.

Even the world and the sun cannot show their two faces at once.

So now we are inextricably woven. I have gathered together all the fragments. I return them to you. You have run with the wind, scattering and dissolving. I have run behind you, like your own shadow, gathering what you have sown in deep coffers.

I AM THE OTHER FACE OF YOU

Our faces are soldered together by soft hair, soldered together, showing two profiles of the same soul. Even when I passed through a room like a breath, I made others uneasy and they knew I had passed.

I was the white flame of your breath, your simoun breath shrivelling the world. I borrowed your visibility and it was through you I made my imprint on the world. I praised my own flame in you.

THIS IS THE BOOK YOU WROTE

AND YOU ARE THE WOMAN

I AM

Only our faces must shine twofold—like day and night—always separated by space and the evolutions of time.

The smoke sent my head to the ceiling: there it hung, looking down upon frog eyes, straw hair, mouth of soiled leather, mirrors of bald heads, furred monkey hands with ham colored palms. The music whipped the past out of its tomb and mummies flagellated my memory.

If Sabina were now a memory; if I should sit here and she should never come again! If I only imagined her one night because the drug made fine incisions and arranged the layers of my body on Persian silk hammocks, tipped with cotton each fine nerve and sent the radium arrows of fantasy through the flesh . . .

I am freezing and my head falls down through a thin film of smoke. I am searching for Sabina again with deep anguish through the faceless crowd.

Jewelle Gomez
(b. 1948)

Jewelle Gomez, an African American lesbian writer, is the author of two poetry collections, *The Lipstick Papers* and *Flamingoes and Bears*, as well as numerous essays and *The Gilda Stories*, from which the following excerpt was taken. *The Gilda Stories*, a novel about an African American lesbian vampire, transforms the horrific nineteenth-century vampire image to be consonant with the positive values of late-twentieth-century lesbian-feminism.

Gomez manages this transformation by first defusing the terror connected with the supernatural. Gomez's lesbian who becomes Gilda is of African heritage. She is unlike individuals whose sensibility is western: She has no desperate need to cling to the rational nor to panic in the face of whatever has no explanation in the western system of logic. She is not terrified by "vodun" or the mysteries of the supernatural, and therefore she "normalizes" those mysteries for the reader.

The lesbian vampire image is further transformed by the "womanist" values Gomez attributes to her vampire characters. They "pursue only life, never bitterness or cruelty." Though they live by sharing the lifeblood of others, they have no need to kill and there is even "a joy to the exchange" they make. They give energy, dreams, and ideas to those from whom they get renewed vitality. The embrace of the vampire as Gomez depicts it is as safe and warm as the embrace of the eternal mother. Gomez's contemporary "co-option" and transformation of the frightening images of the lesbian vampire that moved through literature of the nineteenth century and the first half of the twentieth century is a realization of Bertha Harris's call in her seminal essay, "What We Mean to Say: Notes Toward Defining the Nature of Lesbian Literature," for a lesbian "monster" whose passion and purpose serve her own ends rather than those of patriarchal nightmares.

FURTHER READING: Jewelle Gomez, "Re-Casting the Mythology: Writing Vampire Fiction," *Hot Wire*, 4: 1 (November 1987), 42–43+. Jewelle Gomez, "Imagine a Lesbian—A Black Lesbian," *Trivia*, 12 (1988), 45–60. Jewelle Gomez, *The Gilda Stories* (Ithaca, NY: Firebrand Books, 1991). Sue-Ellen Case, "Tracking the Vampire," *Differences: A Journal of Feminist Cultural Studies*, 3 (Summer 1991), 1–20. Bonnie Zimmerman, " 'Daughters of Darkness': Lesbian Vampires," *Jump Cut*, 24/25 (March 1981), 23–24.

From *The Gilda Stories:* "Louisiana: 1850"

The fields to the north and west of the farmhouse lay fallow, trimmed but unworked. It was land much like the rest in the Delta sphere, warm and moist, almost blue in its richness—blood soil, some said. The not-tall house over the shallow root cellar seemed odd with its distinct aura of life set in the emptiness of the field. Gilda stood at the window looking out to the evening dark as Bird moved around her placing clothes in chests. Gilda tried to pull the strands together, to make a pattern of her life that was recognizable, therefore reinforceable. The farmhouse offered her peace but no answers. It was simply privacy away from the dissembling of the city and relief from the tides, which each noon and night pulled her energy, sucking her breath and leaving her lighter than air. The quietness of the house and its eagerness to hold her safe were like a firm hand on her shoulder. Here Gilda could relax enough to think. She had hardly come through the door before she let go of the world of Woodard's. Still her thoughts always turned back toward the open sea and the burning sun.

The final tie was Bird. Bird, the gentle, stern one who rarely flinched yet held on to her as if she were drowning in life. Too few of their own kind had passed through Woodard's, and none had stayed very long. On their one trip west to visit Sorel, neither could tolerate the dust and noise of his town for more than several weeks. And until the Girl's arrival, Gilda had met no one she sensed was the right one. To leave Bird alone in this world without others like herself would be more cruel than Gilda could ever be. The Girl must stay. She pushed back all doubts: Was the Girl too young? Would she grow to hate the life she'd be given? Would she abandon Bird? The answer was there in the child's eyes. The decision loosened the tight muscles of Gilda's back as if the deed were already done.

The Girl did not know why they had included her in the trip to the farmhouse this time. They rarely brought her along at midseason. The thought that they might want her to leave them made her more anxious than Minta's soft voice. Yet each day Bird and she sat down for their lessons, and in the evening, when Gilda and Bird talked quietly together, they sought her out to join them. She would curl up in the corner, not speaking, only listening to the words that poured from them as they talked of the women back at the house, the politics in town, the war, and told adventurous stories. The Girl thought, at first, that they were made up, but she soon heard in the passion of their voices the truth of the stories Gilda and Bird had lived.

Sometimes one of them would say, "Listen here, this is something you should know." But there was no need for that. The Girl, now tall and lean with adulthood, clung to their words. She enjoyed the contrasting rhythms of their voices and the worlds of mystery they revealed.

She sensed an urgency in Gilda—the stories had to be told, let free from her. And Bird, who also felt the urgency, did not become preoccupied with it but was happy that she and Gilda were spending time together again as it had been before. She unfolded her own history like soft deerskin. Bird gazed at the Girl, wrapped in a cotton shirt, her legs tucked under her on the floor, and felt that her presence gave them an unspoken completeness.

She spoke before she thought. "This is like many times before the fire in my village."

"Ah, and who's to play the part of your toothless elders, me or the Girl?" Gilda asked, smiling widely.

The Girl laughed softly as Bird replied, "Both."

Gilda rose from the dark velvet couch. Her face disappeared out of the low lamplight into the shadow. She stooped, lifted the Girl in her arms, and lay her on the couch. She sat down again and rested the Girl's head in her lap. She stroked the Girl's thick braids as Bird and she continued talking.

In the next silence she asked the Girl, "What do you remember of your mother and sisters?" The Girl did not think of them except at night, just before sleeping, their memory her nightly prayers. She'd never spoken of them to Gilda, only to Bird when they exchanged stories during their reading lessons. Now the litany of names served as memory: Minerva, small, full of energy and questions; Florine, two years older than the Girl, unable to ever meet anyone's eyes; and Martha, the oldest, broad-shouldered like their mother but more solemn. She described the feel of the pallet where she slept with her mother, rising early for breakfast duties—stirring porridge and setting out the rolls. She described the smell of bread, shiny with butter, and the snow-white raw cotton tinged with blood from her fingers.

Of the home their mother spoke about, the Girl was less certain. It was always a dream place—distant, unreal. Except the talk of dancing. The Girl could close her eyes and almost hear the rhythmic shuffling of feet, the bells and gourds. All kept beat inside her body, and the feel of heat from an open fire made the dream place real. Talking of it now, her body rocked slightly as if she had been rewoven into that old circle of dancers. She poured out the images and names, proud of her own ability to weave a story. Bird smiled at her pupil who claimed her past, reassuring her silently.

Each of the days at the farmhouse was much like the others. The Girl rose a bit later than when they were in the city, for there was little work to be done here. She dusted or read, walked in the field watching birds and rabbits. In the late afternoon she would hear Bird and Gilda stirring. They came out to speak to her from the shadows of the porch, but then they returned to their room, where the Girl heard the steady sound of their voices or the quiet scratching of pen on paper.

The special quality of their life did not escape the Girl; it seemed more pronounced at the farmhouse, away from the activity of Woodard's. She had found the large feed bags filled with dirt in the root cellar where she hid so long ago. She had felt the thin depth of soil beneath the carpets and weighted in their cloaks. Although they kept the dinner hour as a gathering time, they had never eaten in front of her. The Girl cooked her own meals, often eating alone, except when Bird prepared a corn pudding or a rabbit she had killed. Then they sat together as the Girl ate and Bird sipped tea. She had seen Gilda and Bird go out late in the night, both wearing breeches and woolen shirts. Sometimes they went together, other times separately. And both spoke to her without voices.

The warning from Minta and the whispers of the secret religion, vodun, still did not frighten her. She had known deep fear and knew she could protect herself when she must. But there was no cause for fear of these two who slept so soundly in each other's arms and treated her with such tenderness.

On the afternoon of the eighth day at the farmhouse the Girl returned from a walk through the fields to get a drink of water from the back pump. She was surprised to hear, through the kitchen window, Gilda's voice drawn tight in argument with Bird. There was silence from the rest of the room, then a burst of laughter from Gilda.

"Do you see that we're fighting only because we love each other? I insist we stop right this minute. I won't have it on such a glorious evening."

The Girl could hear her moving around the small wooden table, pulling back a chair. Gilda did not sit in the chair, instead lowering herself onto Bird's lap. Bird's expression of surprise turned into a laugh, but the tension beneath it was not totally dispelled.

"I'm sick of this talk. You go on about this leaving as if there is somewhere in the world you could go without me."

Her next words were cut short by Gilda's hand on her mouth. And then Gilda's soft, thin lips pressed her back in the chair.

"Please, my love, let's go to our room so I can feel the weight of your body on mine. Let's compare the tones of our skin as we did when we were young."

Bird laughed just as she was expected to do. The little joking references to time and age were their private game. Even knowing there was more to the kisses and games right now, she longed to feel Gilda's skin pressed tightly to her own. She stood up, still clasping Gilda to her breasts, and walked up the stairs with her as if she were a child.

The Girl remained on the porch looking out into the field as the sun dropped quickly behind the trees. She loved the sound of Gilda and Bird laughing, but it seemed they did so only when they thought no others were listening. When it was fully dark she went into the kitchen to make supper for herself. She put on the kettle for tea, certain that Bird and Gilda would want some when they came down. She rooted through the clay jars until she had pulled together a collection of sweet-smelling herbs she thought worthy. She was eager to hear their laughter again.

That evening Bird took the buggy out and called to the Girl to help load the laundry bags inside. The Girl was silent as she lifted the bags up to the buckboard platform to Bird, who kept glancing up at the windows.

"Tell Minta I said hello." The Girl spoke tentatively when the quiet seemed too large. "Tell her not to leave without me." She figured that was a good enough joke since Minta had been deviling everybody with her dreamtalk of going west.

Bird stood straight, dropping the final bundle on the floor of the buckboard, and looked down at the Girl. "What does that mean?"

"I'm teasin'. She keep talkin' about movin' out there with Rachel like I goin' with her."

Bird turned silent, sat, and grasped the reins of the restless horse. The Girl felt more compelled to fill the air. "I'm not goin'."

"You could, you might want to. Eventually you'll want to start your own life, your own family somewhere." Bird's voice was even, but the Girl recognized a false quiet in it from the times she had heard her arguing with Gilda or talking to drunken clients.

"Any family startin' to do will be done right here." The Girl felt safe having finally said what she wanted out loud. She looked up at Bird's face shyly and was pleased to see the flash of Bird's teeth sparking her grin.

Bird climbed up to the seat and spoke casually, the voice of the woman who always kept the house. "I'll stay in town tonight and return tomorrow evening for tea. If there is any danger, you have only to call out to me."

Bird drew the horse out onto the road, leaving the Girl on the porch wondering what danger there might be. Her warning not to have concern was more frightening to her than Minta's cautionary words.

Upstairs, Gilda was silent in her room. She did not join the Girl after Bird was gone but came down later in the evening. She moved about the parlor, making a circle before resting on the arm of the sofa across from the Girl who sat in Bird's favored chair. The Girl's dark face was smooth, her brow wide and square under the braided rows that drew her thick, springy hair to the nape of her neck. Gilda wore pants and a shirt cinched tightly at her waist by soft leather studded with small white beads. She spoke to the Girl in silence. *Do you know how many years I have lived?*

"Many more years than anyone."

Gilda rose and stood over the Girl. "I have Bird's love and yours, I think?" The end of the sentence curled upward in a question.

The Girl had not thought of love until the word was spoken. Yes, she loved them both. The remembered face of her mother was all she had loved until now. Tears slipped down her cheeks. Gilda's sadness washed over her, and she felt the loss of her mother, new and cutting.

"We can talk when I return." Gilda closed the door and was lost in the darkness.

The Girl walked through the house looking at their belongings as if it were the first time she had seen them—their dresses folded smoothly and the delicate linens, the chest that held small tailored breeches and flannel shirts that smelled of earth and lavender water.

She touched the leather spines of the books which she longed to read; some were in languages she did not recognize. Sitting on the edge of the bed that Gilda and Bird shared, she looked patiently at each item in the room, inhaling their scent. The brushes, combs, and jars sat neatly aligned on the dressing table. The coverlet, rugs, and draperies felt thick, luxurious, yet the room was plain. Without Gilda and Bird in the house the rooms seemed incomplete. The Girl walked slowly through each one as if it were new to her, crossing back and forth, searching for something to soothe the unease that crept up into her. Everything appeared just as it had during all the days she had been with Gilda and Bird, except that she felt someone had gone before her as she did now, examining objects, replacing them, pulling out memories, laying them aside.

When the house became cold, the Girl built a fire and curled up on the sofa under her cotton sheet. She fingered the small wooden frame with its rows of beads that Bird had been using to teach her accounting. The clicking of wood on wood was comforting. When Gilda returned she found the Girl asleep, clutching the abacus to her breast as she might a doll. The Girl woke up feeling Gilda's eyes on her and knew it was late by the chill of the air. The fire glowed faintly under fresh logs.

"We can talk now," Gilda said as if she'd never gone out. She sat beside the Girl and held her hand.

"There's a war coming. It's here already, truth be told . . ." She stopped. The effort of getting out those few words left her weary.

"Do you understand when I tell you I can live through no more?"

The Girl did not speak but thought of the night she decided to escape from the plantation.

Gilda continued. "I've been afraid of living too long, and now is the end of my time. The night I found you in the cellar seems only a minute ago. But you were such a child, so full of terror, your journey had been more than the miles of road. When I picked you up your body relaxed into mine, knowing part of your fight was done. I sensed in you a spirit and understanding of the world; that you were the voice lacking among us. Seeing this world with you has given me wonderful years of pleasure. Now my only fear is leaving Bird alone. It's you she needs here with her."

The Girl looked at Gilda's face, the skin drawn tightly across the tiny bones, her eyes glistening with flecks of orange. She wanted to comfort this woman who'd lifted her out of her nightmares.

"You must want to stay. You must need to live. Will you trust me?"

"I never thought to leave you or the house. My home is here as long as you'll have me," the Girl said in a clear voice.

"What I ask is not an easy thing. You may feel you have nothing to go back to, but sooner or later we all want to go back to something. Usually some inconsequential thing to which we've never given much thought before. But it will loom there in our past entreating us cruelly because there is no way to ever go back. In asking this of you, and in the future should you ask it of others, you must be certain that you—that others—are strong enough to withstand the complete loss of those intangibles that make the past so alluring."

The Girl said nothing, not really certain what Gilda meant. She felt a change in the room—the air was taut with energy.

"There are only inadequate words to speak for who we are. The language is crude, the history false. You must look to me and know who I am and if the life I offer is the life you choose. In choosing you must pledge yourself to pursue only life, never bitterness or cruelty."

The Girl peered deeply into the swirling brown and flickering orange of Gilda's eyes, feeling herself opening to ideas and sensations she had never fully admitted before. She drew back, startled at the weight of time she saw behind those eyes.

"Don't be frightened by the idea of death; it is part of life in all things. It will only become worrisome when you decide that its time has come. Power is the frightening thing, not death. And the blood, it is a shared thing. Something we must all learn to share or simply spill onto battlefields." Gilda stopped, feeling the weight of all she wanted to say, knowing it would be too much at once. She would leave the rest to Bird.

The Girl listened to the words. She tried to look again into the world behind Gilda's eyes and understand what was being asked of her. What she saw was open space, no barriers. She saw a dusty road and heard the silence of determination as she felt the tribe close around her as it had closed around Gilda, the child. She saw forests spanning a distance of green too remote for even Gilda to remember.

"My dream was to see the world, over time. The real dream is to make a world—to see the people and still want to make a world."

"I haven't seen much, but what I've seen doesn't give me much appetite," the Girl said, remembering the chill she felt from Bernice's words about the war's aftermath.

"But what of the people?" Gilda's voice rose slightly. "Put aside the faces of those who've hunted you, who've hurt you. What of the people you've loved? Those you could love tomorrow?"

The Girl drew back from the fire in Gilda's voice. Her mother's hands reaching down to pull the cloth up to her chin as she lay on the mattress filled her vision. Her mother's darkened knuckles had loomed large and solid, something she had not articulated her love for. She remembered hearing Bird's voice for the first time below her in the house announcing the entertainment. The deep resonance sent a thrill through her body. Minta's soft warning was all but forgotten, but her tender concern which showed in the bend of her body filled the Girl with joy. The wary, protective way Bernice had watched her grow, their evenings alone in the kitchen talking about the ways of the world—these were things of value. She opened her eyes and looked into Gilda's. She found love there, too. And exhaustion beyond exploration. She could see no future in them although this was what Gilda wanted to promise her.

Reading the thoughts that Gilda tried to communicate, the Girl picked her way through. "You're offerin' me time that's not really time? Time that's gonna leave me by myself?"

"I've seen this world moving on many different paths. I've walked each road with curiosity, anxious to see what we would make of our world. In Europe and to the south of us here have been much the same. When I came here the world was much larger, and the trip I had to make into the new world was as fearful as the one you've made. I was a girl, too, much too young to even be afraid.

"Each time I thought taking a stand, fighting a war would bring the solution to the demons that haunted us. Each time I thought slavery or fanaticism could be banished from the earth with a law or a battle. Each time I've been wrong. I've run out of that youthful caring, and I know we must believe in possibilities in order to go on. I no longer believe. At least for myself."

"But the war is important. People have got to be free to live."

"Yes, and that will no doubt be accomplished. But for men to need war to make freedom . . . I have never understood. Now I am tired of trying to understand. There are those of our kind who kill every time they go out into the night. They say they need this exhilaration in order to live this life. They are simply murderers. They have no special need; they are rabid children. In our life, we who live by sharing the life blood of others have no need to kill. It is through our connection with life, not death, that we live."

Both women were silent. The Girl was uncertain what questions she might even ask. It was like learning a new language. When she looked again into Gilda's eyes she felt the pulsing of blood beneath the skin. She also sensed a rising excitement that was unfamiliar to her.

"There is a joy to the exchange we make. We draw life into ourselves, yet we give life as well. We give what's needed—energy, dreams, ideas. It's a fair exchange in a world full of cheaters. And when we feel it is right, when the need is great on both sides, we can re-create others like ourselves to share life with us. It is not a bad life," Gilda said.

The Girl heard the edge in Gilda's voice but was fascinated by the pulsing blood and the swirling colors in Gilda's eyes.

"I am on the road I've chosen, the one that is right for me. You must choose your path again just as you did when you ran from the plantation in Mississippi. Death or worse might have met you on that road, but you knew it was the one you had to take. Will you trust me?" Gilda closed her eyes and drew back a little, freeing the Girl from her hypnotic gaze.

The Girl felt a chill, as if Gilda's lowered lids had shut off the sun, and for a moment she was afraid. The room was all shadows and unnatural silence as Gilda disappeared behind her closed eyes. Finally, confusion lifted from the Girl who was intent on listening to more than the words: the highs and lows, the pitch, the rhythm were all molded by a kind of faith the Girl hoped she would reach. It was larger than simply a long life. It was a grand adventure for which her flight into freedom had only begun to prepare her.

"Yes," the Girl whispered.

Gilda opened her eyes, and the Girl felt herself drawn into the flowing energy. Her arms and legs became weak. She heard a soft humming that sounded like her mother. She couldn't look away from Gilda's gaze which held her motionless. Yet she felt free and would have laughed if she had had the strength to open her mouth. She sensed rather than felt Gilda pull her into her arms. She closed her eyes, her muscles softened under the touch of Gilda's hand on her arm. She curled her long body in Gilda's lap like a child safe in her mother's arms.

She felt a sharpness at her neck and heard the soothing song. Gilda kissed her on the forehead and neck where the pain had been, catching her in a powerful undertow. She clung to Gilda, sinking deeper into a dream, barely hearing Gilda as she said, "Now you must drink." She held the Girl's head to her breast and in a quick gesture opened the skin of her chest. She pressed the Girl's mouth to the red life that seeped from her.

Soon the flow was a tide that left Gilda weak. She pulled the suckling girl away and closed the wound. Gilda sat with the Girl curled in her lap until the fire died. As the sun crept into the dark room she carried the Girl upstairs to the bedroom, where they slept the day through. Gilda awoke at dusk, the Girl still tight in her arms. She slipped from the bed and went downstairs to put a tub of water to boil. When she returned to finish dressing, the Girl watched her silently.

"I'm not well," the Girl said, feeling the gorge rising in her throat.

"Yes, you'll be fine soon," Gilda said, taking her into her arms and carrying her downstairs and outside. The evening air made the Girl tremble in her thin shirt. Gilda held the Girl's head down over the dirt, then left her sitting alone on the back stairs. She returned with a wet cloth and wiped her mouth and face, then led her inside again. She helped her remove her clothes and lifted her into the large tub standing beside the kitchen table. Then she soaped, rinsed, and massaged the Girl into restfulness, drawing out the fear and pain with her strong, thin hands as she hummed the tune from the Girl's childhood. She dressed her in a fresh gown, one of her own bordered with eyelet lace, smelling of lavender, then put her back to bed.

"Bird will return soon. You mustn't be afraid. You will ask her to complete the circle. It is she who will make you our daughter. Will you remember that?"

"Yes," the Girl said weakly.

"You must also remember, later, when time weighs on you like hard earthenware strapped to your back, it is for love that we do this." Gilda's eyes were fiery and unfocused. The power of them lulled the Girl into sleep, although she felt a pang of unease and hunger inside of her. Gilda's lips again brushed her forehead. Then she slept without dreaming.

She awoke abruptly to find Bird standing over her in darkness shadowed even further by a look of destructive anger, her eyes unblinking and dry.

"When did she leave you?" Bird's voice was tight with control although her hands shook as they clutched several crumpled sheets of paper.

Gilda had said don't be afraid and she wasn't, only anxious to understand what would happen now. "It seems long ago, before dark. She wore her walking clothes and said you would complete the circle. I was to be sure and tell you that."

Bird stalked from the room. Downstairs she stood on the porch, turning east and west as if listening to thoughts on the wind. She ran to the west, through the field, and disappeared for three hours. Her clothes were full of brambles when she returned. She went to the cellar and climbed part way through the door. She could see the new sacks of fresh soil stacked beside the ones she and Gilda had prepared so long ago. She stepped back outside and let the cellar door drop with a resounding thud, then came into the house where the Girl lay weak, unmoving except for her eyes, now dark brown flecked with pale yellow.

Bird looked down at her as if she were a stranger, turned away, and lit a lantern. Again she read the crumpled pages she'd dropped to the floor, then paced, trying not to listen to the Girl's shallow breathing. The darkest part of night passed. Bird stood on the porch again and peered at the stars as if one might signal her.

When the sun began its rise Bird retreated to the shadows of the house, moving anxiously from corner to corner, listening. She was uncertain what to expect, perhaps a ripping sound or scream of pain inside her head. She felt only the Girl weakening upstairs and a cloying uneasiness. In her head she replayed recent conversations with Gilda. Each one came closer and closer to the core.

Gilda had needed Bird to step away so she could end this long life with the peace she sought. And each time Bird had resisted, afraid of losing the love of a woman who was the center of her world. Upstairs was the Girl, now in her charge, the one who'd given that permission for which Gilda had yearned.

Full daylight came behind the closed drapes. Bird stood tense, her body a bronze rod, dull and aching, her full length of flesh and hair calling out for hours. The answer came like the sunlight it was. She felt Gilda lying naked in the water, marveling at its coolness and silence. Then she dove into the darkness of the tide. Without the power of her native soil woven into her breeches, she surrendered easily. The air was squeezed from her lungs and she eagerly embraced her rest. Bird felt a moment of the sun's warmth, her head filled with Gilda's scent. In her ear was the soft sigh of pleasure she recognized from many mornings of their past together, the low whisper of her name, then silence. She knew the knife-edged sun rays stripped the flesh from Gilda's bones. The heat seared through Bird, lightning on her skin and in her marrow. Then, like the gradual receding of menstrual pain, Bird's muscles slackened and her breathing slowed. The crackling was silenced. It was over. Gilda was in the air no more.

Bird went upstairs to the Girl whose face was ashen, her dark eyes now flecked with orange. A frost of perspiration covered her body, and tears ran down the sides of her face. She opened her mouth but no sounds came out. Bird sat against the pillows and pulled the Girl into her arms. She was relieved by the cool tears washing over her brown arm as if she were weeping herself. Bird pulled aside her woolen shirt and bared her breasts.

She made a small incision beneath the right one and pressed the Girl's mouth to it. The throbbing in her chest became synchronous with the Girl's breathing. Soon the strength returned to the Girl's body; she no longer looked so small.

Bird repeated the exchange, taking from her as Gilda had done and returning the blood to complete the process. She finally lay her head back on the pillows, holding the Girl in her arms, and rested. Their breathing and heartbeats sounded as one for an hour or more before their bodies again found their own rhythms. Even then, Bird remained silent.

"She's gone then?" Bird heard her ask. She only nodded and eased her arms from around the Girl's body.

"I'll build a fire," she said and rose quickly from the bed. Alone in the room Bird found the crumpled letter and returned it to the box Gilda had left on the dressing table. She heard the sound of a robe brushing the carpet below as the Girl moved about laying wood on the fire, then settling the kettle atop the stove in the kitchen. She called to Bird to come down. Her voice, now strong and vibrant, was a shock in the late afternoon quiet without Gilda.

They sat in the twilight in front of the low flames, not speaking for some time. Then Bird said, "She wanted you to be called Gilda."

"I know."

"Will you?"

"I don't know."

"It will be dark soon—we must go out. Are you afraid?"

"She said there's little to fear and you'll teach me, as always." They were quiet again.

"She loved you very much, Bird."

"Loved me so much that she traded her life for yours?" Bird almost shouted. In all else there'd been some reasoning, but she could find none in this. Here in the place of the woman to whom she'd given her life sat a child.

"I'm not a child, Bird. If I can hear her words and understand her need, why can't you? I didn't steal her life. She took her road to freedom—just like I did, just like you did. She made a fair exchange. For your sake."

"Fair exchange?" Bird was unnerved by the words she had heard so often in the past when she had been learning the manner of taking the blood and leaving something in return—how to partake of life and be certain not to take life. She chafed under the familiar words and inflection. "You for her?" Bird spit it out. "Hundreds of years of knowledge and wit in exchange for a girl who hasn't lived one lifetime yet."

"It's not just me, it's you. Her life, her freedom for our future. You are as much a part of the bargain as I am. She brought me to this place for your need as well as for mine. It's us seeing the future together that satisfies her needs."

Bird heard the past speaking to her, words she had chosen to ignore. Tonight she stood face to face with their meaning: Gilda's power over her own death was sacred, a decision all others were honor bound to respect. Bird had denied Gilda's right to her quietus and refused to even acknowledge that decision. It was a failure she could not wear easily.

Darkness seeped through the drawn curtains of the parlor. The glow of the almost-steady flame burned orange in the room, creating movement where there was none. The two women sat together as if they were still at their reading lessons. Finally Bird spoke.

"Gilda?"

"Yes."

"It's time now."

They dressed in the warm breeches and dark shirts. Bird took Gilda's hand and looked into the face of the woman who had been her pupil and saw the childlike roundness of her had melted away. Hunger filled her eyes.

"It is done much as it was done here. Your body will speak to you. Do not return to take from anyone too soon again: it can create the hunger in them. They will recover though, if it is not fed. And as you take from them you must reach inside. Feel what they are needing, not what you are hungering for. You leave them with something new and fresh, something wanted. Let their joy fill you. This is the only way to share and not to rob. It will also keep you on your guard so you don't drain life away."

"Yes, these are things she wanted me to know."

"I will teach you how to move about in indirect sunlight, as you've seen us do, and how to take your rest. Already your body sheds its mortal softness. You'll move faster than anyone, have the strength of many. It's that strength that you must learn to control. But we will talk more of these things later. It is better to begin before there is pain."

Gilda and Bird turned west. Their path through the flat field was invisible. Bird pushed aside all thoughts for the moment, remembering only her need to instruct, to insure that the girl gained enough knowledge for her survival. Gilda allowed the feeling of loss to drift through her as they sped into the darkness. Along with it came a sense of completion, too. There was certain knowledge of the world around her, excitement about the unknown that lay ahead, and comfort with her new life. She looked back over her shoulder, but they had moved so quickly that the farmhouse was all but invisible. Inside, the fire was banked low, waiting for their return.

Part IV

In the Closet:
The Literature of
Lesbian Encoding

INTRODUCTION

The French lesbian author Monique Wittig lamented in 1973 regarding her perception of the paucity of lesbian writing:

> Male homosexual literature has a past and a present. Lesbians, in contrast, are silent—just as all women, at all levels, are silent. If you have read the poems of Sappho, Radclyffe Hall's *Well of Loneliness*, the poems of Sylvia Plath [*sic*] and Anaïs Nin, *La batarde* by Violette Leduc, you have read everything.[1]

There was of course a much richer history of writing by women who loved women long before 1973, but, as knowledgeable as Wittig and others have been about literature, that history escaped them for a variety of reasons. One reason that "lesbian literature," or—to be more historically accurate—literature that deals with love between women, has been so difficult to identify is that we have been conditioned to be oblivious to it. If our century has created an outlaw out of the woman who loves women, how can we believe that someone as "respectable" as Louisa May Alcott, for example, was really writing about love between women in novels such as *Work* and *Diana and Persis*? It is much easier to explain her female characters' expressions of passionate intensity about each other as a manifestation of overblown Victorian rhetoric rather than the author's intention to convey same-sex love.

Another reason it has been so difficult to track the literature of love between women is that critics have gone to great pains to deny its existence, as did the scholar who felt compelled to explain of Emily Dickinson's lines "Her heart is fit for home— / I—a Sparrow—build there / Sweet of twigs and twine / My perennial nest" that "the persona is a male sparrow." Such a panic to identify "appropriate" gender, risible as it may seem in our somewhat more enlightened days, has dominated criticism throughout much of the twentieth century.

The most concrete information about a writer's lesbianism has often been ignored or trivialized in biographies, which meant that readers were denied the evidence to confirm what they may have suspected was lesbian subject matter in an author's work. A biography of Edna St. Vincent Millay, for example, squeezes Millay's lesbian experiences (which she continued to have throughout much of her life) into one chapter entitled "Millay's Childhood and Youth," and then organizes each of the subsequent chapters around a male with whom Millay had some relationship. Six men who had relatively little contact with her are treated together in a chapter entitled "Millay's Other Men," although the author admits in that chapter that three of "Millay's other men" were homosexual.

Some well-meaning literary executors continue to try to "protect" the reputation of writers, even in these relatively liberal times. For instance, my attempt to procure eleven poems by Edna St. Vincent Millay for this anthology was rejected by Millay's literary executrix, who wrote me, "These poems are not appropriate for your collection, as Millay did not write lesbian literature. She wrote poetry—pure and simple." Millay's "pure and simple" poetry, however, included verse such as "Evening on Lesbos," in which the speaker laments: "Twice having seen your shingled heads adorable / Side by side, the onyx and the gold, / I know that I have had what I could not hold."

Despite the importance of what can be revealed to the reader about a work when the writer's love of other women is known, biographers have frequently attempted to hide such evidence in the interest of "saving" their respected subject's reputation. Mary Wollstonecraft's novel *Mary* might have been far easier to comprehend had some well-meaning Wollstonecraft scholar not obliterated by hand sixteen lines that Wollstonecraft wrote in a letter apparently discussing her passion for the recently deceased Fanny Blood. In spite of such tampering, the evidence that Wollstonecraft was in love with Fanny Blood is persuasive and quite disturbing to homophobic biographers. One 1970s biographer, after discussing Wollstonecraft's great attachment to Fanny Blood, then seeks frantically to establish Wollstonecraft's heterosexual credentials and comes upon a spurious affair with a Reverend Joshua Waterhouse. The biographer then observes: "In spite of these emotions and professions [to Fanny], a certain secret disloyalty to Fanny did take place. It is rather a relief to discover it" [*sic!*].

But many lesbian writers did not need their biographers to hide the fact of their lesbianism since they assiduously did so themselves, often fabricating a heterosexual past, or sometimes claiming bisexuality, which, in certain eras, was not as shocking as "full-blown lesbianism." Some writers, such as Katherine Mansfield, were indeed bisexual, but while the heterosexual subject matter of their work was forthright, the lesbian material was usually far less so.

The "New Critics" who ruled literary discourse for several decades in the middle of the twentieth century attempted to argue that the text itself was all the reader needed to interpret literature. They insisted that an understanding of the writer's social milieu or literary influences or biography was superfluous to an understanding of the novel or poem. Recent critical thought has pretty well blasted that notion by demonstrating that writing and reading cannot successfully be separated from context. Knowledge about those factors that were considered peripheral by the New Critics is especially crucial to a deciphering of texts that are lesbian. For instance, we can understand a good deal more about Carson McCullers's *The Member of the Wedding* (1946) if we know that McCullers believed that lesbians were men trapped in women's bodies, that she was herself gender dysphoric and a lesbian, and that her main character, Frankie, was largely autobiographical. That knowledge helps reveal to the reader the encoded lesbian material in *The Member of the Wedding*. It explains not only the meaning of Frankie's tomboyism, but also why McCullers presents Frankie as feeling a murderous panic when males try to be sexual with her, why she sees herself as a criminal although she is innocent, and why she feels such joy at the end of the novel when she anticipates her evening with Mary Littlejohn. In the same way, the reader can understand much better the nature of the delirium the main character of Katherine Mansfield's story "Bliss" feels about her husband's mistress once it is known that Mansfield wrote the story when she was in the throes of her bisexual relationships with John Middleton Murry and Ida Baker. The unveiling of the lesbian content in such works often helps to explain what is otherwise inexplicable.

Lesbian material was so veiled throughout much of the twentieth century, before the successes in the 1970s of feminism and the gay and lesbian movement, because writers who were lesbians feared, as many of the headnotes in this section will demonstrate, that if they wrote too clearly as lesbians they would be stigmatized. They believed that their work would be pegged as not universal—not "wording a common cry of many hearts" as Clement Wood[2] said of Amy Lowell's lesbian poetry—and that their words would be discounted by the majority of the population. Therefore, if they saw themselves as writers of "serious" literature they omitted or encoded the lesbian subject matter in their work.

But despite many lesbian authors' attempts at subterfuge, even in their writings that are ostensibly heterosexual or without sexual subject matter,

a lesbian sensibility often reveals itself. That sensibility is suggested sometimes by an expression of strong feminist values—a jaundiced look at
heterosexual institutions such as marriage, a yearning for agency and
independence—coupled with a determined flexibility in the conception of
gender roles. It is suggested more subtly by the gaze that falls lovingly on
the female image and the blurred presentation of the male image. Willa
Cather's fiction, such as *My Ántonia*, for example, can be seen to contain
a lesbian sensibility in these ways, although it has not one word about sex
between women (two female characters in the novel do finally settle down
in a romantic friendship). Clearly not all of Cather's work betrays her
lesbian sensibility: *Death Comes for the Archbishop* and *Shadows on the
Rock*, for example, are without it. But in much of her fiction the lesbian
appears in masquerade, sometimes dressed as a male, sometimes revealed
only in a third-person narrator's gaze.

Twentieth-century lesbian authors obfuscated the lesbian material in
their work both passively and actively. Passively, one way they avoided
writing about the love they know best was simply not to write. As Gloria
Hull has pointed out about the Harlem Renaissance poet Angelina
Grimké,[3] her position in literary history would have been greatly enhanced
had she written more and published more. But, Hull suggests, Grimké censored herself because what she wanted to write were "lines [she did] not
dare." The same might be said of Charlotte Mew, the smallness of whose
literary output, brilliant as it was, has robbed her of a more significant
place in the history of letters. These lesbian writers obfuscated their natural
material by silence.

Another passive means of obfuscating lesbian subject matter which was
employed by many twentieth-century lesbian poets, was simply to omit
gender references altogether and to rely on the social and literary convention that presumes heterosexuality unless specific evidence to the contrary
is provided. If the female speaker in a poem does not address the beloved
as "she," the assumption has always been that the beloved is "he." Once
biographical evidence about a writer's lesbianism is available, of course,
the reader is no longer obliged to assume that a poem with omitted gender
reference is yet another instance of universal heterosexuality. (However,
even if gender reference is omitted and the reader does not know whether
an author is lesbian, the homoeroticism of a work is not necessarily impermeable. For example, in poems that lack a vocal "she" the lesbian inspiration is sometimes betrayed by a reference to the beloved's "sobbing"
or "doing" [her] hair).

Most literary concealment of lesbianism has been active: The lesbian
writer has purposely encoded her lesbian subject matter so that it is veiled
to the majority of the population yet often decipherable by the reader who

has knowledge of the writer's homosexuality and understands her need to hide her lesbian material. Encoding in literature by lesbians has been practiced in multifarious ways. On the most simplistic level, many lesbian writers have simply bearded their pronouns as, for example, May Sarton now admits to having done in her 1961 sonnet sequence "A Divorce of Lovers."[4] Pre-1970s lesbian writers sometimes even wrote an original draft using a feminine pronoun or name and then edited it for publication by supplying a masculine pronoun or name. Much of Gertrude Stein's wacky style can be traced to her need to hide gender. For instance, she often avoids using gendered referents such as "he" or "she" and instead uses the awkward "some" or "one."

The bearded pronoun in lesbian writing may not always have been an attempt to obfuscate. In some cases, such as that of Charlotte Mew, for example, the prevalence of male personae in her love poetry may also be an indication of her transgendered self-perception. Mew's conception of herself as inverted, possessing a male soul, can explain, just as well as her belief that she must hide her lesbianism, why she often spoke in a male voice in her writing. In the absence of concrete proof, it is, of course, difficult to decipher motives from our point in time, but it is possible that the masculine persona did double duty for Mew as well as other writers. It expressed their masculine identification and it also threw homophobic critics off the track.

Still another encoding device that Gertrude Stein used as early as the second decade of the twentieth century was the double entendre, which only those who were homosexual or familiar with the subculture would understand fully. For instance, Stein's "Miss Furr and Miss Skeene" plays on the word "gay," which, before the demystification of the term by the media in the 1970s, would have meant only "merry" to those not privy to the language homosexuals used among themselves. In an era of censorship, she managed to pen with total impunity the most graphic descriptions of lesbian sex through such semihermetic linguistic devices.

Another device, which may be seen in the work of early-twentieth-century poets such as H.D., and perhaps even late-nineteenth-century poets such as the two women who wrote as "Michael Field," was the encoding of contemporary lesbian subject matter through the use of the veil of antiquity. Lesbian poets have often extended Sappho's brief fragments and written whole lesbian poems that were presented, in effect, as attributable not to them but to the long-dead Lesbian. Such a graveyard defusion of the stigma of lesbian love appears in still another variation, in which lesbian poets have written erotically but "safely" about a female beloved who is now dead. The erotic elements of the poem are thus disguised by grief and mourning (see pp. 485 and 486).

Such encoding and obfuscation were not necessarily devices of the trickster, the liar, or the determined survivor. Lesbian writers in the past often believed (and were perhaps authorized in their belief by the convictions of the New Critics about the poet's putative objectivity and search for universalities) that, as May Sarton once argued, "poetry deals in essences not sexes." If it is merely the essence of love that counts in literary representation, the fact of a poem's source in lesbianism could seem irrelevant. In that way, lesbian writers convinced themselves that it was allowable to censor out the lesbian specifics of the inspiration of their work.

The task of decoding lesbian literature is not an easy one. It is, however, rewarding, not only because it helps to set the record straight (or rather unstraight), but also because it allows us to understand dimensions of a work that are otherwise hidden and that make the work far richer. And finally, it helps provide an interesting commentary on the homophobia that forced lesbian authors to invent all manner of tactics, to tell the truth only slant, to contribute to the construction of lesbianism as the love that dare not speak its name.

1. Monique Wittig, quoted in Elaine Marks, "Lesbian Intertextuality," *Homosexualities and French Literature*, eds. Elaine Marks and George Stambolian (Ithaca, N.Y.: Cornell University Press).
2. Clement Wood, *Amy Lowell* (New York: Harold Vinal, 1926).
3. Gloria Hull, "Under the Days: The Buried Life and Poetry of Angelina Weld Grimké," *Conditions: Five* (Autumn 1979).
4. Re. May Sarton: *Conversations with May Sarton*, ed. Earl G. Ingersoll (Jackson, Mississippi: University of Mississippi Press, 1991).

Charlotte Mew
(1869-1928)

Much of Charlotte Mew's poetry focuses passionately and romantically on women, but Mew never permitted herself to create a female persona for these poems. Whenever their gender is identified, her lovers of women speak in the voices of men. Throughout her life, Mew herself loved women, and some of her poems appear to be autobiographical. However, her male personae may not have been merely masks of her intent, since Mew saw herself as being masculine. Despite her small stature, she favored the most tailored clothing—"mannish" jackets, small-sized men's overcoats, collars and ties, porkpie hats. From her schooldays she wore her hair short, cultivated an "ambiguous" gait, and had a voice that broke like that of an adolescent boy. Her British middle-class upbringing was staunchly Victorian, yet she smoked, traveled unchaperoned, and used language "unfit for a lady."

Mew's role model at the age of fourteen was Lucy Harrison, the beloved headmistress of the school Mew attended. Harrison was the first woman Mew had known who wore short hair and cultivated a masculine persona. According to her biographers, when Mew learned that her idol would be leaving the school, "in a wild state of grief [she] began to bang her head against the wall." She persuaded her parents to let her live with Harrison as a boarder and tutee, until Harrison left London two years later to be with her own beloved, another woman teacher. Penelope Fitzgerald speculates that Mew's early sonnet, "Left Behind," commemorates the poet's feelings of loss at this time:

> I wait thy summons on a swaying floor,
>   Within a room half darkness and half glare.
>   I cannot stir—I cannot find the stair—
>   Thrust hands upon my heart—; it clogs my feet,
>   As drop by drop it drains. I stand and beat—
> I stand and beat my heart against the door.

Mew's subsequent loves were not without ambivalence. Ambivalence seems, in fact, to have marked her life. Despite her unabashedly masculine presentation, she felt guilty about her desires. Although she was very attracted to Roman Catholicism, Mew felt she could not join the church because she could not cope with the obligation to confess. She had close ties to the aesthete movement in literature, but she severed her connections with the aesthete journal *The Yellow Book* because Oscar Wilde had been connected with it and she was shocked at his sodomy trial in 1895. She appears to have tried to fight against lesbian temptations, but her success in that battle was imperfect.

Her success in achieving satisfaction as a lesbian was less than imperfect. In an era when there was no easy way for a British lesbian to meet other lesbians, Mew was destined to relive again and again the experiences of frustration in love. In 1894 she fell in love with a writer who was an editorial assistant for *The Yellow Book*, Ella D'Arcy. D'Arcy was aggressively heterosexual, but she encouraged the friendship. Their relationship may have been encoded in Mew's short story "Some Ways of Love," in which the heroine, who is also named Ella, teaches the hero that there are many different ways to love. In 1902 Mew followed D'Arcy to Paris, but finally gave up her pursuit when she understood that D'Arcy would always be far more interested in her own pursuit of men.

Perhaps Mew's most traumatic emotional experience was with the novelist May Sinclair, with whom Mew had a friendship from 1913 to 1916, a time when Sinclair's literary reputation was at its height. It was Sinclair who pursued Mew in the relationship, insisting on their frequent meetings, writing the shy and fearful Mew extremely warm notes, and helping her in the literary world. When Mew finally responded to Sinclair's verbal extravagance, Sinclair rejected her by saying, "My good woman, you are simply wasting your perfectly good passion." Sinclair also delighted in reporting the incident to a number of people. She wrote to Rebecca West that "a lesbian poetess, Charlotte M." had chased her upstairs into the bedroom and "I assure you . . . I had to leap the bed five times." But even after this incident and Sinclair's betrayal, the novelist remained reluctant to give up the relationship and continued sending Mew affectionate notes and pleading for their meeting.

Considering Mew's own rotten luck in selecting people to love, it is not surprising that the lovers in her poetry are generally doomed to frustration. In many of her best poems, such as "The Farmer's Bride," "In Nunhead Cemetery," "Monsieur Qui Passe," and "The Fête," the male speaker experiences only fleeting contact with the beloved. Painful fantasy takes the place of fulfillment. Despite the speakers' inevitable sorrow, however, the appreciation for female erotic beauty in Mew's poetry is intense.

Mew's literary output was very slim, perhaps because, like other lesbian writers of her era, she felt the burden of having to censor her material by masquerade. Mew wrote poems and stories for many of the leading literary journals of her day, but only one book by her, *The Farmer's Bride* (1916), appeared during her lifetime. Despite the paucity of Mew's work, Virginia Woolf had read enough of it so that she could tell Vita Sackville-West in 1924 that Charlotte Mew was "the greatest living poetess." Thomas Hardy agreed, saying that Mew was not only "far and away the best living woman poet," but also that her work "will be read when others are forgotten." In 1928, in despair over the death of her sister Anne, to whom she had been very close, in ill health herself, and unable to write, Charlotte Mew committed suicide.

FURTHER READING: Charlotte Mew, *Collected Poems and Prose*, ed. Val Warner (London: Virago, 1981). T. E. M. Boll, "The Mystery of Charlotte Mew and May Sinclair: An Inquiry," *Bulletin of the New York Public Library*, LXXIV, 3 (September 1970), 445–53. Penelope Fitzgerald, *Charlotte Mew and Her Friends* (New York:

Addison-Wesley, 1988). Alida Monro, "Charlotte Mew—A Memoir" in *Collected Poems of Charlotte Mew* (London: Duckworth, 1953).

MONSIEUR QUI PASSE
(Quai Voltaire)

A purple blot against the dead white door
In my friend's rooms, bathed in their vile pink light,
I had not noticed her before
She snatched my eyes and threw them back to me:
She did not speak till we came out into the night,
Paused at this bench beside the kiosk on the quay.

God knows precisely what she said—
I left to her the twisted skein,
Though here and there I caught a thread,—
Something, at first, about "the lamps along the Seine,
And Paris, with that witching card of Spring
Kept up her sleeve,—why you could see
The trick done on these freezing winter nights!
While half the kisses of the Quay—
Youth, hope,—the whole enchanted string
Of dreams hung on the Seine's long line of lights."

Then suddenly she stripped, the very skin
Came off her soul,—a mere girl clings
Longer to some last rag, however thin,
When she has shown you—well—all sorts of things:
"If it were daylight—oh! one keeps one's head—
But fourteen years!—No one has ever guessed—
The whole thing starts when one gets to bed—
Death?—If the dead would tell us they had rest!
But your eyes held it as I stood there by the door—
One speaks to Christ—one tries to catch His garment's hem—
One hardly says as much to Him—no more:
It was not you, it was your eyes—I spoke to them."

She stopped like a shot bird that flutters still,
And drops, and tries to run again, and swerves.
The tale should end in some walled house upon a hill.
My eyes, at least, won't play such havoc there,—
Or hers—But she had hair!—blood dipped in gold;
And there she left me throwing back the first odd stare.

Some sort of beauty once, but turning yellow, getting old.
Pouah! These women and their nerves!
God! but the night *is* cold!

MY HEART IS LAME

My heart is lame with running after yours so fast
    Such a long way,
Shall we walk slowly home, looking at all the things we passed
    Perhaps to-day?

Home down the quiet evening roads under the quiet skies,
    Not saying much,
You for a moment giving me your eyes
    When you could bear my touch.

But not to-morrow. This has taken all my breath;
    Then, though you look the same,
There may be something lovelier in Love's face in death
As your heart sees it, running back the way we came;
    My heart is lame.

ABSENCE

Sometimes I know the way
   You walk, up over the bay;
It is a wind from that far sea
That blows the fragrance of your hair to me.

Or in this garden when the breeze
   Touches my trees
To stir their dreaming shadows on the grass
   I see you pass.

In sheltered beds, the heart of every rose
   Serenely sleeps to-night. As shut as those
Your guarded heart; as safe as they from the beat, beat
Of hooves that tread dropped roses in the street.

   Turn never again
   On these eyes blind with a wild rain
Your eyes; they were stars to me.—
   There are things stars may not see.

But call, call, and though Christ stands
  Still with scarred hands
Over my mouth, I must answer. So
I will come—He shall let me go!

ON THE ROAD TO THE SEA

We passed each other, turned and stopped for half an hour, then
  went our way,
    I who make other women smile did not make you—
But no man can move mountains in a day.
    So this hard thing is yet to do.

But first I want your life:—before I die I want to see
    The world that lies behind the strangeness of your eyes,
There is nothing gay or green there for my gathering, it may be,
        Yet on brown fields there lies
A haunting purple bloom: is there not something in grey skies
           And in grey sea?
    I want what world there is behind your eyes,
    I want your life and you will not give it me.

Now, if I look, I see you walking down the years,
    Young, and through August fields—a face, a thought, a
      swinging dream
                        perched on a stile—;
    I would have liked (so vile we are!) to have taught you tears
        But most to have made you smile.

    To-day is not enough or yesterday: God sees it all—
Your length on sunny lawns, the wakeful rainy nights—; tell me—;
    (how vain to ask), but it is not a question—just a call—;
Show me then, only your notched inches climbing up the garden
  wall,
        I like you best when you are small.

      Is this a stupid thing to say
      Not having spent with you one day?
   No matter; I shall never touch your hair
   Or hear the little tick behind your breast,
      Still it is there,
      And as a flying bird
Brushes the branches where it may not rest

I have brushed your hand and heard
    The child in you: I like that best
So small, so dark, so sweet; and were you also then too grave and
wise?
        Always I think. Then put your far off little hand in mine;—
                            Oh! let it rest;
I will not stare into the early world beyond the opening eyes,
    Or vex or scare what I love best.
    But I want your life before mine bleeds away—
        Here—not in heavenly hereafters—soon,—
        I want your smile this very afternoon,
    (The last of all my vices, pleasant people used to say,
        I wanted and I sometimes got—the Moon!)

        You know, at dusk, the last bird's cry,
And round the house the flap of the bat's low flight,
    Trees that go black against the sky
And then—how soon the night!

No shadow of you on any bright road again,
And at the darkening end of this—what voice? whose kiss? As if
    you'd say!
It is not I who have walked with you, it will not be I who take
away
    Peace, peace, my little handful of the gleaner's grain
    From your reaped fields at the shut of day.

        Peace! Would you not rather die
    Reeling,—with all the cannons at your ear?
        So, at least, would I,
    And I may not be here
    To-night, to-morrow morning or next year.
    Still I will let you keep your life a little while,
        See dear?
    I have made you smile.

Gertrude Stein
(1874–1946)

Gertrude Stein moved to Paris with her brother Leo in 1903 after dropping out of medical school at Johns Hopkins because of her unhappiness

over a triangular lesbian affair, which she recorded in her first novel, *QED*. The young Steins became interested in Post-Impressionist and modernist art and, supported by a stipend from their wealthy older brother, began buying paintings and befriending painters. Their home at 27 rue de Fleurus soon turned into a salon, with Leo at the center. In 1907, Alice B. Toklas, an American on holiday, appeared at rue de Fleurus, and as Gertrude Stein records in "Didn't Nelly and Lily Love You?" the rest is history. In 1909 Alice moved in with Gertrude and Leo. She served not only as Gertrude's "wife" but also her greatest fan, appreciatively reading her work, typing her manuscripts, sending them out to publishers, keeping all but the most interesting visitors from impinging on Gertrude's time, and, in general, promoting Gertrude as a legend in her own day. Leo moved out in 1914 and left the most popular salon in Paris to the lesbian couple.

By the force of her larger-than-life personality Gertrude Stein became increasingly famous, not only among the literary and artistic expatriates in Paris, but also among less sophisticated Americans back home. When Gertrude and Alice returned to the United States in 1934 to publicize Gertrude's outrageously titled memoirs, *The Autobiography of Alice B. Toklas*, Gertrude and her distinctive prose style were already so well known that New York headlines blared, "Gerty Gerty Stein Stein is Back Home Home Back."

In her life, Gertrude did nothing to hide the fact that she lived with Alice, that they traveled everywhere together, and that they were a team as much as any heterosexual husband and wife could be considered a team. In her writing, however, her lesbian material is often encoded in her hermetic style. Only with the posthumous publication in 1951 of *QED* (which Stein had hidden away in a drawer after writing it in 1903) was it understood by the more astute that much of her writing was specifically lesbian. The critic Edmund Wilson, for example, pointed out that Stein's post-1903 vagueness, such as her lack of distinct referents (her use of "one" and "some" instead of "he" or "she") was due to "a need imposed by the problem of writing about relationships between women of a kind that the standards of the era would not have allowed her to describe more explicitly."

One should not dismiss entirely Stein's claim that she was attempting to do in prose what the modern artists who flocked to her Paris salon were doing in the plastic arts, that is, rid herself of the manacle of representation. But, as Wilson suggests, she also needed to solve the problem of how to deal with the material of her affectional life that her era considered inexpressible. Her advice to Ernest Hemingway on a similar problem is revealing. When the aspiring young writer showed her one of his stories ("Up in Michigan") that refers specifically to his hero's genitalia, Stein advised him that, although the story was good, its graphic detail made it impractical. It was *inaccrochable,* like a painting with salacious subject matter that one could not exhibit. "There is no point" in creating such a work, she insisted, because nothing could be done with it. Of course, her own favorite subject, lesbian love and sex, would have been at least as *inaccrochable* than work that dealt with a discussion of the size of a hero's penis, but with her stylistic "experimentations" Stein had found ways to say what she wanted without worrying about the censors.

Much of Gertrude Stein's work reflects her life with Alice B. Toklas. Stein was influenced in no way by those images of the lesbian as a medical category or a carnivorous flower, which pervaded literature when she began to write. Even in her pre-Toklas novel, *QED,* a remarkable psychological study in the manner of Henry James, the lesbian characters are presented as struggling with moral and emotional subtleties, but their problems stem from the fact that they are complex people rather than congenitally burdened or sinful as a result of their lesbianism. However, Stein quickly realized that literature about lesbians that did not deal with the genesis of the "disease" or the "inevitable" agony caused by the "condition" was not publishable. Therefore, she transformed her lesbians of *QED* into African Americans (thereby retaining the idea of "otherness"), and she published that work in 1910 as "Melanctha."

In order to obviate the need for such transformations, much of her later work employs techniques of obfuscation. Those techniques permitted her to describe graphically what no other published writer felt free to describe for another half-century—for example, orgasm in lesbian sex, as in the prose piece "As a Wife Has a Cow. A Love Story" and the poem "A Third," in which Stein writes:

Climax no climax is necessary
And so near soon.
What and what wives.
Please and pleases.
Extra for them.
Now they have mountains.
She came easy. . . .
It is a very great pleasure altogether.
Softly in a hotel, softly and in a hotel softly in a hotel softly in a hotel.
Next.
Softly in a hotel softly.
When she is through there is nothing more to do when she is through
    everything is done.

In much of the work Stein produced after she met Alice, all or part of her emphasis is on their "marriage," as in "Ada," "Bonne Année," "Sacred Emily," "I Love My Love With a V.," "In This Way Kissing," "The Present," "A Sonatina Followed by Another," "Here: Actualities," "Pay Me," "Water Pipe," and perhaps the longest poem to date about lesbian sex, "Lifting Belly." Stein told all the truth about her life with Alice, but she knew she had to compromise with the censors enough to "tell it slant." In Part II of "Lifting Belly" Stein asks, "Can you read my print?" The uninitiated would undoubtedly have been confounded by the question, but many lesbian readers of her day must have been delighted with their privileged ability to "read her print," to decipher some of her more puzzling work.

"Miss Furr and Miss Skeene," a story about two of Gertrude and Alice's lesbian friends, Miss Mars and Miss Squires, appeared in *Vanity Fair* magazine in 1923. Few heterosexuals in the 1920s understood that the term "gay" was a code word for "homosexual" (even as recently as the 1950s, the subcultural meaning of "gay" was generally not known by the larger society). Thus, the most common critical interpretation of "Miss Furr and Miss Skeene" was that it was an ironic tale about two unhappy old maids whose single state rendered them anything but "gay," that is, merry. The story, an examination not only of a lesbian relationship but of homosexual society in the 1920s, is a striking example of how much Stein could get away with by encoding her lesbian material.

FURTHER READING: Gertrude Stein, *Fernhurst, QED, and Other Early Writings* (New York: Liveright, 1971); *Lifting Belly*, ed. Rebecca Mark (Tallahassee, FL: Naiad, 1989); *Selected Writings of Gertrude Stein*, ed. Carl Van Vechten (New York: Random House, 1962). Richard Bridgman, *Gertrude Stein in Pieces* (New York: Oxford University Press, 1971). Penelope J. Englebrecht, "Lifting Belly is a Language: The Postmodern Lesbian Subject," *Feminist Studies*, 16: 1 (Spring 1990), 85–114. Elizabeth Fifer, "Is Flesh Advisable?: The Interior Theater of Gertrude Stein," *Signs*, 4: 3 (Spring 1979), 472–83. James R. Mellow, *Charmed Circle: Gertrude Stein and Company* (New York: Praeger, 1974). Linda Simon, *The Biography of Alice B. Toklas* (Garden City, NY: Doubleday, 1977). Catharine Stimpson, "Gertrice/Altrude: Stein, Toklas, and the Paradox of the Happy Marriage," in *Mothering the Mind: Twelve Studies of Writers and Their Silent Partners*, eds. Ruth Perry and Martine Brownley, pp. 123–39 (New York: Holmes and Meier, 1984).

Miss Furr and Miss Skeene

Helen Furr had quite a pleasant home. Mrs. Furr was quite a pleasant woman. Mr. Furr was quite a pleasant man. Helen Furr had quite a pleasant voice a voice quite worth cultivating. She did not mind working. She worked to cultivate her voice. She did not find it gay living in the same place where she had always been living. She went to a place where some were cultivating something, voices and other things needing cultivating. She met Georgine Skeene there who was cultivating her voice which some thought was quite a pleasant one. Helen Furr and Georgine Skeene lived together then. Georgine Skeene liked travelling. Helen Furr did not care about travelling, she liked to stay in one place and be gay there. They were together then and travelled to another place and stayed there and were gay there.

They stayed there and were gay there not very gay there, just gay there. They were both gay there, they were regularly working there both of them cultivating their voices there, they were both gay there. Georgine Skeene was gay there and she was regular, regular in being gay, regular in not being gay, regular in being a gay one who was one not being gay longer than was needed to be one being quite a gay one. They were both gay then there and both working there then.

They were in a way both gay there where there were many cultivating something. They were both regular in being gay there. Helen Furr was gay there, she was gayer and gayer there and really she was just gay there, she was gayer and gayer there, that is to say she found ways of being gay there that she was using in being gay there. She was gay there, not gayer and gayer, just gay there, that is to say she was not gayer by using the things she found there that were gay things, she was gay there, always she was gay there.

They were quite regularly gay there, Helen Furr and Georgine Skeene, they were regularly gay there where they were gay. They were very regularly gay.

To be regularly gay was to do every day the gay thing that they did every day. To be regularly gay was to end every day at the same time after they had been regularly gay. They were regularly gay. They were gay every day. They ended every day in the same way, at the same time, and they had been every day regularly gay.

The voice Helen Furr was cultivating was quite a pleasant one. The voice Georgine Skeene was cultivating was, some said, a better one. The voice Helen Furr was cultivating she cultivated and it was quite completely a pleasant enough one then, a cultivated enough one then. The voice Georgine Skeene was cultivating she did not cultivate too much. She cultivated it quite some. She cultivated and she would sometime go on cultivating it and it was not then an unpleasant one, it would not be then an unpleasant one, it would be a quite richly enough cultivated one, it would be quite richly enough to be a pleasant enough one.

They were gay where there were many cultivating something. The two were gay there, were regularly gay there. Georgine Skeene would have liked to do more travelling. They did some travelling, not very much travelling, Georgine Skeene would have liked to do more travelling, Helen Furr did not care about doing travelling, she liked to stay in a place and be gay there.

They stayed in a place and were gay there, both of them stayed there, they stayed together there, they were gay there, they were regularly gay there.

They went quite often, not very often, but they did go back to where Helen Furr had a pleasant enough home and then Georgine Skeene went to a place where her brother had quite some distinction. They both went, every few years, went visiting to where Helen Furr had quite a pleasant home. Certainly Helen Furr would not find it gay to stay, she did not find it gay, she said she would not stay, she said she did not find it gay, she said she would not stay where she did not find it gay, she said she found it gay where she did stay and she did stay there where very many were cultivating something. She did stay there. She always did find it gay there.

She went to see them where she had always been living and where she did not find it gay. She had a pleasant home there, Mrs. Furr was a pleasant enough woman, Mr. Furr was a pleasant enough man, Helen told them and they were not worrying, that she did not find it gay living where she had always been living.

Georgine Skeene and Helen Furr were living where they were both cultivating their voices and they were gay there. They visited where Helen Furr had come from and then they went to where they were living where they were then regularly living.

There were some dark and heavy men there then. There were some who were not so heavy and some who were not so dark. Helen Furr and Georgine Skeene sat regularly with them. They sat regularly with the ones who were dark and heavy. They sat regularly with the ones who were not so dark. They sat regularly with the ones that were not so heavy. They sat with them regularly, sat with some of them. They went with them regularly went with them. They were regular then, they were gay then, they were where they wanted to be then where it was gay to be then, they were regularly gay then. There were men there then who were dark and heavy and they sat with them with Helen Furr and Georgine Skeene and they went with them with Miss Furr and Miss Skeene, and they went with the heavy and dark men Miss Furr and Miss Skeene went with them, and they sat with them, Miss Furr and Miss Skeene sat with them, and there were other men, some were not heavy men and they sat with Miss Furr and Miss

Skeene and Miss Furr and Miss Skeene sat with them, and there were other men who were not dark men and they sat with Miss Furr and Miss Skeene and Miss Furr and Miss Skeene sat with them. Miss Furr and Miss Skeene went with them and they went with Miss Furr and Miss Skeene, some who were not heavy men, some who were not dark men. Miss Furr and Miss Skeene sat regularly, they sat with some men. Miss Furr and Miss Skeene went and there were some men with them. There were men and Miss Furr and Miss Skeene went with them, went somewhere with them, went with some of them.

Helen Furr and Georgine Skeene were regularly living where very many were living and cultivating in themselves something. Helen Furr and Georgine Skeene were living very regularly then, being very regular then in being gay then. They did then learn many ways to be gay and they were then being gay being quite regular in being gay, being gay and they were learning little things, little things in ways of being gay, they were very regular then, they were learning very many little things in ways of being gay, they were being gay and using these little things they were learning to have to be gay with regularly gay with then and they were gay the same amount they had been gay. They were quite gay, they were quite regular, they were learning little things, gay little things, they were gay inside them the same amount they had been gay, they were gay the same length of time they had been gay every day.

They were regular in being gay, they learned little things that are things in being gay, they learned many little things that are things in being gay, they were gay every day, they were regular, they were gay, they were gay the same length of time every day, they were gay, they were quite regularly gay.

Georgine Skeene went away to stay two months with her brother. Helen Furr did not go then to stay with her father and her mother. Helen Furr stayed there where they had been regularly living the two of them and she would then certainly not be lonesome, she would go on being gay. She did go on being gay. She was not any more gay but she was gay longer every day than they had been being gay when they were together being gay. She was gay then quite exactly the same way. She learned a few more little ways of being in being gay. She was quite gay and in the same way, the same way she had been gay and she was gay a little longer in the day, more of each day she was gay. She was gay longer every day than when the two of them had been being gay. She was gay quite in the way they had been gay, quite in the same way.

She was not lonesome then, she was not at all feeling any need of having Georgine Skeene. She was not astonished at this thing. She would have been a little astonished by this thing but she knew she was not astonished at anything and so she was not astonished at this thing not astonished at not feeling any need of having Georgine Skeene.

Helen Furr had quite a completely pleasant voice and it was quite well enough cultivated and she could use it and she did use it but then there was not any way of working at cultivating a completely pleasant voice when it has become a quite completely well enough cultivated one, and there was not much use in using it when one was not wanting it to be helping to make one a gay one. Helen Furr was not needing using her voice to be a gay one. She was gay then and sometimes she used her voice and she was not using it very often. It was quite completely enough cultivated and it was quite completely a pleasant one and she did not use it very often. She was then, she was quite exactly as gay as she had been, she was gay a little longer in the day than she had been.

She was gay exactly the same way. She was never tired of being gay that way. She had learned very many little ways to use in being gay. Very many were telling about using other ways in being gay. She was gay enough, she was always gay exactly the same way, she was always learning little things to use in being gay, she was telling about using other ways in being gay, she was telling about learning other ways in being gay, she was learning other ways in being gay, she would be using other ways in being gay, she would always be gay in the same way, when Georgine Skeene was there not so long each day as when Georgine Skeene was away.

She came to using many ways in being gay, she came to use every way in being gay. She went on living where many were cultivating something and she was gay, she had used every way to be gay.

They did not live together then Helen Furr and Georgine Skeene. Helen Furr lived there the longer where they had been living regularly together. Then neither of them were living there any longer. Helen Furr was living somewhere else then and telling some about being gay and she was gay then and she was living quite regularly then. She was regularly gay then. She was quite regular in being gay then. She remembered all the little ways of being gay. She used all the little ways of being gay. She was quite regularly gay. She told many then the way of being gay, she taught very many then little ways they could use in being gay. She was living very well, she was gay then, she went on living then, she was regular in being gay, she always was living very well and was gay very well and was telling about little ways one could be learning to use in being gay, and later was telling them quite often, telling them again and again.

Amy Lowell
(1874–1925)

Amy Lowell's achievements as a writer and a woman who claimed the right to her preferred lifestyle were all the more remarkable because she came from an extremely prominent, upper-class family. As a child and young woman she made some attempts to behave in the manner expected of her. She went to dancing school from the time she was a subsubdeb, she became a debutante, dated, and even almost became engaged, despite her discomfort in fulfilling such a role.

While the diaries Amy Lowell kept as an adolescent evince an early bisexuality, as she grew older she became less interested in men and finally dared to give up all pretense of heterosexuality. Her fascination with the theater led to her involvement for a time with the musical starlet Lina Abarbanell. It also led her to her first muse, the tragedian Eleonora Duse, whom she saw on stage in 1902. Duse's talent and beauty inspired Lowell to poetry: "It loosed a bolt in my brain and I knew where my true function lay," she later recalled. Her first poem was addressed to the actress and marked the beginning of Lowell's career as a writer.

Like Gertrude Stein (see p. 455), who had in common with her placement in the family (each was the youngest child) and girth (each weighed about 250 pounds), Lowell was a force to be reckoned with by the sheer power of her personality. Also like Stein, Lowell cultivated a pose of eccentricity and was delighted when the *New York Tribune* reported on its front page that she smoked "big black cigars." Actually, it was small, light Manilas, which came elegantly wrapped in tinfoil and tissue paper, that Lowell favored, but she forgave the inaccuracy because she knew the phrase "big, black cigars" would better *épater les bourgeois* than "delicate Manilas."

Not having been blessed with physical beauty herself, Lowell was a great appreciater of it in others. The woman on whom she finally settled her affections when they met in 1909, and who became her mate until Lowell's death, was another beautiful actress, Ada Dwyer Russell. One of Lowell's most often anthologized poems, "A Decade," published in 1919, celebrates their tenth anniversary. Many of her most successful poems, in fact, are about Russell and Lowell's love for her, as she freely admitted to her acquaintances if asked. When Lowell's friend John Livingston Lowes wrote to congratulate her on another frequently anthologized poem, "Madonna of the Evening Flowers," saying that the "beloved" in the poem reminded him of Russell, Lowell responded, "I am very glad indeed that you liked 'Madonna of the Evening Flowers.' How could so exact a portrait remain unrecognized?" The sequence of forty-three poems that comprise the section "Two Speak Together" in *Pictures of the Floating World* (1919), arguably her best poetry, is a document of their life together.

Lowell managed to write and publish lesbian poetry in the teens and twenties of this century because, again like Gertrude Stein, she obfuscated. In 1918 Lowell wrote to D. H. Lawrence, whose patron and champion she was, advising him about his difficulties in finding a publisher since the suppression (primarily for its lesbian scene) of his novel *The Rainbow*:

> I know there is no use in counselling you to make any concessions to public opinions in your books and, although I regret sincerely that you cut yourself off from being published by an outspokenness which the English public does not understand, I regret it not in itself . . . but simply because it keeps the world from knowing what a great novelist you are. I think that you could top them all if you would be a little more reticent on this one subject. You need not change your attitude a particle. You can simply use an india rubber in certain places, and then you can come into your own as it ought to be. . . . When one is surrounded by prejudice and blindness, it seems to me that the only thing to do is to get over in spite of it and not constantly run foul of these same prejudices which, after all, hurts oneself and the spreading of one's work, and does not do a thing to right the prejudice.

As Lowell predicted, there was no use counseling D. H. Lawrence to such action, but Lowell took her own advice. She did not "change [her] attitude a particle." As the autobiographical details in many of her poems suggest, her lyric poetry is often about herself and the women (particularly Ada) who were her lovers. But she encoded just enough to disguise her subject. For example, in the poems of "Two Speak Together" she occasionally, almost perfunctorily, threw in a masculine pronoun or noun in reference to the speaker (who was certainly herself).

Of course those who knew her were not deceived, and despite her care, Lowell eventually paid for her society's prejudice through loss of her literary reputation after her death. Although she won the Pulitzer Prize for her posthumous volume of poems *What's O'Clock*, the attacks on her soon became virulent, as in a particularly scurrilous 1926 book by Clement Wood, *Amy Lowell*, in which he was determined to diminish Lowell's reputation specifically because she was a lesbian. Wood argued that her poetry did not "word a common cry of many hearts," and he concluded that she might qualify "as an impassioned singer of her own desires; and she may well be laureate also of as many as stand beside her," but nonlesbian readers would find nothing in her verse. Of course if an author's heterosexuality is the touchstone of whether his or her writing succeeds in "word[ing] a common cry of many hearts," much of the literature that has generally been accepted in the Euro-American literary canon would have to be thrown out.

Those who did not recognize that Lowell had been a lesbian stigmatized her anyway after her death as an unattractive, overweight woman and an "old maid." An article titled "Amy Lowell as a Poet," which appeared in the *Saturday Review of Literature* in 1927, complained that her poetry was bad because she was "cut off from the prime biological experiences of life by her tragic physical predicament." Because her life was so limited, the critic went on to say (in error and ignorance), her poems are merely decorative, lacking elemental passion: "as always happens when the sources of inspiration are literary and secondary rather than primarily the expression of emotional experience." The nature of the "emotional experience" most of Lowell's lyric poems express needed to be hidden enough to escape the censors, but her insensitive critics notwithstanding, those experiences were the stimulus to some of the most inspired love poetry of the twentieth century.

FURTHER READING: Amy Lowell, *Sword Blades and Poppy Seed* (Boston: Houghton Mifflin, 1914); *Pictures of the Floating World* (Boston: Houghton Mifflin, 1919); *What's O'Clock* (Boston: Houghton Mifflin, 1925); *Ballads for Sale* (Boston: Houghton Mifflin, 1927). S. Foster Damon, *Amy Lowell: A Chronicle, With Extracts from her Correspondence* (Boston: Houghton Mifflin, 1935). Lillian Faderman, "Warding Off the Watch and Ward Society: Amy Lowell's Treatment of the Lesbian Theme," *Gay Books Bibliography*, I: 2 (Summer 1979), 23–27. Jean Gould, *Amy: The World of Amy Lowell and the Imagist Movement* (New York: Dodd Mead, 1975). Susan Gubar, "Sapphistries," *Signs*, 10: 1 (Autumn 1984), 43–62. Glenn Richard Ruihley, *The Thorn of a Rose: Amy Lowell Reconsidered* (Hamden, Conn.: Archon Books, 1975).

From "Two Speak Together"

THE LETTER

Little cramped words scrawling all over the paper
Like draggled fly's legs,
What can you tell of the flaring moon
Through the oak leaves?
Or of my uncurtained window and the bare floor

Spattered with moonlight?
Your silly quirks and twists have nothing in them
Of blossoming hawthorns,
And this paper is dull, crisp, smooth, virgin of loveliness
Beneath my hand.

I am tired, Beloved, of chafing my heart against
The want of you;
Of squeezing it into little inkdrops,
And posting it.
And I scald alone, here, under the fire
Of the great moon.

VENUS TRANSIENS

Tell me,
Was Venus more beautiful
Than you are,
When she topped
The crinkled waves,
Drifting shoreward
On her plaited shell?
Was Botticelli's vision
Fairer than mine;
And were the painted rosebuds
He tossed his lady,
Of better worth
Than the words I blow about you
To cover your too great loveliness
As with a gauze
Of misted silver?
For me,
You stand poised
In the blue and buoyant air,
Cinctured by bright winds,
Treading the sunlight.
And the waves which precede you
Ripple and stir
The sands at my feet.

MADONNA OF THE EVENING FLOWERS

All day long I have been working,
Now I am tired.
I call: "Where are you?"
But there is only the oak-tree rustling in the wind.
The house is very quiet,
The sun shines in on your books,
On your scissors and thimble just put down,
But you are not there.
Suddenly I am lonely:
Where are you?
I go about searching.

Then I see you,
Standing under a spire of pale blue larkspur,
With a basket of roses on your arm.
You are cool, like silver,
And you smile.
I think the Canterbury bells are playing little tunes.

You tell me that the peonies need spraying,
That the columbines have overrun all bounds,
That the pyrus japonica should be cut back and rounded.
You tell me these things.
But I look at you, heart of silver,
White heart-flame of polished silver,
Burning beneath the blue steeples of the larkspur,
And I long to kneel instantly at your feet,
While all about us peal the loud, sweet *Te Deums* of the Canterbury bells.

THE WEATHER-COCK POINTS SOUTH

I put your leaves aside,
One by one:
The stiff, broad outer leaves;
The smaller ones,
Pleasant to touch, veined with purple;
The glazed inner leaves.
One by one
I parted you from your leaves,
Until you stood up like a white flower
Swaying slightly in the evening wind.

White flower,
Flower of wax, of jade, of unstreaked agate;
Flower with surfaces of ice,
With shadows faintly crimson.
Where in all the garden is there such a flower?
The stars crowd through the lilac leaves
To look at you.
The low moon brightens you with silver.

The bud is more than the calyx.
There is nothing to equal a white bud,
Of no colour, and of all,
Burnished by moonlight,
Thrust upon by a softly-swinging wind.

THE ARTIST

Why do you subdue yourself in golds and purples?
Why do you dim yourself with folded silks?
Do you not see that I can buy brocades in any draper's shop,
And that I am choked in the twilight of all these colours?
How pale you would be, and startling,
How quiet;
But your curves would spring upward
Like a clear jet of flung water,
You would quiver like a shot-up spray of water,
You would waver, and relapse, and tremble.
And I too should tremble,
Watching.

Murex-dyes and tinsel—
And yet I think I could bear your beauty unshaded.

THE GARDEN BY MOONLIGHT

A black cat among roses,
Phlox, lilac-misted under a first-quarter moon,
The sweet smells of heliotrope and night-scented stock.
The garden is very still,
It is dazed with moonlight,
Contented with perfume,
Dreaming the opium dreams of its folded poppies.

Firefly lights open and vanish
High as the tip buds of the golden glow
Low as the sweet alyssum flowers at my feet.
Moon-shimmer on leaves and trellises,
Moon-spikes shafting through the snowball bush.
Only the little faces of the ladies' delight are alert and staring,
Only the cat, padding between the roses,
Shakes a branch and breaks the chequered pattern
As water is broken by the falling of a leaf.
Then you come,
And you are quiet like the garden,
And white like the alyssum flowers,
And beautiful as the silent sparks of the fireflies.
Ah, Beloved, do you see those orange lilies?
They knew my mother,
But who belonging to me will they know
When I am gone.

BULLION

My thoughts
Chink against my ribs
And roll about like silver hail-stones.
I should like to spill them out,
And pour them, all shining,
Over you.
But my heart is shut upon them
And holds them straitly.

Come, You! and open my heart;
That my thoughts torment me no longer,
But glitter in your hair.

A SHOWER

That sputter of rain, flipping the hedgerows
And making the highways hiss,
How I love it!
And the touch of you upon my arm
As you press against me that my umbrella
May cover you.

Tinkle of drops on stretched silk.
Wet murmur through green branches.

SUMMER RAIN

All night our room was outer-walled with rain.
Drops fell and flattened on the tin roof,
And rang like little disks of metal.
Ping!—Ping!—and there was not a pinpoint of silence between them.
The rain rattled and clashed,
And the slats of the shutters danced and glittered.
But to me the darkness was red-gold and crocus-coloured
With your brightness,
And the words you whispered to me
Sprang up and flamed—orange torches against the rain.
Torches against the wall of cool, silver rain!

APRIL

A bird chirped at my window this morning,
And over the sky is drawn a light network of clouds.
Come,
Let us go out into the open,
For my heart leaps like a fish that is ready to spawn.

I will lie under the beech-trees,
Under the grey branches of the beech-trees,
In a blueness of little squills and crocuses.
I will lie among the little squills
And be delivered of this overcharge of beauty,
And that which is born shall be a joy to you
Who love me.

LEFT BEHIND

White phlox and white hydrangeas,
High, thin clouds,
A low, warm sun.
So it is this afternoon.
But the phlox will be a drift of petals,

And the hydrangeas stained and fallen
Before you come again.

I cannot look at the flowers,
Nor the lifting leaves of the trees.
Without you, there is no garden,
No bright colours,
No shining leaves.
There is only space,
Stretching endlessly forward—
And I walk, bent, unseeing,
Waiting to catch the first faint scuffle
Of withered leaves.

A SPRIG OF ROSEMARY

I cannot see your face.
When I think of you,
It is your hands which I see.
Your hands
Sewing,
Holding a book,
Resting for a moment on the sill of a window.
My eyes keep always the sight of your hands,
But my heart holds the sound of your voice,
And the soft brightness which is your soul.

PREPARATION

To-day I went into a shop where they sell spectacles.

"Sir," said the shopman, "what can I do for you?
Are you far-sighted or near-sighted?"
"Neither the one nor the other," said I.
"I can read the messages passing along the telegraph wires,
And I can see the antennae of a fly
Perched upon the bridge of my nose."

"Rose-coloured spectacles, perhaps?" suggested the shopman.

"Indeed, no," said I.
"Were I to add them to my natural vision
I should see everything ruined with blood."

"Green spectacles," opined the shopman.

"By no means," said I.
"I am far too prone to that colour at moments.
No. You can give me some smoked glasses
For I have to meet a train this afternoon."

"What a world yours must be, Sir."
Observed the shopman as he wrapped up the spectacles,
"When it requires to be dimmed by smoked glasses."

"Not a world," said I, and laid the money down on the counter,
"Certainly not a world.
Good-day."

A DECADE

When you came, you were like red wine and honey,
And the taste of you burnt my mouth with its sweetness.
Now you are like morning bread,
Smooth and pleasant.
I hardly taste you at all for I know your savour,
But I am completely nourished.

FRIMAIRE

Dearest, we are like two flowers
Blooming last in a yellowing garden,
A purple aster flower and a red one
Standing alone in a withered desolation.

The garden plants are shattered and seeded,
One brittle leaf scrapes against another,
Fiddling echoes of a rush of petals.
Now only you and I nodding together.

Many were with us; they have all faded.
Only we are purple and crimson,
Only we in the dew-clear mornings,
Smarten into colour as the sun rises.

When I scarcely see you in the flat moonlight,
And later when my cold roots tighten,

I am anxious for the morning,
I cannot rest in fear of what may happen.

You or I—and I am a coward.
Surely frost should take the crimson.
Purple is a finer colour,
Very splendid in isolation.

So we nod above the broken
Stems of flowers almost rotted.
Many mornings there cannot be now
For us both. Ah, Dear, I love you!

Katherine Mansfield
(1888–1923)

Katherine Mansfield (pseudonym of Kathleen Beauchamp) often dealt in her work with bisexuality, although her treatment of lesbianism was subtle enough so that critics easily could, and frequently did, permit themselves to miss it. However, as her journals and letters clearly reveal, her bisexuality dominated her life. Her recent biographers, confronted with that material in a more open era, have devoted large portions of their books to her erotic relationships with women. Their thoroughness has enabled contemporary readers to understand better what may have been mystifying to earlier readers, who were not prepared to find lesbian content in the work of a woman who was twice married to men. We know now, for example, that during the writing of her most famous story, "Bliss" (1918), Mansfield was living in France with her long-time woman lover, Ida Baker, and preoccupied with the complications of her triangle with Ida and John Middleton Murry. Such information helps to reveal the bisexual content of the story that critics in the past refused to see.

At her healthiest, Mansfield viewed her bisexuality as a gift. She described it once as the ability to experience "the whole octave of sex." But such a fearless outlook was exceptional in her anxious life. Having internalized the prevailing notion of her day that homosexuality was sinful and abnormal, much like her contemporary Vita Sackville-West (see p. 268), she considered herself divided into a night self and a day self, the former being her lesbian side and the cause of her unhappiness; the latter being the happier heterosexual expression of her personality. In reality, of course, the division of her generally discontented nature was not that clear-cut.

Mansfield's homosexual experiences date back to her days in a New Zealand boarding school, when, as biographer Jeffrey Meyers describes it, she "fell passionately in love with a half-caste Maori princess and heiress," Maata Mahupuka, another student, who was a couple of years older than Mansfield. The relationship is recorded in an unfinished novel, "Maata," written in 1913. In it Mansfield recalls, "Maata felt half suffocated by the strain of the child's little eager body, her smoothering [sic] kisses, her fumbling hands, and yet it comforted her. . . . It was something real and human and safe." Mansfield's description of Maata's very ambivalent reaction to her may be seen to characterize Mansfield's response to her own lesbian experiences throughout her life.

Despite her ambivalence about lesbianism, her women lovers often represented to her the nurturing, loving figure that she felt her mother refused to be. In 1907, at the age of eighteen, she was almost engaged to a young musician, Arnold Trowell (whom she called Caesar), when she fell in love with a woman, Edie Bendall. She wrote in her journal, "Caesar is losing hold of me. Edie is waiting for me. I shall slip into her arms. They are safest. Do you love me?" But another entry about Edie illustrates the terrible conflict Mansfield often suffered in her lesbian relationships:

> Last night I spent in her arms—and to-night I hate her—which, being interpreted, means that I adore her: that I cannot lie in my bed and not feel the magic of her body: which means that sex means as nothing to me. I feel more powerfully all those so-termed sexual impulses with her than I have with any man. She enthrals, enslaves me—and her personal self—her body absolute—is my worship. I feel that to lie with my head on her breast is to feel what life can hold. . . .
>
> In my life—so much Love in imagination; in reality 18 barren years—never pure spontaneous affectionate impulse. Adonis was— dare I seek into the heart of me—nothing but a pose. And now she comes—and pillowed against her, clinging to her hands, her face against mine, I am a child, a woman, and more than half man.

Despite her love-hate reaction to lesbianism, occasional stories, such as "Bains Turc" from *In a German Pension* (1911), focus on what Mansfield showed in this journal entry to be her feelings of comfort and fulfillment through love between women.

In 1903 Mansfield went with her family to England and became a student at Oxford. There she met Ida Baker, a fellow student who soon fell in love with her and with whom Mansfield was to spend much of her life in a stormy relationship. At least in part to escape from her lesbianism,

Mansfield married George Bowden, a man she barely knew. However, Ida accompanied her to the registry office on the day of her marriage, and it was to Ida that Mansfield ran on her wedding night when she decided she did not wish to consummate her marriage. Mansfield's mother, believing (along with Mansfield's husband) that she left the marriage because of her lesbianism, attempted to "cure" her with cold baths. When that did not work, she disinherited Mansfield.

After leaving her husband, Mansfield had numerous affairs with other men—and women. For a time, to support herself she read her works in public and acted on the stage. According to Claire Tomalin in *Katherine Mansfield: A Secret Life*, both Vera Brittain and Rebecca West spoke of Mansfield's appearance in 1913 at a reputedly lesbian nightclub, the Cave of the Golden Calf, where she is said to have performed.

Her relationship with John Middleton Murry began in 1911. According to Murry it was Mansfield who pursued him, who insisted they become lovers, and finally in 1918 insisted that they marry. Through all this time she continued her relationship with Ida, arranging at one point that the three of them live in a *ménage à trois*. When that did not work, Mansfield proposed that she spend six months of the year living with Murry in England and the other six months traveling abroad with Ida. But the tuberculosis that finally caused Mansfield's death at the age of thirty-five made that plan impractical.

Throughout much of her illness Ida stayed with Mansfield as a faithful nurse, despite the almost insane love-hate feelings that often made Mansfield abusive. Typically, in 1919 Mansfield wrote to Murry about her life with Ida: "This *awful relationship* [italics are Mansfield's] living on in its secret corrupt way beside my relationship with you is very extraordinary; no one would believe it. I am two selves—one my true self—the other that she creates in me to destroy my true self." Regardless of such vehemence and venom, and characteristic of her tortured ambivalence, she wrote to Ida the last year of her life, "Try and believe and keep on believing without signs from me that I do love you and want you for my wife."

FURTHER READING: *The Journal of Katherine Mansfield*, Definitive Edition, ed. J. M. Murry (London: Constable, 1954). *The Scrapbook of Katherine Mansfield*, ed. J. M. Murry (New York: Alfred A. Knopf, 1940). Katherine Mansfield, *In a German Pension* (London: Stephen Swift, 1911); *The Aloe*, ed. J. M. Murry (London: Constable, 1930). "The Unpublished Manuscripts of Katherine Mansfield, ed. Margaret Scott, six parts, *Turnbull Library Record* (Wellington), new ser., see esp. "Juliet" (March 1970), Juvenilia from 1906 (November 1970), and two "Maata" fragments (May 1974). C. A. Hankin, *Katherine Mansfield and Her Confessional Stories* (New York: St. Martin's Press, 1983). Jeffrey Meyers, *Katherine Mansfield: A Biography*

(New York: New Directions, 1978). Claire Tomalin, *Katherine Mansfield: A Secret Life* (New York: Alfred A. Knopf, 1988).

Bliss

Although Bertha Young was thirty she still had moments like this when she wanted to run instead of walk, to take dancing steps on and off the pavement, to bowl a hoop, to throw something up in the air and catch it again, or to stand still and laugh at—nothing—at nothing, simply.

What can you do if you are thirty and, turning the corner of your own street, you are overcome, suddenly, by a feeling of bliss—absolute bliss!— as though you'd suddenly swallowed a bright piece of that late afternoon sun and it burned in your bosom, sending out a little shower of sparks into every particle, into every finger and toe? . . .

Oh, is there no way you can express it without being "drunk and disorderly"? How idiotic civilization is! Why be given a body if you have to keep it shut up in a case like a rare, rare fiddle?

"No, that about the fiddle is not quite what I mean," she thought, running up the steps and feeling in her bag for the key—she's forgotten it, as usual—and rattling the letter-box. "It's not what I mean, because— Thank you, Mary"—she went into the hall. "Is nurse back?"

"Yes, M'm."

"And has the fruit come?"

"Yes, M'm. Everything's come."

"Bring the fruit up to the dining-room, will you? I'll arrange it before I go upstairs."

It was dusky in the dining-room and quite chilly. But all the same Bertha threw off her coat; she could not bear the tight clasp of it another moment, and the cold air fell on her arms.

But in her bosom there was still that bright glowing place—that shower of little sparks coming from it. It was almost unbearable. She hardly dared to breathe for fear of fanning it higher, and yet she breathed deeply, deeply. She hardly dared to look into the cold mirror—but she did look, and it gave her back a woman, radiant, with smiling, trembling lips, with big, dark eyes and an air of listening, waiting for something . . . divine to happen . . . that she knew must happen . . . infallibly.

Mary brought in the fruit on a tray and with it a glass bowl, and a blue dish, very lovely, with a strange sheen on it as though it had been dipped in milk.

"Shall I turn on the light, M'm?"

"No, thank you. I can see quite well."

There were tangerines and apples stained with strawberry pink. Some yellow pears, smooth as silk, some white grapes covered with a silver bloom and a big cluster of purple ones. These last she had bought to tone in with the new dining-room carpet. Yes, that did sound rather far-fetched and absurd, but it was really why she had bought them. She had thought in the shop: "I must have some purple ones to bring the carpet up to the table." And it had seemed quite sense at the time.

When she had finished with them and had made two pyramids of these bright round shapes, she stood away from the table to get the effect—and it really was most curious. For the dark table seemed to melt into the dusky light and the glass dish and the blue bowl to float in the air. This, of course in her present mood, was so incredibly beautiful. . . . She began to laugh.

"No, no. I'm getting hysterical." And she seized her bag and coat and ran upstairs to the nursery.

Nurse sat at a low table giving Little B her supper after her bath. The baby had on a white flannel gown and a blue woollen jacket, and her dark, fine hair was brushed up into a funny little peak. She looked up when she saw her mother and began to jump.

"Now, my lovey, eat it up like a good girl," said Nurse, setting her lips in a way that Bertha knew, and that meant she had come into the nursery at another wrong moment.

"Has she been good, Nanny?"

"She's been a little sweet all the afternoon," whispered Nanny. "We went to the park and I sat down on a chair and took her out of the pram and a big dog came along and put his head on my knee and she clutched its ear, tugged it. Oh, you should have seen her."

Bertha wanted to ask if it wasn't rather dangerous to let her clutch at a strange dog's ear. But she did not dare to. She stood watching them, her hands by her side, like the poor little girl in front of the rich little girl with the doll.

The baby looked up at her again, stared, and then smiled so charmingly that Bertha couldn't help crying:

"Oh, Nanny, do let me finish giving her her supper while you put the bath things away."

"Well, M'm, she oughtn't to be changed hands while she's eating," said Nanny, still whispering. "It unsettles her; it's very likely to upset her."

How absurd it was. Why have a baby if it has to be kept—not in a case like a rare, rare fiddle—but in another woman's arms?

"Oh, I must!" said she.

Very offended, Nanny handed her over.

"Now, don't excite her after her supper. You know you do, M'm. And I have such a time with her after!"

Thank heaven! Nanny went out of the room with the bath towels.

"Now I've got you to myself, my little precious," said Bertha, as the baby leaned against her.

She ate delightfully, holding up her lips for the spoon and then waving her hands. Sometimes she wouldn't let the spoon go; and sometimes, just as Bertha had filled it, she waved it away to the four winds.

When the soup was finished Bertha turned round to the fire.

"You're nice—you're very nice!" said she, kissing her warm baby. "I'm fond of you. I like you."

And, indeed, she loved Little B so much—her neck as she bent forward, her exquisite toes as they shone transparent in the firelight—that all her feeling of bliss came back again, and again she didn't know how to express it—what to do with it.

"You're wanted on the telephone," said Nanny, coming back in triumph and seizing *her* Little B.

Down she flew. It was Harry.

"Oh, is that you, Ber? Look here. I'll be late. I'll take a taxi and come along as quickly as I can, but get dinner put back ten minutes—will you? All right?"

"Yes, perfectly. Oh, Harry!"

"Yes?"

What had she to say? She'd nothing to say. She only wanted to get in touch with him for a moment. She couldn't absurdly cry: "Hasn't it been a divine day!"

"What is it?" rapped out the little voice.

"Nothing. *Entendu*," said Bertha, and hung up the receiver, thinking how more than idiotic civilization was.

They had people coming to dinner. The Norman Knights—a very sound couple—he was about to start a theatre, and she was awfully keen on interior decoration, a young man, Eddie Warren, who had just published a little book of poems and whom everybody was asking to dine, and a "find" of Bertha's called Pearl Fulton. What Miss Fulton did, Bertha didn't know. They had met at the club and Bertha had fallen in love with her, as she always did fall in love with beautiful women who had something strange about them.

The provoking thing was that, though they had been about together and met a number of times and really talked, Bertha couldn't yet make her out. Up to a certain point Miss Fulton was rarely, wonderfully frank, but the certain point was there, and beyond that she would not go.

Was there anything beyond it? Harry said "No." Voted her dullish, and "cold like all blond women, with a touch, perhaps, of anaemia of the brain." But Bertha wouldn't agree with him; not yet, at any rate.

"No, the way she has of sitting with her head a little on one side, and smiling, has something behind it, Harry, and I must find out what that something is."

"Most likely it's a good stomach," answered Harry.

He made a point of catching Bertha's heels with replies of that kind . . . "liver frozen, my dear girl," or "pure flatulence," or "kidney disease," . . . and so on. For some strange reason Bertha liked this, and almost admired it in him very much.

She went into the drawing-room and lighted the fire; then, picking up the cushions, one by one, that Mary had disposed so carefully, she threw them back on to the chairs and the couches. That made all the difference; the room came alive at once. As she was about to throw the last one she surprised herself by suddenly hugging it to her, passionately, passionately. But it did not put out the fire in her bosom. Oh, on the contrary!

The windows of the drawing-room opened on to a balcony overlooking the garden. At the far end, against the wall, there was a tall, slender pear tree in fullest, richest bloom; it stood perfect, as though becalmed against the jade-green sky. Bertha couldn't help feeling, even from this distance, that it had not a single bud or a faded petal. Down below, in the garden beds, the red and yellow tulips, heavy with flowers, seemed to lean upon the dusk. A grey cat, dragging its belly, crept across the lawn, and a black one, its shadow, trailed after. The sight of them, so intent and so quick, gave Bertha a curious shiver.

"What creepy things cats are!" she stammered, and she turned away from the window and began walking up and down. . . .

How strong the jonquils smelled in the warm room. Too strong? Oh, no. And yet, as though overcome, she flung down on a couch and pressed her hands to her eyes.

"I'm too happy—too happy!" she murmured.

And she seemed to see on her eyelids the lovely pear tree with its wide open blossoms as a symbol of her own life.

Really—really—she had everything. She was young. Harry and she were as much in love as ever, and they got on together splendidly and were really good pals. She had an adorable baby. They didn't have to worry about money. They had this absolutely satisfactory house and garden. And friends—modern, thrilling friends, writers and painters and poets or people keen on social questions—just the kind of friends they wanted. And then there were books, and there was music, and she had found a wonderful little dressmaker, and they were going abroad in the summer, and their new cook made the most superb omelettes. . . .

"I'm absurd! Absurd!" She sat up; but she felt quite dizzy, quite drunk. It must have been the spring.

Yes, it was the spring. Now she was so tired she could not drag herself upstairs to dress.

A white dress, a string of jade beads, green shoes and stockings. It wasn't intentional. She had thought of this scheme hours before she stood at the drawing-room window.

Her petals rustled softly into the hall, and she kissed Mrs. Norman Knight, who was taking off the most amusing orange coat with a procession of black monkeys round the hem and up the fronts.

". . . Why! Why! Why is the middle-class so stodgy—so utterly without a sense of humour! My dear, it's only by a fluke that I am here at all—Norman being the protective fluke. For my darling monkeys so upset the train that it rose to a man and simply ate me with its eyes. Didn't laugh—wasn't amused—that I should have loved. No, just stared—and bored me through and through."

"But the cream of it was," said Norman, pressing a large tortoiseshell-rimmed monocle into his eye, "you don't mind me telling this, Face, do you?" (In their home and among their friends they called each other Face and Mug.) "The cream of it was when she, being full fed, turned to the woman beside her and said: 'Haven't you ever seen a monkey before?' "

"Oh, yes!" Mrs. Norman Knight joined in the laughter. "Wasn't that too absolutely creamy?"

And a funnier thing still was that now her coat was off she did look like a very intelligent monkey—who had even made that yellow silk dress out of scraped banana skins. And her amber ear-rings; they were like little dangling nuts.

"This is a sad, sad fall!" said Mug, pausing in front of Little B's perambulator. "When the perambulator comes into the hall—" and he waved the rest of the quotation away.

The bell rang. It was lean, pale Eddie Warren (as usual) in a state of acute distress.

"It *is* the right house, *isn't* it?" he pleaded.

"Oh, I think so—I hope so," said Bertha brightly.

"I have had such a *dreadful* experience with a taxi-man; he was *most* sinister. I couldn't get him to *stop*. The *more* I knocked and called the *faster* he went. And *in* the moonlight this *bizarre* figure with the *flattened* head *crouching* over the *lit-tle* wheel. . . ."

He shuddered, taking off an immense white silk scarf. Bertha noticed that his socks were white, too—most charming.

"But how dreadful!" she cried.

"Yes, it really was," said Eddie, following her into the drawing-room. "I saw myself *driving* through Eternity in a *timeless* taxi."

He knew the Norman Knights. In fact, he was going to write a play for N. K. when the theatre scheme came off.

"Well, Warren, how's the play?" said Norman Knight, dropping his monocle and giving his eye a moment in which to rise to the surface before it was screwed down again.

And Mrs. Norman Knight: "Oh, Mr. Warren, what happy socks?"

"I *am* so glad you like them," said he, staring at his feet. "They seem to have got so *much* whiter since the moon rose." And he turned his lean sorrowful young face to Bertha. "There *is* a moon, you know."

She wanted to cry: "I am sure there is—often—often!"

He really was a most attractive person. But so was Face, crouched before the fire in her banana skins, and so was Mug, smoking a cigarette and saying as he flicked the ash: "Why doth the bridegroom tarry?"

"There he is, now."

Bang went the front door open and shut. Harry shouted: "Hullo, you people. Down in five minutes." And they heard him swarm up the stairs. Bertha couldn't help smiling; she knew how he loved doing things at high pressure. What, after all, did an extra five minutes matter? But he would pretend to himself that they mattered beyond measure. And then he would make a great point of coming into the drawing-room, extravagantly cool and collected.

Harry had such a zest for life. Oh, how she appreciated it in him. And his passion for fighting—for seeking in everything that came up against him another test of his power and of his courage—that, too, she understood. Even when it made him just occasionally, to other people, who didn't know him well, a little ridiculous perhaps. . . . For there were moments when he rushed into battle where no battle was. . . . She talked and laughed and positively forgot until he had come in (just as she had imagined) that Pearl Fulton had not turned up.

"I wonder if Miss Fulton has forgotten?"

"I expect so," said Harry. "Is she on the 'phone?"

"Ah! There's a taxi, now." And Bertha smiled with that little air of proprietorship that she always assumed while her women finds were new and mysterious. "She lives in taxis."

"She'll run to fat if she does," said Harry coolly, ringing the bell for dinner. "Frightful danger for blond women."

"Harry—don't," warned Bertha, laughing up at him.

Came another tiny moment, while they waited, laughing and talking, just a trifle too much at their ease, a trifle too unaware. And then Miss Fulton, all in silver, with a silver fillet binding her pale blond hair, came in smiling, her head a little on one side.

"Am I late?"

"No, not at all," said Bertha. "Come along." And she took her arm and they moved into the dining-room.

What was there in the touch of that cool arm that could fan—fan—start blazing—blazing—the fire of bliss that Bertha did not know what to do with?

Miss Fulton did not look at her; but then she seldom did look at people directly. Her heavy eyelids lay upon her eyes and the strange half smile came and went upon her lips as though she lived by listening rather than seeing. But Bertha knew, suddenly, as if the longest, most intimate look had passed between them—as if they had said to each other: "You, too?"—that Pearl Fulton, stirring the beautiful red soup in the grey plate, was feeling just what she was feeling.

And the others? Face and Mug, Eddie and Harry, their spoons rising and falling—dabbing their lips with their napkins, crumbling bread, fiddling with the forks and glasses and talking.

"I met her at the Alpha shore—the weirdest little person. She'd not only cut off her hair, but she seemed to have taken a dreadfully good snip off her legs and arms and her neck and her poor little nose as well."

"Isn't she very *liée* with Michael Oat?"

"The man who wrote *Love in False Teeth*?"

"He wants to write a play for me. One act. One man. Decides to commit suicide. Gives all the reasons why he should and why he shouldn't. And just as he has made up his mind either to do it or not to do it—curtain. Not half a bad idea."

"What's he going to call it—'Stomach Trouble'?"

"I *think* I've come across the *same* idea in a lit-tle French review, *quite* unknown in England."

No, they didn't share it. They were dears—dears—and she loved having them there, at her table, and giving them delicious food and wine. In fact, she longed to tell them how delightful they were, and what a decorative group they made, how they seemed to set one another off and how they reminded her of a play by Tchekof!

Harry was enjoying his dinner. It was part of his—well, not his nature, exactly, and certainly not his pose—his—something or other—to talk about food and to glory in his "shameless passion for the white flesh of the lobster" and "the green of pistachio ices—green and cold like the eyelids of Egyptian dancers."

When he looked up at her and said: "Bertha, this is a very admirable *soufflée!*" she almost could have wept with child-like pleasure.

Oh, why did she feel so tender towards the whole world tonight? Everything was good—was right. All that happened seemed to fill again her brimming cup of bliss.

And still, in the back of her mind, there was the pear tree. It would be silver now, in the light of poor dear Eddie's moon, silver as Miss Fulton, who sat there turning a tangerine in her slender fingers that were so pale a light seemed to come from them.

What she simply couldn't make out—what was miraculous—was how she should have guessed Miss Fulton's mood so exactly and so instantly. For she never doubted for a moment that she was right, and yet what had she to go on? Less than nothing.

"I believe this does happen very, very rarely between women. Never between men," thought Bertha. "But while I am making the coffee in the drawing-room perhaps she will 'give a sign.' "

What she meant by that she did not know, and what would happen after that she could not imagine.

While she thought like this she saw herself talking and laughing. She had to talk because of her desire to laugh.

"I must laugh or die."

But when she noticed Face's funny little habit of tucking something down the front of her bodice—as if she kept a tiny, secret hoard of nuts there, too—Bertha had to dig her nails into her hands—so as not to laugh too much.

It was over at last. And: "Come and see my new coffee machine," said Bertha.

"We only have a new coffee machine once a fortnight," said Harry. Face took her arm this time; Miss Fulton bent her head and followed after.

The fire had died down in the drawing-room to a red, flickering "nest of baby phœnixes," said Face.

"Don't turn up the light for a moment. It is so lovely." And down she crouched by the fire again. She was always cold . . . "without her little red flannel jacket, of course," thought Bertha.

At that moment Miss Fulton "gave the sign."

"Have you a garden?" said the cool, sleepy voice.

This was so exquisite on her part that all Bertha could do was to obey. She crossed the room, pulled the curtains apart, and opened those long windows.

"There!" she breathed.

And the two women stood side by side looking at the slender, flowering tree. Although it was so still it seemed, like the flame of a candle, to stretch up, to point, to quiver in the bright air, to grow taller and taller as they gazed—almost to touch the rim of the round, silver moon.

How long did they stand there? Both, as it were, caught in that circle of unearthly light, understanding each other perfectly, creatures of another world, and wondering what they were to do in this one with all this blissful treasure that burned in their bosoms and dropped, in silver flowers, from their hair and hands?

For ever—for a moment? And did Miss Fulton murmur: "Yes. Just *that*." Or did Bertha dream it?

Then the light was snapped on and Face made the coffee and Harry said: "My dear Mrs. Knight, don't ask me about my baby. I never see her. I shan't feel the slightest interest in her until she has a lover," and Mug took his eye out of the conservatory for a moment and then put it under glass again and Eddie Warren drank his coffee and set down the cup with a face of anguish as though he had drunk and seen the spider.

"What I want to do is to give the young men a show. I believe London is simply teeming with first-chop, unwritten plays. What I want to say to 'em is: 'Here's the theatre. Fire ahead.' "

"You know, my dear, I am going to decorate a room for the Jacob Nathans. Oh, I am so tempted to do a fried-fish scheme, with the backs of the chairs shaped like frying pans and lovely chip potatoes embroidered all over the curtains."

"The trouble with our young writing men is that they are still too romantic. You can't put out to sea without being seasick and wanting a basin. Well, why won't they have the courage of those basins?"

"A *dreadful* poem about a *girl* who was *violated* by a beggar *without* a nose in a lit-tle wood. . . ."

Miss Fulton sank into the lowest, deepest chair and Harry handed round the cigarettes.

From the way he stood in front of her shaking the silver box and saying abruptly: "Egyptian? Turkish? Virginian? They're all mixed up," Bertha realized that she not only bored him; he really disliked her. And she decided from the way Miss Fulton said: "No, thank you, I won't smoke," that she felt it, too, and was hurt.

"Oh, Harry, don't dislike her. You are quite wrong about her. She's wonderful, wonderful. And, besides, how can you feel so differently about some one who means so much to me. I shall try to tell you when we are in bed tonight what has been happening. What she and I have shared."

At those last words something strange and almost terrifying darted into Bertha's mind. And this something blind and smiling whispered to her: "Soon these people will go. The house will be quiet—quiet. The lights will be out. And you and he will be alone together in the dark room—the warm bed. . . ."

She jumped up from her chair and ran over to the piano.

"What a pity some one does not play!" she cried. "What a pity somebody does not play."

For the first time in her life Bertha Young desired her husband.

Oh, she'd loved him—she'd been in love with him, of course, in every other way, but just not in that way. And, equally, of course, she'd understood that he was different. They'd discussed it so often. It had worried her dreadfully at first to find that she was so cold, but after a time it had not seemed to matter. They were so frank with each other—such good pals. That was the best of being modern.

But now—ardently! ardently! The word ached in her ardent body! Was this what that feeling of bliss had been leading up to? But then—then—

"My dear," said Mrs. Norman Knight, "you know our shame. We are the victims of time and train. We live in Hampstead. It's been so nice."

"I'll come with you into the hall," said Bertha. "I love having you. But you must not miss the last train. That's so awful, isn't it?"

"Have a whisky, Knight, before you go?" called Harry.

"No, thanks, old chap."

Bertha squeezed his hand for that as she shook it.

"Good night, good-bye," she cried from the top step, feeling that this self of hers was taking leave of them for ever.

When she got back into the drawing-room the others were on the move.

". . . Then you can come part of the way in my taxi."

"I shall be *so* thankful *not* to have to face *another* drive *alone* after my *dreadful* experience."

"You can get a taxi at the rank just at the end of the street. You won't have to walk more than a few yards."

"That's comfort. I'll go and put on my coat."

Miss Fulton moved towards the hall and Bertha was following when Harry almost pushed past.

"Let me help you."

Bertha knew that he was repenting his rudeness—she let him go. What a boy he was in some ways—so impulsive—so—simple.

And Eddie and she were left by the fire.

"I *wonder* if you have seen Bilks' *new* poem called *Table d'Hôte*," said Eddie softly. "It's *so* wonderful. In the last Anthology. Have you got a copy? I'd *so* like to *show* it to you. It begins with an *incredibly* beautiful line: 'Why Must it Always be Tomato Soup?' "

"Yes," said Bertha. And she moved noiselessly to a table opposite the drawing-room door and Eddie glided noiselessly after her. She picked up the little book and gave it to him; they had not made a sound.

While he looked it up she turned her head towards the hall. And she saw . . . Harry with Miss Fulton's coat in his arms and Miss Fulton with her back turned to him and her head bent. He tossed the coat away, put his hands on her shoulders and turned her violently to him. His lips said: "I adore you," and Miss Fulton laid her moonbeam fingers on his cheeks and smiled her sleepy smile. Harry's nostrils quivered; his lips curled back in a hideous grin while he whispered: "Tomorrow," and with her eyelids Miss Fulton said: "Yes."

"Here it is," said Eddie. " 'Why Must it Always be Tomato Soup?' It's so *deeply* true, don't you feel? Tomato soup is so *dreadfully* eternal."

"If you prefer," said Harry's voice, very loud, from the hall, "I can 'phone you a cab to come to the door."

"Oh, no. It's not necessary," said Miss Fulton, and she came up to Bertha and gave her the slender fingers to hold.

"Good-bye. Thank you so much."

"Good-bye," said Bertha.

Miss Fulton held her hand a moment longer.

"Your lovely pear tree!" she murmured.

And then she was gone, with Eddie following, like the black cat following the grey cat.

"I'll shut up shop," said Harry, extravagantly cool and collected.

"Your lovely pear tree—pear tree—pear tree!"

Bertha simply ran over to the long windows.

"Oh, what is going to happen now?" she cried.

But the pear tree was as lovely as ever and as full of flower and as still.

Angelina Weld Grimké
(1880–1958)

Angelina Weld Grimké's paternal grandmother was born a slave. Her great-aunt was the white abolitionist Angelina Grimké Weld. Her father considered himself a black man, and her mother was born into a prominent white family in Boston. As would have been expected of a writer of such mixed racial background during the era of the Harlem Renaissance, when she was most prolific, most of Angelina Weld Grimké's published work dealt with problems of race. But a significant body of her writing, especially her unpublished poetry, may be read as lesbian.

Grimké's earliest play, *Rachel* (1916), which is about racial injustice in America, was the first successful stage drama written by an African American. Her great public success with *Rachel* was not repeated in subsequent work, but her poetry and short stories were included in almost all the anthologies of African American writers of the Harlem Renaissance and appeared often in African American journals such as *Opportunity*. However, her literary output was not sufficient to enable her to earn a living. Therefore, Grimké, who was a 1902 graduate from Wellesley College, supported herself as a teacher and lived with her father until his death, when she was a middle-aged woman.

There is no evidence of heterosexual involvement in Grimké's life, but extant correspondence does suggest that she was a lover of other women. In an 1896 letter, for example, the young Angelina Grimké asks Mamie Burrill to be her "wife" and exclaims, "Oh Mamie, if you only knew how my heart beats when I think of you and it yearns and pants to gaze, if only for one second upon your lovely face." The letter is signed "Your passionate lover."

Grimké never managed to publish a book during her lifetime, though her numerous poems, published and unpublished, would have provided ample material for more than one volume. The literary critic Gloria Hull suggests that Grimké published so little because the primary stimulus for her writing, apart from the race issue, was her love for other women, and the stigma attached to the subject when Grimké was writing forced her to censor herself. Hull's theory of self-censorship is borne out by the fact that of the hundreds of poems Grimké wrote she attempted to publish not more than three dozen of them. The theory is further borne out by drafts of Grimké's poems that show verses referring to the beloved with a feminine pronoun in the original version and changed in later versions so that the beloved becomes "he." Many of Grimké's love lyrics avoid reference to gender altogether, but their lesbian content is betrayed through telling descriptive words, as in her poem "El Beso," in which the beloved is depicted as "sobbing." Other poems that appear to be lesbian are defused because the beloved in the poem is presented as being dead, thus denying the possibility of lesbian fulfillment.

Hull suggests that Grimké might have been a far more creative and successful poet had she not felt constrained by her society to hide the lesbian impetus and content of her work. "Being a black lesbian poet in America at the beginning of the twentieth century," Hull observes, "meant that one wrote (or half wrote)—in isolation—a lot that she did not show and could not publish. It meant that when one did write to be printed she did so in shackles—chained between the real experience and the conventions that would not give her voice." As Grimké's poem "Rosabel" suggests, lesbian subject matter in her verse appears to have constituted "lines I do not dare":

> Leaves that whisper whisper ever
>   Listen, listen, pray!
> Birds that twitter twitter softly
>   Do not say me nay.
> Winds that breathe about, upon her
>   (Lines I do not dare)
> Whisper, turtle, breathe upon her
>   That I find her fair.

By the 1930s, when African American writers went out of "fashion" as far as publishers were concerned, Grimké, discouraged that her work on race had become no more printable than her work on love, appears to have stopped writing.

FURTHER READING: *Selected Works of Angelina Weld Grimké*, ed. Carolivia Herron (New York: Oxford University Press, 1991). Gloria T. Hull, *Color, Sex and Poetry: Three Women Writers of the Harlem Renaissance* (Bloomington: Indiana University Press, 1987). Gloria T. Hull, "Under the Days: The Buried Life and Poetry of Angelina Weld Grimké," *Conditions: Five, The Black Woman's Issue*, 2: 2 (Autumn 1979).

WHEN THE GREEN LIES OVER THE EARTH

I

When the green lies over the earth, my dear,
A mantle of witching grace;
When the smile and the tear of the young child year
Dimple across its face,
And then flee. When the wind all day is sweet
With the breath of growing things;
When the wooing bird lights on restless feet
And chirrups and trills and sings
        To his lady-love
        In the green above;
Then oh! my dear, when the youth's in the year,
Yours is the face that I long to have near,
        Yours is the face, my dear.
But the green is hiding your curls, my dear,
Your curls so shining and sweet;
And the gold-hearted daisies this many a year

Have bloomed and bloomed at your feet,
And the little birds just above your head
With their voices hushed, my dear,
For you have sung and have prayed and have plead
   This many, many a year.
   And the blossoms fall.
   On the garden wall,
And drift like snow on the green below.
   But the sharp thorn grows
   On the budding rose,
And my heart no more leaps at the sunset glow.
For oh! my dear, when the youth's in the year,
Yours is the face that I long to have near,
Yours is the face, my dear.

A TRIOLET

Molly raised shy eyes to me,
  On an April day;
Close we stood beneath a tree;
Molly raised shy eyes to me,
Shining sweet and wistfully,
Wet and yet quite gay;
Molly raised shy eyes to me,
  On an April day.

BROWN GIRL

In the hot gold sunlight,
  Brown girl, brown girl,
   You smile;
  And in your great eyes,
   Very gold, very bright,
    I see little bells,
   Shaking so lazily,
    (Oh! small they are) . . .
    I hear the bells.
But at fawn dusk
  Brown girl, brown girl,
   I see no smile,
   I hear no bells.

Your great eyes
Are quiet pools;
They have been drinking, drinking,
    All the day,
The hot gold of sunlight.
Your eyes spill sunlight
    Over the dusk.
    Close your eyes,
I hear nothing but the beating of my heart.

YOU

I love your throat, so fragrant, fair,
The little pulses beating there;
Your eye-brows' shy and questioning air;
    I love your shadowed hair.

I love your flame-touched ivory skin;
Your little fingers frail and thin;
Your dimple creeping out and in;
    I love your pointed chin.

I love the way you move, you rise;
Your fluttering gestures, just-caught cries;
I am not sane, I am not wise,
    God! how I love your eyes!

YOUR EYES

Through the downiness of the grey dawn,
    Through its grey gossamer softness—
        Your eyes;
Through the wonder-shine of the one star,
    Beautiful, solitary, in the East—
        Your eyes;

Through the fierceness, the cymbaling of colors,
    Through the whitening glory of the springing sun—
        Your eyes;

Through the chattering of birds, through their songs,
    Delicate, lovely, swaying in the tree-tops,
        Through the softness of little feathered breasts and throats

Through the skitterings of little feet,
Through the whirrings of silken wings—
    Your eyes;

Through the green quiet, the hot languor of noon,
    Sudden, through its cleft peace—
        Your eyes;

Through the slenderness of maiden trees kissed aflame by the mouth of
the Spring,
    Through them standing against a slowly goldening Western sky,
    Through them standing very still, wondering,
    Wistful, waiting—
        Your eyes;

Through the beautiful Dusk, through the beautiful, blue-black hair of
the Dusk,
Through her beautiful parted hair—
    Your eyes,
    Kissing mine.

NAUGHTY NAN

I

    Naughty Nan
    If you can
Tell me how your frowns and smiles,
Sudden tears, and naive wiles,
Linked into a glittering band
Follow swiftly hand in hand?
Tell me wayward April-born,
Child of smiles and tears forlorn,
Have you ever felt the smart
Of a lacerated heart?
Are you but a sprite of moods?
Heartless, that fore'er deludes
    Tell me naughty Nan?

II

    Naughty Nan
    If you can
Tell me why you have such eyes
Gleaming when not drooped in sighs

Or when veiled by falling rain?
Haughty oft but never vain
Sometime wistful orbs of brown,
Sometimes blazing in fierce scorn
But eyes that are never free
From some glance of witchery.
Tell me why you have such lips
Tempting me to stolen sips
Tender, drooping, luring, sad,
Laughing, mocking, madly glad,
    Tell me naughty Nan?

III
Naughty Nan
If you can
Tell me why you play with me,
Take my heart so prettily
In your dainty, slender, hands,
Bruise its tender, loving, bands?
Tell me why your eyes are brown
Mock and glitter when I frown?
Flitting, luring, little, sprite
In a garb of moods bedight,
Dancing here, and dancing there,
Changeling strange, but ever fair
You have caught me in your snare,—
    Naughty Nan.

Virginia Woolf
(1882–1941)

Virginia Woolf grew up in the stimulating intellectual milieu that her father Leslie Stephen, editor of the *Dictionary of National Biography*, was able to provide for her and her eight siblings and half-siblings. The leading lights of the British intelligentsia were regular guests in the Stephens' household, and young Virginia heard in her own home some of the most informative and witty dinner-table talk Victorian England had to offer. However, unlike the males of the family, who were entitled to a prestigious university education, Virginia could only glean whatever she might from her father's very extensive library. Although her autodidacticism resulted in impressive knowledge, she could not help regretting and resenting her lack of formal education. Other shadows were cast on her early years, such as molestation by her two older half-brothers and the death of her mother, Julia Stephen, when Virginia was only thirteen, at which time her father became increasingly morose and peremptory in his demands on his daughters. Virginia's various childhood traumas were probably responsible for her adult depressions and nervous breakdowns, and perhaps even for her suicide at the age of fifty-nine.

Virginia's young adult years were somewhat happier. With her three full siblings she moved to Bloomsbury, and they became the center of an intellectual bohemian community, which included her brother Thoby's Cambridge friends, many of whom were gay men, such as Lytton Strachey and E. M. Forster. Virginia herself had had two powerful same-sex crushes (or what may have been lesbian affairs), one on Madge Vaughan, who was thirteen years older than she, and one on Violet Dickinson, a six-foot-two amazon, who was seventeen years older. But despite her bohemianism, Virginia could not consider adopting a lesbian lifestyle, believing (as was consonant with her times) that a woman who failed to marry was a tragic figure. In 1911 she despairingly wrote about herself to her sister Vanessa, "To be 29 and unmarried—to be a failure—childless—insane too, no writer."

Lytton Strachey, who thought, like many of his homosexual contemporaries, that a gay man should have a marriage of convenience, proposed to Virginia and for a brief twenty-four hours they were actually engaged. However, their Bloomsbury group also included Leonard Woolf, an ostensibly heterosexual Jewish socialist writer, who would make a much more plausible husband, Virginia believed. They married in 1912. Their relationship appears to have been primarily platonic, Leonard nurturing Virginia, encouraging her writing, and, in effect, being the wife that authors of both sexes so much need.

Ten years after their marriage, Virginia Woolf met Vita Sackville-West, with whom she had what was probably the most important erotic relationship of her life. Woolf recorded in various ways Vita's impact on her. In a letter to her sister, for example, teasing Vanessa about her homophobic lack of understanding regarding love between women, Virginia wrote:

> You will never succumb to the charms of any of your sex—what an arid garden the world must be for you! What avenues of stone pavements and iron railings! Greatly though I respect the male mind . . . I cannot see that they have a glowworm's worth of charm about them—the scenery of the world takes no lustre from their presence.

They add of course immensely to its dignity and safety; but when it comes to a little excitement—!

Vita, an amazon like Violet Dickinson, and a dashing aristocrat to boot, provided for Virginia the "charm" and "excitement" that she believed heterosexuality lacked. Although the intensity of their relationship cooled by the end of the 1920s (primarily because Vita engaged in other lesbian affairs), they remained close until Virginia's death in 1941. As much as Virginia had been involved in the relationship, however, it was Vita alone that Virginia considered the real "Sapphist." Where Woolf located herself in a lesbian affair with a "Sapphist" is not entirely clear.

The ambivalent thoughts Virginia Woolf ascribes to Clarissa regarding lesbianism in *Mrs. Dalloway* (1925), written in the midst of her relationship with Vita, might well have been her own feelings: Clarissa "had a scruple picked up Heaven knows where, or, as she felt, sent by Nature (who is invariably wise); yet sometimes she could not resist yielding to the charm of a woman." Young Clarissa had yielded especially to Sally Seton, who was, in fact, modeled on Virginia's girlhood crush Madge Vaughan. And the lines she gives Clarissa with regard to Sally are almost directly out of Virginia's own diary entry in which she remembered her excitement about Madge: "I see myself now standing in the night nursery at Hyde Park Gate, washing my hands, and saying to myself, 'At this moment she is actually under the roof.' "

In 1927 Woolf appears to have wanted to deal with the subject of lesbianism somewhat more extensively. She wrote in her diary that she had "conceived a whole fantasy to be called 'The Jessamy Brides'. . . . Sapphism is to be suggested." Ultimately, Woolf feared to be too direct, perhaps because she could not conceive how directness on that subject would yield anything but bathos (compare the melodrama Radclyffe Hall was writing at that very time, which became *The Well of Loneliness*). Or perhaps she guessed that more directness about lesbianism would have made her work prey to the censors, as *The Well* soon was. Therefore, instead of completing her original idea, Woolf disguised her lesbian subject matter in *Orlando*, a wonderful tour de force about (and to) Vita, which has been rightly described as "the longest and most charming love letter in literature." Vita-Orlando is presented not as a lesbian, however, but as an individual who lives through four centuries, changing gender from male to female and back intermittently. Lesbianism is hinted at in the novel, but generally requires decoding. Virginia wrote Vita that *Orlando* is "all about you and the lusts of your flesh and the lure of your mind." But for the most part, Orlando's relationships are presented as being patently heterosexual.

Still under the influence of her enchantment with Vita, Woolf wrote *A*

Room of One's One, which again hints at lesbianism in passages such as the one in which Woolf toys with the idea that "Chloe liked Olivia." In spite of her subtlety on the lesbian theme, however, Woolf appears to have been nervous about the publication of *A Room of One's Own*. She wrote in her diary, "I shall be attacked for a feminist & hinted at for a Sapphist."

The suggestions of lesbianism in the following short story, "Moments of Being: 'Slaters' Pins Have No Points,' " have been easily overlooked by readers who could believe that the description of Julia as "odd" and "queer" was meant to indicate only that she was an eccentric old maid. Seeing her in those terms, they would have missed the hints of fearful attraction between the younger woman, Fanny, and Julia (who bore Woolf's mother's name and was perhaps no more distant in age from Fanny than Violet or Madge had been from Virginia). It is significant that the story was written in 1928, around the period that Woolf was also at work on *Orlando* and *A Room of One's Own*.

FURTHER READING: Virginia Woolf, *The Diary of Virginia Woolf*, 3 vols., ed. Anne Olivier Bell (New York: Harcourt Brace, 1977–80); *The Letters of Virginia Woolf*, 6 vols. (see esp. vol. III, 1923–1928), eds. Nigel Nicolson and Joanne Trautmann (New York: Harcourt Brace, 1975–1980). Quentin Bell, *Virginia Woolf: A Biography*, 2 vols. (New York: Harcourt Brace, 1972). Barbara Fassler, "Theories of Homosexuality as Sources of Bloomsbury's Androgyny," *Signs*, 5 (1979), 237–51. Sherron E. Knopp, " 'If I Saw You Would You Kiss Me?': Sapphism and Subversiveness in Virginia Woolf's *Orlando*" in *Sexual Sameness: Textual Differences in Lesbian and Gay Writing*, ed. Joseph Bristow (London: Routledge, 1992). Jane Marcus, "Sapphistory: The Woolf and the Well," *Lesbian Texts and Contexts: Radical Revisions*, eds. Karla Jay and Joanne Glasgow (New York: New York University Press, 1990), pp. 164–79. Joanne Trautmann, *The Jessamy Brides: The Friendship of Virginia Woolf and V. Sackville-West* (University Park: Pennsylvania State University Press, 1973). Vita Sackville-West, *The Letters of Vita Sackville-West to Virginia Woolf*, eds. Louise DeSalvo and Mitchell A. Leaska (New York: Morrow, 1984).

Moments of Being: "Slater's Pins Have No Points"

"Slater's pins have no points—don't you always find that?" said Miss Craye, turning round as the rose fell out of Fanny Wilmot's dress, and Fanny stooped with her ears full of the music, to look for the pin on the floor.

The words gave her an extraordinary shock, as Miss Craye struck the last chord of the Bach fugue. Did Miss Craye actually go to Slater's and buy pins then, Fanny Wilmot asked herself, transfixed for a moment? Did she stand at the counter waiting like anybody else, and was she given a bill with coppers wrapped in it, and did she slip them into her purse and then, an hour later, stand by her dressing table and take out the pins? What need had she of pins? For she was not so much dressed as cased, like a beetle compactly in its sheath, blue in winter, green in summer. What need had she of pins—Julia Craye—who lived, it seemed, in the cool, glassy world of Bach fugues, playing to herself what she liked and only consenting to take one or two pupils at the Archer Street College of Music (so the Principal, Miss Kingston said) as a special favour to herself, who had "the greatest admiration for her in every way." Miss Craye was left badly off, Miss Kingston was afraid, at her brother's death. Oh, they used to have such lovely things, when they lived at Salisbury and her brother Julius was, of course, a very well-known man: a famous archaeologist. It was a great privilege to stay with them, Miss Kingston said ("My family had always known them—they were regular Salisbury people," Miss Kingston said), but a little frightening for a child; one had to be careful not to slam the door or bounce into the room unexpectedly. Miss Kingston, who gave little character sketches like this on the first day of term while she received cheques and wrote out receipts for them, smiled here. Yes, she had been rather a tomboy; she had bounced in and set all those green Roman glasses and things jumping in their case. The Crayes were none of them married. The Crayes were not used to children. They kept cats. The cats, one used to feel, knew as much about the Roman urns and things as anybody.

"Far more than I did!" said Miss Kingston brightly, writing her name across the stamp, in her dashing, cheerful, full-bodied hand, for she had always been practical.

Perhaps then, Fanny Wilmot thought, looking for the pin, Miss Craye said that about "Slater's pins having no points," at a venture. None of the Crayes had ever married. She knew nothing about pins—nothing whatever. But she wanted to break the spell that had fallen on the house; to break the pane of glass which separated them from other people. When Polly Kingston, that merry little girl, had slammed the door and made the Roman vases jump, Julius, seeing that no harm was done (that would be his first instinct) looked, for the case was stood in the window, at Polly skipping home across the fields; looked with the look his sister often had, that lingering, desiring look.

"Stars, sun, moon," it seemed to say, "the daisy in the grass, fires, frost on the window pane, my heart goes out to you. But," it always seemed to add, "you break, you pass, you go." And simultaneously it covered the intensity of both these states of mind with "I can't reach you—I can't get at you," spoken wistfully, frustratedly. And the stars faded, and the child went.

That was the kind of spell, that was the glassy surface that Miss Craye wanted to break by showing, when she had played Bach beautifully as a reward to a favourite pupil (Fanny Wilmot knew that she was Miss Craye's favourite pupil) that she too felt as other people felt about pins. Slater's pins had no points.

Yes, the "famous archaeologist" had looked like that, too. "The famous archaeologist"—as she said that endorsing cheques, ascertaining the day of the month, speaking so brightly and frankly, there was in Miss Kingston's voice an indescribable tone which hinted at something odd, something queer, in Julius Craye. It was the very same thing that was odd perhaps in Julia too. One could have sworn, thought Fanny Wilmot, as she looked for the pin, that at parties, meetings (Miss Kingston's father was a clergyman) she had picked up some piece of gossip, or it might only have been a smile, or a tone when his name was mentioned, which had given her "a feeling" about Julius Craye. Needless to say, she had never spoken about it to anybody. Probably she scarcely knew what she meant by it. But whenever she spoke of Julius, or heard him mentioned, that was the first thought that came to mind: there was something odd about Julius Craye.

It was so that Julia looked too, as she sat half turned on the music stool, smiling. It's on the field, it's on the pane, it's in the sky—beauty; and I can't get at it; I can't have it—I, she seemed to add, with that little clutch of the hand which was so characteristic, who adore it so passionately, would give the whole world to possess it! And she picked up the carnation which had fallen on the floor, while Fanny searched for the pin. She crushed it, Fanny felt, voluptuously in her smooth, veined hands stuck about with water-coloured rings set in pearls. The pressure of her fingers seemed to increase all that was most brilliant in the flower; to set it off; to make it more frilled, fresh, immaculate. What was odd in her, and perhaps in her brother too, was that this crush and grasp of the fingers was combined with a perpetual frustration. So it was even now with the carnation. She had her hands on it; she pressed it; but she did not possess it, enjoy it, not altogether.

None of the Crayes had married, Fanny Wilmot remembered. She had in mind how one evening when the lesson had lasted longer than usual and it was dark, Julia Craye had said, "It's the use of men, surely, to protect us," smiling at her that same odd smile, as she stood fastening her cloak, which made her, like the flower, conscious to her finger tips of youth and brilliance, but, like the flower too, Fanny suspected, inhibited.

"Oh, but I don't want protection," Fanny had laughed, and when Julia Craye, fixing on her that extraordinary look, had said she was not so sure of that, Fanny positively blushed under the admiration in her eyes.

It was the only use of men, she had said. Was it for that reason then, Fanny wondered, with her eyes on the floor, that she had never married?

After all, she had not lived all her life in Salisbury. "Much the nicest part of London," she had said once, "(but I'm speaking of fifteen or twenty years ago) is Kensington. One was in the Gardens in ten minutes—it was like the heart of the country. One could dine out in one's slippers without catching cold. Kensington—it was like a village then, you know," she had said.

Here she had broken off, to denounce acridly, the draughts in the Tubes.

"It was the use of men," she had said, with a queer, wry acerbity. Did that throw any light on the problem why she had not married? One could imagine every sort of scene in her youth, when with her good, blue eyes, her straight, firm nose, her piano playing, her rose flowering with chaste passion in the bosom of her muslin dress, she had attracted first the young men to whom such things, and the china tea-cups and the silver candlesticks, and the inlaid tables (for the Crayes had such nice things) were wonderful; young men not sufficiently distinguished; young men of the Cathedral town with ambitions. She had attracted them first, and then her brother's friends from Oxford or Cambridge. They would come down in the summer, row her up the river, continue the argument about Browning by letter, and arrange perhaps on the rare occasions when she stayed in London to show her—Kensington Gardens?

"Much the nicest part of London—Kensington. I'm speaking of fifteen or twenty years ago," she had said once. "One was in the Gardens in ten minutes—in the heart of the country." One could make that yield what one liked, Fanny Wilmot thought, single out for instance, Mr. Sherman, the painter, an old friend of hers; make him call for her by appointment one sunny day in June; take her to have tea under the trees. (They had met, too, at those parties to which one tripped in slippers without fear of catching cold.) The aunt or other elderly relative was to wait there while they looked at the Serpentine. They looked at the Serpentine. He may have rowed her across. They compared it with the Avon. She would have considered the comparison very seriously, for views of rivers were important to her. She sat hunched a little, a little angular, though she was graceful then, steering. At the critical moment, for he had determined that he must speak now—it was his only chance of getting her alone—he was speaking with his head turned at an absurd angle, in his great nervousness, over his shoulder—at that very moment she interrupted fiercely. He would have them into the Bridge, she cried. It was a moment of horror, of disillusionment, of revelation for both of them. I can't have it, I can't possess it, she thought. He could not see why she had come then. With a great splash of his oar he pulled the boat round. Merely to snub him? He rowed her back and said good-bye to her.

The setting of that scene could be varied as one chose, Fanny Wilmot reflected. (Where had that pin fallen?) It might be Ravenna—or Edinburgh, where she had kept house for her brother. The scene could be changed and the young man and the exact manner of it all; but one thing was constant—her refusal and her frown and her anger with herself afterwards and her argument, and her relief—yes, certainly her immense relief. The very next day perhaps she would get up at six, put on her cloak, and walk all the way from Kensington to the river. She was so thankful that she had not sacrificed her right to go and look at things when they are at their best—before people are up, that is to say. She could have her breakfast in bed if she liked. She had not sacrificed her independence.

Yes, Fanny Wilmot smiled, Julia had not endangered her habits. They remained safe, and her habits would have suffered if she had married. "They're ogres," she had said one evening, half laughing, when another pupil, a girl lately married, suddenly bethinking her that she would miss her husband, had rushed off in haste.

"They're ogres," she had said, laughing grimly. An ogre would have interfered perhaps with breakfast in bed; with walks at dawn down to the river. What would have happened (but one could hardly conceive this) had she had children? She took astonishing precautions against chills, fatigue, rich food, the wrong food, draughts, heated rooms, journeys in the Tube, for she could never determine which of these it was exactly that brought on those terrible headaches that gave her life the semblance of a battlefield. She was always engaged in outwitting the enemy, until it seemed as if the pursuit had its interest; could she have beaten the enemy finally she would have found life a little dull. As it was, the tug-of-war was perpetual—on one side the nightingale or the view which she loved with passion—yes, for views and birds she felt nothing less than passion; on the other, the damp path or the horrid long drag up a steep hill which would certainly make her good for nothing next day and bring on one of her headaches. When, therefore, from time to time, she managed her forces adroitly and brought off a visit to Hampton Court the week the crocuses (those glossy bright flowers were her favourites) were at their best, it was a victory. It was something that lasted; something that mattered for ever. She strung the afternoon on the necklace of memorable days, which was not too long for her to be able to recall this one or that one; this view, that city; to finger it, to feel it, to savour, sighing, the quality that made it unique.

"It was so beautiful last Friday," she said, "that I determined I must go there." So she had gone off to Waterloo on her great undertaking—to visit Hampton Court—alone. Naturally, but perhaps foolishly, one pitied her for the thing she never asked pity for (indeed she was reticent habitually, speaking of her health only as a warrior might speak of his foe)—one pitied her for always doing everything alone. Her brother was dead. Her sister was asthmatic. She found the climate of Edinburgh good for her. It was too bleak for Julia. Perhaps too she found the associations painful, for her brother, the famous archaeologist, had died there; and she had loved her brother. She lived in a little house off the Brompton Road entirely alone.

Fanny Wilmot saw the pin on the carpet; she picked it up. She looked at Miss Craye. Was Miss Craye so lonely? No, Miss Craye was steadily, blissfully, if only for a moment, a happy woman. Fanny had surprised her in a moment of ecstasy. She sat there, half turned away from the piano, with her hands clasped in her lap holding the carnation upright, while behind her was the sharp square of the window, uncurtained, purple in the evening, intensely purple after the brilliant electric lights which burnt unshaded in the bare music room. Julia Craye sitting hunched and compact holding her flower seemed to emerge out of the London night, seemed to fling it like a cloak behind her. It seemed in its bareness and intensity the effluence of her spirit, something she had made which surrounded her, which was her. Fanny stared.

All seemed transparent for a moment to the gaze of Fanny Wilmot, as if looking through Miss Craye, she saw the very fountain of her being spurt up in pure, silver drops. She saw back and back into the past behind her. She saw the green Roman vases stood in their case; heard the choristers playing cricket; saw Julia quietly descend the curving steps on to the lawn; saw her pour out tea beneath the cedar tree; softly enclose the old man's hand in hers; saw her going round and about the corridors of that ancient Cathedral dwelling place with towels in her hand to mark them; lamenting as she went the pettiness of daily life; and slowly ageing, and putting away clothes when summer came, because at her age they were too bright to wear; and tending her father's sickness; and cleaving her way ever more definitely as her will stiffened towards her solitary goal; travelling frugally; counting the cost and measuring out of her tight shut purse the sum needed for this journey, or for that old mirror; obstinately adhering whatever people might say in choosing her pleasures for herself. She saw Julia—

She saw Julia open her arms; saw her blaze; saw her kindle. Out of the night she burnt like a dead white star. Julia kissed her. Julia possessed her.

"Slater's pins have no points," Miss Craye said, laughing queerly and relaxing her arms, as Fanny Wilmot pinned the flower to her breast with trembling fingers.

H.D. (Hilda Doolittle)
(1886–1961)

The bisexual American writer H.D. became an expatriate in 1911 when she went to Europe with another aspiring young poet, Frances Josepha Gregg, the woman to whom she wrote her first pastoral love poems. Frances returned to the United States the following year under pressure from her family, but Hilda Doolittle remained in England and renewed her acquaintance with Ezra Pound, to whom she had been almost engaged when he was a young student at the University of Pennsylvania. The intimacy between her and Pound did not last long, but through his influence she was able to publish her imagist poems, and it was he who gave her the *nom du plume* H.D., Imagiste. H.D.'s work as an imagist poet brought her considerable fame (before the advent of women's studies, she was often one of the few female writers to be included in American literature anthologies), but it also limited her reputation, her other works having been generally ignored by critics. In recent years, however, feminist scholars have begun to study her long poetic narratives and especially her autobiographical novels, which contain extensive lesbian subject matter.

In 1913 H.D. married the British novelist Richard Aldington. By agreement the marriage was to be an open one. Aldington was well aware of her lesbian relationships, and as he approvingly observed to a correspondent in later years: "I think women are quite often bisexual, having affairs with women without in the least losing pleasure in men; and some of the women I have been with longest have gone to be with other women quite frankly, and with no disturbance. Both my wives did it." While Aldington did not disapprove of H.D.'s lesbian affairs, he did disapprove when she had an affair with a young music critic, Cecil Gray, and became pregnant by him.

Aldington virtually cast H.D. out, claiming her child was Gray's responsibility. Gray did not wish to take that responsibility. H.D.'s problems were exacerbated because in the midst of her solitary pregnancy she caught double pneumonia. Fortunately for her, she had recently met a twenty-four-year-old woman with literary ambitions who admired her work and soon worshiped her. Winifred Ellerman (who later published under the name of Bryher), was the daughter of one of the wealthiest shipping magnates in England. When it was thought that H.D. was close to death, she told Bryher, "If I could walk to Delphi I should be healed." And Bryher promised, "I will take you to Greece as soon as you are well." This began their lifelong intimate relationship, which lasted more than forty years, until

H.D.'s death. Bryher adopted H.D.'s daughter, who was born in 1919, and the two women traveled throughout Europe, the Middle East, and America together. Bryher cared for H.D. through all her subsequent ups and downs and settled the equivalent of several million dollars on her in 1940. They had a lesbian "open marriage," which often included heterosexual affairs on H.D.'s part, but she and Bryher appear to have been the primary relationship in each other's lives.

Despite her many affairs with men, H.D. believed that heterosexuality was antithetical to a woman's ability to create artistically. She associated her writing with her lesbianism and, like a later poet, May Sarton, she insisted to the end of her life that it was the women she loved, "the Mother" in various forms, that was for her "the Muse, the Creator." Despite that conviction and her need to record such ideas in her writing, H.D. also felt it was necessary to practice some degree of self-censorship in what she published. The poetry that was published in her lifetime occasionally touched on lesbianism, but in those poems she often hid behind a persona, especially the mask of Sappho, and the distance of antiquity.

Like many of her lesbian and bisexual contemporaries, H.D. appears to have prevaricated, to herself perhaps more than to anyone else, about the meaning of her self-censorship. In 1934 Sylvia Dobson, a young woman who was her lover for a time, expressed discomfort at the thought of being categorized as "lesbian" in medical terms. H.D. responded with an argument she probably often used to explain to herself the "unimportance" of publishing her lesbian material:

> It is hardly a question of your being, as you say, A2 or B3 Lesbian.
> . . . But it's a matter of something infinitely bigger than Lesbian A2
> or anything. The Lesbian or the homo-sexual content is only a symbol-note, I did not say a "symptom." *That* is not very important.
> *How* you love is more important than WHO you love.

But in fact, H.D. understood that for her the WHO was indeed important because only by loving a woman could she free her creative impulses. She was also all too aware that from society's perspective the WHO had phenomenal importance, which was the reason she so often censored the lesbian content of her writing.

With regard to the lesbian material in her fiction, H.D. practiced this self-censorship in diverse ways. For example, in *Palimpsest*, one of the few autobiographical novels that she allowed to be published during her life, she not only used the device of a setting in the ancient world to screen her autobiographical content, but she also assigned a masculine gender to those aspects of herself that were not conventionally female, and she downplayed the importance of the lesbian relationship that appears in this work, hiding it in the subtext or in a depiction of "female bonding."

But her greatest self-censorship was her refusal to make public those autobiographical novels in which the theme of lesbianism is important and clear. *Paint It To-day*, for example, written in 1921 (and only recently published), presents an idealized lesbian relationship that is central to the character's achievement of her identity as an artist. It is only lesbian love in this novel that can cure the stifling effects of traditional heterosexual socialization. H.D.'s first pair of lesbian lovers in *Paint It To-day* are Josepha (Frances Gregg's middle name was Josepha) and Midget (H.D.). The two young women, who are both writers, go off to Europe together and aspire to (re)invent women's poetry, to eschew men's "large, epic pictures" and create instead "songs that cut like swallow-wing the high untainted ether." The relationship between the two ends when Josepha's mother insists she return to the States and marry a man. The novel then focuses on Midget's own marriage in Europe (a relationship that H.D. describes as "remote and unbelievable"), her pregnancy, and finally her happy rescue by a woman who represents Bryher.

Another unpublished novel, *Asphodel* (completed in 1922), covers similar ground, focusing on a young American woman who goes to Europe, marries a European, becomes pregnant by another man, and meets a Bryher character who rescues her and forms a lesbian family with her and her child. *HERmione*, written in 1926–27 and finally published in 1981, twenty years after H.D.'s death, focuses further on the Frances Gregg material, describing H.D.'s meeting and affair with Frances (Fayne Rabb) as well as her engagement to Ezra Pound (George Lowndes) and his response to her lesbian relationship with Frances. As in *Paint It To-day*, it is the lesbian lovers who help each other assume their identities as artists.

FURTHER READING: H.D., *Collected Poems, 1912–1944*, Louis L. Martz, ed. (New York: New Directions, 1983); *HERmione* (New York: New Directions, 1981); *Paint It To-day* (New York: New York University Press, 1992). Diana Collecott, "What Is Not Said: A Study in Textual Inversion," *Sexual Sameness: Textual Differences in Lesbian and Gay Writing*, ed. Joseph Bristow (London: Routledge, 1992). Rachel Blau DuPlessis, *H.D.: The Career of That Struggle* (Bloomington: Indiana University Press, 1986). Susan Stanford Friedman, *Penelope's Web: Gender, Modernity, H.D.'s Fiction* (New York: Cambridge University Press, 1990). Barbara Guest, *Herself Defined: The Poet H.D. and Her World* (Garden City, NY: Doubleday, 1984). Caroline Zilboorg, *Richard Aldington and H.D.: The Early Years in Letters* (Bloomington: Indiana University Press, 1992).

FRAGMENT THIRTY-SIX
I know not what to do: my mind is divided.
        —Sappho

I know not what to do,
my mind is reft:
is song's gift best?
is love's gift loveliest?
I know not what to do,
now sleep has pressed
weight on your eyelids.

Shall I break your rest,
devouring, eager?
is love's gift best?
nay, song's the loveliest:
yet were you lost,
what rapture
could I take from song?
what song were left?

I know not what to do:
to turn and slake
the rage that burns,
with my breath burn
and trouble your cool breath?
so shall I turn and take
snow in my arms?
(is love's gift best?)
yet flake on flake
of snow were comfortless,
did you lie wondering,
wakened yet unawake.

Shall I turn and take
comfortless snow within my arms?
press lips to lips
that answer not,
press lips to flesh
that shudders not nor breaks?
Is love's gift best?
shall I turn and slake
all the wild longing?
O I am eager for you!

as the Pleiads shake
white light in whiter water
so shall I take you?

My mind is quite divided,
my minds hesitate,
so perfect matched,
I know not what to do:
each strives with each
as two white wrestlers
standing for a match,
ready to turn and clutch
yet never shake muscle nor nerve nor tendon;
so my mind waits
to grapple with my mind,
yet I lie quiet,
I would seem at rest.

I know not what to do:
strain upon strain,
sound surging upon sound
makes my brain blind;
as a wave-line may wait to fall
yet (waiting for its falling)
still the wind may take
from off its crest,
white flake on flake of foam,
that rises,
seeming to dart and pulse
and rend the light,
so my mind hesitates
above the passion
quivering yet to break,
so my mind hesitates
above my mind,
listening to song's delight.

I know not what to do:
will the sound break,
rending the night
with rift on rift of rose
and scattered light?
will the sound break at last

as the wave hesitant,
or will the whole night pass
and I lie listening awake?

THE GIFT

Instead of pearls—a wrought clasp—
a bracelet—will you accept this?

You know the script—
you will start, wonder:
what is left, what phrase
after last night? This:

The world is yet unspoiled for you,
you wait, expectant—
you are like the children
who haunt your own steps
for chance bits—a comb
that may have slipped,
a gold tassel, unravelled,
plucked from your scarf,
twirled by your slight fingers
into the street—
a flower dropped.

Do not think me unaware,
I who have snatched at you
as the street-child clutched
at the seed-pearls you spilt
that hot day
when your necklace snapped.

Do not dream that I speak
as one defrauded of delight,
sick, shaken by each heart-beat
or paralyzed, stretched at length,
who gasps:
these ripe pears
are bitter to the taste,
this spiced wine, poison, corrupt.
I cannot walk—
who would walk?

Life is a scavenger's pit—I escape—
I only, rejecting it,
lying here on this couch.

Your garden sloped to the beach,
myrtle overran the paths,
honey and amber flecked each leaf,
the citron-lily head—
one among many—
weighed there, over-sweet.

The myrrh-hyacinth
spread across low slopes,
violets streaked black ridges
through the grass.
The house, too, was like this,
over painted, over lovely—
the world is like this.

Sleepless nights,
I remember the initiates,
their gesture, their calm glance.
I have heard how in rapt thought,
in vision, they speak
with another race,
more beautiful, more intense than this.
I could laugh—
more beautiful, more intense?

Perhaps that other life
is contrast always to this.
I reason:
I have lived as they
in their inmost rites—
they endure the tense nerves
through the moment of ritual.
I endure from moment to moment—
days pass all alike,
tortured, intense.

This I forgot last night:
you must not be blamed,
it is not your fault;
as a child, a flower—any flower

tore my breast—
meadow-chicory, a common grass-tip,
a leaf shadow, a flower tint
unexpected on a winter-branch.

I reason:
another life holds what this lacks,
a sea, unmoving, quiet—
not forcing our strength
to rise to it, beat on beat—
a stretch of sand,
no garden beyond, strangling
with its myrrh-lilies—
a hill, not set with black violets
but stones, stones, bare rocks,
dwarf-trees, twisted, no beauty
to distract—to crowd
madness upon madness.

Only a still place
and perhaps some outer horror
some hideousness to stamp beauty,
a mark—no changing it now—
on our hearts.

I send no string of pearls,
no bracelet—accept this.

AT BAIA

I should have thought
in a dream you would have brought
some lovely, perilous thing,
orchids piled in a great sheath,
as who would say (in a dream)
I send you this,
who left the blue veins
of your throat unkissed.

Why was it that your hands
(that never took mine)
your hands that I could see
drift over the orchid heads

so carefully,
your hands, so fragile, sure to lift
so gently, the fragile flower stuff—
ah, ah, how was it

You never sent (in a dream)
the very form, the very scent,
not heavy, not sensuous,
but perilous—perilous—
of orchids, piled in a great sheath,
and folded underneath on a bright scroll
some word:

Flower sent to flower;
for white hands, the lesser white,
less lovely of flower leaf,

or

Lover to lover, no kiss,
no touch, but forever and ever this.

Carson McCullers
(1917–67)

When Carson McCullers published her first novel, *The Heart Is a Lonely Hunter* (1940), at the age of twenty-three, she was touted by Houghton Mifflin's publicists and taken into the public heart as a *Wunderkind*, whose body language and predilection for men's pants and shirts represented a cute tomboyishness. Despite the ten-year difference between them, she could be seen as an incarnation of Mick, the "sexless" adolescent protagonist of her novel. If it occurred to many among her public that Carson looked and acted like a baby butch, that suspicion must have been quickly allayed by the well-publicized fact that her marriage to a man, Reeves McCullers, was already in its third year.

However, careful lesbian readers of McCullers would soon have sufficient clues that the publicists' presentation of her did not tell all the story. Heterosexual lovers were rare in her fiction. The illicit sexual passion in her second novel, *Reflections in a Golden Eye* (1941), between Leonora and Langdon (who are presented as being stupid and insensitive) is not repeated in any other novel by McCullers. Most often, the possibility of male-female sexual interest does not exist in the universe that McCullers constructs, or it is glanced over, or it is shown as dangerous, destructive, or quite beside the point of female existence.

Although McCullers's lesbian material is generally encoded, her treatment of male homosexuality is more direct. Her familiarity with gay male culture dates back to her youthful days in Columbus, Georgia, where, in male attire and the only female in the group, she would accompany her men friends to homosexual hangouts. Gay male luminaries, including W. H. Auden, Tennessee Williams, Truman Capote, and Benjamin Britten were later among her closest friends. Most of her novels—*The Heart Is a Lonely Hunter, Reflections in a Golden Eye, The Ballad of the Sad Café, Clock Without Hands* (1961)—focus on male-male sexual interest.

Her lesbian material generally excludes references to sexual interest, but its content may be seen as lesbian nonetheless. Like many homosexuals of her era and earlier who were influenced by the definitions of the sexologists, McCullers conflated gender role identification and sexual orientation. She was a lesbian, as she explained to her friends, because she was born a man in a woman's body. What appears to have come first in her psychosexual development was not her sexual feelings for other women (though as an adolescent she experienced a powerful and long-lasting crush on her piano teacher), but rather her anger and discomfort at being female. Like her characters Frankie and Mick, she quickly dropped her ignominiously feminine first name, Lula, in childhood and demanded to be called by her more androgynous middle name, Carson. Her childhood friend at the age of nine, Helen Jackson, recalled in an interview with McCullers's definitive biographer, Virginia Spencer Carr, that Carson "hated more than anything else being made to do 'sissy things with sissy little girls.' She much preferred kick-the-can and football."

Like several of McCullers's female characters, what thrilled adolescent girls, such as attending "proms" (house parties for the thirteen-year-old set at which there were opportunities to hold hands with or kiss boys), could not thrill her. She was uncurvaceous and long (5 feet 8½ inches before adolescence), much too smart to be a convincing southern belle, and, of course, not popular with the boys when she became too old to play the role of tomboy. As a teenager she made her peers uncomfortable. In high school she was once attacked with jeers and rocks by female classmates, who called her "freakish-looking" and "queer." But she seems to have clung to difference. In the 1930s, for example, when even bulldaggers in Harlem and Greenwich Village were dressing like women from the waist down (that is, sporting skirts and stockings), Carson, residing in a small southern town, often wore men's pants. She never "outgrew" that sartorial preference.

Like many lesbians and bisexuals of her day, McCullers married a bisexual man, Reeves McCullers. They divorced four years later in 1941, and married again in 1945, but the relationship was primarily one of companionship. They called each other "Brother" and "Sister." Both had numerous affairs with people of their own sex. A few days after Carson and Reeves arrived in New York in 1940, shortly after the publication of her first novel, she fell madly in love with Annemarie Clarac-Schwarzenbach, a beautiful Swiss writer. Although Annemarie never reciprocated McCullers's intensity, she appears to have been the great passion of her life. The relationship was cut short a couple of years later when Annemarie died in a bicycle accident. The other important love of McCullers's life was Mary Mercer, a child psychiatrist, whom she met in 1958 and with whom she remained until her death in 1967.

The following story, "Like That," which was not published until four years after McCullers's death, was written while she was still a teenager. Its narrator, who represents one of McCullers's autobiographical portraits of "butchy" adolescents, may have been the fictional original for her later depictions of characters such as Mick and Frankie. Like Mick, who vows, after learning about heterosexual sex, "I never will marry with any boy," the narrator of "Like That" decides after observing the effect of heterosexual experience on her sister, "I never would let any fuss with any boy make me feel or look like that."

However, while Mick's inversion appears to be congenital, the narrator of "Like That" is as she is because of environmental influences. Before the action of the story begins, the narrator has already been traumatized by her knowledge that heterosexual sex leads to death. Her aunt's death in childbirth is followed almost immediately by the narrator's discovery about menstruation and its implications. With her sister's affair with Tuck the trauma is renewed. The narrator sees that heterosexuality spells the destruction of female wholeness and integrity and it signals the end of the Edenic relationship females can share.

FURTHER READING: Carson McCullers, The Heart Is a Lonely Hunter (Boston: Houghton Mifflin, 1940). Carson McCullers, The Ballad of the Sad Café (1943; reprint, New York: Bantam, 1976); The Member of the Wedding (1946; reprint, New York: Bantam, 1986). Panthea Reid Broughton, "Rejection of the Feminine in Carson McCullers's Ballad of the Sad Café," Twentieth Century Literature 20: 1 (January 1974). Virginia Spencer Carr, The Lonely Hunter: A Biography of Carson McCullers (Garden City, NY: Doubleday, 1975). Louise Westling, Sacred Groves and Ravaged Gardens: The Fiction of Eudora Welty, Carson McCullers and Flannery O'Connor (Athens: University of Georgia Press, 1985).

Like That

Even if Sis is five years older than me and eighteen we used always to be closer and have more fun together than most sisters. It was about the same with us and our brother Dan, too. In the summer we'd all go swimming together. At nights in the wintertime maybe we'd sit around the fire in the living room and play three-handed bridge or Michigan, with everybody putting up a nickel or a dime to the winner. The three of us could have more fun by ourselves than any family I know. That's the way it always was before this.

Not that Sis was playing down to me, either. She's smart as she can be and has read more books than anybody I ever knew—even school teachers. But in High School she never did like to priss up flirty and ride around in cars with girls and pick up the boys and park at the drug store and all that sort of thing. When she wasn't reading she'd just like to play around with me and Dan. She wasn't too grown up to fuss over a chocolate bar in the refrigerator or to stay awake most of Christmas Eve night either, say, with excitement. In some ways it was like I was heaps older than her. Even when Tuck started coming around last summer I'd sometimes have to tell her she shouldn't wear ankle socks because they might go down town or she ought to pluck out her eyebrows above her nose like the other girls do.

In one more year, next June, Tuck'll be graduated from college. He's a lanky boy with an eager look to his face. At college he's so smart he has a free scholarship. He started coming to see Sis the last summer before this one, riding in his family's car when he could get it, wearing crispy white linen suits. He came a lot last year but this summer he came even more often—before he left he was coming around for Sis every night. Tuck's O.K.

It began getting different between Sis and me a while back, I guess, although I didn't notice it at the time. It was only after a certain night this summer that I had the idea that things maybe were bound to end like they are now.

It was late when I woke up that night. When I opened my eyes I thought for a minute it must be about dawn and I was scared when I saw Sis wasn't on her side of the bed. But it was only the moonlight that shone cool looking and white outside the window and made the oak leaves hanging down over the front yard pitch black and separate seeming. It was around the first of September, but I didn't feel hot looking at the moonlight. I pulled the sheet over me and let my eyes roam around the black shapes of the furniture in our room.

I'd waked up lots of times in the night this summer. You see Sis and I have always had this room together and when she would come in and turn on the light to find her nightgown or something it woke me. I liked it. In the summer when school was out I didn't have to get up early in the morning. We would lie and talk sometimes for a good while. I'd like to hear about the places she and Tuck had been or to laugh over different things. Lots of times before that night she had talked to me privately about Tuck just like I was her age—asking me if I thought she should have said this or that when he called and giving me a hug, maybe, after. Sis was really crazy about Tuck. Once she said to me: "He's so lovely—I never in the world thought I'd know anyone like him—"

We would talk about our brother too. Dan's seventeen years old and was planning to take the co-op course at Tech in the fall. Dan had gotten older by this summer. One night he came in at four o'clock and he'd been drinking. Dad sure had it in for him the next week. So he hiked out to the country and camped with some boys for a few days. He used to talk to me and Sis about Diesel motors and going away to South America and all that, but by this summer he was quiet and not saying much to anybody in the family. Dan's real tall and thin as a rail. He has bumps on his face now and is clumsy and not very good looking. At nights sometimes I know he wanders all around by himself, maybe going out beyond the city limits sign into the pine woods.

Thinking about such things I lay in bed wondering what time it was and when Sis would be in. That night after Sis and Dan had left I had gone down to the corner with some of the kids in the neighborhood to chunk rocks at the street light and try to kill a bat up there. At first I had the shivers and imagined it was a smallish bat like the kind in Dracula. When I saw it looked just like a moth I didn't care if they killed it or not. I was just sitting there on the curb drawing with a stick on the dusty street when Sis and Tuck rode by slowly in his car. She was sitting over very close to him. They weren't talking or smiling—just riding slowly down the street, sitting close, looking ahead. When they passed and I saw who it was I hollered to them. "Hey, Sis!" I yelled.

The car just went on slowly and nobody hollered back. I just stood there in the middle of the street feeling sort of silly with all the other kids standing around.

That hateful little old Bubber from down on the other block came up to me. "That your sister?" he asked.

I said yes.

"She sure was sitting up close to her beau," he said.

I was mad all over like I get sometimes. I hauled off and chunked all the rocks in my hand right at him. He's three years younger than me and it wasn't nice, but I couldn't stand him in the first place and he thought he was being so cute about Sis. He started holding his neck and bellering and I walked off and left them and went home and got ready to go to bed.

When I woke up I finally began to think of that too and old Bubber Davis was still in my mind when I heard the sound of a car coming up the block. Our room faces the street with only a short front yard between. You can see and hear everything from the sidewalk and the street. The car was creeping down in front of our walk and the light went slow and white along the walls of the room. It stopped on Sis's writing desk, showed up the books there plainly and half a pack of chewing gum. Then the room was dark and there was only the moonlight outside.

The door of the car didn't open but I could hear them talking. Him, that is. His voice was low and I couldn't catch any words but it was like he was explaining something over and over again. I never heard Sis say a word.

I was still awake when I heard the car door open. I heard her say, "Don't come out." And then the door slammed and there was the sound of her heels clopping up the walk, fast and light like she was running.

Mama met Sis in the hall outside our room. She had heard the front door close. She always listens out for Sis and Dan and never goes to sleep when they're still out. I sometimes wonder how she can just lie there in the dark for hours without going to sleep.

"It's one-thirty, Marian," she said. "You ought to get in before this."

Sis didn't say anything.

"Did you have a nice time?"

That's the way Mama is. I could imagine her standing there with her nightgown blowing out fat around her and her dead white legs and the blue veins showing, looking all messed up. Mama's nicer when she's dressed to go out.

"Yes, we had a grand time," Sis said. Her voice was funny—sort of like the piano in the gym at school, high and sharp on your ear. Funny.

Mama was asking more questions. Where did they go? Did they see anybody they knew? All that sort of stuff. That's the way she is.

"Goodnight," said Sis in that out of tune voice.

She opened the door of our room real quick and closed it. I started to let her know I was awake but changed my mind. Her breathing was quick and loud in the dark and she did not move at all. After a few minutes she felt in the closet for her nightgown and got in the bed. I could hear her crying.

"Did you and Tuck have a fuss?" I asked.

"No," she answered. Then she seemed to change her mind. "Yeah, it was a fuss."

There's one thing that gives me the creeps sure enough—and that's to hear somebody cry. "I wouldn't let it bother me. You'll be making up tomorrow."

The moon was coming in the window and I could see her moving her jaw from one side to the other and staring up at the ceiling. I watched her for a long time. The moonlight was cool looking and there was a wettish wind coming cool from the window. I moved over like I sometimes do to snug up with her, thinking maybe that would stop her from moving her jaw like that and crying.

She was trembling all over. When I got close to her she jumped like I'd pinched her and pushed me over quick and kicked my legs over. "Don't," she said. "Don't."

Maybe Sis had suddenly gone batty, I was thinking. She was crying in a slower and sharper way. I was a little scared and I got up to go to the bathroom a minute. While I was in there I looked out the window, down toward the corner where the street light is. I saw something then that I knew Sis would want to know about.

"You know what?" I asked when I was back in the bed.

She was lying over close to the edge as she could get, stiff. She didn't answer.

"Tuck's car is parked down by the street light. Just drawn up to the curb. I could tell because of the box and the two tires on the back. I could see it from the bathroom window."

She didn't even move.

"He must be just sitting out there. What ails you and him?"

She didn't say anything at all.

"I couldn't see him but he's probably just sitting there in the car under the street light. Just sitting there."

It was like she didn't care or had known it all along. She was as far over the edge of the bed as she could get, her legs stretched out stiff and her hands holding tight to the edge and her face on one arm.

She used always to sleep all sprawled over on my side so I'd have to push at her when it was hot and sometimes turn on the light and draw the line down the middle and show her how she really was on my side. I wouldn't have to draw any line that night, I was thinking. I felt bad. I looked out at the moonlight a long time before I could get to sleep again.

The next day was Sunday and Mama and Dad went in the morning to church because it was the anniversary of the day my aunt died. Sis said she didn't feel well and stayed in bed. Dan was out and I was there by myself so naturally I went into our room where Sis was. Her face was white as the pillow and there were circles under her eyes. There was a muscle jumping on one side of her jaw like she was chewing. She hadn't combed her hair and it flopped over the pillow, glinty red and messy and pretty. She was reading with a book held up close to her face. Her eyes didn't move when I came in. I don't think they even moved across the page.

It was roasting hot that morning. The sun made everything blazing outside so that it hurt your eyes to look. Our room was so hot that you could almost touch the air with your finger. But Sis had the sheet pulled up clear to her shoulders.

"Is Tuck coming today?" I asked. I was trying to say something that would make her look more cheerful.

"Gosh! Can't a person have *any* peace in this house?"

She never did used to say mean things like that out of a clear sky. Mean things, maybe, but not grouchy ones.

"Sure," I said. "Nobody's going to notice you."

I set down and pretended to read. When footsteps passed on the street Sis would hold onto the book tighter and I knew she was listening hard as she could. I can tell between footsteps easy. I can even tell without looking if the person who passes is colored or not. Colored people mostly make a slurry sound between the steps. When the steps would pass Sis would loosen the hold on the book and bite at her mouth. It was the same way with passing cars.

I felt sorry for Sis. I decided then and there that I never would let any fuss with any boy make me feel or look like that. But I wanted Sis and me to get back like we'd always been. Sunday mornings are bad enough without having any other trouble.

"We fuss a lots less than most sisters do," I said. "And when we do it's all over quick, isn't it?"

She mumbled and kept staring at the same spot on the book.

"That's one good thing," I said.

She was moving her head slightly from side to side—over and over again, with her face not changing. "We never do have any real long fusses like Bubber Davis's two sisters have—"

"No." She answered like she wasn't thinking about what I'd said.

"Not one real one like that since I can remember."

In a minute she looked up the first time. "I remember one," she said suddenly.

"When?"

Her eyes looked green in the blackness under them and like they were nailing themselves into what they saw. "You had to stay in every afternoon for a week. It was a long time ago."

All of a sudden I remembered. I'd forgotten it for a long time. I hadn't wanted to remember. When she said that it came back to me all complete.

It was really a long time ago—when Sis was about thirteen. If I remember right I was mean and even more hardboiled than I am now. My aunt who I'd liked better than all my other aunts put together had had a dead baby and she had died. After the funeral Mama had told Sis and me about it. Always the things I've learned new and didn't like have made me mad—mad clean through and scared.

That wasn't what Sis was talking about, though. It was a few mornings after that when Sis started with what every big girl has each month, and of course I found out and was scared to death. Mama then explained to me about it and what she had to wear. I felt then like I'd felt about my aunt, only ten times worse. I felt different toward Sis, too, and was so mad I wanted to pitch into people and hit.

I never will forget it. Sis was standing in our room before the dresser mirror. When I remembered her face it was white like Sis's there on the pillow and with the circles under her eyes and the glinty hair to her shoulders—it was only younger.

I was sitting on the bed, biting hard at my knee. "It shows," I said. "It does too!"

She had on a sweater and a blue pleated skirt and she was so skinny all over that it did show a little.

"Anybody can tell. Right off the bat. Just to look at you anybody can tell."

Her face was white in the mirror and did not move.

"It looks terrible. I wouldn't ever ever be like that. It shows and everything."

She started crying then and told Mother and said she wasn't going back to school and such. She cried a long time. That's how ugly and hardboiled I used to be and am still sometimes. That's why I had to stay in the house every afternoon for a week a long time ago. . . .

Tuck came by in his car that Sunday morning before dinner time. Sis got up and dressed in a hurry and didn't even put on any lipstick. She said they were going out to dinner. Nearly every Sunday all of us in the family stay together all day, so that was a little funny. They didn't get home until almost dark. The rest of us were sitting on the front porch drinking ice tea because of the heat when the car drove up again. After they got out of the car Dad, who had been in a very good mood all day, insisted Tuck stay for a glass of tea.

Tuck sat on the swing with Sis and he didn't lean back and his heels didn't rest on the floor—as though he was all ready to get up again. He kept changing the glass from one hand to the other and starting new conversations. He and Sis didn't look at each other except on the sly, and then it wasn't at all like they were crazy about each other. It was a funny look. Almost like they were afraid of something. Tuck left soon.

"Come sit by your Dad a minute, Puss," Dad said. Puss is a nickname he calls Sis when he feels in a specially good mood. He still likes to pet us.

She went and sat on the arm of his chair. She sat stiff like Tuck had, holding herself off a little so Dad's arm hardly went around her waist. Dad smoked his cigar and looked out on the front yard and the trees that were beginning to melt into the early dark.

"How's my big girl getting along these days?" Dad still likes to hug us up when he feels good and treat us, even Sis, like kids.

"O.K.," she said. She twisted a little bit like she wanted to get up and didn't know how to without hurting his feelings.

"You and Tuck have had a nice time together this summer, haven't you, Puss?"

"Yeah," she said. She had begun to see-saw her lower jaw again. I wanted to say something but couldn't think of anything.

Dad said: "He ought to be getting back to Tech about now, oughtn't he? When's he leaving?"

"Less than a week," she said. She got up so quick that she knocked Dad's cigar out of his fingers. She didn't even pick it up but flounced on through the front door. I could hear her half running to our room and the sound the door made when she shut it. I knew she was going to cry.

It was hotter than ever. The lawn was beginning to grow dark and the locusts were droning out so shrill and steady that you wouldn't notice them unless you thought to. The sky was bluish grey and the trees in the vacant lot across the street were dark. I kept on sitting on the front porch with Mama and Papa and hearing their low talk without listening to the words. I wanted to go in our room with Sis but I was afraid to. I wanted to ask her what was really the matter. Was hers and Tuck's fuss so bad as that or was it that she was so crazy about him that she was sad because he was leaving? For a minute I didn't think it was either one of those things. I wanted to know but I was scared to ask. I just sat there with the grown people. I never have been so lonesome as I was that night. If ever I think about being sad I just remember how it was then—sitting there looking at the long bluish shadows across the lawn and feeling like I was the only child left in the family and that Sis and Dan were dead or gone for good.

It's October now and the sun shines bright and a little cool and the sky is the color of my turquoise ring. Dan's gone to Tech. So has Tuck gone. It's not at all like it was last fall, though. I come in from High School (I go there now) and Sis maybe is just sitting by the window reading or writing to Tuck or just looking out. Sis is thinner and sometimes to me she looks in the face like a grown person. Or like, in a way, something has suddenly hurt her hard. We don't do any of the things we used to. It's good weather for fudge or for doing so many things. But no she just sits around or goes for long walks in the chilly late afternoon by herself. Sometimes she'll smile in a way that really gripes—like I was such a kid and all. Sometimes I want to cry or to hit her.

But I'm hardboiled as the next person. I can get along by myself if Sis or anybody else wants to. I'm glad I'm thirteen and still wear socks and can do what I please. I don't want to be any older if I'd get like Sis has. But I wouldn't. I wouldn't like any boy in the world as much as she does Tuck. I'd never let any boy or any thing make me act like she does. I'm not going to waste my time and try to make Sis be like she used to be. I get lonesome—sure—but I don't care. I know there's no way I can make myself stay thirteen all my life, but I know I'd never let anything really change me at all—no matter what it is.

I skate and ride my bike and go to the school football games every Friday. But when one afternoon the kids all got quiet in the gym basement and then started telling certain things—about being married and all—I got up quick so I wouldn't hear and went up and played basketball. And when some of the kids said they were going to start wearing lipstick and stockings I said I wouldn't for a hundred dollars.

You see I'd never be like Sis is now. I wouldn't. Anybody could know that if they knew me. I just wouldn't, that's all. I don't want to grow up —if it's like that.

Jane (Auer) Bowles
(1917–73)

When she was eighteen Jane Auer went on dates with the "nice Jewish boys" her mother picked out for her, but after they brought her home she would sneak out again and finish the evening in a lesbian bar in Greenwich Village or engaged in some other lesbian adventure. By the time she met Paul Bowles in 1937 she had cut her hair short and was smoking little Cuban cigars. Paul, a promising young composer, was a bisexual who was enamored of the witty, talented, lively Jane. She told him that she had affairs only with women but that of course she intended someday to marry a man. Heterosexual marriage would bring her a small inheritance from her family, it would permit her to escape from her overly binding mother, and it would remedy her unwelcome solitude (she told a gay composer friend, David Diamond, at that time, "Honey, I'm so lonely"). Heterosexual marriages of convenience in the 1930s were very common among lesbians. Paul Bowles also believed, despite his interest in men, that "one gets married." He recalled to biographer Millicent Dillon, "Jane and I used to spin fantasies about how amusing it would be to get married and horrify everyone, above all our respective families." They married in 1938.

Their relationship, which lasted for thirty-five years, was more than a marriage of convenience, despite the fact that it ceased to be sexual by 1940. Both had primarily homosexual affairs, yet remained in close contact with each other, often traveling around the world together and sometimes living together. Although among Jane's many lovers were a couple of men, she generally refrained from heterosexual affairs because she knew that Paul did not mind her lesbian relationships but would be "very hurt" if she got involved with another male. Jane now saw herself as being emotionally split. She wrote a friend in 1950 about her fulfilling relationship in Paris with a woman, "Marty": "Having known Marty, I will not die still searching and feeling cheated." But in the same letter she lamented, "Some days I am in misery because I seem to feel two equally strong destinies, and one of them is to be with Paul."

Paul Bowles functioned much like Harold Nicolson in Vita Sackville-West's life. While both women saw themselves as preferring a sexual relationship (and all its concomitant adventures) with another woman, their husbands apparently represented to them a kind of safety and stability that lesbians in the pre-lesbian-feminist era had little reason to believe they could find with another woman. During a time when Jane was alone in Morocco, in hot (and ostensibly useless) pursuit of two women while Paul was working and having affairs with men in New York, she wrote him, "I cannot imagine a better time really than being in a place we both liked and each of us being free and having adventures. Even if mine were frustrating, they would be more amusing, naturally, if you were here."

Their relationship was not always constructive. When Jane, who often suffered from writer's block, was agonizing over her inability to finish a piece, Paul told her that the only way to write was to sit down and do it. He, who had hitherto been only a composer, quickly wrote first several stories and then *The Sheltering Sky* (a "heterosexualized" novel that features his relationship with Jane), which became a best-seller. He continued to be a productive fiction writer through much of his life. The effect on Jane was to intensify her writer's block.

Although she was able to finish one novel, one full-length play, and several short stories in the course of their marriage, much of her most promising work, such as the intriguing fragments of a lesbian novel, *Going to Massachusetts,* remained unfinished. She may have been unable to complete her more explicitly lesbian writing because of fear of censorship, but it also appears that in addition to being intimidated by Paul's success she had an overwhelming need for his reassurance, and when it was not easily forthcoming she felt lost. She wrote him in 1948 about her work as an author, "Would I bother if you didn't exist? It is awful not to know what one would do if one were utterly alone in the world. You could do just what you've always done . . . but I don't exist independently."

Despite what she saw as a great need for Bowles in her life, her lesbian affairs were numerous and never hidden from him. On their honeymoon in Paris, Jane left Paul to go off to Le Monocle, a notorious lesbian bar, where she fell into mad lust over the butch proprietress, Bobbie. Her stormy affair with a woman twenty-two years her senior, Helvetia Perkins, lasted for seven years, during which Jane often lived with Helvetia but saw Paul every day when they were in the same city. (The relationship with Helvetia is recorded in Jane Bowles's short play *A Quarreling Pair* [1944], which encodes the lesbian material by presenting the women as sisters instead of lovers.) After the affair with Helvetia was over, when Paul was traveling in 1947, Jane wrote him, "I wish to hell I could find some woman still so that I wouldn't always be alone at night." She was often not alone, having been involved with a proprietress of an American tea shop, as well as with a daughter of an English countess, the wife of an Italian prince, and many others.

Her longest, and most difficult, lesbian relationship was with a Moroccan peasant woman, Cherifa, whom she met when she went to join Paul in Morocco in 1948. When Paul returned to New York to write the music for the Broadway production of a new play, *Summer and Smoke,* by his gay friend Tennessee Williams, Jane remained in Morocco in order to pursue Cherifa, a grain seller in the Tangier marketplace, who sported a downy mustache and wore jeans and golf shoes under her long red-and-white-striped Berber blanket. Although Cherifa looked like a Western lesbian, she was having a sexual relationship with an Arab man when Jane met her. Cherifa also had emotional and sensual relationships with other women, attachments that the Western world in another era would have dubbed romantic friendships—but Jane knew nothing of romantic friendship and assumed that what she was seeing was lesbianism. It caused considerable confusion, which was compounded by Jane's secondary romantic interest in Tetum, another masculine-looking woman who sold grain in the marketplace. Jane dubbed Tetum the "mountain dyke," although again the woman was innocent of Western-style lesbianism.

It is difficult to tell what Jane's pursuit of these Arab women meant to her. She wrote Paul that her courtship of them gave her the feeling of "being on the edge of something." She had witnessed Paul and his gay male friends who, while visiting Morocco, acquired easy access into the male Arab culture by their ability to buy young Arab men for sex and thus to insinuate themselves into their lives. In that less sensitive era, such a money-sex exchange was seldom analyzed for its unfortunate colonial implications.

To Jane, the exoticism of the adventure was enviable. She discovered, however, that as a Western woman it was much less easy to make such contacts and inroads into the culture of Arab women.

For years Jane continued her pursuit with incredible tenacity, in between several lesbian affairs with Westerners. She managed eventually to see a bit of the culture by buying dinners for Cherifa's family, giving her money, clothes, even paying her doctor bills—and expending similar generosity on Tetum. In the mid-1950s, she persuaded Cherifa to live with her, with the understanding that she would deed a house that she and Paul bought in Morocco to the Arab woman. Jane told a gay male friend that she and Cherifa finally did have something of an erotic exchange, though Jane "had to teach Cherifa to make love." Their sexual relationship lasted for only about a year. In 1967 Jane was hospitalized for depression, and Paul, holding Cherifa responsible for Jane's illness, managed to get Cherifa out of her life to a significant extent. (It was said by Moroccans that Cherifa performed black magic hexes on Jane.) Jane was finally committed to a mental hospital in Málaga, where she died in 1973.

The following selections, a letter to two American lesbian friends and a short story, both tell of Jane's frustrations as a Western lesbian attempting to relate to Arab women, though the lesbian content of the story is much more encoded than that of the letter. Like Carson McCullers, Jane Bowles felt more comfortable dealing openly in her writing with gay men than with lesbians, as her (incomplete) novella, *Andrew,* illustrates. Her only completed novel, *Two Serious Ladies* (1943), had been criticized by her mother, as well as Paul's family, Helvetia, and others for being "too obviously lesbian." Thus in most of her subsequent works, with the exception of the aborted *Going to Massachusetts,* she hid the lesbian subject matter, though not the lesbian sensibility.

FURTHER READING: Jane Bowles, *My Sister's Hand in Mine: The Collected Works of Jane Bowles* (New York: Ecco Press, 1978); *Out in the World: Selected Letters of Jane Bowles, 1935–1970,* ed. Millicent Dillon (Santa Barbara, CA: Black Sparrow Press, 1985). Millicent Dillon, *A Little Original Sin: The Life and Work of Jane Bowles* (New York: Holt, Rinehart, 1981). Michelle Green, *The Dream at the End of the World: Paul Bowles and the Literary Renegades in Tangier* (New York: HarperCollins, 1991).

Selected Letters

From Jane Bowles to Natasha von Hoershelman &
Katharine Hamill, from Tangier, June 1954

Darling Natasha and Katharine,
I never stop thinking about you but too much happened. Please forgive me
if this is not an amusing letter. . . . I think I had better simply write you a
gross factual résumé of what has happened. Then if I have any sense I shall
keep notes. Because what is happening is interesting and funny in itself. I
am a fool to have lost two whole months of it. I have no memory—only
a subconscious memory which I am afraid translates everything into something else, and so I shall have to take notes. I have a very pretty leather
book for that purpose.

The day you left I was terribly terribly sad. I still miss you—in the sense
that I keep thinking through it all that you should be here and how sorry
I am that you left before I could truly take you into some of the life that
I love.

. . . I went down that long street, way down in, and landed in a room
filled with eighteen women—and a dozen or two little babies wearing knitted capes and hoods. One lady had on a peach satin evening dress and
over it the jacket of a man's business suit. (A Spanish business suit.) I had
been searching for Cherifa—and having been to about three houses all
belonging to her family I finally landed there. I thought I was in a
bordello—the room was very plush—filled with hideous blue and white
chenille cushions made in Manchester England. Cherifa wore a pale blue
sateen skirt down to the ground and a grayish Spanish sweater—a kind of
school sweater but not sporty. She seemed to be constantly flirting with a
woman in a pale blue kaftan (our hostess), and finally she sat next to her
and encircled her waist. C. looked like a child. The woman weighed about
160 pounds and was loaded with rouge and eye makeup. Now I know her.
An alcoholic named Fat Zohra and one of two wives. She is married to a
kind of criminal whom I believe knifed his own brother over a card game
and spent five years in jail. The other wife lives in a different house and
does all the child-bearing. Fat Zohra is barren. There was one pale-looking
girl (very light green), whom I thought was surely the richest and the most
distinguished of the lot. She wore a wonderful embroidered kaftan—a rich
spinach green with a leaf design. Her face was rather sour—thin compressed lips and a long mean-looking nose. I was sad while they played the
drums and did their lewd belly dances because I thought, my God if you
had only stayed a day longer but of course if you had perhaps they
wouldn't have asked you in (Cherifa I mean); they are so leery of strangers.

In any case at the end of the afternoon, (and part of my sadness was an aching jealousy of the woman in the blue kaftan), Cherifa took me to the doorway and into the blue courtyard where two boring pigeons were squatting and asked me whether or not I was going to live in my house. The drums were still beating and I had sticky cakes in my hand—those I couldn't eat. (I stuffed down as many as I could; I loathe them) but I was really too jealous and also sad because you had left to get down very many. I said I would of course but not before I found a maid. She told me to wait and a minute later came out with the distinguished pale green one; Here's your maid, she said. "A very poor girl."

Anyway a month and a half later she became my maid. I call her sour pickle and she has stolen roughly about one thousand four hundred pesetas from me. I told C. about it who advised me not to keep any money in the house. She is a wonderful maid—an excellent cook and sleeps with me here. . . .

One day before Ramadan and before Paul had typhoid I went to the market and sat in a gloom about Indo-China and the Moroccan situation and every other thing in the world that was a situation outside my own. Soon I cheered up a little. I was in the part where Tetum sits in among the coal and the mules and the chickens. Two little boy musicians came by. I gave them some money and Tetum ordered songs. Soon we had a big crowd around us, one of those Marrakech circles. Everybody stopped working (working?) and we had one half-hour of music, myself and everybody else, in that part of the market—(you know). And people gathered from round about—just like Tiflis. Tetum was in good spirits. She told me that Cherifa had a girlfriend who was fat and white. I recognized fat Zohra—though I shall never know whether or not I put the fat white picture in her mind or not. I might have said "Is she fat and white?" I don't know. Then she asked me if I wouldn't drive her out to Sidi Menarie—one of the sacred groves around here where Sidi Menarie (a saint) is buried. They like to visit as many saints as possible of course because it gives them extra gold stars for heaven. I thought—"Natasha and Katharine will be angry." They told me to stick to Cherifa but then they didn't know about fat Zohra. After saying this in my head I felt free to offer Tetum a trip to the grove without making you angry.

Of course it turned out that she wanted to take not only one but two neighbors and their children. We were to leave at eight-thirty A.M., *she insisted*. The next day when I got to Tetum's house on the Marshan with Temsamany (nearly an hour late) Tetum came to the door in a grey bathrobe. I was very surprised. Underneath she was dressed in a long zugdun and under that she wore other things. I can't describe a zugdun but it is quite enough to wear without adding on a bathrobe. But when they wear our night clothes they wear them over or under their own (which are simply the underpeelings or first three layers of their day clothes, like in Tiflis). She yanked me into her house, tickled my palm, shouted to her neighbor (asleep on the other side of a thin curtain) and in general pranced about the room. She dressed me up in a hideous half-Arab half-Spanish cotton dress which came to my ankles and had no shape at all. Just a little round neck. She belted it and said "—now go back to the hotel and show your husband how pretty you look." I said I would some other day; and what about our trip to the saint's tomb? She said yes yes—but she had to go and fetch the other two women who both lived in a different part of the town. I said would they be ready and she said something like, "Bacai—shouay." Which means just nothing. Finally I arranged to come back for her at three. Rather infuriated because I had gotten Temsamany up at the crack. But I was not surprised—nor was he. Tetum took me to her gate. "If you are not here at three," she said in sudden anger, "I shall walk to the grove myself on my own legs." (Five hours, roughly.) We went back at three and the laundry bags were ready and the children and Tetum.

"We are going to two saints," Tetum said. "First Sidi Menarie and then we'll stop at the other saint's on the way back. He's buried on the edge of town and we've got to take the children to him and cut their throats because they have whooping cough." She poked one of the laundry bundles who showed me a knife. I was getting rather nervous because Paul of course was expecting us back roughly around seven and I know how long those things can take. We drove along the awful road (the one that frightened you) toward the grove—only we went on and on much further out and the road began to bother me a little after a while. You would have hated it. The knife of course served for the symbolic cutting of the children's throat though at first I had thought they were going to draw some blood, if not a great deal. I didn't think they were actually going to kill the children or I wouldn't have taken them on the ride. We reached the sacred grove which is not far from the lighthouse one can see coming into the harbor. Unfortunately they have built some ugly restaurants around and about the lighthouse, and not far from the sacred grove so that sedans are now constantly passing on the highway. The grove itself is very beautiful and if one goes far enough inside it, far away from the road, one does not see the cars passing. We didn't penetrate very far into the grove because being a Christian, (oy!) I can't sit within the vicinity of the saint's tomb. Temsamany spread the tarpaulin on the ground and the endless tea equipment they had brought with them and they were off to the saint's leaving Temsamany and myself behind. He said, "I shall make a fire and then when they come back the water will be boiling." They came back. God knows when. The water was boiling—we had used up a lot of dead olive branches. They sat down and lowered their veils so that they hung under their chins like ugly bibs. They had bought an excellent sponge cake. As usual something sweet. I thought, "Romance here is impossible." Tetum's neighbors were ugly. One in particular—"Like a turtle," Temsamany said. She kept looking down into her lap. Tetum the captain of the group said to the turtle, "Look at the world. Look at the world." "I am looking at the world," the other woman said, but she kept looking down into her lap. They cut up all the sponge cake. I said, "Stop—leave it, we'll never eat it all." Temsamany said, "I'm going to roller skate." He went off and we could see him through the trees. After a while the conversation stopped. Even Tetum was at a loss. There was a little excitement when they spotted the woman who runs the toilets under the grain market—seated not far off—with a group, somewhat larger than ours—but nothing else happened.

I went to look for Temsamany on the highway. He had roller skated out of sight. I felt that all my pursuits here were hopeless. I looked back over my shoulder into the grove. Tetum was swinging upside down from an olive tree, her knees hooked over a branch, and she is, after all, forty-five and veiled and a miser.

There is more to this day but I see now that I have done exactly what I did not want to do. I have gone into great detail about one incident, which is probably of no interest.

But as a result of that day Cherifa and I have been much closer. In fact she spends two or three nights here a week in dungarees and Haymaker shirts. She asked for five thousand pesetas (about one hundred and fifteen dollars), so that she could fill her grain stall to the brim. I have given her so far fifteen hundred pesetas. She sleeps in dungarees and several things underneath. I shall have to write you a whole other letter about this—in fact I waited and waited before writing because foolishly I hoped that I could write you "I have or have not—Cherifa." The awful thing is that I don't even know. I don't know what they do. I don't know how much they feel. Sometimes I think that I am just up against that awful hard-to-get Virgin block. Sometimes I think they just don't know. I—it is difficult to explain. So hard to know what is clever maneuvering on her part—what is a lack of passion—and what is fear—just plain fear of losing all her marketable value and that I won't care once I've had her. She is terribly affectionate at times and kissing is heaven. However I don't know quite how soon or if I should clamp down. I simply don't know. All the rules for playing the game are given me by Paul or else Temsamany. Both are men. T. says if you don't get them the first two times you never will. A frightening thought. But then he is a man. I told Paul one couldn't buy desire and he said desire can come but only with habit. And never does it mean what it means to us—rather less than holding hands supposedly. Everything is very preliminary and pleasant like the beginning of a love affair between a virgin and her boyfriend in some automobile. Then when we are finally in bed she says, "Now sleep." Then comes either "Goodbye" or a little Arabic blessing which I repeat after her. There we lie like two logs—one log with open eyes. I take sleeping pill after sleeping pill. Yet I'm afraid to strike the bargain. "If you do this I will give you all of the money—if not—" It is very difficult for me. Particularly as her affection and tenderness seem so terribly real. I'm not even sure that this isn't the most romantic experience in a sense that I have ever had and it is all so miraculous compared to what little went on before. I hesitate to rush it— to be brutal in my own eyes—even if she would understand it perfectly. I think love and *sex*—that is tenderness and sex beyond kissing and less caresses—may be forever separate in their minds, so that one might be going toward something less rather than more than what one had in the beginning. According to the few people I have spoken to . . . they have absolutely no aftermath. Lying back relaxing—all that which is more pleasant than the thing itself if one is in love (and only then) is nonexistent. Just quickly "O.K.? now we sleep." Or a rush for six water bowls—to wash the sin away. I'm not even sure I haven't in a way slept with C. Because I did get "Safi—naasu?" ("O.K. now we sleep.") But it does not mean always the same thing. I am up too many trees and cannot write you all obviously. Since I cannot seem to bring myself to the point of striking a verbal bargain—(cowardice, delicacy, love?) I don't know—but I simply can't—not yet. I shall have to wait until I find the situation more impossible than pleasant—until my nerves are shot and I am screaming with exasperation. It will come—but I don't believe I can say anything before I feel that way. It would only sound fake. My hunch is she would go away saying never. Then eventually come back. At the moment, no matter what, I am so much happier than I was. She seems to be getting a habit of the house. Last night she said, "It's strange that I can't eat eggs in my own house but here I eat them." Later she said that her bed at home was not as good as mine. Mine by the way is *something*—lumpy with no springs—just on straw—a thin wool mattress, on straw. At home she sleeps in a room with her great-aunt. The great-aunt on the floor. Cherifa on the bed, natch. She's that kind. I find her completely beautiful. A little smaller than myself—but with strong shoulders—strong legs with a good deal of hair on them—at the same time soft soft skin—and twenty-eight years old. Last night we went up on the topmost terrace and looked at all of Tangier. The boats and the stars and the long curved line of lights along the beach. There was a cold wind blowing and Cherifa was shivering. I kissed her just a little. Later downstairs she said the roof was very beautiful, and she wondered whether or not God had seen us. I wonder. I could go on about this, dear Katharine and Natasha, and I will some other time. I wish to Christ you were here. I can talk to Paul and he is interested but not that interested because we are all women. We see each other almost daily—his house is not far from here. And it is a lovely walk. Outside the walls of the Casbah—overlooking the beach and the ocean. Most of my time is taken up with him or Cherifa—or the house and now work. I am beginning again to work. Before she came I was such a nervous wreck I couldn't do any-thing. Also I was in despair about all the world news and as I told you Paul's illness—everything was a mess. Now I am in a panic about money and though I will write a play—I must write other things too for immediate cash. Not that I don't have any for a while but I must not use it all up before I have completed at least enough of a play for an advance. Thank God I am in a house and not in a hotel. Although the house has cost me a good deal until now it won't henceforth because I've bought most ev-erything I needed except a new bed for upstairs. I shall fill the house with beds—traps for a virgin. I feel happier now that I've written you. All the time I have been saying—I should write about *this* to N. and K. but it seemed impossible—utterly impossible to make a résumé of all that hap-pened before. And as you see, it was impossible. I have not even found it possible to write in this letter why Tetum swinging from an olive tree in her cloak and hood should have precipitated all this—but it did. I think Cherifa got worried about losing me to Tetum—she was so worried she asked me for a kaftan right off. Then started a conversation, a bargaining conversation which resulted in her coming here after Ramadan to spend the night. But I can't go into that now. I always let Fatima (sour pickle) decide what we are to eat. It is all so terribly simple—all in one dish. Either lamb with olives or with raisins, and onions, or chicken with the same or ground meat on skewers or beef or lamb on skewers (you remember how wonderful they taste). Or a fried potato omelet with onions, or boiled noodles with butter or eggs fried in oil and always lots of black bread and wine at five pesetas a quart (excellent). I've had guests once, Tennessee in fact, white beans in oil and with salt pork like the ones I cooked for you. Lots of salad—cucumber, tomato and onion, all chopped up, almost daily. Fresh figs, bananas, cherries. Whatever fruit is in season. Wonderful bowls of Turkish coffee in the morning which is brought to our bed (when she is here as she happens to be now for a kind of a week-end) or to me alone. And piles of toast soaked in butter. At noon we eat very little. Usually if Cherifa isn't here (she supposedly comes twice a week but that can include two afternoons) I go over to Paul's for lunch—cxccpt that he never eats until three thirty—sometimes four. I get up at seven and by then I am so hungry I don't even care but I like seeing him. We eat soup and bread and butter and cheese and tuna fish. For me tuna fish is the main diet. I love this life and I'm terrified of the day when my money runs out. The sex thing aside—it is as if I had dreamed this life before I was born. Perhaps I will work hard to keep it. I cannot keep Cherifa without money, or even myself, after all. Paul told Cherifa that without working I would never have any money so she is constantly sending me up into my little work room. A good thing. Naturally I think of her in terms of a long long time. How one can do this and at the same time fully realize the fact that money is of paramount importance to one's friend and etc. etc., that if there is to be much sleeping it will most likely be against their will or something they will do to please one—I simply don't know. Possibly if it came to that I might lose interest in the sleeping part, possibly why I keep putting off the bargaining—but the money I know is paramount. Yet they are not like we are. Someone behaving in the same way—who was not an Arab I couldn't bear. All this will have to wait for some other letter. Perhaps it is all a bore, if so tell me. But I thought since you have seen her and Tangier that it would interest you. . . .

Please write. I shall worry now about this messy letter.

All my love, always,
J. Bowles.

Everything Is Nice

The highest street in the blue Moslem town skirted the edge of a cliff. She walked over to the thick protecting wall and looked down. The tide was out, and the flat dirty rocks below were swarming with skinny boys. A Moslem woman came up to the blue wall and stood next to her, grazing her hip with the basket she was carrying. She pretended not to notice her, and kept her eyes fixed on a white dog that had just slipped down the side of a rock and plunged into a crater of sea water. The sound of its bark was earsplitting. Then the woman jabbed the basket firmly into her ribs, and she looked up.

"That one is a porcupine," said the woman, pointing a henna-stained finger into the basket.

This was true. A large dead porcupine lay there, with a pair of new yellow socks folded on top of it.

She looked again at the woman. She was dressed in a haik, and the white cloth covering the lower half of her face was loose, about to fall down.

"I am Zodelia," she announced in a high voice. "And you are Betsoul's friend." The loose cloth slipped below her chin and hung there like a bib. She did not pull it up.

"You sit in her house and you sleep in her house and you eat in her house," the woman went on, and she nodded in agreement. "Your name is Jeanie and you live in a hotel with other Nazarenes. How much does the hotel cost you?"

A loaf of bread shaped like a disc flopped on to the ground from inside the folds of the woman's haik, and she did not have to answer her question. With some difficulty the woman picked the loaf up and stuffed it in between the quills of the porcupine and the basket handle. Then she set the basket down on the top of the blue wall and turned to her with bright eyes.

"I am the people in the hotel," she said. "Watch me."

She was pleased because she knew that the woman who called herself Zodelia was about to present her with a little skit. It would be delightful to watch, since all the people of the town spoke and gesticulated as though they had studied at the *Comédie Française*.

"The people in the hotel," Zodelia announced, formally beginning her skit. "I am the people in the hotel."

" 'Good-bye, Jeanie, good-bye. Where are you going?'

" 'I am going to a Moslem house to visit my Moslem friends, Betsoul and her family. I will sit in a Moslem room and eat Moslem food and sleep on a Moslem bed.'

" 'Jeanie, Jeanie, when will you come back to us in the hotel and sleep in your own room?'

" 'I will come back to you in three days. I will come back and sit in a Nazarene room and eat Nazarene food and sleep on a Nazarene bed. I will spend half the week with Moslem friends and half with Nazarenes.' "

The woman's voice had a triumphant ring as she finished her sentence; then, without announcing the end of the sketch, she walked over to the wall and put one arm around her basket.

Down below, just at the edge of the cliff's shadow, a Moslem woman was seated on a rock, washing her legs in one of the holes filled with sea water. Her haik was piled on her lap and she was huddled over it, examining her feet.

"She is looking at the ocean," said Zodelia.

She was not looking at the ocean; with her head down and the mass of cloth in her lap she could not possibly have seen it; she would have had to straighten up and turn around.

"She is *not* looking at the ocean," she said.

"She is looking at the ocean," Zodelia repeated, as if she had not spoken.

She decided to change the subject. "Why do you have a porcupine with you?" she asked her, although she knew that some of the Moslems, particularly the country people, enjoyed eating them.

"It is a present for my aunt. Do you like it?"

"Yes," she said. "I like porcupines. I like big porcupines and little ones, too."

Zodelia seemed bewildered, and then bored, and she decided she had somehow ruined the conversation by mentioning small porcupines.

"Where is your mother?" Zodelia said at length.

"My mother is in her country in her own house," she said automatically; she had answered the question a hundred times.

"Why don't you write her a letter and tell her to come here? You can take her on a promenade and show her the ocean. After that she can go back to her own country and sit in her house." She picked up her basket and adjusted the strip of cloth over her mouth. "Would you like to go to a wedding?" she asked her.

She said she would love to go to a wedding, and they started off down the crooked blue street, heading into the wind. As they passed a small shop Zodelia stopped. "Stand here," she said. "I want to buy something."

After studying the display for a minute or two Zodelia poked her and pointed to some cakes inside a square box with glass sides. "Nice?" she asked her. "Or not nice?"

The cakes were dusty and coated with a thin, ugly-colored icing. They were called *Galletas Ortiz*.

"They are very nice," she replied, and bought her a dozen of them. Zodelia thanked her briefly and they walked on. Presently they turned off the street into a narrow alley and started downhill. Soon Zodelia stopped at a door on the right, and lifted the heavy brass knocker in the form of a fist.

"The wedding is here?" she said to her.

Zodelia shook her head and looked grave. "There is no wedding here," she said.

A child opened the door and quickly hid behind it, covering her face. She followed Zodelia across the black and white tile floor of the closed patio. The walls were washed in blue, and a cold light shone through the broken panes of glass far above their heads. There was a door on each side of the patio. Outside one of them, barring the threshold, was a row of pointed slippers. Zodelia stepped out of her own shoes and set them down near the others.

She stood behind Zodelia and began to take off her own shoes. It took her a long time because there was a knot in one of her laces. When she was ready, Zodelia took her hand and pulled her along with her into a dimly lit room, where she led her over to a mattress which lay against the wall.

"Sit," she told her, and she obeyed. Then, without further comment she walked off, heading for the far end of the room. Because her eyes had not grown used to the dimness, she had the impression of a figure disappearing down a long corridor. Then she began to see the brass bars of a bed, glowing weakly in the darkness.

Only a few feet away, in the middle of the carpet, sat an old lady in a dress made of green and purple curtain fabric. Through the many rents in the material she could see the printed cotton dress and the tan sweater underneath. Across the room several women sat along another mattress, and further along the mattress three babies were sleeping in a row, each one close against the wall with its head resting on a fancy cushion.

"Is it nice here?" It was Zodelia, who had returned without her haik. Her black crepe European dress hung unbelted down to her ankles, almost grazing her bare feet. The hem was lopsided. "Is it nice here?" she asked again, crouching on her haunches in front of her and pointing at the old woman. "That one is Tetum," she said. The old lady plunged both hands into a bowl of raw chopped meat and began shaping the stuff into little balls.

"Tetum," echoed the ladies on the mattress.

"This Nazarene," said Zodelia, gesturing in her direction, "spends half her time in a Moslem house with Moslem friends and the other half in a Nazarene hotel with other Nazarenes."

"That's nice," said the women opposite. "Half with Moslem friends and half with Nazarenes."

The old lady looked very stern. She noticed that her bony cheeks were tattooed with tiny blue crosses.

"Why?" asked the old lady abruptly in a deep voice. "*Why* does she spend half her time with Moslem friends and half with Nazarenes?" She fixed her eye on Zodelia, never ceasing to shape the meat with her swift fingers. Now she saw that her knuckles were also tattooed with blue crosses.

Zodelia stared back at her stupidly. "I don't know why," she said, shrugging one fat shoulder. It was clear that the picture she had been painting for them had suddenly lost all its charm for her.

"Is she crazy?" the old lady asked.

"No," Zodelia answered listlessly. "She is not crazy." There were shrieks of laughter from the mattress.

The old lady fastened her sharp eyes on the visitor, and she saw that they were heavily outlined in black. "Where is your husband?" she demanded.

"He's traveling in the desert."

"Selling things," Zodelia put in. This was the popular explanation for her husband's trips; she did not try to contradict it.

"Where is your mother?" the old lady asked.

"My mother is in our country in her own house."

"Why don't you go and sit with your mother in her own house?" she scolded. "The hotel costs a lot of money."

"In the city where I was born," she began, "there are many, many automobiles and many, many trucks."

The women on the mattress were smiling pleasantly. "Is that true?" remarked the one in the center in a tone of polite interest.

"I hate trucks," she told the woman with feeling.

The old lady lifted the bowl of meat off her lap and set it down on the carpet. "Trucks are nice," she said severely.

"That's true," the woman agreed, after only a moment's hesitation. "Trucks are very nice."

"Do *you* like trucks?" she asked Zodelia, thinking that because of their relatively greater intimacy she might perhaps agree with her.

"Yes," she said. "They are nice. Trucks are very nice." She seemed lost in meditation, but only for an instant. "Everything is nice," she announced, with a look of triumph.

"It's the truth," the women said from their mattress. "Everything is nice."

They all looked happy, but the old lady was still frowning. "Aicha!" she yelled, twisting her neck so that her voice could be heard in the patio. "Bring the tea!"

Several little girls came into the room carrying the tea things and a low round table.

"Pass the cakes to the Nazarene," she told the smallest child, who was carrying a cut-glass dish piled with cakes. She saw that they were the ones she had bought for Zodelia; she did not want any of them. She wanted to go home.

"Eat!" the women called out from their mattress. "Eat the cakes."

The child pushed the glass dish forward.

"The dinner at the hotel is ready," she said, standing up.

"Drink tea," said the old woman scornfully. "Later you will sit with the other Nazarenes and eat their food."

"The Nazarenes will be angry if I'm late." She realized that she was lying stupidly, but she could not stop. "They will hit me!" She tried to look wild and frightened.

"Drink tea. They will not hit you," the old woman told her. "Sit down and drink tea."

The child was still offering her the glass dish as she backed away toward the door. Outside she sat down on the black and white tiles to lace her shoes. Only Zodelia followed her into the patio.

"Come back," the others were calling. "Come back into the room."

Then she noticed the porcupine basket standing nearby against the wall. "Is that old lady in the room your aunt? Is she the one you were bringing the porcupine to?" she asked her.

"No. She is not my aunt."

"Where *is* your aunt?"

"My aunt is in her own house."

"When will you take the porcupine to her?" She wanted to keep talking, so that Zodelia would be distracted and forget to fuss about her departure.

"The porcupine sits here," she said firmly. "In my own house."

She decided not to ask her again about the wedding.

When they reached the door Zodelia opened it just enough to let her through. "Good-bye," she said behind her. "I shall see you tomorrow, if Allah wills it."

"When?"

"Four o'clock." It was obvious that she had chosen the first figure that had come into her head. Before closing the door she reached out and pressed two of the dry Spanish cakes into her hand. "Eat them," she said graciously. "Eat them at the hotel with the other Nazarenes."

She started up the steep alley, headed once again for the walk along the cliff. The houses on either side of her were so close that she could smell the dampness of the walls and feel it on her cheeks like a thicker air.

When she reached the place where she had met Zodelia she went over to the wall and leaned on it. Although the sun had sunk behind the houses, the sky was still luminous and the blue of the wall had deepened. She rubbed her fingers along it: the wash was fresh and a little of the powdery stuff came off. And she remembered how once she had reached out to touch the face of a clown because it had awakened some longing. It had happened at a little circus, but not when she was a child.

Muriel Rukeyser

(1913–80)

Muriel Rukeyser was known throughout much of her life as a social activist and a poet who incorporated into her work her interest in liberal political causes. However, although she was bisexual, not until late in her career did homosexuality appear to her to be a political issue. In fact, in one early poem she exclaimed, "Not Sappho, Sacco," referring to the unjust political executions of the American left-wing heroes, Sacco and Vanzetti, and rejecting themes of lesbian love as inappropriate to her poetry. Rukeyser believed—like many women of her generation, including her fellow student at Vassar, Elizabeth Bishop, another lesbian poet who carefully avoided the subject of lesbianism—that homosexuality was and should remain the love that dare not speak its name. Unlike Bishop, however, Rukeyser, who was championed by the feminist movement of the 1970s for the antipatriarchal sentiments that were reflected in her poetry, internalized some of the tenets of radical feminism. In 1978 she even agreed to be included in a reading of lesbian poets at the Modern Language Association convention, though illness finally prevented her from attending. (She died less than two years later.) Her work is now regularly included in anthologies of lesbian poetry, such as Elly Bulkin and Joan Larkin's 1981 collection, *Lesbian Poetry,* and Carl Morse and Joan Larkin's 1988 collection, *Gay and Lesbian Poetry in Our Time.*

Though she long avoided in her writing an emulation of their occasional treatment of homosexual themes, Rukeyser's poetic models were the gay poets Walt Whitman and W. H. Auden. What she emulated was their broad embrace of humanity and the ways in which they used poetry to promote social consciousness. Her own social consciousness drove her to cover the Scottsboro trial (of nine young African American men who had been arrested for the alleged rape of two white women), to travel to Spain in support of the antifascists during the Spanish Civil War, to travel to Seoul to protest the death sentence of the poet Kim Chi-Ha, to participate in the anti–Vietnam War movement, and to campaign against the spread of nuclear power. Finally, the rise of a gay-liberation movement obliged and permitted her to write poems such as "Despisals," in which she championed homosexuality and vowed "Never to despise in myself what I have been taught / to despise."

Rukeyser was married to a man in 1945, but the marriage was annulled a few months later. She was known also to have had other heterosexual love affairs, as well as lesbian relationships. She became pregnant out of wedlock in 1947 and chose to raise the child as a single mother. Although she had been very prolific as a poet since 1935, when her first book, *Theory of Flight,* won the Yale Younger Poets Award, she produced little in the 1950s because, according to her biographers, she was busy with the duties of motherhood. She resumed her prolific output in 1962 with *Waterlily Fire.*

Rukeyser's 1968 volume, *Speed of Darkness,* has been identified by lesbian critics as a celebration of "coming out," but her message is so subtle that any but the most determined lesbian reader could easily miss it. In one poem in this volume, Rukeyser calls for "No more masks! No more mythologies," but she is herself unable to toss away her mask of presumptive heterosexuality in most of these poems, perhaps because of her internalized homophobia. She seems to have feared unknown reprisals as she suggested in her poem "Kathe Kollwitz": "What would happen if one woman told the truth about her life? / The world would split open."

However, in her 1973 volume, *Breaking Open,* Rukeyser, by approaching a telling of the "truth" about her lesbianism, does dare the world to split open. In poems such as "Looking at Each Other," for example, she reveals something of lesbian sexuality not only by lines such as "Yes, our breasts saw each other's breasts," but by the rhythm and pace of the lovemaking that is being described. With regard to her entire canon, however, lesbianism is well encoded in Rukeyser's writing. Yet knowing to look for such references, the reader becomes privy to important dimensions of those poems that must have been entirely veiled to those who knew nothing of Rukeyser's lesbianism.

FURTHER READING: Muriel Rukeyser, *The Collected Poems of Muriel Rukeyser* (New York: McGraw-Hill, 1978). Eloise Klein Healy, "Muriel Rukeyser," in *Contemporary Lesbian Writers of the United States: A Bio-Bibliographical Critical Sourcebook,* eds. Denise Knight and Sondra Pollack (forthcoming, Westport, CT: Greenwood Publishing). Louise Kertesz, *The Poetic Vision of Muriel Rukeyser* (Baton Rouge: Louisiana State University Press, 1980). Liz Yorke, "Constructing a Lesbian Poetic for Survival: Broumas, Rukeyser, H.D., Rich, Lorde," in *Sexual Sameness: Textual Differences in Lesbian and Gay Writing,* ed. Joseph Bristow (London: Routledge, 1992).

DESPISALS

In the human cities, never again to
despise the backside of the city, the ghetto,
or build it again as we build the despised
backsides of houses.   Look at your own building.
You are the city.

Among our secrecies, not to despise our Jews
(that is, ourselves) or our darkness, our blacks,
or in our sexuality   wherever it takes us
and we now know we are productive
too productive, too reproductive
for our present invention—never to despise
the homosexual who goes building another

with touch   with touch   (not to despise any touch)
each like himself, like herself each.
You are this.
                              In the body's ghetto
never to go despising the asshole ·
nor the useful shit that is our clean clue
to what we need.   Never to despise
the clitoris in her least speech.

Never to despise in myself what I have been taught
to despise.   Not to despise the other.
Not to despise the *it*.   To make this relation
with the it : to know that I am it.

LOOKING AT EACH OTHER

Yes, we were looking at each other
Yes, we knew each other very well
Yes, we had made love with each other many times
Yes, we had heard music together
Yes, we had gone to the sea together
Yes, we had cooked and eaten together
Yes, we had laughed often day and night
Yes, we fought violence and knew violence
Yes, we hated the inner and outer oppression
Yes, that day we were looking at each other
Yes, we saw the sunlight pouring down
Yes, the corner of the table was between us
Yes, bread and flowers were on the table
Yes, our eyes saw each other's eyes
Yes, our mouths saw each other's mouth
Yes, our breasts saw each other's breasts
Yes, our bodies entire saw each other
Yes, it was beginning in each
Yes, it threw waves across our lives
Yes, the pulses were becoming very strong
Yes, the beating became very delicate
Yes, the calling   the arousal
Yes, the arriving   the coming
Yes, there it was for both entire
Yes, we were looking at each other

CRIES FROM CHIAPAS

Hunger
   of mountains
         spoke
            from a tiger's throat.
Tiger-tooth peaks.
         The moon.
             A thousand mists
turning.
     Desires of mountains
           like the desires of women,
moon-drawn,
      distant,
         clear black among
             confusions of silver.
Women of Chiapas!
        Dream-borne
           voices of women.
Splinters of mountains,
         broken obsidian,
             silver.
White tigers
    haunting
        your forehead here
            sloped in shadow—
black hungers of women,
         confusion
           turning like tigers
And your voice—

I am
   almost asleep
      almost awake
         in your arms.

May Swenson

(1913–89)

May Swenson was born in Logan, Utah, the oldest child in a Mormon family. She described herself in a 1982 interview with lesbian writer Lee Hudson as having been uncomfortable with the "feminine" responsibilities for her siblings that were foisted on her when she was young: "I would rather be myself and be making my poems than be changing diapers. Well, why couldn't I change the diapers and then make a poem? I don't know —I didn't want to do it." She left Utah and Mormonism and lived much of her adult life in lesbian relationships. For many years before her death her partner was R. R. Knudson, a writer of lesbian novels for adolescents and young adults.

Much of Swenson's work encodes lesbian themes. As a writer who began publishing books in the homophobic 1950s, Swenson learned to be cagey about her subject matter. In her interview with Hudson, who apparently understood but did not name the hidden lesbian subject matter in Swenson's poetry, Swenson assumed the closeted lesbian coyness of her era. "I don't write confessional poetry, do I?" she said. "At least not in the usual sense. It's likely that there are confessions in my work but they are masked. They're hidden." When Hudson, a product of a much younger generation, asked, "Why do you hide them?" Swenson responded, "I don't know. You tell me. I don't know everything about myself."

That habit of circumspection, which was so characteristic of lesbian poets of her generation, continued in much of her poetry, even in more liberal times, though occasionally Swenson came to relax her guard. "I don't write about people very much . . ." she said in the 1980s. "I do but in a hidden way. Some of my poems that seem to be about animals or other things are actually about people in a disguised way." Those "people," in her animal and flower poems such as "Poet to Tiger," and "A Trellis for R.," appear most often to be women, and they are the object of the erotic regard of the (ungendered) speaker, who is agent and perpetrator of the gaze.

Swenson uses numerous other devices to encode her lesbian subject matter. Often she lets slip just the slightest hint, for example, alluding to an androgynous lover's dreamed-of baby book that is both "pink and blue" or describing the beloved's delicate skin. The roles, both domestic and sexual, played by lover and beloved in many of her poems are interchangeable, as they frequently are in lesbian relationships. In "You Are," for example, the speaker is presented first as being vine to the beloved's vial and "twining inside" the beloved, and then it is the speaker who becomes the vial.

FURTHER READING: May Swenson, *Iconographs* (New York: Charles Scribner's Sons, 1970; *In Other Words* (New York: Alfred Knopf, 1987); *The Love Poems of May Swenson* (Boston: Houghton, Mifflin, 1991). Lee Hudson, "A Conversation with May Swenson," *Literature in Performance*, 3: 2 (April 1983), 55–66. Sue Russell, "A Mysterious and Lavish Power: How Things Continue to Take Place in the Work of May Swenson," *Kenyon Review* (forthcoming, Summer 1994).

POET TO TIGER

The Hair

You went downstairs
saw a hair in the sink
and squeezed my toothpaste by the neck.
You roared. My ribs are sore.
This morning even my pencil's got your toothmarks.
Big Cat Eye cocked on me you see bird bones.
Snuggled in the rug of your belly
your breath so warm
I smell delicious fear.
Come breathe on me rough pard
put soft paws here.

The Salt

You don't put salt on anything
so I'm eating without.
Honey on the eggs is all right
mustard on the toast.
I'm not complaining I'm saying I'm
living with *you.*
You like your meat raw
don't care if it's cold.
Your stomach must have tastebuds
you swallow so fast.
Night falls early. It's foggy. Just now

I found another of your bite marks in the cheese.
I'm hungry. Please
come bounding home
I'll hand you the wine to open

with your teeth.
Scorch me a steak unsalted
boil my coffee twice
say the blessing to a jingle on the blue TV.
Under the lap robe on our chilly couch
look behind my ears "for welps"
and hug me.

The Sand

You're right I brought a grain
or two of sand
into bed I guess in my socks.
But it was you pushed them off
along with everything else.

Asleep you flip
over roll
everything under
you and off
me. I'm always grabbing
for my share of the sheets.

Or else you wake me every hour with sudden
growled I-love-yous
trapping my face between those plushy
shoulders. All my float-dreams turn spins
and never finish. I'm thinner
now. My watch keeps running fast.
But best is when we're riding pillion
my hips within your lap. You let me steer.
Your hand and arm go clear
around my ribs your moist
dream teeth fastened on my nape.

A grain of sand in the bed upsets you or
a hair on the floor.
But you'll get
in slick and wet from the shower if I let
you. Or with your wool cap
and skiing jacket on
if it's cold.
Tiger don't scold me
don't make me comb my hair outdoors.

Cuff me careful. Lick don't
crunch. Make last what's yours.

The Dream

You get into the tub holding *The Naked Ape*
in your teeth. You wet that blond
three-cornered pelt lie back wide
chest afloat. You're reading
in the rising steam and I'm
drinking coffee from your tiger cup.
You say you dreamed
I had your baby book
and it was pink and blue.
I pointed to a page and there
was your face with a cub grin.

You put your paws in your armpits
make a tiger-moo.
Then you say: "Come here
Poet and take
this hair
off me." I do.
It's one of mine. I carefully
kill it and carry
it outside. And stamp on it
and bury it.
In the begonia bed.
And then take off my shoes
not to bring a grain
of sand in to get
into our bed.
I'm going to
do the cooking
now instead
of you.
And sneak some salt in
when you're not looking.

A TRELLIS FOR R.

B   Pink lips the serrate
L   folds taste smooth
U   and R
E but you are R   o
         o   s
         s   e
         e too   h
and buttermilk but with blood   i
dots showing through.   p round the center
A little salty your white   bud I suck. I milknip

nape boy-wide. Glinting hairs shoot   your two B
back of your ears' R   l
         o   u
         s   e skeined blown R
         e that   o
tongue likes to feel   s
the maze of slip into   e
the funnel tell a thunder whisper to. beauties too to sniff their
When I kiss   berries' blood up stiff pink tips.
                                       You're white

your eyes' straight lashes
down crisp go like doll's
blond straws. Glazed
iris R
   o
   s
   e
   s your lids unclose
to B
  l
  u
  e ringed targets their dark
sheen spokes almost green. I sink in
B
l
u
e black R
      o
      s
      e heart holes until
you blink.

in patches only mostly R
                 o
                 s
                 e
buck skin and salty
speckled like a sky. I
love your spots your white neck R
                                   o
                                   s
                                   e
your hair's wild straw splash
silk spools for your ears.
But where white spouts out spills

on your brow to clear
eyepools wheel shafts of light
R
o
s
e you are B
         l
         u
         e.

YOU ARE

you are my mirror
in your eye's well I float
my reality proven
        I dwell
        in you
        and so
        I know
        I am
no one
can be sure
by himself
of his own being
        and the world's seeing
      the fleeting mirrors of others' eyes

cloudy abstracted remote
or too bright convex false directly smiling
or crepuscular under their lids
crawling the ground like snails
or narrowed
nervously hooked to the distance
                    is suspect
do I live
does the world live
do I live in it
or does it live in me?
                    because you believe I exist I exist
                    I exist in your verdant garden
                            you have planted me
                            I am glad to grow
I dream of your hands by day
all day I dream of evening
when you will open the gate
come out of the noisy world
to tend me
                            to pour at my roots
                            the clear the flashing water
                            of your love
and exclaim over my new leaf
and stroke it with a broad finger
as if a god surprised fondled his first earth-sprig

                            once I thought
                            to seek the limits
                            of all being
            I believed
            in my own eyes' seeing
            then
                            to find pattern purpose aim
                            thus forget death
                            or forgive it
then I thought
to plumb the heart of death
to cicatrize that spot
and plot abolishment
                    so that pattern shape and purpose
                    would not gall me

I would be its part forever
content in never falling
from its web

                now I know
                beginning and end
                are one
                and slay each other
but their offspring is what *is*
not was or will be
                am I? yes
                and never was
                until you made me
                crying there you are!
                and I unfurled in your rich soil
I am the genie
in your eye's well
crouching there
so that you must take me with you everywhere
an underwater plant in a secret cylinder
                you the vial
                and I the vine
                and I twining inside you
and you glad
to hold me
floating there
                for if I live in you
                you live holding me
                enfolding me you *are*
it is proven and the universe exists!
                one reflects the other
                man mirrors god
                image in eye affirms its sight
                green stem in earth attests
                its right to spin
                in palpable roundness
is this then
what is meant
that god is love
and is that all?
                how simple and how sure
                at the very hub of hazard

so seeming fearful fragile insecure
two threads
in the web of chaos
lashed by the dark daemonic wind
crossed upon each other
therefore fixed and still
axial in the bursting void
are perpetual each according to the other
I am
then I am a garden too
and tend you

                my eye is a mirror
                in which you float
                a well where you dwell smiling

      I the vial
      hold you
      a vine a twining genie
I enfold you
and secrete the liquid
of your being
in that I love you
and you live *in* me

Part V

Amazons:
The Literature of
Lesbian-Feminism

INTRODUCTION

The lesbian-feminist movement took root in America in the late 1960s and flourished for almost two decades, spreading eventually to the United Kingdom and other areas of Western Europe such as France, Germany, and Holland. In contrast to the lesbian literary images produced during other periods, which originated in Europe and were then adopted by American authors, the first lesbian-feminist writers were primarily American. Their work provided strong influences for European lesbian-feminists and has been responsible for the proliferation of a dramatically different tradition of lesbian literature in the Western world.

Many of the women who called themselves lesbian-feminists had had a history of heterosexuality, but in the 1960s and '70s they had become radical feminists. Their analysis of male domination and patriarchal behavior led them to reject their old bonds with men. Those women challenged the prevailing notion of the first half of the twentieth century that homosexuality is either inborn or developed in early childhood. Lesbianism was to them a happy social and political choice that any woman could and should make. Once a woman understood enough about the evils of patriarchy to commit herself to radical feminism, they insisted, lesbianism was her only logical next step.

The new movement, whose founders were primarily young women in their twenties and thirties, was fueled by a phenomenal energy. With the commitment and enthusiasm born of their youth, they longed to refashion the whole world to make it a better place for women. They hoped to design a lesbian-feminist culture (a "woman's culture," they called it) that would be woman-affirming, self-sufficient, healthy, and joyous in its celebration of sisterly and sexual love between women. While their movement did not bring about the vast social changes these young women had envisioned, in terms of literature they succeeded very well, creating a whole new genre of fiction and poetry that represented an immense break with most of the earlier literary images of love between women.

The slogan of lesbian-feminism became "Feminism is the theory; lesbianism is the practice." The identity politics of lesbian-feminists usually encompassed the whole of their emotional and erotic lives. They considered women who worked in the feminist movement and then went home at night to sleep in the enemy camp to be foolishly or dangerously deluded. They saw themselves as "women-identified women," whose lesbianism was a natural outgrowth of their desire to make *woman* prime in their lives. They wanted to invest other women with their love and energies rather than continuing to support a male-centered and chauvinistic society. Their definition of "lesbian" expanded to include even women who had little or no sexual contact with other females but who devoted their political and personal lives to the promotion of women rather than men. Bonding together with other women against male tyranny, sharing a rich inner life with them, exchanging support with other women, all qualified a woman to take her place in the "lesbian continuum."

The young women who came to lesbianism through radical feminism were joined in their movement by older women who had been lesbians long before the rebirth of the feminist movement in the 1960s. Many of those "old gays" realized that feminism had always been for them an unarticulated principle and the new movement gave them a voice. Some of the women who joined the lesbian-feminist movement had been lesbians in gay liberation for a time and left because their new feminist awareness convinced them that the men with whom they worked in gay liberation were interested only in promoting their own agenda and were insensitive to lesbians' needs. The diversity of sexual backgrounds alone, in addition to differences in class, race, and other issues, made unanimity of sentiments within the lesbian-feminist movement unlikely, but all its members agreed that love between women was superior to heterosexuality, and lesbian-feminist literature reflected that conviction.

Regardless of why women came to lesbian-feminism, they built a flourishing culture that expressed lesbian-feminist ideals. Throughout the 1970s there emerged all over North America, the United Kingdom, and in Western Europe numerous lesbian-feminist bookstores, journals, publishing houses, and a large audience of lesbian readers who craved works that promulgated feminism and presented positive literary images of love between women. Lesbian-feminist readers not only demanded the literary creation of lesbian heroes (or "heras") but they angrily rejected older literature that treated lesbians as men trapped in women's bodies or carnivorous flowers. They also had little interest in literature in which the subject of lesbianism was encoded; they required instead that authors be open and affirming about love between women. The new publishing houses that were established to produce literature for the community, such as Naiad Press, Diana Press, and Daughters, generally sought for publication work that reflected the philosophy of the movement. Not all lesbian-feminist writing ended with the lovers drifting off into old age together, but in those works in which lesbian love failed it was made clear that the obstacles to happiness were not the women's sicknesses or sins but rather the difficulties placed in their way by a sick world.

From its inception, with defiant and often hilarious works such as Judy Grahn's *Edward the Dyke* (1971) and Rita Mae Brown's *Rubyfruit Jungle* (1973), lesbian-feminist writing constituted an unprecedented shift from what had been a largely male-influenced depiction of lesbianism to a literature that demanded that women define entirely for themselves what lesbianism meant. In lesbian-feminist writing, lesbianism usually meant relationships of harmony and happiness, an escape from the horrors of heterosexuality, a promise of self-fulfillment and healthy independence. The darkness and despair that cursed a woman who was a lesbian in earlier literature were visited, in lesbian-feminist writing, on heterosexual women who had not yet seen the light. In the past, humor had been used against the lesbian to satirize love between women; in lesbian-feminist writing, humor was used to depict the silliness of patriarchy or homophobia.

If the new literary conception of love between women had any analogues in earlier writing they were to be found in some of the literature of romantic friendship that presented women as kindred spirits, loving and nurturing each other in relationships of equality. Lesbian-feminist literature was different from the literature of romantic friendship, however, because it was born in a post-Freudian era when the erotic implications of same-sex love could not be ignored. But unlike the erotic writing that was influenced by nineteenth-century French Decadent literature, lesbian-feminist writing presented sex between women as mutually fulfilling, guilt-free, constructive, and a cause for celebration.

The lesbian-feminist community and the writers who represented it believed that lesbian-feminists could create a new meaning for love between women. Borrowing the title of a 1973 book by Jill Johnston, lesbian-feminists sought to erect (either figuratively or in fact) what they called a "Lesbian Nation," a society that would move beyond the sadistic and hegemonic world that men had created. Such a society would have to be constructed from scratch. "No one has imagined us," Adrienne Rich said in "Twenty-One Love Poems." "Whatever we do together is pure invention / The maps they gave us were out of date / by years." This new and better society was to be accomplished by a welding of social and political idealism with lesbianism. As lesbian-feminist poet Fran Winant characterized it in a poem of the 1970s, the secret to the construction of a peaceful amazon world was to "eat rice, have faith in women." Lesbian-feminist writers, whether poets, essayists, novelists, or songwriters, were valued as the prophets, architects, and social midwives whose artistic productions would help birth this new world.

As Jane Rule's story "In the Attic" suggests, lesbian-feminists compared themselves with lesbians of earlier generations and considered their predecessors unevolved, products of a dark age. Lesbian-feminists generally believed that the older lesbian subcultures promoted self-destructive behavior. They were critical of lesbian lives that had been played out in gay bars, where evils such as alcoholism had been encouraged, or in hiding, which had made lesbians fearful and full of self-loathing. Lesbian-feminists saw the earlier lesbian society as having been a product of male chauvinism and homophobia, and they determined to change it. That determination was reflected by their writers, whose presentation of lesbian relationships generally avoided, for example, depictions of butch-femme relationships (which lesbian-feminists considered an unfortunate emulation of heterosexuality), which had been so popular in the pulps of the 1950s and early '60s.

Much of the writing that came out of the lesbian-feminist movement betrayed a tremendous anger at the old man-made world. What had radicalized many of these women in the first place was their conviction that females, even in the best of circumstances, suffered social and personal oppressions—rape, legal discrimination, economic injustices—from which most males were free. It was men, they pointed out in writings such as Judy Grahn's "A Woman Is Talking to Death," who invented crimes, punishments, and all the other horrors of the world. Lesbian-feminist literature often focused on the physical and emotional violence men perpetrated against women as much as on women's love for each other.

In their work the writers sometimes despaired over women's difficulties in creating a peaceful and loving community when they had to endure as a backdrop for their creation the frightening male-dominated world. Perhaps because of their despair, lesbian-feminist science fiction, such as Katherine Forrest's *Daughters of a Coral Dawn,* Sally Gearhart's *Wanderground,* and Joanna Russ's "When It Changed," became a favorite genre among lesbian-feminists. That genre envisioned possible worlds in which men might be deprived of their dangerous powers over women or even banished, and women would be free to govern themselves and create a perfect society. Lesbian-feminist science fiction even anticipated the 1980s proliferation of lesbian couples' mothering via artificial insemination. It sometimes imagined, as Joanna Russ's story does, an all-female world in which women pairs have children by the merging of their ova.

In the midst of the great flowering of lesbian-feminist culture, however, considerable dissension emerged. One area of controversy revolved around the issues of race and ethnicity. "Third World lesbians" (as some lesbians of color called themselves in the 1970s) felt that the lesbian-feminist movement and the literature connected to it provided little place for them. They believed that the white, middle-class-dominated lesbian-feminist movement had imported the racism of the parent culture into their subculture. Lesbians of color also felt disconnected from the popular tenets of lesbian separatism, which demanded that lesbians cut off all associations with men. Many Third World lesbians believed that their male relatives suffered as much as women from oppression and discrimination, and that in the likely event of racial conflict it would be their families, including their male relatives, on whom they would have to rely. Lesbian separatism seemed to them to be a middle-class white woman's luxury. Though some of the most important voices of lesbian-feminism were African American, even they had some ambivalence about the movement, as may be seen, for example, in the poetry of Pat Parker. To the credit of white lesbian-feminists, they heeded such voices and attempted increasingly to encourage more writers who were lesbians of color to speak to the lesbian-feminist movement. By the 1980s they had succeeded (see Part VI).

But there was dissension among white lesbian authors as well. Some writers, even those with strong lesbian-feminist identification, felt occasionally something of a tyranny in their audience's demands. The 1970s poet Martha Shelley, for example, in her poem "Reading at the Village Gate," expressed her befuddlement and resentment that her lesbian-feminist audience cheered whenever she used the word "lesbian," regardless of the merit or message of the poems in which that term appeared: "A world of words—they wanted only one," she laments.

Other lesbian writers who hoped to attract this new large audience of lesbian readers felt frustrated by what they perceived to be the "political correctness" in their readers' requirements, the demands that literature about lesbians be invariably "positive" and wholesome and designed to counter the earlier damaging stereotypes of lesbians as men trapped in women's bodies or carnivorous flowers. Some 1970s writers, such as Bertha Harris, feared that lesbian literature was being sanitized, and that the kind of work that most lesbian-feminist publishing houses and readers were encouraging was not lesbian literature. "People who write from a 'lesbian sensibility' write against the rules," Harris insisted, while, ironically, lesbian-feminism was developing a stringent set of rules about what could and could not be said in lesbian literature.

But despite such battles, the 1970s marked a time when lesbian writers wrested from homophobic writers, whose influence had prevailed through much of the history of lesbian literature, the right to define who the lesbian was. Though lesbian-feminist definitions came to be seen as too confining by the end of the 1980s, lesbian authors no longer felt obliged to cut their characters to match the pattern that had been fabricated in other centuries by writers who were largely male and heterosexual.

Rita Mae Brown
(b. 1944)

Rita Mae Brown became a civil-rights and gay-rights activist in her early twenties. When she was expelled from the University of Florida for her activism and lesbianism she went to New York, where, in 1967, she helped found one of the first gay and lesbian student organizations in the country, the Student Homophile League at Columbia University. In the 1960s and '70s Brown was often the center of controversy. Her membership in the National Organization of Women was cut short when she came into conflict with the group because they tried to silence her on the issue of lesbianism. She went on to become a member of one of the early lesbian-feminist separatist collectives, the Furies, which published a newspaper by that name whose circulation was small but whose impact on the views of the new movement became significant. In the early 1970s Brown, with her great energy and charisma, was perhaps the most effective spokeswoman for lesbian-feminism in America, declaring that lesbianism was a social and political choice which any woman could make:

> I became a lesbian because the culture that I live in is violently anti-woman. How could I, a woman, participate in a culture that denies my humanity? . . . To give a man support and love before giving it to a sister is to support that culture, that power system.

Such declarations became a rallying cry for thousands of women who came to lesbianism through radical feminism.

Brown's first novel, *Rubyfruit Jungle,* which was published in 1973 by Daughters, a lesbian-feminist press, began a new genre of lesbian literature. Unlike earlier novels such as Compton Mackenzie's *Extraordinary Women* (1928), which attempted to deal humorously with lesbianism by laughing at lesbians, Brown's comic lesbian novel laughs at heterosexuals. She creates a superhero of Molly Bolt, who is morally superior to, and much prettier, smarter, and stronger than, all the straight people she encounters. The rights to *Rubyfruit Jungle* were soon bought by Bantam, a mass-circulation publisher, and the book became a best-seller, rivaling *The Well of Loneliness* as the best-known lesbian novel ever to be published. Her later novels, such as *Sudden Death* (thought to be a *roman à clef* about the tennis career of her former lover, Martina Navratilova), share with her early work a focus on lesbians, feminism, and slapstick humor, but they are less concerned with the radical principles of lesbian-feminism.

FURTHER READING: Rita Mae Brown, *The Hand That Cradles the Rock* (New York: New York University Press, 1971); *Rubyfruit Jungle* (Plainfield, VT: Daughters, 1973); *Songs to a Handsome Woman* (Oakland, CA: Diana Press, 1973); *In Her Day* (Plainfield, VT: Daughters, 1976); *A Plain Brown Rapper* (Oakland, CA: Diana Press, 1977); *Six of One* (New York: Harper & Row, 1978). Leslie Fishbein, "*Rubyfruit Jungle*: Lesbianism, Feminism, and Narcissism," *International Journal of Women's Studies*, 7:2 (March–April 1984), 155–59. Kathleen Martindale, "Rita Mae Brown's *Six of One* and Anne Cameron's *The Journey*: Fictional Contributions to the Ethics of Feminist Non-violence," *Atlantis*, 12: 1 (Fall 1986), 103–10.

From *Rubyfruit Jungle*: Violet Hill Elementary School

Leota B. Bisland sat next to me that year in sixth grade, and Leroy sat behind. Leota was the most beautiful girl I had ever seen. She was tall and slender with creamy skin and deep, green eyes. She was quiet and shy so I spent most of sixth grade concentrating on making Leota laugh. Miss Potter wasn't too pleased with my performance in the first row but she was a sweet old soul and only made me stand in the hall once. That didn't work out because I kept returning to the doorway to dance when Miss Potter's head was turned. I also made the finger at Leroy. Right when I was in the middle of shooting the bird, Miss Potter turns from the blackboard, "Molly, since you enjoy performing so much I'm going to make you the star of the Christmas play this year." Leroy asked whether the play was going to be *The Creature from the Black Lagoon*. Naturally everybody screamed. Miss Potter said no, it was a play about the nativity of Jesus and I was to be Virgin Mary.

Cheryl Spiegelglass got so mad she jumped up and said, "But Miss Potter, the Virgin Mary was the mother of little Lord Jesus and she was the most perfect woman on earth. Virgin Mary has to be played by a good girl and Molly isn't good. Yesterday she stuck a wad of bubble gum in

Audrey's hair." Cheryl was bucking to be Virgin Mary, that was clear. Miss Potter said that we had to consider dramatic talent not just whether a person was good or not. Besides, maybe if I played Virgin Mary some of her goodness would rub off.

Leota was a lady of Bethlehem so she was in the play too. And Cheryl was Joseph. Miss Potter said this would be a great challenge to Cheryl. She was also in charge of costumes, probably because her father would donate them. Anyway she got her name in the program twice in big letters.

Leroy was a Wise Man, and he wore a long beard with Little Lulu curls on it. We all had to stay after school every day to remember our lines and rehearse. Miss Potter was right! I was so busy trying to get everything perfect that I didn't have time to get into trouble or think about anything else except Leota. I began to wonder if girls could marry girls, because I was sure I wanted to marry Leota and look in her green eyes forever. But I would only marry her if I didn't have to do the housework. I was certain of that. But if Leota really didn't want to do it either, I guessed I'd do it. I'd do anything for Leota.

Leroy began to get mad that I was paying so much attention to a mere village inhabitant and he was a Wise Man. He forgot it as soon as I gave him my penknife with the naked lady on it that I clipped from Earl Stambach.

The Christmas pageant was an enormous production. All the mothers came, and it was so important that the fathers even took off work and Cheryl's was sitting right in the front row in the seat of honor. Carrie and Florence showed up to marvel at me being Virgin Mary and at Leroy in robes. Leroy and I were so excited we could barely stand it, and we got to wear makeup, rouge and red lipstick. Getting painted was so much fun that Leroy confessed he liked it too, although boys aren't supposed to, of course. I told him not to worry about it, because he had a beard and if you had a beard, it must be all right to wear lipstick if you wanted to because everyone will know you're a man. He thought that sounded reasonable and we made a pact to run away as soon as we were old enough and go be famous actors. Then we could wear pretty clothes all the time, never pick potato bugs and wear lipstick whenever we felt like it. We vowed to be so wonderful in this show that our fame would spread to the people who run theaters.

Cheryl overheard our plans and sneered, "You can do all you please, but everyone is going to look at me because I have the most beautiful blue cloak in the whole show."

"Nobody's gonna know it's you because you're playing Joseph and that'll throw them off. Ha." Leroy gloated.

"That's just why they'll all notice me, because I'll have to be specially skilled to be a good Joseph. Anyway, who is going to notice Virgin Mary, all she does is sit by the crib and rock Baby Jesus. She doesn't say much. Any dumb person can be Virgin Mary, all you have to do is put a halo over her head. It takes real talent to be Joseph, especially when you're a girl."

The conversation didn't get finished because Miss Potter bustled backstage. "Hush, children, curtain's almost ready to go up. Molly, Cheryl, get in your places."

When the curtain was raised there was a rustle of anticipation in the maternal audience. Megaphone Mouth said above all the whispers, "Isn't she dear up there?"

And dear I was. I looked at Baby Jesus with the tenderest looks I could manufacture and all the while my antagonist, Cheryl, had her hand on my shoulder digging me with her fingernails and a staff in her right hand. A record went on the phonograph and "Noël" began to play. The Wise Men came in most solemnly. Leroy carried a big gold box and presented it to me. I said, "Thank you, O King, for you have traveled far." And Cheryl, that rat, says, "And traveled far," as loud as she could. She wasn't supposed to say that. She started saying whatever came in her head and sounded religious. Leroy was choking in his beard and I was rocking the cradle so hard that the Jesus doll fell on the floor. So I decided two can play this game. I leaned over the doll and said in my most gentle voice, "O dearest babe, I hope you have not hurt yourself. Come, let Mother put you back to bed." Well, Leroy was near to dying of perplexity and he started to say something too, but Cheryl cut him off with, "Don't worry, Mary, babies fall out of the cradle all the time." That wasn't enough for greedy-guts, she then goes on about how she was a carpenter in a foreign land and how we had to travel many miles just so I could have my baby. She rattled on and on. All that time she spent in Sunday school was paying off because she had one story after another. I couldn't stand it any longer so I blurted out in the middle of her tale about the tax collectors, "Joseph, you shut up or you'll wake the baby." Miss Potter was aghast in the wings, and the shepherds didn't know what to do because they were back there waiting to come on. As soon as I told Joseph to shut up, Miss Potter pushed the shepherds on the stage. "We saw a star from afar," Robert Prather warbled, "and we came to worship the newborn Prince." Just then Barry Aldridge, another shepherd, peed right there on the stage he was so scared. Joseph saw her chance and said in an imperious voice, "You can't pee in front of little Lord Jesus, go back to the hills." That made me mad. "He can pee where he wants to, this is a stable, ain't it?" Joseph stretched to her full height and began to push Barry off the stage with her staff. I jumped out of my chair and wrenched the staff out of her hand. She grabbed it back, "Go sit down, you're supposed to watch out for the baby. What kind of mother are you?" "I ain't sittin nowhere until you button your fat lip and do this right." We struggled and pushed each other until I caught her off balance and she tripped on her long cloak. As she started to fall, I gave her a shove and she sailed off the stage into the audience. Miss Potter flew out on the stage, took my hand and said in a calm voice, "Now ladies and gentlemen, let's sing songs appropriate to the season." Miss Martin at the piano struck up "Oh Come All Ye Faithful."

Cheryl was down there among the folding chairs bawling her eyes out. Miss Potter pulled me off stage where I had started to sing. I knew I was in for it.

"Now Molly, Cheryl did wrong to talk out of turn, but you shouldn't have shoved her off the stage." Then she let me go, not even a little slap. Leroy was as surprised as I was. "It's a good thing she ain't mad but wait until Aunt Carrie and Florence get a hold of you."

True enough, Carrie nearly lost her liver with rage and I had to stay in the house for a solid week and all that time I had to do the chores: dishes, ironing, wash, even cooking. That made me give up the idea of marrying Leota B. Bisland if she wouldn't do the chores or at least half of them. I had to figure out a way to find out what Leota would agree to.

That week I thought of how to ask Leota to marry me. I'd die in front of her and ask her in my last breath. If she said yes, I'd miraculously recover. I'd send her a note on colored paper with a white dove. I'd ride over to her house on Barry Aldridge's horse, sing her a song like in the movies, then she'd get on the back of the horse and we'd ride off into the sunset. None of them seemed right so I decided to come straight out and ask.

Next Monday after school Leroy, Leota and I were walking home. I gave Leroy a dime and told him to go on ahead to Mrs. Hershener's for an ice cream. He offered no resistance as his stomach always came first.

"Leota, you thought about getting married?"

"Yeah, I'll get married and have six children and wear an apron like my mother. Only my husband will be handsome."

"Who you gonna marry?"

"I don't know yet."

"Why don't you marry me? I'm not handsome but I'm pretty."

"Girls can't get married."

"Says who?"

"It's a rule."

"It's a dumb rule. Anyway, you like me better than anybody, don't you? I like you better than anybody."

"I like you best but I still think girls can't get married."

"Look, if we want to get married we can get married. It don't matter what anybody says. Besides Leroy and I are running away to be famous actors. We'll have lots of money and clothes and we can do what we want. Nobody dares tell you what to do if you're famous. Now ain't that a lot better than sitting around here with an apron on?"

"Yes."

"Good. Then let's kiss like in the movies and we'll be engaged." We threw our arms around each other and kissed. My stomach felt funny.

"Does your stomach feel strange?"

"Kinda."

"Let's do it again."

We kissed again and my stomach felt worse. After that, Leota and I went off by ourselves each day after school. Somehow we knew enough not to go around kissing in front of everyone, so we went into the woods and kissed until it was time to go home. Leroy was beside himself because I didn't walk home with him anymore. One day he trailed us into the woods and burst in on us like a triumphant police sergeant.

"Kissing. You two come out here kissing. I'm gonna tell everyone in the whole world."

"Well now, Leroy Denman, what you want to tell for? Maybe you ought to try it before you shoot your big mouth off. You might want to come here after school too."

Temptation shone in Leroy's eyes, he never wanted to miss anything, but he hedged, "I don't want to go kissing girls."

"Kiss the cows then, Leroy. There's nothin else to kiss. It feels good. You're sure missing some fun!"

He began to weaken, "Do I have to close my eyes if I kiss you?"

"Yes. You can't kiss and keep your eyes open, they'll cross forever."

"I don't want to close my eyes."

"All right then, stupid, keep your eyes open. What do I care if you got cross-eyes. It's not my problem if you don't want to do it right."

"Who do I kiss first?"

"Whoever you want."

"I'll kiss you first since I know you better." Leroy puckered up and gave me a kiss like Florence gives at night.

"Leroy, that ain't right. You got your mouth all screwed up. Don't squinch it together like that."

Leota was laughing and she reached out to Leroy with a long arm, drew him to her and gave him a fat kiss. Leroy began to get the idea.

"Watch us," Leota advised. We finished a kiss then I gave Leroy another one. He was getting a little better at it although he was still stiff.

"How's your stomach feel?"

"Hungry, why?"

"Don't your stomach feel funny at all?" Leota asked.

"No."

"Maybe it's different for boys," she said.

After that the three of us went off after school. It was ok having Leroy around but he never did get to be an accomplished kisser. There were times when I felt kissing Leota wasn't enough, but I wasn't sure what the next step would be. So until I knew, I settled for kissing. I knew about fucking and getting stuck together like dogs and I didn't want to get stuck like that. It was very confusing. Leota was full of ideas. Once she laid down on top of me to give me a kiss and I knew that was a step in the right direction, until Leroy piled on and my lungs near caved in. I thought maybe we'd do it again when Leroy wasn't around.

Leroy convinced me not to tell anyone that we were kissing and all going to be famous. He figured it was another one of those rules and the grown-ups would keep us from running away to act. And the grown-ups did keep us three from running away together, but not because we were kissing in the woods.

One bitter night in February with the oven on and the gas heaters going, all the adults asked us into the kitchen. They told us we were moving to Florida as soon as school was over. There'd be warm weather all year round, and you could pick oranges right off the trees. I didn't believe it, of course. It can't be warm all year round. Another trick, but I didn't say anything. Carrie assured us we'd like it because we could swim in the ocean, and jobs were easier to find so there'd be something for everybody. Then they put us all to bed. Going to Florida wasn't so bad. They didn't have to tell lies to get me to go, I just didn't want to leave Leota, that's all.

The next day I told Leota the news and she didn't like it any more than I did, but there seemed to be nothing we could do about it. We promised to write each other and to keep going out into the woods until the very last day.

Spring came late that year and the roads were muddy. Carrie and Florence had already gone through the house, throwing things out, packing things we didn't need for everyday use. By May everything was ready to go save for a few kitchen utensils, the clothes we wore and a few pieces of furniture in the living room. Every day I felt a little worse. Even Leroy started to feel the pinch, and he didn't care about Leota or kissing quite the way I did. It seemed like if I was going to leave I ought to leave knowing more than kissing. Leota wasn't far from the same conclusion. One week before school ended she asked me to spend the night with her. She had a bedroom all to herself so we wouldn't have to share it with her little sister, and her mother said it was fine. This was one time things worked in my favor. There was no question that Leroy could be asked to spend the night. If Carrie wouldn't let me sleep in Leroy's room, it was a sure bet that nobody was going to let Leroy spend the night at Leota's. Leroy didn't care much anyway. Sleep was sleep to Leroy.

I put my toothbrush, pajamas and comb in a paper bag and walked down the road to the Bislands. You could see their house from far away because they had a TV aerial on it. We stayed up and watched the *Milton Berle Show*. He kept getting pies in the face and everyone thought that was so funny. I didn't think it was so funny. They should have eaten the pies instead of throwing them at each other. If they were mad why didn't they just knock the crap out of each other? It made no sense to me but it was fun to watch. I didn't care if Milton Berle didn't know better.

After the show, we got into bed and pulled up the sheets. Leota's mother closed the door and shut off the lights because they were still watching TV. That was fine with us. Soon as the door was shut we started kissing. We must have kissed for hours but I couldn't really tell because I didn't think about anything except kissing. We did hear her parents turn off the TV and go to bed. Then Leota decided we'd try lying on top of one another. We did that but it made my stomach feel terrible.

"Molly, let's take our pajamas off and do that."

"Ok, but we got to remember to put them back on before morning."

It was much better without the pajamas. I could feel her cool skin all over my body. That really was a lot better. Leota started kissing me with her mouth open. Now my stomach was going to fall out on the floor. Great, I am found dead in the Bisland home with my stomach hanging outa my mouth. "Leota, that makes my stomach hurt a lot more but it's kinda good too."

"Mine too."

We kept on. If we were going to die from stomach trouble we were resolved to die together. She began to touch me all over and I knew I was really going to die. Leota was bold. She wasn't afraid to touch anything and where her knowledge came from was a secret but she knew what she was after. And I soon found out.

The next morning we went to school like any two sixth-grade girls. I fell asleep during fractions. Leroy gave me a poke and snickered. Leota looked at me with those dreamy eyes and I hurt all over again. We couldn't move to Florida, we just couldn't.

But we did.

Audre Lorde
(1934–92)

Audre Lorde, born in New York of Caribbean parents, was a pioneering and powerful voice of black lesbian-feminism for twenty years, from the early 1970s until her untimely death in 1992. The beginning of her long struggle with breast cancer is recorded in *The Cancer Journals* (1980). Recognition of Lorde's literary achievement went well beyond the lesbian-feminist community. Her volume of poetry *From a Land Where Other People Live* (1973) was a finalist for the National Book Award. She was one of the few (and perhaps token) women of color whose work could not be ignored in black and women's studies classes even at the inception of such courses in the early 1970s, when problems of homophobia, racism, and sexism had barely begun to be addressed in the college curriculum.

Lorde's poetry and prose deal with her own battles against racism, sexism, and homophobia. Her work often demonstrates the anger and determined hope for change that led her to characterize herself as a "warrior poet." But it also celebrates lesbian love, and specifically lesbian eroticism. In her influential essay "The Uses of the Erotic" she sees lesbian sexuality as a source of great potential power for women. In her "biomythography," as she calls her somewhat fictionalized life story *Zami: A New Spelling of My Name* (1982), Lorde adopts the lesbian-feminist definition of lesbianism as being synonymous with strength. She insisted, against the denials of the African American heterosexual community at the time: "I believe there have always been Black dykes around—in the sense of powerful and women-oriented women." She recognizes that most of those "dykes" would not have willingly claimed the name for themselves, but nevertheless their "dykiness" and their power were one. Using that lesbian-feminist definition of the dyke, Lorde proudly traces her own lesbianism back to her mother, who was also powerful and woman-identified.

FURTHER READING: Audre Lorde, *Zami: A New Spelling of My Name* (Watertown, MA: Persephone, 1982); *Chosen Poems: Old and New* (New York: Norton, 1982); *Sister Outsider: Essays and Speeches* (Trumansburg, NY: Crossing Press, 1984). Erin G. Carlston, "*Zami* and the Politics of Plural Identity," in *Sexual Practice, Textual Theory: Lesbian Cultural Criticism*, eds. Susan J. Wolfe and Julia Penelope (Cambridge, MA: Blackwell, 1993). Anita Cornwell, " 'So Who's Giving Guarantees'?: An Interview with Audre Lorde," *Sinister Wisdom* (Fall 1977), 15–21. Barbara Christian, "No More Buried Lives—The Theme of Lesbianism in Lorde, Naylor, Shange and Walker," *Feminist Issues* 5 (Spring 1985), 3–20. Anna Wilson, "Audre Lorde and the African-American Tradition: When the Family Is Not Enough," *New Lesbian Criticism*, ed. Sally Munt (New York: Columbia University Press, 1992), 75–93.

From *Zami: A New Spelling of My Name*

To whom do I owe the power behind my voice, what strength I have become, yeasting up like sudden blood from under the bruised skin's blister?

My father leaves his psychic print upon me, silent, intense, and unforgiving. But his is a distant lightning. Images of women flaming like torches adorn and define the borders of my journey, stand like dykes between me and the chaos. It is the images of women, kind and cruel, that lead me home.

To whom do I owe the symbols of my survival?

Days from pumpkin until the year's midnight, when my sisters and I hovered indoors, playing potsy on holes in the rosy linoleum that covered the living-room floor. On Saturdays we fought each other for the stray errand out of doors, fought each other for the emptied Quaker Oats boxes, fought each other for the last turn in the bathroom at nightfall, and for who would be the first one of us to get chickenpox.

The smell of the filled Harlem streets during summer, after a brief shower or the spraying drizzle of the watering trucks released the rank smell of the pavements back to the sun. I ran to the corner to fetch milk and bread from the Short-Neck Store-Man, stopping to search for some blades of grass to bring home for my mother. Stopping to search for hidden pennies winking like kittens under the subway gratings. I was always bending over to tie my shoes, delaying, trying to figure out something. How to get at the money, how to peep out the secret that some women carried like a swollen threat, under the gathers of their flowered blouses.

To whom do I owe the woman I have become?

DeLois lived up the block on 142nd Street and never had her hair done, and all the neighborhood women sucked their teeth as she walked by. Her crispy hair twinkled in the summer sun as her big proud stomach moved her on down the block while I watched, not caring whether or not she was a poem. Even though I tied my shoes and tried to peep under her blouse as she passed by, I never spoke to DeLois, because my mother didn't. But I loved her, because she moved like she felt she was somebody special, like she was somebody I'd like to know someday. She moved like how I thought god's mother must have moved, and my mother, once upon a time, and someday maybe me.

Hot noon threw a ring of sunlight like a halo on the top of DeLois's stomach, like a spotlight, making me sorry that I was so flat and could only feel the sun on my head and shoulders. I'd have to lie down on my back before the sun could shine down like that on my belly.

I loved DeLois because she was big and Black and special and seemed to laugh all over. I was scared of DeLois for those very same reasons. One day I watched DeLois step off the curb of 142nd Street against the light, slow and deliberate. A high yaller dude in a white Cadillac passed by and leaned out and yelled at her, "Hurry up, you flat-footed, nappy-headed, funny-looking bitch!" The car almost knocking her down. DeLois kept right on about her leisurely business and never so much as looked around.

To Louise Briscoe who died in my mother's house as a tenant in a furnished room with cooking privileges—no linens supplied. I brought her a glass of warm milk that she wouldn't drink, and she laughed at me when I wanted to change her sheets and call a doctor. "No reason to call him unless he's real cute," said Miz Briscoe. "Ain't nobody sent for me to come, I got here all by myself. And I'm going back the same way. So I only need him if he's cute, real cute." And the room smelled like she was lying.

"Miz Briscoe," I said, "I'm really worried about you."

She looked up at me out of the corner of her eyes, like I was making her a proposition which she had to reject, but which she appreciated all the same. Her huge bloated body was quiet beneath the grey sheet, as she grinned knowingly.

"Why, that's all right, honey. I don't hold it against you. I know you can't help it, it's just in your nature, that's all."

To the white woman I dreamed standing behind me in an airport, silently watching while her child deliberately bumps into me over and over again. When I turn around to tell this woman that if she doesn't restrain her kid I'm going to punch her in the mouth, I see that she's been punched in the mouth already. Both she and her child are battered, with bruised faces and blackened eyes. I turn, and walk away from them in sadness and fury.

To the pale girl who ran up to my car in a Staten Island midnight with only a nightgown and bare feet, screaming and crying, "Lady, please help me oh please take me to the hospital, lady . . ." Her voice was a mixture of overripe peaches and doorchimes; she was the age of my daughter, running along the woody curves of Van Duzer Street.

I stopped the car quickly, and leaned over to open the door. It was high summer. "Yes, yes, I'll try to help you," I said. "Get in."

And when she saw my face in the streetlamp her own collapsed into terror.

"Oh no!" she wailed. "Not you!" then whirled around and started to run again.

What could she have seen in my Black face that was worth holding onto such horror? Wasting me in the gulf between who I was and her vision of me. Left with no help.

I drove on.

In the rear-view mirror I saw the substance of her nightmare catch up with her at the corner—leather jacket and boots, male and white.

I drove on, knowing she would probably die stupid.

To the first woman I ever courted and left. She taught me that women who want without needing are expensive and sometimes wasteful, but women who need without wanting are dangerous—they suck you in and pretend not to notice.

To the battalion of arms where I often retreated for shelter and sometimes found it. To the other's who helped, pushing me into the merciless sun—I, coming out blackened and whole.

To the journeywoman pieces of myself.
Becoming.
Afrekete.

How I Became a Poet

"Wherever the bird with no feet flew she found trees with no limbs."

When the strongest words for what I have to offer come out of me sounding like words I remember from my mother's mouth, then I either have to reassess the meaning of everything I have to say now, or re-examine the worth of her old words.

My mother had a special and secret relationship with words, taken for granted as language because it was always there. I did not speak until I was four. When I was three, the dazzling world of strange lights and fascinating shapes which I inhabited resolved itself in mundane definitions, and I learned another nature of things as seen through eyeglasses. This perception of things was less colorful and confusing but much more comfortable than the one native to my nearsighted and unevenly focused eyes.

I remember trundling along Lenox Avenue with my mother, on our way to school to pick up Phyllis and Helen for lunch. It was late spring because my legs felt light and real, unencumbered by bulky snowpants. I dawdled along the fence around the public playground, inside of which grew one stunted plane tree. Enthralled, I stared up at the sudden revelation of each single and particular leaf of green, precisely shaped and laced about with unmixed light. Before my glasses, I had known trees as tall brown pillars ending in fat puffy swirls of paling greens, much like the pictures of them I perused in my sisters' storybooks from which I learned so much of my visual world.

But out of my mother's mouth a world of comment came cascading when she felt at ease or in her element, full of picaresque constructions and surreal scenes.

We were never dressed too lightly, but rather "in next kin to nothing." *Neck skin to nothing?* Impassable and impossible distances were measured by the distance "from Hog to Kick 'em Jenny." *Hog? Kick 'em Jenny?* Who knew until I was sane and grown a poet with a mouthful of stars, that these were two little reefs in the Grenadines, between Grenada and Carriacou.

The euphemisms of body were equally puzzling, if no less colorful. A mild reprimand was accompanied not by a slap on the behind, but a "smack on the backass," or on the "bamsy." You sat on your "bam-bam," but anything between your hip-bones and upper thighs was consigned to the "lower-region," a word I always imagined to have french origins, as in "Don't forget to wash your *l'oregión* before you go to bed." For more clinical and precise descriptions, there was always "between your legs"— whispered.

The sensual content of life was masked and cryptic, but attended in well-coded phrases. Somehow all the cousins knew that Uncle Cyril couldn't lift heavy things because of his "bam-bam-coo," and the lowered voice in which this hernia was spoken of warned us that it had something to do with "down there." And on the infrequent but magical occasions when mother performed her delicious laying on of hands for a crick in the neck or a pulled muscle, she didn't massage your backbone, she "raised your zandalee."

I never caught cold, but "got co-hum, co-hum," and then everything turned "cro-bo-so," topsy-turvy, or at least, a bit askew.

I am a reflection of my mother's secret poetry as well as of her hidden angers.

Sitting between my mother's spread legs, her strong knees gripping my shoulders tightly like some well-attended drum, my head in her lap, while she brushed and combed and oiled and braided. I feel my mother's strong, rough hands all up in my unruly hair, while I'm squirming around on a low stool or on a folded towel on the floor, my rebellious shoulders hunched and jerking against the inexorable sharp-toothed comb. After each springy portion is combed and braided, she pats it tenderly and proceeds to the next.

I hear the interjection of *sotto voce* admonitions that punctuated whatever discussion she and my father were having.

"Hold your back up, now! Deenie, keep still! Put your head so!" Scratch, scratch. "When last you wash your hair? Look the dandruff!" Scratch, scratch, the comb's truth setting my own teeth on edge. Yet, these were some of the moments I missed most sorely when our real wars began.

I remember the warm mother smell caught between her legs, and the intimacy of our physical touching nestled inside of the anxiety/pain like a nutmeg nestled inside its covering of mace.

The radio, the scratching comb, the smell of petroleum jelly, the grip of her knees and my stinging scalp all fall into—*the rhythms of a litany, the rituals of Black women combing their daughters' hair.*

Saturday morning. The one morning of the week my mother does not leap from bed to prepare me and my sisters for school or church. I wake in the cot in their bedroom, knowing only it is one of those lucky days when she is still in bed, and alone. My father is in the kitchen. The sound of pots and the slightly off-smell of frying bacon mixes with the smell of percolating Bokar coffee.

The click of her wedding ring against the wooden headboard. She is awake. I get up and go over and crawl into my mother's bed. Her smile. Her glycerine-flannel smell. The warmth. She reclines upon her back and side, one arm extended, the other flung across her forehead. A hot-water bottle wrapped in body-temperature flannel, which she used to quiet her gall-bladder pains during the night. Her large soft breasts beneath the buttoned flannel of her nightgown. Below, the rounded swell of her stomach, silent and inviting touch.

I crawl against her, playing with the enflanneled, warm, rubber bag, pummeling it, tossing it, sliding it down the roundness of her stomach to the warm sheet between the bend of her elbow and the curve of her waist below her breasts, flopping sideward inside the printed cloth. Under the covers, the morning smells soft and sunny and full of promise.

I frolic with the liquid-filled water bottle, patting and rubbing its firm giving softness. I shake it slowly, rocking it back and forth, lost in sudden tenderness, at the same time gently rubbing against my mother's quiet body. Warm milky smells of morning surround us.

Feeling the smooth deep firmness of her breasts against my shoulders, my pajama'd back, sometimes, more daringly, against my ears and the sides of my cheeks. Tossing, tumbling, the soft gurgle of the water within its rubber casing. Sometimes the thin sound of her ring against the bedstead as she moves her hand up over my head. Her arm comes down across me, holding me to her for a moment, then quiets my frisking.

"All right, now."

I nuzzle against her sweetness, pretending not to hear.

"All right, now, I said; stop it. It's time to get up from this bed. Look lively, and mind you spill that water."

Before I can say anything she is gone in a great deliberate heave. The purposeful whip of her chenille robe over her warm flannel gown and the bed already growing cold beside me.

"Wherever the bird with no feet flew she found trees with no limbs."

MEET

Woman when we met on the solstice
high over halfway between your world and mine
rimmed with full moon and no more excuses
your red hair burned my fingers as I spread you
tasting your ruff down to sweetness
and I forgot to tell you
I have heard you calling across this land
in my blood before meeting
and I greet you again
on the beaches in mines lying on platforms
in trees full of tail-tail birds flicking
and deep in your caves of decomposed granite
even over my own laterite hills
after a long journey
licking your sons
while you wrinkle your nose at the stench.

Coming to rest
in open mirrors of your demanded body
I will be black light as you lie against me
I will be heavy as August over your hair
our rivers flow from the same sea

and I promise to leave you again
full of amazement and our illuminations
dealt through the short tongues of color
or the taste of each other's skin when it hung
from our childhood mouths.

When we meet again
will you put your hands upon me
will I ride you over our lands
will we sleep beneath trees in the rain?
You shall get young as I lick your stomach
hot and at rest before we move off again
you will be white fury in my navel
I will be sweeping night
Mawulisa foretells our bodies
as our hands touch and learn
from each other's hurt.
Taste my milk in the ditches of Chile and Ouagadougou
in Tema's bright port while the priestess of Larteh
protects us
in the high meat stalls of Palmyra and Abomey-Calavi
now you are my child and my mother
we have always been sisters in pain.

Come in the curve of the lion's bulging stomach
lie for a season out of the judging rain
we have mated we have cubbed
we have high time for work and another meeting
women exchanging blood
in the innermost rooms of moment
we must taste of each other's fruit
at least once
before we shall both be slain.

LOVE POEM

Speak earth and bless me
with what is richest
make sky flow honey out of my hips
rigid as mountains
spread over a valley
carved out by the mouth of rain.

And I knew when I entered her   I was
high wind in her forest's hollow
fingers whispering sound
honey flowed   from the split cup
impaled on a lance of tongues
on the tips of her breasts   on her navel
and my breath   howling into her entrances
through lungs of pain.

Greedy as herring-gulls
or a child
I swing out   over the earth
over and over   again.

ON A NIGHT OF THE FULL MOON

I

Out of my flesh that hungers
and my mouth that knows
comes the shape I am seeking
for reason.
The curve of your waiting body
fits my waiting hand
your breasts warm as sunlight
your lips quick as young birds
between your thighs the sweet
sharp taste of limes.

Thus I hold you
frank in my heart's eye
in my skin's knowing
as my fingers conceive your warmth
I feel your stomach
move against mine.

Before the moon wanes again
we shall come together.

II

And I would be the moon
spoken over your beckoning flesh
breaking against reservations
beaching thought
my hands at your high tide
over and under inside you
and the passing of hungers
attended   forgotten.

Darkly risen
the moon speaks
my eyes
judging   your roundness
delightful.

Adrienne Rich
(b. 1929)

When Adrienne Rich won the Yale Younger Poets Award in 1951 for her
first book, *A Change of World*, she became recognized as a poet in the
establishment (that is, masculine) tradition which was valorized at midcen-
tury. W. H. Auden praised her early verse for its New Critical values of
detached control and restraint—though poems from the 1951 volume
such as "Aunt Jennifer's Tigers" and her 1963 collection *Snapshots of a
Daughter-in-Law* reveal an early and what had been largely unnoticed feminism. Rich married a Harvard economist in 1953 and had three sons.
Together with her husband, she became involved in the civil-rights and
antiwar movements, and she taught in a program for disadvantaged young
people. These activities steered her toward writing poetry that was even
more a direct expression of her social and political consciousness.

In 1970 Rich left her husband and soon identified herself as a lesbian.
Her 1976 essay "It Is the Lesbian in Us" defines what lesbian-feminism has
meant to her: "a sense of desiring oneself, choosing oneself; it was also a
primary intensity between women, an intensity which in the world at large
was trivialized, caricatured, or invested with evil. . . . I believe it is the
lesbian in every woman who is compelled by female energy, who gravitates
toward strong women, who seeks a literature that will express that energy
and strength." Rich has lived for many years with the Caribbean lesbian-

feminist writer Michelle Cliff, with whom she edited the lesbian-feminist journal *Sinister Wisdom*.

Rich's 1970s work reflected very directly her commitment to lesbianism and feminism. When she won the National Book Award in 1974 for *Diving Into the Wreck* she accepted the honor in the name of all women. For the last twenty years Rich has been considered one of the most prominent and influential poets among feminists, both lesbian and nonlesbian. Her prose writings, which include her study of motherhood, *Of Woman Born* (1976), her essays in *On Lies, Secrets, and Silence* (1979), and especially the essay "Compulsory Heterosexuality and Lesbian Existence" (1980), have also been central in influencing lesbian and feminist thought.

Her post-1970s work has focused somewhat less on lesbian-feminism and more on various other abiding personal and political concerns. For example, her most recent volumes of poetry, *Your Native Land, Your Life* (1986) and *An Atlas of a Difficult World* (1991), explore a problem she began to examine in the early 1980s in her essay "Split at the Root"—what it means to her to have been born half-Jewish. She is a founding member of an editorial collective which publishes *Bridges: A Journal for Jewish Feminists and Our Friends*.

FURTHER READING: *Norton Critical Edition of Adrienne Rich's Poetry*, eds. Barbara Charlesworth Gelpi and Albert Gelpi (New York: Norton, 1975). Adrienne Rich, *The Dream of a Common Language* (New York: Norton, 1978): *A Wild Patience Has Taken Me This Far* (New York: Norton, 1981). Elly Bulkin, "An Interview With Adrienne Rich," part I: *Conditions*, 1: 1 (April 1977), 50–65; part II: *Conditions*, 1: 2 (October 1977), 53–66. Marilyn Farwell, "Toward a Definition of the Lesbian Literary Imagination," *Signs*, 14: 1 (Autumn 1988), 100–18. Susan Stanford Friedman, "I Go Where I Love: An Intertextual Study of H. D. and Adrienne Rich," *Signs*, 9: 2 (Winter 1983), 228–45. Judith McDaniel, "To Be of Use: Politics and Vision in Adrienne Rich's Poetry," *Sinister Wisdom*, 7 (Fall 1978), 92–99. Catharine Stimpson, "Adrienne Rich and Lesbian/Feminist Poetry," *Where the Meanings Are: Feminism and Cultural Spaces* (New York: Methuen, 1988).

From TWENTY-ONE LOVE POEMS

❧

Wherever in this city, screens flicker
with pornography, with science-fiction vampires,
victimized hirelings bending to the lash,
we also have to walk . . . if simply as we walk
through the rainsoaked garbage, the tabloid cruelties
of our own neighborhoods.

We need to grasp our lives inseparable
from those rancid dreams, that blurt of metal, those disgraces,
and the red begonia perilously flashing
from a tenement sill six stories high,
or the long-legged young girls playing ball
in the junior highschool playground.
No one has imagined us. We want to live like trees,
sycamores blazing through the sulfuric air,
dappled with scars, still exuberantly budding,
our animal passion rooted in the city.

&

I wake up in your bed. I know I have been dreaming.
Much earlier, the alarm broke us from each other,
you've been at your desk for hours. I know what I dreamed:
our friend the poet comes into my room
where I've been writing for days,
drafts, carbons, poems are scattered everywhere,
and I want to show her one poem
which is the poem of my life. But I hesitate,
and wake. You've kissed my hair
to wake me. *I dreamed you were a poem,*
I say, *a poem I wanted to show someone . . .*
and I laugh and fall dreaming again
of the desire to show you to everyone I love,
to move openly together
in the pull of gravity, which is not simple,
which carries the feathered grass a long way down the upbreathing air.

&

Since we're not young, weeks have to do time
for years of missing each other. Yet only this odd warp
in time tells me we're not young.
Did I ever walk the morning streets at twenty,
my limbs streaming with a purer joy?
did I lean from any window over the city
listening for the future
as I listen here with nerves tuned for your ring?
And you, you move toward me with the same tempo.
Your eyes are everlasting, the green spark

of the blue-eyed grass of early summer,
the green-blue wild cress washed by the spring.
At twenty, yes: we thought we'd live forever.
At forty-five, I want to know even our limits.
I touch you knowing we weren't born tomorrow,
and somehow, each of us will help the other live,
and somewhere, each of us must help the other die.

&

I come home from you through the early light of spring
flashing off ordinary walls, the Pez Dorado,
the Discount Wares, the shoe-store. . . . I'm lugging my sack
of groceries, I dash for the elevator
where a man, taut, elderly, carefully composed
lets the door almost close on me.—*For god's sake hold it!*
I croak at him.—*Hysterical,*—he breathes my way.
I let myself into the kitchen, unload my bundles,
make coffee, open the window, put on Nina Simone
singing *Here comes the sun.* . . . I open the mail,
drinking delicious coffee, delicious music,
my body still both light and heavy with you. The mail
lets fall a Xerox of something written by a man
aged 27, a hostage, tortured in prison:
My genitals have been the object of such a sadistic display
they keep me constantly awake with the pain. . . .
Do whatever you can to survive.
You know, I think that men love wars. . . .
And my incurable anger, my unmendable wounds
break open further with tears, I am crying helplessly,
and they still control the world, and you are not in my arms.

&

Your small hands, precisely equal to my own—
only the thumb is larger, longer—in these hands
I could trust the world, or in many hands like these,
handling power-tools or steering-wheel
or touching a human face. . . . Such hands could turn
the unborn child rightways in the birth canal
or pilot the exploratory rescue-ship
through icebergs, or piece together

the fine, needle-like sherds of a great krater-cup
bearing on its sides
figures of ecstatic women striding
to the sibyl's den or the Eleusinian cave—
such hands might carry out an unavoidable violence
with such restraint, with such a grasp
of the range and limits of violence
that violence ever after would be obsolete.

ॐ

(THE FLOATING POEM, UNNUMBERED)

Whatever happens with us, your body
will haunt mine—tender, delicate
your lovemaking, like the half-curled frond
of the fiddlehead fern in forests
just washed by sun. Your traveled, generous thighs
between which my whole face has come and come—
the innocence and wisdom of the place my tongue has found there—
the live, insatiate dance of your nipples in my mouth—
your touch on me, firm, protective, searching
me out, your strong tongue and slender fingers
reaching where I had been waiting years for you
in my rose-wet cave—whatever happens, this is.

Judy Grahn
(b. 1940)

Judy Grahn, one of the first poets to be identified with the lesbian-feminist
movement, was a co-founder of the Woman's Press Collective, an early
lesbian-feminist publishing house, which issued Grahn's first books of
poetry. Through her roles of poet and publisher, Grahn was tremendously
influential in the development of the genre of lesbian-feminist poetry that
gave voice to "The Common Woman," as Grahn described her heroes in
her book by that name. Grahn, who is white but who attended an African
American college, has worked as a waitress, a meat packer, a maid, and a
secretary. Many of the experiences of the working-class women she wrote
about were her own. She chose as the title for the St. Martin's Press edition
of her collected poems in 1978 *The Work of a Common Woman*. Grahn's

1974 volume, *A Woman Is Talking to Death*, also reveals her identification with the powerless and outcasts of history and the present. Her working-class, lesbian-feminist identity politics remains implicit or explicit in much of her poetry.

In addition to her common-woman persona, Grahn has consistently attempted to construct a mythology for lesbians that would counter that which had been devised by the homophobic parent culture. In her prose writing, such as *Another Mother Tongue: Gay Words, Gay Worlds* (1984) and *The Highest Apple: Sappho and the Lesbian Poetic Tradition* (1985), Grahn creates compelling (if not always academically persuasive) cultural histories in which the lesbian is valorized. She speculates, for example, that the word "dyke" may have heroic roots in the name of the early British queen Boadicea, or the Greek goddess of balance, natural justice, and storms, Dike.

Grahn's prose poem *Edward the Dyke*, which was published in 1971, two years before the American Psychiatric Association agreed to expunge homosexuality from its list of mental illnesses, was revolutionary for its time. Grahn insisted in *Edward the Dyke*, which is about a young lesbian who finds herself on a psychiatrist's couch, that lesbians are not sick but rather that the "mental health" profession is greedy and has therefore managed to convince homosexuals that they are "vile" and need curing. When asked what her lesbianism means to her, Edward the Dyke responds with a free-association rhapsody about love and women's liberation such as characterized the lesbian-feminist ideal in the early 1970s: "Love flowers pearl, of delighted arms. Warm and water. Melting of vanilla wafer in the pants. Pink petal roses trembling overdew on the lips, soft and juicy fruit. . . . Cinnamon toast poetry. Justice equality higher wages. Independent angel song. It means I can do what I want."

FURTHER READING: Judy Grahn, *The Work of a Common Woman: The Collected Poetry of Judy Grahn, 1964–1977* (includes *Edward the Dyke*, "The Common Woman," and other volumes originally published by the Women's Press Collective. Introduction by Adrienne Rich, New York: St. Martin's Press, 1978); *Another Mother Tongue: Gay Words, Gay Worlds* (Boston: Beacon, 1984). Katharyn Machan Aal, "Judy Grahn on Women's Poetry Readings: History and Performance," *Sinister Wisdom*, part I: 25 (Winter 1984), 67–76; part II: 27 (Fall 1984), 54–61. Amitai Avi-Ram, "The Politics of the Refrain in Judy Grahn's *A Woman Is Talking to Death*," *Women and Language*, 10: 2 (Spring 1987), 38–43. Mary J. Carruthers, "The Re-Vision of the Muse: Adrienne Rich, Audre Lorde, Judy Grahn, Olga Broumas," *Hudson Review*, 36: 2 (Summer 1983), 293–322.

A WOMAN IS TALKING TO DEATH

One
Testimony in trials that never got heard

my lovers teeth are white geese flying above me
my lovers muscles are rope ladders under my hands

we were driving home slow
my lover and I, across the long Bay Bridge,
one February midnight, when midway
over in the far left lane, I saw a strange scene:

one small young man standing by the rail,
and in the lane itself, parked straight across
as if it could stop anything, a large young
man upon a stalled motorcycle, perfectly
relaxed as if he'd stopped at a hamburger stand;
he was wearing a peacoat and levis, and
he had his head back, roaring, you
could almost hear the laugh, it
was so real.

"Look at that fool," I said, "in the
middle of the bridge like that," a very
womanly remark.

Then we heard the meaning of the noise
of metal on a concrete bridge at 50
miles an hour, and the far left lane
filled up with a big car that had a
motorcycle jammed on its front bumper, like
the whole thing would explode, the friction
sparks shot up bright orange for many feet
into the air, and the racket still sets
my teeth on edge.

When the car stopped we stopped parallel
and Wendy headed for the callbox while I
ducked across those 6 lanes like a mouse
in the bowling alley. "Are you hurt?" I said,
the middle-aged driver had the greyest black face,
"I couldn't stop, I couldn't stop, what happened?"

Then I remembered. "Somebody," I said, "was *on*
the motorcycle." I ran back,

one block? two blocks? the space for walking
on the bridge is maybe 18 inches, whoever
engineered this arrogance. In the dark
stiff wind it seemed I would
be pushed over the rail, would fall down
screaming onto the hard surface of
the bay, but I did not, I found the tall young man
who thought he owned the bridge, now lying on
his stomach, head cradled in his broken arm.

He had glasses on, but somewhere he had lost
most of his levis, where were they?
and his shoes. Two short cuts on his buttocks,
that was the only mark except his thin white
seminal tubes were all strung out behind; no
child left *in* him; and he looked asleep.

I plucked wildly at his wrist, then put it
down; there were two long haired women
holding back the traffic just behind me
with their bare hands, the machines came
down like mad bulls, I was scared, much
more than usual, I felt easily squished
like the earthworms crawling on a busy
sidewalk after the rain; *I wanted to*
leave. And met the driver, walking back.

"The guy is dead." I gripped his hand,
the wind was going to blow us off the bridge.

"Oh my God," he said, "haven't I had enough
trouble in my life?" He raised his head,
and for a second was enraged and yelling,
at the top of the bridge—"I was just driving
home!" His head fell down. "My God, and
now I've killed somebody."

I looked down at my own peacoat and levis,
then over at the dead man's friend, who
was bawling and blubbering, what they would
call hysteria in a woman. "It isn't possible"
he wailed, but it was possible, it was
indeed, accomplished and unfeeling, snoring
in its peacoat, and without its levis on.

He died laughing: that's a fact.

I had a woman waiting for me,
in her car and in the middle of the bridge,
I'm frightened, I said.
I'm afraid, he said, stay with me,
please don't go, stay with me, be
my witness—"No," I said, "I'll be your
witness—later," and I took his name
and number, "but I can't stay with you,
I'm too frightened of the bridge, besides
I have a woman waiting
and no license—
and no tail lights—"
So I left—
as I have left so many of my lovers.

we drove home
shaking, Wendy's face greyer
than any white person's I have ever seen.
maybe he beat his wife, maybe he once
drove taxi, and raped a lover
of mine—how to know these things?
we do each other in, that's a fact.

who will be my witness?
death wastes our time with drunkenness
and depression
death, who keeps us from our
lovers.
he had a woman waiting for him,
I found out when I called the number
days later

"Where is he" she said, "he's disappeared."
"He'll be all right" I said, "*we* could
have hit the guy as easy as anybody, it
wasn't anybody's fault, they'll know that,"
women so often say dumb things like that,
they teach us to be sweet and reassuring,
and say ignorant things, because we dont invent
the crime, the punishment, the bridges
that same week I looked into the mirror
and nobody was there to testify;

how clear, an unemployed queer woman
makes no witness at all,
nobody at all was there for
those two questions: what does
she do, and who is she married to?

I am the woman who stopped on the bridge
and this is the man who was there
our lovers teeth are white geese flying
above us, but we ourselves are
easily squished.

keep the women small and weak
and off the street, and off the
bridges, that's the way, brother
one day I will leave you there,
as I have left you there before,
working for death.

we found out later
what we left him to.
Six big policemen answered the call,
all white, and no child *in* them.
they put the driver up against his car
and beat the hell out of him.
What did you kill that poor kid for?
you mutherfucking nigger.
that's a fact.

Death only uses violence
when there is any kind of resistance,
the rest of the time a slow
weardown will do.

They took him to 4 different hospitals
til they got a drunk test report to fit their
case, and held him five days in jail
without a phone call.
how many lovers have we left.

there are as many contradictions to the game,
as there are players.
a woman is talking to death,
though talk is cheap, and life takes a long time
to make

right. He got a cheesy lawyer
who had him cop a plea, 15 to 20
instead of life
Did I say life?

the arrogant young man who thought he
owned the bridge, and fell asleep on it
he died laughing: that's a fact.
the driver sits out his time
off the street somewhere,
does he have the most vacant of
eyes, will he die laughing?

Two
They don't have to lynch the women anymore

death sits on my doorstep
cleaning his revolver
death cripples my feet and sends me out
to wait for the bus alone,
then comes by driving a taxi.

the woman on our block with 6 young children
has the most vacant of eyes
death sits in her bedroom, loading
his revolver

they don't have to lynch the women
very often anymore, although
they used to—the lord and his men
went through the villages at night, beating &
killing every woman caught
outdoors.
the European witch trials took away
the independent people; two different villages
—after the trials were through that year—
had left in them, each—
one living woman:
one

What were those other women up to? had they
run over someone? stopped on the wrong bridge?
did they have teeth like

any kind of geese, or children
in them?

Three
This woman is a lesbian be careful

In the military hospital where I worked
as a nurse's aide, the walls of the halls
were lined with howling women
waiting to deliver
or to have some parts removed.
One of the big private rooms contained
the general's wife, who needed
a wart taken off her nose.
we were instructed to give her special attention
not because of her wart or her nose
but because of her husband, the general.

as many women as men die, and that's a fact.

At work there was one friendly patient, already
claimed, a young woman burnt apart with X-ray,
she had long white tubes instead of openings;
rectum, bladder, vagina—I combed her hair, it
was my job, but she took care of me as if
nobody's touch could spoil her.

ho ho death, ho death
have you seen the twinkle in the dead woman's eye?

when you are a nurse's aide
someone suddenly notices you
and yells about the patient's bed,
and tears the sheets apart so you
can do it over, and over
while the patient waits
doubled over in her pain
for you to make the bed *again*
and no one ever looks at you,
only at what you do not do
Here, general, hold this soldier's bed pan
for a moment, hold it for a year—
then we'll promote you to making his bed.
we believe you wouldn't make such messes

if you had to clean up after them.

that's a fantasy.
this woman is a lesbian, be careful.

When I was arrested and being thrown out
of the military, the order went out: dont anybody
speak to this woman, and for those three
long months, almost nobody did;   the dayroom, when
I entered it, fell silent til I had gone; they
were afraid, they knew the wind would blow
them over the rail, the cops would come,
the water would run into their lungs.
Everything I touched
was spoiled. They were my lovers, those
women, but nobody had taught us to swim.
I drowned, I took 3 or 4 others down
when I signed the confession of what we
had done   together.

No one will ever speak to me again.

I read this somewhere; I wasn't there:
in WW II the US army had invented some floating
amphibian tanks, and took them over to
the coast of Europe to unload them,
the landing ships all drawn up in a fleet,
and everybody watching. Each tank had a
crew of 6 and there were 25 tanks.
The first went down the landing planks
and sank, the second, the third, the
fourth, the fifth, the sixth went down
and sank. They weren't supposed
to sink, the engineers had
made a mistake. The crews looked around
wildly for the order to quit,
but none came, and in the sight of
thousands of men, each 6 crewmen
saluted his officers, battened down
his hatch in turn and drove into the
sea, and drowned, until all 25 tanks
were gone. did they have vacant
eyes, die laughing, or what? what

did they talk about, those men,
as the water came in?

was the general their lover?

Four
A Mock Interrogation

Have you ever held hands with a woman?

Yes, many times—women about to deliver, women about to
have breasts removed, wombs removed, miscarriages, women
having epileptic fits, having asthma, cancer, women having
breast bone marrow sucked out of them by nervous or
indifferent interns, women with heart condition, who were
vomiting, overdosed, depressed, drunk, lonely to the point
of extinction: women who had been run over, beaten up.
deserted. starved. women who had been bitten by rats; and
women who were happy, who were celebrating, who were
dancing with me in large circles or alone, women who were
climbing mountains or up and down walls, or trucks or roofs
and needed a boost up, or I did; women who simply wanted
to hold my hand because they liked me, some women who
wanted to hold my hand because they liked me better than
anyone.

These were many women?

Yes.   many.

What about kissing? Have you kissed any women?

I have kissed many women.

When was the first woman you kissed with serious feeling?

The first woman ever I kissed was Josie, who I had loved at
such a distance for months. Josie was not only beautiful,
she was tough and handsome too. Josie had black hair and
white teeth and strong brown muscles. Then she dropped
out of school unexplained. When she came back she came
back for one day only, to finish the term, and there was a
child in her. She was all shame, pain, and defiance. Her eyes
were dark as the water under a bridge and no one would
talk to her, they laughed and threw things at her. In the
afternoon I walked across the front of the class and look-

ed deep into Josie's eyes and I picked up her chin with my
hand, because I loved her, because nothing like her trouble
would ever happen to me, because I hated it that she was
pregnant and unhappy, and an outcast. We were thirteen.

You didn't kiss her?

How does it feel to be thirteen and having a baby?

You didn't actually kiss her?

Not in fact.

You have kissed other women?

Yes, many, some of the finest women I know, I have kissed.
women who were lonely, women I didn't know and didn't
want to, but kissed because that was a way to say yes we are
still alive and loveable, though separate, women who recognized a loneliness in me, women who were hurt, I confess to
kissing the top of a 55 year old woman's head in the snow in
boston, who was hurt more deeply than I have ever been
hurt, and I wanted her as a very few people have wanted
me—I wanted her and me to own and control and run the
city we lived in, to staff the hospital I knew would mistreat
her, to drive the transportation system that had betrayed
her, to patrol the streets controlling the men who would
murder or disfigure or disrupt us, not accidentally with machines, but
on purpose, because we are not allowed out
on the street alone—

Have you ever committed any indecent acts with women?

Yes, many. I am guilty of allowing suicidal women to die
before my eyes or in my ears or under my hands because I
thought I could do nothing, I am guilty of leaving a prostitute who held a knife to my friend's throat to keep us from
leaving, because we would not sleep with her, we thought
she was old and fat and ugly; I am guilty of not loving her
who needed me; I regret all the women I have not slept with
or comforted, who pulled themselves away from me for lack
of something I had not the courage to fight for, for us, our
life, our planet, our city, our meat and potatoes, our love.
These are indecent acts, lacking courage, lacking a certain
fire behind the eyes, which is the symbol, the raised fist, the

sharing of resources, the resistance that tells death he will
starve for lack of the fat of us, our extra. Yes I have committed acts of indecency with women and most of them were
acts of omission. I regret them bitterly.

Five
Bless this day oh cat our house

"I was allowed to go
3 places, growing up," she said—
"3 places, no more.
there was a straight line from my house
to school, a straight line from my house
to church, a straight line from my house
to the corner store."
her parents thought something might happen to her.
but nothing   ever   did.

my lovers teeth are white geese flying above me
my lovers muscles are rope ladders under my hands
we are the river of life and the fat of the land
death, do you tell me I cannot touch this woman?
if we use each other up
on each other
that's a little bit less for you
a little bit less for you, ho
death, ho ho death.

Bless this day oh cat our house
help me be not such a mouse
death tells the woman to stay home
and then breaks in the window.

I read this somewhere, I wasn't there:
In feudal Europe, if a woman committed adultery
her husband would sometimes tie her
down, catch a mouse and trap it
under a cup on her bare belly, until
it gnawed itself out, now are you
afraid of mice?

Six
Dressed as I am, a young man once called
me names in Spanish

a woman who talks to death
is a dirty traitor

inside a hamburger joint and
dressed as I am, a young man once called me
names in Spanish
then he called me queer and slugged me.
first I thought the ceiling had fallen down
but there was the counterman making a ham
sandwich, and there was I spread out on his
counter.

For God's sake I said when
I could talk, this guy is beating me up
can't you call the police or something,
can't you stop him? he looked up from
working on his sandwich, which was *my*
sandwich, I had ordered it. He liked
the way I looked. "There's a pay phone
right across the street" he said.

I couldn't listen to the Spanish language
for weeks afterward, without feeling the
most murderous of urges, the simple
association of one thing to another,
so damned simple.

The next day I went to the police station
to become an outraged citizen
Six big policemen stood in the hall,
all white and dressed as they do
they were well pleased with my story, pleased
at what had gotten beat out of me, so
I left them laughing, went home fast
and locked my door.
For several nights I fantasized the scene
again, this time grabbing a chair
and smashing it over the bastard's head,
killing him. I called him a spic, and
killed him. My face healed, his didnt.
no child *in* me.

now when I remember I think:
maybe *he* was Josie's baby.

all the chickens come home to roost,
all of them.

Seven
Death and disfiguration

One Christmas eve my lovers and I
we left the bar, driving home slow
there was a woman lying in the snow
by the side of the road. She was wearing
a bathrobe and no shoes, where were
her shoes? she had turned the snow
pink, under her feet. she was an Asian
woman, didnt speak much English, but
she said a taxi driver beat her up
and raped her, throwing her out of his
car.
what on earth was she doing there
on a street she helped to pay for
but doesn't own?
doesn't she know to stay home?

I am a pervert, therefore I've learned
to keep my hands to myself in public
but I was so drunk that night,
I actually did something loving
I took her in my arms, this woman,
until she could breathe right, and
my friends who are perverts too
they touched her too
we all touched her
"You're going to be all right"
we lied. She started to cry
"I'm 55 years old" she said
and that said everything.

Six big policemen answered the call
no child *in* them.
they seemed afraid to touch her,
then grabbed her like a corpse and heaved her
on their metal stretcher into the van,
crashing and clumsy.
She was more frightened than before.

they were cold and bored.
'don't leave me' she said.
'she'll be all right' they said.
we left, as we have left all of our lovers
as all lovers leave all lovers
much too soon to get the real loving done.

Eight
a mock interrogation

Why did you get into the cab with him, dressed as you are?

I wanted to go somewhere.

Did you know what the cab driver might do
if you got into the cab with him?

I just wanted to go somewhere.

How many times did you
get into the cab with him?

I dont remember.

If you dont remember, how do you know it happened to
you?

Nine
Hey you death

ho and ho poor death
our lovers teeth are white geese flying above us
our lovers muscles are rope ladders under our hands
even though no women yet go down to the sea in ships
except in their dreams.

only the arrogant invent a quick and meaningful end
for themselves, of their own choosing.
everyone else knows how very slow it happens
how the woman's existence bleeds out her years,
how the child shoots up at ten and is arrested and old
how the man carries a murderous shell within him
and passes it on.

we are the fat of the land, and
we all have our list of casualties

to my lovers I bequeath
the rest of my life

I want nothing left of me for you, ho death
except some fertilizer
for the next batch of us
who do not hold hands with you
who do not embrace you
who try not to work for you
or sacrifice themselves or trust
or believe you, ho ignorant
death, how do you know
we happened to you?

wherever our meat hangs on our own bones
for our own use
your pot is so empty
death, ho death
you shall be poor

Joanna Russ
(b. 1937)

Joanna Russ is best known as a writer of science fiction, a genre that she says became important to her in college when she realized that as a woman she was necessarily outside the experiences that were reflected in the "serious" male literary tradition. She recalls, however, that it was not until 1969 that she became a radical feminist. As a writer she elected to record her own lesbian and feminist reality, which she would disguise as science fiction. The female characters in her work are heroic and often in battle against men, who are seen as corrupted by their chauvinism and corrupters of any society in which they have power. She depicts marriage as being oppressive but child rearing and the education of the young as a noble endeavor.

In addition to her important feminist and lesbian science-fiction writings, such as "When It Changed" (1972), *The Female Man* (1975), *The Adventures of Alyx* (1976), and *The Two of Them* (1978), she has written feminist criticism, including *How to Suppress Women's Writing* (1983) and *Magic Mamas, Trembling Sisters, Puritans & Perverts* (1985).

FURTHER READING: Joanna Russ, *The Female Man* (New York: Bantam, 1975); *On Strike Against God* (New York: Out and Out Books, 1980); *Magic Mamas, Trembling Sisters, Puritans & Perverts* (Freedom, CA: The Crossing Press, 1985). Samuel R. Delaney, "The Order of Chaos," *Science Fiction Studies*, 6 (1979). Natalie M. Rosinsky, "A Female Man? The 'Medusan' Humor of Joanna Russ," *Extrapolation*, 23: 1 (Spring 1982).

When It Changed

Katy drives like a maniac; we must have been doing over 120 km/hr on those turns. She's good, though, extremely good, and I've seen her take the whole car apart and put it together again in a day. My birthplace on Whileaway was largely given to farm machinery and I refused to wrestle with a five-gear shift at unholy speeds, not having been brought up to it, but even on those turns in the middle of the night, on a country road as bad as only our district can make them, Katy's driving didn't scare me. The funny thing about my wife, though: she will not handle guns. She has even gone hiking in the forests above the 48th parallel without firearms, for days at a time. And that *does* scare me.

Katy and I have three children between us, one of hers and two of mine. Yuriko, my eldest, was asleep in the back seat, dreaming twelve-year-old dreams of love and war: running away to sea, hunting in the North, dreams of strangely beautiful people in strangely beautiful places, all the wonderful guff you think up when you're turning twelve and the glands start going. Some day soon, like all of them, she will disappear for weeks on end to come back grimy and proud, having knifed her first cougar or shot her first bear, dragging some abominably dangerous dead beastie behind her, which I will never forgive for what it might have done to my daughter. Yuriko says Katy's driving puts her to sleep.

For someone who has fought three duels, I am afraid of far, far too much. I'm getting old. I told this to my wife.

"You're thirty-four," she said. Laconic to the point of silence, that one. She flipped the lights on, on the dash—three km. to go and the road getting worse all the time. Far out in the country. Electric-green trees rushed into our headlights and around the car. I reached down next to me where we bolt the carrier panel to the door and eased my rifle into my lap. Yuriko stirred in the back. My height but Katy's eyes, Katy's face. The car engine is so quiet, Katy says, that you can hear breathing in the back seat. Yuki had been alone in the car when the message came, enthusiastically decoding her dot-dashes (silly to mount a wide-frequency transceiver near an I.C. engine, but most of Whileaway is on steam). She had thrown herself out of the car, my gangly and gaudy offspring, shouting at the top of her lungs, so of course she had had to come along. We've been intellectually prepared for this ever since the Colony was founded, ever since it was abandoned, but this is different. This is awful.

"Men!" Yuki had screamed, leaping over the car door. "They've come back! Real Earth men!"

We met them in the kitchen of the farmhouse near the place where they had landed; the windows were open, the night air very mild. We had passed all sorts of transportation when we parked outside, steam tractors, trucks, an I.C. flatbed, even a bicycle. Lydia, the district biologist, had come out of her Northern taciturnity long enough to take blood and urine samples and was sitting in a corner of the kitchen shaking her head in astonishment over the results; she even forced herself (very big, very fair, very shy, always painfully blushing) to dig up the old language manuals—though I can talk the old tongues in my sleep. And do. Lydia is uneasy with us; we're Southerners and too flamboyant. I counted twenty people in that kitchen, all the brains of North Continent, Phyllis Spet, I think, had come in by glider. Yuki was the only child there.

Then I saw the four of them.

They are bigger than we are. They are bigger and broader. Two were taller than me, and I am extremely tall, 1m, 80cm in my bare feet. They are obviously of our species but *off*, indescribably off, and as my eyes could not and still cannot quite comprehend the lines of those alien bodies, I could not, then, bring myself to touch them, though the one who spoke Russian—what voices they have!—wanted to "shake hands," a custom from the past, I imagine. I can only say they were apes with human faces. He seemed to mean well, but I found myself shuddering back almost the length of the kitchen—and then I laughed apologetically—and then to set a good example (*interstellar amity,* I thought) did "shake hands" finally. A hard, hard hand. They are heavy as draft horses. Blurred, deep voices. Yuriko had sneaked in between the adults and was gazing at *the men* with her mouth open.

He turned *his* head—those words have not been in our language for six hundred years—and said, in bad Russian:

."Who's that?"

"My daughter," I said, and added (with that irrational attention to good manners we sometimes employ in moments of insanity), "My daughter, Yuriko Janetson. We use the patronymic. You would say matronymic."

He laughed, involuntarily. Yuki exclaimed, "I thought they would be good-looking!" greatly disappointed at this reception of herself. Phyllis Helgason Spet, whom someday I shall kill, gave me across the room a cold, level, venomous look, as if to say: *Watch what you say. You know what I can do.* It's true that I have little formal status, but Madam President will get herself in serious trouble with both me and her own staff if she continues to consider industrial espionage good clean fun. Wars and rumors of wars, as it says in one of our ancestors' books. I translated Yuki's words into *the man's* dog-Russian, once our *lingua franca,* and *the man* laughed again.

"Where are all your people?" he said conversationally.

I translated again and watched the faces around the room; Lydia embarrassed (as usual), Spet narrowing her eyes with some damned scheme, Katy very pale.

"This is Whileaway," I said.

He continued to look unenlightened.

"Whileaway," I said. "Do you remember? Do you have records? There was a plague on Whileaway."

He looked moderately interested. Heads turned in the back of the room, and I caught a glimpse of the local professions-parliament delegate; by morning every town meeting, every district caucus, would be in full session.

"Plague?" he said. "That's most unfortunate."

"Yes," I said. "Most unfortunate. We lost half our population in one generation."

He looked properly impressed.

"Whileaway was lucky," I said. "We had a big initial gene pool, we had been chosen for extreme intelligence, we had a high technology and a large remaining population in which every adult was two-or-three experts in one. The soil is good. The climate is blessedly easy. There are thirty millions of us now. Things are beginning to snowball in industry—do you understand?—give us seventy years and we'll have more than one real city, more than a few industrial centers, full-time professions, full-time radio operators, full-time machinists, give us seventy years and not everyone will have to spend three quarters of a lifetime on the farm." And I tried to explain how hard it is when artists can practice full-time only in old age, when there are so few, so very few who can be free, like Katy and myself. I tried also to outline our government, the two houses, the one by professions and the geographic one; I told him the district caucuses handled problems too big for the individual towns. And that population control was not a political issue, not yet, though give us time and it would be. This was a delicate point in our history; give us time. There was no need to sacrifice the quality of life for an insane rush into industrialization. Let us go our own pace. Give us time.

"Where are all the people?" said that monomaniac.

I realized then that he did not mean people, he meant *men,* and he was giving the word the meaning it had not had on Whileaway for six centuries.

"They died," I said. "Thirty generations ago."

I thought we had poleaxed him. He caught his breath. He made as if to get out of the chair he was sitting in; he put his hand to his chest; he looked around at us with the strangest blend of awe and sentimental tenderness. Then he said, solemnly and earnestly:

"A great tragedy."

I waited, not quite understanding.

"Yes," he said, catching his breath again with that queer smile, that adult-to-child smile that tells you something is being hidden and will be presently produced with cries of encouragement and joy, "a great tragedy. But it's over." And again he looked around at all of us with the strangest deference. As if we were invalids.

"You've adapted amazingly," he said.

"To what?" I said. He looked embarrassed. He looked inane. Finally he said, "Where I come from, the women don't dress so plainly."

"Like you?" I said, "Like a bride?" for the men were wearing silver from head to foot. I had never seen anything so gaudy. He made as if to answer and then apparently thought better of it; he laughed at me again. With an odd exhilaration—as if we were something childish and something wonderful, as if he were doing us an enormous favor—he took one shaky breath and said, "Well, we're here."

I looked at Spet, Spet looked at Lydia, Lydia looked at Amalia, who is the head of the local town meeting, Amalia looked at I don't know who. My throat was raw. I cannot stand local beer, which the farmers swill as if their stomachs had iridium linings, but I took it anyway, from Amalia (it was her bicycle we had seen outside as we parked), and swallowed it all. This was going to take a long time. I said, "Yes, here you are," and smiled (feeling like a fool), and wondered seriously if male Earth people's minds worked so very differently from female Earth people's minds, but that couldn't be so or the race would have died out long ago. The radio network had got the news around-planet by now and we had another Russian speaker, flown in from Varna; I decided to cut out when *the man* passed around pictures of his wife, who looked like the priestess of some arcane cult. He proposed to question Yuki, so I barreled her into a back room in spite of her furious protests, and went out on the front porch. As I left, Lydia was explaining the difference between parthenogenesis (which is so easy that anyone can practice it) and what we do, which is the merging of ova. That is why Katy's baby looks like me. Lydia went on to the Ansky Process and Katy Ansky, our one full-polymath genius and the great-great-I don't know how many times great-grandmother of my own Katharina.

A dot-dash transmitter in one of the outbuildings chattered faintly to itself: operators flirting and passing jokes down the line.

There was a man on the porch. The other tall man. I watched him for a few minutes—I can move very quietly when I want to—and when I allowed him to see me, he stopped talking into the little machine hung around his neck. Then he said calmly, in excellent Russian, "Did you know that sexual equality has been re-established on Earth?"

"You're the real one," I said, "aren't you? The other one's for show." It was a great relief to get things cleared up. He nodded affably.

"As a people, we are not very bright," he said. "There's been too much genetic damage in the last few centuries. Radiation. Drugs. We can use Whileaway's genes, Janet." Strangers do not call strangers by the first name.

"You can have cells enough to drown in," I said. "Breed your own."

He smiled. "That's not the way we want to do it." Behind him I saw Katy come into the square light that was the screened-in door. He went on, low and urbane, not mocking me, I think, but with the self-confidence of someone who has always had money and strength to spare; who doesn't know what it is to be second-class or provincial. Which is very odd, because the day before, I would have said that was an exact description of me.

"I'm talking to you, Janet," he said, "because I suspect you have more popular influence than anyone else here. You know as well as I do that parthenogenetic culture has all sorts of inherent defects, and we do not— if we can help it—mean to use you for anything of the sort. Pardon me; I should not have said 'use.' But surely you can see that this kind of society is unnatural."

"Humanity is unnatural," said Katy. She had my rifle under her left arm. The top of that silky head does not quite come up to my collar-bone, but she is as tough as steel; he began to move, again with that queer smiling deference (which his fellow had showed to me but he had not) and the gun slid into Katy's grip as if she had shot with it all her life.

"I agree," said the man. "Humanity is unnatural. I should know. I have metal in my teeth and metal pins here." He touched his shoulder. "Seals are harem animals," he added, "and so are men; apes are promiscuous and so are men; doves are monogamous and so are men; there are even celibate men and homosexual men. There are homosexual cows, I believe. But Whileaway is still missing something." He gave a dry chuckle. I will give him the credit of believing that it had something to do with nerves.

"I miss nothing," said Katy, "except that life isn't endless."

"You are—?" said the man, nodding from me to her.

"Wives," said Katy. "We're married." Again the dry chuckle.

"A good economic arrangement," he said, "for working and taking care of the children. And as good an arrangement as any for randomizing heredity, if your reproduction is made to follow the same pattern. But think, Katharina Michaelason, if there isn't something better that you might secure for your daughters. I believe in instincts, even in Man, and I can't think that the two of you—a machinist, are you? and I gather you are some sort of chief of police—don't feel somehow what even you must miss. You know it intellectually, of course. There is only half a species here. Men must come back to Whileaway."

Katy said nothing.

"I should think, Katharina Michaelason," said the man gently, "that you, of all people, would benefit most from such a change," and he walked past Katy's rifle into the square of light coming from the door. I think it was then that he noticed my scar, which really does not show unless the light is from the side: a fine line that runs from temple to chin. Most people don't even know about it.

"Where did you get that?" he said, and I answered with an involuntary grin, "In my last duel." We stood there bristling at each other for several seconds (this is absurd but true) until he went inside and shut the screen door behind him. Katy said in a brittle voice, "You damned fool, don't you know when we've been insulted?" and swung up the rifle to shoot him through the screen, but I got to her before she could fire and knocked the rifle out of aim; it burned a hole through the porch floor. Katy was shaking. She kept whispering over and over, "That's why I never touched it, because I knew I'd kill someone, I knew I'd kill someone." The first man—the one I'd spoken with first—was still talking inside the house, something about the grand movement to re-colonize and re-discover all that Earth had lost. He stressed the advantages to Whileaway: trade, exchange of ideas, education. He too said that sexual equality had been re-established on Earth.

Katy was right, of course; we should have burned them down where they stood. Men are coming to Whileaway. When one culture has the big guns and the other has none, there is a certain predictability about the outcome. Maybe men would have come eventually in any case. I like to think that a hundred years from now my great-grandchildren could have stood them off or fought them to a standstill, but even that's no odds; I will remember all my life those four people I first met who were muscled like bulls and who made me—if only for a moment—feel small. A neurotic reaction, Katy says. I remember everything that happened that night; I remember Yuki's excitement in the car, I remember Katy's sobbing when we got home as if her heart would break, I remember her lovemaking, a little peremptory as always, but wonderfully soothing and comforting. I remember prowling restlessly around the house after Katy fell asleep with one bare arm flung into a patch of light from the hall. The muscles of her forearms are like metal bars from all that driving and testing of her machines. Sometimes I dream about Katy's arms. I remember wandering into the nursery and picking up my wife's baby, dozing for a while with the poignant, amazing warmth of an infant in my lap, and finally returning to the kitchen to find Yuriko fixing herself a late snack. My daughter eats like a Great Dane.

"Yuki," I said, "do you think you could fall in love with a man?" and she whooped derisively. "With a ten-foot toad!" said my tactful child.

But men are coming to Whileaway. Lately I sit up nights and worry about the men who will come to this planet, about my two daughters and Betta Katharinason, about what will happen to Katy, to me, to my life. Our ancestors' journals are one long cry of pain and I suppose I ought to be glad now but one can't throw away six centuries, or even (as I have lately discovered) thirty-four years. Sometimes I laugh at the question those four men hedged about all evening and never quite dared to ask, looking at the lot of us, hicks in overalls, farmers in canvas pants and plain shirts: *Which of you plays the role of the man?* As if we had to produce a carbon copy of their mistakes! I doubt very much that sexual equality has been re-established on Earth. I do not like to think of myself mocked, of Katy deferred to as if she were weak, of Yuki made to feel unimportant or silly, of my other children cheated of their full humanity or turned into strangers. And I'm afraid that my own achievements will dwindle from what they were—or what I thought they were—to the not-very-interesting curiosa of the human race, the oddities you read about in the back of the book, things to laugh at sometimes because they are so exotic, quaint but not impressive, charming but not useful. I find this more painful than I can say. You will agree that for a woman who has fought three duels, all of them kills, indulging in such fears is ludicrous. But what's around the corner now is a duel so big that I don't think I have the guts for it; in Faust's words: *Verweile doch, du bist so schoen!* Keep it as it is. Don't change.

Sometimes at night I remember the original name of this planet, changed by the first generation of our ancestors, those curious women for whom, I suppose, the real name was too painful a reminder after the men died. I find it amusing, in a grim way, to see it all so completely turned around. This too shall pass. All good things must come to an end.

Take my life but don't take away the meaning of my life.

For-A-While.

Jane Chambers
(1937–83)

Jane Chambers died of brain cancer at the height of her career as a lesbian-feminist playwright. Her most successful play, *Last Summer at Bluefish Cove,* was produced in 1980 in New York at the Actors Playhouse and toured throughout the United States, bringing lesbian-feminism to the stage even in regional theaters. *Last Summer at Bluefish Cove* reflects many of the values of the lesbian-feminist movement and lifestyle (and sometimes gently laughs at them). The play depicts a cohesive group of old friends who are productive, strong, funny, and kind to each other. They provide good models for a previously heterosexual woman who learns through lesbian love to overcome the timidity and dependency that lesbian-feminists associated with straight life. The play illustrates the lesbian-feminist conviction that "any woman can."

Chambers's other produced plays with lesbian themes included *A Late Snow* (1979) and *My Blue Heaven* (1982). Her 1978 novel *Burning* depicts the witch of earlier centuries as a lesbian-feminist foremother. The plot of the novel revolves around two modern women who find themselves reexperiencing the lives of two women lovers who were persecuted as witches in seventeenth-century Salem. Chambers's volume of poems, *Warrior at Rest,* which is also largely lesbian-feminist, was published posthumously in 1984.

FURTHER READING: Jane Chambers, *A Late Snow* (New York: Avon, 1979); *My Blue Heaven* (New York: JH Press, 1982); *Burning* (New York: Jove, 1978). Claudia Allen, "As You Like It: Lesbian Plays," *Hot Wire,* 5: 3 (September 1989), 38–39+. Harriet Ellenberger, "The Dream Is the Bridge: In Search of Lesbian Theatre," *Trivia* (Fall 1984), 17–59. Peggy M. Landau, "Jane Chambers: In Memoriam," *Women and Performance,* 1: 2 (Winter 1984), 55–57.

Last Summer at Bluefish Cove

ACT ONE

(Early summer at Bluefish Cove, an isolated beach area near the city. In the foreground, there is a pebble beach. At the apron, a jutting rock rears its head above the sea, speckled with seaweed and colonies of clutching mussels. Upstage, a flight of weathered wooden steps lead to a one-room

rustic cabin with a living/sleeping area and a kitchenette. A door leads off the room to an unseen bathroom. There is also a door to a closet, upstage.

At rise, the cottage is dimly lit and our attention is focused on the rock and beach. A pair of rubber sandals and a well-worn workshirt are tossed carelessly at the foot of the steps. On the rock, barefoot, clad in worn cutoffs and frayed halter is LIL ZALINSKI, *sitting [or standing] and squinting into the afternoon sun as she waits impatiently for a fish to bite. From her handling of the pole, we can see she is an experienced fisherwoman.)*

LIL: Come on, you mother, bite. (*Pause.*) I see you circling down there. Come on, sweetheart. (*She jiggles bait*). Damn. You obviously don't know who you're dealing with here. I won the 1960 All American Girl Scout Fish-Off. I was the champeen. Sixteen bass and twelve blowfish. Of course I was just a kid then but I've gotten better with the years. (*She pulls in the line, checks the bait.*)

(EVA MARGOLIS *enters, unseen by* LIL. EVA *is walking quietly along the beach. She is dressed in proper resort clothing—everything about her says upper middle class. She watches* LIL, *unseen, with interest and amusement.)*

LIL: (*Wiggles line.*) If you were a person, you know what we'd call you? A C.T. You nuzzle the bait but you don't put out. Now, I'm going to try a different approach, it's called courting. You're going to love it. Here's how it goes. You're a terrific looking fish, you know that, sweetheart? You're a real knockout. Now, don't get me wrong, it's not just your body I'm after. I love your mind, your sense of humor, your intellect, your politics. . . . Aha, I'm getting your attention, huh? I respect you, darling. I love you. Now, bite, baby, bite.

(EVA *who, unnoticed by* LIL, *has been listening, speaks.)*

EVA: I'd fall for that. It's a good line.

LIL: (*Surprised.*) Would you mind telling that to the bluefish? (*She notes that* EVA *is an attractive woman and turns on the charm.*) I usually do pretty well with that line, I must be losing my touch.

EVA: (*Not picking up on* LIL's *flirtatiousness.*) Maybe you need to change your strategy. (*She walks to water's edge and peers in at fish.*) You could try caveman tactics. Hit it on the head with a stick.

LIL: (*Still charming.*) Not my style. I prefer a classier approach.

EVA: (*Still innocent.*) Have you tried poetry? (*To fish.*) "Shall I compare thee to a summer's day? Thou art more lovely and more temperate."

LIL: (*Peers into water.*) It's gone. Gone. You've driven that fish right back to the Atlantic.

EVA: (*Shrugs.*) As my mother always tells me, there are other fish in the sea.

LIL: That's a practical philosophy. Coldhearted but practical.

EVA: You're getting a bad sunburn. Is that your shirt? Better put it on.

   (EVA *picks up* LIL's *shirt from the steps, tosses it to her.* LIL *takes this as a sign of interest from* EVA *but* EVA *is only being friendly and proceeds to exit down the beach.*)

LIL: Thanks.

EVA: (*Going.*) Don't lose heart. Maybe you'll catch that fish tomorrow.

LIL: Hey—(EVA *turns.*) I'm Lillian Zalinski. Everybody calls me Lil.

EVA: Eva Margolis. I'm the pink cabin for the summer. (*She continues to leave.*)

LIL: (*Trying to stop her.*) Holly House. We call it Holly House. I'm in Crabapple, right up there. We've all been wondering who rented Holly House this season. The couple who had it the last two years split up. You're the only newcomer on the Cove this year, the other cabins are the same old gang. Are you alone?

EVA: Yes. The other cabins are all rented to couples?

LIL: (*Meaning herself.*) All but one.

EVA: I guess I'll have to get used to being odd man out.

LIL: More like New Girl In Town. You'll get lots of attention, I guarantee it.

EVA: (*Still misunderstanding.*) Well, I could use some attention. You're married, of course?

LIL: Not me. I'm the other one who's not a couple.

   (EVA *senses that* LIL *is not an ordinary person—that there is some subtext in this repartee but she can't identify it, so she asks:*)

EVA: Are you one of those swinging singles I've read about?

LIL: (*Teasing.*) Well, that depends . . .

EVA: (*Thinking she's got it.*) I bet you're an artist—or a writer!

LIL: No. I used to sell time for a television station—but I'm taking the summer off.

EVA: You and I are the only singles?

LIL: That's right. (LIL, *of course, is pleased at that.*) ·

EVA: (*Disappointed.*) Well, it's going to be a long summer. I hope you play chess. (*She starts to leave again.*)

LIL: I hate it. I like to fish.

EVA: You can't fish at night.

LIL: I could fish at night but I prefer to do more interesting things. (EVA *still looks blank.*) Hey, would you toss me those sandals? This beach is murder on the feet. (EVA *brings her the sandals.*) You'll have to come to the opening of the season bash tonight. It's at my cabin, right up there. Music, food, booze, dancing. (EVA *is trying to size* LIL *up.*)

EVA: Were you ever married?

LIL: (*Cavalierly.*) Oh, sure. Lots of times.

EVA: I was only married once. For twelve years.

LIL: (*Stunned.*) Twelve years? I had one that made it two years and eight months. Eight long months. Rae and Annie will approve of you. They've been together nine.

EVA: How many times were you really married?

LIL: Oh God, I don't know—a dozen? Who counts?

EVA: Come on. A dozen husbands?

LIL: (*Realizing.*) Husbands?

EVA: Husbands. You know the guy in the tuxedo, he's waiting at the altar when you come down the aisle.

LIL: Husbands.

EVA: Husbands.

LIL: How did you come to rent Holly House?

EVA: Oh, it was a godsend. I walked out on George on Wednesday, just packed the suitcases and left. It gave me such pleasure to leave him stranded with a paisley overnight bag and a Board of Directors meeting in Chicago the next day. He'd go naked before he'd carry a paisley bag into a Board of Directors meeting—no, he wouldn't go naked. He thinks he's underdeveloped—for all I know, he may be. I married him when I was still in college so my basis for comparison is limited. Is six inches small? This book I'm reading says size doesn't matter. It's all in how he uses it. Foreplay is everything—this book says. It's called *The Female Sexual Imperative*. It's written by a woman doctor. Have you read it?

LIL: (*Still stunned.*) I've seen it.

EVA: (*Enjoying this conversation.*) Well, you probably know everything that's in it, anyway. I can't believe I've gotten to be this old and I don't know anything.

LIL: How did you get Holly House?

EVA: I left George on Wednesday and drove until dark. I wasn't heading any place in particular, I was just leaving George. I wound up in the village over there and checked into the Holiday Inn. The desk clerk—he was one of those sweet young men, you know the kind—handed me the room key and I burst into tears. I realized that I was going to spend the night alone, away from home, for the first time in my life.

LIL: How did you get *here?*

EVA: To Bluefish Cove? Well, the desk clerk—actually, he was quite nice in spite of his predilections—he said there was a place right down the street where I could get a drink and not be approached by mashers, a place where mostly businesswomen went. . . .

LIL: He sent you to Molly Pitcher's?

EVA: And I met this nice lady at the bar—she's a real estate agent—

LIL: Margery Eaton.

EVA: She handles the rentals for Bluefish Cove. I suppose you know her.

LIL: Very well.

EVA: I told her I needed quiet, some place to get myself together—she was wonderful. She didn't question me or ask for references, she didn't even ask me if I had a husband or kids. She just took my money and handed me the lease. I think she's a feminist. She assumed I was in charge of my own life.

LIL: She assumed something, that's for sure.

EVA: And it's working out wonderfully. It's beautiful here—and maybe I'll make some new friends. This party tonight, it's at your cabin?

LIL: (*Quickly.*) But you don't have to come.

EVA: Oh, but I want to. I've been holed up in my cabin for days now reading *The Female Sexual Imperative.* A party tonight would be just perfect, Lil. It's time for me to make my debut as a single woman.

LIL: (*Trying to ease out gracefully.*) Eva, you might feel out of place.

EVA: (*Misunderstanding.*) Because I'm single? Well, you are, too. Of course, I've been married so long I've forgotten how to flirt—but then you said it's mostly couples here—still, somebody might have a single houseguest or a bachelor brother, you never know, we might get lucky. I don't even remember how to hold a conversation with a man. (*She sees that* LIL *is uncomfortable.*) I promise not to cut in on your territory.

LIL: Somehow I'm not worried about that. It's just a bunch of beach bums, just the residents of the Cove. It's no big thing.

EVA: It is to me. I'm going to a party—by myself! I feel like a teenager again. When I was in high school, my best friend Joan and I always had a pow-wow before going to a party—I would never have dreamed of picking out a dress—or a boyfriend—without getting Joan's approval first. (*Touching* LIL's *hand.*) This book is right. It is possible for grown women to be friends. (*She feels slightly awkward at the sudden closeness and turns to leave.*) Thank you, Lil. I'll see you tonight!

LIL: (*As* EVA *goes,* LIL *glances toward the cabin.*) Oh, dear. Oh, dear.

(*Lights go down on the beach.* LIL *sits on the steps in the darkness and begins to clean fish quietly. We do not notice her because the lights go up in the cabin—there is music and chatter.* ANNIE *and* RAE *are dancing,* KITTY *paces as* RITA *watches. It is several hours later.*)

KITTY: Damn Marge Eaton!

RITA: She might have been drunk.

RAE: I think she made a perfectly reasonable assumption.

ANNIE: Walks like a duck, talks like a duck, hangs out with ducks, must be a duck.

KITTY: How could Marge do this to me?

RAE: If you meet a woman in a gay bar, you naturally assume she's gay.

KITTY: This could ruin my career!

RAE: Annie has just as much to lose as you have, Kitty. Annie's famous, too.

ANNIE: Rae . . .

RAE: Well, you are, darling. Annie was famous when you (*Meaning* KITTY.) were still delivering babies at that clinic in Brooklyn.

KITTY: It's not the same thing. Annie's a sculptor.

RAE: Sculptress. We take pride in the feminine gender.

KITTY: Well, you shouldn't. It's diminutive. Sculptor is generic. And nobody cares who a sculptor . . .

RAE: Sculptress.

ANNIE: Honey . . .

KITTY: Who a sculptor goes to bed with.

RITA: Kitty is developing a new language. She's going to write a dictionary of nonsexist language.

KITTY: (*To* ANNIE.) Nobody cares who you go to bed with.

RAE: I do. (RAE *turns off the record player, busies herself in the kitchen.* ANNIE *tends the bar.*)

KITTY: I have a new book coming out!

RITA: It's even better than *The Female Sexual Imperative.* It's called *Coming Together: The Search for Connubial Equality.* It's a play on words.

KITTY: I'm trying to liberate American women.

RITA: *Publishers Weekly* gave her an award. "Literature's Most Credible Women's Libber."

ANNIE: Don't worry, Kitty. If your career blows up, we'll give you an award. (*She hands* KITTY *a drink.*) "Bluefish Cove's Most Incredible Dyke."

KITTY: It isn't funny. I'll lose my credibility.

ANNIE: Not to mention your royalties.

KITTY: I'm dependent on my royalties! (*About* RITA.) We're dependent on my royalties. I gave up a career in medicine, remember, to devote myself to The Movement.

RAE: Why is it every time Kitty says "The Movement," it sounds like a disturbance of the lower colon?

KITTY: I don't know why I come back here every summer—I don't know why I put up with the bunch of you—I'm dedicating my life to a worthy cause—

RITA: We didn't have to come here this summer. The Swedish government offered Kitty a grant to go there and write.

ANNIE: Kitty, m'dear, we are your old friends. We recognize that you gave up long gory hours in the operating room in order to make a million writing books; we recall how you sacrificed day after day of peering up dark vaginas with a penlight in order to become a national celebrity. Our hearts bleed for you when we see your handsome face on the cover of *Ms.* or tune into Phil Donahue and listen to you instructing American women to grab their sexuality—

RAE: No, honey. "Seize their sexuality," that's what she said on Donahue. "Seize your sexuality," she said. Some woman in the audience thought she was advocating masturbation.

RITA: She does advocate masturbation. There's a whole chapter on it in this new book.

ANNIE: We are aware of your achievements and cognizant of your sacrifices. We have watched you fall in and out of love, in and out of lust, in and out of hangovers, we have tolerated and accepted you when you were young, dedicated and struggling, we tolerate and accept you now that you are rich, famous and arrogant. Bluefish Cove is more than just a lesbian beach colony, Kitty, it's family. And that's why you keep coming back.

RITA: Kitty is not arrogant. She's brilliant.

ANNIE: She's both. And she depends on us to keep her from becoming totally obnoxious.

KITTY: I wouldn't take that from anybody else, you know.

ANNIE: I know. That's why I said it.

RAE: What are families for?

KITTY: (*Calling out to steps.*) Lil, how can you do this to me? My career is in jeopardy! A straight woman in Bluefish Cove. I can't believe it. Is nothing sacred any more?

ANNIE: Kitty, don't get in a snit and screw up this summer, huh? Have some consideration, will you? (*She nods toward the door where* LIL *sits outside.*)

RAE: It's just one woman. One simple, little woman. She's not going to rent the Goodyear blimp and fly cross-country with a banner announcing that Dr. Kitty Cochrane is a lesbian.

KITTY: It only takes one person to start a rumor that can ruin a career.

ANNIE: Lil has the right to invite anybody she wants, anybody at all, to her own cabin for her own party.

KITTY: What difference does it make to Lil? She hasn't got anything to lose.

RAE: Kitty.

KITTY: I didn't mean it like that. I just mean—we're dealing with the rest of my life.

ANNIE: We're dealing with the rest of Lil's life, too.

RAE: We all agreed we were going to make this summer perfect. Nobody is going to fight—

ANNIE: (*To* KITTY.)—or fuck around.

RITA: Kitty never fucks around.

RAE: Love is blind.

ANNIE: (*To* KITTY *and* RITA.) Please, think about Lil.

RITA: (*Helpfully.*) Well, maybe it won't be so bad, Kitty. She is a straight woman. She'll be source material for your new book.

KITTY: Well, I can't see any other way of doing this: we'll all just have to pretend we're straight.

(RAE *shakes her head helplessly.* ANNIE, *who has poured a drink for* LIL, *takes both glasses and heads for door, disgusted.*)

ANNIE: I'm just about to give up on you, Kitty.

KITTY: I can say Rita's my cousin.

RITA: You could say I'm your secretary. I am your secretary.

KITTY: But, darling, she's bound to come into our cabin sometime during the summer and celebrities don't sleep in a double bed with their secretaries—but if you're my cousin—

RAE: Incest is preferable to being gay.

KITTY: (*To* RAE.) Annie could be your—sister-in-law. You can say you're divorced, which is true, you wouldn't have to lie, and you can say Annie's husband died valiantly in Viet Nam. Donna can say she's Sue's daughter.

RAE: I don't want to be around when you suggest that to Sue. Sue's slightly paranoid about that age difference, anyway.

RITA: But Kitty, we'd have to lie all the time. I mean, if the woman is living in Holly House, she's going to see us everywhere, every day, on the beach, at the picnic tables, in the glen, on the path . . .

RAE: Kitty, the woman may be straight but I haven't heard that she's retarded.

RITA: I don't know if we could carry it off, Kitty. Someone's bound to make a slip.

KITTY: Oh, shut up, Rita. I know that. They wouldn't do it, anyway. Nobody cares about my career! The whole thing is hideous and impossible. (*She wails and sinks into further depression.*) Sooner or later, it's your friends who do you in. My father used to say that.

(*Lights dim on the cabin, up on beach.* ANNIE *has descended the steps and sits just above* LIL.)

ANNIE: Need some help?

LIL: No thanks, I'm almost finished.

ANNIE: Why didn't you have them cleaned at the market?

LIL: How'd you know I didn't catch these?

ANNIE: I was looking out the window this afternoon when you came up the stairs with an empty bucket.

LIL: Don't rat on me. I have a reputation to uphold.

ANNIE: My lips are sealed.

LIL: Actually, I don't mind cleaning them. It releases my hostilities. (ANNIE *hands* LIL *the drink.*) Thanks. Has Kitty offended anyone yet?

ANNIE: Everyone. Right off.

LIL: Good. It's the opening of the season initiation. Kitty offends everyone, everyone puts Kitty in her place. Then we can settle in for the long, hot summer. Same thing, every year. When I lived with Kitty, it was a nightly ritual, putting Kitty in her place. She thrives on it, you know.

606 CHLOE PLUS OLIVIA

ANNIE: She's having a temper tantrum about your asking the straight lady to the party tonight.

LIL: I never would have if I'd known she was straight—but by the time I found out, it was too late. Well, she'll have to face it sooner or later—she might as well know right now, at the beginning of the season, she's smack in the middle of a bunch of dykes.

ANNIE: Kitty would prefer she never finds that out.

LIL: Kitty may change her mind when she sees her. She's nice looking.

ANNIE: I saw her. From the window.

LIL: Ah-ah.

ANNIE: Not me. I'm a married lady.

LIL: Maybe she'll turn out to be a nice, straight lady for Kitty to chase around after all summer. Kitty has never made it through a summer at Bluefish Cove without at least one side affair.

ANNIE: Not true. She never fooled around the two years she lived with you. You were the one who fooled around.

LIL: She called me an alley cat.

ANNIE: I remember. You had that fling with Donna. . . .

LIL: But I denied it. I swore, Girl-Scout's Honor, I hadn't laid a finger on Donna.

ANNIE: She didn't believe you. Kitty may be a pain in the ass but she's nobody's fool.

LIL: She set the answering machine to monitor and record. She bugged our goddam telephone.

ANNIE: And you, dummy, made a date to meet Donna at a motel—

LIL: Well, where else? She was living with Sue, I was living with Kitty— I'm too old to do it in the back of a car.

ANNIE: Didn't Kitty follow you to the motel?

LIL: Pounded on the door, made a complete ass of herself. Donna and I jumped out the window, bare-assed, with our clothes under our arms. Good thing we were on the first floor.

ANNIE: And Kitty never let you back in your apartment.

LIL: Never. Changed the locks and put my things out in the hallway like an Indian matriarch divorcing her husband.

ANNIE: You ever wish you'd stayed with Kitty?

LIL: It never would have worked.

ANNIE: It might have. I wouldn't have believed, nine years ago, that Rae and I would make it—but we have. And it's better now than it ever was.

LIL: (Shrugs.) I'm not a long-distance runner, Annie.

ANNIE: You were in love with Kitty.

LIL: Oh, for a minute, maybe. But I had a lust for freedom and she had a lust for fame and fortune. . . . Kitty's all right. Don't go so hard on her.

ANNIE: I'll try to remember that.

LIL: Someday sculptures by Anne Joseph will be in the Metropolitan and dedicated little art students will pry into your life, long-nosed intense professors will refer to you as the Master of Free Form. . . .

ANNIE: You think so?

LIL: I know it. And books by Dr. Kitty Cochrane will be on library shelves a hundred years from now. How long will your sculptures last?

ANNIE: (Uneasily.) Indefinitely.

LIL: Thousands of years. And Rae has two grown children and they'll have children. That's a kind of immortality. (Pause.) Alley cats just come and go.

(LIL stands with the bucket and fish heads and bones, then runs down the steps onto the beach, tossing the fish remains against the rock, into the sea. ANNIE watches her with love and sadness.)

ANNIE: Hey, Lil! (LIL looks up.) I love you.

LIL: (Laughs and starts to climb the stairs.) Don't you start that. We made a pact years ago in a dormitory room, never lovers, always friends.

ANNIE: I didn't mean that, dummy. I only meant you're my good buddy and I love you.

LIL: Come on, cut the crap. How many drinks have you had?

(Lights rise on cabin. RAE opens the door for them.)

RAE: I hope you didn't bring the heads and guts in with you.

LIL: Nope. Threw them in the sea. From the sea we come, to the sea we returneth. . . .

RAE: I don't mind cooking them but I sure hate to clean them. (RAE *takes fish, goes about preparing them.*)

LIL: (*Patting* RAE's *ass.*) Just like a woman.

ANNIE: Watch that, buddy.

RAE: There's nothing more disgusting than a male chauvinist dyke.

   (LIL *and* ANNIE *go into living room.*)

LIL: (*Approaching* KITTY *from behind.*) Don't tell me! Yes! It must be! It is! Dr. Kitty Cochrane, High Priestess of Feminism, right in my very own living room. May I have your autograph? (KITTY *looks at her coolly.*) Come on, Kitty.

RITA: She's upset that you invited that straight woman.

LIL: Eva? She's just a nice, naive little lady, Kitty. We're going to be a lot more upsetting to her than she is to us.

ANNIE: Ah, but she has invaded our secret Isle of Lesbos. The enemy is in our camp, a traitor moves among us. . . .

RITA: Kitty does have to be very careful.

LIL: She seems like a nice woman. She's all right, Kitty, it's going to be okay. (*Pause.*) Knock, knock, Kitty, can you hear me through the closet door?

KITTY: If this woman blows my cover, if she goes to the media and announces Dr. Kitty Cochrane is a dyke (*She wags her finger at* LIL.) do you know how David Susskind would love to get hold of that?

LIL: Deny it, Kitty. Deny everything. You're so good at that.

KITTY: The public is not ready. The public is still trying to accept the concepts of equal rights and the clitoral orgasm. It would be a catastrophe for me to come out of the closet now. It would be as incredible as if—Gloria Steinem announced her intention to marry—Marlo Thomas. The entire Movement would shudder and collapse.

RITA: Kitty is a figurehead, jutting boldly and courageously from the prow of the ship of human rights sailing through the treacherous sea of prejudice and ignorance. . . .

LIL: (*To* KITTY.) You didn't write that?

RITA: Yes, she did.

KITTY: I didn't use it. It was a first draft. Rita, how could you remember that?

RITA: I remember everything you write, Kitty. I have to type it four times. She does four drafts of everything.

LIL: (*To* KITTY.) I think I liked you better when you practiced medicine. You always looked so sexy in that white coat. (LIL, *tired, sits.*)

KITTY: How're you feeling, Lil?

LIL: Terrific.

KITTY: Really.

LIL: Don't start on me. You're not my doctor.

KITTY: You're under my supervision.

LIL: Bullshit. You have my records, that's all. I only agreed to that because my doctor wouldn't let me spend the summer out here otherwise. If I suddenly turn fuchsia and collapse, do something. Otherwise, keep your distance, understand?

RITA: Kitty just wants to help you.

LIL: (*To* KITTY.) You don't even practice medicine any more.

RITA: She didn't go to Sweden this summer so she could stay here with you.

KITTY: Rita! That's not true, Lil. I never did like Sweden and I wouldn't miss a summer at the Cove for anything. (*She feels* LIL's *forehead.*) You're overdoing. You cannot stay on that beach all day. You can't take that much sun.

LIL: You try to take my pulse and I'll break your fingers. I'm fine. I feel just fine.

(EVA *is approaching on the beach.*)

RAE: Hey, here she comes.

ANNIE: (*Wiggling her eyebrows.*) Nice. Very nice. You always did have good taste, Lil.

RAE: (*To* ANNIE.) Get in here and butter this skillet before I break it over your head.

ANNIE: I love a possessive woman.

RAE: Well, you've got one. (*About* EVA.) She's skinny and she's got blue eyes—and if I catch you looking crocksided at her, I'll snatch you bald-headed.

EVA: (*Calling.*) Lil?

ANNIE: (*At the door.*) You've got the right place. Come on up.

RAE: (*To* ANNIE.) You're a married woman.

ANNIE: I can dream, can't I?

RAE: Skinny with blue eyes. Revs up her motor every time. Get in here. (*She hauls* ANNIE *in by her britches pocket. This is a game between* RAE *and* ANNIE. *They are devoted to each other.*)

EVA: (*At door.*) Lil?

(LIL, *who shows evidence of being tired, goes to the door.*)

LIL: Hi, Eva.

EVA: I didn't hear much noise but I was too excited to wait. I've been dressed and ready for an hour.

LIL: Donna and Sue are late, as usual, but everybody else is here. Come on in.

EVA: Do I look all right?

ANNIE: I think you look terrific. (*To* RAE.) Doesn't she look terrific?

RAE: Wonderful.

KITTY: (*Inside, to* RITA.) I hope she doesn't introduce us by last names.

RAE: (*Wipes her hand on towel and extends it.*) I'm Rae. Welcome to Blue-fish Cove. The Li'l Abner character here is Annie Joseph.

ANNIE: Hi. We've been looking forward to meeting you. Lil told us all about you.

LIL: Not all. I don't know everything.

ANNIE: Hey, what are you drinking? Besides being assistant chef, I'm also the official barkeep.

EVA: Scotch and water, do you have that?

ANNIE: Sure. Coming up.

LIL: Rita Sanderson, Eva Margolis.

EVA: Hi.

KITTY: (*Quickly.*) I'm Katherine.

EVA: Hello.

ANNIE: You want this Scotch heavy or light?

EVA: Oh, light, please, I'm not a big drinker. Did you say your name is Annie Joseph?

ANNIE: That's right.

EVA: Are you the sculptress?

KITTY: Sculp*tor*.

ANNIE: It doesn't matter. I make sculptures.

EVA: I took a class in art appreciation last year—we studied you.

ANNIE: Thank you.

EVA: I never met a sculptress (*She hesitates, anxious to please, and glances towards* KITTY's *back.*)—sculptor?—(*But* KITTY *doesn't respond.*)—before.

RITA: (*Being helpful.*) Sculptress sounds like she does a little less of it a little less well.

RAE: Bull!

KITTY: (*To* RAE.) We really need a new word altogether. We need to develop our own language.

EVA: (*To* KITTY.) You must be a feminist! I'm trying to become one. I'm reading that new book by Dr. Cochrane right now: *The Female Sexual Imperative.* (KITTY *has turned her face away from* EVA, *so* EVA *addresses* ANNIE.) Have you read it?

ANNIE: (*To* LIL.) Do I have to answer that?

EVA: Oh, do. You'll love it. It'll change your life. I know most men get very uptight about their wives reading feminist literature—George nearly went wild when I bought this book by Dr. Cochrane. He said his secretary read it and got so uppity he had to fire her. And of course he blames Dr. Cochrane and her book for the fact I left him.

RAE: It wouldn't be the first time Dr. Cochrane's been blamed for a breakup.

EVA: But it's not true. It's really not. I would have eventually left, anyway. I mean, our marriage just wasn't working. We tried everything. We really did. (*To* RITA.) Have you read Dr. Cochrane's book?

RITA: Well, yes, I have.

EVA: She's wonderful.

RITA: She's marvelous.

EVA: I would have left George anyway but Dr. Cochrane's book made me feel good about it—as if it were a beginning, not an end.

KITTY: What a lovely thing to say.

RITA: (*To* ANNIE.) You see? She is a figurehead, jutting boldly and courageously from the prow of the ship of human rights.

EVA: She's the most important woman in the twentieth century, that's what I think. Kitty Cochrane is going to change the world.

ANNIE: (*To* LIL.) She can't hold out against this kind of flattery—I give her fifteen more minutes.

LIL: Fifteen more seconds. Bet you ten bucks.

EVA: If any of you haven't read the book, I'll let you have my copy when I'm finished. Just don't tell your husbands where you got it from. I'm in the last chapter now and I have savored every word. I'm telling you, you don't know what it is to be a woman until you've read Dr. Kitty Cochrane.

KITTY: I'm really thrilled the book has had such meaning for you.

LIL: (*Nudges* ANNIE.) See?

EVA: Oh, it has. It saved my life.

KITTY: Really?

EVA: Oh, *yes.*

LIL: (*To* ANNIE.) Watch this. (KITTY *hesitates a moment.*) Now.

KITTY: I am Dr. Kitty Cochrane.

LIL: (*To* ANNIE.) Ten bucks. Fork over.

EVA: (*Stunned.*) Really?

RITA: But Kitty, you said . . .

KITTY: Rita, I have an obligation to my public.

EVA: How terribly exciting.

(RAE, *who has missed much of the previous interchange because she was taking food out of the oven, rises, plates in hand.*)

RAE: (*Handing out plates.*) Okay, group, soup's on.

EVA: But everybody's not here. . . .

RAE: Like I used to say to my kids, you get here on time or your plate goes in the oven.

EVA: (*To* RAE.) When is your husband coming?

RAE: My husband? Coming? Oh, he's not. He won't be here. We were divorced nine years ago.

EVA: Oh. What about your children?

RAE: What about them?

ANNIE: They're on their own. One of them's bumming around Oregon and the other one's in summer school in the city.

EVA: You have children, too?

ANNIE: No, I just feel like Rae's are half mine.

EVA: (*Befuddled.*) You're neighbors.

RAE: No, we live together.

EVA: Oh. I don't have children now. We had a son but—(*To* KITTY, *who is cringing.*)—you have children?

KITTY: Oh, no, I don't. (*Quickly.*) I delivered 273 of them, however, and what a glorious thing it is to bring new life into the world.

RITA: I almost had a baby once. (*Everyone stares at her, surprised.*) I was pregnant when I was in college. The boy was very considerate. He paid for the abortion. It was a little girl.

EVA: I used to want a little girl. I wanted her to look just like me. My immortality, I guess. (*To* KITTY.) Your book says a woman has the right to control her own body. My husband, George, thinks that's a mortal sin. George thinks a lot of things are mortal sins. Like the things you say in your book about marital sex—

(*The lights are fading on that scene and coming up on the beach where* SUE, *a homely woman in her mid-40s, is helping* DONNA, *a beauty in her 20s, cross the rocky beach.* SUE *is obviously old money and wears frayed jeans and torn sneakers with the ease of the very rich.* DONNA *is very conscious of her good looks. She's a flirt and a social climber and does both with charm.)*

DONNA: Wait, Sue!

SUE: Honey, I told you that you couldn't walk this beach in those sandals. If you'd wear sensible sneakers. . . .

DONNA: The sandals make my ankles look thinner.

SUE: If your ankles got any thinner, your feet would break off. Come on.

DONNA: The sandals are sexier. Too bad Gucci isn't imprinted on the back of them.

SUE: I could stamp Saks Fifth Avenue on your ass.

DONNA: I'd like to have a pair of these in white, too. Can we order them by phone?

SUE: On one condition. Don't flirt with Lil tonight.

DONNA: Flirt with Lil?

SUE: Don't look dumb. You always flirt with Lil.

DONNA: Oh, Sue.

SUE: Ever since you had that brief affair with her . . .

DONNA: I never had an affair with Lil.

SUE: Don't lie to me. Kitty told me all about it. You and Lil leaping out a motel window.

DONNA: Kitty made up that story.

SUE: Why would Kitty make up a story like that?

DONNA: I don't know but she did. Why on earth would I want Lil Zalinski when I've got you? I bet Lil never made more than fifteen thousand dollars a year in her whole life.

SUE: She's good looking. She's reputed to be dynamite in the sack. She had you once and dropped you like a hot potato. My baby doesn't like to get dumped.

DONNA: They have these sandals in blue, too.

SUE: Have a heart, will you?

DONNA: I saw a terrific denim pantsuit in Lord & Taylor.

SUE: Whatever you want, Donna, just don't flirt with Lil tonight. I may be a fool but I don't want to look like one. Leave me some pride, huh?

DONNA: Don't you even feel sorry for Lil? Don't you feel guilty? You're ten years older than she is and you're still healthy as a horse.

SUE: When you're born into my financial bracket, you feel sorry for everybody, guilty about everything—and you learn very quickly that you can't do a damn thing about other people's bad luck. Two pairs of sandals and a pantsuit, that's all you want? You have a tragic flaw, Donna. You never gamble for high enough stakes. I might have gone for a Mercedes. (*She pats* DONNA's *rump.*) Keep moving, honey. We're late already. Go on.

DONNA: (*Climbing steps.*) YOO-HOO!

SUE: (*As they enter.*) Only an hour late, we're improving.

RAE: Come on in, your plates are in the oven.

ANNIE: (*To* EVA.) They're always late. Donna has to change clothes twenty times.

EVA: I changed clothes four times tonight, myself.

RAE: Sue McMillan, Donna Atterly, Eva Margolis. Eva's got Holly House this season.

SUE: Welcome. The two who had it last year fought nightly, kept the whole Cove in a state of crisis. I hope you're happily paired up with someone.

EVA: No, I'm not. (DONNA *takes an interested look.*)

SUE: Oh, dear. I was hoping for some peace and quiet.

RITA: Eva just broke up—

SUE: Well, we've all been through that—

RITA: With her husband. She's been married for twelve years.

DONNA: To a man?

EVA: What else? (*There is an awkward silence.*) Well, don't worry, I won't burden you with the boring details. Other people's divorces are a dull subject of conversation.

RAE: We were just discussing our children.

DONNA: Children?

RAE: Well, I do have two, you know.

EVA: (*To* DONNA.) Do you have children?

DONNA: Me?

EVA: Well, I'm sure you will. You're young yet. Are you married?

DONNA: Married? Me?

ANNIE: (*To* DONNA.) You're not married.

DONNA: No, I'm not married.

EVA: But your last name is different from your mother's.

DONNA: My mother?

LIL: She's not her mother.

DONNA: Sue? No, she's not my mother.

EVA: I'm sorry.

SUE: It's all right. It's an understandable mistake.

DONNA: You didn't think it was understandable when the maitre d' at Lutèce said it. You nearly bit his head off.

EVA: I'm sorry. I just assumed . . .

SUE: Forget it. All right? (*She moves to the window, embarrassed.*)

ANNIE: Honey, did you put coffee on?

DONNA: (*To* EVA.) Now see what you've done? She'll give me a hard time for the rest of the night.

EVA: I've apologized. I don't know what else to do.

DONNA: Well, it was a dumb thing to say.

LIL: Donna!

EVA: I thought it was a perfectly reasonable assumption. What is she, your aunt?

DONNA: Are you putting me on? (*To* LIL.) Where'd you find her?

KITTY: (*Quickly.*) I have a new book coming out. In the fall.

DONNA: (*To* EVA.) She's going to give me hell all night because of you.

RITA: Kitty's new book is really very exciting. I've read it, you know. I typed it.

DONNA: Jesus H. Christ. (*She glances toward* SUE.)

RAE: (*Seizing the situation.*) Look how clear it is tonight. You can see Connecticut! (*She goes to window and puts her arm around* SUE, *comfortingly.*) I bet it's beautiful from the beach. Lil, why don't you take Eva down and show her the Connecticut skyline from the beach? Coffee will be another ten minutes.

LIL: (*To* EVA.) Would you like that?

EVA: (*Anxious to get out of there.*) Yes. Yes, I would.

DONNA: (*To* EVA.) You better get your act together or this summer is going to be a real mess.

ANNIE: Be careful on the steps, it's dark and those planks are older than both of you. (LIL *leads* EVA *down the steps.*)

KITTY: (*Watching them go.*) Dear God in Heaven.

ANNIE: Speak to her for us, Kitty. She listens to you.

KITTY: Sue, you've got to do something about her. (*She means* DONNA.)

DONNA: About me? You better do something about her. Is Lil making it with her or what?

ANNIE: Poor Eva. She doesn't know what the hell is going on.

RAE: It must be awful for her.

DONNA: Awful for her? She hurt Sue's feelings.

SUE: Since when have you cared about that?

DONNA: I care. I've stuck around three years, I must care.

SUE: (*Touched.*) Come on then, give your old Mom a hug and kiss.

DONNA: Just a minute. I want to see what Lil's up to down there.

SUE: That's none of your business.

ANNIE: (*Looking out the window.*) That's what I'd say if they were doing something but they're not doing anything.

KITTY: Give Lil time.

RAE: I don't think that's what Lil has on her mind this summer.

ANNIE: Why not? If I were Lil, that's exactly what I'd have on my mind.

RAE: Kitty? Is she going to make it through the summer?

KITTY: The chemotherapy appears to have had a positive effect. There's no sign of new growth.

ANNIE: So she could get well and live for years.

KITTY: She could.

RITA: But, Kitty, you said that practically never happens, not with that kind of cancer. You said it moves so fast.

KITTY: (*Snaps.*) There is no indication of new growth at the present time.

RITA: But you said . . .

KITTY: It doesn't matter what I said, Rita. The practice of medicine is not an exact science. And I'm no expert in this field, don't ask me!

RITA: You are an expert, Kitty. You were an expert.

KITTY: Never.

RITA: It was your field of specialty!

KITTY: Don't tell me what I did, Rita!

RITA: You said you couldn't stand to watch people dying. You said you had to lie all the time and give people hope when you didn't think there was any.

KITTY: Rita, for God's sake!

RITA: These are your friends, Kitty, and they ought to know—she's not pushy and self-centered the way you think. She's kind and sensitive and caring. . . .

KITTY: Rita, Rita! What am I going to do with you?

RITA: I'm telling them because I love you.

KITTY: I know that! I just don't know how to shut you up!

RITA: She's angry at me that I told her secret.

RAE: It's not a secret, honey.

SUE: It's a charade. She wants us to play it with her, so we do.

DONNA: It's not all a charade. Kitty can be very pushy and self-centered. And mean. She can be very mean.

KITTY: And loud. I can be very loud. You can hear me clear through a motel room door.

DONNA: I haven't the foggiest notion what you're talking about.

RAE: Hold it! RING! Into your corners, ladies. We all agreed no fights this summer. We're going to make this summer perfect: this one's for Lil.

DONNA: What is she doing down there?

SUE: Will you get away from that window?

DONNA: I'm not flirting with her. I'm watching her.

SUE: Well, don't.

RAE: Hey, hey, take it easy, Sue.

DONNA: She can't help herself, she's menopausal.

KITTY: (*Clinically.*) Are you really?

DONNA: She has no interest in sex, she flies off the handle all the time.

RAE: According to Kitty's book, none of those symptoms come with menopause. That's an old wives' tale.

DONNA: Sue says she's menopausal, says it herself.

RAE: Kitty's book says . . .

SUE: Fuck what Kitty's book says. How would Kitty know? (*To* KITTY.) Have you *been* menopausal?

KITTY: Don't get so upset, Sue. There's nothing to get so upset about.

SUE: She makes me feel so completely inadequate.

DONNA: I don't make you feel any way—don't blame me for your own insecurities.

ANNIE: (*To* SUE.) Why do you continue to put up with that?

SUE: Because I love her.

DONNA: Do you really? Say that again. I like to hear you say that.

SUE: I can't. Donna, you're driving me crazy! (SUE *exits to bathroom.*)

DONNA: Hey, *wait!* Sue! I was only kidding! Where's your sense of humor?

KITTY: (*At window, looking down at beach.*) I don't like the looks of that.

ANNIE: (*Looking, too.*) Naw, they're just talking.

KITTY: They've been talking too long. Straight ladies can be very dangerous. They tend to toy with our affections.

ANNIE: Well, you're certainly the expert on that subject.

KITTY: (*Starchily.*) Lil does not need to be toyed with this summer.

RITA: I had a college roommate like that. We'd make out all night and then she'd get up in the morning and babble on about how she loved her boyfriend. I thought for months I was hallucinating.

KITTY: I want this summer to be as pleasant and serene as possible.

ANNIE: Lil can take care of herself. She can. I think she can.

   (*Lights down on cabin, up on beach.*)

LIL: (*As though concluding a description.*) . . . and to the left, that's the yacht basin. July 4th, they'll race, a hundred boats with spinnakers—it's really breathtaking.

EVA: You love it here, don't you?

LIL: It's my favorite place in all the world. I wish I'd found it sooner. This is only my fourth summer at the Cove.

EVA: Well, think of it this way. You have forty summers ahead of you. I think I'll head back to my cabin now. Thanks for inviting me.

LIL: It was awful for you, wasn't it? I'm sorry. The whole thing was just a terrible mistake.

EVA: I don't understand! I tried to be polite and sociable. I tried to say the right things. I've never felt so left out in my life. I might as well have been speaking another language.

LIL: You were speaking another language.

EVA: I thought I had it figured out—no men, no husbands—then Rae started talking about her children.

LIL: Lesbians have children, too. Some lesbians do.

EVA: I feel like such a fool. Why didn't you just tell me?

LIL: I couldn't. I couldn't just say, all the women in this cove are lesbians —because I don't have the right to make that kind of announcement for them. They have to make the decision to tell that themselves and everybody doesn't make the same decision at the same time—it's a mess, that's what it is, a mess. It's hard on us and it's hard on you. I'm sorry.

EVA: They're probably up there right now, laughing at what an idiot I made of myself.

LIL: No, nobody wanted to hurt you or embarrass you, Eva. I should never have invited you tonight—but at the time I asked you, I thought you were one of us.

EVA: You what?

LIL: It was a logical assumption. Marge Eaton has never, in recorded history, rented a cabin in Bluefish Cove to a heterosexual.

EVA: Never?

LIL: Bluefish Cove has been a gay women's haven for thirty years or more. These cabins were built by two elderly "maiden ladies"—that's what the locals called them. One of them's still alive in a nursing home, up island. Couple of years ago, a bunch of us drove up to see her. Annie took some photographs of the yacht race on the Sound and Rae brought her a bouquet of lavender. She never did understand who we were or why we were there. She kept staring at us and twice she looked around as though there were someone standing behind her and she said, "Elizabeth, I believe we have some company." Elizabeth was her lover's name, I guess. I don't know what will happen to the Cove when the old lady dies.

EVA: You could buy it. You could all get together and buy it.

LIL: Maybe Sue will buy it. She has the money to do it. Or Kitty.

EVA: I can't believe that Kitty Cochrane . . .

LIL: Yeah, well, don't talk about it, huh? It really could hurt her career.

EVA: George always claimed that women's libbers were a bunch of . . .

LIL: Dykes? Not all—but some. After all, dykes are women, too. I'll call Marge tomorrow. I'll explain to her and maybe she'll cancel your rental contract.

EVA: I don't know where else to go. I need a friend now. I'd wanted it to be you.

LIL: I'm not a vampire, for heaven's sake. I don't go around pouncing on pretty women. I know how to be friends. But you won't be comfortable here, Eva. You're out of place.

EVA: I'm out of place everywhere, Lil. I'm out of place here, in my marriage, in my life. And I'm terrified to be alone. I've never been alone.

LIL: Everybody's alone, Eva, sooner or later—we do all the important things alone.

EVA: Not me.

LIL: You're alone getting born, giving birth, dying. Oh, people may be standing around you, watching you, but you do the thing alone. You fall in love alone. Yes, you do. It's not like dancing the tango, two people don't fall in love in lockstep. One falls first, one falls later and maybe one never falls at all. You say Kitty's book changed your life—it didn't. It might have given you some courage but you're the one who changed your life, Eva. You rented the cabin, you spoke to me on the beach, you asked me to be your friend—you're not nearly so dependent as you think you are, Eva. Wherever you go this summer, I expect you'll do just fine.

EVA: Those women in your cabin tonight, they all seem so independent. And you, you don't need anybody. I admire that. You're not afraid of anything. George says women can't get along without men. Ha. I wish he could have seen what I saw tonight.

LIL: Eva, forget what you saw tonight, huh? Go back to your cabin, get a good night's sleep and I'll call Marge for you in the morning. Go on. Oh Jesus, don't start crying.

EVA: I'm not crying! I'm mad. I'm scared. You don't want me here and I don't know where to go . . . you were going to be my friend . . .

LIL: Eva, I am your friend. Everything's going to be just fine, you'll see. Now, go on. It's freezing out here. Good night.

(Reluctantly, EVA leaves. LIL watches, then turns and mounts stairs to cabin. Lights up in cabin.)

ANNIE: Here she comes.

KITTY: Alone?

RAE: Well, hey there. We were getting worried about you.

LIL: Sorry. She was pretty upset. This has been a stinking party, hasn't it?

DONNA: It's early yet. We can still party.

SUE: (Exiting bathroom.) We're going home now, Donna.

DONNA: Why?

SUE: I'm tired. I'm menopausal!

DONNA: What a drag!

SUE: We'll see you on the beach tomorrow, okay? Donna?

DONNA: Lil, want to go sailing tomorrow?

SUE: Donna.

DONNA: You don't like to sail. It makes you seasick. Lil?

LIL: (*Her attention is toward the window.*) I'll take a raincheck, Donna.

SUE: Donna, come on.

DONNA: If you change your mind, Lil . . .

SUE: Donna. (*They exit.*)

ANNIE: I'd like to strangle that kid. What a cunt.

KITTY: Annie! Never use a woman's genitalia as a derogatory word. What kind of feminism is that?

ANNIE: Kitty, m'dear, it has been my experience that in any group of men you will find a number of pricks. And occasionally, mind you, occasionally, in a group of fine upstanding women like ourselves, you will find a cunt. Donna is one. She wants Lil's body.

KITTY: She's had Lil's body.

ANNIE: Well, apparently she didn't get enough of it.

LIL: How could she? Kitty was breaking down the motel room door.

KITTY: She isn't good for you.

LIL: Don't worry. I can't be bothered. I haven't the energy or time.

RAE: That's the most sensible thing I've heard you say since I've known you.

(KITTY *is preparing to leave.* RITA *follows suit.*)

KITTY: (*At door.*) All right, gang. I'm going into town at ten a.m. tomorrow morning. If you want anything, write it down and attach cash. Last year, I managed to lose a lot of money. "Oh, Kitty, pick up some aspirin for me, will you?" "Toothpaste, we're nearly out of toothpaste." "Tampax, I forgot to get Tampax." This year, Rita's keeping track and I'm going to bill you.

LIL: Once a nitpicker, always a nitpicker; becoming famous hasn't changed you one damn bit.

KITTY: Last chance. Night all.

RITA: Thank you. It was a lovely dinner, Rae.

(They exit. RAE *picks up the cups and stacks them in the sink.* LIL *stares out the window.)*

RAE: That Rita's got good manners. She's the only one who said how good the meal was, the only one. The rest of you bums just took it for granted.

ANNIE: I never take you for granted, love, never. My life with you is a glorious adventure.

RAE: Are you making that up?

ANNIE: My nights are rich with mystery, my dreams breathless with expectation.

RAE: You read that somewhere!

ANNIE: I think I read it in a Kitty Cochrane book. (RAE *smacks her with dishtowel.*) On the other hand, maybe I overheard Lil saying that to Donna! (*Again, a smack.*)

ANNIE: (*Sees* LIL.) Are you okay, Lil?

LIL: Just tired.

ANNIE: Well, they told you to expect that, didn't they? Maybe you should take a nap in the afternoon.

LIL: I don't have time to take a nap.

ANNIE: Hey. (*She tries to comfort* LIL *but* LIL *brushes her off.*) You like her, huh? I know you. Do I know you or do I know you? I know you. You like her, huh? Huh? Am I right? You like her! Uh-huh!

LIL: (*Laughs.*) Kind of.

ANNIE: See there? Who knows you? I know you. Nobody knows you like I do. Right?

LIL: Right.

ANNIE: I love you, good buddy.

LIL: You said that earlier. Don't get mushy.

ANNIE: I know. My loving you is not enough. But just the same, I do. (*Calls to* RAE.) Come on, ol' lady, we're going home. Don Juan here is plumb wore out.

RAE: All right, all right, I'm just finishing up.

ANNIE: You need anything, Lil?

LIL: Yeah. Time.

ANNIE: You really like her.

LIL: She needs somebody. So do I.

ANNIE: Well then?

LIL: No. Wouldn't work.

ANNIE: Never say never.

LIL: She's straight.

ANNIE: Maybe she is and maybe she isn't.

LIL: She is.

ANNIE: I thought Rae was, too. Married lady with chubby babies hanging on her skirt. Then she attacked me.

LIL: It's not the same thing. You could offer her a life together.

ANNIE: You don't know yet what you could offer her—it's not the quantity of time, Lil, it's the quality—and you've got lots of quality, my friend.

LIL: You know, the one thing I've always had going for me is I know who I am. I know who I am, what I am, and what I'm capable of doing. Most of the time, I actually know what I want.

ANNIE: And?

LIL: She doesn't. She doesn't know a thing about herself. I don't make brass sculptures that last forever. I never wrote a book or had a baby. I'd like to pass something on.

RAE: (To ANNIE.) Okay, hot shot, let's go.

ANNIE: We'll see you in the morning?

LIL: Thanks, both of you.

RAE: When you get to feeling better, you can cook for us and wash our dishes.

LIL: That's a deal.

ANNIE: Get some sleep, will you?

LIL: I'll try. I get tired but my mind won't stop. I don't want to waste time sleeping.

ANNIE: I bet you could work up a terrific erotic dream tonight. Now, I don't consider that a waste of time!

LIL: (*Grins.*) You may be right about that.

ANNIE: Do I know you, huh?

LIL: Will you get outta here? (*They exit.* LIL *straightens up, unmakes the bed, sits on it, despondent. To herself.*) It isn't fair. (*She examines* ANNIE's *sculpture on table, replaces it, lights a cigarette, then hurls the ashtray on the floor.*) Goddammit. (*She bursts into tears and races into the bathroom.*)

(*Lights slowly down on cabin, up on beach. A passage of time.* EVA, *wrapped in jacket and shivering against the sea breeze, enters. She looks up at the cabin and begins to mount the stairs.* LIL, *coming out of the bathroom, is startled by the knock.*)

LIL: Who is it?

EVA: I'm too upset to sleep.

LIL: (*Not going to door.*) It's late, Eva. I'm very tired.

EVA: But I need to talk.

LIL: (*Reluctantly coming to door.*) We'll talk tomorrow. Life doesn't look so damned dramatic in the sunlight.

EVA: Have you been crying? Your face is swollen.

LIL: Naw. Catching a cold or something.

EVA: Your eyes are puffy.

LIL: Probably an allergic reaction to the sun. I stayed on the beach too long this afternoon.

EVA: I warned you. Bet your shoulders are blistered.

LIL: No, they're fine.

(EVA *touches* LIL's *shoulder;* LIL *winces.*)

EVA: See? You ought to put something on them. You have some Noxzema?

LIL: No, Eva. I'm just fine. I'm terrific, wonderful. Good night.

EVA: It gets cold here at night, doesn't it? (*She shivers visibly.*) That sea breeze . . .

LIL: All right, Eva, but not for long. I've got to get some sleep.

(She lets her in. LIL *keeps her distance.* EVA *sits awkwardly.)*

EVA: I used to talk to my little boy, Lenny, late at night like this. I'd sit by his bed and talk and he'd listen to me. He lived to be six years old. I taught him to read—he loved to read. He'd read to me out loud. I'd never been much of a reader myself, until Lenny came along. Then I started going to the library and bookstores to get books for him—and I'd pick up something for myself. In a way, you could say Lenny taught me to read. I think George thought he was somehow responsible for Lenny's heart. George thinks he's responsible for everything. He's not a mean man, he's just set in his ways. My mother wanted me to márry an adventurer—she was always dreaming about adventures. Going places no one else had gone, doing things no one had done—she never went anywhere herself, of course, it all happened in her mind. She wanted me to have adventures for her. And I haven't had one. . . .

LIL: Oh, I'm sure you have, Eva. Coming to the party tonight was a kind of adventure, wasn't it? Maybe not a pleasant one, but—

EVA: I bet you have adventures all the time.

LIL: Don't make a heroine out of me, Eva.

EVA: But I admire you.

LIL: I've done a whole lot of things in my life which were not in the least bit admirable. Ask Kitty Cochrane, she'll give you an earful.

EVA: Were you and Kitty . . .

LIL: For a while.

EVA: But now, you're not . . .

LIL: It's not a time for me to make commitments. I was never much for making commitments, anyway.

EVA: How did you know you were?

LIL: *(Challenging her.)* What?

EVA: *(Forcing herself to say it.)* Gay.

LIL: I fell in love with a woman. *(Snaps.)* What is this, twenty questions?

EVA: I'm sorry—I just don't know anything about it and—

LIL: Okay. I knew very early, some people do. I knew when I couldn't take my eyes off my high school English teacher, when my knees quivered every time my chemistry lab partner brushed her elbow against mine. When I could hardly wait for double dates to end so my girlfriend and I could cuddle in her bed together and demonstrate to one another what the boys had done to us. I knew it didn't mean a thing to her—that when I touched her, she was pretending that I was a boy. But I wasn't pretending. She was the real thing for me. I didn't know there were so many others like me until I got to college and met Annie. Annie swears that she was born gay. She was playing doctor with little girls in kindergarten. She's never had the slightest heterosexual tendency.

EVA: So, it was you and Annie?

LIL: Oh, goodness, no. Never. Annie and I are best buddies. It was Annie who showed me the gay bars and restaurants, the gay resort areas—we gays are kind of like the hobbits—no matter how repressive earthlings get, we continue to thrive in Middle Earth. We're survivors. We straddle both worlds and try to keep our balance.

EVA: Kitty Cochrane's book says you can be bisexual. She says it's the most natural way to be.

LIL: (*Sardonically.*) She does, huh?

EVA: I'd really never thought about that before.

LIL: (*Knowing what is coming.*) Well, Kitty also claims a mature person should not expect their partner to remain monogamous, that jealousy is an immature response. And I'm here to tell you that what Kitty says and what Kitty does are not the same thing. Kitty is a very possessive lady.

EVA: You don't like her, do you? You're always putting her down.

LIL: Like Kitty? I adore Kitty. She's my good friend. I might poke a little fun at Dr. Kitty Cochrane, feminist soothsayer, but that's just a mask she wears. The real Kitty is an old-time friend of mine. We've been through a lot together. Kitty's all right. I can count on Kitty to come through.

EVA: Lil, were you ever attracted to a man?

LIL: Are you writing a book or what? It's after midnight!

EVA: (*Flustered.*) No, I'm just trying to . . .

LIL: (*Challenging.*) To *what*?

EVA: (*Quietly.*) To understand. You think I'm boring, don't you?

LIL: No . . .

EVA: Just another runaway housewife.

LIL: I don't think you're boring, Eva. You're lonely, vulnerable, curious—and that combination scares the hell out of me. (LIL *smiles at* EVA.)

EVA: (*Shyly.*) I thought about you ever since I saw you on the beach today—at the party tonight, I could feel you watching me. I thought I could. (LIL *shrugs, admitting it.*) I sensed something was happening between us, I mean, I've never felt this kind of thing with a woman and I didn't know how to . . . I don't know how to . . . I mean, I've never . . . I wasn't even sure, I'm not sure . . . (LIL *begins to grin, watching* EVA *stammer through this.*) (*Quietly smiling.*) Are you just going to let me stand here and make a fool out of myself?

LIL: I'm not a curiosity, Eva. I'm not an experiment, not an adventure. On the other hand, I have never, repeat *never,* gone shopping with anybody for matching sheets and drapes at Bloomingdale's.

EVA: I understand.

LIL: (*Touching her face.*) Do you?

EVA: (*Bravely.*) I'm not as naive as you think I am.

LIL: You're not? (LIL *touches* EVA *seductively.*)

EVA: All right, I am.

LIL: Uh-huh. (*She guides* EVA *toward door.*) Go home, Eva. It's late, I'm tired, I'll see you on the beach tomorrow. We'll spend the afternoon together on the beach, all right? (*She touches* EVA's *lips with her fingers. Sighs.*) My mother must have told me fifty times, never kiss on the first date.

EVA: You're a puritan.

LIL: No, but my mother is. This is the first time I've ever taken her advice. Goodnight. (EVA *starts to descend stairs, looks back.*) Goodnight, Eva.

(LIL *smiles as* EVA *exits, but the smile fades to anxiety as*)

BLACKOUT

ACT TWO

(*Midsummer now.* KITTY, RITA, RAE *and* DONNA *are sunbathing on the beach.* DONNA *wears her useless sandals and a giant beach hat and the smallest possible bikini.* RAE, KITTY *and* RITA *wear ordinary bathing suits and are passing around a thermos of martinis.* ANNIE, *in ragged cutoffs and a shirt with the sleeves ripped out of it, is barefooted on the rock, fishing.* SUE *is with her.* DONNA *struts back and forth, displaying her body and glancing up at the cabin with irritation.)*

DONNA: Don't they ever get out of bed?

RAE: Why don't you mind your own business?

DONNA: Well, they can't be doing it all the time. It's physically impossible.

RITA: Kitty says women are capable of many multiple orgasms. Men aren't but women are.

DONNA: Well, I think it's perverted. We've hardly seen Lil all summer.

RAE: It's Lil's summer. If she wants to spend it in bed, let her.

DONNA: Well, it isn't fair.

KITTY: You'd think it was fair enough if you were the one in bed with her. (SUE *turns and catches* KITTY's *eye. To* SUE.) Sorry.

   (DONNA *climbs partway up the stairs, looking.* SUE *watches her.)*

ANNIE: (*To* SUE.) You deserve better than that, Sue.

SUE: Do I?

ANNIE: Yes. She uses you.

SUE: They all do. She's not the first pretty young thing I've kept. I don't expect she'll be the last.

ANNIE: You're a nice lady. You don't have to buy love.

SUE: I have never known, in fact, who loved me and who loved my bankbook—except with this one. I don't have to lie awake nights saying to myself, "But she said this," or, "She did this," and, "Maybe that does mean she loves me"—with Donna, I know exactly where I stand. (*Lightly.*) It hurts less that way, Annie.

KITTY: (*Calling to* DONNA.) Come down from there, leave her alone.

DONNA: None of you are concerned about Lil. (*She comes down.*) You don't care whether you see her this summer or not. You don't care if you ever see her again.

RAE: Of course we care.

DONNA: Any day could be her last.

KITTY: Oh, don't be so dramatic, Donna. People in Lil's condition just don't keel over suddenly. She'll have adequate warning and so will we.

RAE: I saw them walking on the beach this morning. Lil looked fine, her color's good. And I don't know when I've seen her look so happy.

RITA: I saw Eva in the supermarket. She looks good, too. She was all excited about moving into Lil's apartment in the city—she said they'd signed a lease to take the cabin again next summer.

KITTY: She said what?

RAE: She hasn't told her!

KITTY: Why didn't you tell me that?

RITA: I told you I saw her.

KITTY: But you didn't tell me that.

RITA: You were writing. I didn't want to break your concentration.

RAE: Annie! (ANNIE *leaps from rock to shore, turns to offer* SUE *a hand.*)

ANNIE: Yeah. I don't know what it is Lil does to catch fish off this rock but I don't seem to have any luck at all.

RAE: Did you know that Lil hasn't told Eva?

ANNIE: Hasn't told her what? (*Pauses, realizes.*) She hasn't?

KITTY: I understand it but I'm not happy about it. Lil's going through denial. It's natural—but in these circumstances—

ANNIE: I wouldn't tell her, either.

DONNA: I would—it would be so—romantic. Like Camille.

SUE: Will you shut up?

ANNIE: (*To* SUE.) Thank you. That's a step in the right direction, Sue.

RAE: But it isn't right, not to tell her. Eva ought to know.

ANNIE: As long as Lil feels good, I don't see why she has to tell her. Lil doesn't want to be looked on as a dying woman, for Christ's sake. Would you? She's in love, she feels wonderful, she wants to live. Leave her alone.

DONNA: You'd think she'd want to spend her last days with her friends. She just met Eva—she's known us for years.

ANNIE: (*To* SUE.) Will you do something about that brat before I drown her?

DONNA: I don't have to take that from you. I don't have to stand here and be insulted by a bunch of dykes.

ANNIE: Oh, and what are you, sweetheart, chopped liver?

DONNA: I'm bisexual. Or I could be if I wanted to. When we took that cruise to St. John's last year, I could have had every man on shipboard, couldn't I, Sue?

SUE: To tell the truth, dear, I thought you did.

DONNA: Well, I didn't! But nobody could blame me if I had. I certainly don't get any at home!

RAE: Donna!

DONNA: (*To* ANNIE.) You don't care about Lil. You're just going to let her stay up in that cabin with that stranger all summer long. She's going to die and we'll never see her again and you don't care. I'm going back to the cabin, Sue. (*She hobbles off.*) Sue? I'm going back to the cabin, aren't you coming? (*No answer.*) Sue!

SUE: (*Not moving.*) No. You're a big girl, Donna. You can get here to there alone. (DONNA *is stunned.*) Go on. (DONNA, *puzzled and disgruntled, hobbles off.*)

ANNIE: (*To* SUE.) Good girl.

SUE: She's spoiled rotten. And I'm the one who spoiled her. She was a perfectly ordinary little girl from Brooklyn when I met her. Oh, she'd gone to modeling school but she worked as a trainee on the Information Desk at Bloomingdale's. I was looking for the sale in Sportswear and she directed me first to Home Furnishings and then to Men's Outerwear and finally to Lingerie. She had a wonderful sense of humor about her inefficiency and never once apologized for sending me on wild goose chases all over the store. Donna was not always what she is now. I played a part in creating the monster. And like Dr. Frankenstein, I am somewhat reluctant to release my creation on the world.

(*Lights dim on beach, up in cabin.* EVA *is sitting on the unmade bed. She has a pad of paper in her lap; she is making a list.* LIL *is not in sight.*)

EVA: How big is your dining room?

LIL: (*Sticking her head out the bathroom door, washing her face.*) What?

EVA: Your dining room?

LIL: *Our* dining room.

EVA: How big is it?

LIL: (*Coming out, still scrubbing her face.*) It's very tiny. Actually, it's not a dining room, it's an alcove. It's, oh, I don't know, about like—I don't know, honey, it's little.

EVA: Will it hold an oak table and six bentwood chairs?

LIL: Sweetheart, this is a very small apartment.

EVA: But I have so much gorgeous furniture. Do I have to leave it all for George? (LIL *goes back to bathroom.*) We can get a bigger apartment.

LIL: (*Returning.*) Honey, I can afford *this* apartment.

EVA: Well, I can get a job. Some kind of job. Can't I? Do you want me to work?

LIL: (*From bathroom.*) It's not what I want, Eva, it's what *you* want. What do you want? (LIL *exits the bathroom, finished.*) What do you want?

EVA: I wish you'd stop asking me that.

LIL: I don't want you to do anything to please me. Just please yourself.

EVA: But I don't know what I want. Except you. I want you. Always.

LIL: (*Efficiently.*) It may come as a big surprise to you, my darling, but there is more to life than—(EVA *kisses her lightly, seductively, then moves away.*)—uhhhh. (LIL *follows. The following dialogue occurs during a slow-moving chase*—EVA *seducing,* LIL *reaching out,* EVA *moving away. It's a lovers' dance.*)

EVA: More to life than what?

LIL: Don't listen to me. I don't know what I'm talking about.

EVA: More to life than sex?

LIL: Some people say that but they lie. It's a pack of lies.

EVA: You mean love does make the world go round?

LIL: Oh, definitely.

EVA: Resolves all problems?

LIL: Absolutely.

EVA: Love conquers all?

LIL: No doubt about it.

EVA: My mother used to tell me, "Marry a rich man. Love doesn't pay the rent."

LIL: Your mother is a callous woman.

EVA: Will a six-foot couch fit in your living room?

LIL: *Our* living room.

EVA: Will it?

LIL: Honey, a six-foot person will hardly fit in that living room.

EVA: What am I supposed to do with all my furniture?

LIL: Sell it, store it, give it to George, give it to your mother, give it to the Salvation Army, burn it, just stop talking about it, put that damn list away and come here.

EVA: My mother always told me to plan for the future.

LIL: I can see your mother and I are not going to get along.

EVA: We have so much future to plan for, Lil—so many years together, so many things to do—do you ski?

LIL: Do I ski? I was the college downhill champion.

EVA: I'm the snowplow queen myself. You can follow my trail by the sitz-marks. But I love it. Imagine riding beside you in a chairlift. I've always had a fantasy about making love in a chairlift. Everybody on the mountain's craning their necks looking but they can't get to me and my lover, we're isolated, out of reach, oblivious to their stares and shouts, caught in the frenzy of our insatiable desire. Want to try that?

LIL: Nope. You might have gotten away with doing that with George but if you and I tried it, there'd be a sheriff waiting on the platform.

EVA: I never did it with George. George was never even in that fantasy.

LIL: But it was a man in the fantasy.

EVA: Well, I didn't know any better. Let's go to Switzerland and ski the Alps. And Spain. You want to go to Spain? I've never been to Spain.

LIL: Nope. I don't want to go to Spain. They throw homosexuals in jail in Spain. They'll take one look at the way my knees quiver when you look at me and they'll put me in the hoosegow and throw away the key. Let's go to Amsterdam. We can get married in Amsterdam.

EVA: Really?

LIL: Yep, we're nice and legal there, just like ordinary folks. Want to marry me?

EVA: Ah, you say that to all your girls.

LIL: I never said it before in my whole life. Girl-Scout's honor. It might make your mother happy. She sounds like the kind of woman who doesn't want you to live in sin.

EVA: What am I going to tell her?

LIL: That you've left George.

EVA: I've already told her that. I called her the night I did it. She was hysterical for twenty minutes but she got over it. She and George never got along. I'm sure she's already called her friends to elicit names of suitable eligible men.

LIL: Tell her you have a roommate.

EVA: What if I tell her the truth?

LIL: Don't.

EVA: Why not?

LIL: Does she vote a liberal ticket? Did she march for civil rights? Did she protest the war in Viet Nam? Did she boycott grapes and support the draft evaders?

EVA: No.

LIL: Don't tell her then. It's ten to one she'll disown you as a pervert.

EVA: She wouldn't.

LIL: Mine did. Just say you have a roommate and keep your mouth shut. Unless, of course, you get off on verbal flagellation and suicide threats.

EVA: I don't want to have to lie to my mother. I've never lied to my mother.

LIL: Everybody has lied to their mother.

EVA: Well, not about anything important.

LIL: Annie's mother won't allow Rae in the house. Sue's brothers won't allow her to visit her nieces and nephews. Rita was trained to be a teacher, you know, junior high school math. Her father called the school board and reported her. My mother feigned a suicide attempt and then had a nervous breakdown. Her shrink finally convinced her that my sexuality was not her fault and now she has disowned me. She wipes her hands of me, she says. She says I have faulty genes and I'm a malicious pervert. I keep reading stories in the gay press about how eighteen-year-olds announce it to their families over Christmas dinner and everybody hugs each other and it's all hunky-dory. Well, maybe that happens to eighteen-year-olds but it's never happened to anybody I know. The only one I know who has remained unscathed by their family is Kitty Cochrane—and that's because she has remained safely inside the closet.

EVA: I don't want to lose my family—but I don't want to lie to them, either. I want them to share my happiness. I want them to know you and love you. . . .

LIL: Don't count on it, Eva. Don't tell them unless you're prepared to lose them. I don't think you should tell them anything at all, not yet. I mean, we're very new, you and me, and what if you change your mind, what if something happens—next year this time you could be married to some upstanding dentist in Westchester.

EVA: Lil! You don't mean that.

LIL: Why not?

EVA: I love you! This may have started out to be a summer fling but it's much more than that now—what's the matter with you?

LIL: I'm trying to be realistic, Eva. Things change, people change.

EVA: But you love me—you said you love me. Or is that just part of the game, part of the malicious perversion?

LIL: (*Embraces* EVA.) I love you more than I have ever loved anyone. For the first time in my life, I understand why knights rode miles to slay a dragon for their lady's hand.

EVA: (*Half-crying, half-laughing.*) Lil.

LIL: And all those songs with "moon" and "June" and "croon," I thought they were pretty silly. Now, I'm whistling those tunes in the shower. Remember that song, "You're My Everything"? I used to hear that and say to myself, now what the hell does that mean, "You're my everything"? Nobody's anybody's everything. I was wrong.

EVA: Lil?

LIL: Yes, angel?

EVA: Are you ashamed of me? Do I embarrass you?

LIL: What?

EVA: You don't see your friends any more. Since I've been living here, you don't ever ask them over. I see them on the path and they ask how you are—they look at me funny as though I've taken you away from them.

LIL: I'd rather be alone with you.

EVA: At first I thought they didn't like me. And maybe you were embarrassed about me. That first party—it was awful. I know I made a bad impression.

LIL: Eva—I'm proud of you.

EVA: Do you know what tomorrow is?

LIL: Saturday?

EVA: It's our first anniversary. One month.

LIL: Oh, dear. If you cry because I forgot our first anniversary . . .

EVA: Let's celebrate tomorrow night.

LIL: All right.

EVA: Invite your friends?

LIL: Not just the two of us?

EVA: We can't live in a vacuum forever. Besides, I want to show off. I want all your friends to see how much in love we are. I'm not such a dummy as they thought.

LIL: All right, you asked for it! (*She opens the door, runs partway down the steps.*) Hey gang! Hey, down there! We're throwing a beach party tomorrow night—steamed clams and crabs and lobsters! It's our first anniversary! Bring your own booze—

(*The lights fade on the cabin and we hear the sound of a transistor radio on the beach. It's the night of the party, the beach is lit by moonlight.* DONNA, SUE, RITA *and* KITTY *go to the edges of the stage, collecting driftwood for the fire.* LIL *joins* ANNIE *on the beach—they are laying the firewood.* RAE *climbs the stairs to help* EVA *prepare the party food in the cabin kitchen.*)

LIL: Next year I'm going to buy some of that fire-starter, that stuff in cans. Trying to light a fire this big with drift and matches is an exercise in frustration.

ANNIE: I thought you were a Girl Scout, you got a merit badge in beach survival.

LIL: I did, I did, but I think I must have cheated—damned if I can remember how I did it.

ANNIE: You probably didn't do it at all. You charmed some little redhead into doing it for you.

LIL: That's not unlikely. That's how I passed Home Economics. Priscilla Miller, who could sew a seam straight as a ruler and fry an egg without breaking the yolk, lives forever in my grateful heart. (*She stands up, breathes the sea air.*) Annie, I feel terrific. I never felt so good in my whole life.

ANNIE: I'm glad, Lil. I'm happy for you. For both of you.

LIL: Doctors aren't infallible, you know. Sometimes these things just stop —the condition arrests itself, recedes, it goes away. When I was going to the clinic for chemotherapy, I met this woman whose tumor'd just stopped, disappeared, seventeen years ago. Then it came back—but she had a seventeen-year reprieve. It happens. She said she knew she couldn't die because she had to raise three kids—so she didn't die. And for seventeen years, until her kids were grown, she felt fine. It's all in having something to live for, Annie. I have Eva to live for now.

ANNIE: I've known you for a long time, Lil, and I don't think I've ever seen you in love before. Not like this.

LIL: It's never been like this. I didn't know it could be like this. Is it like this for you and Rae?

ANNIE: Well, probably not exactly—well, yes, I guess so. I mean, we've kind of passed that stage where we can't keep our hands off each other, thank goodness. You mellow out after a while, you know.

LIL: You mean the honeymoon ends.

ANNIE: Yeah—but that's when the good stuff starts.

LIL: Couldn't be any better than this. In ten years, we'll match notes, okay?

ANNIE: You haven't told Eva, have you?

LIL: She asked about the scar. I told her I had a hysterectomy. Which is true. She doesn't need to know any more than that—what more is there? I feel terrific. They told me I'd start having short-term pain. I haven't felt a thing. I'm telling you, Annie, it's gone. I know it is.

(DONNA *approaches* LIL *with an armful of firewood.*)

DONNA: This is getting my shirt all dirty. (LIL *takes the wood,* DONNA *brushes at her shirt.*)

LIL: Come on, gang, keep the driftwood coming.

SUE: (*Depositing her load and collapsing on the beach.*) Enough already!

RAE: (*Out the cabin door.*) Hey, we could use some help up here!

SUE: I volunteer! Anything to get out of this! (*She gratefully climbs the steps.*)

KITTY: (*Dumping driftwood.*) I really think this is enough, Lil. We're cooking seafood, not signalling for rescue.

LIL: One more. One more armful.

KITTY: You overdo, Lil. You always overdo.

(RITA *is staggering up with her armload.*)

RITA: (*To* KITTY.) Is this it?

KITTY: She says one more. (*Contemplates* RITA'*s pile.*) I'll take half of this, she'll never know the difference.

(*Lights down on beach, up in cabin.*)

SUE: (*Peering in pot.*) Jesus, that thing's alive!

RAE: They're all alive. That's how you cook them, alive.

SUE: Well, I know that, but I thought you drugged them or something first.

RAE: Nope. Right into the fire, alive.

SUE: I wish I hadn't seen it. It looked directly at me.

EVA: I take it you don't cook.

SUE: Only under duress. If push comes to shove, I can put a TV dinner in the oven.

EVA: Donna does the cooking?

SUE: Are you kidding? In the city, the cook does the cooking. When we travel, the hotel does the cooking and out here, we eat two meals a day at Molly Pitcher's.

RAE: Can you count to eight? Then count out the paper napkins, forks, spoons, glasses, paper plates—put them in that box and carry them downstairs. (SUE *grimaces and proceeds to do so.*)

EVA: (*To* SUE.) You travel all year round from place to place?

SUE: All my life. When I was growing up, it was Bar Harbor in the summer, a Massachusetts girls' school in the fall, Christmas in London, back to school for the winter, spring in Paris or Switzerland, back to Bar Harbor. There was a townhouse in the city we called home—my father lived there most of the time but the rest of us wafted in and out, on our way to somewhere else.

EVA: That's the kind of life my mother always said she wished that she could give me.

SUE: It was a nightmare.

EVA: I never went away to school. I went to a local college and lived at home. When George and I first married, we lived with his family for a year before we bought a place of our own. My mother was never crazy about George. She said that he was dull. If Lil were male, my mother would approve her as the perfect choice. We're going to travel, we're going to ski the Alps and Lil wants to take me to Amsterdam. Did you know you can get married in Amsterdam?

SUE: I thought you could get married anywhere.

EVA: A man and woman can get married anywhere. I mean Lil and me. We could get married in Amsterdam.

RAE: Whatever for?

EVA: Well, it would be kind of romantic.

SUE: For god's sake, don't tell Donna about it. She'd marry me, divorce me and wipe me out.

EVA: Oh, no she wouldn't.

RAE: Oh, yes she would.

EVA: Well, I'm glad I married George—I spent twelve years with him. If I'd just lived with him, if I didn't have a marriage contract, I wouldn't get a thing.

RAE: You may not get a thing. I didn't. Not one red cent. I put him through school, raised two kids, kept his house—now if he'd left me, I'd have had him by the short hairs. But I left him, see, and I left him for a woman. The only way he'd agree to let me keep the kids was if I forfeited my suit for child support. Annie's putting my kids through college.

EVA: But George and I bought that house together, we furnished it together, he made investments in the market for both of us.

RAE: In your name?

EVA: I don't know. George took care of those things.

RAE: Did he beat you up?

EVA: No!

RAE: Have a mistress?

EVA: Not that I know of—maybe.

RAE: Unless you can prove abuse or adultery, you're probably out of luck, sweetheart. At least in this state. You left him. And for heaven's sake, don't ever let him know you left him for a woman. Zilch. You'll get zilch.

EVA: But I never had to earn a living. George made good money. I don't know how to be anything but a housewife.

RAE: Me, either. And I'm good at it. I like to make a home, I like to shop, cook, clean. When my kids act up or Annie and I have a fight, I like to get down on my knees with a scrub-brush and wash that kitchen floor until it squeaks. It's a blasphemous thing to say in this age of Kitty Cochrane feminism, but I like creating an environment that's warm and pretty for the people I love.

EVA: Do your kids understand—about you and Annie?

RAE: Oh, we worried ourselves sick about that. We practiced just how we were going to tell the kids. Before we got up the courage to do it, they told us. They'd known it all along. My daughter went through a bad period about it when she was thirteen, fourteen—you know girls that age can't stand to be the least bit different—having a lesbian mother was an embarrassment, I guess. Even now, I'm not as close to her as I'd like to be—we get along all right but something's missing between us. My boy, it didn't faze him. He's a good kid, hair down to his ass but a mother can't have everything. (*She changes the subject abruptly.*) Okay, Eva, grab that pot, will you? And can you carry this box, too? Be careful with that, hold it upright.

EVA: (*Looking in box.*) What is it?

RAE: Get your nose out of there. It's a surprise.

EVA: It's a cake!

SUE: (*Looking.*) "Happy Number One. And Many More."

RAE: *And many more.*

EVA: Well, I should hope so. It's only a month. I expect us to stay together until we're ninety.

(*They gather up the boxes and bags and start downstairs as the lights dim in the cabin and come up on beach.* DONNA *is sitting on the stairs, watching. The others have finished preparing the fire.*)

ANNIE: Fire's going good.

DONNA: At last.

LIL: You haven't done a thing to help.

DONNA: I did so. I carried wood.

SUE: (*Calls from above.*) Donna! I could use some help with this.

DONNA: (*Mimicking.*) "Donna," "Donna."

ANNIE: Give her a break, will you? She's damned nice to you. Show some appreciation.

DONNA: She doesn't want me to be nice to her, don't you know that? If I were nice to her, she'd drop me in a minute. (DONNA *goes to help.*)

ANNIE: (*To* KITTY.) You understand that?

KITTY: Yes.

ANNIE: You would.

KITTY: (*As though from a textbook.*) Sue lacks self-esteem so she asks Donna to reinforce that she, Sue, is, in fact, not worthy of receiving love. If Donna were to demonstrate affection for Sue, Sue would feel betrayed and her emotional dependence on Donna would no doubt cease. It's a classic interaction between neurotics—the symptoms vary from battering to emotional flagellation. It is not infrequently found in parent/child and employer/employee relationships as well as those of mates. In the case of Donna and Sue, Donna, as the flagellator, also experiences guilt because she does, in fact, harbor affection for Sue but she senses, accurately, that to demonstrate that affection would jeopardize the game on which their relationship is based. It is this guilt which causes Donna to act promiscuously as in the case of Lil where Donna wishes Lil to punish her in the same way Donna has punished Sue.

LIL: (*To* ANNIE.) I'm sorry you asked that.

ANNIE: Not as sorry as I am.

RITA: (*Who has been following this carefully.*) You mean that Donna wants Lil to beat her up?

KITTY: Emotionally, dear, emotionally.

RITA: Because she feels guilty because she's so nasty to Sue.

KITTY: That's right.

RITA: Well, why *is* she so nasty to Sue? (KITTY *opens her mouth to explain.* ANNIE *stops her.*)

ANNIE: Don't you say that again. I got a headache the first time. (*To* RITA.) Donna is nasty to Sue because Sue's a sap and Donna's a cunt. (*She dares* KITTY *to challenge that.*)

KITTY: Well, I suppose that's another way of putting it.

(*The others arrive on the beach and unload beside the fire.*)

LIL: Where's the beer? You forgot the beer!

RAE: I set it on the counter. The big red cooler. I thought you had it, Sue.

SUE: I thought Donna got it.

DONNA: I only carried what you handed to me, Sue. I'm not a mind reader.

EVA: I'll go back up.

LIL: No, I'll go, honey.

ANNIE: Oh, no you don't. I'll go.

KITTY: (*To* LIL.) Let Annie go. That cooler's heavy.

LIL: (*Challenging her.*) So what?

KITTY: Lil. Let Annie go.

LIL: No. I said I'm going.

ANNIE: (*Pushing her aside gently.*) Out of the way, pal.

LIL: (*Seizing her.*) I said I'm going. (*Meanwhile,* EVA *is completely bewildered by all this.*)

DONNA: (*Grabbing* LIL.) Listen to Kitty, she's your doctor.

LIL: She's not my doctor. There's nothing wrong with me! Let me go, Annie. (ANNIE *looks at* KITTY.) Don't do this to me, Kitty.

KITTY: (*To* ANNIE.) Let her go. (LIL *races up the stairs.*)

EVA: What was that about?

RAE: Rita? Give me a hand here, will you? Push back those coals, Annie, so we can dump the clams in.

EVA: (*To* RAE.) What happened?

RAE: (*Pats* EVA'*s hand.*) Nothing, honey, nothing happened. Sue?

SUE: Don't you ask me to pick up one of those evil-looking critters.

EVA: (*Persistent.*) Something happened but I didn't understand.

ANNIE: (*To* KITTY.) She swears she feels fine.

KITTY: Maybe she does.

ANNIE: She says being in love has cured her.

KITTY: Oh, Annie, I hope that's true. I really want to believe in miracles— I want a miracle for her.

(LIL *appears at the top of the stairs with the cooler. She lifts it over her head and, showing off, descends the stairs.*)

ANNIE: Jesus, Lil!

LIL: I'm an Amazon! I can lift bull elephants above my head. I can slay dragons to win my lady's hand. (ANNIE *starts to help her.*) Don't, Annie, you'll upset my balance. (ANNIE *stops. They all watch breathlessly as* LIL *successfully completes the steps and presents the cooler at* EVA'*s feet.*) Voila! (*She takes a deep bow. To* ANNIE.) See? (*To* KITTY.) Now get the hell off my back.

RITA: She's only trying to help you!

LIL: I don't need her help. (*But at that moment the abdominal pain strikes and bends her double.*)

ANNIE: Lil!

LIL: Don't touch me! I'm all right! I'm going to be all right! (*It hits her again.*) Eva! (EVA, *bewildered, frightened, reaches out to* LIL.) I'm going to be fine, Eva. It's nothing, really. I'm going to be just fine. (*It hits again.*)

KITTY: (*To* ANNIE.) Help me get her up the stairs. (*They move to do so.*)

EVA: What's wrong? What's the matter with her? Lil?

KITTY: (*To* ANNIE.) You get her shoulders. (*As they straighten her up,* LIL *cries with pain.*)

ANNIE: Take it easy, pal, we got you.

EVA: What's wrong? What are you doing to her?

LIL: Eva!

KITTY: Sorry, Eva, out of the way.

EVA: Lil!

(*As they carry* LIL *upstairs, the lights fade on the beach. There is a complete blackout and when the lights come up, one week has passed. On the stage is an open overnight case.* KITTY *and* LIL's *voices come from the bathroom.*)

KITTY: (*From bathroom.*) Lil, listen to me.

LIL: (*From bathroom.*) You're wasting your breath, Kitty.

KITTY: (*From bathroom.*) Lil, you're stubborn as a mule.

(*During this,* ANNIE *comes out of closet where she has been hanging up* LIL's *nightshirt. She returns to open overnight bag and continues to unpack. She takes out robe and hangs it in closet, returns to take out slippers, toothpaste, etc.*)

LIL: (*From bathroom.*) Don't lecture me, Kitty.

KITTY: (*From bathroom.*) Put on your bathrobe. (*Out door, to* ANNIE.) Where's her robe? (ANNIE *hands it to* KITTY.)

LIL: (*From bathroom.*) Go to hell.

KITTY: (*In bathroom.*) Put it on. You just got out of the hospital, for Christ's sake, Lil. You're going to lie down and rest if I have to tie you to the bed. (KITTY, *irritated, exits bathroom. To* ANNIE.) Can't you talk some sense into her.

ANNIE: I'm her best friend, not her keeper.

KITTY: She wants to go fishing.

LIL: (*From bathroom, hollers.*) I feel fine!

ANNIE: (*To* KITTY *about overnight bag.*) I'm unpacking this.

KITTY: (*Irritated.*) I see you are.

ANNIE: She said to unpack it.

LIL: (*Entering, wearing robe halfheartedly.*) I'm not going back to the hospital, Kitty.

(ANNIE *unpacks cigarettes from bag and puts them tentatively on counter.* KITTY *reaches for them but* LIL *slaps her hand protectively across them.*)

KITTY: You're self-destructive.

LIL: My lungs are fine. My lungs have always been fine. Pink and healthy as a baby's. (LIL *reaches for a drink.*) My liver's fine, too.

KITTY: Lie down, Lil. Please.

LIL: Stop trying to turn me into an invalid!

KITTY: Just *walked* out of the hospital. *Walked* out.

LIL: I'm an adult human being. I have a few civil rights left.

KITTY: Lil, you're not being reasonable.

LIL: Fuck reasonable! This is my body, my life. I'll decide what's going to happen to me.

ANNIE: Lil . . .

LIL: (*To* ANNIE.) Don't you start on me. You're supposed to be on *my* side.

KITTY: There are no sides. You need surgery.

LIL: Sure. I need surgery this month and I'll need it again next month and again in two months—you know the statistics, Kitty.

KITTY: It will prolong your life, Lil.

LIL: In a hospital bed? No thanks.

ANNIE: You could let them try the cobalt again. . . .

KITTY: You responded very well to chemotherapy last spring.

LIL: For six weeks I was nauseated all day, my hair started falling out, I broke out in blotches, I was so weak I could hardly get from one room to another—Annie and Rae were waiting on me day and night. . . .

ANNIE: We didn't mind!

LIL: I mind!

KITTY: But the treatments helped. You felt wonderful until last week on the beach. . . .

LIL: And I feel fine again now. Without operations, without treatments, I feel fine.

KITTY: Bullshit, Lil.

LIL: They've already got my ovaries, uterus, tubes—if I'm going, I'm going with my hair, guts, breasts, whatever I've got left. I'm going as a person, not a patient. I'm going wanting to live, not wishing I were dead.

KITTY: You are stubborn and bullheaded—and you won't let anybody help you! There's a part of you I've never reached, Lil. You always close the door!

LIL: (*Lightly.*) You and I were terrible together, Kitty. Just terrible. We competed with each other all the time. Our relationship was an exercise in "can you top this?"

KITTY: (*To* ANNIE.) She thought I was a coward when I stopped practicing medicine.

LIL: (*Lying, glances at* ANNIE.) No, I didn't.

ANNIE: (*Backing her up.*) She didn't.

KITTY: (*To both of them.*) I know.

LIL: Well, my mother always wanted me to marry a doctor.

ANNIE: And she thought you looked sexy in that white coat. I could never see it myself.

KITTY: Those two years with you, Lil, they were special.

LIL: Well, try to remember the good parts, will you?

KITTY: I don't ever want to forget beating on that door of that motel room. Every time I take myself seriously, I want to think of that. I must have looked like twelve kinds of a jackass.

LIL: You did. (*To* ANNIE.) She did. (*They laugh together.*)

KITTY: (*Through the laughter, to* ANNIE.) Don't let me forget that.

ANNIE: Count on it.

(*The laughter awkwardly peters out. A moment of silence falls.*)

LIL: (*Quietly.*) How much time do I have left, Kitty? (KITTY *can't answer.* ANNIE *turns away suddenly, about to cry.* LIL *puts her hand on* ANNIE'*s shoulder. To* ANNIE.) Don't you go soft on me. I need you now.

ANNIE: (*Holding herself together.*) I'm here. I'm right here. (LIL *keeps her hand on* ANNIE *as though for support.*)

LIL: Answer me, Kitty.

KITTY: What are you asking me, Lil? How long on your feet and pain-free?

LIL: Yes. I have to know. I have to plan.

KITTY: Lil, there's new growth. It could accelerate—or you could go into remission again.

LIL: Is that likely?

KITTY: It happens sometimes.

LIL: The worst that could happen, Kitty. The bottom line.

KITTY: Don't put me in this position, Lil.

LIL: Six months?

ANNIE: Answer her, Kitty.

KITTY: Less.

LIL: Three?

KITTY: (*Hedging.*) Maybe.

LIL: Six weeks of feeling good?

KITTY: At least.

LIL: (*She'd expected more time—she is stunned.*) Why is this happening to me, Kitty? Why isn't it happening to you or Annie or Rita or Rae? Why not Donna, why not Sue? Are you all so much worthier than I am? I'm in love—for the first time in my life, I feel totally alive. Damn you! (KITTY *is helpless.*)

ANNIE: (*To* KITTY.) Do something. Help her. (*But* KITTY *can't.*)

LIL: (*Seeing* KITTY'*s helplessness.*) It's all right.

ANNIE: (*Angry.*) It's not all right!

LIL: (*Comforting* ANNIE.) I'm going to fish with you, my friend, out on that rock—we're going to smoke the best stuff we can buy—and every day, the first one to catch two blues buys lunch and drinks at Molly Pitcher's.

ANNIE: (*Trying to be light.*) I'm not much good at fishing.

LIL: I'll teach you all my tricks. (*To* KITTY.) And you, you never beat me in a game of poker yet.

KITTY: (*Trying to be light.*) That's because you cheat.

LIL: Me? The Girl Scout? Cheat? Eight o'clock tonight—I'm going to teach you how to fake. Quarters.

KITTY: Aw, Lil. *Pennies.*

LIL: *Quarters,* Kitty. Tightwad. Geez. (*To* ANNIE.) I'm offering her trade secrets and she's hassling me over quarters. Now I ask you, is that gratitude?

(*During the above sequence,* RITA, RAE *and* EVA *enter.* EVA *is carrying a container of soup.*)

RAE: Don't slosh that. It's hot.

RITA: Her hands are shaking. (*She takes container from* EVA. *To* RAE.) Smells delicious.

(*Onstage,* LIL, ANNIE *and* KITTY *are continuing their moment of closeness. As this scene on the beach concludes, they move awkwardly apart on stage.*)

RAE: Actually, it's very bland. Kitty said to make something easy on her stomach. They've got her on a lot of medication. Don't let her load it with salt.

EVA: (*Uncomfortably close to the stairs.*) I wish someone had told me. . . . (RAE *touches* EVA *supportively.*)

RITA: Would it have made a difference?

EVA: I don't know. It might have. (*She takes bowl from* RITA *and steps onto the stairs, calls.*) Lil! (*The group onstage responds immediately.*)

ANNIE: (*To* LIL.) Hey, it's Eva.

KITTY: (*Admitting* EVA, RAE *and* RITA.) It took you that long to open a can of chicken noodle?

RAE: I made it from scratch! Only the best for Lil.

KITTY: She could have starved while we were waiting.

(*EVA sees* LIL—*they look at one another for a moment.*)

EVA: Soup. Rae made it for you. (*EVA puts it on counter.*)

LIL: Fuck Rae's soup. (*She opens her arms and* EVA *goes into them. They cling to one another.*)

RAE: (*In response to* LIL*'s line.*) Gee, thanks.

RITA: (*To* LIL.) Welcome home.

(*RITA and* RAE *attempt to welcome* LIL, *touching her shoulder, kissing her cheek, but she's oblivious to them, her attentions are all on* EVA.)

RAE: Ditto. (*But there is no response from* LIL.)

ANNIE: (*Having stuck her finger in the soup.*) This needs salt.

KITTY: She shouldn't have salt.

ANNIE: (*To* RAE.) It's too bland, honey, has no taste.

RAE: (*Observing* LIL *and* EVA.) Anybody get the feeling we're not wanted?

(*The others agree and they start to move out. As they go:*)

ANNIE: (*To* LIL.) Stay away from that soup, it's terrible.

KITTY: If you need me, Lil, I'll be on the beach.

RITA: (*Calls.*) She'll be in the cabin. (*To* KITTY.) You're going to bed. You've been at that hospital day and night.

KITTY: (*Stubbornly.*) I'll be on the beach, Lil.

RITA: (*Lovingly.*) Kitty, we haven't been alone together for a week. . . .

KITTY: (*Getting the picture.*) I'll be in the cabin, Lil.

ANNIE: (*As they exit, to* RAE.) Why don't we go to Molly Pitcher's and have lunch with Sue and Donna?

RAE: Because there's a pot of soup this big on the stove.

ANNIE: I was afraid of that.

(*They are all offstage.*)

LIL: (*Holding* EVA *apart and looking at her.*) Well, I'm back. Fit as a fiddle.

EVA: You're going to be just fine.

LIL: Oh, yeah, I always said I could lick this thing.

EVA: (*Uncomfortable.*) Don't let the soup get cold.

LIL: (*Aware of* EVA's *discomfort.*) You didn't know you were getting damaged merchandise, did you? I'm sorry, Eva.

EVA: Stop that.

LIL: It changes everything.

EVA: No, it doesn't. (*But it does.*) Soon as you get to feeling better, we'll go to Europe just like we planned.

LIL: Sure.

EVA: We'll go to Switzerland—we don't have to ski.

LIL: I couldn't tell you.

EVA: I know. (*Pause.*) We can still ride the chairlift up the Alps.

LIL: I just couldn't tell you.

EVA: Tiny villages sparkling in the snow . . .

LIL: (*Sharply.*) There's no snow in Switzerland this time of year.

EVA: (*Forging ahead.*) We'll go to Amsterdam then. Maybe Rae and Annie will come with us. Somebody has to give me away.

LIL: Nobody can give you away, Eva. You don't belong to anybody but yourself.

EVA: You're upset. You're not feeling well.

LIL: I feel fine. Alley cats recover very quickly.

EVA: We'll travel for a while, then maybe rent a cottage in New England this fall—we can go to the movies and read books together—I can read your favorite books to you—

LIL: Do yourself a favor, Eva. Leave me.

EVA: You don't mean that.

LIL: I do. I bet I've had a hundred women in my life—what makes you think I'd want to spend the rest of my life with you? And your memories of George and your goddam furniture and your uptight mother?

EVA: Lil, don't.

LIL: I want to do some living before I die. (*She goes to door.*) Hey, anybody down there? Where's Donna? I want to see Donna! (*She turns to* EVA *coldly.*) Get out of here, Eva. Get out of my life. (EVA *doesn't budge.*)

EVA: That's always worked for you, hasn't it? One act of bravado and you're off the hook. (LIL *is stunned.*) You have to catch the biggest fish, take every card game, seduce all the women you encounter—as long as you're winning, Lil, you're just fine. But when things get difficult, you leap out the motel window. We love each other, Lil. That's a commitment.

LIL: (*Quietly.*) Next summer, someone else will be standing at this window watching a July sunset—and Rae and Annie will be sitting over there, sipping drinks, and they'll say to this stranger at the window— "Beautiful sunset, huh? Lil loved that view. She thought God put that rock down there for her. When she stood on it with the surf pounding against it, spraying salt so high that she could taste it on her lips, she was Queen of Bluefish Cove."—I can't say goodbye to that beach out there, Eva. I can't say goodbye to Annie or to Kitty. How can I say goodbye to you? (LIL *goes to* EVA, *lets* EVA *hold her.* EVA *is now the strong one.*)

(*As the lights dim to black, we hear* KITTY *and* RITA's *voices.*)

RITA: The wind's so strong. I had no idea it got so cold along the beach.

KITTY: Well, we've never had the occasion to be out here in late fall.

RITA: Pull that scarf around your neck, darling, I don't want you to catch cold. You start the promotion tour for your new book next week and it would be disastrous if you developed laryngitis.

KITTY: What would you think if I were to open up my office again. . . .

RITA: You mean go back to practicing?

KITTY: Lil always felt that I was copping out.

(*The lights are now up on the cabin and the beach.* KITTY *and* RITA, *dressed for winter, walk to the stairs;* RAE, *also dressed for winter, sits on the stairs.* ANNIE *stands on the rock, looking out to sea.* RITA *and* KITTY *mount the stairs.*)

RAE: (*Glancing at her watch.*) I guess it's over now in Michigan. The service was at one o'clock.

RITA: I don't understand how they could take her. She wanted to be buried here.

KITTY: They're her family, honey. They have the legal right.

RITA: Her mother and father had disowned her.

KITTY: Well, they did fly here and stay by her at the end.

RITA: Stay by her? They guarded her from us.

(At the top of the stairs, they enter the cabin and begin to stack boxes and fold clothing for packing. EVA enters from the bathroom, carrying a box.)

SUE: I don't know what to do with all this stuff. Toothpaste, aspirin, bubblebath—

EVA: I promised Marge Eaton we'd clear this place out. Just put it over there, Sue.

KITTY: Lil asked me to give these clothes to the women's center. Some of them are pretty raggedy.

RITA: You can't give that workshirt to anybody. It's torn in half a dozen places.

KITTY: Well, throw it away then.

EVA: No. *(She takes it.)* I'd like to have that.

RITA: We could store these toiletries in our cabin for the winter—it's a shame to throw it all away.

SUE: What about this tackle box?

EVA: She wanted Annie to have that.

RITA: I'll take it down to her. *(She goes downstairs.)*

EVA: I wonder who'll have this place next summer?

KITTY: How about you, Eva?

EVA: I don't think so, Kitty. I couldn't afford it, anyway.

KITTY: You can always visit us.

EVA: I hope I'll be working next summer. I finish that office management course in January, thanks to Sue.

KITTY: If I open my practice again, I'll need an office manager.

EVA: (*Gratefully.*) Thanks. I've filled out applications for several big corporations with offices in Europe. I'd really like to travel. (*Smiles.*) Have some adventures.

KITTY: She loved you very much.

EVA: (*Pulling herself together.*) I know.

KITTY: (*Changing the subject.*) I expected to see Donna here today.

SUE: I don't think she knows, Kitty. I don't know where to contact her.

KITTY: That was the healthiest thing you ever did, Sue.

SUE: If you say so.

EVA: (*Looking around.*) Well, I think that's it. We can start carrying it down.

SUE: (*Calls.*) Hey, Rae, Rita, let's go.

(RAE *and* RITA *come upstairs and take bundles from* KITTY. *One by one, they begin to come down the stairs, arms loaded.* ANNIE *is squatting by* LIL's *tackle box, picking out the lures. As others come down the stairs, she leaps to the rock, holding one lure in her hand.*)

RAE: What is that, honey?

ANNIE: It's her favorite lure. She always used it for the bluefish. (*Puts lure in tackle box.*) Next year, we're going to build a barbecue pit down here. It'll be our summer project.

RAE: My summer project is going to be to lie in the sun with my feet up.

KITTY: I don't know how much time I'll be able to spend out here next year—if I open up my practice, I'll have office hours weekdays—

RITA: I think I'll hate it when you're on call, you'll be tired all the time.

SUE: I wouldn't miss a summer at Bluefish Cove for anything—it somehow puts my whole year in perspective.

(*They are off now except* ANNIE *and* RAE. *They look up at* EVA *in cabin.*)

RAE: You coming, Eva?

EVA: (*Lowering blinds.*) Yes, I'm coming.

ANNIE: You need a hand?

EVA: No thanks, Annie. I can make it by myself.

(She lowers the blind between herself and audience. RAE *and* ANNIE *exit, knowing* EVA *will soon follow.)*

BLACKOUT

Jane Rule
(b. 1931)

Jane Rule, born in the United States, has lived in British Columbia with her partner, Helen Sonthoff, since 1956. It was in Canada that Rule became a writer of lesbian fiction and essays. Her first novel, *Desert of the Heart* (1964), had the rare distinction in the early sixties of presenting lesbian characters who did not end in murder, suicide, or drowned in a well of loneliness. Her main character goes to Reno for a divorce, meets a younger woman who is a lesbian, and falls in love. The novel ends with the promise of their happy life together. It was made into a popular film, *Desert Hearts*, in the 1980s. Rule's 1970 novel *This Is Not for You* did not share the optimism of the earlier novel, depicting instead a woman who is too caught up in conventionality to be able to live as a lesbian.

With the growth of the lesbian-feminist movement in the 1970s, however, Rule resumed her earlier optimism. The following story, "In the Attic of the House," from her collection *Theme for Diverse Instruments* (1975), depicts a new generation of lesbians, who are confident and happy in the society they have built. They find the timidity of the previous generation virtually incomprehensible.

Although Rule's plots in novels such as *Against the Season* (1971) and *The Young in One Another's Arms* (1977) do not always revolve around the subject of lesbianism, lesbian characters generally play some role. Her collection of essays, *Lesbian Images* (1975), was a groundbreaking attempt to recover literary lesbian foremothers. The title of her 1985 essay collection, *A Hot-Eyed Moderate,* suggests where she usually positioned herself in the midst of the passions of the lesbian-feminist movement.

FURTHER READING: Jane Rule, *Desert of the Heart* (1964; reprint, Tallahassee: Naiad Press, 1982); *Lesbian Images* (New York: Doubleday, 1975); *Theme for Diverse Instruments* (1975; Naiad Press, Tallahassee, 1990). Maureen Brady, " 'A Vision of Central Value': The Novels of Jane Rule," *Resources for Feminist Research*, 12: 1 (March 1983), 13–16. Judith Niemi, "Jane Rule and the Reviewers," *Margins*, 23 (August 1975), 34–37. Marilyn R. Schuster," Strategies for Survival: The Subtle Subversion of Jane Rule," *Feminist Studies*, 7 (Fall 1981), 431–50. Gillian Spraggs, "Hell and the Mirror: A Reading of *Desert of the Heart*," in *New Lesbian Criticism: Literary and Cultural Readings*, ed. Sally Munt (New York: Columbia University Press, 1992).

In the Attic of the House

Alice hadn't joined women's liberation; she had only rented it the main floor of her house. It might turn out to be the alternative to burning it down, which she had threatened to do sober and had nearly accomplished when she was drunk. Since none of the four young women who moved in either drank or smoked, they might be able to save Alice from inadvertence. That was all. And the money helped. Alice had not imagined she would ever be sixty-five to have to worry about it. Now the years left were the fingers of one hand. She was going to turn out to be one of the ones too mean to die.

"I'm a lifer," she said at the beer parlor and laughed until her lungs came to a boil.

"Don't sound like it, Al. If the weed don't get you, the traffic will."

"Naw," Alice said. "Only danger on the road is the amateur drunks, who can't drive when they're sober either. I always get home."

The rules were simple: stay in your own lane, and don't honk your horn. Alice was so small she peered through rather than over her steering wheel and might more easily have been arrested as a runaway kid than a drunk. But she'd never caught hell from anyone but Harriet, rest her goddamned soul. Until these females moved in.

"Come have a cup of tea," one of them would say just as Alice was making a sedate attempt at the stairs.

There she'd have to sit in what had been her own kitchen for thirty years, a guest drinking Red Zinger or some other Kool-Aid-colored wash they called tea, squinting at them through the steam: Bett, the giant postie; Trudy and Jill, who worked at the women's garage without a grease mark under their fingernails; Angel, who was unemployed; young, all of them, incredibly young, killing her with kindness. Sober, she could refuse them with, "I never learned to eat a whole beet with chopsticks," or "Brown rice sticks to my dentures," but once she was drunk and dignified, she was caught having to prove that point and failing as she'd always failed, except that now there was the new test of the stairs.

"Do you mind having to live in the attic of your own house?" Bett asked as she offered Alice a steadying hand.

"Mind? Living on top of it is a lot better than living in the middle of it ever was. I don't think I was meant for the ground floor," Alice confessed, her spinning head pressed against Bett's enormous bosom until they reached the top stair.

"You all right now? Can you manage?"

"Sleep like a baby. Always have."

Alice began to have infantile dreams about those breasts, though awake and sober she found them comically alarming rather than erotic, eye-level as she was with them. Alice liked Bett and was glad, though she didn't hold with women taking over everything, that Bett delivered the mail. Bett had not only yellow hair but yellow eyebrows, a sunny sort of face for carrying the burden of bills as well as the promise of love letters and surprise legacies. And everyone was able to see at a glance that this postie was a woman.

Angel was probably Bett's girl, though Alice couldn't tell for sure. Sometimes Alice imagined four-way orgies going on downstairs, but it could as easily be a karate lesson. It was obvious that none of them was interested in men.

"We don't hate men because we don't need them," said Trudy, the one who memorized slogans; who, once she could fix a car, couldn't imagine what other use men were ever put to.

Hating men, for this crew, would be like hating astronauts, too remote an exercise to be meaningful. Alice knew lots of men, was more comfortable with them than with women at the beer parlor or in the employees' lounge at Safeway, where she worked. As a group, she needed them far more than she needed women. Working among them and drinking among them had always been her self-esteem.

"Aren't you ashamed to sit home on a Saturday night?" Alice asked.

"We don't drink; the bars aren't our scene."

Alice certainly couldn't imagine them at her beer parlor, looking young enough to be jail bait and dressed so badly men who had taken the time to shave and change into good clothes couldn't help taking offense. Even Alice, with her close-cropped hair, put on a nice blouse over good slacks, even sometimes a skirt, and she didn't forget her lipstick.

"Do you buy all your clothes at the Sally Ann?" Alice asked, studying one remarkably holey and faded tank top Jill was wearing.

"Somebody gave me this one," Jill admitted irritably. "Why should you mind? You're the only one of any sex who has a haircut like that."

"Don't you like it?" Alice asked.

"It's sort of male chauvinist," Trudy put in, "as if you wanted to come on very heavy."

"I don't come on," Alice said. "I broke the switch."

At the beer parlor someone might have said, "Then I'll screw you in," or something else amiable, but this Trudy was full of sudden sympathy and instruction about coming to terms with your own body, as if she were about to invent sex, not for Alice, just for instance.

"Do you know how old I am?"

"We're not ageists here," Jill said.

"I'm old enough to be your grandmother."

"Not if you're still working at Safeway, you're not. My grandma's got the old-age pension."

"When I was young, we had some respect for old people."

"Everybody should respect everybody," Angel said.

"I have every respect for you," Alice said with dignity. "Even about sex."

"You know what you should do, Alice?" Angel asked. "It's not too late . . . is come out."

"Come out?" Alice demanded. "Of where? This is my house after all. You're just renting the main floor. Come out? To whom? Everyone I know is dead!"

Harriet, rest her goddamned soul. Alice mostly pretended that she never spoke Harriet's name. In fact, she almost always waited to do it until she had drunk that amount which would let her forget what she had said so that she could say it over and over again. "Killed herself in my bathtub. Is that any way to win an argument? Is it?"

"What argument?" Trudy would ask.

"This bathtub?" Jill tried to confirm.

"How?" Angel wanted to know.

Later, on her unsteady way upstairs, Alice would resent most Bett's asking, "Were you in love with Harriet?"

"In love?" Alice demanded. "Christ! I lived with her for thirty years."

Never in those thirty years had Alice ever spoken as openly to Harriet as she was expected to speak with these females. Never in the last twenty years had Alice and Harriet so much as touched, though they slept in the same bed. At first Alice had come home drunk and pleading. Then she came home drunk and mean, sometimes threatening rape, sometimes in a jeering moral rage.

"What have you got to be guilty about? You never so much as soil your hand. I'm the one that should be crawling off to church, for Christ's sake!"

Sometimes that kind of abuse would weaken Harriet's resolve and she would submit, whimpering like a child anticipating a beating, weeping like a lost soul when it was over.

Finally Alice simply came home drunk and slept in a drunken stupor. She learned from the beer parlor how many men did the same thing.

"Scruples," one man explained. "They've got scruples."

"Scruples, shit! On Friday night I go home with the dollars and say, 'You want this? You put out for it.' "

"So what are you doing down here? It's Friday, isn't it?"

"Yeh, well, we split. . . ."

Harriet had her own money. She was a legal secretary. Alice remembered the first time she ever saw Harriet in the beer parlor wearing a prim gray suit, looking obviously out of place. Some cousin had brought her and left her for unrelated pleasures. After they'd talked a while, Alice suggested a walk along the beach. It was summer; there was still light in the sky.

Years later, Harriet would say, "You took advantage. I'd been jilted."

Sometimes, when Alice was very drunk, she could remember how appealing the young Harriet had been, how willingly she had been coaxed from kisses to petting of her shapely little breasts, protesting with no more than, "You're as bad as a boy, Al, you really are." "Do you like it?" "Well, I'm not supposed to say so, am I?" Alice also remembered the indrawn breath of surprise when she first laid her finger on that wet pulse, the moment of wonder and triumph before the first crying, "Oh, it must be terrible what we're doing! We're going to burn in hell!"

Harriet could frighten Alice then with her guilt and terror. Once Alice promised that they'd never again, as Harriet called it, "go all the way," if they could still kiss, touch. Guiltily, oh so guiltily, weeks later, when Alice thought Harriet had gone to sleep, very gently she pressed open Harriet's thighs and touched that forbidden center. Harriet sighed in sleeping pleasure. Three or four times a week for several years Alice waited for the breathing signal that meant Harriet was no longer officially aware of what was happening. Alice could mount her, suck at her breasts, stroke and enter her, bring her to wet coming, and hold her until she breathed in natural sleeping. Then Alice would go to the bathroom and masturbate to the simple fantasy of Harriet making love to her.

It wasn't Harriet who finally quit on it. It was Alice, shaking her and shouting, "You goddamned hypocrite! You think as long as you take pleasure and never give it, you'll escape. But you won't. You'll be in hell long before I will, you goddamned *woman!*"

"We're looking for role models," Angel said. "Anybody who lived with anybody for thirty years . . ."

"I don't know what you're talking about," Alice said soberly on her way to work, but late that night she was willing enough. "Thirty years is longer than reality, you know that? A lifetime guarantee on a watch is only twenty. Nothing should last longer than that. Harriet should have killed herself ten years earlier, rest her goddamned soul. I always told her she'd get to hell long before I did."

"What was Harriet like?" Bett asked on the way upstairs.

"Like? I don't know. I thought she was pretty. She never thought so."

"It must be lonely for you now."

"I've never had so much company in all my damned life."

To be alone in the attic was a luxury Alice could hardly believe. It had been her resigned expectation that Harriet, whose soul had obviously not been at rest, would move up the stairs with her. She had not. If she haunted the tenants as she had haunted Alice, they didn't say so. The first time Trudy and Jill took a bath together probably exorcised the ghost from that room, and Harriet obviously wouldn't have any more taste for the vegetarian fare in the dining room than Alice did. As for what probably went on in the various beds, one night of that could finally have sent Harriet to hell where she belonged.

Alice understood, as she never had before, why suicide was an unforgivable sin. Harriet was simply out of the range of forgiveness, as she hadn't been for all her other sins from hoarding garbage to having what she called a platonic relationship with that little tart of a switchboard operator in her office.

"If you knew anything about Plato . . ." Alice had bellowed, knowing only that.

Killing herself was the ultimate conversation stopper, the final saying, "No backs."

"The trouble with ghosts," Alice confided to Bett, "is that they're only good for replays. You can't break any new ground."

Bett leaned down and kissed Alice good night.

"Better watch out for me," Alice said, but only after Bett had gone downstairs. "I'm a holy terror."

That night Harriet came to her in a dream, not blood-filled as all the others had been but full of light. "I can still forgive you," she said.

"For what?" Alice cried, waking. "What did I ever do but love you, tell me that!"

That was the kind of talk she heard at the beer parlor from her male companions, all of whom had wives and girl friends who spent their time inventing sins and then forgiving them.

"My wife is so good at forgiving, she's even forgiven me for not being the Shah of Iran, how do you like that?"

"I like it. It has dignity. My old lady forgives my beard for growing in the middle of the night."

They had also all lived for years with threats of suicide.

"She's going to kill herself if I don't eat her apricot sponge, if I don't cut the lawn, if I don't kiss her mother's ass. I tell her it's okay with me as long as she figures out a cheap way of doing it."

Alice was never drunk enough or off her guard enough until she got home to say, "Harriet did. She killed herself in my bathtub." Nobody at the beer parlor or at work knew that Harriet was dead.

"I didn't ever tell them she was alive," she said to Bett. "So what's the point of saying she's dead?"

"Why do you drink with those people?" Bett asked. "They can't be your real friends."

"How can you say a thing like that?"

"They don't know who you are."

"Do you?" Alice demanded. "What has a woman bleeding to death in my bathtub got to do with who I am?"

Bett was pressing Alice's drunken head against her breast.

That night Alice fell asleep with a cigarette in her hand. When she woke, the rug was on fire. She let out a bellow of terror and began to try to stamp out the flames with her bare feet.

Jill was the first one to reach her, half drag, half carry her out of the room. Trudy and Bett went in with buckets of water while Angel phoned the fire department.

"Don't let the firemen in," Alice moaned, sitting on Harriet's old chair in their old living room. "They'll wreck the place."

The fire was out by the time the truck arrived. After the men had checked the room and praised presence of mind and quick action for saving the house, the fire chief said, "Just the same, one of these nights she's going to do it. This is the third time we know of."

Jill, with the intention of confronting Alice with that fact, was distracted with discovering that Alice's feet were badly burned.

The pain killers gave Alice hallucinations: the floor of her hospital room on fire, her nurse's hair on fire, the tent of blankets at the foot of her bed burning, and Harriet was shouting at her, "We're going to burn in hell."

"Please," Alice begged. "I'd rather have the pain."

In pain, she made too much noise, swore, demanded whiskey, threatened to set herself on fire again and be done with it, until she was held down and given another shot.

Her coworkers from Safeway sent her flowers, but no one she worked with came to see her. No one she drank with knew what had happened. From the house, only Bett came at the end of work, still dressed in her uniform.

"Get me out of here," Alice begged. "Can't you get me out of here?"

In the night, with fire crackling all around her, Alice knew she was in hell, and there was no escape, Bett with her sunny face and great breasts the cruelest hallucination of all.

Even on the day when Bett came to take her home, Alice was half-convinced Bett was only a devilish trick to deliver her to greater torment, but Alice also knew she was still half-crazy with drugs or pain. There the house still stood, and Bett carried her up the stairs into an attic so clean and fresh she hardly recognized it. Alice began to believe in delivery.

"This bell by your bed," Bett explained, "all you need to do is ring it, and Angel will come."

Alice laughed until her coughing stopped her.

"It's a sort of miracle you're alive," Trudy said when she and Jill came home from work and up to see her.

"I'm indestructible," Alice said, a great world-weariness in her voice.

"This place was a rat's nest," Jill complained. "You can't have thrown out a paper since we moved in—or an empty yogurt carton. Is that all you eat?"

"I eat out," Alice said, "for whatever business of yours it is. And nobody asked you to clean up after me."

"It scared us pretty badly," Trudy said. "We all came close to being killed."

"Sometimes you remind me a little of Harriet," Alice said with slow malice. "That's a friend of mine who killed herself."

"We know who Harriet is," Jill said. "Al, if we can't talk about this, we're all going to have to move out."

"Move out? What for?"

"Because we don't want to be burned to death in our sleep."

"You've got to promise us that you won't drink when you're smoking or smoke when you're drinking," Trudy said.

"This is my house. I'm the landlady. You're the tenants," Alice announced.

"We realize that. There's nothing we can do unless you'll be reasonable."

Bett came into the room with a dinner tray.

"Get out, all of you!" Alice shouted. "And take that muck with you!"

Jill and Trudy were twins in obedience. Bett didn't budge.

"I got you out because I promised we'd feed you."

"What you eat is swill!"

"Look, Angel even cooked you some hamburger."

"You can't make conditions for me in my own house."

"I know that; so do the others. Al, I don't want to leave. I don't want to leave you. I love you. I want you to do it for yourself."

"Don't say that to me unless I'm drunk. I can't handle it."

"Yes, you can. You don't have to drink."

"What in hell else am I supposed to do to pass the time?" Alice demanded.

"Read, watch t.v., make friends, make love."

"Don't taunt me!" Alice cried into the tray of food on her lap.

"I'm not taunting," Bett said. "I want to help."

Until Alice could walk well enough to get out of the house on her own, there was no question of drinking. She kept nothing in the house, having always used drink as an excuse to escape Harriet. There was nothing to steal from her tenants. She was too proud to ask even Bett to bring her a bottle. The few cigarettes she'd brought home with her from the hospital would have to be her comfort. She found herself opening a window every time she had one and emptying and washing the ashtray when she was through.

"You're turning me into a sneak!" she shouted at Bett.

"It all looks nice and tidy to me," Bett said. "Trudy says you're so male-identified that you can't take care of yourself. I'm going to tell her she's wrong."

Alice threw a clean ashtray at her, and she ducked and laughed.

"You're getting better, you really are."

Alice returned to the beer parlor before she returned to work. She wasn't walking well, but she was walking. She had been missed. When she told about stamping out the fire with her own bare feet, she was assured of more free beer than she could drink in an evening even when she was in practice. How good it tasted and how companionable these friends who never asked questions and therefore didn't analyze the answers, who made connection with yarns and jokes. Alice had hung onto a couple of the best hospital stories and told them before she was drunk enough to lose her way or the punch line. She only laughed enough to cough at other people's jokes, which, as the evening wore on, were less well told and not as funny. Drink did not anesthetize the pain in Alice's healing feet, and that made her critical. Getting a tit caught in a wringer wasn't funny; it hurt.

"And here's one for those tenants of yours, Al, hey? How can you stem the tide of women's liberation? Put your finger in the dyke!"

It was an ugly face shoved into her own. Alice suddenly realized why a man must be forgiven his beard growing in the night, forgiven over and over again, too, for not being the prince of a fellow you wished he were. Alice didn't forgive. She laughed until she was near to spitting blood, finished her beer and her cigarette, and went out to find her car. As on so many other nights, even a few minutes after she got home, she couldn't remember the drive, but she knew she'd done it quietly and well.

"Come on," Bett said. "Those feet hurt. I'm going to carry you up."

Drunk in the arms of the sunny Amazon, Alice said, "Do you know how to stem the tide of women's liberation? Do you?"

"Does anyone want to?" Bett asked, making her careful, slow way up the stairs.

"Sure. Lots of people. You put your finger . . ."

"In the dyke, yeah, I know."

"Don't you think that's funny?"

"No."

"I don't either," Alice agreed.

Bett carried Alice over to her bed, which had been turned down, probably by Angel.

"Now, I want you to hand over the rest of your cigarettes," Bett said. "I'll leave them for you in the hall."

"Take them," Alice said.

"All right," Bett agreed and reached into Alice's blouse where she kept a pack tucked into her bra when she didn't have a pocket.

Alice half bit, half kissed the hand, then pressed herself up against those marvelous breasts, a hand on each, and felt the nipples, under the thin cloth of Bett's shirt, harden. Bett had the cigarettes, but she did not move away. Instead, with her free hand, she unbuttoned her shirt and gave Alice her dream.

As in a dream, Alice's vision floated above the scene, and she saw her own close-cropped head, hardly bigger than a baby's, her aging, liver-spotted face, her denture-deformed mouth, sucking like an obscene incubus at a young magnificence of breast which belonged to Angel. Then she saw Bett's face, serene with pity. Alice pulled herself away and spat.

"You pity me! What do you know about it? What could you know? Harriet, rest her goddamned soul, lived in *mortal sin* with me. She *killed herself* for me. It's not to *pity!* Get out! Get out, all of you right now because I'm going to burn this house down when I damned well please."

"All right," Bett said.

"It's my hell. I earned it."

"All right," Bett said, her face as bright as a never-to-come morning.

Alice didn't begin to cry until Bett had left the room, tears as hot with pain and loss as fire, that burned and burned and burned.

Monique Wittig

(b. 1936)

Monique Wittig, who has made her home in America for many years, was considered a leading figure in the French women's liberation movement in the 1970s. Her reputation was based not only on her fiction but also on her contributions to lesbian-feminist theory and politics. Her essays, such as "One Is Not Born a Woman" (1980) and "The Straight Mind" (1980), anticipated much of the social constructionist-essentialist debate of the 1980s by insisting that femininity and heterosexuality are not natural but rather social constructs. The linguistic innovations in Wittig's writings, through which she hopes to reclaim language, divesting it of its patriarchal nature, have been preserved to a large extent in most of their English translations. Elaine Marks characterizes Wittig's linguistic experiments as an attempt to "create a language capable of speaking the unspoken in Western literature," especially with regard to lesbian sexuality.

Wittig's first novel, *The Opoponax* (1966), is about a lesbian relationship between two French girls at school. Wittig's later fiction became increasingly experimental and radical. Both *Les guérillères* (1969) and *The Lesbian Body* (1973) deal with all-women communities, but while the earlier novel holds out some hope of reconciliation with men, heterosexuality is totally irrelevant in the latter. Wittig plays with the Amazon legend in both works, but she sets *The Lesbian Body* in what appears to be a fictive Lesbos (Sappho's name is invoked more than twenty times). In *The Lesbian Body* Wittig fashions a female universe devoted to the exploration of the physical fact of the bodies of the women lovers. She has no interest in the usual Western and male-centered descriptions of love. Every cell of the (lesbian) female body receives focus—to be taken apart and recreated again in love and erotic passion. Her coauthored book *Lesbian Peoples* (1979) is a dictionary of lesbian-feminist history and language.

FURTHER READING: Monique Wittig, *The Opoponax* (New York: Simon and Schuster, 1966); *The Lesbian Body* (1973; translation, New York: Morrow, 1975). Monique Wittig and Sande Zeig, *Lesbian Peoples: Material for a Dictionary* (New York: Avon, 1979). Elaine Marks, "Lesbian Intertextuality," *Homosexualities and French Literature*, eds. George Stambolian and Elaine Marks (Ithaca, NY: Cornell University Press, 1979). Martha Rosenfeld, "Language and the Vision of a Lesbian-Feminist Utopia in Wittig's *Les Guérillères, Frontiers*, 6: 1–2 (Spring-Summer 1981), 6–9. Namascar Shaktini, "A Revolutionary Signifier: *The Lesbian Body*," *Lesbian Texts and Contexts*, eds. Karla Jay and Joanne Glasgow (New York: New York University Press, 1990).

From *The Lesbian Body*

The city where you live is surrounded by a labyrinth where the unaccredited are lost who do not announce themselves by blowing the siren-voiced crescent-shaped trumpet fastened across the breasts by a leather thong as you all do. For a long time now *I* have been walking seeking to find the way in each of the slanting paths overcome by the scent of the flowers determined not to raise m/y trumpet to m/y mouth to rejoin you in the utmost secrecy. Grey-headed finches with blue bellies are ranked one against the other on the spreading branches of the limes at hand's height. *I* have so often traversed this garden eyes bandaged you holding m/e by the shoulders to guide m/e refusing whenever *I* asked you to give m/e a clue to m/y whereabouts. *I* recall your bites on the nape of m/y neck, the distress that afflicts m/e each time you halt leaving m/e alone in the dark, *I* recall your laughter m/y confusion when the bandage removed *I* have lost sight of you, *I* recall the torment that seizes m/e waiting for you seeking you along the sandy paths, *I* recall the cries you wrench from m/e surprising m/e from behind the persistence with which you continue to put the bandage round m/e forbidding m/e to discover how to arrive alone. Now *I* have lost heart, *I* stay seated in a grove of pink lilac. At a given moment some little girls in the treetops amuse themselves by throwing oranges at m/e. They answer m/y pleas with mockery. *I* start off again, *I* see island dwellings clearly visible in apparently quite accessible places, *I* see them withdraw whenever *I* approach them. *I* lose patience at m/y inability to draw near them on this horizontal surface where every point seems given at the first glance. A moment comes towards evening when m/y legs can no longer carry m/e, then *I* lie down bringing the coiled trumpet to m/y mouth to announce m/y surrender and fall asleep.

The bandage keeps m/y eyes closed. *I* am in darkness. A glitter sometimes an orange dazzle enters between m/y eyelids and m/y eyes firmly pressed on by the ligature. From time to time you m/y best-beloved you increase the pressure by applying your two palms to m/y eyeballs and rolling them under your fingers. A great shudder seizes m/e in the flawless night in which *I* am plunged, m/y thighs m/y legs m/y ankles are pervaded by a tingling, m/y sex especially is smarting, tiny movements take place on m/y belly, there is a pullulation on m/y breasts, the movements invade m/y skin by thousands, an increasingly intolerable formication spreads over m/e, it affects m/e up to the armpits, m/y arms are involved on both their aspects, it gains m/y neck m/y shoulders, m/y mouth m/y flanks are assailed. *I* have gooseflesh over m/y entire surface. Suddenly *I* am perforated by bites in numerous places where m/y skin has been touched. Then you, you begin to sing in a very soft voice m/y ravisher while *I* am no longer able to remain still, *I* begin to struggle, while *I* perceive the movements with heightened intensity. The bandage is suddenly removed by your hands. *I* discover that *I* am absolutely covered over m/y entire naked body with great black spiders from the feet to the hair m/y skin all eaten away creviced full of bites of purplish swellings vile. Your fingers rest on m/y mouth brushing away several of the creatures to prevent m/e from crying out. You look at m/e, you smile at m/e infinitely, m/y eyes are apposed to your eyes, I am seized by unnameable joy and horror, thus I abase m/yself m/y head supported by your hands.

The women lead m/e to your scattered fragments, there is an arm, there is a foot, the neck and head are together, your eyelids are closed, your detached ears are somewhere, your eyeballs have rolled in the mud, I see them side by side, your fingers have been cut off and thrown to one side, I perceive your pelvis, your bust is elsewhere, several fragments of forearms the thighs and tibiae are missing. M/y vision blurs at this sight, the women support m/e under the shoulders, m/y knees give way, m/y cries are stifled in m/y breast, they ask m/e where you should be interred in what order to collect your fragments which makes m/e recoil shrieking, I pronounce a ban on the recording of your death so that the traitress responsible for your being torn to pieces may not be alerted. I announce that you are here alive though cut to pieces, I search hastily for your fragments in the mud, m/y nails scrabble at the small stones and pebbles, I find your nose a part of your vulva your labia your clitoris, I find your ears one tibia then the other, I assemble you part by part, I reconstruct you, I put your eyes back in place, I appose the separated skin edge to edge, I hurriedly produce tears vaginal juice saliva in the requisite amount, I smear you with them at all your lacerations, I put m/y breath in your mouth, I warm your ears your hands your breasts, I introduce all m/y air into your lungs, I stand erect to sing, far off I perceive the island shore and the sun shining on the sea, I turn away the goddesses of death squatting on their heels around you, I begin a violent dance around your body, m/y heels dig into the ground, I arrange your hair on the clumps of grass, I Isis the all-powerful I decree that you live as in the past Osiris m/y most cherished m/y most enfeebled I say that as in the past we shall succeed together in making the little girls who will come after us, then you m/y Osiris m/y most beautiful you smile at m/e undone exhausted.

Your palms are against m/y palms a faintness overcomes m/e, weakness affects the hollows of m/y knees, you are face to face with m/e the soft inward of your arms pressed against m/y arms, then a formication spreads in m/y epidermis, I see m/y pores dilate, I see your pores do likewise, open they secrete fine hairs in thousands the colour and consistence of those of the crania, they grow at full speed, I feel them fall from your arms on to m/y arms, *I* cannot distinguish yours from m/ine they are so mingled as they multiply, the two faces remain naked, but they develop below the chin on the shoulders on the breasts the back, the arms the forearms are covered with them, they emerge from the breasts, they emerge from the loins, they emerge from the bellies thighs legs, they reach our feet, only the vulvas and the pubic fleeces are unaltered, they are so numerous that they create the effect of a pelt with very long hairs of tenuous consistence, *I* clasp you m/y hands buried in your hairs, *I* begin to weep because *I* can no longer touch your bare skin. You on the contrary you laugh, you bend m/e in your arms, you show m/e how to catch the wind, you seek a current, all the hairs stretch out on either side, they raise us up, they enable us to fly away, *I* wipe m/y tears against you m/y furred one, *I* float m/y arms on your arms, the wind mingles our hairs, it combs them, it brushes them, it gives them lustre, farewell dark continent you steer for the isle of the living.

Olga Broumas
(b. 1949)

Olga Broumas was born in Greece on the Aegean island of Syros and became a resident of the United States in 1967. Her poetry, with its references to Greek myth, landscape, and literary tradition, often reflects her Greek background. For many of her poems Broumas also finds sources in fairy tales, much as Anne Sexton has. Regardless of its sources, however, Broumas's poetry is unabashedly lesbian—both erotically and politically.

Like many lesbian-feminist writers of the 1970s, Broumas often took a defiant stance, depicting her lesbian lovers as transgressive and joyous in their social transgressions, crossing streets on the red and "kissing against the light, singing." Lesbianism is presented as being unarguably superior to heterosexuality, both morally and sexually. Thus, it was a remarkable tribute to her talent that despite what was (correctly) construed by the judges as her lesbian chauvinism, Broumas won the Yale Younger Poets Award in 1977 for her first volume, *Beginning With O*. Stanley Kunitz, who wrote the preface for the award edition of the book, could not forbear to point out that "her poems may be considered outrageous in some quarters," and "I detect a note of stridency in her voice, a hint of doctrinal overkill," though he opined that her "high style and musical form" provided compensation. What Kunitz characterized as "stridency," Broumas's lesbian-feminist readers prized as her courage to tell the truth.

FURTHER READING: Olga Broumas, *Beginning With O* (New Haven, Conn.: Yale University Press, 1977); *Soie Sauvage* (Port Townsend, WA: Copper Canyon, 1980); *Pastoral Jazz* (Port Townsend, WA: Copper Canyon, 1983). Mary J. Carruthers, "The Re-Vision of the Muse: Adrienne Rich, Audre Lorde, Judy Grahn, Olga Broumas," *Hudson Review*, 36: 2 (Summer 1983), 293–322. Liz Yorke, "Constructing a Lesbian Poetic for Survival: Broumas, Rukeyser, H.D., Rich, Lorde," *Sexual Sameness: Textual Differences in Lesbian and Gay Writing*, ed. Joseph Bristow (New York: Routledge, 1992).

AMAZON TWINS

I.

You wanted to compare, and there
we were, eyes on each eye, the lower
lids
squinting
suddenly awake

though the light was dim.   Looking away
some time ago, you'd said
    the eyes are live
    animals, domiciled in our head
but more than the head

is crustacean-like.   Marine
eyes, marine
odors. Everything live
(tongue, clitoris, lip and lip)
swells in its moist shell.   I remember the light

warped round our bodies finally
crustal, striated with sweat.

II.

In the gazebo-like café, you gave
me food from your plate, alert
to my blood-sweet hungers
double edged
in the glare of the sun's
and our own
twin heat.   Yes, there
we were, breasts on each side, Amazons
adolescent at twentynine

privileged
to keep the bulbs and to feel the blade
swell, breath-sharp
on either side. In that public place

in that public place.

SLEEPING BEAUTY

I sleep, I sleep
too long, sheer hours
hound me, out
of bed and into clothes, I wake
still later, breathless, heart
racing, sleep
peeling off like a hairless
glutton, momentarily
slaked.   Cold

water shocks me
back from the dream.   I see
lovebites like fossils: *something*
that did exist

dreamlike, though
dreams have the perfect alibi, no
fingerprints, evidence
that a mirror could float
back in your own face, gleaming
its silver eye.   Lovebites like fossils. Evidence.
Strewn

round my neck like a ceremonial
necklace, suddenly
snapped apart.

•

Blood.   Tears.   The vital
salt of our body.   Each
other's mouth.
Dreamlike
the taste of you
sharpens my tongue like a thousand shells,
bitter, metallic.   I know

as I sleep
that my blood runs clear
as salt
in your mouth, my eyes.

City-center, mid-
traffic, I
wake to your public kiss.   Your name
is Judith, your kiss a sign

to the shocked pedestrians, gathered
beneath the light that means
stop
in our culture
where red is a warning, and men
threaten each other with final violence: *I will drink
your blood.*   Your kiss
is for them

a sign of betrayal, your red
lips suspect, unspeakable
liberties as
we cross the street, kissing
against the light, singing, *This
is the woman I woke from sleep, the woman that woke
me sleeping.*

RAPUNZEL
A woman who loves a woman is forever young.
Anne Sexton

Climb
through my hair, climb in
to me, love

hovers here like a mother's wish.
You might have been, though you're not
my mother.   You let loose like hair, like static
her stilled wish, relentless
in me and constant as
tropical growth.   Every hair

on my skin curled up, my spine
an enraptured circuit, a loop of memory, your first

private touch.   How many women
have yearned
for our lush perennial, found

themselves pregnant, and had
to subdue their heat, drown out their appetite
with pickles and harsh weeds.   How many
grew to confuse greed
with hunger, learned to grow thin on the bitter
root, the mandrake, on their sills.   *Old*

bitch, young
darling.   May those who speak them
choke on their words, their hunger freeze
in their veins like lard.
Less innocent
in my public youth
than you, less forbearing, I'll break the hush
of our cloistered garden, our harvest continuous
as a moan, the tilled bed luminous
with the future
yield.   Red

vows like tulips.   Rows
upon rows of kisses from all lips.

SNOW WHITE
I could never want her (my mother) until I myself
had been wanted. By a woman. Sue Silvermarie

Three women
on a marriage bed, two
mothers and two daughters.
All through the war we slept
like this, grand-
mother, mother, daughter.   Each night
between you, you pushed and pulled
me, willing
from warmth to warmth.

Later we fought so
bitterly through the peace
that father blanched in his uniform,
battlelined forehead milky
beneath the khaki brim.

We fought like mad-
women till the house-
hold shuddered, crockery fell, the bed-
clothes heaved in the only passion
they were, those maddening
peacetime years,
to know.

                              •

  A woman
  who loves a woman
  who loves a woman
  who loves a man.
                    If the circle
              be unbroken . . .
                    Three years
into my marriage I woke with this
from an unspeakable dream
about you, fingers
electric, magnetized, repelling
my husband's flesh.   Blond, clean,
miraculous, this alien
instrument I had learned to hone,
to prize, to pride myself on, instrument
for a music I couldn't dance,
cry or lose
anything to.
                    A curious
music, an un-
catalogued rhyme, mother / daughter, we lay
the both of us awake
that night you straddled
two continents and the wet
opulent ocean to visit us, bringing
your gifts.
                    Like two halves
of a two-colored apple-red
with discovery, green with fear—we lay
hugging the wall between us, whitewash
leaving its telltale tracks.
                              Already
some part of me had begun
the tally, dividing

the married spoils, claiming
your every gift.
Don't curse me, Mother, I couldn't bear
the bath
of your bitter spittle.
                          No salve
no ointment in a doctor's tube, no brew
in a witch's kettle, no lover's mouth, no friend
or god could heal me
if your heart
turned in anathema, grew stone
against me.
                          Defenseless
and naked as the day
I slid from you
twin voices keening and the cord
pulsing our common protest, I'm coming back
back to you
woman, flesh
of your woman's flesh, your fairest, most
faithful mirror,
                          my love
transversing me like a filament
wired to the noonday sun.

Receive
me, Mother.

Irena Klepfisz

(b. 1941)

Irena Klepfisz, a Jewish lesbian-feminist writer, was born in Warsaw in the
midst of World War II. After the war, she emigrated with her mother to
Sweden in 1946 and then to the United States in 1949. Klepfisz was among
the earliest lesbian-feminist authors to explore ethnicity in her writing—in
her case, what it means to be a Jew who is also a lesbian-feminist. Her
work, particularly the poems in her collection *Keeper of Accounts* (1982),
often depicts her perception of the similarity between Jewishness and
lesbian-feminism, suggesting that they both have served to create her as an

outsider with a vision of alienation, though, ironically, they are also seen as being in diametrical opposition to each other.

Throughout her career Klepfisz has been equally active in Jewish and lesbian-feminist communities. She was a founding editor of *Conditions* in 1977 and she has been a contributing editor for *Sinister Wisdom*, both lesbian-feminist journals. She is also coeditor of *The Tribe of Dina: A Jewish Woman's Anthology* (1986) and is the author of *Dreams of an Insomniac: Jewish Feminist Essays, Speeches and Diatribes* (1990).

FURTHER READING: Irena Klepfisz, *Keeper of Accounts* (Berkeley, CA: Sinister Wisdom Books, 1982); *Different Enclosures: The Poetry and Prose of Irena Klepfisz* (London: Onlywomen Press, 1985); *A Few Words in the Mother Tongue: Poems Selected and New, 1971–1990* (Portland, Oregon: Eighth Mountain Press, 1990). Evelyn Torton Beck, "From Nightmare to Vision: An Introduction to the Essays of Irena Klepfisz," *Belles Lettres*, 6: 1 (Fall 1990), 2–5. Janis Kelly and Amy Stone, "Irene Klepfisz Interview," *off our backs*, 13: 11 (December 1983), 10–11.

THEY DID NOT BUILD WINGS FOR THEM

they did not build wings for them
the unmarried aunts;   instead they
crammed them into old maids' rooms
or placed them as nannies with
the younger children;   mostly they
ate in the kitchen, but sometimes
were permitted to dine with the family
for which they were grateful and
smiled graciously as the food was passed.
they would eat slowly never filling
their plates and their hearts would
sink at the evening's end when it was
time to retreat into an upstairs corner.

but there were some who did not smile
who never wished to be grafted on
the bursting houses.   these few remained
indifferent to the family gatherings
preferring the aloneness of their small rooms
which they decorated with odd objects
found on long walks.   they collected
bird feathers and skulls unafraid to clean
them to whiteness;   stones which resembled
humped bears or the more common tiger and

wolf;   dried leaves whose brilliant colors
never faded;   pieces of wood still covered
with fresh moss and earth which retained
their moisture and continued flourishing.
these they placed by their dresser mirror
in arrangements reminiscent of secret rites
or hung over delicate watercolors of unruly
trees whose branches were about to snap
with the wind.

it happened sometimes that among these
one would venture even further.   periodically
would be heard vague tales of a woman
withdrawn and inaccessible suddenly disappearing
one autumn night leaving her room bare
of herself.   women gossiped about a man.
but eventually word would come back
she had moved north to the ocean and lived
alone.   she was still collecting
but now her house was filled with crab
and lobster shells;   discolored claws
which looked like grinning south american
parrots trapped in fish nets decorated
the walls;   skulls of unidentifiable
creatures were arranged in geometric patterns
and soft reeds in tall green bottles
lined the window sills.   one room
in the back with totally bare walls
was a workshop.   here she sorted colored
shells and pasted them on wooden boards
in the shape of common flowers.   these she sold
without sentiment.

such a one might also disappear inland.
rumor would claim she had travelled in
men's clothing.   two years later it would
be reported she had settled in the woods
on some cleared land.   she ran a small farm
mainly for supplying herself with food
and wore strangely patched dresses and shawls
of oddly matched materials.   but aloneness
was her real distinction.   the house was neat
and the pantry full.   seascapes and pastoral

scenes hung on the walls.   the garden was
well kept and the flower beds clearly defined
by color: red   yellow   blue.   in the woods
five miles from the house she had an orchard.
here she secretly grafted and crossed varieties
creating singular fruit of shades and scents
never thought possible.   her experiments rarely
failed and each spring she waited eagerly to see
what new forms would hang from the trees.
here the world was a passionate place and she
would visit it at night baring her breasts
to the moon.

DINOSAURS AND LARGER ISSUES
for rachel

1. & 2.   the first two nights
she lay   diagonally across
the bed   clutching at the blankets
she refused me   room & warmth

3.   the third night
she told me   i can't handle
this   i can't handle   it
i slept   in the living room

4.   the fourth night
she said   this has to be
the last night   & moved
close to me

5.   the fifth night
she did not speak   about
it.

ETLEKHE VERTER OYF MAME-LOSHN /
A FEW WORDS IN THE MOTHER TONGUE

lemoshl: for example

di kurve   the whore
a woman who acknowledges her passions

di yidene   the Jewess   the Jewish woman
ignorant   overbearing
let's face it: every woman is one

di yente   the gossip   the busybody
who knows what's what
and is never caught off guard

di lezbianke   the one with
a roommate   though we never used
the word

dos vaybl   the wife
or the little woman

·

in der heym   at home
where she does everything to keep
yidishkayt alive

yidishkayt   a way of being
Jewish   always arguable

in mark   where she buys
di kartofl un khalah
(yes, potatoes and challah)

di kartofl   the material counterpart of *yidishkayt*

mit tsibeles   with onions
that bring *trern tsu di oygn*
tears to her eyes   when she sees
how little it all is
veyniker un veyniker
less and less

di khalah   braided
vi ir hor far der khasene
like her hair before the wedding
when she was *aza sheyn meydl*
such a pretty girl

di lange shvartse hor
the long black hair
di lange shvartse hor

•

a froy kholmt   a woman
dreams *ir ort oyf der velt*
her place in this world
un zi hot moyre   and she is afraid
so afraid of the words
kurve
yidene
yente
lezbianke
vaybl

zi kholmt   she dreams
un zi hot moyre   and she is afraid
ir ort
di velt
di heym
der mark

a meydl kholmt
a kurve kholmt
a yidene kholmt
a yente kholmt
a lezbianke kholmt

a vaybl kholmt
di kartofl
di khalah

yidishkayt

zi kholmt
di hor
di lange shvartse hor

zi kholmt
zi kholmt
zi kholmt

Pat Parker
(1944–89)

Pat Parker, an African American, began writing poetry in the mid-1960s as an expression of her involvement in various social movements, including the civil-rights and black-liberation movements. In the next decade she turned her attention to the gay-liberation and feminist movements, and then to lesbian-feminism. Her writing remained an expression of her social convictions throughout her career, and she was considered among lesbian-feminist critics to be one of the most effective poets of identity politics. Much of her poetry was written to be read aloud. With her charisma and wry wit Parker was immensely successful in solo and concert reading performances for lesbian-feminist audiences across the country. In 1976 the lesbian-feminist record company, Olivia Records, released a recording of Pat Parker and Judy Grahn reading their work: *Where Would I Be Without You: The Poetry of Pat Parker and Judy Grahn.*

As a "Third World lesbian" in the lesbian-feminist movement, Parker found herself to be part of a tiny minority within a minority. Lesbian-feminists were very receptive to her work, and she often wrote for lesbian-feminist journals; all her volumes of poetry were published by lesbian-feminist publishing houses. However, like many African American women in the 1970s, Parker maintained reservations about the movement because she felt that the racism of the larger society was often manifested among the women who proclaimed themselves her white sisters. Because she believed that racial problems in the world at large mandated that blacks retain family unity, she was especially critical of white lesbian separatists who rejected the possibility that male relatives and friends could be a part of their community.

FURTHER READING: Pat Parker, *Child of Myself* (Berkeley, CA: Shameless Hussy Press, 1972); *Pit Stop* (Oakland, CA: The Woman's Press Collective, 1973); *Womanslaughter* (Oakland, CA: Diana Press, 1978). Brett Beemyn, "Bibliography of Works by and About Pat Parker (1944–1989)," *Sage*, 6: 1 (Summer 1989), 81–82. Barbara Smith, "Naming the UnNameable: The Poetry of Pat Parker," *Conditions*, 1: 3 (Spring 1978), 99–103. Joanne Stato, "Pat Parker, 1944–1989," *off our backs*, 19: 8 (August/Sept. 1989), 1+.

FOR WILLYCE

When i make love to you
  i try
    with each stroke of my tongue
      to say i love you
      to tease i love you
      to hammer   i love you
      to melt i love you

  & your sounds drift down
    oh god!
      oh jesus!
    and I think—
here it is, some dude's
getting credit for what
    a woman
      has done,
        again.

MY LADY AIN'T NO LADY

my lady ain't no lady

she doesn't flow into a room—
she enters & her presence is felt.
she doesn't sit small—
she takes all her space.
she doesn't partake of meals—
she eats—replenishes herself.

my lady ain't no lady—

she has been known
  to speak in loud voice,
  to pick her nose,
  stumble on a sidewalk,
  swear at her cats,
  swear at me,
  scream obscenities at men,
  paint rooms,
  repair houses,
  tote garbage,
  play basketball,

& numerous other
un lady like things.

my lady is definitely no lady
which is fine with me,

cause i ain't no gentleman.

•

*"How do we know that the panthers will accept a
gift from white—middle—class—women?"*

Have you ever tried to hide?
    In a group
                of women
                            hide
            yourself
slide between the floor boards
slide yourself away child
    away from this room
        & your sister
before she notices
    your black self &
her white mind
                slide your eyes

                down
away from the other blacks
    afraid—a meeting of eyes
& pain would travel between you—
        change like milk to buttermilk
        a silent rage.
            SISTER!   your foot's smaller,
but it's still on my neck.

BROTHER
for Blackberri

I

It is a simple ritual.
Phone rings
Berri's voice
low, husky
'What's you're doing?'

'Not a thing,
you coming over?'
'Well, I thought I'd
come by.'
A simple ritual.
He comes
we eat
watch television
play cards
play video games
some nights
he sleeps over
others
he goes home
sometimes
he brings a friend
more often
he doesn't.
A simple ritual.

II

It's a pause that alerts me
tells me this time
is hard time
the pain has risen
to the water line
we rarely verbalize
there is no need.

Within this lifestyle
there is much to undo you.
Hey look at the faggot!
When I was a child
our paper boy was Claude
every day
seven days a week
he bared the Texas weather
the rain that never stopped
walked through the Black section
where sidewalks had not
yet been invented

and ditches filled with water.
Walk careful Claude
across the plank
that served as sidewalk
sometime tips into the murky water
or heat
wet heat
that covers your pores
cascades rivulets of
stinging sweat down your body.
Our paper boy Claude
bared the weather well
each day he came
and each Saturday at dusk
he would come to collect.

My parents liked Claude.
Each Saturday Claude polite
would come
always said thank you
whether we had the money
or not.
Each Saturday
my father would say
Claude is a nice boy
works hard
goes to church
gives his money to his mother
and each Sunday
we would go to church
and there would be Claude
in his choir robes
til the Sunday
when he didn't come.

Hey look at the faggot!

Some young men howled at him
ran in a pack
reverted to some ancient form
they took Claude
took his money
yelled faggot

as they cast his body
in front of a car.

III

How many cars have you dodged Berri?
How many ancient young men have you met?
Perhaps your size saved you
but then you were not always this size
perhaps your fleetness
perhaps
there are no more ancient young men.

Ah! Within this lifestyle
we have chosen.
Sing?
What do you mean
you wanna be a singer?
Best get a good government job
maybe sing on the side.
You heard the words:
Be responsible
Be respectable
Be stable
Be secure
Be normal, boy.

How many quarter-filled rooms
have you sang your soul to
then washed away with
blended whiskey?

I told my booking agent one year
book me a tour
Blackberri and I
will travel this land
together
take our Black Queerness
into the face
of this place and say

Hey, here we are
a faggot & a dyke, Black
we make good music

& write good poems
We Be—Something Else.

My agent couldn't book us.
It seemed my lesbian audiences
were not ready for my faggot
brother
and I remembered
a law conference
in San Francisco
where women
women who loved women
threw boos and tomatoes
at a woman who dared
to have a man in her band.

What is this world we have?
Is my house the only safe place
for us?
And I am rage
all the low-paying gigs
all the uncut records
all the dodged cars
all the fear escaping
all the unclaimed love
so I offer my bosom
and food
and shudder
fearful of the time
when it will not be
enough
fearful of the time
when the ritual
ends.

Part VI

FLOWERINGS:
POST-LESBIAN-FEMINIST
LITERATURE

INTRODUCTION

While lesbian-feminist thought continued to influence lesbian literature throughout the 1980s and even into the '90s, a new generation of writers has worked to modify that thought. Sometimes this younger generation of lesbian authors simply takes for granted lesbian-feminist principles rather than foregrounding them in their work. For example, lesbian love poetry is less likely now to be presented in a political context than it was during the height of lesbian-feminism, and more likely to focus exclusively on women's sexual passion for each other (compare, for example, the 1970s poems of Adrienne Rich and the mid-1980s poems of Marilyn Hacker). Such recent literature assumes the victories without naming the battles that lesbian-feminists fought. Contemporary lesbian writers may even divorce themselves explicitly from any allegiance to lesbian-feminism while nevertheless taking as a "given" in their work many of the ideas that lesbian-feminists propounded, such as the legitimacy of lesbian love or a woman's right to autonomy.

The younger generation of lesbian writers may be said to exhibit some "anxiety of influence," having learned a good deal from their lesbian-feminist predecessors yet determined to find new ways to express themselves as lesbian writers and to effect a break with their foremothers. Post–lesbian-feminist writers are often satirical in their presentation of what they perceive to be the deadly seriousness of many lesbian-feminists. The younger generation frequently attempts a lighter tone and a looser set of prescriptions for behavior. They are by-and-large less critical of males, believing, in view of the many successes of feminism, that women are not invariably victimized by men. The younger writers generally consider lesbian separatism to be unnecessary as a strategy for protecting women from putative male corruption. Many post–lesbian-feminists even see themselves as forming alliances with men, especially gay men, with whom they share common enemies, and whose suffering from the AIDS epidemic they view with grief and compassion.

Both lesbian-feminist and post–lesbian-feminist writers have busied themselves in redefining the content and tone of lesbian literature rather than accepting the imposition of earlier models, many of which were not created by lesbians. But the most recent shifts with regard to what is to be satirized, valorized, or foregrounded in lesbian literature have not been effected without conflict between the older generation and the new. Those older lesbian-feminists who have not embraced the shifts themselves (and many of them have) point out that the revolution is unfinished, that men still subjugate women in the real world, that lesbians are swallowed up in the coalitions they make with gay men, and that literature still needs to reflect these problems. However, their voices have gotten considerably weaker since the start of the 1990s.

Perhaps the greatest conflict between the older generation of writers and post–lesbian-feminists concerns the literary representations of lesbian sexuality. Actually, the conflict was first articulated by writers who were part of the lesbian-feminist movement, such as Joan Nestle, Pat Califia, and Susie Bright, but who came to feel that lesbian-feminism was colorless as well as repressive in its treatment of lesbian sexuality. They sometimes claimed for lesbian sexuality a bold and passionate history, and they criticized the lesbian-feminist conception of sexuality for excluding, in its attempt to be politically correct, a whole panoply of fulfilling and important sexual expressions.

Younger writers took up their criticism, demanding that lesbian literature deal with the sexually "forbidden": butch-femme, s/m, and other varieties of sexual relationships and role play, penetration with or without dildoes, desire that is divorced from politics. But unlike Decadent literature, which often focused on the moral dangers of unorthodox sexual relating (while simultaneously titillating the voyeuristic reader), post–lesbian-feminist literature, sharing in the temper of our times, has no notion of moral danger with regard to sexuality. "Danger" is present in such work only as a stimulant to pleasure—and it is finally the lesbian reader who is to be pleasured by this literature rather than the straight male, who was often the targeted reader of literature about lesbians in other eras.

The miserable women who are doomed by their inappropriate and excessive sexual appetites in the work of Baudelaire and his literary descendants have no place in contemporary lesbian literature. Lesbian sexual appetite is now often celebrated—and the more, the better. The sexual outlaw is a hero in post–lesbian-feminist literature. Contemporary lesbian writers have taken many of the male-created images of lesbians that were employed in a condemnation of love between women, and have coopted them for their own delectation. For example, the lesbian vampire who was a staple in earlier literature that villainized the lesbian, becomes a cultural icon, a force for good, in the work of contemporary lesbian writers such as Katherine Forrest and Jewelle Gomez.

Graphic literature of unorthodox lesbian sexuality such as sado-masochism has become the center of heated debate among lesbians. Some argue that it is an imitation of the models created by men that exploit women and even lead to violence against women; others argue that lesbians have a right to any sexual expression that has significance for them, and that feminists who wish to "save women from themselves" by censoring their reading and their activities are no better than men who have tried to restrain female sexuality for their own purposes. Those who align them-selves with the "pro-sex" side believe that female empowerment is depen-dent, at least in part, on a woman's right to sexual exploration, experimentation, and expression. The support for such sexual radicalism in the lesbian community is suggested by the popularity of lesbian porno magazines first published in the mid-1980s, such as *On Our Backs* (the title is an ironic answer to the lesbian-feminist newspaper *off our backs*), *Quim,* and *Bad Attitude.* There have also been numerous anthologies of lesbian erotica, published both in America and abroad since the second half of the 1980s, such as *Serious Pleasures, More Serious Pleasures, Erotica, The Naiad Erotica, Bushfire,* and *An Intimate Wilderness.*

The sex debates are only one manifestation of the younger generation's divorce from the tenets of their lesbian-feminist predecessors. Many young lesbian writers no longer see themselves as "lesbian" at all but rather as "queer," for both aesthetic and ethical reasons. That confrontational term and all it stands for evolved from the politics of anger that America's ne-glect of the AIDS crisis triggered in the gay male community and its lesbian supporters. Groups such as ACT UP challenged American complacency by noisy interventions, such as the invasion of St. Patrick's Cathedral in New York during mass in order to protest the clergy's homophobia and lack of sympathy for people with AIDS. The concept of Queer Nation, with its zaps, kiss-ins, and general militancy grew out of ACT UP organizations in the United States and spread abroad (reaffirming the influence, first seen in the 1970s, that American concepts of homosexuality now have on Western Europe, as compared to earlier eras in which European concepts influenced America).

Queer Nation became the harbinger of queer style, with its "in your face" approach to homophobes and all forms of orthodox thinking. Queer aesthetics are a calculated attempt to outrage the conventional and complacent by unorthodox dress, music, writing, and other cultural expressions. Queer style represents a determination to redefine what it means to be a sexual outlaw. The queer aesthetic is self-consciously colorful and untame. It calls attention to itself, challenging what queers see (with only partial accuracy) as the complacency of the older generation of gays' willingness to merge with the dominant culture in exchange for a few civil rights. It is manifested in literature by outrageous subject matter and a queer chauvinism.

Queer ethics are as critical of the older generation as are queer aesthetics, claiming that gay liberation was a male-dominated, white, middle-class movement and that lesbian-feminism was barely better, in its exclusions or oversights of people of color, the working class, and all "queers" who didn't fit their narrow precepts. "Queer" is meant to be inclusive of not only forward-thinking lesbians and gays but all manner of sexual outlaws. As an anonymous 1991 London pamphlet that called for "Queer Power Now" conceptualized it: "Queer means to fuck with gender. There are straight queers, bi-queers, tranny [transvestite and transsexual] queers, lez queers, fag queers, SM queers, fisting queers." Queers are critical of gays' attempts to homogenize sexual nonconformists under their label. Queers claim that they are an *alliance of differences.*

The New Queers refuse to believe in the simple binary division between homo and hetero just as much as they refuse to believe in appropriate gender behavior; therefore, a lez queer and a fag queer can have sex together, she dressed in a jock strap and he in lace panties. Queers often play with gender, viewing it as little more than performance. No rules hold, no sacred assumption is impermeable to challenge and parody. Literary postmodernism, with its questioning of stable categories, its disbelief in a set reality, its refusal to engage in binary thinking, would, of course, have considerable appeal for queer writers and their readers. Many of the most interesting contemporary lesbian writers, such as Sarah Schulman and Jeanette Winterson, are literary postmodernists and speak to a community of queer readers.

Contemporary lesbian writers and their audiences are interested not only in the sexual outlaw's "difference" but in other forms of difference as well. Much of contemporary writing examines the intersections of race, sex, and gender in order to illustrate the facts of difference. Lesbians of color have found a significant voice in the new climate, speaking not only to other lesbians of color but also to white lesbians who are eager to understand racial and ethnic difference. Much of the literature of lesbians of color explores the difficulties in bridging their various differences as both lesbians and members of racial communities. Latina, Asian, African, and Native American lesbians ask where they must place their first allegiances.

How can they trust either their racial or lesbian communities when they suspect the former of being homophobic and the latter of being racist? Is it possible to obviate these problems by aligning themselves first and most strongly with a lesbians-of-color community?

Since the publication of the ground-breaking anthology *This Bridge Called My Back* (1981), which brought together the work of women of color, many of whom were lesbian, there has been a great flowering of literature that explores such questions. That flowering has included a pro-liferation of writing by groups that were almost silent in earlier eras, such as Asian and Native American lesbians. To the white lesbian reader this literature is a call to conscience as well as a revelation of forms of oppres-sion different from, yet similar to, their own.

The flowering of lesbian literature is also manifested by other inclusions that were largely absent from earlier literature. Gay men, for example, are now likely to be subjects in lesbian writing. Lesbian mothers and their children—especially male children, who were often regarded with as much suspicion as were males in general by the lesbian-feminist community—are now sympathetic figures in lesbian literature. The cast of credible heroes and supporting actors in lesbian literature has expanded tremendously in the last decade. Contemporary lesbian literature mirrors contemporary les-bian life in its reflection of far greater inclusiveness in the definition of community.

Chrystos
(b. 1946)

Chrystos was born in San Francisco of a Menominee father and a European mother. Chrystos is "part of a group called 'Urban Indians' by the govern-ment," she writes. She sees herself as having been shaped by her experiences in a multicultural society, but especially by her father and "the pain that white culture has caused [him]." Much of her poetry is informed by her anger over the treatment of Native Americans by the white world, but the lesbian content in her work has been significant and sexually graphic enough so that right-wing politicians protested when she was awarded an NEA grant. She has identified herself as a lesbian since the age of seventeen. Her poetry, even when the content is not specifically Native American, often employs the imagery and spiritual sensibility associated with Native American culture. Thus her lesbian voice frequently merges with her Native American voice in her work.

FURTHER READING: Chrystos, *Not Vanishing* (Vancouver, B.C.: Press Gang Publishers, 1988); *Dream On* (1991): "Nidishenok (Sisters)," *Maenad*, 2: 2 (Winter 1982), 23–32. Karen Claudia and Lorraine Sorrel, "Chrystos: Not Vanishing—&In Person," *off our backs*, 19: 3 (March 1989), 18–19.

FOR SHAROL GRAVES

Deep breath   Inhale the drums   Feet begin
We sway in fringed shawls
sparkling beadwork   deerskin leggings
to the voice of the South Drum singing
gently tin cones tingle   Whispers of women
as we wheel around the sun
wearing jewel-colored velvet skirts
moccasins only for dancing
holding eagle feather fans   family blankets
Beyond us   the men leap & prance shaking bells
their roaches bob
We're a circle apart
within
First time you and I have danced together
In the distance
big silver cans steam with stew
drunks reel
children eat fry bread dripping with honey & butter
Our feet pass over the earth with soft thuds
Your otter fur braids swish
You've worked all year
on the Thunderbird belt & ribbonwork skirt
for this day
Your beauty echoes
beyond drums
Holds me
here now in my kitchen as I remember
dancing with you washed in light
Our spirits whirl
Step into
the still center
of a friendship drum

DREAM LESBIAN LOVER

is there when I get home from work but allows me silence
to unravel or better yet   isn't there
but has left a note & a little surprise
She rubs my feet for hours
She wants to love me till I can't stand no more
& she rolls over to me so sweet
Dream lover cooks me hot meals & washes up after
Never arrives without flowers & only brings my favorites
Dream lover has long fingers   a patient playful tongue
& thrives on five hours sleep a night
She could play the harmonica   weave pine needle baskets
bead me a wedding sash   write me lust poems & love poems
Dream lover has eyes deep as the sky   feels herself in others
feels our connecting bones   Rises early in the morning
to make the best rich coffee
Aah she could bring you to your knees with a look
& does
Dreamy woman has a bed of lace & roses & home
She could build a fire in the rain
Could always fix my car for free
Could call the dentist to make my appointment
Iron my shirt when I'm in a hurry
Knows how to make chocolate mousse   chocolate silk pie
black bottom cupcakes   molasses cookies   sour cream cake
lemon pound cake & fresh mango ice cream
O such a creamy dreamy one
She's showing up tonight with a butch pout & a femme slink
a tough stance & a long knowing
Dream lover
she won't have any other girlfriends
but won't mind
if I do

a *Personals Ad* with tongue in cheek

GETTING DOWN

to the bone place where blood is made
and every moon's a mother
your hands & tongue

in me a brush fire I wake up wanting you
Shrill cry of a dawn bird between my legs
memories of your sweet brown breasts
brushing my thighs
You go
where no one
has gone before until I'm weeping laughing
as you murmur in my wet ear
your husky voice like hot blood   *I love you*
My hair in your mouth burns for you
your lips nibble my lips my breasts
think they can't live without you
Between moments of you I'm a bird
who flies out of vision
You come
like the first bird breaking open the night with dawn
stars bursting into day sucking you I'm made
a moon sweet with light
Crying in the bone & blood place where you make me
yours

YOUR TONGUE SPARKLES

sun on water now in my mouth memory rich as real
kisses I understand to my root   to bone ancestors where red
& so new   you speak without calluses despite our scars
Woman down my throat you stir my heart nectar where bitterness
has fought to seed
O you rainy tongue   you amaryllis tongue   you early spring
tongue   you smooth black leather tongue   you firemoon tongue
you goosebumps tongue   you soft bites tongue   you feather
tongue   you take me all in tongue   you fill me up tongue
you butter tongue   you maple syrup tongue   you rising
wind tongue   you creamy silky tongue
you fine fine tongue
you knows the way
tongue

NIGHT VISITS

in clear stars bringing silver corn
her radiance full of memories
ways of those whose bones shape our time
A path opens: My feet are rainbow wolves running
calling a cool song through the caves
down to the crystal blue pool
where I was born softly
My eyes open dark as beginning
There were feathers in a clump in white snow
faint flecks of blood   I felt her hunger
as I passed the startled place of death
rushing over rocks
Bare trees echoed with her loneliness
I was her corn in bad winters
I wanted to be
so much more

Beth Brant (Degonwadonti)
(b. 1941)

Beth Brant is a Bay of Quinte Mohawk whose work often deals with lesbianism as well the experiences of Native Americans. Brant says she became an author during a trip to Mohawk Valley, when a bald eagle flew in front of her car, sat in a tree, and instructed her to write. She is a mother and a grandmother, and has lived with her lesbian partner for many years. Her 1983 anthology, *A Gathering of Spirits,* was the first book that brought together works by Native American women, many of whom were lesbian. Her own fiction and poetry, which combines the subject of lesbianism and Native American experience, has often appeared in lesbian journals and anthologies and is collected in *Mohawk Trail.*

FURTHER READING: Beth Brant, *Mohawk Trail* (Ithaca, NY: Firebrand, 1985); "Seeking My Own Vision: Two Remembrances," *Common Lives/Lesbian Lives,* 2 (Winter 1981), 5–8; "Third World Women's Writing," *Sinister Wisdom,* 19 (1982), 32–36; Beth Brant, "Lesbian Alliances: Heterosexism in the Eighties—The Call of the Heron," *Sojourner,* 14: 3 (November 1988), 15.

HER NAME IS HELEN

Her name is Helen.
She came from Washington State twenty years ago through
broken routes
of Hollywood, California,
Gallup, New Mexico,
Las Vegas, Nevada,
ended up in Detroit, Michigan where she lives in #413
in the gut of the city.
She worked in a factory for ten years, six months, making
carburetors for Cadillacs.
She loved factory work.
She made good money, took vacations to New Orleans.
"A real party town."

She wears a cowboy hat with pretty feathers.
Can't wear cowboy boots because of the arthritis
that twists her feet.
She wears beige vinyl wedgies. In the winter she pulls on
heavy socks to protect her bent toes from the slush and rain.

Helen takes pictures of herself.

Everytime she passes those Polaroid booths,
one picture for a dollar,
she closes the curtain and the camera flashes.

When she was laid off from the factory
she got a job in a bar, serving up shots and beer.
Instead of tips, she gets presents from her customers.
Little wooden statues of Indians in headdress.
Naked pictures of squaws with braided hair.
Feather roach clips in fuchsia and chartreuse.
Everybody loves Helen.
She's such a good guy. An honest-to-god Indian.

Helen doesn't kiss.
She allows her body to be held when she's had enough
vodkas and Lite beer.
She's had lots of girlfriends.
White women who wanted to take care of her,
who liked Indians,
who think she's a tragedy.

Helen takes pictures of herself.
She has a picture on a keychain, along with a baby's shoe
and a feathered roach clip.
She wears her keys on a leather belt.
Helen sounds like a chime, moving behind the bar.

Her girlfriends took care of her.
Told her what to wear
what to say
how to act more like an Indian.
"You should be proud of your Indian heritage.
Wear more jewelry.
Go to the Indian Center."

Helen doesn't talk much.
Except when she's had enough
vodkas and Lite beer.
Then she talks about home,
about her mom,
about the boarding schools,
the foster homes,
about wanting to go back to see her people
before she dies.
Helen says she's going to die when she's fifty.

She's forty-two now.
Eight years to go.

Helen doesn't kiss.
Doesn't talk much.
Takes pictures of herself.

She touches women who are white.
She is touched by their hands.

Helen can't imagine that she is beautiful.
That her skin is warm
like redwood and fire.
That her thick black hair moves like a current.
That her large body speaks in languages stolen from her.
That her mouth is wide and full and when she smiles
people catch their breath.

"I'm a gay Indian girl.
A dumb Indian.

A fat, ugly squaw."
This is what Helen says.

She wears a t-shirt with the legend
Detroit
splashed in glitter across her large breasts.
Her breasts that white women have sucked
and molded to fit their mouths.

Helen can't imagine that there are women
who see her.
That there are women
who want to taste her breath and salt.
Who want a speech to be created between their tongues.
Who want to go deep inside her
touch places that are dark, wet,
muscle and spirit.
Who want to swell, expand two bodies into a word
of our own making.

Helen can't imagine that she is beautiful.

She doesn't kiss.
Doesn't talk much.
Takes pictures of herself so she will know she is there.

Takes pictures of herself to prove she is alive.

Helen takes pictures of herself.

Kitty Tsui
(b. 1953)

Kitty Tsui was raised in Hong Kong and England and settled in the United
States as a teenager. She came out as a lesbian during the 1970s, in the
midst of the feminist movement. Her work, which has been frequently anthologized, often deals with the conflicts between being Asian and being
lesbian—an identity that her conservative Asian community refuses to recognize. While her writing expresses pride in her Chinese heritage, especially
as it relates to her grandmother, who had been a star of the Chinese opera,
it also illustrates her distaste for the nature of male-female relationships in
traditional Asian culture. Similarly, her identification in her work is

strongly lesbian but uncomfortable with the white lesbian community, which, she believes, has been insensitive to Asian lesbians. The theme of the difficulty the Asian lesbian experiences in situating herself is recurrent in Tsui's work.

Tsui is a founding member of the collective Unbound Feet and an editor of *New Phoenix Rising: The Asian/Pacific Lesbian Newsletter*. *The Words of a Woman Who Breathes Fire* is a collection of her poetry and prose.

FURTHER READING: Kitty Tsui, *The Words of a Woman Who Breathes Fire* (San Francisco: Spinsters, Ink, 1983).

A CHINESE BANQUET
for the one who was not invited

it was not a very formal affair but
all the women over twelve
wore long gowns and a corsage,
except for me.

it was not a very formal affair, just
the family getting together,
poa poa, kuw fu without *kuw mow**
(her excuse this year is a headache).

aunts and uncles and cousins,
the grandson who is a dentist,
the one who drives a mercedes benz,
sitting down for shark's fin soup.

they talk about buying a house and
taking a two week vacation in beijing.
i suck on shrimp and squab,
dreaming of the cloudscape in your eyes.

my mother, her voice beaded with sarcasm:
you're twenty six and not getting younger.
it's about time you got a decent job.
she no longer asks when i'm getting married.

you're twenty six and not getting younger.
what are you doing with your life?

---

* *kuw fu:* uncle
   kuw mow: aunt

you've got to make a living.
why don't you study computer programming?

she no longer asks when i'm getting married.
one day, wanting desperately to
bridge the boundaries that separate us,
wanting desperately to touch her,

tell her: mother, i'm gay,
mother i'm gay and so happy with her.
but she will not listen,
she shakes her head.

she sits across from me,
emotions invading her face.
her eyes are wet but
she will not let tears fall.

mother, i say,
you love a man.
i love a woman.
it is not what she wants to hear.

aunts and uncles and cousins,
very much a family affair.
but you are not invited,
being neither my husband nor my wife.

aunts and uncles and cousins
eating longevity noodles
fragrant with ham inquire:
sold that old car of yours yet?

i want to tell them: my back is healing,
i dream of dragons and water.
my home is in her arms,
our bedroom ceiling the wide open sky.

HOW CAN I SHOW THIS POEM
TO GERALDINE?

1.

you have been talking about
your celibacy
for months.

while snorting cocaine
and shooting a film with your best friend.

last night i wanted to talk.
i went to your house.
the front door was open.
i entered and found you
drinking wine with a bearded poet.
in a moment of anger
i wanted to scream at you
and drive insults like
nails into your skin.

we have been friends for years,
drinking at jigoku,
you stealing all the dances
that night at cesar's
and at intervals telling me
the hassles with alejandro,
with roberto.
hustling drinks,
smiling under your panama
your lips deep with color
and open,
like a persimmon i sank my teeth into.

we have been friends for years.
you are a woman i know
but have never known before.
i would be a liar
if i were to say
i do not regret
i am not a man

for you.

2.

you have been talking about
your celibacy
for months.
while having problems with your sportscar
and buying burritos in the mission.

i read the loneliness
in your poetry
though your face is soft
and we reminisce
about the woman we know
who drinks red wine
and cries silently
behind her typewriter in the kitchen
when the guests are gone.

some nights
i leave my lover for you,
giving excuses like
she's really depressed tonight,
i gotta go over.

we sit at la rondalla
and drink courvoisier
and are quiet with much to say.

it is storming outside
and as we leave
water from the neon sign
falls on your black hair.
but you are unaware of it.
you are doing the mambo
with alejandro
on sultry caribbean shores

and you smile that seductive smile.

IT'S IN THE NAME

i've been called sway
                    sue
                    suey
                    suzy
                    tissue
                    ha-chiew.

my father pronounced it choy
so i grew up saying choy,
always careful to add: t-s-u-i.

the first name is kit fan,
fragrant purity.
but can also mean
marriage.
in chinese, choy
can also mean hurry, fast, *faidee*.

i am constantly
chased by the chant
hurry to get married . . .

if it's not bad enough
it's in the name
it's also in the face.

one day a woman instructor
insisted i had been
one of her guest speakers
in a class.

she was so sure of herself
she had me convinced
it was during my alcohol days
when memory was gone.

genny lim was the speaker.

it happens all the time.
orientals so hard to tell apart.
the same day
a woman stopped
to wish me a good opening.

i was not in a play or an art show.

zand gee, nancy hom and stephanie lowe
had a three-woman show.

that's not all.
i've been called
willyce kim,
canyon sam,
louise low.

it happens all the time.

a newspaper woman thought
i was willyce kim for months.
willyce kim gets called susan kwong.
nellie wong is made nellie kim
or not mentioned by name at all.
merle woo is called merle wong
or smeared as yellow woman
in a gay male publication.

it happens all the time.
it's in the name.
it's in the face.

orientals so hard to tell apart.

our faces,
strong, brown,
different as
the bumps
on the skin of
bittermelon.
our tongues,
sharp and fragrant
as ginger,
telling our history,
our experiences
as asian american women,
workers and poets,
cutting the ropes
that bind us,
breaking from
the silence of centuries

to write
our dreams into action,
give voice to our visions
and tongues
to our foreparents,
those who entered
at chinese hospital
or the paper sons
who came by way of
angel island,

forced to take
false names.

the sewing shop worker,
the secretary,
the doctor,
the *deem sum* girl,
the lesbian,
the bike messenger,
the typesetter,
the boxer,
the student.

each with a name.
each with a face,

blood, bone, breath.

Suniti Namjoshi (b. 1941)
Gillian Hanscombe (b. 1945)

Suniti Namjoshi was born in Bombay and educated in India and America. Her poetry and fables often draw on her Indian roots and its storytelling and oral traditions. Namjoshi's work is frequently lesbian-feminist in its sensibility, especially its celebration of egalitarian lesbian love, but it is at least as interested in the subject of what it means to be a lesbian of Indian background, from a country in which, as she and her lover say in the poem "We Can Compose Ourselves," "we wither, having no word," that is, no name for their lesbian love. Namjoshi has published several volumes of fables, including *Feminist Fables* (1981) and *Aditi and the One-Eyed Monkey* (1986), as well as four books of poetry, beginning with *The Jackass and the Lady* (1980).

Gillian Hanscombe was born in Australia but moved to England at the age of twenty-five. Her work is strongly informed by a lesbian and feminist consciousness. In addition to writing poetry and nonfiction prose, such as *Between Friends* (1982), she has produced several literary studies, including a work on the bisexual British writer Dorothy Richardson, and a coauthored work, *Writing for their Lives: The Modernist Women, 1910–1940* (1987).

The following poems are from *Flesh and Paper*, a volume by Namjoshi and Hanscombe, which records their love relationship between 1984 and

1986. Many of the poems were taken out of the letters between them and woven into an interconnecting text. One section of the work consists of poems written about a visit they made together to Namjoshi's home in India. In its structure it is a dialogue between two lesbian lovers who are trying to bridge the gap they experience when they must make sense of their love in a culture that is not only entirely foreign to one of them, and has become foreign while yet remaining disturbingly familiar to the other, but also that does not even acknowledge their existence.

FURTHER READING: Gillian Hanscombe, *Between Friends* (Boston: Alyson, 1982). Gillian Hanscombe and Suniti Namjoshi, *Flesh and Paper* (Devon: Jezebel, 1986). Suniti Namjoshi, *Because of India* (London: Onlywomen Press, 1989).

WAS IT QUITE LIKE THAT?

i

And so you said, "Well, which goddess then?"
I replied, "Come to the country of which
my bones are made up, I mean, the minerals,
the dust and ashes, the named chemicals. Our gods
inhabit birds and beasts and our ruined temples
are still functioning." So we went to India
where a stone is a god—if you say it is—
and where a great many stones are carved with gods,
but just lying about, because, as I told you,
the whole country is a gigantic junk heap.
When we walked about, both reverent and casual,
you were undisturbed. How shall I say it?
You were like me. Did you exercise caution
O my dearest love? You did not question my kinship.

ii

Was it quite like that?

We stop for coffee. No
tigers about. And the room air-conditioned. "The
context . . ." I mumble, break off inanely.
"Yes." You're businesslike.

"Your people show up badly here."

Is that it?
I'm white. I'm Western civilization. I'm Christendom,
their blood running in rivers. I'm capitalist

imperialism, overlording their lords. I'm
barbarism: misplacing, renaming. I'm us, not them.
"And the lesbians . . ." I try again. Mrs. Moore, alone
in the cave, lost her bearings. But that's a fiction
and the writer was one of us.

"We must go," you say gently. I make the coffee
taste just like home.

iii

But we were late for lunch. . . .
                    My mother
might wait. In any event
                all the servants
would be kept waiting. Why
                make an issue
over time for coffee? Time
                    together—
that was the issue. But we were
                    together,
not face to face, side by side. . . .
    And behind the explanations
the frightening admission:
                in this kind country
of exact relationships, there is
                    no word
for you and me.
                Come lover,
they are my kin
                and I their alien,
share the bloodied bonds with me.

IN THAT PARTICULAR TEMPLE

In that particular temple
                a god slept
and a goddess danced,
                and in another
a goddess slept and a god
                    danced.
Do I dare say it? Perhaps—
                it is possible—

that it's all the same?
                    That rapt
and dispassionate stare,
                    the flaring curve
of the gorgeous hip
                    and the round
and unashamed breasts,
                    I have worshipped
before. When we make love
                    you and I
are both sacred and secular.
                    The goddess' limbs
begin to move.
                    Balanced underfoot
the world spins.

BECAUSE OF INDIA

Because of India, before and after,
what could we uncover?
the history not for taking:
the family not for joining:
the cause not for naming:

and lover, what could we discover
in any country or poetry? (being

visitors; and seemly); we can

can

only take the goddess, carry her about,
plait for her a new liturgy (because

of India you came and I return). We can

—I/you can—press dreams and theories, bellies,
breasts, hair, hips, lips; and words; all
plaited now, until tomorrow. I have
told her, lover, to expect
fresh flowers for her feet.

WE CAN COMPOSE OURSELVES

We can compose an ocean if we like;
deck it about with sand dunes, a
mountain or two, some trees.
Or we can compose ourselves.
But a politics? To invent, just we two,
a view? How to think? What to do?
And a country?

                In yours, though the
climate is warm, the buildings fabulous,
though even the rocks have names,
we wither, having no word.

                     And in mine,
the word is so raw it bleeds; and from
fury of pain, it attacks; and would
maim us daily. We can compose ourselves;
but it's our bodies, not our passports,
fit so uncommonly well.

Cherríe (Lawrence) Moraga
(b. 1952)

Cherríe Moraga was born in California of an Anglo father and a Chicana mother. Although she began writing under her patronymic, "Lawrence," she soon assumed her mother's name. Much of her writing deals with her attempts to reconcile her lesbianism and her Latina roots, and with the class differences that divide women. In Moraga's collection of poetry and prose, *Loving in the War Years* (1983), she equates her love for women with a reclamation of her mother's race. Moraga's 1986 theatrical piece, *Giving Up the Ghost,* focuses on women's desire for sexual independence.

Moraga has been central to the formation of a Latina literary tradition, not only through her own writing, but also through the anthologies she helped coedit, including *This Bridge Called My Back* (1981) and *Cuentos: Stories by Latinas* (1983).

FURTHER READING: Cherríe Moraga, *Loving in the War Years* (Boston: South End Press, 1983); *Giving Up the Ghost* (Los Angeles: West End Press, 1986); "A Unified Rainbow of Strength," *off our backs*, 12: 2 (February 1982), 4–6. Cherríe Moraga and Barbara Smith, "Lesbian Literature: A Third World Perspective," *Radical Teacher*, 24

(1983), 12–14. Lorraine Sorrel, "This Bridge Moves Feminists," *off our backs*, 12: 4 (April 1982), 4–5+.

LATER, SHE MET JOYCE

1

Later, she met Joyce
and after they had been friends for a whole
school year, formed their own
girls' gang with code words & rhymes
that played itself coolly
on *this* side of trouble
they got separated by the summer.

　　　Joyce, without a phone
　　　and so far away
　　　into the bordering
　　　town.

But just once, they rendezvoused
on the front porch of a pair
of old white folks, friends of the family.
　　　"Come see me," Joyce whispered
over the telephone line. "I'm
only a few blocks away."

And without expecting to, Cecilia climbed
right up those steps and straight into Joyce's
arms and she would never forget the shape
of the girl's chest, a good one
and a half years older and
how her own small chest & cheek
sunk into it.
　　　　　It spread through her body
the cool breath and release
of a tightness she didn't know
she had held back, waiting
for the summer's end.
Waiting to look
into Joyce's round-like-an-olive
face and see it, full of tears, too.
It was the first time for both of them.
And Cecilia thought, *so this is love.*

2

Later, she met Joyce
who didn't come back
to cath-lic school
it being too hard she guessed
(there *was* no telephone)
in a big winter coat
after mass one sunday
looking more like a momma
than her childhood friend.
Rounder than Cecilia had ever seen her
hair teased high off her head.

　"Hi," Cecilia said.
　"Eh, ésa, 'ow you doing? Whadchu say, man?"

Joyce moved back and forth, her suedes
toeing the ground, talking that talk
that Cecilia's momma called
a difernt claz o' people
that had something to do with your tongue
going thick on you, wearing
shiny clothes and never getting
to college.

Seems in other people's eyes
Joyce was a fat half-breed
that flunked close-to-twice
in other people's eyes
in other people's eyes.

In Joyce's eyes that morning
Cecilia looked for a sign,

C'mon Joyce　be kidding　please
you remember me　you remember
me　you remember
please
　　　and thought she detected
some trace there between the two thick lines
of turquoise, of the brown eyes that cried
over missing her.

Missing Joyce turned
pachuca on her, walking away
talking about the "guyz"
she would like to have
ride her low
through the valley floor.

3

Later that year,
Cecilia was picked
by the smart
white
girls
for president.

LA DULCE CULPA

What kind of lover have you made me, mother
who drew me into bed with you at six at sixteen
oh, even at sixty-six you do still
lifting up the blanket with one arm
lining out the space for my body with the other

    as if our bodies still beat
    inside the same skin
    as if you never noticed
    when they cut me
    out
    from you.

What kind of lover have you made me, mother
who took belts to wipe this memory from me

    the memory of your passion
    dark & starving, spilling
    out of rooms, driving
    into my skin, cracking
    & cussing in spanish
    the thick dark *f* sounds
    hard *c*'s splitting
    the air like blows

you would get a rise out of me
you knew it in our blood
the vision, of my rebellion

What kind of lover have you made me, mother
who put your passion on a plate for me
nearly digestible. Still trying to swallow
the fact that we lived most of our lives
with the death of a man
whose touch ran
across the surface of your skin
never landing nightly
where you begged it
to fall

    to hold your desire
    in the palm of his hand

    for you to rest there
    for you to continue.

What kind of lover have you made me, mother
so in love
with what is left
unrequited.

LOVING IN THE WAR YEARS

Loving you is like living
in the war years
I *do* think of Bogart & Bergman
not clear who's who
but still singin a long smoky
mood into the piano bar
drinks straight up
the last bottle in the house
while bombs split
outside, a broken
world.

A world war going on
but you and I still insisting
in each our own heads
still thinkin how

if I could only make some contact
with that woman across the keyboard
we size each other up
       yes . . .

Loving you has this kind of desperation
to it, like do or die, I
having eyed you from the first
time you made the decision to move
from your stool
to live dangerously.

All on the hunch
that in our exchange of photos
of old girlfriends, names
of cities and memories
back in the states
the fronts we've manned
out here on the continent
all this on the hunch
that *this* time there'll be
no need for resistance.

Loving in the war years
calls for this kind of risking
without a home to call our own
I've got to take you as you come
to me, each time like a stranger
all over again. Not knowing
what deaths you saw today
I've got to take you
as you come, battle bruised
refusing our enemy, fear.

We're all we've got. You and I

maintaining
this war time morality
where being queer
and female is as rude
as we can get.

Emma Pérez
(b. 1954)

Emma Pérez received her Ph.D. from UCLA and is a professor of History and Literature at the University of Texas in El Paso. She is concerned in her scholarly work with the social history of Chicanas and with formulating theories of Chicana lesbian-feminism. In her fiction she hopes to fuse literature and history. She insists that history also needs to be read as literature—that historical accounts are invariably dependent on interpretation, and the socially and politically weak have had history interpreted against them.

"Gulf Dreams" is an excerpt from an autobiographical novel in progress. Pérez examines in this work the vicissitudes of growing up Chicana in a class-ridden and racist Texas town. Her autobiographical character learns about making coalitions with the "different," understanding the uses and misuses of history, and coming to terms with lesbianism.

Gulf Dreams

There is one woman whom fate has destined for each of us.
If we miss her we are saved.
—Anonymous

I met her in my summer of restless dreams. It was a time when infatuation emerges erotic and pure in a young girl's dreams. She was a small girl, a young woman. Her eyes revealed secrets, mysteries I yearned to know long after that summer ended.

My eldest sister introduced us. The young woman, the sister of my sister's best friend, became my friend. At our first meeting we went to the park. We walked, then stood under a cottonwood tree for hours, exchanging glances that bordered on awkward embarrassment. I remember we avoided the clarity of the afternoon. In a few moments, after her eyes sank tenderly into mine, she caressed a part of me that I never knew existed.

At fifteen, I hadn't known love. I don't know if I fell in love that day. I know I felt her deeply and reassuringly. Without a touch, her passion traced the outline of my face. I wanted to brush her cheek lightly with my hand, but I, too frightened, spoke in riddles, euphemistic yearnings: the sun so hot; the trees so full; the earth pressed beneath me.

Weeks passed before I saw her again. During those long nights, I dreamt but did not sleep. Lying in my bed next to an open window, the breezes aroused me. They made me feel a peculiar edginess, mixed with calm. It rained. A soft drizzle fell on my face through the netted screen. I dreamt of her fingers brushing my skin, lightly smoothing over breasts, neck, back, all that ached for her. A fifteen-year-old body ached from loneliness and desire, so unsure of the certainties that her body felt. Nights like this would bring her to me. Never sleeping, half-awake to ensure that it was she embracing me. In those dreams we touched carefully. By morning, I rose exhausted. For those few weeks, sleepless, restless dreams exhausted me.

The day I would see her again held me in fear and anticipation. Far more than these emotions, I felt relief. I felt relieved because to see her would satisfy me, if only momentarily. To see her again, my body spoke to me. To see her eyes envelop mine. I had to remember their color. I had to see the olive hands that caused so much delight. I had to know that I had not invented her for dreams.

It was morning. A hot, dusty, gravel road linked our homes. My eldest sister drove to the young girl's house to see her own best friend. I sat, the passenger, staring out at fields, rows of cotton balls, white on green, passing quickly, the motion dizzying my head and stomach. My sister, familiar with my nausea in moving vehicles, had wrapped a wet face cloth in a plastic bag. The coolness of the moist rag soothed my forehead. As an additional precaution, I had stuffed two brown paper bags, one inside the other, under the car seat.

When we arrived, she was sitting on a porch swing hanging from a worn, wooden house, the paint peeling with no memory of color. Our sisters hugged, went into the kitchen, poured coffee and prepared for gratifying gossip. We were not alone; brothers, sisters, a mother, faces and names I can't recall—the introductions necessary, trusting, unsuspecting. No one knew why I had come. To see my new friend, they thought. To link families with four sisters who would be friends longer than their lifetimes, through children who would bond them at baptismal rites. *Comadres*. We would become intimate friends, sharing coffee, gossip and heartaches. We would endure the female life cycle—adolescence, marriage, menopause, death, and even divorce, before or after menopause.

I had not come for that. I had come for her kiss.

We walked through tall grass. Silent. A path led to the shade of a tree. I watched her waist and hips, rhythmic, broad, swaying. At sixteen, her hips and breasts were a woman's. Under the tree, we avoided eyes, avoided touch, avoided that which I hoped we both wanted. I stared at her. She grabbed handfuls of dry leaves, sifting them through her fingers, methodically repeating in her exercise. For an instant, I forgot her name. I could not place her. She was foreign, a stranger. The memory loss buffered my pain. So painful to watch the distance between us. I left that day without renewal. I knew the dreams would cease. I began to repair the damage. I revived the mundane. I sought its refuge.

The dreams did not cease. I saw her with him. That day under the shaded tree, she had spoken about a young boy. She craved his delicious expert mouth, she said. She told me he had sucked her nipples. He was careful not to hurt her or impregnate her. Instead, he licked her moistness. He loved her. No other boy had ever licked her softness.

Those were my dreams. The morning I lost my memory, forgot her name, I watched her lips relive desire for him. At night, they appeared in my bedroom. Invaded my bed. Even there, she belonged to him.

I did not envy him. I despised him, his coarseness, his anxious determination. She longed for someone to arouse her soul. Each time she dared to look directly into my eyes, she quickly averted hers. She alerted the passion, then repressed it immediately, her fear a reproach against me.

Her desire for him pierced me. Still, I wanted her. I wanted her to come alone at night just as she had those first two weeks when exhaustion fulfilled me.

We became friends. The promise of female rituals enraged me. We met weekly, then monthly, then not at all. Her boy became her cause. Often, I spotted him in the fields. His strong, brown back bending over to pick the cotton that filled the trailing sack. A perfectly beautiful back, I thought. She was in love with a beautifully strong, muscular, brown back.

As a young woman of fifteen in a nearly coastal Texas town, I didn't recognize love. In a town where humidity bred hostility, I memorized hate. Bronze in the summer, with hair and eyes so light that I could pass through doors that shut out my sisters and brother, I envied their dark color and brown eyes. I grew to resent my own because they set me apart from my family. At four, my sisters convinced me I was adopted. Eyes so green, this was not my family. At five, I took a butcher knife, sat calmly, sadly, on the pink chenille bedspread, threatening to slice away at tanned skin. I remember the scene like a dream. Always the sad child, burdened.

When I stared into cameras, I didn't smile, laugh, or clown as children do, so unfamiliar to me how my cousins giggled with each other. My mother framed photographs that captured the sadness, held it squarely like a package with a time bomb that would not explode for years. Right now the sadness only watched. There was one photograph. Not yet one year old and I laughed openly and happily. Evidence of childhood. I wondered, when did the sadness begin?

Racial conflict epitomized the Texas town with a Spanish name. Anglo Texans arrogantly mispronounced its name, giving it an ugly, abbreviated, sound. El Pueblo became L Peblo. I liked the sound in Spanish but felt humiliated to say it aloud in a town with a white conscience. The white conscience followed me to public places. It tried to invade our home, but my mother and father resisted. We learned at Anglo schools the skill of separation. The language of survival. Somehow, we learned to sustain a separation that allowed a semblance of happiness at home. Out there, a white world sneered at our tortilla lunches, our second-hand clothes, our culture's survival habits. Inside our home, white habits, like white friends, felt unwelcome.

Pronunciation divided the two worlds. In a school where students' names ranged from Hodges and Hutchins, to a sprinkling of Garza and González, teachers rejected Spanish phonetics. They taught me to enunciate strange foreign sounds. The sounds had migrated from East to West a century earlier; sounds which imposed authority; sounds which brutalized names, towns, words, street signs, life that was here three hundred years before Anglo invasion.

With an imposing southern drawl, the teacher taught English sounds to Mexican children. "Church," she said.

"Shursh," I repeated.

"Church," she spoke, slower and louder.

"Shursh," I pronounced, quickly and softly, unskilled at the language of survival. But I would learn.

I missed her. Daily, hourly, I missed her. Since that meeting under the tree, I had retrieved pride to dismiss longing. The pride surfaced. It guided me through the day. It stopped me from climbing into my sister's white Dodge. Weekly, my sister traveled that gravel road to confer with her *comadre*.

One Saturday morning I tucked away pride, answered longing and sat, the passenger, the victim. She half-expected me. Took my hand, led me to her bedroom, sat me down on her twin bed next to her. She spoke reasonably. She had missed me. Why had I stopped coming? Why had I stayed away so long? She relied on my friendship, a passionate friendship, she called it. Mute, I looked away, paralyzed, embarrassed, hurt. She played at my emotions under the guise of friendship. We had moved far beyond that first day when we refused to acknowledge clarity.

A knock on the door, the interruption was inevitable. Through the door, her mother announced his intrusion. He waited on the porch swing, waited to take her for a ride in a borrowed black Chevy, waited to drive her to deserted fields and back roads where boys tested their virility.

Her eyes sparkled. He gave them an amused sparkle. She examined my face searching for jealousy. At an early age, I learned to exhibit indifference with sad eyes. She misinterpreted the sadness and chose jealousy. I watched through the window. It framed them, froze them like a photograph. He wrapped his arm around her waist. The black Chevy rolled away, rocks crackling under the wheels, dust spreading, leaving a brown film on my sister's white Dodge.

I would not see her again for a year.

My mother's house rested behind my father's workshop. My older sisters told me there had been a house before this one where they and my brother had lived. I even lived there until my first birthday. Then, my father moved us closer to the railroad tracks, next to the cotton gin.

I memorized the routine of caring in that two bedroom home for six people. My cousins thought we were rich to live in a house my father bought with the G.I. bill. They lived in timeworn rented houses. Ours was newer, but hidden behind an aluminum building, my father's upholstery shop, my favorite playground. It became our favorite playground. Among the stripped chairs and couches waiting for floral designs to hide the bare frames, among the velour scraps and sharp nails, my brother and I played. My father's hammering was our financial security, his love proven over and over. Sometimes he hammered for sixteen hours daily, stopping only for ice water and saltine crackers. My brother and I were messengers, carriers delivering our mother's tenderness to our father down a worn path from the house to the shop.

I distrusted and even despised some brown-skinned men when I was fifteen. But I know I loved my father. A strong, broad-shouldered man with black, curly hair, he adored my mother's beauty. He raged jealously when she walked into town with her sisters. Men would stare at her creamy light skin, curved waist and hips, and her thick, black hair. She feared my father's jealousy like abuse, and often, stayed home to appease. I misunderstood her compliance. In time, I recognized her strength, his weakness.

Long before the summer of restless dreams, I watched my sisters dress, paint their cheeks and lips, file nails, and emerge perfumed and shapely for brown-skinned boys. They each picked one. The eldest chose a small, cynical one. The younger chose a dark, brooding boxer. They would both become my friends. They would both deceive my sisters, hence lose my trust. Men and deception became one fused realization. Yet, like myself, they only sought understanding—selfish understanding and constant adoration from women.

My brother became the necessary companion throughout childhood. *Los cuates,* the twins, our family named us. Inseparable. He, small boned, petite, eternally naive, was younger than I in every way but years. Accustomed to his companionship, I resented how he shunned my invitations to films or parties as we grew older. Maybe he resented me. I, bigger, light-skinned, had caught up with him in school, made friends and passing grades. Maybe I reminded him too much of the white world outside our home. Maybe, in mastering the language of survival, I too became an outsider. He no longer allowed me to share his dreams. Long before, I had stopped listening to them.

At fifteen, I didn't hate boys. I even liked some of them. Between the young gigglers with hard-ons and the older cat-callers with hard-ons, the choices were few. Finally, I chose one. I chose an outsider, white-skinned, blue-eyed, so blond his hair was white. In two years together, through daily phone calls, weekly films, and obligatory kisses, I refused to let him inside. Years later, after we ended daily phone calls, when his wife was at work, I mounted him as he lay on his living room floor. Too guilty to take me to a white woman's bed, too ashamed to make love, his face flushed. In seconds, it was over. A beginning and an end were wrapped in one humiliating afternoon. The afternoon on his living room floor punctuated the end of a romance. The end mimicked the beginning.

When I was fifteen and chose him, he released a numbness that had protected me from her. The protection gone, the numbness lifted, the dreams revived. She returned alone at night, to soothe, to nurture, to explain why we loved only in dreams. I fell deeper. She would never leave, not as long as he stayed. Now she protected me from passage into female rites.

He wore pain. His face a grimace, his voice unctuous. He loved to wear pain. A young boy of seventeen from Alabama, he mistrusted his mother's anger. He and his father colluded. They misunderstood her thick, white body, her callused hands, her bitterness. Domestic service in Alabama was black women's work. In Texas, Mexican women cleaned white women's homes. Her white skin had not guaranteed that privilege.

She did not marry above her family. She married a poor boy, a hard worker like herself. The man she married spotted a strong build for healthy babies and a double salary. He raised her son to despise her strength. The son took her bitterness and made it his own. How could she have known a son would deceive her? He would bond with male prerogative to abandon the female, the womb.

When I met him, I inherited his contempt for a mother he neither respected nor pitied. I inherited him the moment when a boy's ambivalence turns cocksure. Arrogance takes over, tenderness cannot be public. Maleness, so convinced of its superiority to the feminine, evolves.

Instinctively, relationships became predictable and I became cold, withdrawn. Only she could break through. I resisted as long as I could. Frozen. Her glance, a smile, a playful word would melt me. Once again, longing disrupted me.

The year without her, before age sixteen, I preoccupied myself with the boy from Alabama. The town disapproved of brown and white holding hands. Since my childhood, racial insults were common in supermarkets, restaurants, laundromats, barber shops, and gas station bathrooms. The Texaco near my grandmother's house announced on its bathroom door, "For Colored Only."

I was born in 1954, the year civil rights was initiated once again through "Brown vs. the Board of Education" in Topeka, Kansas. In the 1950s, pretension superseded reality. McCarthy must have frightened some Mexicans into patriotic idiocies. How many turned their back on *mojados*? The wetbacks of ancestry forgotten. How many got caught in the American dilemma of scapegoats, communists, and be-bop? In that Texas town there were no civil rights marches, no activists. Only rice paddies and cotton fields where Mexicans and Blacks couldn't even earn a livelihood. El Pueblo was far from Washington and closer to Kansas. Distance, however, was inconsequential, El Pueblo only slept.

Cold war residue infiltrated the town's schoolyards. In the first grade, two six-year-olds worried that Russian airplanes might bomb the school. Their enemy across the ocean crept up on their comfortable lives, but only in their ridiculous reasoning. My enemy was nearer. My enemy sat across the aisle whispering to an accomplice. Two blond, big-boned girls conspired as they stared down at brown skin. Their parents had told them to sit apart from Mexicans with *piojos*. The lice would hatch from eggs exploding like little bombs in their hair. That would happen if they sat too close to a Mexican. I was their target of fear and ridicule, a bearer of filth and disgust, a non-person. I wasn't as defiant as my friends Josefina y Susana. Josie and Susie would run up close to the *bolillitas* and shove a brown head of hair next to a blond one and then run away. The white girls would scream. My friends would laugh victorious at the game they invented to balance injustices. But the game only lasted in the playground. In class, the Anglo teacher bonded with the white students who wore freshly pressed cotton. To all of them, the handful of Mexicans were as alien as Russians. To us, they were even stranger.

The cold war heated up as the years passed. Alliances were made for survival. Josie and Susie were my allies, but there was another one. A girl who walked home alone each day, and although she lived in a brick home where the rich *bolillos* lived, they treated her differently. I didn't understand why. She dressed in up-to-date clothes, not hand-me-downs. She seemed just like them, but her hair was so black it looked blue like her eyes. Once, I overheard the *bolillitas* talking about her. She, too, was an outcast, but without *piojos.* The people at her church had murdered Jesus Christ, they said. I wondered. She didn't look like an accomplice, she wasn't like the white girls who could kill in an instant as they determined one's social standing. If you were like them you could join their clique and have the power to determine who was, and who was not, popular. Even in grade school, they prepared for the Junior League and sororities.

Sue, the one they called a Jesus killer, became my friend. I never questioned her about the rumor. Her kindness and our silent pledge defied children's cruel jokes. Josie and Susie didn't want me to hang around Sue. She was different, not brown like us and she didn't even know Spanish, they said. She was too odd to be in our safe trio. But I recognized a loner, a quiet self-contained girl who didn't have friends and didn't seem to care. Our friendship was restricted to holding hands on the playground the way best friends would do. But in the afternoon, I'd walk home with Josie and Susie because we all lived in the same poor neighborhood just beyond the railroad tracks. They'd laugh and ridicule kids on the sidewalk—the way they walked or talked. I enjoyed laughter with them. They didn't bother me about Sue anymore. It was as if they understood that she and I were alike in some off-colored way.

In grade school, I found myself apologizing repeatedly. The apologetic fool enraged by my own passivity and powerlessness. I remember the obligatory trip to the Principal's office. Long hallways, my stomach churned. He signed an absentee slip. I apologized. Did not want to trouble such a busy man. I thanked him. Neglected to call him "sir." The neglect mustered more apologies. Insistent, he asked that I repeat after him, "Yes sir." "Yes sir, I'm sorry, sir." His bald, ivory head reflected sun rays through the office window.

My father didn't teach his children to say "sir." To him, that title implied emotional distance. He showed us that the outside was deceitful. He, like his children, faced hierarchy out there in the whiteness of El Pueblo. He refused to enforce that imposition. When he walked through our door each evening, he cursed white "sirs" to hell for withholding wages.

In that school, I learned the origin of *maldiciones,* the curse of the Alamo. In the seventh grade, the teacher taught us to absorb the conqueror's lies in history books. The Battle of the Alamo, she said, represented the valor of the founding fathers, men who gave their lives for freedom. The devil dictator Santa Anna and hundreds of Mexicans massacred the brave heroes, Bowie and Crockett. She turned to me, a grey-haired, plump, one-armed woman, challenging my patriotism. Josie, Susie and I speculated on the loss of her arm. We made up our own incredulous myths, a farm accident, or a jealous lover.

She glared at me, "What do you think of the Alamo?" And then, "Are you glad that Texas is in America?"

I hesitated. Closed minds and open eyes waited. I understood that my dignity stood trial. For them, the sins of their ancestors were in question. But they didn't know that. Like the one-armed teacher, thick, witless patriotism blinded them. The lies were as blatant as her missing arm, the one they all chose to ignore. No one examined the stump. No one asked what happened. What was the injustice she had suffered as a child or a young woman? Did she inherit this indignity at birth? No. They all pretended to know what they couldn't possibly understand.

And, at that moment, I took my most unyielding stand against the Alamo.

"I don't know."

I spoke eloquently, "I don't have all the facts."

In the seventh grade I wasn't prepared to argue history but I refused to renounce my *mestizaje,* my parents, my Mexican ancestry, to comfort Anglos. I wouldn't let them win this battle so easily. I sought truth and the textbooks hid it, I suspected.

In 1967, the Southwest rocked with Chicanismo. The explosive movement would change my future, but now, the Alamo rearranged my present. It was a metaphor for masculinity in a region where destiny had been stolen.

I spotted her in a local market. The clerk, an elderly Anglo from Louisiana with an emphatic Southern drawl, harassed her. She placed a loaf of white bread on the counter. He refused to add the thirty-three cents to her family's account. Their payment was late again. She argued with him, then pleaded. I enjoyed watching her argue, resented her pleading. It minimized her pride. Finally, the store manager, a middle-aged, pot-bellied man and son of the clerk, walked to the check-out stand. His eyes seduced her body. Her smile convinced him. Promptly, he added thirty-three cents to her bill. She had begun payment with a smile. It found her in his shabby, filthy, office on a cot that stunk like mildew. I judged her. I would continue to judge her until I too stripped for men whose power robbed my dignity.

When I began to dream that night, I saw her on the store manager's cot, lying on her stomach, her buttocks smooth and firm. His hand moved across her back, finding her soft, heart-shaped ass. He rubbed up and down, then in circles, enjoying her muscular flesh. But it was me who kissed her eyes. And it was she who encircled my nipples with her tongue. Awakened from the dream, I quivered. I felt her go to him, her boy, the one she nurtured. I felt her loving him again. She would not leave him easily. I knew that.

Routine and books comforted me. The summer over, fall gave me hope. I studied. I sublimated. I worked at K-Mart.

Persistent patterns from my past still paint my future. I sought protection. I know now that his white skin stood like armor between me and an unjust town. I liked this boy from Alabama whose blue eyes witnessed poverty in his own home. I liked his big shoulders, his tight, freckled forearms. We became lovers who kissed on Friday nights at drive-in theaters where I avoided sex.

Fatigue overtook my strength. His demands doubled. Familiarity gave him license to give me orders. My resistance led to petty arguments, so typically the high school sweetheart's drama. He was muscular, popular, a straight-A white student; and I was Mexican, but smart and somewhat pretty, therefore acceptable. After a year, his habits bored me. The kisses no longer stimulated. My eyes wandered to neighborhood boys, to *pachucos,* so coolly sexy, so dangerously off-limits. My eyes wandered but at night I waited for her.

I think I realized that I had always been in love the moment I saw her again. My heart sank. I fought tears. While I had busied myself with the boy from Alabama, she had grown more beautiful. Being in love, I thought, has made her more beautiful. Her hair fell around her face. She saw me. We had not spoken since that day in her bedroom. She smiled. She walked in my direction. I tried to smile but my lips deceived me. My expression puzzled her. When she hugged me, she buried her head between my neck and shoulder, resting comfortably, feeling like just yesterday we had lain in each other's arms.

The smell of her hair, I had only imagined its scent for so long. Why was she holding me? She asked how I had been. She had seen me often, she said. She had seen me at school, the park, in town, with the boy from Alabama. She questioned me seeking answers. Was I happy? Did I love him? Her voice bubbled. Quickly, I masked my emotions. I hid behind him. I pretended that he was special. I don't think I lied when I said I loved him. I felt love for him. I had hidden behind that type of love for so long. Yet, seeing her reminded me that I had only practiced at love. I practiced kisses and language with him. The smell of her hair woke me. Realization struck. She was different.

I'm not sure how she was different, but she felt unlike before. But then, I hadn't really felt her. I carried her around inside me always, but physically, I'd never really touched her. I imagined entering her, enjoying that ration of her, but only when and if she wanted me.

I could not compete with her past, nor could she with mine. There was no competition, only commonality. Our souls touched before in a life where my love for her was not forbidden.

How can I explain that she was the core of me? I say this over and over, to you, to myself. We merged before birth, entwined in each other's souls, wrapped together like a bubble of mist, floating freely, reflecting rainbows. This was before flesh, before bones crushed each other foolishly trying to join mortal bodies, before the outline of skin shielded us from one another. We both knew this, that we came from the same place, that we were joined in a place so uncommon that this world, which bound us in limitations, could not understand the bond that flesh frustrated.

We became intimate friends again, desperately engaged. This time she stared longingly after me when I walked by with the boy from Alabama. She began to love me. I had not stopped loving her, nor would I stop.

I thought that writing this years later would finally release me from her. But I feel no reprieve. Not yet. Maybe the only resolution is in the act of loving. Maybe I had to love her enough to let her go. I had to begin to love her more than I loved my selfishness. I knew what I had to do but I wasn't ready. I cried.

We became enraptured and entrapped. We were addicted to each other's eroticism. A kiss on the cheek inflamed me for hours. I witnessed her greed. Teasing reached new heights. Could I let go of my addiction to her, to her body, to her words? Would I let go? The desire to desire her—my weakness. I didn't care. I risked seeing her every day despite the moodiness she provoked. Her boyfriend grew more and more threatened each time I appeared. His hostility sharpened. Mine became silent and distant when he saw her approach. She and I, trapped in social circumstances. Propriety kept us apart.

Some women exude sex simultaneously with erotic movements. She was that woman. Her scent alone emitted sensuality. I learned how boys had damaged her. I felt her damage. She punished me when I refused to continue the pattern with which she was so familiar. When I denied her the fight she sought, she would finally look elsewhere. So accustomed to brutality, she chose to play the victim. We sensed that dynamic in each other. She knew that if the game didn't work the first time, eventually I would play anyway. I couldn't resist her when I saw her agonizing. After running to him, he would oblige by hurting her, then she would come to me. And I rescued her, then resented my duty to her. And so we played this deceitful game, angry because we didn't know how to stop the pattern. I would spit fierce words at her. I abused her in long paragraphs filled with accusations. Sometimes, without uttering a sound, I hurt her. I manipulated just as she did.

I couldn't let go. Whatever bound us went beyond friendship. And through our games I recognized when she would leave me again, each time she would be gone a little longer. She returned to him, the boy with the strong brown back. I almost faced him on the path that routinely led me to her. I watched motionless from the street. The fog, the dull sky and the cold air warned me. He opened the door that I had opened so often. I couldn't cry. I stood, the numbed observer. Long before he traced my steps to her door, I knew. I knew that it was over again. She was tired of repeating the pain, the pleasure, then more pain. I was tired of her lies. I listened when she lied to him on the telephone while I sat on her bed. Only now did I hear that the lies were for me. I wanted truth, but I believed her lies because I believed my heart.

Another phase over. I refused to say good-bye. It is far better not to know when something is over. It is far better not to imprint that image permanently in one's mind. I prefer to walk through the habits of the day, treating good-bye as if it were not that at all, as if tomorrow we'll meet again for coffee. I began to mourn her. I don't know when I said good-bye, but I anticipated the moment. And it happened. The image marked in a memory that I shielded from myself for years. I had to forget that predetermined second. So much more is stamped in my mind—her smile, her breath, her persistence. She wore me out. I needed rest.

Jeanette Winterson
(b. 1959)

Jeanette Winterson's literary techniques and focus—her experimentations with narrative voice and extraordinary language, her philosophical inquiries into the meaning of desire, her play with gender—place her among the most sophisticated writers of contemporary lesbian fiction. Winterson's childhood in a British pentecostal evangelical family into which she had been adopted is the subject of her first novel, *Oranges Are Not the Only Fruit* (1985), and a 1990 television drama that she based on the novel. Winterson explores in that work her fundamentalist upbringing, her discovery of lesbian love, and the violent reaction of the religious community when her sexual orientation is unveiled. Both her novel and video play won prestigious awards, as have her subsequent novels, *The Passion* (1987) and *Sexing the Cherry* (1989).

The following excerpt, taken from *The Passion*, is set in early-nineteenth-century Venice. But *The Passion* is postmodernist in its view of the flexibility of gender, its refusal to see biological sex as a reliable signifier, and its assumption of universal bisexuality. Winterson examines the shared properties of all passion, whether it be manifested in the form of hero worship, religion, heterosexuality, or homosexuality.

Winterson's work continues to present philosophical dissections of gender. Her latest novel, *Written on the Body* (1992), goes even beyond *The Passion* in her questioning of the rigidity of our gendered society. For example, Winterson offers enough hints to suggest that *Written on the Body* is a lesbian novel; but she also teases by leaving the gender of the narrator undetermined and by dangling before the reader provocative and purposely confusing evidence. A reference to the narrator's "ex-boyfriend," for example, raises the question of whether the narrator is really a lesbian. Perhaps she's a bisexual woman? A bisexual man? The reader's certainties about biological sex and sexual orientation are thus exploded and the notion of gender is destabilized.

FURTHER READING: Jeanette Winterson, *Oranges Are Not the Only Fruit* (1985; New York: Atlantic Monthly Press, 1988); *The Passion* (1987; reprint, New York: Atlantic Monthly Press, 1988); *Written on the Body* (New York: Alfred Knopf, 1992). Jackie Kay, "Unnatural Passions," *Spare Rib*, 209 (February 1990), 26–29. Suzanne Scott and Lynne M. Constantine, "Interview with Jeanette Winterson," *Belles Lettres*, 5: 4 (Summer 1990), 24–26.

From *The Passion:* "The Queen of Spades"

Nowadays, the night is designed for the pleasure-seekers and tonight, by their reckoning, is a *tour de force*. There are fire-eaters frothing at the mouth with yellow tongues. There is a dancing bear. There is a troupe of little girls, their sweet bodies hairless and pink, carrying sugared almonds in copper dishes. There are women of every kind and not all of them are women. In the centre of the square, the workers on Murano have fashioned a huge glass slipper that is constantly filled and re-filled with champagne. To drink from it you must lap like a dog and how these visitors love it. One has already drowned, but what is one death in the midst of so much life?

From the wooden frame above where the gunpowder waits there are also suspended a number of nets and trapezes. From here acrobats swing over the square, casting grotesque shadows on the dancers below. Now and again, one will dangle by the knees and snatch a kiss from whoever is standing below. I like such kisses. They fill the mouth and leave the body free. To kiss well one must kiss solely. No groping hands or stammering hearts. The lips and the lips alone are the pleasure. Passion is sweeter split strand by strand. Divided and re-divided like mercury then gathered up only at the last moment.

You see, I am no stranger to love.

It's getting late, who comes here with a mask over her face? Will she try the cards?

She does. She holds a coin in her palm so that I have to pick it out. Her skin is warm. I spread the cards. She chooses. The ten of diamonds. The three of clubs. Then the Queen of spades.

"A lucky card. The symbol of Venice. You win."

She smiled at me and pulling away her mask revealed a pair of grey-green eyes with flecks of gold. Her cheekbones were high and rouged. Her hair, darker and redder than mine.

"Play again?"

She shook her head and had a waiter bring over a bottle of champagne. Not any champagne. Madame Clicquot. The only good thing to come out of France. She held the glass in a silent toast, perhaps to her own good fortune. The Queen of spades is a serious win and one we are usually careful to avoid. Still she did not speak, but watched me through the crystal and suddenly draining her glass stroked the side of my face. Only for a second she touched me and then she was gone and I was left with my heart smashing at my chest and three-quarters of a bottle of the best champagne. I was careful to conceal both.

I am pragmatic about love and have taken my pleasure with both men and women, but I have never needed a guard for my heart. My heart is a reliable organ.

At midnight the gunpowder was triggered and the sky above St. Mark's broke into a million coloured pieces. The fireworks lasted perhaps half an hour and during that time I was able to finger enough money to bribe a friend to take over my booth for a while. I slipped through the press towards the still bubbling glass slipper looking for her.

She had vanished. There were faces and dresses and masks and kisses to be had and a hand at every turn but she was not there. I was detained by an infantryman who held up two glass balls and asked if I would exchange them for mine. But I was in no mood for charming games and pushed past him, my eyes begging for a sign.

The roulette table. The gaming table. The fortune tellers. The fabulous three-breasted woman. The singing ape. The double-speed dominoes and the tarot.

She was not there.

She was nowhere.

My time was up and I went back to the booth of chance full of champagne and an empty heart.

"There was a woman looking for you," said my friend. "She left this."

On the table was an earring. Roman by the look of it, curiously shaped, made of that distinct old yellow gold that these times do not know.

I put it in my ear and, spreading the cards in a perfect fan, took out the Queen of spades. No one else should win tonight. I would keep her card until she needed it.

Gaiety soon ages.

By three o'clock the revellers were drifting away through the arches around St. Mark's or lying in piles by the cafés, opening early to provide strong coffee. The gaming was over. The Casino tellers were packing away their gaudy stripes and optimistic baize. I was off-duty and it was almost dawn. Usually, I go straight home and meet my stepfather on his way to the bakery. He slaps me about the shoulder and makes some joke about how much money I'm making. He's a curious man; a shrug of the shoulders and a wink and that's him. He's never thought it odd that his daughter cross-dresses for a living and sells second-hand purses on the side. But then, he's never thought it odd that his daughter was born with webbed feet.

"There are stranger things," he said.

And I suppose there are.

This morning, there's no going home. I'm bolt upright, my legs are restless and the only sensible thing is to borrow a boat and calm myself in the Venetian way; on the water.

The Grand Canal is already busy with vegetable boats. I am the only one who seems intent on recreation and the others eye me curiously, in between steadying a load or arguing with a friend. These are my people, they can eye me as much as they wish.

I push on, under the Rialto, that strange half-bridge that can be drawn up to stop one half of this city warring with the other. They'll seal it eventually and we'll be brothers and mothers. But that will be the doom of paradox.

Bridges join but they also separate.

Out now, past the houses that lean into the water. Past the Casino itself. Past the money-lenders and the churches and the buildings of state. Out now into the lagoon with only the wind and the seagulls for company.

There is a certainty that comes with the oars, with the sense of generation after generation standing up like this and rowing like this with rhythm and ease. This city is littered with ghosts seeing to their own. No family would be complete without its ancestors.

Our ancestors. Our belonging. The future is foretold from the past and the future is only possible because of the past. Without past and future, the present is partial. All time is eternally present and so all time is ours. There is no sense in forgetting and every sense in dreaming. Thus the present is made rich. Thus the present is made whole. On the lagoon this morning, with the past at my elbow, rowing beside me, I see the future glittering on the water. I catch sight of myself in the water and see in the distortions of my face what I might become.

If I find her, how will my future be?

I will find her.

Somewhere between fear and sex passion is.

Passion is not so much an emotion as a destiny. What choice have I in the face of this wind but to put up sail and rest my oars?

Dawn breaks.

I spent the weeks that followed in a hectic stupor.

Is there such a thing? There is. It is the condition that most resembles a particular kind of mental disorder. I have seen ones like me in San Servelo. It manifests itself as a compulsion to be forever doing something, however meaningless. The body must move but the mind is blank.

I walked the streets, rowed circles around Venice, woke up in the middle of the night with my covers in impossible knots and my muscles rigid. I took to working double shifts at the Casino, dressing as a woman in the afternoon and a young man in the evenings. I ate when food was put in front of me and slept when my body was throbbing with exhaustion.

I lost weight.

I found myself staring into space, forgetting where I was going.

I was cold.

I never go to confession; God doesn't want us to confess, he wants us to challenge him, but for a while I went into our churches because they were built from the heart. Improbable hearts that I had never understood before. Hearts so full of longing that these old stones still cry out with their extasy. These are warm churches, built in the sun.

I sat at the back, listening to the music or mumbling through the service. I'm never tempted by God but I like his trappings. Not tempted but I begin to understand why others are. With this feeling inside, with this wild love that threatens, what safe places might there be? Where do you store gun-powder? How do you sleep at night again? If I were a little different I might turn passion into something holy and then I would sleep again. And then my extasy would be my extasy but I would not be afraid. . . .

November in Venice is the beginning of the catarrh season. Catarrh is part of our heritage like St. Mark's. Long ago, when the Council of Three ruled in mysterious ways, any traitor or hapless one done away with was usually announced to have died of catarrh. In this way, no one was embarrassed. It's the fog that rolls in from the lagoon and hides one end of the Piazza from another that brings on our hateful congestion. It rains too, mournfully and quietly, and the boatmen sit under sodden rags and stare helplessly into the canals. Such weather drives away the foreigners and that's the only good thing that can be said of it. Even the brilliant water-gate at the Fenice turns grey.

On an afternoon when the Casino didn't want me and I didn't want myself, I went to Florian's to drink and gaze at the Square. It's a fulfilling pastime.

I had been sitting perhaps an hour when I had the feeling of being watched. There was no one near me, but there was someone behind a screen a little way off. I let my mind retreat again. What did it matter? We are always watching or watched. The waiter came over to me with a packet in his hand.

I opened it. It was an earring. It was the pair.

And she stood before me and I realised I was dressed as I had been that night because I was waiting to work. My hand went to my lip.

"You shaved it off," she said.

I smiled. I couldn't speak.

She invited me to dine with her the following evening and I took her address and accepted.

In the Casino that night I tried to decide what to do. She thought I was a young man. I was not. Should I go to see her as myself and joke about the mistake and leave gracefully? My heart shrivelled at this thought. To lose her again so soon. And what was myself? Was this breeches and boots self any less real than my garters? What was it about me that inter-ested her?

You play, you win. You play, you lose. You play.

I was careful to steal enough to buy a bottle of the best champagne.

Lovers are not at their best when it matters. Mouths dry up, palms sweat, conversation flags and all the time the heart is threatening to fly from the body once and for all. Lovers have been known to have heart attacks.

Lovers drink too much from nervousness and cannot perform. They eat too little and faint during their fervently wished consummation. They do not stroke the favoured cat and their face-paint comes loose. This is not all. Whatever you have set store by, your dress, your dinner, your poetry, will go wrong.

Her house was gracious, standing on a quiet waterway, fashionable but not vulgar. The drawing-room, enormous with great windows at either end and a fireplace that would have suited an idle wolfhound. It was simply furnished; an oval table and a *chaise-longue*. A few Chinese ornaments that she liked to collect when the ships came through. She had also a strange assortment of dead insects mounted in cases on the wall. I had never seen such things before and wondered about this enthusiasm.

She stood close to me as she took me through the house, pointing out certain pictures and books. Her hand guided my elbow at the stairs and when we sat down to eat she did not arrange us formally but put me beside her, the bottle in between.

We talked about the opera and the theatre and the visitors and the weather and ourselves. I told her that my real father had been a boatman and she laughed and asked could it be true that we had webbed feet?

"Of course," I said and she laughed the more at this joke.

We had eaten. The bottle was empty. She said she had married late in life, had not expected to marry at all being stubborn and of independent means. Her husband dealt in rare books and manuscripts from the east. Ancient maps that showed the lairs of griffins and the haunts of whales. Treasure maps that claimed to know the whereabouts of the Holy Grail. He was a quiet and cultured man of whom she was fond.

He was away.

We had eaten, the bottle was empty. There was nothing more that could be said without strain or repetition. I had been with her more than five hours already and it was time to leave. As we stood up and she moved to get something I stretched out my arm, that was all, and she turned back into my arms so that my hands were on her shoulder blades and hers along my spine. We stayed thus for a few moments until I had courage enough to kiss her neck very lightly. She did not pull away. I grew bolder and kissed her mouth, biting a little at the lower lip.

She kissed me.

"I can't make love to you," she said.

Relief and despair.

"But I can kiss you."

And so, from the first, we separated our pleasure. She lay on the rug and I lay at right angles to her so that only our lips might meet. Kissing in this way is the strangest of distractions. The greedy body that clamours for satisfaction is forced to content itself with a single sensation and, just as the blind hear more acutely and the deaf can feel the grass grow, so the mouth becomes the focus of love and all things pass through it and are re-defined. It is a sweet and precise torture.

When I left her house some time later, I did not set off straight away, but watched her moving from room to room extinguishing the lights. Up-wards she went, closing the dark behind her until there was only one light left and that was her own. She said she often read into the small hours while her husband was away. Tonight she did not read. She paused briefly at the window and then the house was black.

What was she thinking?

What was she feeling?

I walked slowly through the silent squares and across the Rialto, where the mist was brooding above the water. The boats were covered and empty apart from the cats that make their homes under the seat boards. There was no one, not even the beggars who fold themselves and their rags into any doorway.

How is it that one day life is orderly and you are content, a little cynical perhaps but on the whole just so, and then without warning you find the solid floor is a trapdoor and you are now in another place whose geography is uncertain and whose customs are strange?

Travellers at least have a choice. Those who set sail know that things will not be the same as at home. Explorers are prepared. But for us, who travel along the blood vessels, who come to the cities of the interior by chance, there is no preparation. We who were fluent find life is a foreign language. Somewhere between the swamp and the mountains. Somewhere between fear and sex. Somewhere between God and the Devil passion is and the way there is sudden and the way back is worse.

I'm surprised at myself talking in this way. I'm young, the world is before me, there will be others. I feel my first streak of defiance since I met her. My first upsurge of self. I won't see her again. I can go home, throw aside these clothes and move on. I can move out if I like. . . .

Passion, I spit on it.

I spat into the canal. . . .

The surface of the canal had the look of polished jet. I took off my boots slowly, pulling the laces loose and easing them free. Enfolded between each toe were my own moons. Pale and opaque. Unused. I had often played with them but I never thought they might be real. My mother wouldn't even tell me if the rumours were real and I have no boating cousins. My brothers are gone away.

Could I walk on that water?

Could I?

I faltered at the slippery steps leading into the dark. It was November, after all. I might die if I fell in. I tried balancing my foot on the surface and it dropped beneath into the cold nothingness.

Could a woman love a woman for more than a night?

I stepped out and in the morning they say a beggar was running round the Rialto talking about a young man who'd walked across the canal like it was solid.

I'm telling you stories. Trust me.

When we met again I had borrowed an officer's uniform. Or, more precisely, stolen it.

This is what happened.

At the Casino, well after midnight, a soldier had approached me and suggested an unusual wager. If I could beat him at billiards he would make me a present of his purse. He held it up before me. It was round and nicely padded and there must be some of my father's blood in me because I have never been able to resist a purse.

And if I lost? I was to make him a present of my purse. There was no mistaking his meaning.

We played, cheered on by a dozen bored gamblers and, to my surprise, the soldier played well. After a few hours at the Casino nobody plays anything well.

I lost.

We went to his room and he was a man who liked his women face down, arms outstretched like the crucified Christ. He was able and easy and soon fell asleep. He was also about my height. I left him his shirt and boots and took the rest.

She greeted me like an old friend and asked me straight away about the uniform.

"You're not a soldier."

"It's fancy dress."

I began to feel like Sarpi, that Venetian priest and diplomat, who said he never told a lie but didn't tell the truth to everyone. Many times that evening as we ate and drank and played dice I prepared to explain. But my tongue thickened and my heart rose up in self-defence.

"Feet," she said.

"What?"

"Let me stroke your feet."

Sweet Madonna, not my feet.

"I never take off my boots away from home. It's a nervous habit."

"Then take off your shirt instead."

Not my shirt, if I raised my shirt she'd find my breasts.

"In this inhospitable weather it would not be wise. Everyone has catarrh. Think of the fog."

I saw her eyes stray lower. Did she expect my desire to be obvious? What could I allow; my knees?

Instead I leaned forward and began to kiss her neck. She buried my head in her hair and I became her creature. Her smell, my atmosphere, and later when I was alone I cursed my nostrils for breathing the everyday air and emptying my body of her.

As I was leaving she said, "My husband returns tomorrow."

Oh.

As I was leaving she said, "I don't know when I will see you again."

Does she do this often? Does she walk the streets, when her husband goes away, looking for someone like me? Everyone in Venice has their weakness and their vice. Perhaps not only in Venice. Does she invite them to supper and hold them with her eyes and explain, a little sadly, that she can't make love? Perhaps this is her passion. Passion out of passion's obstacles. And me? Every game threatens a wild card. The unpredictable, the out of control. Even with a steady hand and a crystal ball we couldn't rule the world the way we wanted it. There are storms at sea and there are other storms inland. Only the convent windows lock serenely out on both.

I went back to her house and banged on the door. She opened it a little. She looked surprised.

"I'm a woman," I said, lifting up my shirt and risking the catarrh.

She smiled. "I know."

I didn't go home. I stayed.

Sarah Schulman

(b. 1958)

Sarah Schulman, who began writing for the feminist, gay, and left-wing presses in 1980, has become a leading postmodernist lesbian author in recent years and one of the most talented of those who are being identified as the "new queer writers" of the 1990s. Her first novel, *The Sophie Horowitz Story* (1984), about an investigative reporter for a small-circulation feminist newspaper, was already postmodernist in its sense of play and parody, its refusal to hold sacred all the sanctities of lesbian-feminism, its questions about simplistic concepts of identity, and its preference for multiple interpretations of phenomena. Schulman laughs, for example, at the political correctness and habit of trashing within the lesbian-feminist movement by having Sophie describe a group called "Women Against Bad Things," who had "some kind of politics which none of us understood. Whatever we did, they didn't like."

Schulman's subsequent work has continued in the same postmodernist vein. In *Girls, Visions, and Everything* (1986), a novel about a Jewish lesbian who sees herself as an outlaw on the loose in New York City, Schulman often tricks the reader by presenting an ostensible realism, which she quickly undercuts with parody. In *After Delores* (1988), a novel with a lesbian sleuth, she again presents what appears to be realistic, and then destabilizes it by the unexpected. Unlike the usual detective novel, lesbian or otherwise, although the mystery is solved, there is no closure. The lesbian hero is an antihero, whose lonely life or moral stature isn't improved by the successful sleuthing that permits her to catch a male villain.

People in Trouble (1990), which reflects Schulman's concerns as a longtime AIDS activist, is somewhat more realistic than her earlier work, insisting on the importance of queer political action. Nevertheless, it too plays occasionally with surrealism and parody. Her latest novel, *Empathy* (1992), may also be considered postmodern in the ways it examines the complexities and uncertainties of character and events. Schulman often parodies the icons of culture in this novel. For example, she steals from and laughs at Freud by naming her two lesbian lovers Anna O and Dora. Despite Schulman's rejection of political orthodoxy, and in apparent contradiction to her postmodernist detachment, her work never lacks a social consciousness, just as her postfeminism always betrays something of a feminist sensibility.

FURTHER READING: Sarah Schulman, *The Sophie Horowitz Story* (Tallahassee, FL: Naiad, 1984); *Girls, Visions and Everything* (Seattle: Seal Press, 1986); *After Delores* (New York: Dutton, 1988); *Empathy* (New York: Dutton, 1992). Christi Cassidy, "A Conversation with Sarah Schulman," *Visibilities*, 3: 1 (Jan.-Feb. 1989), 8+. Denise Kulp, "Sarah Schulman: 'On the Road to . . . ,'" *off our backs*, 16: 11 (December 1986), 20–1+. Sally Munt, " 'Somewhere Over the Rainbow . . .': Postmodernism and the Fiction of Sarah Schulman," *New Lesbian Criticism*, ed. Sally Munt (New York: Columbia University Press, 1992).

The Penis Story

The night before they sat in their usual spots. Jesse's hair was like torrents of black oil plunging into the sea. Ann watched her, remembering standing in the butcher shop looking at smoked meat, smelling the grease, imagining Jesse's tongue on her labia. She was starving.

"I'm just waiting for a man to rescue me," Jesse said.

"Look, Jess," Ann answered. "Why don't we put a timeline on this thing. Let's say, forty. If no man rescues you by the time you're forty, we'll take it from a different angle. What do you say?"

"I say I'll be in a mental hospital by the time I'm forty."

Jesse was thirty-two. This was a realistic possibility.

"Jesse, if instead of being two women, you and I were a woman and a man, would we be lovers by now?"

"Yes." Jesse had to answer yes because it was so obviously true.

"So what's not there for you in us being two women? Is it something concrete about a man, or is it the idea of a man?"

"I don't think it's anything physical. I think it is the idea of a man. I want to know that my lover is a man. I need to be able to say that."

Ann started to shake and covered her legs with a blanket so it wouldn't be so obvious. She felt like a child. She put her head on Jesse's shoulder feeling weak and ridiculous. Then they kissed. It felt so familiar. They'd been doing that for months. Each knew how the other kissed. Ann felt Jesse's hand on her waist and back and chest. Jesse reached her hand to Ann's bra. She'd done this before too. First tentatively, then more directly, she brushed her hands and face against Ann's breasts. Ann kissed her skin and licked it. She sucked her fingers, knowing those nails would have to be cut if Jesse were to ever put her fingers into Ann's body. She looked at Jesse's skin, at her acne scars and blackheads. She wanted to kiss her a hundred times. Then, as always, Jesse became disturbed, agitated. "I'm nervous again," she said. "Like, *oh no—now I'm going to have to fuck.*"

Suddenly Ann remembered that their sexual life together was a piece of glass. She put on her shirt and went home. This was the middle of the night in New York City.

When Ann awoke the next morning from unsettling dreams, she saw that a new attitude had dawned with the new day. She felt accepting, not proud. She felt ready to face adjustment and compromise. She was ready for change. Even though she was fully awake her eyes had not adjusted to the morning. She reached for glasses but found them inadequate. Then she looked down and saw that she had a penis.

Surprisingly, she didn't panic. Ann's mind, even under normal circumstances, worked differently than the minds of many of those around her. She was able to think three thoughts at the same time, and as a result often suffered from headaches, disconnected conversation, and too many ideas. However, at this moment she only had two thoughts: "What is it going to be like to have a penis?" and "I will never be the same again."

It didn't behave the way most penises do. It rather seemed to be trying to find its own way. It swayed a bit as she walked to the bathroom mirror, careful not to let her legs interfere, feeling off balance, as if she had an itch and couldn't scratch it. She tried to sit back on her hips, for she still had hips, and walk pelvis first, for she still had her pelvis. In fact, everything appeared to be the same except that she had no vagina. Except that she had a prick.

"I am a prick," she said to herself.

The first thing she needed to do was piss and that was fun, standing up seeing it hit the water, but it got all over the toilet seat and she had to clean up the yellow drops.

"I am a woman with a penis and I am still cleaning up piss."

This gave her a sense of historical consistency. Now it was time to get dressed.

She knew immediately she didn't want to hide her penis from the world. Ann had never hidden anything else, no matter how controversial. There was nothing wrong with having a penis. Men had them and now she did too. She wasn't going to let her penis keep her from the rest of humanity. She chose a pair of button-up Levi's and stuffed her penis into her pants where it bulged pretty obviously. Then she put on a t-shirt that showed off her breasts and her muscles and headed toward the F train to Shelley's house to meet her friends for lunch.

By the time Ann finished riding on the F train she had developed a fairly integrated view of her new self. She was a lesbian with a penis. She was not a man with breasts. She was a woman. This was not androgyny, she'd never liked that word. Women had always been whole to Ann, not half of something waiting to be completed.

They sat in Shelley's living room eating lunch. These were her most attentive friends, the ones who knew best how she lived. They sat around joking until Shelley finally asked, "What's that between your legs?"

"That's my penis," Ann said.

"Oh, so now you have a penis."

"I got it this morning. I woke up and it was there."

They didn't think much of Ann's humor usually, so the conversation moved on to other topics. Judith lit a joint. They got high and said funny things, but they did keep coming back to Ann's penis.

"What are you going to do with it?" Shelley asked.

"I don't know."

"If you really have a penis, why don't you show it to us?" Roberta said. She was always provocative.

Ann remained sitting in her chair but unbuttoned her jeans and pulled her penis out of her panties. She had balls too.

"Is that real?"

Roberta came over and put her face in Ann's crotch. She held Ann's penis in her hand. It just lay there.

"Yup, Ann's got a penis all right."

"Did you eat anything strange yesterday?" Judith asked.

"Maybe it's from masturbating," Roberta suggested, but they all knew that couldn't be true.

"Well, Ann, let me know if you need anything, but I have to say I'm glad we're not lovers anymore because I don't think I could handle this." Judith bit her lip.

"I'm sure you'd do fine," Ann replied in her usual charming way.

Ann put on her flaming electronic lipstick. It smudged accidentally, but she liked the effect. This was preparation for the big event. Ann was ready to have sex. Thanks to her lifelong habit of masturbating before she went to sleep, Ann had sufficiently experimented with erections and come. She'd seen enough men do it and knew how to do it for them, so she had no trouble doing it for herself. Sooner or later she would connect with another person. Now was that time. She wore her t-shirt that said, "Just visiting from another planet." Judith had given it to her and giggled, nervously.

The Central Park Ramble used to be a bird and wildlife sanctuary. Because it's hidden, and therefore foreboding, gay men use it to have sex, and that's where Ann wanted to be. Before she had a penis, Ann used to imagine sometimes while making love that she and her girlfriend were two gay men. Now that she had this penis, she felt open to different kinds of people and new ideas, too.

She saw a gay man walking through the park in his little gym suit. He had a nice tan like Ann did and a gold earring like she did too. His t-shirt also had writing on it. It said, "All-American Boy." His ass stuck out like a mating call.

"Hi," she said.

"Hi," he said.

"Do you want to smoke a joint?" she asked very sweetly.

He looked around suspiciously.

"Don't worry, I'm gay too."

"OK honey, why not. There's nothing much happening anyway."

So, they sat down and smoked a couple of joints and laughed and told about the different boyfriends and girlfriends that they had had, and which ones had gone straight and which ones had broken their hearts. Then Ann produced two beers and they drank those and told about the hearts that they had broken. It was hot and pretty in the park.

Ann mustered up all her courage and said.

"I have a cock."

"You look pretty good for a mid-op," he said.

His name was Mike.

"No, I'm not a transsexual. I'm a lesbian with a penis. I know this is unusual, but would you suck my cock?"

Ann had always wanted to say "suck my cock" because it was one thing a lot of people said to her and she never said to anyone. Once she and her friends made little stickers that said "End Violence in the Lives of Women," which they stuck up all over the subway. Many mornings when she was riding to work, Ann would see that different people had written over them "suck my cock." It seemed like an appropriate response given the world in which we all live.

Mike thought this was out of the ordinary, but he prided himself on taking risks. So he decided "what the hell" and went down on her like an expert.

Well, it did feel nice. It didn't feel like floating in hot water, which is what Ann sometimes thought of when a woman made love to her well with her mouth, but it did feel good. She started thinking about other things. She tried the two-gay-men image but it had lost its magic. Then she remembered Jesse. She saw them together in Jesse's apartment. Each in their usual spots.

"What's the matter, Annie? Your face is giving you away."

"This is such a bastardized version of how I'd like to be relating to you right now."

"Well," said Jesse. "What would it be like?"

"Oh, I'd be sitting here and you'd say 'I'm ready' and I'd say, 'ready for what?' and you'd say, 'I'm ready to make love to you Annie.' Then I'd say 'Why don't we go to your bed?' and we would."

"Yes," Jesse said. "I would smell your smell Annie. I would put my arms on your neck and down over your breasts. I would unbutton your shirt, Annie, and pull it off your shoulders. I would run my fingers down your neck and over your nipples. I would lick your breasts, Annie, I would run my tongue down your neck to your breasts."

Ann could feel Jess's wild hair like the ocean passing over her chest. Jesse's mouth was on her nipples licking, her soft face against Ann's skin.

She was licking, licking then sucking harder and faster until Jesse clung to her breasts harder and harder.

"You taste just like my wife," Mike said after she came.

"What?"

Ann's heart was beating. The ocean was crashing in her ears.

"I said, you taste just like my wife, when you come I mean. You don't come sperm, you know, you come women's cum, like pussy."

"Oh thank God."

Ann was relieved.

Another morning Ann woke up and her fingers were all sticky. It was still dark. First she thought she'd had a wet dream, but when she turned on her reading lamp she saw blood all over her hands. Instinctively she put her fingers in her mouth. It was gooey, full of membrane and salty. It was her period. She guessed it had no other place to come out, so it flowed from under her fingernails. She spent the next three and a half days wearing black plastic gloves.

The feeling of her uterine lining coming out of her hands gave Ann some hope. After living with her penis for nearly a month, she was beginning to experience it as a loss, not an acquisition. She was grieving for her former self.

One interesting item was that Ann was suddenly in enormous sexual demand. More women than had ever wanted to make love with her wanted her now. But most of them didn't want anyone to know, so she said no.

There was one woman, though, to whom she said yes. Her name was Muriel. Muriel dreamed that she made love to a woman with a penis and it was called "glancing." So she looked high and low until she found Ann, who she believed had a rare and powerful gift and should be honored.

Ann and Muriel became lovers and Ann learned many new things from this experience. She realized that when you meet a woman, you see the parts of her body that she's going to use to make love to you. You see her mouth and teeth and tongue and fingers. You see her fingers comb her hair, play the piano, wash the dishes, write a letter. You watch her mouth eat and whistle and quiver and scream and kiss. When she makes love to you she brings all this movement and activity with her into your body.

Ann liked this. With her penis, however, it wasn't the same. She had to keep it private. She also didn't like fucking Muriel very much. She missed the old way. Putting her penis into a woman's body was so confusing. Ann knew it wasn't making love "to" Muriel and it certainly wasn't Muriel making love "to" her. It was more like making love "from" Muriel and that just didn't sit right.

One day Ann told Muriel about Jesse.

"I give her everything within my capacity to give and she gives me everything within her capacity to give—only my capacity is larger than hers."

In response Muriel took her to the Museum of Modern Art and pointed to a sculpture by Louise Bourgeois. Ann spent most of the afternoon in front of the large piece, an angry ocean of black penises which rose and crashed, carrying a little box house. The piece was called "Womanhouse." She looked at the penises, their little round heads, their black metal trunks, how they moved together to make waves, and she understood something completely new.

They got together the next day in a bar. As soon as she walked in Ann felt nauseous. She couldn't eat a thing. The smell of grease from Jesse's chicken dinner came in waves to Ann's side of the table. She kept her nose in the beer to cut the stench.

"You're dividing me against myself, Jesse."

Jesse offered her some chicken.

"No thanks, I really don't want any. Look, I can't keep making out with you on a couch because that's as far as you're willing to go before this turns into a lesbian relationship. It makes me feel like nothing."

Ann didn't mention that she had a penis.

"Annie, I can't say I don't love being physical with you because it wouldn't be true."

"I know."

"I feel something ferocious when I smell you. I love kissing you. That's why it's got to stop. I didn't realize when I started this that I was going to want it so much."

"Why is that a problem?"

"Why is that a problem? Why is that a problem?"

Jesse was licking the skin off the bone with her fingers. Slivers of meat stuck out of her long fingernails. She didn't know the answer.

"Jesse, what would happen if someone offered you a woman with a penis?"

Jesse wasn't surprised by this question, because Ann often raised issues from new and interesting perspectives.

"It wouldn't surprise me."

"Why not?"

"Well, Annie, I've never told you this before, actually it's just a secret between me and my therapist, but I feel as though I do have a penis. It's a theoretical penis, in my head. I've got a penis in my head and it's all mine."

"You're right," Ann said. "You do have a penis in your head because you have been totally mind-fucked. You've got an eight-inch cock between your ears."

With that she left the restaurant and left Jesse with the bill.

Soon Ann decided she wanted her clitoris back and she started to consult with doctors who did transsexual surgery. Since Ann had seen, tasted, and touched many clitorises in her short but full life, she knew that each one had its own unique way and wanted her very own cunt back just the way it had always been. So, she called together every woman who had ever made love to her. There was her French professor from college, her brother's girlfriend, her cousin Clarisse, her best friend from high school, Judith, Claudette, Kate, and Jane and assorted others. They all came to a big party at Shelley's house where they got high and drank beer and ate lasagna and when they all felt fine, Ann put a giant piece of white paper on the wall. By committee, they reconstructed Ann's cunt from memory. Some people had been more attentive than others, but they were all willing to make the effort. After a few hours and a couple of arguments as to the exact color tone and how many wrinkles on the left side, they finished the blueprints. "Pussy prints," the figure skater from Iowa City called them.

The following Monday Ann went in for surgery reflecting on the time she had spent with her penis. When you're different, you really have to think about things. You have a lot of information about how the mainstream lives, but they don't know much about you. They also don't know that they don't know, which they don't. Ann wanted one thing, to be a whole woman again. She never wanted to be mutilated by being cut off from herself and she knew that would be a hard thing to overcome, but Ann was willing to try.

Marilyn Hacker
(b. 1942)

Marilyn Hacker's *Presentation Piece* won the National Book Award for poetry in 1975. Hacker plays with all manner of traditional poetic forms, including the sestina, rondeau, and sonnet, presenting them in modern urban idiom. In terms of technique, she is one of the most polished of contemporary lesbian poets. *Love, Death and the Changing of the Seasons* (1986), from which the following poems were taken, is a book-length sonnet sequence, a novel in verse in its effect, that deals with the birth, flowering, and death of a lesbian love affair between a young woman and the much older speaker.

Love, Death and the Changing of the Seasons has been compared by critics to Adrienne Rich's "Twenty-One Love Poems," but the differences between the two works can serve perhaps as an illustration of the significantly different eras in which they were written. Rich's 1970s sequence places her lesbian love relationship, both its fulfillment and its defeat, in a political context. Hacker's lovers of the mid-1980s exist largely outside of politics (though Hacker was the editor of the feminist literary magazine *13th Moon* from 1982 to 1986). Her focus in these poems is on romance, intense sexual desire, and what has been construed in modern times as a universal (and hence apolitical) fact that shared sexual excitement generally does not last forever.

FURTHER READING: Marilyn Hacker, *Taking Notice* (New York: Knopf, 1981); *Love, Death and the Changing of the Seasons* (New York: Arbor House, 1986). Karla Hammond, "An Interview With Marilyn Hacker," *Frontiers*, 5: 3 (Fall 1980), 22–27.

RUNAWAYS CAFÉ I

You hailed a cab outside the nondescript
yuppie bar on Lexington to go
downtown. Hug; hug: this time I brushed my lips
just across yours, and fire down below
in February flared. O bless and curse
what's waking up no wiser than it was.
I will not go to bed with you because
I want to very much. If that's perverse,
there are, you'll guess, perversions I'd prefer:
fill the lacunae in: one; two; three; four . . .
I did, cab gone. While my late bus didn't come,
desire ticked over like a metronome.
For you, someone was waiting up at home.
For me, I might dare more if someone were.

FEBRUARY 25

Dear Bill, I dawdled answering your letter.
My punishment—the postal rates were raised.
The mail piled on this table has me fazed.
I think of it as clearing up the clutter.

There's somebody I like better and better
—she's someone else's lover, though; not mine.
She hides her blushes in her leonine
hair, that was more like tinsel than like butter
when I ruffled it—the feminine
of *avuncular*. She's twenty-five,
but age is not the muddle of the matter
whose damp wings are unfolding now, alive
out of the chrysalis that I felt shatter
when I kissed her till heat split my spine.

Well, damn, it's a relief to be a slut
after such lengths of "Man delights not me,
nor woman neither," that I honestly
wondered if I'd outgrown it. Chocolate
or wine, a cashmere scarf, a cigarette,
had more to do with sensuality
than what's between my belly and my butt
that yearns toward you now unabashedly.
I'd love to grip your head between my thighs
while yours tense toward your moment on my ears,
but I'll still be thankful for this surprise
if things turn out entirely otherwise,
and we're bar buddies who, in a few years,
will giggle about this after two beers.

FUTURE CONDITIONAL

After the supper dishes, let us start
where we left off, my knees between your knees,
half in the window seat. O let me, please,
hands in your hair, drink in your mouth. Sweetheart,
your body is a text I need the art
to be constructed by. I halfway kneel
to your lap, propped by your thighs, and feel
burning my hand, your privacy, your part
armor underwear. This time I'll loose
each button from its hole; I'll find the hook,
release promised abundance to this want,
while your hands, please, here and here, exigent
and certain, open this; it is, this book,
made for your hands to read, your mouth to use.

SATURDAY MORNING

While you sleep off the brandy, little one,
my hand could find its way back to the place
it knows so well, now. Even with your face
turned away from me, sleeping in till noon,
you move right through me. After we were done
talking (thence the brandy) until four
AM, you, in the dark, played three songs for
me while I dozed—so tired I couldn't come
when you'd tried for me. So you sat on the floor
with the guitar, beside me, troubadour,
and then, naked, you woke me to you, brought me
down on your mouth, brought it down and caught me
in the gray dawn, whose sunburst was your name
like brandy in my mouth as I came and came.

BLOOMINGDALE'S I

"If I weren't working, I'd sleep next to you
an hour or two more. Then we'd get the car
and drive a while, out of Manhattan, to
a quiet Bloomingdale's in Westchester.
If we saw anything we liked, we'd buy it!
We'd try things on, first, in one cubicle.
You'd need to make an effort to be quiet
when I knelt down and got my fingers full
of you, my mouth on you, against the wall.
You'd pull my hair. You'd have to bite your tongue.
I'd hold your ass so that you wouldn't fall.
Later, we'd take a peaceful walk along
the aisles, letting our hands touch every chance
they got, among the bras and underpants."

Pat Califia
(b. 1954)

Pat Califia's writing has stirred controversy in the lesbian-feminist community since the late 1970s when her essays propounding lesbian sadomasochistic sexual acts began appearing in *The Advocate,* a newspaper read primarily by gay men. Her 1981 sex manual for lesbians, *Sapphistry,* was also a center of debate in the lesbian sex wars that became heated in the mid-1980s. Sexual radicals, led by Califia and others, defended a more aggressive and adventurous lesbian sexuality against lesbian-feminists who were concerned that the tools of such sexuality (for example, pornography and role playing) encouraged the victimization of women no less than did men's aggressive sexual behavior. Califia's "in your face" volume of lesbian sex stories, *Macho Sluts* (1988), fueled the debates once again by presenting (as the title suggests) the most politically incorrect images of lesbian sexuality Califia could devise, such as mother-daughter incest, group sex, sadomasochism, and lesbian–gay male sex.

"The Finishing School," from *Macho Sluts,* is interesting, however, not only as an example of Califia's confrontational response to what she sees as lesbian-feminist pieties. It also demonstrates how some contemporary lesbian writers have attempted to reclaim the genres of pornography and Decadent literature for the delectation of the lesbian reader rather than the male voyeur. Califia appropriates all the staples of those genres, such as intergenerational exploitation, victimization of the innocent, whips and leather and cruelty. But she reverses the implicit or explicit moral tone usually connected with such a presentation by showing that neither exploitation, victimization, innocence, nor cruelty are what they seem, and whips and leather are only props for an exchange of pleasure between the equally gratified sexual sadist and sexual masochist.

FURTHER READING: Pat Califia, *Macho Sluts* (Boston: Alyson, 1988); "We Know What We Want: Lesbian Literature Meets the Sexual Revolution," *Sinister Wisdom,* 1: 2 (Fall 1976), 67–72; "Feminism and Sadomasochism," *Heresies,* 3: 4 (1981), 30–34. Rose Collis, "Pleasure Is a Risky Business," *Spare Rib,* 191 (June 1988), 10–12. Irene Diamond and Lee Quinby, "The Feminist Sexuality Debates," *Signs,* 10: 1 (Autumn 1984), 119–25. Jyanni Steffensen, "Things Change . . . And About Time Too: A Critical Review of Women's Erotic Writing," *Hecate,* 15: 2 (1989), 26–33.

The Finishing School

It was dusk, but the heavy drapes had not yet been drawn. Outside, the late afternoon breeze had freshened into a gusty wind which was marching up and down the driveway, interrogating the two rows of young poplars on either side of the drive. The slender, lacy trees betrayed their agitation and bowed in submission again, and again.

Inside, the woman, Berenice, was seated on a brown (mocha, actually) velvet sofa. Despite the fire leaping from log to log in the grate, she tucked her feet under an embroidered cushion and drew her red satin dressing gown a little tighter to her breast. She was in her early forties, a tall woman with a fine head of short and curly dark hair. When in motion, she gave an impression of grace and strength. In repose, she seemed remarkably self-possessed and alert. One could not imagine anything that would surprise or offend her. A silver tea service on a small mahogany table emitted steam and the smell of chocolate and spice. Berenice inhaled this friendly odor and smiled at the stirring spectacle the windows presented. The girl, Clarissa, was seated on the floor. Everything was in its place. Her universe was in order; complete.

She put a hand out and stroked the fair head, which had been bowed in misery for the past half-hour. A little, tear-streaked face soon turned to stare up at her. She laid a warning finger on those sweet full lips, a ripe cherry.

"Don't," she instructed. The girl bowed her head again, and her shoulders trembled. The woman resumed stroking her hair, lifting handfuls of the champagne tresses and slowly releasing them. Her little beauty was wearing a black velvet corset, cinched just tight enough to set off her small waist and plump up the perfect round cheeks of her behind. It also held her breasts, which were just beginning to bud, up and together. The nipples were so tiny and pink that they were barely visible. A pair of black silk stockings encased her coltish legs, trimmed with lace garters with black rosettes, and disappeared into a pair of black velvet high-heeled shoes. Each shoe had a tiny silver ring in the back, just above the heel. A fine silver chain ran from ring to ring, constraining the length of steps Clarissa could take and the positions she could arrange her limbs in when at rest. In addition, a silver chain was looped in a figure-eight about each instep and heel, securing the shoes to Clarissa's feet.

Berenice tightened her grip on the little one's hair and drew her head back. Her fingertips traced the course of a single tear down the cheek, the throat, the heaving bosom. "My sweet," she said tenderly, "you will spoil your complexion and give yourself a headache. Wouldn't you like your cocoa now?"

Clarissa's head was firmly held. She stared into wise, brown eyes. They were calm, loving, and quite merciless. She bit her lower lip and managed a timid, "Yes, please."

"I'll pour tonight," the woman said, and slid off the couch. She tipped a small amount of brandy from a crystal decanter into one of the cups, then added cocoa and stirred. For herself she poured a balloon of the same brandy. "This will do you good," she said briskly. Clarissa took the cup with both hands.

Berenice put her brandy on a side table and went over to the window to close the drapes. She added another log to the fire. It caught immediately, so that the room brightened and grew quite warm. Her robe had no sash. As she moved about, it fell open from time to time and displayed the full lines of her figure. Her skin was slightly brown, her hips generous, the whole effect sensuous and maternal. Well aware of Clarissa's attention, she came back to the sofa and curled herself up as before.

They sat in companionable silence, sipping and watching the fire. Some color returned to Clarissa's face. She let go one shuddering sigh and then carefully set her cup and saucer on a low table. Turning, she put her hands beneath the cushion and sought out her mistress's supple feet.

"May I warm them?" she pleaded.

"If it will comfort you."

Clarissa chafed them tenderly between her soft hands, held them to her breast, then gently laid them down and began to kiss the toes and insteps. Suddenly her misery returned in full force, and she wept over those beautiful feet, kissing the tears away and drying them with her hair. "Oh! I'm sorry," she hiccupped, "but—but—"

Strong arms gathered her in, the red satin robe opened to receive her, and she was enthroned in her lover's lap. "I'm not sorry to learn that you will miss me," Berenice said. That wonderful husky voice!

Clarissa thought, how much I love her, and sobbed, "Oh, I shall— ever so!"

". . . as long as this outburst is no sign that you intend to disobey me."

"No! No, I'll do whatever you want. Only let me come back. I know you won't have me if I'm bad. But if I am good, you will let me come back, won't you?"

"Of course, silly girl. This is your home. It's only six months of school, not a lifetime sentence of permanent exile. If you tried to run away, I would seek you with all my powers and bring you back, even from the ends of the earth."

Clarissa snuggled between her breasts. In their shelter, she was almost reassured. "Six months isn't such a long time," she murmured, trying to sound grown-up.

"Are you sleepy?"

"No."

"Fetch my brandy. Elise is doing your packing. We'll spend your last night home together, in the discipline chamber."

Clarissa shivered, then slipped off her lap and took up the snifter of brandy. The lamplight shone through the liqueur so that a small amber circle floated, shimmering, below her clavicle. Berenice remained seated, enjoying the sight of the tiny steps permitted by the silver chain (which was thin enough to break) and the high-heeled shoes. She was proud of this fair child, and determined not to spoil her by slacking in correction or stinting in affection. Seeing that Clarissa was prepared to mince after her, she strode out of the room and down the hall. The discipline chamber, that shrine to domestic tranquillity, was only a short distance away.

Berenice surveyed the room from the threshold. Everything was in good order. Elise, the maid, was meticulous. She reminded herself that while Clarissa was away at finishing school, she would have more time to spend with Elise. Her maid was too well trained to complain about neglect, but the performance of any loved one will slacken and become slovenly if they are left unsupervised too long. Clarissa's absence would not be intolerable, she told herself firmly. They must all be separated if Clarissa was to become a grown woman. The school was the next logical step in the development of her sexuality. Elise would be very entertaining, she promised herself. There were certain things one could not demand of a mere child. Perhaps it was time to throw another party for their friends. Elise had been kept so busy at the last one. Quite the belle of the ball.

The chamber was paneled with dark wood. One wall and the ceiling contained large mirrors. A Persian carpet of intricate design, brightly and sensuously colored, covered the floor. In the middle of the room was a device that resembled a large sawhorse. The top bar and legs were well padded and covered with black leather. There were rings at the head and foot and along the legs. One pair of legs had leather stirrups nailed to it about a foot and a half from the floor. In one corner of the room, a complicated arrangement of ropes and pulleys dangled from the ceiling. A set of stocks had been pushed against one wall, next to a huge, lacquered chest. In the corner behind the door, an ivory-and-gold umbrella stand held an assortment of canes, switches, riding crops, dog whips, and bundles of birch twigs. Berenice straightened these as one would a flower arrangement, reminding herself of what was there. Then she went to the carved Chinese chest and removed four silver bracelets, four short pieces of medium-weight silver chain, and several finely crafted silver locks. These she arranged on the lid of the chest, then fished in her robe for the necklace she always wore, and reassured herself that the key to the locks was on her person.

Clarissa arrived with the brandy. She knelt and offered it, head turned to the side, eyes cast down. Her mournful, pouting mouth and red eyes gave the traditional pose a dash of extra delight. Berenice left her in that position while she stoked the fire, then came and took the snifter from her. "Up on the horse," she ordered.

Clarissa swung onto its back with the skill of a gymnast—which, indeed, she was. Berenice removed the jewelry chain that held her feet together, but left her shoes on. There was a bracelet for each wrist and ankle.

These were quickly locked in place. By caresses, she directed Clarissa to stretch out along the length of the beam, belly down, arms over her head, legs spread, feet in the stirrups. Deftly, efficiently, Clarissa was chained to the horse. As soon as the last lock clicked into place, she began to moan and twist on the beam.

"I'm afraid," she said. "But I want to please you!"

"We will see which frightens you more, the pain or my displeasure."

Berenice approached her trembling, girlish victim, hiding something in her hand. "Close your eyes," she ordered. Despite whimpers and some insubordinate squirming, she blindfolded Clarissa with a mink-lined sleeping shade. She had already selected her first instrument of chastisement: a carriage whip with a brand new cracker. It made a good deal more noise than anything else. In her other hand, she took up an ostrich plume. A rabbit's fur glove and a currying comb were also nearby, ready for her use. By alternating all of these devices, causing both pain and pleasure with each of them, she soon had Clarissa relaxed and completely vulnerable, jumping and moaning, her skin sensitized, her nerves trained to soothe any hurt or discomfort and blend it quickly into her growing sexual arousal. Even when correcting serious misdeeds, Berenice was not brutal. She loved helplessness, she craved the sight of a female body abandoning all decency and self-control. These things are not granted save in loving trust. Dominance is not created without complicity. A well-trained slave is hopelessly in love with her mistress and will weep for days if a fault is not reprimanded. If no punishment is forthcoming, she will ask for it—even administer it herself as proof of her devotion.

Berenice stroked the inside of Clarissa's thighs with the fur glove and allowed her to feel the first few contractions of an orgasm. Then she withdrew and removed the blindfold. Clarissa protested vociferously. "There's no pleasing you," Berenice laughed. "You don't like it on and you don't like it off. Perverse little monkey." She fondled her. "Pretty thing. I'll do as I like with you. Won't I? Won't I?" And she forced eloquent, clarion agreement from her chained virgin slave. Her caresses wandered near the most sensitive areas of the poor child's body. "Can you guess what I want to do? Hmm? My almost-grown-up girl? Something we don't do very often, you and I." Her fingers trespassed, tempted, and retreated. "A little serious flagellation, my pet. A really good, thorough beating. Can you, for me?"

"Oh—please," panted Clarissa.

Berenice selected a short cat from the umbrella stand and began to lightly switch Clarissa's shoulders and backside. The lashes flicked her tender thighs as well, leaving red stripes that quickly faded. She alternated the blows with moments of loving praise and encouragement, during which time she would tickle Clarissa between the legs with the whip handle. She soon had her writhing upon the horse, her behind plunging up and down like a lusty mare. The girl gasped for breath and clenched and unclenched her tiny hands.

"You're blushing," Berenice said. She ran a cool hand over Clarissa's hindquarters. She struck again, harder. "Hush. This is nothing. Hush. Nothing." She walked to the head of the horse and took possession of the bound girl's mouth. "More? Yes. More." She resumed her position at the foot of the horse and landed several well-aimed blows. "Now you can go ahead. Sing. I like to hear you. God, I'd love to flog the skin off your dimpled, pink behind." The cat whished through the air, creating a small breeze that stirred Berenice's curls.

Clarissa snorted and snuffled. Her hair hung in wet strands, and her body was shimmering with perspiration. A streak of more viscous moisture stained the division of her pubic fleece. "I can take more," she said as Berenice appeared by her head.

Berenice smiled. "So sweet," she murmured. "You are so sweet."

"Kiss?"

"Oh, yes."

Berenice's penetrating tongue was so strong! Clarissa forgot herself and began to nip and swallow at it. Berenice laughed at her and withdrew.

"Oh—more!" Clarissa wailed. "I'm on fire from head to toe. Don't leave me!"

"Naughty girl," said Berenice. "Salacious little slut. Biting at my mouth like a common streetwalker. We must punish the baggage, or she will go from bad to worse. Isn't that so, my darling?"

Clarissa fought back her agreement, and remained silent.

"Oh? She wants to argue with her betters. Impudence on top of a sensuous disposition. This is a frightful combination. Tell me this, rebellious miss, did you or did you not nip at me? Eh?"

"I—I did," Clarissa confessed.

"And was it out of pain or fright?"

"Nooo."

"Then we must conclude that you were overwhelmed by carnal impulses. And you know that cannot be tolerated."

"Yes," Clarissa admitted, defeated. "I know."

"Well, then. Let's have no more vain attempts to avoid just punishment. Ooh, just you wait till I get my hands on you. Baggage! Tart!" While calling the wrath of heaven down upon her disobedient child, Berenice gave her a sip or two of brandy, then she visited the lacquer chest again. She glanced quickly over the tray that perched on top of its other contents, a tray that originally had contained velvet boxes full of strands of pearls, earrings, diamond brooches, and the like. Now it held another sort of jewelry. She selected one of the trinkets, diabolical miniatures that winked at her. Then she took it over to Clarissa, for her inspection. "My grandmother brought these back from the Orient," she said. "She used them to fasten her opera cape. Aren't they pretty?" She showed Clarissa a pair of silver clasps, each in the form of a dragon whose jaw moved to grip the edge of a cloak . . . or whatever was placed in its rapacious mouth. The clasps were connected by a few inches of chain.

The beam was so narrow that Clarissa's breasts peeked out on either side of it. Berenice petted them, making the little girl so lascivious that she thought she must go mad if she were not granted some reprieve. A pinch on each nipple only increased her need. "You are so cruel," she wept.

Berenice twisted the nearest nipple. "Mind your tongue," she said, and pressed the cold, grinning dragon against her soft skin. "Do you know what I'm going to do with this?" she asked. "Have you already guessed?"

"No," Clarissa lied.

Berenice opened one of the clamps, pulled slightly on Clarissa's nipple, and left the mythical beast hanging from her breast. In another moment, its twin was swinging from the other breast. The chain was so short that it almost made her nipples touch.

Clarissa sounded as if she were crying, but no tears were coming from her eyes, and she was attempting to rub her female parts against the beam. The stiffness of her corset prevented her from achieving full freedom of movement, and the slight contact she was able to achieve with the leather only titillated her further.

Berenice went to the foot of the beam and petted her again, spreading her love dew from the clitoris up to the perineum, anointing each side of the inner lips, even rubbing it on her tightest, smallest hole. Then she bent down and blew on the moisture, and Clarissa groaned, "I feel as if I'm nothing but wetness, nothing but the thing between my legs. What are you going to do to me?"

"What does it matter to you?"

"It doesn't—only don't leave me—please take me, use me—oh!" she cried as Berenice once again spread the thick juices, smeared them onto her thighs and between the cheeks of her behind, and expelled her hot breath on the inflamed, liquid parts.

When Clarissa was quite incoherent, Berenice selected her third and final weapon: a long, flexible, yellow cane. Before beginning, she administered more brandy and a few sharp tugs on the grinning dragons.

Thus far, she had inflicted moderate pain and reddened the skin until it was warm and slightly swollen to the touch, but she had not bruised it. She was not in the habit of marking Clarissa, preferring her skin smooth and unblemished. Clarissa coveted the welts on Elise's body and often reproached Berenice for withholding them. Tonight, she informed her young charge, she would leave her with visible tokens of the whipping.

"I have to give you enough to last six months. Remember that, if you think you've had enough. Six long, lonely months." Though she seriously doubted Clarissa would go without comfort, company, or chastisement at this particular school. Sternly, she repressed a pang of jealousy. She had kept Clarissa all to herself for years. The love between them was genuine, but might not survive her adolescence. Even this sweet submission might fade and something hostile, domineering, or indifferent grow up in its place.

Clarissa was waiting patiently for her to resume talking or begin the caning. Berenice collected herself, and returned to the task at hand. She must think of nothing else. No scattered concentration could be allowed to make her hand waver.

"The marks will move up your legs from the back of the knee to the top of your hips. They will be evenly spaced and parallel to each other. You will not move."

Berenice's voice was calm and deadly. Clarissa froze. Training exercises performed in previous sessions had convinced her that, when explicitly ordered not to move, she had best not stir even one-eighth of one inch.

A few seconds to allow tension to build, to gather and slow her breathing, to take the most careful aim—then—swick! swick! swick! Each stripe was awful. Berenice alternated sides so that each thigh would match. She paused before marking Clarissa's behind, to give them both a chance to take courage. Then she struck out like a tigress and left her with a perfect row of weals from the tender roll of baby fat just beneath the buttock to the thin, tightly stretched skin at the tip of her tailbone.

Clarissa babbled pleas for forgiveness and release. Berenice fingered her lightly, evoking a pitiful moan. She repeated her caress, more insistently, and Clarissa's whole body begged for more. "Please go into me," Clarissa cried. "Take my maidenhead. I don't want to give it to anyone else but you, Mother. Elise says she loves having you inside her, more than anything. I can't stand it when you won't give me what you give her. Please! Please!"

Berenice frowned. "You're jealous," she said. "I find that very unattractive. Do you think you can coerce me into anything? Hmm?" She tickled her pudenda, applied light pressure over her hymen, but would not enter. Then she returned to Clarissa's pink pearl and took her to the brink of orgasm. "Apologize," she said through gritted teeth. "And you'd better make me believe it, or I'll deny you satisfaction and send you to school in a chastity belt!"

Their voices raised to shouts, a disjointed cacophony of curses and humiliating confessions, they urged each other on. "I'm nothing," Clarissa cried in ecstasy. "I deserve nothing but the most brutal and rigorous punishment. I beg your forgiveness, your clemency, your correction. I plead for the opportunity to expunge my guilt, to redress my failing. Oh—I am sorry, sorry, sorry, sorry!"

"Ah, yes, that. Will a little more of this do it? It usually does," spat Berenice. "Yes, my little abused angel. Come to me. You will come to me. Now. Yes, now."

The chains and the horse protested as Clarissa flung her body from side to side and drenched Berenice's hand with profuse evidence of her pleasure. Then she was deathly still. Berenice moved to her head and petted her as one would a frightened animal. "There, there," she said. Clarissa lifted her head. Her eyes were overflowing. "Am I still here?" she whispered. "Oh, thank you, dearest Mother. Please don't leave me. Don't ever stop loving me."

"Hush, darling. I'm going to take you down." As she plied her key among the tiny locks, Berenice instructed Clarissa on the behavior that would be expected of her at the school. "You must show your headmistress and teachers the same respect and cheerful obedience that you give me. I'll read your reports every month," she concluded, working on the chains that locked the spike heels onto Clarissa's feet. "If they are satisfactory, when you return I will deflower you, if that is your wish and your maidenhead is still intact."

"It will be," Clarissa said. "I pro—"

"Hush. Don't promise me anything. You're too young to vow constancy. Wait until you've met the headmistress of Hightowers, then see if you bring your heart back to me in one piece—let alone your little oyster, my love."

Clarissa could barely comprehend the woe and distress in that bitter speech. Before she could compose a reassuring reply, Berenice gathered her limp body up in her arms, kicked the door open, and called down the hallway, "Elise! Draw a bath for two. Lay out plenty of towels and the birching ointment. I want a tray of cordials and a cold supper laid out in my room. Then you may retire for the night."

"Yes, madam," was the civil reply that floated back to her. The sound of running water came faintly from the other side of the house—Elise was adding boiling water to the tub she had already filled. Berenice took a fresh grip on Clarissa, who was patting her face and murmuring endearments in French, and carried her away from the room. Elise would clean up. Reliable, invaluable Elise!

By the time they arrived, the bath was prepared. Fresh, snowy towels were heaped on a little cart along with an open jar of ointment, two cakes of fragrant soap, and a saucer on which chilled segments of tangerine had been arranged. Beside the saucer was a crystal pitcher of ice water and two cut glass tumblers. The tub—large, round, deep enough to stand in—was full to the brim and steaming. On the surface of the water floated a single gardenia.

Berenice eased Clarissa down, unlaced and removed the corset, then helped her climb into the tub. The little girl winced when the hot water made contact with her bottom, then an expression of happy pride lit up her face. "You marked me!" she exclaimed. "I won't be able to sit down on the train tomorrow."

"You may not," Berenice said ruefully, hanging her robe on a bronze hook, "but I couldn't resist your plump little hot cross buns. Let's relax and refresh ourselves."

She climbed into the tub beside Clarissa. There were marble shelves inside the tub at the right height for them to sit down and still have their shoulders covered by the lovely hot water. While they soaked, they fed each other slices of tangerine and took tiny sips of the cold water. Clarissa recovered quickly, and was the first out of the tub. She dried herself, then held out a thick towel to receive Berenice. She dried her mistress carefully, daring to kiss her shoulders and the place between her breasts. She brushed against the older woman, hugged her tight, and whispered, "Will you take me into your bed tonight?"

Berenice considered this request. She felt a certain lassitude, the cynical melancholy that overcame her when she was exhausted. Then she contemplated Clarissa's enthusiasm, her fresh face, her hope and affection, and could not bear to disappoint her. Perhaps the maraschino cherry mouth and the dove-like hands could arouse her interest and restore her contentment.

But they could not go like this, like a pair of simple-minded, medieval shepherdesses slipping hand-in-hand into the nearest patch of willows. She seized Clarissa by the hair and dragged her closer, until the tips of her toes barely touched the thick white carpet. "Oh, yes," she threatened. "I'll take you into my bed tonight. And you won't get any sleep at all—not a wink." Forgetting her robe (but not the birching ointment), she hauled Clarissa out of the bathroom and pushed her toward the stairs. "Let's see what your gratitude is worth," she sneered.

They got as far as the landing before Clarissa broke away, sank to her knees, and buried her face between Berenice's thighs. From the bottom of the stairs, Elise (on her way to tidy up the disciplinary chamber) caught a glimpse of the beautiful pose. She smiled wistfully, shook out her feather duster, and went in solitary pursuit of her domestic duties.

Berenice did not quite keep her word. She fell asleep an hour before dawn. Clarissa watched the first light of day suffuse the room, and contemplated this small betrayal of her love. Her eyes seemed to be full of fine sand. Invisible wrinkles in the bedclothes plagued her, and she was afraid her backside would hurt in an ugly way if she thought too much about it. It was odd, how little it took to satisfy Berenice's lust once the whipping or other punishment was over. She, Clarissa, could not say, "Remember you will be six months without me. Surely you need a little more of me to last those six long months." She wore two dozen welts, some of which were bleeding, but she had not dared leave a love-bite in the hollow of her lover's shoulder. Clarissa could not swallow her indignation. It left a dry lump in her throat. She had tried to prolong the sweetness, reaching for Berenice's breasts with her lips and hands, but Berenice had pushed her down between her thighs, relegating her to genital service, withholding her breasts. Even then, Clarissa had teased and toyed with her, postponing the particular tongue-flickers that would bring her mistress to the peak of pleasure. But Berenice had grown angry with her and threatened to bring herself to climax if Clarissa did not give immediate satisfaction. Now she could only sigh and twist the sheet in her hands and try to fend off the miserable thought of leaving home. She could not even find a trace of Berenice's musk on her fingertips or beneath her tongue.

"Be still," Berenice ordered her. Her voice was surprisingly clear for someone who had just been awakened. Clarissa froze, appalled at herself. Berenice drew her closer, put one arm beneath her shoulder, and used her other hand to trap Clarissa's wrists. It was not long before both of them slumbered, after that.

But it seemed to Clarissa that this deep peace lasted only a few moments before Elise reached under the covers, scooped her up, and took her away from Berenice's side.

"I'm to get you dressed and ready for the train," Elise explained in a whisper, putting her down so she could close the bedroom door.

"But Elise—"

"Hush, child. The mistress isn't coming to see you off. She said so herself. I'm to see you packed and on your way. Your aunt will be motoring up for you shortly. Her niece will be going to school with you."

Clarissa nodded, dumb with shock. Elise sighed in sympathy. "I'll make you strawberry waffles," she said. "There's even whipped cream. And you can have coffee this morning, since you were up so late." She took Clarissa by the hand and led her toward the kitchen. "Do you want to wash up and dress first? I've already packed your bags."

"Would you mind if I just ran around this way for a little while? I'll wash my hands and face at the kitchen tap."

"Well—it's a fine, warm day. No harm in it I suppose. Let's go, then. You and I don't often have the morning to ourselves."

Clarissa brightened. "Oh, Elise," she said, flinging her arms around the maid's neck, "you are so good to me."

They embraced. Then Elise drew her down the stairs and into the sunny kitchen. Strings of garlic and peppers hung from the rafters. There was the big, cast-iron, wood-burning stove, the huge white sink with its brass taps, the shelves of glass mixing bowls (each a different color), the racks of herbs and measuring cups and knives—all the magic implements of the chef's art.

"She did you with quite a heavy hand," Elise said enviously.

"Ooh!" Clarissa squealed. "Does it show?"

"Look in the mirror by the china closet. Here, climb up on this chair. See?" Elise's fingers traced the perfectly even stripes. The center of each weal was raised a little.

"How will I ever sit down?" Clarissa gloated, sweeping strands of pale hair over her shoulder so she could get a better look.

"I'll give you my traveling pillow. People will think you want to raise yourself up enough to see out the window. When Berenice gave it to me, Mamma praised her lavishly for her sisterly concern. She would have fainted if she had lifted my skirt and discovered what I was sitting on. It's nice to keep something like that in the family. Maybe someday you can pass the pillow on to your little girl."

Bored with this genealogical sentimentality, Clarissa was smacking her own behind and wincing at the sensations. "Are these fine marks, Elise?" she asked, getting the conversation back into more interesting channels.

"They look as deep and even as any I've received from her hands," Elise said, catering to the youngster's vanity. "I swear it." She took her hands off the young, tender bottom with regret. Her own needs, ignored for so many weeks, stirred and made her itch. "You admire yourself as long as you like. I've got to mix up these waffles."

Clarissa stayed bent over in front of the mirror, one hand parting her buttocks, for only a few more seconds. Then she straightened, tossed the hair out of her eyes, and jumped down. After replacing the chair at the table, she went over to the steaming urn and poured a large mug of coffee for each of them.

"Tell me a story," she said, bringing the blue-and-white cups to Elise. She cleared away the broken eggshells and disposed of them, then dragged a high stool over to the counter. Elise was mixing batter in a green glass bowl. "I'll hull the strawberries while you talk to me."

Elise was charming in her short black uniform, white apron, and lacy cap. Clarissa admired the ruler-straight seams that ran up the backs of her legs, the high spike heels (two inches higher than her own training shoes), and stared at the rings that pierced Elise's dainty ears and the fine chains that ran from each earlobe to the rings in each side of her nose. She wondered if Berenice would give her rings when she grew up, or let her wear a little uniform like that. It was darling, so short that it showed off Elise's bottom every time she bent or moved. Really, her black silk panties were very tight.

It never occurred to Clarissa that she might be Berenice's favorite, despite the fact that Berenice regularly caressed her sex and rarely touched Elise at all (except with a bundle of birch twigs or the nasty lithe cane). She was terribly jealous of Elise's rings and uniform and the sophisticated psychological games Berenice would play with her. Also, Elise was allowed to wait on the parties. These occasions excited Clarissa to a fever pitch, but she was always sent up to bed after a brief presentation and demonstration of her newest feat of obedience. Elise got to greet the little groups of elegantly dressed women at the door, take their wraps, serve them drinks, bring out trays of canapés, escort their slaves into the cells in the dungeon, worship their high boots, kiss their knees and hands, perform every menial and intimate service they required. On one occasion, she had been relieved of her serving duties and used solely as an ashtray. Clarissa made a resolution to do very well at this awful school they were sending her to, to make Berenice love her the best of all.

"What do you want a story about?" Elise said briskly. Her cheeks were flaming red. She was a little out of breath, and not from being too tightly corseted or stirring batter too vigorously. The child had such a direct, piercing gaze! Must she look at her that way, at the hem of her skirt and the chains that brushed her cheeks, with such unflinching calm? It was unnerving. Really, that itch was getting worse. She smothered an image of Clarissa slowly lifting her short, black skirt and slowly pulling down her damnably tight silk panties and firmly bending her over the counter for a vigorous spanking. Then Clarissa would take one of the long wooden spoons and . . . oh, she had been kept waiting for so long. Would Berenice ever take pity on her, perhaps today?

"Tell me about you and Mother and how she enslaved you and you lost her and found her and laid your fortune at her feet so you could wear a maid's uniform every day and she had me, and you both decided to bring me up without any of the flaws that were present in your early education and—"

"Oh, that's quite a long story!" Elise laughed. "You won't have time to hear all that before you leave for the train."

"I'll eat two waffles, at least, and we will too have time, if you start now while everything's cooking. I must have a story, Elise, please, I was so good last night and they probably won't tell the little girls any stories at this dismal place you're shipping me off to."

"You know perfectly well that Hightowers is a fine institution, the very best finishing school we could find for you, and you will hardly suffer any—"

"Elise," wailed Clarissa, "pleeeease!"

"Well! Yes, if you promise not to interrupt."

"Goody!" Clarissa wielded the silver strawberry huller with enthusiasm, making a small mountain of green tops, and plopped berry after berry into the colander. "Come on, tell me, tell me!"

"I'm pouring. Don't distract me." Elise held the bowl over the hot waffle iron. She ladled batter onto the black teeth, then closed the lid and turned over her timer. The timer was a small sculpture: two women, one upside down, bound together by their hair. The sand ran down a crystal column, which they were also bound to by their long, flowing locks.

"Your grandmamma—my mother—was an opera singer," she began. "We never stopped traveling, and we never knew what the next train stop would bring. Sometimes Mamma was a success, her role would be all the rage, she would be the most fashionable woman in town. Then we were well received. We would stay in expensive hotels and life would be a mad whirl, a series of gala events. Mysterious messengers would deliver letters, flowers, perfume, and even more exotic gifts. We would receive a constant stream of visitors—millionaires, society matrons, opium-eaters, pretty young men who would eye Mamma's paint-pots and costumes with thinly concealed longing. There were always conspiracies, music, candy, wine, new sights to see, a blooming passion or a plot to crush some enterprising social climber's hopes. I can't remember sleeping during any of Mamma's popular periods. I can't even remember lying down."

"But it wasn't always that way, was it?" prompted Clarissa.

"No," Elise said, shaking her head. "Sometimes Mamma was out of voice. Then we would stay in cheap, dirty hotels or arrive uninvited at the homes of old friends. We would scrimp and scheme to save just one fine outfit apiece, to go calling on Mamma's old backers and composers and fellow singers. We would be cold and hungry, and Berenice would struggle to keep Mamma's spirits up so she would not begin to drink and lose her voice altogether, and all our hopes with it.

"It was an exciting, stormy life, and I could enjoy the ups and downs only because there was an eye in the storm: my older sister, Berenice. She was the one who packed my trunk, found my missing glove, somehow got me dinner if we arrived late and the hotel kitchen was closed, nursed me when I was ill, taught me my alphabet and my embroidery stitches, and petted my little cunny when I could not sleep. Mamma would often talk of hiring a governess, but our circumstances were too irregular to make it practical. We had sporadic lessons from a series of tutors, usually hired and fired by Berenice.

"In the beginning, Berenice would report me to Mamma when I was bad, and Mamma would punish me. Even as a child, I realized that Berenice would sometimes set traps for me and present false evidence of sins I had never committed. She would always arrange to be present when I was corrected. I could not understand why the sister I loved and trusted found pleasure in this sort of injustice. I was further confused because when Mamma heard that I had been misbehaving, her reactions were completely unpredictable. If a suitor were in the room, she might want to get rid of me as quickly as possible, so she would scold me a little, give me an indulgent kiss of forgiveness, and send me back to Berenice, who would be enraged and treat me coldly for days. If she had just read a sarcastic review or had lost a lover to a rival, she might come at me with her fan or a slipper and leave me devastated.

"I finally went to Berenice and implored her to spare me from this round of false accusations, cruel punishments for small faults, and undeserved forgiveness for grave errors. I pleaded that I was dependent upon her love and justice to make my life bearable, and that without her I would sink into despair. Then I burst into tears. She listened to me weep for a very long time before she raised me to my feet, dried my tears, and told me she had a solution to propose. I stammered that I would agree to anything, but she forbade me to agree before I heard her out. She put me on the hassock at her feet, while she sat in a big, overstuffed chair, and she offered me the following terms. I listened raptly, staring at the high, black boots she insisted on wearing regardless of the fashions of the moment."

Elise opened the waffle iron, removed the crisp, brown square, and popped it onto the plate Clarissa held out. The greedy girl smacked her lips. "You start eating now," Elise said. "I'll have one myself, then make you another. The whipped cream is in the icebox."

"More story," Clarissa insisted, her mouth full.

"Yes, more story. Well, Berenice told me that nothing pleased her more than caring for me, seeing to my education, and setting standards for my behavior. She confessed that she could not help tricking Mamma into punishing me, because it gave her such pleasure to see me wriggle and cry and struggle when I was slapped on the face or spanked with a hairbrush. She said it troubled her conscience somewhat, but not excessively, since I often got off scot-free when I had been a regular little hellion. She asked me if I remembered how kind she was after such punishments, and if I had noticed how quickly she took possession of my body as soon as we were alone. I replied that these passionate moments surprised and flattered me, but I had not realized her excitement was caused by my suffering. She said she regretted the injustice of this treatment, and begged my pardon. I freely forgave her. I added that I did not mind being punished, if I had in fact done something wrong, and that until I was properly punished for a misdeed, my conscience gave me no rest. Berenice then said she would cease to bring any complaints at all to Mamma, who was erratic and ineffectual, if I would agree to submit to her discipline. She promised to be fair as well as strict, and to act with my best welfare in mind. By this means, she hoped to make us both happier. She promised to release me from this contract at any point if that was my wish."

Elise took her own waffle from the iron and spread strawberries and cream on it. She told the next installment of the story between bites. "I agreed at once, even though the idea was a novel one. I adored my mother—we both did—but she treated us more like a permanent audience than a family. Berenice already had all the responsibility for mothering me. It seemed fair that she should have power and authority as well. So Berenice kissed me on the forehead, gave me a bonbon, then put me on the sofa with my sewing box and a glove that needed mending. After she left the room, I fell into a reverie. I was exhausted by my tears and without meaning to, I fell sound asleep. I was awakened by Berenice, calling me to dress for dinner. When she saw I had not completed the sewing, she was not angry, but said calmly that it looked as if I needed a demonstration of the terms of our agreement.

"We went to dinner with Mamma and a railroad magnate who was trying to get her to star in a light musical comedy written by his oldest son. That very evening, Berenice tied me to our bed and spanked me with her own hand, on my bare bottom! I was terribly humiliated. I had never been tied up before, and certainly never been struck on my naked flesh. After she untied me, she insisted on being thanked and ordered me to kiss her all over. Instead of refusing or performing a perfunctory job, I found myself crying out passionately, fondling myself while I knelt and suckled, pleading with her to possess me completely. 'That is just what I intend to do,' she told me. 'I don't know exactly how yet, but I will learn. I will learn from you how to keep you under my dominance and make you love me, and we will never be parted, dear sister. You will always belong to me.' "

Elise stopped to pour another waffle for Clarissa and refill their mugs with hot coffee. Clarissa jiggled impatiently in her chair until Elise was settled once more at the table and ready to resume her tale. "Hurry," she urged. "I don't want Aunt Jennifer to come and spoil the story."

Elise smiled. "I'll try to finish. But I told you it was long. Let me see. Where was I? Oh, yes. Well, in the days that followed, I tried to please her in the smallest thing. But when the mood was on her to see me cry out and struggle, she could always detect some fault that required correction. Gradually, we began to play the game of discipline for its own sake. I fell more and more in love with Berenice, and would endure the most ingenious and barbaric tortures for the sake of her kiss and smile. Mamma was very pleased with the change in us. We no longer bothered her with our petty quarrels, and everyone could tell how fond we were of each other.

"The idyll continued until I was eighteen. Mamma came home early from the theater one evening and caught Berenice in the act of whipping me with a handful of long-stemmed roses. This could have been passed off as bizarre but well-intentioned corporal punishment, and Berenice would have received no more than a scolding for being too severe. But she had stuffed a peeled persimmon up me before beginning the flagellation, and I was so frightened when I saw Mamma that it tumbled out, rolled across the floor, and came to rest at her feet.

"Our mamma, who could pass the most loathsome beggers on the street without distress, was enraged and disgusted by the sight of our love-play. Because I was apparently the victim—tied and bleeding from the thorns— she did not blame me, but she flew at Berenice and tried to claw her eyes out, ignoring my screams for mercy and my shouts that it was all my fault, I could explain, please stop! Berenice seized her wrists and held her, weeping and cursing, at arm's length.

"Mamma vowed to disinherit her, turn her out with nothing but the clothes on her back. Luckily, it was near dawn, and a group of Mamma's friends who had been out all night drinking and singing in the cafés burst in on us and insisted that we accompany them to breakfast. Mamma, surrounded by her drunk and bawdy friends, found it hard to enforce this harsh sentence immediately. Berenice stood in the doorway of our suite, pale and still. I ran into our room, rifled my jewelry and Mamma's purse, found a heavy cloak, stuffed extra underthings, a nightgown, and another dress into a small case, and brought these gifts to her. Mamma's face darkened when she saw me put the bag at Berenice's feet and slip the cloak around her shoulders, but she was simultaneously fending a hand away from her bodice and being told a really scandalous story about her deadliest enemy.

" 'Don't worry about me,' Berenice said, kissing my tear-stained cheeks. 'Perhaps this should have happened earlier. You and I had gone as far as we could under her roof. I know someone in Paris who can get me started on my own. A woman who knows how to wield a whip won't have any trouble making her living in Paris. So come to me when you can, my love. I'll wait for you there.' And so we were parted."

"This is so sad," breathed Clarissa. "Isn't my waffle ready yet?"

"Oh. Yes, I suppose it must be. Give me your plate. You'll have to eat this in a hurry, now."

"I will, I will. Tell me how sad it was!"

"Well, I thought I would die. My whole world had been ruined. But despite my misery, I stayed with Mamma. Often I would chastise myself for not having Berenice's independent fire. But I had a premonition that my role was necessary and important, and that I would recover my long-lost love all in good time. Because there was nothing else to do, I waited on Mamma patiently. My devotion was not rewarded by anything like Berenice's fiery and thorough ministrations. Occasionally it became too much for me, and I would whip myself in front of my dressing glass.

"During those unhappy years, I learned to detest the men who followed Mamma about, fickle fools who were attracted by her dynamic personality but always attempted to quench her fire. They never stood by her when she was despondent or out of work. I began to take charge of Mamma's engagements and income, and invested everything I could. I became quite fussy and boring, obsessed with interest rates, real estate and securities. I also obtained a reputation for being an indomitable virago when negotiating Mamma's contracts and appearances.

"We were in, of all cities, Paris, when Mamma had her greatest triumph. She sang her favorite role in *The Bird of Paradise,* Flavia, the girl who sells tropical birds on the wharf of Florence, who is impregnated by the heir-apparent of the Doge, and kills herself on the eve of his betrothal so she will not be tempted to disrupt his wedding, not knowing that it was not her lover in whom she confided the news of her conception, but his evil twin brother who was thought to be dead, who has returned to the city and trained all her birds to peck out the prince's eyes when they are released in one brilliant flock at his coronation, which was her deathbed request.

"Mamma sang as she had never sung before. But she caught influenza while two counts, one French and one Italian, were making love to her in an open carriage on her way back to our hotel. They were quite piqued because her fever made her delirious before she could tell them which of their countries had won her accolade for amative skill. She died before the week was up, leaving me with her estate.

"Would you believe that with all that money at my disposal, it took me a month to find Berenice? A month of harrowing anxiety and sickening fear. I could hardly see to the funeral. But my search finally bore fruit. I found my sister, your mother, in the grimmest section of the city. She was ill, carrying you, dear child, and in desperate need. She had been a minor light of the Parisian underworld, caning some of the most regal buttocks on the continent, but the police and her competitors combined to betray and undo her. She did not have the vicious character one needs to survive in such a sordid world; she was not a criminal. She could hardly believe I had come for her, and embraced me until I thought my ribs would crack.

I took her away and found this home for us, a simple country estate with excellent drainage, adjoining tenant farms, and a high resale value, where we can practice our love as the fancy takes us and provide a home for you. And we will stay here forever and ever, or as long as it makes us happy."

Clarissa applauded. "Oh, what a beautiful story," she said. "I love the way your eyes sparkle when you tell it. Now tell me about the time when Mother gave you away to Aunt Jennifer and—"

"Absolutely not! Up the stairs with you and into your traveling clothes. I've already laid the dress and shoes out on your bed. Your aunt will be here any minute now. Wear the peach satin corset that laces up the front. Hurry, while I clean up. And be sure to put on every one of your crinolines, young lady—don't think you can fool me by stuffing one down the laundry chute! Shoo!"

Cheryl Clarke
(b. 1947)

Cheryl Clarke's first volume of poetry, *Narratives* (1983), revealed its focus in the subtitle: *poems in the tradition of black women.* Her subsequent volumes continue to be poems in the tradition of black women. Her 1986 lyric collection, *Living as a Lesbian,* from which the following poems were taken, was followed in 1989 by another collection of narrative verse, *Humid Pitch.* Cheryl Clarke's poetry often concerns itself with the unsung lesbian heroes of her African American background, and it frequently echoes the cadences of African American jazz or the lyrics of the blues. Her heritage is a vital source of her verse.

But her poetry also demonstrates some movement beyond the earlier political concerns that characterized her work as a member since 1981 of the editorial collective of the lesbian-feminist magazine *Conditions.* While difference continues to be an important theme in Clarke's poetry, many of her poems assume rather than dissect issues of race and difference. Lesbian sensuality and sexuality, and their concomitant complications and joys, are a major focus. As she reveals in an article on her work, one of her primary interests as a writer has been in "creating sexual poetry."

FURTHER READING: Cheryl Clarke, *Narratives: poems in the tradition of black women* (Kitchen Table: Women of Color Press, 1983); *Living as a Lesbian* (Ithaca, NY: Firebrand, 1986); *Humid Pitch* (Ithaca, NY: Firebrand, 1989); "Inspiration: Seven Stories of Creating Art—Creating Sexual Poetry," *Hot Wire,* 4: 1 (November 1987),

28–29. Jennie Ruby, "The Black Diaspora," *off our backs*, 18: 8 (August–September 1988), 10.

KITTATINNY

I wanna love and treat you, love and treat you right.
BOB MARLEY

Kittatinny Tunnel in that holy place you let me hit
I push on toward your darker part.
I'll take you there and mean it.

In my car, by the road, in a tent, in a pit
stop, and practice a funkier art,
Kittatinny Tunnel of that holy place you let me hit.

Shout, cry, promise, beg, cajole, go limp, or spit
on me with dirty words to test my heart.
I'll take you there and mean it.

Crawl from me, pitch a fit,
stand, hug the wall, bend, and direct me part
and penetrate Kittatinny, that holy place you let me hit.

And take it, take it, take it.
Call it bitch, whore, slave, tart.
I'll take you there and mean it.

Tribad, dildo, lick your clit-
oris. Come, pee, shit, or fart,
I'll take you there and mean it,
Kittatinny Tunnel of that holy place you let me hit.

WHAT GOES AROUND COMES AROUND, OR THE PROOF IS IN THE PUDDING

*Truthfulness, honor, is not something which springs
ablaze of itself; it has to be created between people. . . .*
ADRIENNE RICH, "WOMEN AND HONOR"

A woman in my shower crying.
All I can do is make potato salad
and wish I hadn't been caught lying.

I dust the chicken for frying
pretending my real feelings too much a challenge
to the woman in my shower crying.

I forget to boil the eggs, time is flying,
my feet are tired, my nerves frazzled,
and I wish I hadn't been caught lying.

Secondary relationships are trying.
I'd rather roll dough than be hassled
by women in my shower crying.

Truth is clarifying.
Pity it's not more like butter.
I wish I hadn't been caught lying.

Ain't no point denying,
my soufflé won't even flutter.
I withhold from the woman in my shower crying
afraid of the void I filled with lying.

SAN JUAN: 1979

first night:
I am reaffirmed in the dissipating lushness
of this steamy city
where dark men people its sidewalks
and coffee houses,
where pasty gringos meander in twos like nuns
arrogant in their ignorance of the language.

restaurant:
A mulatto waiter seats me resentfully.
Two dark women with Asian eyes seat themselves.
I watch the one. Her eyes go soft and dark at the
other over the candle.

hotel lobby:
I am smug in this scene of seasonal affection
and evening gear, as two dark women with Asian eyes
skate across the marble lobby.
The other is laughing with the one whose eyes went
soft and dark over the candle.

departure:
I am on the tourist shuttle.
Through my Pentax, my eye catches them
in a gray blue blur of three-piece suits

and luggage.
My finger is sluggish.
The unruly head of a tourist
blocks the potential print.
The jitney jerks into gear.

resolution:
I am reaffirmed and ramified
in this noisy, polluted, disappointing city.
Sidewalks crowded with delicate dark men
and sun sick gringos who think the language
quaint and unimportant.

Frankie Hucklenbroich
(b. 1939)

Frankie Hucklenbroich dropped out of high school in 1956 and sold magazines door to door around the United States. The following year she came out into the working-class-bar culture as a butch. She has been an office worker, a janitor, a madam in a house of prostitution, a housebreaker, and a jail inmate. In the 1970s Hucklenbroich passed a high school equivalency exam and was admitted to college, from which she graduated *cum laude* after two years. She became a lesbian-feminist at that time and her poetry was published in numerous lesbian-feminist journals and anthologies. In the climate of the 1980s she reclaimed her butch identity.

"Crystal Diary" is a section of a novel in progress, which Hucklenbroich compares to John Rechy's *City of Night,* an autobiographical novel about his experiences as a gay male hustler migrating from city to city around the United States. Hucklenbroich's honest account of her life as a crystal addict owes its tone to a post–lesbian-feminist era that confronts a variety of convictions about correct behavior. She resurrects raw images of lesbian life, such as were prevalent in Decadent literature of the nineteenth century or the pulps of the 1950s. However, Hucklenbroich presents her material without the inevitable moralizations of the earlier literature.

A Crystal Diary

The cops are still watching me through their binoculars.

They're perched on top of a smokestack a few blocks away and from where they are they have a straight view right into this room. We live on the third floor. There isnt a window shade.

If I hang a sheet up in the window now theyll just get agitated. After all weve been here for a couple of months without bothering to cover the window and it would look suspicious to suddenly go around hanging curtains. The last thing I want is for those cops up there to get more pissed off than they already are.

I wonder where they got the smokestack idea? I wonder how they ran us down?

I havent left this room for some time. At least a couple of days but maybe more. At first I just didnt have any reason to split. I was doing some writing, a long poem for Diane, and getting into my books. Then yesterday morning I spotted them up there on the smokestack and now Im scared to leave. Last night I didnt turn any lights on. I just sat by the window all night in the dark watching the sidewalk in front of the hotel. I thought the cops might climb down the stack and then come sliding through the foggy streets. Sneaking up on me.

But nothing happened except there was a nasty fight between two hookers outside the bar on the corner. One of the hookers sliced open the other one's face with a straight razor and in the pink light from the neons the blood that sprayed everywhere looked like wine. Only one prowl car showed up for the fight and when its black-and-white snub nose came around the corner the crowd watching the fight and the hookers too all melted away like magic. The one with her face laid open ran up the street with her hands pinching her new lips together and blood pouring down her arms and dripping from her elbows and then she dodged into an alley between two buildings. When I saw the prowl car I held my breath but the car just went on past the hotel and turned into the alley after the injured hooker, and the fog turned and swirled in its headlights.

When the sun came up this morning my own cops were still up on the smokestack. Still in place. They think theyve got me fooled but they dont. Each time they pass the binoculars back and forth the beautiful San Francisco sun glints off the lenses. I can keep easy track of them and know theyre still up there and not fanning around the hotel. As long as I see those flashes of light Im okay. But Im surprised they didnt think of something so basic and rub dust or something onto the glass.

Just now I saw the outline of one of their heads. Tiny. Like the head of an ant.

For their sake I sure hope they're not waiting for me to go to sleep. I can go a long time without sleep. A long long time.

I wonder: are they plainclothes or just harness bulls?

I know what they're after.

They're after Diane.

They're waiting for Diane to come home or for me to hit the bricks and eventually lead them to her. I'll never give them Diane. Never. Never. If they finally do crash the room they can bust me, take me in, jack me around, whatever they want but I wont give them Diane. In another day or two something will happen to make them lose interest. Or else they'll come in and roust me. One or the other. Unless she comes home Diane will be safe either way. She'll be so safe she wont even know what I had to go through to keep her that way unless she has to send somebody to bail me out.

Honor among thieves and all that shit.

Right now Diane is probably at Hanks place on Folsom Street dry-fucking her brains out. Thats how she gets her crystal. Our crystal. By fucking Hank. He's the biggest crystal dealer in town and Diane—with her butterscotch-colored hair and smoky voice and mad eyes—backfired on him. I could tell him that the voice is just from using so much crystal but he probably already knows that and if hes like me his fingertips still tingle and his groin melts like wax when she talks to him. He loves her. He still uses her for a runner but he actually loves her which impresses me. Hanks hurt some people really bad and the word on the street is that hes offed a couple of people as well and you wouldnt expect someone like Hank to get all soft about a chick, any chick, even Diane. So we both love her. She has a power and she uses it.

Diane uses. She uses. Crystal. Hank. Me. Anybody anytime for anything. Ive seen her operate and she can knock you out with one slashing lift of eyebrow. She has a power and she uses. But its okay.

There go the little sparks of sun off the ends of the binoculars again. Theres a woman up there too. A lady cop. Probably gay. Probably butch. (I cant see a femme climbing up there.) Diane might. If she was a cop.

What a thought!

But there has to be a woman up there. I feel that. My scalp and the back of my neck have the same electric feeling I used to get whenever a woman was watching me in one of the bars and I was pretending not to know it.

Diane left me two full tablespoons. Packed tight, not fluffed up. Even with my tolerance two measured spoons should last me until she can come back. She has her faults but shes never let me run dry yet. Not since the first time she slid a needle into my vein and showed me the cosmic lights.

And she never complains.

I know Im expensive. It takes a lot of fucking for a lot of crystal, for her to feed my arm. She takes care of things. Diane says I should look at Hank as nothing but a trick and fucking a trick is just her job. But I hate Hank. Just as a matter of principle.

She says Thats silly, what about the hookers youve been with? You took *their* money. Did you hate their tricks? I tell her No but they didnt mean anything to me and you do. Then she just laughs and says You cant say I didnt warn you baby.

And sometimes I even feel kind of sorry for Hank. He just won't believe Diane's really gay. He thinks if he ignores me long enough I'll go away. He thinks if he *doesnt* ignore me the idea of competition from a woman will make him less of a man.

I dont know what I think anymore.

Until the cops came to the smokestack I was speeding so high and fine. Now I'd be crawling walls if I didnt have my writing to settle into. Im that worried. And I *need* to trip.

I know its July. I dont know anything else about the month. Which week or whether its Wednesday or Sunday. I sure dont know the date. Im going to keep on writing and use x's to mark off sections. The x's won't mean dates, just thoughts and different things. Then I can put them together sometime and maybe start a journal. A crystal diary. X will mean "entry."

We hocked my typewriter. Also my stereo and my tape recorder and my television and my black star sapphire and diamond pinkie ring. Later on we sold the pawn tickets. We dont keep anything very long. Now I have to write longhand but I've got leftover typing paper and plenty of pencils. Writing is normal for me. I love it. Someday Im going to put it all together. Get published. For now the cops will just see me scribbling innocently away. They wont have any idea Im onto them. I can look out the window at the smokestack like Im searching for inspiration.

And maybe someone will come over and I can get a message on the street warning Diane to stay away. Yesterday people knocked on the door five or six times but I ignored them. Today I'll answer if the voice on the other side sounds okay.

X   One of the first things Diane ever said to me was Everybody uses everybody Frankie. I still didnt believe that even after my time on the streets. Another thing she said when I first knew her was You're too butch for me, I like to control my situation. We're going to have to change your head around some. I remember I just laughed. I didnt believe that either.

I was the one who was going to change Diane.

I was going to save her. From Hank. From crystal. From the vultures that were always surrounding her with their hands out. From the headgames. From herself. I had a blindness for Diane. She told me and I wouldnt listen. I wouldnt see.

I thought I was Sir Lancelot and she was my Guinevere. I just needed to convince her. Wonderful me was going to show her wonderful her. My hand to god I looked at that woman and white picket fences were nailed on my eyes. I looked at her and I wanted to enter a little cottage after a hard days work at some factory and holler Honey Im home! I wanted us to buy a poodle and a Volkswagen. I wanted her to start wearing aprons in and high heels out. Diane would cook. I would mow the lawn and dump the trash and change any flat tires on the car. Meanwhile I'd write reams of excellent lesbian poetry in the evenings, each word a modest offering to her. I would then preen beneath her fulsome praise. And I'd bury my grateful face between her legs at least nightly. Thats how it was going to be for us.

I was beside myself. Besotted. She made me snort and whinny and paw the sand.

Know what I mean?

After we got together and I moved in with her almost without her knowing it and I started using out of curiosity and also to prove to her that crystal can be done for fun without changing your whole life and I promptly got hooked almost without my knowing it I grew to understand her better. Or maybe less. Maybe they're both the same thing.

XX   Hanks street name is Big Man but not because of his size, as he is just a short black meaneyed middleaged guy with skinny arms and legs. The color of his flesh is that same black that you find at the point of a purple Crayola. "Big Man" refers to the incredible amount of crystal he controls and also to the people he bought his franchise from, who take care of him. Everyone on the streets except me and Diane is afraid of him and I might be leery of him too if I didn't have Diane standing between us. Big Man truly dislikes me.

On the other hand if it wasnt for Diane I probably wouldnt even know Hank much less have spent so many afternoons sitting in the chair by the window and watching him fuck her into the mattress while she smiled at me over his shoulder or from under her arm (if they were fucking doggy style) or from whatever position they were busy licking sucking fucking gulping slapping biting mauling and grunting unh! unh! unh! Im no watchfreak.

Being there was bad. Being somewhere else would have been worse.

There is a small rose with two delicate green leaves tattooed on her shoulder. The tracks on her arms are like ropes.

Dont get me wrong. I could have left them alone. Nobody asked me to stay. It was just that one minute there we'd all be, sitting around bagging crystal into nickel and dime and quarter bags and twenty-dollar spoons, fluffing it up through a couple of flour sifters to make it go further and not talking much but just concentrating on the count and the scales and business, and the next minute they'd be rolling around on the floor or the bed and pulling at each others clothes and it was *our* bed. *Our* floor. *My* woman. And I couldnt just say Oh excuse me I see that you're fucking, well I think I'll just run down to the corner for a carton of milk. This was the way things were. Hank was our bread-and-butter man. Our insurance we'd never have to worry about where our next bag was coming from. But I wasnt about to let him drive me out of the pad.

It was home after all.

So I'd shoot up and I'd hang out. Sometimes I'd try to read or draw but mostly I just watched, waiting for Hank to throw his head back so far it almost touched his spine while his eyes rolled up and his knobby little body went stiff and thrummed like a jerked wire and Diane kept working her snatch or hips or lips fast as an engine going into third gear as she finally (FINALLY!) got his rocks off. Now and then the sonofabitch would want to go two or three times.

Those were rough afternoons.

I stayed fried and kept my face nice and bland even when he'd turn his piggy eyes back to me and grin. I just maintained my cool. He'd be pulling his clothes on and I'd pop open a couple of frosty longnecks and say Ready for a beer? handing him one. I'd take a long casual swallow from the other one and pass it to Diane.

One time when they were in the middle of fucking Hank turned his head and looked at me and said Come on Frankie you ride my pony for a change. I got room for two. And he pulled his big wet dick out of Diane and used his hand to wag it back and forth at me like the tail of a dog. Come on Mr. Butch he said. Come on over here girl.

Instant paranoia. What to do? What to do?

But Diane reached up real fast and grabbed his face in her fingers and turned him back to her and said Let her alone Daddy, maybe I dont want to share you. Hank laughed and rolled her onto her stomach.

And I thought Thanks baby.

They finished fucking. Hank said he had some business and Diane should meet him later on that night. Coltrane was blowing at a club in North Beach and Hank wanted them to go down and take him in. While he dressed Diane ran around the room naked gathering up his watch and his hat and the briefcase he uses for a stashbag and when he went out the door he pecked her on the cheek like some square john headed for the office and said Catch you later honey and I wanted to kill him. I wanted a truck to spread him across about a block of asphalt or one of his buddies to drive him down to the docks and blow him away. But then my very next thought was But what about our habits? See between the two of us Diane and I are hitting up a good eighty/ninety bucks worth a day. And its rising.

Crystal is the Great Simplifier.

Then Diane went into the bathroom and I listened to her spitting in the sink and brushing her teeth for a long time and then I heard the water running in the tub and the sound her body made hitting the water as she climbed in and sat down and stretched her legs out and then I didnt hear anything for quite a while so I knew she was just soaking. And then she was splashing around and making noises and when she started to hum I knew she was washing her hair. While she was in the tub I wrote a poem about her: So you were the lovely stranger/whose bellbottom jeans smelled of danger/who fucked like a frog and slept like a log/or a hog or a dog in the manger.

Diane, with her crazy eyes.

XXX   Finally one day I told her she'd have to figure some way to keep Hank away from our place. I told her the fuck sessions brought me down. Completely bummed my high. Diane understood that. But we both knew it meant she'd wind up having to spend a lot more time away from home. I figured in the long haul it'd be worth it. If only for my inner peace and quiet. She told Hank their relationship was too important to her and she wanted her time with him to be more private. The asshole loved it. Ate it up. I guess he thought he finally had a chance.

Yet even when I didnt have to look at Hanks ugly face or ass anymore I'd still go off on a tangent now and then. Even while we were sitting there feeding our arms I'd start in telling her how rotten what a scumbag Hank was for giving her crystal—bags and bags of it—plenty to sell for him and plenty left over for us. Diane would just listen and smile at me while I went on and on and on. One day she asked me What makes you any better than Hank?

My mouth dropped open.

Think about it she said. Hanks taking care of us both. I do the fucking but we both get our dope and a place and the cigarettes and the food and the beer. I fuck for us. And youre letting me. You take from me just like I take from him. Lets get real here she said. She lit a cigarette and flipped the dead match into a corner. Hanks my trick she went on. My chump. Tell me Im not yours Frankie.

I stared at her and I couldnt say anything.

Thats why I just shake my head when you talk about how you love me she grinned. She hiked a leg across mine so she could sit on my lap. What does that word mean to you? I know what it means to me. When I say it I mean I'll take care of you and I'll keep you high and I'll cover your back and I wont let anybody jack you around but me. Youre different. Youre a romantic. Baby if you really felt the way you *think* you do youd *have* to take off. You know Im not gonna change and you wouldnt be able to stand what I do. With or without the crystal you'd split.

Youre wrong I said. I love you.

Whatever. Hey! Dont feel so bad! Its all a tradeoff. You know?

Then I had to ask: Do you *want* me to leave?

She reached out a finger and touched my shoulder and then the side of my face. Ah Frankie. Ive done a real number on you huh? Jesus!

That pissed me off. I pulled away so she had to stand up.

Very serious and very earnest she said Look baby youre just a junkie. Okay? Just a speed freak. Just like me. Thats who we are. Were just better at it than most. And she said Youre not going anywhere. We both know that. Dont we?

I felt myself nodding.

Now! she said brightly. Mamas gonna take care of you! I know what'll make you feel better. . . . We'll do a hit. Then we'll go outside and play. Okay? I'll even hit you myself instead of you doing it.

No way was I turning down an offer like that. I allowed myself to be pacified. It was easy.

XXXX   *This is what its like to do crystal.*

Diane goes to the dresser for our works. Damn! she says. We need to pick up fresh points. Yours are all dull. Want to try one of mine?

I shake my head. She uses #24s but I need #26s as my veins are smaller. Once I got an abscess with a #24. (But you cant use a dull point either. A burred needle can catch the vein and pull a tiny piece right out through your skin which leaves you with a real sore arm for a while.) Sharpen one up for me I tell her.

She nods and rubs the tip of a needle back and forth across the striker of a matchbook until it sharpens up some. She sucks off the grit and runs a bit of copper wire about as thick as a hair down through the inside to clear away any dirt or old blood. Then she runs the point under the bathroom faucet for a while.

Already I am sweating with impatience: that sharp, sour sweat users call "the slicks."

She comes out of the bathroom and glancing at me she says Just another minute babe and taps a fat pile of powder from the bag into a teaspoon. Adds half a dropperful of water and stirs with the tip of a finger until the crystal dissolves. Then she strikes a match and holds the flame to the bottom of the spoon until little heat bubbles dance in its bowl. I am rolling a thumbnail-sized piece of cotton into a tight ball. When Diane shakes out the match I lean toward her and lay the cotton easy into the spoon. I push the plastic end of the point onto the dropper and hand the 'fit to her.

Diane squeezes the rubber bulb and touches the needle to the wet cotton, relaxing the bulb so that suction makes the hit begin to climb up into the dropper. She winks at me and smiles. Powerhouse she says and I grin as the level of fluid in the 'fit rises until there is a dropperful of crystal so strong that its cloudy gray instead of clear.

I roll up my shirtsleeve and use a belt to tie off the crook of my left arm. I have to slap the vein a few times to make it jump to the surface of my skin. I have rollers and floaters for veins and theyll fall right off the end of the point if theyre not standing up high enough. And then its a skinpop, the whole hit is wasted. Just a big sac of liquid loose and burning inside my muscle. So Im careful to get the vein as high and still as I can.

Diane taps the dropper until a bubble of air forms inside and breaks and then she slides the needle deep into my arm and I undo the tie and a thin string of blood floats lazily up into the 'fit like red seaweed, showing a register first try. She relaxes the bulb suddenly and crystal and blood shoot back up to the top of the 'fit and she squeezes and relaxes/squeezes and relaxes, jacking off the hit without ever fully pumping it into the vein until the 'fit is full of half blood and half crystal and she does this and its like waiting to come and she finally drives it all home for me and I feel first a metallic taste rising in the back of my throat and then my snatch burning and then my brain explodes and the rush is better than sex better than love you squares have never had anything so good. Theres just no way for you to know. And now I am Alice flying up toward the ceiling with my hands and arms reaching into the corners of the room and I rock with pleasure and while all this is happening my brain opens suddenly like a wide dark flower and the rush is so good so good so much better than poems music sky sunsets family friends self oh! much better than anything that ever was or ever could be amen amen amen better and better hold on to her hand while I use my fingers to press my eyes back into my skull better breathe *hard!* and catch up with the rest of me ah pant and shiver and drip with sweat and let the rush ease off, ease off, ease off now, slow and warm and sweet and no there's nothing like it nothing not anything as good as this Diane.

She pulled the needle out and pressed her thumb against my arm to stop the bleeding. I was still panting and still rushing a little and she laughed and said See what I mean babe?

I laughed back.

Then she hit herself up. And then we sat around rapping about this and that, anything and everything, until somebody who wanted to make a buy started beating on the door.

XXXXX   If the cops on the smokestack really knew what they were doing they'd just walk up here nice and polite and offer me my own five-pound bag. Im not saying Id give Diane over. But Id be tempted.

XXXXXX   Gypsy came by looking for Diane. I told him I wasnt sure when she would be back. So then he wanted me to front him a dime bag. Gypsy like everybody else knows Diane always leaves me a good stash when she takes off. I said I didnt have anything but he just grinned and parked himself in the chair and started jacking his greasy jaws about nothing bullshit stupid stuff as if I could be interested in anything he had to say. I knew he'd hang out until I either turned him on to some crystal or he brought me down. So I gave up and told him Id let him have a fix but after that I wanted the place to myself. I would of kicked him out but for some reason Diane really likes the guy and I didnt want to hassle with her later about how I treat her friends.

I went ahead and cooked us up a couple of hits and we did them in the john. I didnt say why and he looked at me like I was nuts. But I dont care what Gypsy thinks. I just didnt want the cops to see us fixing. Maybe even film us or something.

Afterward he still tried to talk me into fronting him a bag but I said No way Gypsy. You still owe us from the last time.

I thought the asshole was going to cry.

Come on Frankie! *Diane* would do it he said.

I said Fuck you Gypsy. Im not Diane.

So he left pissed off anyway. He stole my red windbreaker off the bed and I didnt even see him go near there. I wont tell Diane about the jacket.

She'll just laugh and say giving him the dime bag would've been cheaper. And then I'll have to pay for being mean to him.

Everybody knows Gypsy is a ripoff artist. He steals something whenever he comes over. Always something small. One time a little leather manicure case. He makes his living stealing things from cars. He'll walk up bold as you please and pop the locks with a Slimjim. Take his time going through the gloveboxes and seats. He'll go to parking lots and hit ten/twelve cars in a row. He gets money, cameras, radios, tape recorders, one time a nickelplated two-shot derringer he brought around to trade for crystal. We sold it later on to Monkey Bob who finally shot some chick with it.

Diane says Gypsy steals from his friends for the human touch he doesnt get when he rips off anonymous cars. I think he's just a spider. A real lowlife. Seven or eight months ago he almost got himself killed. He started dealing a little crystal and then he suddenly picked up a nice chunk of the action. His stuff was so good it took the top of your head off. It was even better than Big Mans. Diane kept warning him to take his business across town but he wouldnt listen and she got real worried about him. Hank was ready to step on him and Diane didnt know how long she could talk Hank out of breaking his legs or worse. But before Hank got around to doing something people found out Gypsy was cutting his stuff with meat tenderizer and he had to leave town. So Hank let it slide. Meat tenderizer! What a rotten trick! He could have really hurt somebody. He's only been back in town about a month.

Wouldnt you know Diane would forgive and forget?

Before he left I made Gypsy promise that if he ran into Diane he'd tell her to call me. Theres a pay phone in the hall that we use.

I want to warn her about the cops on the smokestack.

XXXXXXX   The smokestack belongs to a brewery on Van Ness, right near Mel's Drive-in where I worked as a carhop when I first hit San Francisco. That was back when Dawn and I broke up. I'm almost thirty now. Between Dawn and Diane I played the field. Strippers. Hookers. Cocktail waitresses. A bellydancer. Even a couple of "nice" women. Joe Studley, that was me.

Dawn and I lasted over four years. Before that I was with Kim for three years. Before *that* I also played the field, learning about women and gay life and how to be a butch. And before that I was with Lil but only for six weeks until she dumped me. Lil was the very first woman I ever really went to bed with. She brought me out and didnt even know it. I was ashamed to tell her. I was just this great galumping girl from Missouri, on my own in Los Angeles and in love for the first time in my life. I knew what I wanted but I had only the haziest idea of how to get there. So I tried to fake it and of course I failed dismally and so she dumped me and later on she married a faggot to get out of her moms house. We were both babies back then. But god I thought she hung the moon.

Except for Diane I dont know where any of them are now.

I miss that.

XXXXXXXX   The way I met Dawn was I walked into this place in Hollywood called The Cellar because it was below street level. You opened a door and had to go down a flight of concrete steps to get to the bar and some rinkydink tables and a small dancefloor. There she was. Dancing with a stocky young dude with very white skin and dark hair. Later I'd find out he was her highschool sweetheart and they were engaged. Great for my ego.

Anyway they were just a pair of straights or so my soft internal push of instinct told me but as I reached the bottom of the steps he spun her and she wound up facing me. We were so close I could have touched her and the butch in me and the bitch in her said Well hello there! and when the music stopped I walked by their table to see what they were drinking. Both had Coors.

I bought three bottles at the bar and went over and just pulled up a chair and sat down.

They played it very sophisticated. Thanked me for the brews and we all exchanged names and then I asked them What are you two doing in a gay joint?

Bob said they didnt know it was gay when they came in and once they ordered they figured they might as well stay and dance a few sets.

A little local color? I grinned.

Dawn laughed but Bob just smiled at me over the rim of his glass. He was a very nice guy. Very mellow and laidback. Dawn and I kept looking at each other but Bob didnt seem to notice or maybe he just felt secure. I thought about how Dawn moved like a young tiger on the dancefloor.

We made chitchat. Dawn was going to Chouinard's School of Art. Bob was down visiting. They were both from Vegas. The Mormon part. Bob laughed. He told me all about his job at the Tropicana on the Vegas Strip and about how he made good money just screwing lightbulbs into the big fancy signs on the outside of the club whenever they burned out. I thought that was a really a neat way to make a living. Dawn talked about the things she liked to paint. Finally Bob got up to use the john. I looked over at Dawn and I could feel my heart pounding like a kids but (very suave) I just said Come home with me. She stood up and picked up her purse and followed me outside and we ran to the cabstand on the corner and I took her home for the next four years. The point of all this is that there are times and people—just a few—that happen to you without warning, leave you stunned and change your whole life.

Even after they're gone you're different because of what you became when you were with them.

XXXXXXXXX   Every woman who ever really mattered to me showed up in some crazy accidental way and then it was always an immediate thing. Lil in the Marlin Inn. Kim in Coffee Dan's. I found Diane in Chukkers.

Chukkers is on Turk and Taylor down in the middle of the San Francisco Tenderloin and it was quiet that night which is not usual even at four A.M. Id left a party over in North Beach but I was feeling pretty good and not yet ready to wrap it up so I swung by Chukkers to see what was shaking. It looked like nothing was. A couple of bulldykes were at one of the tables. A femme we used to call Lean Doreen because she was so skinny lay stretched out and snoring in a booth. A local junkie was nodding in a corner. An old queen with a really bad red toupee sat at another table watching the door. That was it.

I took a table and the waiter swished over and I said Whats up Candy? Looks like a morgue in here.

No booze! he said, *very* annoyed. Cant run an afterhours with no *booze!* Cops raided earlier. Closed us for three goddamn hours! *Some*body forgot to take *care* of somebody. . . . Come back tomorrow. We'll be set by then. How bout a Coke for now?

I said Okay but when I got the Coke it was lukewarm and I was sorry I ordered. I was just getting ready to leave when Diane walked in.

Hair falling in her eyes. Cheekbones like knives. A long bruise on her throat. But proud and beautiful in sandals and bellbottoms and a black velvet blouse that looked like a medieval tunic. Silver bangles on her wrists and a silver cord tied tight around her waist for a belt. She didnt look around and scope the place out like people do. As far as she was concerned Chukkers was empty. She climbed up on a barstool and laid a big purse on the bar and began taking things out and examining them with care and putting them back in the purse again.

Candy walked down the bar and spoke to her and I saw her shake her head No. When I caught his eye I waved him over.

Who is *that?* I said.

Diane Ferrari and she's bad news. Dont go looking to get burned my friend.

Me? Get burned? Candy. Surely you jest.

He gave me a look. This one you should pass on he said.

So how come I never saw her around before?

Sometimes shes here every night for a few hours. Then she disappears for weeks. Or months. I dont know where else she hangs out. Candy pursed his lips. She's a busy lady he said.

Yeah? Whats her story?

A speedfreak. Real heavy-duty. Nice lady but messed up bigtime. Smart too.

Whaddaya mean smart?

Books he said. She always carries three or four in that saddlebag of hers. Sometimes she'll sit by the jukebox—I mean right *by* it—so she can get enough light to read by. Whole place is jumpin and there she sits reading away. I hear she's gay but I never seen her with a woman. Just junkie fags or alone.

Smart huh? Bring me another Coke okay?

Candy shrugged. You're making a mistake Dear he sang.

I just grinned at him from the top of my ego. I said Mine to make. Tell you what . . . I'll pick the Coke up at the bar. A cold one this time okay?

I walked over with him and got my Coke and then I moved down the bar and stood next to her. She glanced at me and went back to digging through her purse.

I said What are you reading tonight?

She turned to face me and her look was definitely not friendly. What do *you* want? she said.

Now I was not used to this kind of a reception. I didnt know whether to be annoyed or amused. So I settled for intrigued and decided to try direct with this one. I'll be honest with you I answered. I asked Candy about you. Your name's Diane and youre bright as well as goodlooking. You like to read. Me too. I dont know what I want yet but when I do I'll tell you. If we're on speaking terms. Are we?

She was glaring at me so I tilted my head and smiled to show her how harmless I could be. Just a sheep in wolfs clothing.

You're being honest with me huh?

Thats right. I am.

Dont you know—and the mad lights I'd get to know so well were dancing in her eyes even in that dark place—that honesty is just another word for a certain subtle ignorance?

She actually said that. Who *is* this? I thought. Out loud of course I had to say Look, lets go for breakfast and talk about books. You can explain honesty to me. Or ignorance. Okay?

We stared at each other. She said Im reading Rilke. Steppenwolf. Also The Duino Elegies. Do you know who Rilke is?

I nodded and I saw her smile for the first time. The next thing she said was Good. We'll skip breakfast. What I'd really rather do is take a shower with you.

Right then I knew I was a goner.

XXXXXXXXXX   Diane has finally called. Gypsy saw her and gave her my message. When I told her about the cops on the smokestack she was quiet for a while. Then she asked me to go over it again. So I did.

Baby she said. On the smokestack Frankie? And then she asked Are they harness bulls or are they in suits and ties?

I told her I couldnt see them, just the sparks flashing from their binoculars and the occasional outline of a head.

She said Do you really think there are cops on the smokestack Frankie?

I said What do you mean? I've been watching them for two days.

Listen she said. You know you're just paranoid. Dont you? You're hallucinating baby.

I told her No Im not. They've been there since early yesterday morning. Dont come home.

She made a disgusted noise and told me Sit in a warm tub. Take some downers. Get some sleep. I'll see you sometime tomorrow morning.

Where are you at? I asked. What are you doing hon?

Her voice sounded a million miles away. Taking care of business she said. Dont do anything freaky okay? Then she hung up. Diane is one of those people who when youre doing your best for her is always trying to put you down.

She's crazy if she thinks Im going to sleep. Thats what they're waiting for. Paranoid my ass! I know what I know.

I think I'll have another taste. And then a nice cold beer after the rush.

XXXXXXXXXXX   I dont recall what I was doing when Monroe died. I just remember that when Dawn and I saw her in The Misfits she made me feel sorry for her. Not her character but Marilyn. Herself. Then we heard she killed herself or got murdered. That was five years ago.

I know just what I was doing when Kennedy was shot. We were driving from Vegas back to LA and we were in the middle of that long and dreary desert stretch when Dawn flipped on the radio for some sounds only instead of music a man's voice said "—report is true. President Kennedy has been shot. The President has been shot in Dallas Texas." Its a joke I said. Like Welles' War of the Worlds. Its just a joke. Some joke! Dawn said and went to another station and another and another. Then we knew it was true.

We pulled off the road and just sat there in the deadly heat and held each other and cried.

The following year in the course of our breaking up Dawn tried very hard to run me down with her car. A lot can change in a year.

One year ago I cruised this town in spitshined boots and suedefront sweaters. My shirts went out to the laundry and came back with heavy starch in the body and extra heavy in the collars and cuffs. I wore ascots with stickpins and black ski pants with the straps under the insteps so I'd have a sharp line from the top of my boot to my waist. I was always clean. I wasnt disposed to having another "relationship." I was the stonest of stone butches and loving every minute of it. My address book was thicker than most people's skins are. I put rows of stars by the best names.

Now I have Diane.

Our relationship is monogamous according to her. According to her Hank doesnt matter because he just fucks her. She says fucking is business and eating pussy is emotional and nobody eats her pussy but me. Its funny but I dont even do that much anymore. We're always so busy. Selling crystal. Scoring crystal. Shooting crystal. Tripping. Its like we're celibating.

Diane only goes out doing business or dealing crystal. Everything else we really need is inside this room. We can go on like this forever.

Thats fine with me.

One time she told me her power over me is that she's so weak it makes her stronger than I am. I tripped on that for days.

XXXXXXXXXXXX   There was still some orange juice in the icebox and a couple of slices of rye bread. I had that and another beer. Then I hit up some more crystal but I can tell Im getting ready to crash hard because the rush was still great only I dont have any of the wired energy I should have. But I want to stay awake for Diane. Maybe I'll clean up and then stroll on over to the smokestack and yell I'm right down here you motherfuckers! Come and get me! Or maybe they'll leave first and then Diane can come home and I'll still be here.

Its getting pretty dark out now. Outside the neons are all winking on, slicing the air with red and green and hot pink and blue. The squares have gone home from their jobs and the traffic is all pimp cars and cop cars and cars holding tricks looking for sex and cars driven by people who were headed somewhere else and got lost down here. The street people are taking over the night. All the hookers and hustlers and winos and junkies and the fools who still think they're just slumming. I have to stop writing soon or turn on a light and I dont think Im ready for more light. Im tired. Im tired. My eyelids feel like sandpaper when I blink.

During the early time when we were first together and I was just chipping with crystal and hadnt even learned how to hit myself yet and Diane still had a hefty habit but wasnt using quite as much as she does now and Hank wasnt as big a part of our life we used to laugh a lot and talk for hours and go places and hold each other but we weren't as close as we are now. Crystal makes you close. Close. You read each other. Youre in each others skins.

Youre like those little blades of grass that push their way up through cement, that uncurl in back alleys where the bricks are covered with garbage and bits of broken glass, that somehow wind up waving from the ledges of buildings high above peoples heads. Crystal teaches you that everything really matters but nothing else is important and if you can understand that my friend then youre another user. You already know that a spoonful of crystal holds all pleasure and balm and weal. There is a simple order in such focus.

Diane says I just like being an outlaw. Maybe so. But if I had to choose between a good rush and almost anything else I'd be tying off my arm without a thought. I know people whove been doing crystal for years. I never yet met anybody who quit.

Diane.

Dorothy Allison
(b. 1949)

Dorothy Allison was born out of wedlock to a working-class teenager in South Carolina. Her roots are often the subject of her poetry and prose. The tone of her work, as she describes it, is "hard assed," as even the titles of her books of fiction suggest. Allison's short stories, collected as *Trash* (1988), reflect the violence of her childhood and life in the South as well as her ties to the female survivors of her family and her lesbianism. Her autobiographical novel, *Bastard Out of Carolina* (1992), continues her exploration of what it means to be a working-class female, a victim of violence and incest, and a determined survivor.

Allison often assumes in her work an "attitude" which may be considered characteristic of post–lesbian-feminism. She presents, for example, an angry challenge to lesbian-feminist notions about appropriate sexual behavior (she is a defender of lesbian s/m), a fierce pride of (working) class, and an "in your face" stance.

FURTHER READING: Dorothy Allison, *The Women Who Hate Me* (Ithaca, NY: Fire-brand Books, 1983); *Trash* (Ithaca, NY: Firebrand Books, 1988); *Bastard Out of Carolina* (New York: Dutton, 1992).

THE WOMEN WHO HATE ME

1.

The women who do not know me.

The women who, not knowing me, hate me
mark my life, rise in my dreams and shake their loose hair
throw out their thin wrists, narrow their already sharp eyes
say   *Who do you think you are?*

Lazy, useless, cuntsucking, scared, stupid
What you scared of anyway?
Their eyes, their hands, their voices.
Terrifying.

The women who hate me cut me
as men can't.   Men don't count.
I can handle men. Never expected better
of any man   anyway.
                              But the women,
shallow-cheeked young girls the world was made for
safe little girls who think nothing of bravado
who never got over by playing it tough.

What do they know of my fear?

What do they know of the women in my body?
My weakening hips, sharp good teeth,
angry nightmares, scarred cheeks,
fat thighs, fat everything.

Don't smile too wide. You look like a fool.
Don't want too much. You an't gonna get it.

An't   gonna   get   it.
Goddamn.

Say goddamn and kick somebody's ass
that I am not even half what I should be,
full of terrified angry bravado.

BRAVADO.
The women who hate me
don't know
can't imagine
life-saving, precious bravado.

2.

God on their right shoulder
righteousness on their left,
the women who hate me never use words
like hate   speak instead of nature
of the spirit not housed in the flesh
as if my body, a temple of sin,
didn't mirror their own.

Their measured careful words echo
earlier coarser stuff   say

What do you think you're doing?
Who do you think you are?

Whitetrash
no-count
bastard
mean-eyed
garbage-mouth
cuntsucker
cuntsucker
no good to anybody, never did diddlyshit anyway.

You figured out yet who you an't gonna be?

The women who hate me hate
their insistent desires, their fat lusts
swallowed and hidden, disciplined to nothing
narrowed to bone and dry hot dreams.
The women who hate me deny
hunger and appetite,
the cream delight
of a scream
that arches the thighs and fills
the mouth with singing.

3.

Something hides here
a secret thing shameful and complicated.
Something hides in a tight mouth
a life too easily rendered
a childhood of inappropriate longing
a girl's desire to grow into a man
a boyish desire to stretch and sweat.

Every three years I discover again
that   no,   I knew nothing before.
Everything must be dragged out,
looked over again. The unexamined life
is the lie, but still
must I every time deny
everything I knew before?

4.

My older sister tells me flatly
she don't care who I take to my bed
what I do there.   Tells me finally
she sees no difference between
her husbands, my lovers. Behind it all
we are too much the same to deny.

My little sister thinks my older crazy
thinks me sick
more shameful to be queer than crazy
as if her years hustling ass,
her pitiful junky whiteboy
saved through methadone and marriage, all that
asslicking interspersed with asskicking,
all those pragmatic family skills we share mean nothing
measured against the little difference
of who and what I am.

My little sister   too
is one of the women who hate me.

5.

I measure it differently, what's shared,
what's denied, what no one wants recognized.

My first lover's skill at mystery,
how one day she was there, the next gone;
the woman with whom I lived for eight years
but slept with less than one;
the lover who tied me to the foot of her bed
when I didn't really want that
but didn't really know
what else I could get.

What else can I get?
Must I rewrite my life
edit it down to a parable where everything
turns out for the best?

But then what would I do with the lovers
too powerful to disappear   the women
too hard to melt to soft stuff?
Now that I know that soft stuff
was never where I wanted to put my hand.

6.

The women who hate me
hate   too   my older sister
with her many children, her weakness for
good whiskey, country music, bad men.
She says the thing *women's lib* has given her
is a sense she don't have to stay too long
though she does
still she does
much too long.

7.

I am not so sure anymore of the difference.
I do not believe anymore in the natural superiority
of the lesbian, the difference between my sisters and me.

Fact is, for all I tell my sisters
I turned out terrific at it myself:
sucking cunt, stroking ego, provoking,
manipulating, comforting, keeping.
Plotting my life around mothering
other women's desperation
the way my sisters
build their lives
around their men.
Till I found myself   sitting at the kitchen table
shattered glass, blood in my lap and her
the good one with her stern insistence
just standing there wanting me
to explain it to her   save her from being
alone with herself.

Or that other one
another baby-butch wounded girl
    How can any of us forget how wounded
    any of us have to be to get that hard?
Never to forget that working class says nothing
does not say who she was   how she was
fucking me helpless. Her hand on my arm
raising lust to my throat   that lust
everyone says does not happen
though it goes on happening
all the time.

How can I speak of her, us together?
Her touch drawing heat from my crotch to my face
her face, terrifying, wonderful.
Me saying, "Yeah, goddamn it, yeah,
put it to me, ease me, fuck me, anything . . ."
till the one thing I refused
then back up against a wall
her rage ugly in the muscles of her neck
her fist swinging up to make a wind
a wind blowing back to my mama's cheek
past my stepfather's arm.

I ask myself over and over how I
came to be standing in such a wind?
How I came to be held up like my mama

with my jeans, my shoes locked in a drawer
and the woman I loved breathing on me,
   "You bitch.   You damned fool."

   "You want to try it?"
   "You want to walk to Brooklyn
     barefooted?"
   "You want to try it
     mothernaked?"

Which meant   of course   I had to decide
how naked   I was willing to go   where.

Do I forget all that?
Deny all that?
Pretend I am not
my mama's daughter
my sister's mirror?
Pretend I have not
at least as much lust
in my life   as pain?

Where   then   will I find the country
where women never wrong women
where we will sit knee to knee
finally listening
to the whole
naked truth
of our lives?

Minnie Bruce Pratt
(b. 1946)

Minnie Bruce Pratt, a Southern writer, was an early member of Feminary,
a radical feminist editorial collective, as well as a member of the lesbian-
feminist action group LIPS. Much of her poetry, which is collected in her
1981 volume, *The Sound of One Fork,* and her 1985 volume, *We Say We
Love Each Other,* continues in the lesbian-feminist tradition of the 1970s.
But her most recent volume, *Crimes Against Nature* (1990), sounds a note
that was largely neglected in the 1970s. Pratt focuses in that volume on the

struggles of lesbian mothers and her personal anguish as a mother of two boys from whom she was separated when her ex-husband discovered she was a lesbian.

Crimes Against Nature received the Lamont Prize, awarded by the Academy of American Poets, as well as the Lambda Literary Award, a recognition from the gay and lesbian literary community. The success of *Crimes Against Nature* in the lesbian community is indicative perhaps of the burgeoning interest in lesbian motherhood throughout the 1980s and early 1990s. Its popular reception also suggests a growing toleration within the community for all manner of women, including those who retain deep emotional ties with their male offspring.

FURTHER READING: Minnie Bruce Pratt, *The Sound of One Fork* (Night Heron, 1981); *We Say We Love Each Other* (San Francisco: Spinsters / Aunt Lute, 1985); *Crimes Against Nature* (Ithaca, NY: Firebrand, 1990).

ALL THE WOMEN CAUGHT IN FLARING LIGHT

1.

A grey day, drenched, humid, the sun-
flowers bowed with rain.   I walk aimless
to think about this poem.   Clear water runs
as if in a streambed, middle of the alley,
a ripple over bricks and sandy residue,
for a few feet pristine as a little creek
in some bottomland, but then I corner
into the dumped trash, mattresses, a stew
of old clothes. I pull out a wooden fold-up
chair, red vinyl seat, useful for my room,
while water seeps into my shoes.   A day to
be inside, cozy.   Well, let's pick a room:

Imagine a big room of women doing anything,
playing cards, having a meeting, the rattle
of paper or coffee cups or chairs pushed back,
the loud and quiet murmur of their voices,
women leaning their heads together.   If we
leaned in at the door and I said, *Those women
are mothers,* you wouldn't be surprised, except
at me for pointing out the obvious fact.

Women *are* mothers, aren't they?   So obvious.

Say we walked around to 8th or 11th Street
to drop in on a roomful of women, smiling, intense,
playing pool, the green baize like moss.   One
lights another's cigarette, oblique glance.
Others dance by twos under twirling silver moons
that rain light down in glittering drops.
If I said in your ear, through metallic guitars,
These women are mothers, you wouldn't believe me,
would you?   Not really, not even if you had come
to be one of the women in that room.   You'd say:
Well, maybe, one or two, a few.   It's what we say.

Here, we hardly call our children's names out loud.
We've lost them once, or fear we may.   We're careful
what we say.   In the clanging silence, pain falls
on our hearts, year in and out, like water cutting
a groove in stone, seeking a channel, a way out,
pain running like water through the glittering room.

2.

I often think of a poem as a door that opens
into a room where I want to go.   But to go in

here is to enter where my own suffering exists
as an almost unheard low note in the music,
amplified, almost unbearable, by the presence
of us all, reverberant pain, circular, endless,

which we speak of hardly at all, unless a woman
in the dim privacy tells me a story of her child
lost, now or twenty years ago, her words sliding
like a snapshot out of her billfold, faded outline
glanced at and away from, the story elliptic, oblique
to avoid the dangers of grief.   The flashes of story
brilliant and grim as strobe lights in the dark,
the dance shown as grimace, head thrown back in pain.

Edie's hands, tendons tense as wire, spread, beseeched,
how she'd raised them, seven years, and now not even
a visit, Martha said she'd never see the baby again,
her skinny brown arms folded against her flat breasts,

flat-assed in blue jeans, a dyke looking hard as a hammer:
And who would call her a mother?
                                    Or tall pale Connie,
rainbow skirts twirling, her sailing-away plans, islands,
women plaiting straw with shells: Who would have known
until the night, head down on my shoulder, she cried out
for her children shoved behind the father, shadows
who heard him curse her from the door, hell's fire
as she waited for them in the shriveled yard?

All the women caught in flaring light, glimpsed
in mystery: The red-lipped, red-fingertipped woman
who dances by, sparkling like fire, is she here on the sly,
four girls and a husband she'll never leave from fear?
The butch in black denim, elegant as ashes, her son
perhaps sent back, a winter of no heat, a woman's salary.
The quiet woman drinking gin, thinking of being sixteen,
the baby wrinkled as wet clothes, seen once, never again.

Loud music, hard to talk, and we're careful what we say.
A few words, some gesture of our hands, some bit of story
cryptic as the mark gleaming on our hands, the ink
tattoo, the sign that admits us to this room, iridescent
in certain kinds of light, then vanishing, invisible.

3.

If suffering were no more than a song's refrain
played through four times with its sad lyric,
only half-heard in the noisy room, then done with,
I could write the poem I imagined: All the women
here see their lost children come into the dim room,
the lights brighten, we are in the happy ending,
no more hiding, we are ourselves and they are here
with us, a reconciliation, a commotion of voices.

I've seen it happen. I have stories from Carla,
Wanda.   I have my own: the hammering at authority,
the years of driving round and round for a glimpse,
for anything, and finally the child, big, awkward,
comes with you, to walk somewhere arm in arm.

But things have been done to us that can never be
undone.　The woman in the corner smiling at friends,
the one with black hair glinting white, remembers
the brown baby girl's weight relaxed into her lap,
the bottle in her right hand, cigarette in her left,
the older blonde girl pressed tense at her shoulder,
the waves' slap on the rowboat, the way she squinted
as the other woman, her lover, took some snapshots,
the baby sucking and grunting rhythmic as the water.

The brown-eyed baby who flirted before she talked,
taken and sent away twenty years ago, no recourse,
to a tidy man-and-wife to serve as daughter.
If she stood in the door, the woman would not know her,
and the child would have no memory of the woman,
not of lying on her knees nor at her breast, leaving
a hidden mark, pain grooved and etched on the heart.

The woman's told her friends about the baby.　They
keep forgetting.　Her story drifts away like smoke,
like vague words in a song, a paper scrap in the water.
When they talk about mothers, they never think of her.

No easy ending to this pain.　At midnight we go home
to silent houses, or perhaps to clamorous rooms full
of those who are now our family.　Perhaps we sit alone,
heavy with the past, and there are tears running bitter
and steady as rain in the night.　Mostly we just go on.

A WAVING HAND

Last night of the visit, the youngest put his head
down, saying, *Again and again and again and again
and again,* his head down on the bed.
　　　　　　　　　　　　　　　I said
we should get a medal for every time we say good-bye,
like a purple heart;　or we could have a waving hand
(*Like the one in the windows of roaring trucks,*
he says.)
　　　　　　　　Our chests would be heavy with
medals, heavy waving hands:　pendulum:

we come back, we say hello.　He cheered up, then.

THE PLACE LOST AND GONE, THE PLACE FOUND

One low yellow light, the back room a cave,
musty sleeping bags, us huddled on the floor.
We pretend we're camped somewhere with no calendar,
distant from morning when I will leave and leave
them motherless children again.   The oldest travels
into sleep, holds my hand while I listen, left,
to a huge wind come up in my hollow ears, my breath,
pain, and me asking: What are we besides this pain,
this frail momentary clasp?

        At the window next day
the face of the youngest stiff with grief, and at my desk
beside me years after, his face, clear, fixed,
like a photo set in a paperweight, crystal heavy pain.
Pick it up, unable to put it down.

          Yet woven,
still twined in my hand, his sinewy fingers like twigs
in the tree we climbed the first day:

          As soon as I jumped
from the car and hugged them, each a small *oomph*,
they rushed me to climb their tree, maple in the jumbled
wild green strip of land between houses and lawns,
up, feet there, there's the nest, rumpled,
suspended.   They long for the hidden bird.   We talk
about what I can't remember, nothing but words.   We drop
seeds into light, translucent silent whirligigs,
better than copters, they say, and gently rock
the branch I sit on with their long scratched legs.

They have asked me into their tree and, satisfied,
we sit rather large in its airy room.   Their house
slides away across the lawn to the edge.   Now
we are in the middle.   Now they show me the inside.
If I see a small grass motion, it's probably voles.
That muddy excavation will be dug bigger, longer,
for a cave, for a hideout with a tin roof.   And all
paths, distinct or vague in the rank weeds, go
places.   The oldest leads me to his, a pond
sunk, hedged, and forgotten.   No one else comes.
He watches in the morning (silver), in the evening (gold).
For what?   For the birds, to be the one who sees
and takes the bird away, but only with his eyes.

The youngest boy takes me to the smallest creek.
We see the crawfish towers squiggled in the mud.
We see dim passageways down to hidden creatures,
mysteries.   We follow scarce water under a road
into sun.   They show me jewelweed, touch-me-not,
dangling red-orange tiny ears, and the brown pods,
how seed rattles and springs and scatters if you fling
out your hand, even carelessly.   They show me everything,
saying, with no words, they have thought of me here,
and here I am with them in the in-between places.

THE LAUGHING PLACE

There was the time I got mad and hired a detective,
I told the oldest boy one night he asked for more
stories.   The cluttered supper table rattled and shook
like a car in low gear as he teetered back his chair:

It was spring after the fall I left your father,
and you, in the old brick house with the weedy yard.
He was after me, threats like boots and knives:
Sign the papers or never see your children again.
I was rabbit-scared foolish as if I'd slipped the pen
and, lolloping toward the bushes, heard the man's hands
about to snatch me by my hind legs up and skin me alive.

All spring I was in a sorry crouch, shank-shaking,
waiting.   Maybe he'd get tired of whack, whack
at such stupid red-eyed game.   I went and came
back for nervous visits, sprung free a bit by quick
tizzies of wind investigating the leaves that proved

summer.   Then one day your brother, smooth-cheeked
innocent, crow-eyed, told me about the strange woman
sleeping cozy overnight like a plump feather pillow
in his father's bed.   At first I was just aggravated,

and then, then, I got light-headed, hot-fingered mad at
this young Mr. Buck, laying down the law, do-as-I-say-
not-as-I-do two-faced deceitful man out to lambast
me for doing what I please, doing as he does but with a
different woman.   That's how I got hissing mad as a cat
and called the detective up out of the yellow phonebook

into the snackbar red vinyl booth, a little slick-haired
weasel-worded gold-toothed man, *yes ma'm, no ma'm,*
in his lime polyester suit, green as slime, his promise
of a trail, a furtive gleam at the lit, lidded windows
of the house I later imagined him snoozing in front of,
easy in his rusty Chevy as a mole deep in his hole,
asleep in an earth of dirt, and not a speck of evidence,
mud or rock, to throw, nothing out of him for my money,

except the idea of slinking in dark moonlight to pounce.

So that's what I did, with my lover, in her car.   Sneaked
up the street to lurk and look for any pointed proof
I could use, mean as claws.   We snouted, hooted, prowled
around the house, sniffed, flitted, plotted, but rooted
out only this: a bit of courage in my heart, canny,
cunning, that I could outsmart threat.   Which I did.

I went to the hmmph-hmmphing lawyer and said, *Listen,
I have a story*, told until he slowly picked the phone
up and called the man off me with *Careful, stones, stones
and people in glass houses.*   I'd thought I needed hard
evidence, a rock in the hand. I'd thought the house
was brick.   I'd thought I did not know how to fight,
and all the years after I've believed I did nothing
but tremble there for him to steal, kill, eat my life.

Now, telling you this, I've remembered: Those nights
I slipped around, playing the detective, making my escape.

Then the boy and I at the kitchen table both began to grin.

Jackie Kay

(b. 1961)

The poet and dramatist Jackie Kay is a black Scottish lesbian who was
adopted as a child by white parents, a subject she explores in her book of
poems, *The Adoption Papers* (1991). Her plays and television films deal
with the subjects of pornography, AIDS, and people of color as well as
lesbianism. Her work is almost always politically engaged and often concerned with the interrelationship of sex, race, and gender.
  In her poetry Kay is representative of a new generation of lesbian au-

thors whose writing has moved beyond what they consider the confines of the "appropriate" subjects of lesbian-feminist literature. Kay focuses in her award-winning collection on a variety of topics, such as transracial adoption and its effect on a black child, artificial insemination and the lesbian family, the tragedies caused by AIDS for gay men and those who love them, the psychology of male transvestites, and male homosexuals who hide in heterosexual marriages. Her interest is less in addressing an orthodox community of lesbians than in speaking to a community of queers.

FURTHER READING: Jackie Kay, *The Adoption Papers* (Newcastle-upon-Tyne, England: Bloodaxe Books, 1991).

PHOTO IN THE LOCKET
(for Louise)
I

There are things I don't tell her
private things, a garnet necklace
slipped between black silk and cotton.
My new friend gives me an African name
writes letters often; once she sent one
with a spicy bun, a can of black grape
and an old photo of her and her sister—
two black girls side by side
in identical white lace dresses,
big bows on their nappy (a word
I've just learnt) hair and ankle socks.
So clean. Black people are hot on hygiene.
White people sleep with cats and dogs.

I don't talk about these things.
My past is locked in a travelling trunk.
Inside: Sabena, my nanny, my mother
her long black fingers shine
like reefs lit by moonlight;
my house; the swimming pool;
my old white public school.
I'm ashamed. I didn't think much.
Sometimes I see the black man's face
at the window, coming to get us.

My mother is white. My father is white.
My lover is white. At night we lie
like spoons breathing the same cold air
inside the room with two outside walls.
We snuggle under blankets, sometimes
turn in unison our bodies all
mixed up.
We can only meet here in bed—
my fingers inside her high tide,
she making a rivulet run through me
in a rush, a gush till we are both
beached up.

When my family first met her
they thought I was undoing my past
through her. It's not like that.
I love her. Not like I loved Sabena.
I love lying next to her
the dark of her skin, the pale of mine.
Sometimes I want to tell her,
if you knew what it was really like:
servants living in corrugated huts outside
no electricity, no running water
you wouldn't be lying here kissing my breasts.

I keep it hidden. Locked—a photo
inside a locket that never opens

In the morning I wake before you
the pale winter light peeps through
our skin; side by side, in sharp relief.
Something I've been reading in *Midnight Birds*
makes me feel like Judas;
I get up make toast and tea.

I am five years old again
looking out this kitchen window.
Somebody turns the palm of my hand
up and asks why it isn't black.
Is your bottom black someone sniggers.
Then they all laugh. I put loose leaves
in the tea-pot. Let them brew.
Last night we talked into the small
hours again. You said they used to call

you specky. The toast burns.
I pull it out furious. It is not
the same. It is not the same.
I don't want to play it out on you.
You get up for breakfast:
"I'm always making the fucking toast,"
before you rub the sleep out of your eyes.

Yesterday I said a terrible thing.
My tongue is full of old ideas.
Sometimes they slip like falling rocks.
Warning. Landslide. I can't repeat it.
She'll repeat it for me.
Often. So that I don't forget.

This is the nightmare: the soft laughter
then this sudden storm. I don't know where
we go wrong. I am all that. True.
I lived it. Now I live with her. Together.
Not as servant and Madam. No.
Not like that, I don't believe her.
As lovers, as lovers, as lovers.
Words chase me like bullets overhead.
Kaffir. Wog. Kaffir. Wog.
Between tight teeth I whisper.

I hug say sorry let's go back
to bed. We're too young. This
is too heavy. I'd like to stop seeing
white like whitewash on hospital walls
like a blank projection screen;
black like onyx stones or moist earth.

What am I doing with you
if all I want is to make you
eat shit for your ancestors?

It's better for her now down here
in London. Yet still with her friends
I shake a little when I'm pouring tea.
Waiting for discovery. They disapprove
I'm sure of the two of us together.

At clubs we separate for the evening,
come back together in bed much later,
where no eyes watch like marbles.

Tonight while she sleeps
I lie thinking of home.
I miss the land. The red dust roads.
The jacaranda tree, picking ripe avocados
or mangoes. I miss the words; the whole tutti.
I don't talk of this. Even memories
lead to trouble. Especially memories.

Which school. What house. Which friend.
We were brought up on different worlds:
she on mince and potatoes, drizzle, midges;
me on mealies, thunderstorms, chongalolas.

II

Now I tell you almost everything.
Something shifted like sand
a while ago and the sea thrashed
out and in, carrying my secrets back
with the eventide. And my tongue
returned to the cave in my mouth.

You tell me when you were wee
you stood on a baby chick, squashed it,
how you felt it for years underfoot.
I tell you our rabbit Harvey
was strangled and buried in
our very own back garden.

Now, some of your memories are mine.
We move on. We don't forget.
We change not like amoebas
more like plants keeping the same stem.

Now we are light years away.
Sometime ago I opened my trunk
and showed her a photo of Sabena.
Then it all came out. My strawberry dress.
The school assembly. Hot rain on dust.

Bit by bit we sat and picked till
I laughed and cried like some huge
waterfall—giggling and howling.

HE TOLD US HE WANTED A BLACK COFFIN
(for Margaret McAllister)

I phoned up the funeral director,
he said it would cost us a fortune
so we bought an ordinary pine one
painted it black matt like his furniture.
It looked smashing. He went out
like Charles Rennie Mackintosh—
a single bunch of white lilies on top.
None but Derek's flowers.

These past few days I can't stop thinking
how I wanted to take the abscess out
of his five year old mouth and put it in mine;
I wanted to fall off that wall in Greig Street;
the day I swore at Mrs. Calder
for calling my son a poof in front of hers.
I always knew from when he was thirteen
and he cried when Gavin moved to Aberdeen.

No morphine no morphine no morphine
I want to be alive when I'm alive
dead when I'm dead know what I mean.
No first aid box to fetch,
No oil of cloves, no germolene
nothing, nothing—his hand in mine
his thumb tap tapping my palm
me saying you're all right son

Everything is all messed up.
The boy careening down the hill in the park
his sledge a huge pair of wings, scarf flying.
The man in my kitchen laughing at my bad jokes
(who'll laugh now?) The man in the hospital bed
the size of the boy; his face a person from Belsen.
The song he sang at the school concert
(what was it?) It doesn't seem that long ago.

MUMMY AND DONOR AND DEIRDRE

I went to school today.
I wore my new trainers, laces undone.
A nice boy called Tunde sat next to me.
In the playground he gave me a Monster
Munch; I gave him a bite of my apple.

We both went with him to school.
Took the day off. It was awful
long. It's happened so fast.
All day the hands of the clock moved in secret.
At last—his face at the gate. "And then and then."

He said my daddy is an underground man
What is your daddy? I said I don't have a daddy;
I have a mummy and a donor and a Deirdre.
Deirdre has hair the colour of that tree.
She helps people with no money.

I don't think we'll both go to parents' night.
I don't want things harder than they are.
I want to protect him from the names and stones.
I'd love it all to be different—Deirdre and me
in the PTA. Us on school holidays. No big deal.

Tunde said Do you know who your daddy is?
I said yes he's a friend of a friend of mummy's.
He has curly hair. He looks after animals.
I've got a picture. Come home and I'll show you.
We can play blockblusters. Don't you dare go away.

I was awful lucky. Third time with the syringe.
I didn't want Deirdre to do it with me.
I made myself all cosy. Lit a candle.
Had a body shop bath. Glass of Aqua Libre.
Wine's bad with sperm apparently.

I told Tunde some kids come from
their daddys using the penis; others from
their mummys using frozen sperm;
others because their mummys get the seed
put it in a syringe and put it in the vagina.

I wiped the tears from his face.
I kept saying don't cry, never mind.

Tunde won't play with him any more.
Are they dirty words, he asks me.
What am I supposed to say? Tell me.

Today Tunde and I said we won't tell
anybody else what we tell each other.
It will all be secret. I gave him a chocolate.
He gave me a Monster Munch.
Tunde has the same thing to eat everyday.

DRESSING UP
(for Toby)

My family's all so squalid
I'm trying to put it behind
me—real typical working class
Scottish: Da beats Ma drinks it off.
I couldn't stomach it, banging

doors, turning ma music up top
blast. I told ma ma years ago. She'd
rather I murdered somebody than
that. She wasn't joking either.
Nobody gets hurt, it's not for

the image even I'm just dead
childish. Mascara I like, rouge,
putting it on after powder.
I love wearing lots of layers.
Ma ma always dresses boring

No frills. See at Christmas I had
on black stockings Santa would kill
for and even Quentin Crisp would
look drab beside my beautiful
feather boa—bright fucking red.

Ma ma didn't touch her turkey
Finally she said What did I do
I know what they call you, transvite.
You look a bloody mess you do.
She had a black eye, a navy dress.

Copyright Acknowledgments